The Handbook of Contemporary Semantic Theory

Edited by

Shalom Lappin

Copyright © Blackwell Publishers Ltd 1996, 1997

First published 1996

First published in paperback 1997

Blackwell Publishers Ltd
108 Cowley Road
Oxford OX4 1JF, UK

Blackwell Publishers Inc
350 Main Street
Malden, Massachusetts 02148, USA

British Library Cataloguing in Publication Data
A CIP catalogue record for this book is available from the British Library

Library of Congress Cataloging in Publication Data has been applied for

ISBN   0–631–18752–9 (Hbk) — ISBN   0–631–20749–X (Pbk)

Typeset in 10 on 12pt Palatino
by Graphicraft Typesetters Limited, Hong Kong
Printed and bound in Great Britain
by Hartnolls Ltd, Bodmin, Cornwall

This book is printed on acid-free paper

6/2/19

The ~~Handbook of Contemporary~~
Sema~~~~ 1/01   Tel. 504505

**BLACKPOOL AND
THE FYLDE COLLEGE**
An Associate College of Lancaster University

This book must be returned to the
College Library on or before the last date stamped below

SOUTH L R C

☎ 01253 504505

𝕀𝔹

Blackwell Handbooks in Linguistics

This outstanding multi-volume series covers all of the major sub-disciplines within linguistics today and, when complete, will offer a comprehensive, critical and authoritative survey of linguistics as a whole.

Already published

1 **The Handbook of Phonological Theory**
   Edited by John A. Goldsmith

2 **The Handbook of Child Language**
   Edited by Paul Fletcher and Brian MacWhinney

3 **The Handbook of Contemporary Semantic Theory**
   Edited by Shalom Lappin

4 **The Handbook of Phonetic Sciences**
   Edited by William Hardcastle and John Laver

5 **The Handbook of Sociolinguistics**
   Edited by Florian Coulmas

Forthcoming

The Handbook of Contemporary Syntactic Theory
Edited by Mark R. Baltin and Chris Collins

The Handbook of Morphology
Edited by Andrew Spencer and Arnold M. Zwicky

The Handbook of Historical Linguistics
Edited by Brian D. Joseph and Richard D. Janda

Do not say anything which cannot be understood in the hope that in the end it will be understood.

Hillel, *Pirkei Avot*, Perek Bet, Pasuk Hey (Chapter 2:5)

To my parents, Adah and Ben Lappin, who introduced me to natural language and inspired me to investigate it

Contents

Notes on Contributors   xi
Preface   xvii
Introduction   1

I   Formal Semantics in Linguistics   9

1. The Development of Formal Semantics in Linguistic Theory   11
BARBARA H. PARTEE

II   Generalized Quantifier Theory   39

2. The Semantics of Determiners   41
EDWARD L. KEENAN

3. The Role of Situations in Generalized Quantifiers   65
ROBIN COOPER

III   The Interface between Syntax and Semantics   87

4. The Syntax/Semantics Interface in Categorial Grammar   89
PAULINE JACOBSON

5. Anaphora and Identity   117
ROBERT FIENGO and ROBERT MAY

6. The Interpretation of Ellipsis   145
SHALOM LAPPIN

IV   Anaphora, Discourse and Modality   177

7. Coreference and Modality   179
JEROEN GROENENDIJK, MARTIN STOKHOF and FRANK VELTMAN

8. Anaphora in Intensional Contexts   215
CRAIGE ROBERTS

9. Quantification, Quantificational Domains and Dynamic Logic   247
JEAN MARK GAWRON

V   Focus, Presupposition and Negation   269

10. Focus   271
MATS ROOTH

11. Presupposition and Implicature   299
LAURENCE R. HORN

12. Negation and Polarity Items   321
WILLIAM A. LADUSAW

VI   Tense   343

13. Tense and Modality   345
MÜRVET ENÇ

VII   Questions   359

14. The Semantics of Questions   361
JAMES HIGGINBOTHAM

15. Interrogatives: Questions, Facts and Dialogue   385
JONATHAN GINZBURG

VIII   Plurals   423

16. Plurality   425
FRED LANDMAN

IX   Computational Semantics   459

17. Computational Semantics – Linguistics and Processing   461
JOHN NERBONNE

X   Lexical Semantics   485

18. Lexical Semantics and Syntactic Structure   487
BETH LEVIN and MALKA RAPPAPORT HOVAV

XI   Semantics and Related Domains   509

19. Semantics and Logic   511
GILA Y. SHER

20. Semantics and Cognition   539
RAY JACKENDOFF

21. Semantics, Pragmatics, and Natural-Language Interpretation   561
RUTH M. KEMPSON

22. Semantics in Linguistics and Philosophy: An Intensionalist
    Perspective   599
JERROLD J. KATZ

References   617

Index   653

Notes on Contributors

Robin Cooper is Reader in Cognitive Science and Principal Investigator in the Human Communication Research Center at the University of Edinburgh. His publications are mainly in the area of natural language semantics and recently he has been concerned with computational semantics. His book *Quantification and Syntactic Theory* (Reidel) appeared in 1983. He has recently co-edited and contributed to a four-volume survey of formal and computational semantics produced for the FraCas (Framework for Computational Semantics) Consortium.

Mürvet Enç is Associate Professor of Linguistics at the University of Wisconsin, Madison. She has written articles on the semantics of tense and temporal expressions, including 'Towards a Referential Analysis of Temporal Expressions', *Linguistics and Philosophy*, 1986 and 'Anchoring Conditions for Tense', *Linguistic Inquiry*, 1987.

Robert Fiengo received his Ph.D. from MIT in 1974. He is Professor of Linguistics at Queens College and the Graduate Center, City University of New York. He is the author of *Surface Structure* (Harvard University Press, 1980) and, with Robert May, *Indices and Identity* (MIT Press, 1994).

Jean Mark Gawron is a research linguist at the Artificial Intelligence Center at SRI in Menlo Park, California. He is co-author with Stanley Peters of *Anaphora and Quantification in Situation Semantics* (CSLI, 1990) and is also a writer of fiction. His interests include lexical semantics, quantification and anaphora, indexicals, comparatives, and superlatives.

Jonathan Ginzburg is currently a research follow at the Human Communication Research Centre, University of Edinburgh. He gained a B.Sc. in mathematics from the Hebrew University of Jerusalem and a Ph.D. in linguistics from Stanford University. His interests include the syntax through pragmatics of interrogatives, propositional attitudes, and the semantics of dialogue.

Jeroen Groenendijk teaches logic and linguistics at the University of Amsterdam. He is affiliated with both the Institute for Logic, Language and Computation and the Department of Philosophy. Together with Martin Stokhof he has published papers on dynamic semantics, including 'Dynamic Montague Grammar' in L. Kalman and L. Polos (eds) *Papers from the Second Symposium on Logic and Language* (Akademiai Kiado, Budapest, 1990) and 'Dynamic Predicate Logic', *Linguistics and Philosophy*, 1991. He is also an Associate Editor of *Linguistics and Philosophy*.

Laurence R. Horn is Professor and Director of Graduate and Undergraduate Studies in the Department of Linguistics at Yale University. His publications include *A Natural History of Negation* (Chicago University Press, 1989) and numerous philosophical articles. His primary research area lies within the union (if not the intersection) of traditional logic, lexical semantics, neo-Gricean pragmatic theory, and the analysis of negation. Other research interests include functional syntax, grammatical relations, and language, sex, and gender.

James Higginbotham is Professor of General Linguistics, University of Oxford and formerly Professor of Philosophy and Linguistics, MIT. His publications include articles on syntactic and semantic theory and the philosophy of language and linguistics.

Malka Rappaport Hovav is Associate Professor in the Department of English at Bar-Ilan University, where she has worked since 1984. She has also been affiliated with the Lexicon project of the MIT Center for Cognitive Science. Her major research interests are lexical semantics and morphology, and their interaction with syntax. She is co-author with Beth Levin of *Unaccusativity: At the Syntax-Lexical Semantics Interface* (MIT Press, 1995).

Ray Jackendoff is Professor of Linguistics at Brandeis University. He is the author of *Semantics and Cognition* (MIT Press, 1983), *Consciousness and the Computational Mind* (MIT Press, 1987), *Semantic Structures* (MIT Press, 1990) and, with Fred Lordhal, *A Generative Theory of Tonal Music* (MIT Press, 1983). His most recent book, *Patterns in the Mind: Language and Human Nature* (Basic Books, 1994), presents the *Weltanschauung* of contemporary generative linguistics and psycholinguistics in a fashion accessible to the lay reader.

Pauline Jacobson is Professor of Cognitive and Linguistic Sciences at Brown University. Her research centers on the syntax/semantics interface and is carried out primarily within the tradition of Categorical Grammar. Recent publications include articles in E. Bach et al. (eds) *Quantification in Natural Language* (Kluwer, 1995) and in A. Szabolcsi and I. Sag (eds) *Lexical Matters* (CLSI, 1992).

Jerrold J. Katz received his Ph.D. in philosophy from Princeton University. Having taught at Princeton, MIT, the City University of New York, and King's

College London, he is currently Distinguished Professor in the Philosophy and Linguistics Programs at The Graduate Center of the City University of New York. He has written articles and books on philosophy and linguistics, including *Semantic Theory* (Harper and Row, 1972), *Propositional Structure and Illocutionary Force* (Harvester, 1977), *Language and other Abstract Objects* (Rowman and Littlefield, 1981), *Cogitations* (OUP, 1986), and *The Metaphysics of Meaning* (MIT Press, 1990). He is currently working on a book on the philosophy of mathematics. His major research interests are philosophy of language, semantics, philosophy of linguistics, philosophy of mathematics, and metaphysics.

Edward L. Keenan received his Ph.D. from the University of Pennsylvania. He is Professor of Linguistics at UCLA, and has written a series of papers in generalized quantifier theory and Boolean semantics. He has also published, with Leonard Falz, *Boolean Semantics for Natural Language* (Reidel, 1985).

Ruth M. Kempson is Professor of Linguistics at the School of Oriental and African Studies at the University of London. She is the author of *Presupposition and the Delimitation of Semantics* (CUP, 1975), Semantic Theory (CUP, 1977) and editor of *Mental Representations* (CUP, 1988). Her research interests include the interface of syntax, semantics, and pragmatics, language and proof theory, labelled deduction and natural language interpretation.

William A. Ladusaw gained his Ph.D. from the University of Texas at Austin. He is Associate Professor of Linguistics at the University of California, Santa Cruz. His research interests are in semantics and the syntax-semantics interface, with a particular interest in negation. He has published papers on negation, negative polarity items, and logical form.

Fred Landman is Associate Professor of Semantics in the Linguistics Department at Tel Aviv University. He is the author of *Towards a Theory of Information: The Status of Partial Objects in Semantics* (Foris Publications, 1984) and *Structures for Semantics* (Kluwer, 1991), and of various articles on semantics. Unlike everyone else, he was not born in a scenic spot, but in a dump of a baby clinic in Amsterdam, which (fortunately) no longer exists.

Shalom Lappin is Professor of Linguistics at the School of Oriental and African Studies, University of London. He was formerly a Research Staff Member at IBM T. J. Watson Research Center in Hawthorne, New York. His teaching and research interests are in formal semantics, formal syntax, and computational linguistics. He is the author of *Sorts, Ontology, and Metaphor: The Semantics of Sortal Structure* (de Gruyter, 1981) and, with Asa Kasher, *Philosophical Linguistics* (Scriptor, 1977). His most recent publications include articles in *Linguistics and Philosophy* and *Computational Linguistics*.

Beth Levin is Associate Professor in the Department of Linguistics at Northwestern University. Her research investigates the lexical representation of verb meaning, as well as the interactions between lexical semantics, syntax, and morphology. She is the author of *English Verb Classes and Alternations: A Preliminary Investigation* (University of Chicago Press, 1993) and co-author with Malka Rappaport Hovav of *Unaccusativity: At the Syntax-Lexical Semantic Interface* (MIT Press, 1995). Prior to coming to Northwestern, she had major responsibility for directing the Lexicon Project of the MIT Center for Cognitive Science.

Robert May received his Ph.D. in 1977 from MIT, and has taught at Barnard College, Columbia University and the University of California, Irvine, where he is currently Professor of Linguistics. He is the author of *Logical Form: Its Structure and Derivation* (MIT Press, 1985) and, with Robert Fiengo, *Indices and Identity* (MIT Press, 1994).

John Nerbonne is a computational linguist who has worked on inheritance-based lexicons, computational semantics, and applied linguistics. He has worked at Hewlett-Packard Laboratories and at the German Artificial Intelligence Center. He is currently Professor of Computational Linguistics and Chair of Humanities Computing at the Rijksuniversiteit Gronigen. He has published articles in a number of journals, including *Computational Linguistics, Annals of Mathematics and Artificial Intelligence, Künstliche Intelligenz* and *Machine Translation*.

Barbara H. Partee is Distinguished University Professor of Linguistics and Philosophy at the University of Massachusetts, Amherst. She has published numerous books and articles on formal semantics and mathematical linguistics. Her most recent book, co-edited with A. Ter Meulen and R. Wall, is *Mathematical Methods in Linguistics* (Kluwer, 1989).

Mats Rooth is Professor of Linguistics in the Institute for Computational Linguistics, University of Stuttgart. He has worked on focus and the semantics of noun phrases. His recent papers include 'Noun Phrase Interpretation in Montague Grammar, File Change Semantics, and Situation Semantics' in P. Gärdenfors (ed.), *Generalized Quantifier Theory* (Reidel 1987) and 'A Theory of Focus Interpretation', *Natural Language Semantics*, 1992.

Craige Roberts is Associate Professor of Linguistics at the Ohio State University, Columbus. She has published papers on anaphora, modality, and pragmatics. Among her recent articles are 'Modal Subordination and Pronominal Anaphora in Discourse', *Linguistics and Philosophy*, 1989 and 'Domain Restriction in Dynamic Interpretation' in E. Bach et al. (eds.) (1995).

Gila Y. Sher is Associate Professor of Philosophy at the University of California, San Diego. Among her publications are *The Bounds of Logic; A Generalized Veiwpoint* (MIT, 1991) and articles in *The Pacific Philosophical Quarterly, The Journal of Philosophical Logic, and Linguistics and Philosophy*. Her current research centers on the theory of truth.

Martin Stokhof teaches logic and linguistics at the University of Amsterdam. He is affiliated with both the Institute for Logic, Language and Computation and the Department of Philosophy. Together with Jeroen Groenendijk he has published papers on dynamic semantics, including 'Dynamic Montague Grammar' in L. Kalman and L. Polos (eds) *Papers from the Second Symposium on Logic and Language* (Akademiai Kiado, Budapest, 1990) and 'Dynamic Predicate Logic', *Linguistics and Philosophy*, 1991. He is also an Associate Editor of *Linguistics and Philosophy*.

Frank Veltman is Associate Professor in Logic at the Department of Philosophy of the University of Amsterdam. He has published several papers on the borderline between semantics and logic. The topics dealt with include conditionals, modalities, defaults, and vagueness.

Preface

Work on this handbook began in 1992, when I was a Research Staff Member in the Computer Science Department at IBM T.J. Watson Research Center in Hawthorne, New York. The book came along when I moved to London in the summer of 1993 to take up a position in the Linguistics Department at the School of Oriental and African Studies, University of London. That it was finished is due, in no small measure, to the help and support which I received from numerous people.

I am grateful to the contributors for their cooperation and patience during the extended process of assembling and editing the papers in the volume. Reading and discussing their articles with them has given me a wonderful perspective on the depth and range of current research at the frontiers of contemporary semantic theory. My editors at Blackwell, Philip Carpenter, Steven Smith, and Bridget Jennings, have provided much help, advice, and encouragement. I would like to thank Robert May for very useful advice on the design and structure of the Handbook. Ruth Kempson has given me invaluable support and critical discussion. I am grateful to my wife, Elena, whose love and good natured tolerance have been indispensable to the completion of this project. She carries heavy editorial responsibilities of her own, but never failed to display full understanding of the demands which the handbook involved. Finally, I must thank my children, Miriam, Yaakov, Yoni, and Shira, for being themselves, and for putting up with the long periods during which I was working on the handbook. Part of the time required for this work rightfully belongs to them, and I will now try to repay some of what I owe them.

Shalom Lappin
London, February, 1995

Introduction

In the past twenty-five years semantics has moved from a peripheral status in the theory of grammar to a central role in linguistic research. At the beginning of the 1970s most linguists working within generative grammar regarded linguistic semantics as an underdeveloped field without a clearly specified formal framework or a well-defined research programme. The following comment from Chomsky (1971) reflects this widely held view.

> In the domain of semantics there are, needless to say, problems of fact and principle that have barely been approached, and there is no reasonably concrete or well-defined "theory of semantic representation" to which one can refer. I will, however, assume here that such a system can be developed, and that it makes sense to speak of the ways in which the inherent meaning of a sentence, characterized in some still-to-be-discovered system of representation, is related to various aspects of its form. (p.183)

The situation changed soon after the publication of Chomsky's paper. The appearance of Montague's "Proper Treatment of Quantification in Ordinary English" (PTQ) in 1973 provided a model for developing a formal semantic theory of natural language. Specifically, Montague constructed a theory of semantic representation in which the model theoretic interpretations of natural language sentences (and expressions generally) are built up by rules operating in strict correspondence with the syntactic operations that generate their structural representations. Montague's work established the foundations for research in formal semantics for the next two decades. At approximately the same time, Jackendoff (1972) proposed a system for representing lexical semantic relations within generative grammar. This system (and its subsequent refinements) has provided the basis for a considerable amount of work on the relation between lexical meaning and syntax. In the past few years a variety of innovative formal developments have extended both the empirical coverage and the explanatory power of current semantic theories. Genuine progress has been made in the analysis of difficult semantic problems which have, until now, resisted solution. Thus, for example, while classical Montague Grammar adopts an essentially static, sentence-bound view of meaning, the investigation of dynamic processes of interpretation has yielded proposals for modelling the incremental flow of information through discourse. Similarly, by extending model theory to represent the internal structure of discourse situations, situation-based theories have provided precise accounts of the respective roles played by certain aspects of extra-linguistic context and the context-independent components of sentence meaning in generating complete interpretations for sentences.

The papers in this handbook address the major areas of current semantic research. Taken together, they offer an overview of the state of the art in semantic theory. The handbook is not intended to provide an exhaustive account of the issues it deals with. Nor does it purport to be an introductory textbook. Each paper gives a brief introductory sketch of previous work on the problem addressed and includes all the relevant references. This introduction serves as a guide for readers interested in pursuing the background to the problem in greater detail. In most cases, the author devotes the greater part of the article to the presentation of his/her current work on the topic.

The book is organized thematically rather than by theoretical approach. Each chapter concerns a particular problem or area of research. This allows the reader to appreciate the issues which constitute the research domain of contemporary semantics, rather than encouraging him/her to partition the field into competing schools. Fortunately, as the papers in this volume show, paradigm boundaries in current semantic theory tend to be porous, and there is a high degree of mutual interaction among researchers across these boundaries. This indicates the existence of a significant core of shared assumptions among many semanticists concerning the objectives of semantic theory and the set of phenomena to which it applies. However, the major theoretical paradigms are well represented, and the set of contributors encompasses a broad spectrum of views. The contributors are leading figures in the field, whose research has shaped current thinking on the issues which they take up here. Therefore, the articles in the handbook present a view of the central issues and major theoretical developments which are driving work in contemporary semantic theory.

In Section I Partee provides a history of formal semantics in linguistic theory. Given the fact that she has played a key role in the introduction of Montague Grammar (MG) into generative linguistics and contributed to the subsequent emergence of this model as the dominant framework for formal semantics, she is uniquely placed to present this historical account. In her paper, Partee traces the roots of MG to ideas in logic, model theory and the philosophy of language. She discusses the development of MG and the evolution of several post-Montague approaches to formal semantics, such as Discourse Representation Theory (DRT) (Kamp (1981), Kamp and Reyle (1993), and Heim (1982)), Situation Semantics (Barwise and Perry (1983)) and Dynamic Montague Grammar (Groenendijk and Stokhof (1990a)).

Section II is concerned with Generalized Quantifier (GQ) theory, which occupies a central place in formal semantics. On the GQ approach, NPs are analyzed as belonging to a unified syntactic category and corresponding semantic type. A GQ is generally taken to denote a set of sets, and a determiner is characterized as denoting a relation between sets. Keenan gives a survey of GQ theory, and presents the results of some of his recent work on the semantics of determiners. This work develops the ideas on Boolean semantics for determiners in, for example, Keenan and Moss (1985), Keenan and Stavi (1986) and Keenan (1987b). Cooper argues for a formulation of GQ theory which employs situation-theoretic notions in specifying the interpretation of quantified NPs. This analysis involves a significant revision of the classical version of GQ theory presented in Barwise and Cooper (1981).

The papers in Section III take up the question of how to characterize the interface between syntactic structure and semantic representation. Jacobson indicates how the interface is characterized within the framework of Categorial Grammar (CG). The CG approach sustains Montague's programme for specifying a homomorphism between syntactic categories and semantic types, where both categories and types are either basic elements or functions on objects built up from these elements. Jacobson's version of CG dispenses with empty syntactic categories and semantic variables. The relations which they are intended to capture are expressed by complex syntactic functions and the semantic functions which correspond to them. Fiengo and May take up the syntax-semantics interface in the context of determining how syntactic factors contribute to the interpretation of anaphoric relations. The guiding principle which informs their investigation is that identity of syntactic structure implies identity of semantic interpretation. This principle leads them to formulate a set of criteria for recognizing when two expressions exhibit the same syntactic structure, and so stand in the relation of (syntactic) *reconstruction* to each other. In my paper, I explore the interface question from the perspective of ellipsis resolution. I consider three types of constituent fragment (only two of which are genuine instances of ellipsis), and I argue that it is not possible to apply a single strategy of either syntactic or semantic reconstruction to all of them. Each fragment type requires a distinct reconstruction procedure which generates an interpretation at a different level of representation.

Section IV is devoted to the dynamic interpretation of anaphoric elements in discourse. Groenendijk, Stokhof and Veltman propose an account of pronominal anaphora which combines aspects of the dynamic semantics proposed in Groenendijk and Stokhof (1990a) and (1991) with Veltman's (forthcoming) update semantics. The account seeks to model the way in which a speaker's assertion of a sentence can modify an information state that existed prior to the assertion. Their analysis extends their previous work in order to capture the anaphoric possibilities of pronouns in modal contexts. Craige Roberts deals with a similar range of issues. She suggests an analysis of pronominal anaphora in intensional contexts which relies on both the notions of modal subordination (Roberts (1987) and (1989)) and the accommodation of a presupposition

(Lewis (1979)). Mark Gawron is concerned with the way in which the domain of a quantified NP is specified and updated in discourse. He maintains that the setting and modification of a quantificational domain is subject to dynamic factors of a sort analogous to those which determine the interpretation of pronouns in conversation. Gawron constructs a dynamic logic to represent the processes involved in domain update.

Section V contains papers on focus, presupposition, and negation. Rooth characterizes the focus of a sentence in terms of a set of alternative propositions which are obtained by substituting different values for a variable corresponding to the focused constituent. This analysis develops the proposals of Rooth (1985) and (1992). Horn gives a history of the semantic and pragmatic concepts of presupposition and their respective connections with the pragmatic notion of conversational implicature. He relates these issues to current research on discourse processing, specifically to Sperber and Wilson's (1986) work on Relevance Theory. Ladusaw discusses the semantics of clausal negation in connection with the distribution of negative polarity items and negative concord. He extends the account of negative polarity suggested in Ladusaw (1979) to take account of the role of pragmatic factors in determining the interpretation of negative polarity structures.

Section VI addresses the semantics of tense. Enç discusses the relationship between tense and modals. She argues that in English, the past is the only genuine tense, while the future is, in fact, interpreted as a modal and the present is the absence of tense specification.

Section VII consists of two papers on the semantics of questions. Higginbotham proposes that a question is interpreted as a space of possibilities, and a relevant answer to a question is a statement which eliminates some but not all of the possibilities in this space. He uses this account of questions to define the notion of a partial answer and to characterize the presupposition of a question. The analysis is developed within the framework of intensional logic, and it extends the account given in Higginbotham (1993). Ginzburg offers a situation-theoretic analysis of interrogatives on which a question is a partially specified situation type that generates a set of information structures (states of affairs) each of which potentially resolves the question. The notion of resolvedness is, in part, discourse dependent and invokes the informational state of the questioner. Ginzburg applies this treatment of interrogatives to construct a model of question-answer dialogues.

In Section VIII Landman gives an account of plurality on which both cumulative and distributive readings of a plural NP are identified as cases in which the NP denotes a sum (a plural entity), and does not receive a thematic role in the predication determined by the verb of which the NP is an argument. By contrast, a collective reading involves the assignment of a thematic role to an NP which denotes a group (an individual entity). The theory of plurals which Landman presents here develops and significantly modifies the analysis in Landman (1989a) and (1989b).

In Section IX Nerbonne presents a computational model of semantic interpretation within the framework of a unification-based approach to grammar (he uses HPSG to illustrate this approach). He specifies the interpretation process as unification of semantic feature structures. Unification involves the generation of composite feature representations from the structures of constituent expressions, in accordance with the constraints that the constituent feature structures impose. Nerbonne argues that compositionality need not hold in this model of interpretation.

Section X is devoted to lexical semantics. Levin and Rappaport take up the problem of how to determine the linking rules which specify the correspondence between the lexical semantic representation of a verb and its syntactic argument structure. They adopt the view that the argument structure of a verb is, in general, projected from its lexical semantic representation. They explore the relation between verbs of sound and verbs of manner of motion, in connection with the syntactic property of unaccusativity, in order to provide a case study which motivates this view.

Finally, Section XI takes up the connections between semantics and related disciplines. While it is firmly anchored in the theory of grammar, semantics, more than most other areas of linguistic research, is a focus for interdisciplinary activity. Computer science, logic, philosophy, pragmatics and psychology have all contributed important ideas to linguistic semantics and have been influenced by developments in semantic theory. Sher discusses the development of first-order logic and GQ theory within the framework of Tarskian semantics. She proposes a generalized concept of logicality based upon Mostowski's idea of invariance of interpretation under permutation of the elements of a model. She specifies Tarskian interpretations for various classes of GQs within an extended first-order system. Her paper provides an interesting perspective on some of the formal issues in GQ theory raised in Keenan's paper. Jackendoff describes the framework for representing lexical conceptual structures which he has developed and refined in recent work (such as Jackendoff (1990) and (1992)). He identifies these structures as the point of interface between grammar and cognition. He maintains that they provide the level of representation at which the universal conceptual relations underlying semantically coherent lexical (specifically verb) classes are expressed. Jackendoff's theory of lexical conceptual structure relates directly to the issues which Levin and Rappaport address in their paper. Kempson considers the traditional separation of semantics and pragmatics. She argues that this distinction should be discarded in favour of a unified model of interpretation which incorporates both context-dependent and context-independent aspects of meaning. She proposes a proof theoretic system in which the interpretation of a sentence is built up incrementally through a species of natural deduction. Her approach is similar in spirit to that of the dynamic semantic theories presented in Section IV. Katz discusses the influence of extensionalist theories of meaning developed by philosophers like Carnap, Quine and Davidson on formal semantics, and he offers a critique of these theories. He suggests an alternative view of meaning on which the intension of an expression is not characterized in denotational terms, but through decomposition into a complex of universal semantic features. Katz deals with issues that are also taken up in the papers by Partee and by Jackendoff. The non-denotational version of intensionalism which he presents develops ideas from Katz (1990b) and (1992).

The papers in this volume indicate the prominence of at least five major themes in contemporary semantic theory. First, the concern to model interpretation as a dynamic process involving the successive modification of an information state through discourse (which began with Kamp's DRT (1981)) has emerged as a primary line of research. Dynamic semantic theories are yielding increasingly sophisticated representations of the information states attributed to discourse participants, and progressively refined accounts of the procedures through which these states are modified in response to contributions to a discourse. As a result, the classical notion of interpretation as the specification of a model for a set of sentences has given way to the view that interpretation applies to a sequence of sentences, and evolves as each element of the sequence is processed.

Second, there has been a considerable expansion in the formal resources of both the type theories applied to natural language and the model theories used to specify interpretations. An example of the former development is the introduction of flexibly determined grammatical categories with corresponding types, as well as the adoption of various type shifting operations in CG. The use of n-ary $(2 \leq n)$ determiner functions and resumptive quantifiers in the representation of GQs in natural language provides a second example.[1] The extension of models, in situation semantics, to include situation types is an instance of the latter phenomenon. Another case where classical models are enriched is the introduction of algebraic structure into the domain of elements to permit the definition of composite individuals in order to represent the denotations of certain plural expressions.[2] These increases in the expressive power of both instantiated type theory and model theory are intended to capture semantic properties of expressions which cannot be accommodated in more classical frameworks. To the extent that these enrichments are well motivated, they indicate that the semantic interpretation of natural languages requires a type theory and a model theory that are considerably more complex than the system of Intensional Logic that Montague employed for the PTQ fragment.

Third, two main approaches to the syntax-semantics interface have shaped discussion of the relation between syntactic structure and semantic interpretation. On the first, an abstract syntactic level of Logical Form (LF) is derived by non-overt operations of raising that apply to quantified NPs and *in situ* *wh*-phrases to generate operator-variable structures. LF is the level of syntactic representation to which rules of semantic interpretation apply.[3] The second approach identifies the interface level with a structure in which all constituents appear in their surface positions.[4] Each view represents a certain type of choice in determining the relative complexity of syntactic representation and procedures of semantic interpretation. In general, a richer syntactic structure permits a simpler and more straightforward mapping of the interface structure onto a semantic interpretation. Conversely, a more impoverished syntactic representation which is closer to the lexically realized surface form requires more powerful semantic devices to generate an appropriate interpretation (or set of interpretations). Both empirical factors and theory-internal considerations play a role in deciding how to weight this balance.

The fourth theme concerns the question of whether there is an autonomous level of semantic representation which intervenes between the syntactic structure of a sentence and its model theoretic interpretation. Such a level has no place in MG, where interpreting a sentence consists entirely in computing its denotation relative to a model on the basis of the denotations (relative to the model) of its constituents. However, at least some dynamic approaches assign a representation to a sentence which corresponds to the informational state that it produces, and which is, in turn, mapped into a model.[5] The current emphasis on the semantic processing of sentences in a discourse sequence and the fine grained specification of context-dependent factors has given rise to theories which seek to represent the interaction of discourse participants and the states of affairs they talk about. The focus on informational processing has resulted in a strong tendency to posit independent semantic structures which are essentially models of cognitive states. This trend reflects the growing recognition of the psychological and computational dimensions of semantic interpretation.

Finally, the fifth issue is the absence of a common theoretical framework which can accommodate the sort of research currently being done in lexical semantics on one hand and in formal semantics on the other. The decompositional lexical conceptual structures which Jackendoff and other lexical semanticists employ cannot express the insights of formal semantics with respect to the properties of quantified NPs (and other scope defining elements), referential terms, and anaphoric expressions. They also seem unable to represent presuppositions. Formal theorists, for their part, have generally relied on meaning postulates to express lexical semantic relations. They have not managed to incorporate into their frameworks the systematic and subtle generalizations of lexical semanticists concerning the meaning relations which hold for different subclasses of lexical items. Some important work has been done by formal semanticists on the model theoretic treatment of the concepts and regularities that have emerged in lexical semanticists.[6] However, this is an area where much remains to be done. Specifically, what is required is a framework which will express the relationship between the "internal" semantic properties of a lexical item and its contribution to the denotation of a sentence in which it appears.

The issues connected with these five research themes will undoubtedly continue to provide focal points for much future work in semantic theory. If the papers in this handbook succeed in giving a sense of the directions which current research in semantics is pursuing and the vitality of this research, then the handbook will have achieved its purpose.

NOTES

1   See, for example, Keenan (1987b), van Benthem (1989), and May (1989) on n-ary and resumptive quantifiers.
2   See Link (1983) and (1987b), and Landman (1989a) and (1989b).
3   For the role of LF in the grammar see May (1985). Chomsky (1993) proposes a minimalist model of syntax in which LF is the only level of syntactic structure to which syntactic constraints apply, and so it is the only level of syntactic representation.
4   Variants of this view are developed in, for example, CG, HPSG (Pollard and Sag (1994)), and in Lappin (1991), (1993a), and (forthcoming).
5   This view is explicitly adopted in DRT, and it appears to be implicit in the dynamic semantics presented by Groenendijk, et al. in this volume. Moreover, the respective situation theoretic analyses which Cooper, Gawron and Ginzburg propose in this volume also suggest a representationalist approach. It should be noted that not all dynamic theories assume a level of semantic representation which is distinct from the interpretation of a sentence in a model. Thus, Lappin (1989), Lappin and Francez (1994) and Heim (1990) propose E-type accounts of donkey pronouns which are dynamic in that the domain and range of E-type functions are determined by prior expressions in discourse. However, none of these accounts posits a discourse representation apart from the model theoretic structures in terms of which the denotations of expressions are specified.
6   Carlson (1984), and Dowty (1989) and (1991) propose formal reconstructions of thematic roles and linking rules. Zwarts and Verkuyl (1994) offer a model theoretic formulation of Jackendoff's lexical conceptual structures.

I Formal Semantics in Linguistics

1 The Development of Formal Semantics in Linguistic Theory

BARBARA H. PARTEE

1 Earlier Traditions in Semantics

Formal semantics has roots in several disciplines, most importantly logic, philosophy, and linguistics. The most important figure in its history was Richard Montague, a logician and philosopher whose seminal works in this area date from the late 1960s and the beginning of the 1970s; its subsequent development has been a story of fruitful interdisciplinary collaboration among linguists, philosophers, logicians, and others, and by now formal semantics can be pursued entirely within linguistics as well as in various interdisciplinary settings.

At the time of Montague's work, semantics had been a lively and controversial field of research for centuries, and radically different approaches to it could be found across various disciplines. One source of deep differences was (and still is) the selection of the object of study: the central questions of semantics may come out quite differently if one focusses on language and thought, or on language and communication, on language and truth, or on language "structure" per se. A more accidental but no less profound source of differences is the research methodology prevalent in the field within which one approaches questions of semantics. Thus early generative linguists concentrated first on "semantic features", using methodology influenced by phonology to study questions of lexical meaning borrowed in part from psychology (which emphasized concept discrimination and principles for scaling semantic fields) and structuralist anthropology. A central goal in such approaches to lexical semantics was and still is to identify semantic "distinctive features" or semantic "atoms" which combine to form lexical meanings, with never-ending debates about whether total decomposability into such atoms is possible at all and about the universality or non-universality of the "semantic primitives" of natural languages. The increasingly dominant impact of syntax on the whole field soon led to focus on questions such as the relation between syntactic and semantic ambiguity, the issue of whether transformations preserve meaning, and other such structural questions which can be explored relatively independently of the issue of "what meanings are." Semantic representations were often modelled on syntactic tree structures (sometimes influenced by the syntax of some logic), and in some theories were (and are) taken to be identical with some level of syntactic structures (e.g. the underlying structures of Generative Semantics or the level of Logical Form of GB syntax.)

In the first years of generative grammar, the key semantic properties of sentences were taken to be ambiguity, anomaly, and synonymy, analyzed in terms of how many readings a given sentence has, and which sentences share which readings (Katz and Fodor 1963, Chomsky 1965). The impact of philosophy and logic on semantics in linguistic work of the 1950s and 1960s was limited; many linguists knew some first-order logic, aspects of which began to be borrowed into linguists' "semantic representations," and there was gradually increasing awareness of the work of some philosophers of language.[1] Generative semanticists in the late sixties and early seventies in particular started giving serious attention to issues of "logical form" in relation to grammar, and to propose ever more abstract underlying representations intended to serve simultaneously as unambiguous semantic representations and as input to the transformational mapping from meaning to surface form (see, for instance, Bach 1968, Fillmore 1968, Karttunen 1969, Lakoff 1968, 1971, 1972). But these semantic representations were generally not suggested to be in need of further interpretation, and truth-conditions and entailment relations were never explicitly mentioned as an object of study in the indigenously linguistic traditions that existed before formal semantics came into linguistics in the 1970s.

The truth-conditional tradition in semantics has its source in the work of those logicians and philosophers of language who viewed semantics as the study of the relation between language on the one hand and whatever language is *about* on the other, some domain of interpretation which might be the real world or a part of it, or a hypothesized model of it, or might be some constructed model in the case of an artificial language. Such philosophers and logicians, at least since Frege, have tended strongly to view semantics non-psychologistically, making a distinction between language and our knowledge of it, and generally taking such notions as reference, truth-conditions, and entailment relations as principal data which a semantic description has to get right to reach even the most minimal standards of adequacy.

Before Montague, most logicians and most linguists (with important exceptions such as Reichenbach 1947) had agreed, for different reasons, that the apparatus developed by logicians for the syntax and semantics of formal languages was inapplicable to the analysis of natural languages. Logicians considered natural languages too unsystematic, too full of vagueness, ambiguity, and irrelevant syntactic idiosyncrasies to be amenable to formalization. Those linguists who took note of logicians' formalizations of the syntax and semantics of formal languages tended to reject the logicians' approach for either or both of two reasons: (1) the formal languages invented and studied by the logicians appeared to be structurally so different from any natural language as to fall outside the bounds of the class of possible human languages and hence to be irrelevant to linguistics,[2] or (2) logicians generally eschewed the concern for psychological reality which is so important to most linguists; not only is this difference noticeable in what the notion of "possible language" means to a logician versus a linguist, but also in the question of whether properties like truth-conditions and entailment relations are or are not relevant to linguistics, given that speakers of a natural language do not always (in fact cannot always) have reliable intuitions about them.

2 Montague and "English as a Formal Language"

2.1 The rise of model-theoretic semantics in philosophy and logic

Within philosophical logic, the foundational work of Frege, Carnap and Tarski led to a flowering in the middle third of this century of work on modal logic and on tense logic, on conditionals, on referential opacity, and on the analysis of other philosophically interesting natural language phenomena. The competition among different modal logics characterized by different axiom systems had led some philosophers like Quine to reject modal and intensional notions as incurably unclear; but the field was revolutionized when Kripke (1959) and Kanger (1957a,b) argued for the importance of distinguishing between possible models of a language (the basis for the semantical definition of entailment) and possible worlds (possible states of affairs, different ways things might be or might have been) as elements that should be included within a given model to be used in giving a model-theoretic semantics for modal notions.[3] The distinction between models and worlds is an important one for the semantics of all intensional constructions, but one that is still not always clearly appreciated; see discussion in Gamut (1991, Chapter 2). (The distinction between moments or intervals of time and models is intuitively much clearer, so it can be helpful to recall the analogy between the role of times in models of tensed languages and the role of possible worlds in models of modal languages, an analogy noted below as one of Montague's contributions to the field.)

The resulting extension of model-theoretic techniques into the realm of modal logic led to a great expansion of work in logic and the philosophy of language in quantified modal logic, tense logic, the logic of indexicals and demonstratives, studies of adjectives and adverbs, propositional attitude verbs, conditional sentences, and intensionality more generally. With few exceptions, most of this work followed the earlier tradition of not formalizing the relation between the natural language constructions being studied and their logico-semantic analyses: the philosopher-analyst served as a bilingual speaker of both English and the formal language used for analysis; only the formal language would be provided with a model-theoretic semantics.

2.2 *Montague*

Montague was himself an important contributor to these developments in philosophical logic. Montague had been a student of Tarski's (along with Dana Scott, with whom he corresponded while working out his intensional logic), and as a faculty member at UCLA was a teacher and then a colleague of David Kaplan, co-authored a logic textbook with his colleague Donald Kalish, and was an active part of a strong logic group spanning the departments of philosophy and mathematics. He did important work on intensional logic, including the unification of tense logic and modal logic and more generally the unification of "formal pragmatics" with intensional logic (Montague 1968, 1970a.) This was accomplished in part by treating both worlds and times as components of "indices" and intensions as functions from indices (not just possible worlds) to extensions. He also generalized the intensional notions of property, proposition, individual concept, etc., into a fully typed intensional logic, extending the work of Carnap (1956), Church (1951), and Kaplan (1964), putting together the function-argument structure common to type theories since Russell with the treatment of intensions as functions to extensions.[4]

Although linguists have focussed on Montague's last three papers, and it is those that most directly set the framework for formal semantics, a considerable amount of Montague's earlier work was on areas of philosophical logic of direct relevance to issues in semantics and on the logico-philosophical analysis of various concepts that have traditionally been of concern in the philosophy of language: the logic of knowledge and belief, the interpretation of embedded *that*-clauses, syntactic vs. semantic analysis of modal operators, the analysis of events as properties of moments of time, and the analysis of obligations and other "philosophical entities" discussed in Montague (NCPE 1969). It was reportedly[5] the experience of co-authoring Kalish and Montague (1964), a logic textbook, that gave Montague the idea that English should after all be amenable to the same kind of formal treatment as the formal languages of logic. Kalish and Montague took pains to give students explicit guidance in the process of translation from English to first-order logic: rather than the usual informal explanations and examples, they produced an algorithm for step-by-step conversion of sentences of (a subset of) English into formulas of first-order logic. Montague reportedly then reasoned that if translation from English into logic could be formalized, it must also be possible to formalize the syntax and semantics of English directly, without proceeding via an intermediate logical language. This led to the provocatively titled paper "English as a Formal Language" (Montague EFL 1970b), which begins with the famous sentence, "I reject the contention that an important theoretical difference exists between formal and natural languages." (in Montague 1974, p.188.) As noted by Bach (1989), the term "theoretical" here must be understood from a logician's perspective and not from a linguist's. What Montague was denying was the logicians' and philosophers' common belief that natural languages were too unruly to be amenable to formalization; what he was proposing, in this paper and even more systematically in Montague (1970c), was a framework for describing syntax and semantics and the relation between them that he considered compatible with existing practice for formal languages and an improvement on existing practice for the description of natural language. The central properties of this framework are the subject of the next subsection.

2.3   Montague's theory of grammar

Montague's paper "Universal Grammar" [UG] (Montague 1970c) contains the most general statement of Montague's formal framework for the description of language[6,7]. The central idea is that anything that should count as a grammar should be able to be cast in the following form: the syntax is an algebra, the semantics is an algebra, and there is a homomorphism mapping elements of the syntactic algebra onto elements of the semantic algebra. This very general definition leaves a great deal of freedom as to what sorts of things the elements and the operations of these algebras are. As for the syntactic algebra, in the case of a typical logical language the elements can be the well-formed expressions, but in the case of a natural language, ambiguity makes that impossible, since the homomorphism requirement means that each element of the syntactic algebra must be mapped onto a unique element of the semantic algebra[8] (the shorthand terminology for this is that the syntax must provide a "disambiguated language"). In the PTQ grammar for a fragment of English, the syntax is not explicitly presented as an algebra, but if it were transformed into one, the elements would be the analysis trees.

The relation between a linguist's syntactic component and syntax as an algebra is not always easy to see, and it can be non-trivial to determine whether and how a given syntax can be presented as an algebra, and more particularly, as an algebra homomorphic to a corresponding semantic algebra. The core issue is compositionality, since for Montague, the central function of syntax is not simply to generate the well-formed expressions of a language but to do so in such as way as to provide the necessary structural basis for their semantic interpretation.[9] GPSG and the various categorial grammar frameworks currently under exploration are among the clearest examples of "linguists' grammars" that are more or less consistent with the requirements of Montague's UG, since context-free grammars are easily converted to equivalent algebras (their surface phrase-structure trees being isomorphic to their derivation trees.)

The choice for the semantic elements is totally free, as long as they make up an algebra, i.e. as long as there is a well-defined set of elements and well-defined operations that have elements of the algebra as operands and values. The semantic elements, or "semantic values" as they are often called, could be taken to be the model-theoretic constructs of possible-worlds semantics as in Montague's fragments of English and most "classical" formal semantics, or the file change potentials of Heim (1982), or the game strategies of game-theoretical semantics, or the simple extensional domains of first-order logic, or hypothesized psychological concepts, or expressions in a "language of thought", or anything else. What is constrained is not the "substance" of the semantics but some properties of its structure and of its relation to syntactic structure.

It is the homomorphism requirement, which is in effect the compositionality requirement, that provides the most important constraint on UG in Montague's sense, and it is therefore appropriate that compositionality is frequently at the heart of controversies concerning formal semantics; see Section 3.5 below.

"Universal Grammar" presents formal frameworks for both "direct" and "indirect" semantic interpretation, the latter proceeding via translation into an intermediate language, as in Montague's grammars for fragments of English in UG and PTQ; only in his EFL fragment did he provide a direct model-theoretic interpretation of the natural language syntactic rules. (Examples of direct interpretation can also be found in the work of Cresswell, von Stechow, and Kratzer.) For "indirect" semantic interpretation, the notion of compositional translation is defined. As expected, this involves a requirement of homo-morphism between two syntactic algebras; the process is therefore iterable and any number of intermediate languages could be invoked (see the application of this idea in Rosetta 1994). When both translation into an intermediate language and the semantic interpretation of that intermediate language are compositional, the intermediate language is in principle dispensable, since the composition of those two homomorphisms amounts to a direct compositional interpretation of the original language. Montague viewed the use of an inter-mediate language as motivated by increased perspicuity in presentation; linguists with a Chomskyan background tend to be interested in the psycho-logical reality of some level of "semantic representation", but direct evidence for or against such levels has been scarce.

The paper of Montague's that had the most impact on linguists was "PTQ" (Montague 1973), and to many linguists, "Montague Grammar" has probably meant what Montague did in PTQ (and what subsequent linguists and phi-losophers did following the model of PTQ with greater and lesser innovations; the term therefore has a vague boundary with the broader term "formal se-mantics"), although it is the broader algebraic framework of UG that consti-tutes Montague's theory of grammar. Properties of PTQ that are not required by UG include the use of a version of categorial grammar in the syntax; the use of the lambda-calculus, an extremely important[10] tool for helping to make compositionality realizable; Montague's IL' (Intensional Logic) as an interme-diate language (with its particular possible-worlds interpretation of proposi-tions, properties, etc.); function-argument application as the interpretation of virtually all basic grammatical relations; the exclusive use of unary functions and concomitant use of strictly binary-branching (where branching at all) analysis trees; the introduction of individual concepts;[11] the very important and influential analysis of noun phrases as uniformly denoting generalized quantifiers,[12] about which more will be said below; a particular treatment of quantifier scope, of *de dicto* and *de re* readings of NPs in opaque contexts, and of pronouns as bound variables (embodying Montague's solution to important problems about quantifying into opaque contexts raised by Quine 1960); and the generalizing of virtually all argument-taking expressions to "intensional versions", part of the strategy illustrated in PTQ of "generalizing to the worst case" in order to achieve uniformity of semantic type for each syntactic category. I have just summarized key properties of PTQ at breakneck speed in an extremely abbreviated form; pedagogical introductions and fuller discussions are readily available elsewhere (e.g. Partee 1973c, 1975a, Thomason 1974, Dowty et al. 1981, Link 1979, Gamut 1991; see Zimmermann 1981 for an insightful review of three German Montague Grammar textbooks including Link 1979).

One important principle required by the UG framework and at the heart of Montague's semantics, inherited from the traditions of logic and model theory and transmitted as one of the defining principles of formal semantics, is the principle that truth-conditions and entailment relations are the basic semantic data, the phenomena that have to be accounted for to reach observational adequacy. Cresswell (1978) has put this in the form of his "Most Certain Principle": we may not know what meanings are, but we know that if two sentences are such that we can imagine a situation in which one of them is true and the other false, then they do not have the same meaning. (Cresswell shows how many decisions about semantic analysis, both in general architecture and in particular instances, can be seen to follow from that principle.) The adoption of truth conditions and entailment relations as basic semantic data is not innocuous from a foundational perspective (see Section 3.2). Nevertheless it has proved so helpful in making semantic proposals more explicit than they had previously been that it has become widely (although not universally) adopted, especially, but not only, among formal semanticists. It may be hard to remember or realize how surprising and controversial an idea it was to linguists in the early 1970s.

Another interesting feature of Montague's work which was novel to linguists and became quite influential methodologically was the "method of fragments". "Fragment" has become almost a technical term of formal semantics. What is meant is simply writing a complete syntax and semantics for a limited subset ("fragment") of a language, rather than, say, writing rules for the syntax and semantics of relative clauses or some other construction of interest while making implicit assumptions about the grammar of the rest of the language. Linguists have traditionally given small (but interesting) fragments of analyses of various aspects of complete natural languages; Montague gave complete analyses of small (but interesting) fragments of natural languages.[13]

Montague did not work single-handedly or in a vacuum; his papers include acknowledgements to suggestions from David Lewis, David Kaplan, Dana Scott, Rudolph Carnap, Alonzo Church, Terence Parsons, Hans Kamp, Dan

Gallin, the author, and others. And there were other important early contributors to the development of formal semantics as well, several of whom have
been mentioned and/or will be mentioned in Section 3 below.

3   "Montague Grammar" and Linguistics

3.1   *The introduction of Montague's work into linguistics*

Montague was doing his work on natural language at the height of the "linguistic wars" between generative and interpretive semantics (see Fodor 1980,
Newmeyer 1980, Harris 1993), though Montague and the semanticists in linguistics had no awareness of one another. (Montague was aware of Chomsky's
work and respected its aim for rigor but was skeptical about the fruitfulness
of studying syntax in isolation from semantics (see Note 9, Section 2.3).) As
argued in Partee (1973c, 1975a), one of the potential attractions of Montague's
work for linguistics was that it offered an interestingly different view of the
relation between syntax and semantics that might be able to accommodate the
best aspects of both of the warring approaches. The PTQ instantiation of
Montague's algebraic theory illustrates what Bach (1976) christened the "rule-
by-rule" approach to syntax-semantics correspondence: syntactic rules put
expressions (or expressions-cum-structures, see Partee 1975a) together to form
more complex expressions, and corresponding semantic rules interpret the
whole as a function of the interpretations of the corresponding parts. This is
quite different from both generative and interpretive semantics, which were
framed in terms of the prevailing conception of syntactic derivations from some
kind of phrase-structure-generated underlying structures via transformations
to surface structures, with the debate centered on which level(s) of syntactic
representations provided the basis for semantic interpretation. The closest linguistic analog to Montague's rule-by-rule approach was in Katz and Fodor's
(1963) proposal for compositional interpretation of Chomsky's T-markers (deep
structure P-markers plus transformational history), but that approach was
abandoned as too unrestrictive once Katz and Postal (1964) had introduced the
hypothesis that transformations might be meaning-preserving, a hypothesis
that in a sense defines generative semantics. Interpretive semantics did not go
back to the derivational T-marker correspondence of early Katz and Fodor,[14]
but rather focussed on the level of surface structure and the question of what
other levels of syntactic representation might have to feed into semantic interpretation (Jackendoff 1972).
   The earliest introduction of Montague's work to linguists came via Partee
(1973a, 1973c, 1975a) and Thomason (1974),[15] where it was argued that
Montague's work might allow the syntactic structures generated to be relatively conservative ("syntactically motivated") and with relatively minimal departure from direct generation of surface structure, while offering a principled

way to address the semantic concerns such as scope ambiguity that motivated some of the best work in generative semantics.

While "Montague Grammar" was undoubtedly the principal vehicle by which the influence of model-theoretic semantics came into linguistics, there were other more or less connected lines of similar research which contributed to the ensuing cooperative linguistics-philosophy enterprise. The work of David Lewis is important in this regard, both because Lewis, who knew the work of Chomsky and other linguists quite well, was an important influence on Montague's own work via conversations and his participation in Montague's seminars, and because Lewis (1968, 1969, 1970) presented many of the same kinds of ideas in a form much more accessible to linguists. Cresswell (1973) was another related work, a book-length treatment of a similar semantic program, with a great deal of valuable discussion of both foundational issues and many specific grammatical constructions. Also Parsons (ms. 1972), Keenan (1971a,b), and Thomason and Stalnaker (1973) were early and active contributors to linguistics-logic-philosophy exchanges.

By the middle of the 1970s, "Montague Grammar" and related work in formal semantics was flourishing as a cooperative linguistics-and-philosophy enterprise in parts of the US, the Netherlands, Germany, Scandinavia, and New Zealand, and among individual scholars elsewhere. (By the late seventies it was no longer possible to keep track.) The first published collection, Partee (ed., 1976), contained contributions by Lewis, Partee, Thomason, Bennett, Rodman, Delacruz, Dowty, Hamblin, Cresswell, Siegel, and Cooper and Parsons; the first issue of *Linguistics and Philosophy* contained Karttunen (1977) as its first article; the biennial Amsterdam Colloquia, still a major forum for new results in formal semantics, started up in the mid-seventies and opened its doors to scholars from outside Europe by the late seventies. Other conferences and workshops on or including Montague Grammar were held in various places in the U.S. and Europe from the mid-seventies onward.

3.2   An example: NP interpretation

A good example of the interesting novelty to linguists of Montague's analysis was his treatment of NPs in PTQ. One exciting idea was the uniform interpretation of all NPs as generalized quantifiers (which may have been suggested to him by David Lewis; see Note 12), which allowed one to be explicit about their important semantic differences, as in generative semantics treatments, while having a single semantic constituent corresponding to the syntactic NP constituent, unlike the distribution of pieces of NP-meanings all over the tree as required by the first-order-logic-like analyses linguists had been trying to work with (because linguists generally knew nothing about type theory, certainly nothing about generalized quantifiers). Dependence on first-order logic had made it impossible for linguists to imagine giving an explicit semantic interpretation for "the" or "a" or "every" or "no" that didn't require a great deal of structural decomposition into formulas with quantifiers and connectives, more or less the translations one finds in logic textbooks. The generative semanticists embraced such structures and made underlying structure look more like first-order logic, while the Chomskyites rejected such aspects of meaning as not belonging to any linguistic level and gave no explicit account of them at all. One can speculate that the rift might never have grown so large if linguists had known about generalized quantifiers earlier. The productive teamwork of Barwise and Cooper (1981) is a beautiful example of how formal properties and linguistic constraints and explanations can be fruitfully explored in tandem with the combined insights and methodologies of model theory and linguistics, and generalized quantifiers have continued to be a fertile domain for further linguistically insightful work exploiting formal tools (see the papers on Generalized Quantifier Theory by Keenan and Cooper in this volume).

A second important aspect of NP interpretation in PTQ is the handling of scope via differences in analysis trees. The treatment (and sometimes even the existence) of the scope ambiguity of (1) was a matter of considerable controversy in the interpretive/generative semantics debates. PTQ used a "Quantifying-In" rule which resulted in a single syntactic tree structure for (1) but two different analysis trees,[16] an important illustration of the "rule-by-rule" approach:

(1)   A unicorn eats every fish

McCawley (1981) points out the similarity between Montague's Quantifying-In rules and the generative semantics Quantifier-Lowering rule, and there are indeed important similarities between what one might look at as a command relation in a Montagovian analysis tree and a command relation in a generative semantics underlying structure or a GB LF. The differences in conception are nevertheless interesting and important, with Montague's approach more like the old "item-and-process" (vs. "item-and-arrangement") grammars or like Zellig Harris's underappreciated algebraic work (e.g. Harris 1968) which also treats structural similarity between languages in terms of "history of rules applied in derivations" rather than in geometrical configurations at selected levels of representation. Montague's Quantifying-In rule was in fact outside the bounds of what linguists would have called a single rule, since it simultaneously substituted a full NP for one occurrence of a given "variable" (he_n) and pronouns of appropriate gender, case, and number for all other occurrences of that same variable.

The proper treatment of scope ambiguity and the binding of pronouns is of course a continuing area of controversy with profound implications for the nature of the syntactic and semantic components of grammar and their interface. Cooper (1975) invented "Cooper storage", with its concomitant weakening of compositionality, as a means to avoid even a derivational ambiguity in a sentence for which there is no independent syntactic motivation for positing ambiguity. Scope ambiguity is also the only known phenomenon for which GPSG (Gazdar et al. 1985) had to choose between abandoning context-freeness or abandoning compositionality; they opted for the latter in quietly presupposing Cooper storage for quantifier scope. May (1977) introduced Quantifier Raising, approximately the mirror image of the generative semantics rule of Quantifier Lowering, and then made the startling proposal that c-command at LF does not in fact disambiguate quantifier scope, thereby abandoning the otherwise respected principle that the input to semantic interpretation must be a disambiguated syntax, and that whatever "logical form" may mean, being truth-conditionally disambiguated is part of it. Other proposals for dealing with quantifier scope can be found in contemporary literature, including the "Flexible Categorial Grammar" approach of Hendriks (1987, 1993) and others. This has been and undoubtedly will continue to be an important arena for exploring consequences of various conceptions of rules and representations and the connections among them, as are the equally varied and controversial proposals concerning the syntax and semantics of pronouns and other "bindable" expressions.[17] The integration of psycholinguistics and formal semantics requires some resolution of the problem of combinatorial explosion that comes with the disambiguation of such pervasive ambiguities as scope ambiguities; see Johnson-Laird (1983), Fodor (1982). It is hard to imagine all the ways in which recent linguistic history might be different if quantifier scope did not have to be worried about at all, but as long as systematic truth-conditional differences are regarded as semantic differences, quantifier scope possibilities must be accounted for. (See the papers in this book on Anaphora, Scope, Binding and Ellipsis for some of the contemporary ramifications of these issues.)

3.3 Function-argument structure and the reinvigoration of categorial grammar, and lambdas

Another important legacy of Montague's work, one which has become so thoroughly absorbed into linguistics that its novelty in the early 1970s is easily forgotten, is the idea of seeing function-argument structure as the basic semantic glue by which meanings are combined. What did we think before that? In early work such as Katz and Fodor (1963) or Katz and Postal (1964) one sees attempts to represent meanings by means of bundles of features and meaning combinations as the manipulations of such feature-bundles; there were obvious problems with any semantic combinations that didn't amount to predicate-conjunction. Later logically-oriented linguists working on semantics invoked representations that looked more or less like first-order logic augmented by various "operators" (this was equally true for generative and interpretive semantics), and more generally the practice of linguists dealt in "semantic representations" without explicit attention to the interpretation of those representations. This was the practice David Lewis was deploring on the first page of his 1970 paper "General Semantics":

> But we can know the Markerese translation of an English sentence without knowing the first thing about the meaning of the English sentence: namely, the conditions under which it would be true. Semantics with no treatment of truth conditions is not semantics. Translation into Markerese is at best a substitute for real semantics, relying either on our tacit competence (at some future date) as speakers of Markerese or on our ability to do real semantics at least for the one language Markerese. (D. Lewis (1970), p.18)

I believe linguists did presuppose tacit competence in Markerese, and moreover took it to represent a hypothesis about a universal and innate representation, what Jerry Fodor later dubbed the Language of Thought (e.g. Fodor 1975), and therefore not in need of further interpretation. The problems that resulted and still result, however, from making up names for operators like "CAUSE" or features like "AGENT" without addressing the formidable problems of defining what they might mean, are evident whenever one looks at disputes that involve the "same" operators as conceived by different linguists or in the analysis of different languages or even different constructions in the same language.

But let us come back to "real semantics" and the impact of seeing semantic interpretation as involving a great deal of function-argument structure (something also emphasized early by Lewis, Cresswell, and Parsons, and traceable to the work of Frege, Tarski, and Carnap.) The idea of an "intensional transitive verb" like Montague's treatment of *seek* had apparently not occurred to linguists or philosophers before: opacity was seen as embedding under some sentential operator, and to make the opacity of a verb like *seek* explicit required engaging in lexical decomposition (as suggested, for instance, in Quine 1960) to make the opacity-producing operator overt. Similarly, linguists had never thought to analyze adjectives as functions applying to nouns. "Normal" adjectives were all assumed to originate as predicates and get to prenominal position via relative-clause reduction (Bach (1968) went so far as to get nouns into their head positions via relative-clause reduction as well, thereby providing a clausal structure that could contain temporal operators in order to account for temporal ambiguity in superficially tenseless expressions like "the president"), and linguists who noticed the non-predicate-like behavior of adjectives like *former* and *alleged* also noted the existence of cognate adverbs which were taken to be their sources through syntactically complex derivational relations (or equally complex derivations in an interpretivist treatment, where the "more logical" representation was derived, not underlying).

Function-argument structure and a rich type theory go naturally together in the treatment of natural language, given the fairly rich array of kinds of constituents that natural languages contain. Even if Chierchia (1984) is correct in hypothesizing that the productive categories, those which have corresponding *wh*-words and/or pro-forms and are not limited to a small finite set of exemplars (criteria which may not always exactly agree, but a good start), are never higher than second-order in their types, that is still a much richer type structure than was found in the classical predicate logic, which has so little diversity of types (sentence, entity, and n-place first-order predicates) as to leave linguists who employed it unaware of types at all, and to make it understandable why explicit semantics before Montague Grammar seemed to require so much lexical decomposition. (See Dowty 1979 for illuminating discussion by a generative semanticist who became a leading Montague grammarian.)

The appreciation of the importance of function-argument structure also helped linguists understand much more of the original motivation of categorial grammar, a formalism which was invented and developed by Polish logicians (Lesniewski 1929, Ajdukiewicz 1935) but which was dismissed by linguists as soon as it was proven to be equivalent in generative power to context-free phrase-structure grammar. Linguists had seen it only as an alternative syntactic formalism, either not knowing or not caring that one of its central features is the way its category names encode an intimate correspondence between syntactic category and semantic type. Categorial grammars are therefore very attractive from the point of view of compositionality; this was pointed out by Lyons (1968) and Lewis (1970); Montague (1973) used a modified categorial grammar, and Cresswell (1973) used what he christened a lambda-categorial grammar. The problem of the (supposed) non-context-freeness of English and the context-freeness of standard categorial grammar was addressed in three different ways by those four authors. Lyons and Lewis added a (meaning-preserving) transformational component to a categorial base. Montague used categorial grammar nomenclature to establish the homomorphic category-to-type correspondence among generated expressions but allowed syntactic operations much more powerful than concatenation for putting expressions together (as with the Quantifying-In rule mentioned above). Cresswell added free permutations to his categorial grammar, thereby generating a superset of English, with disclaimers about syntactic adequacy and suggestions about possible filters that might be added.

As linguists (and other philosophers and logicians; see especially the work of van Benthem and his colleagues and students) have taken up the challenge of adapting categorial grammars to the demands of natural languages, a great deal of interesting work has resulted, and there would undoubtedly be even more if it were not impeded by the current tendency of GB-centrism to crowd out development of other syntactic frameworks. Luckily, there has been a substantial amount of very high-quality work in this area and it can be expected that leading ideas will continue to make their way into the dominant framework, at the least. (See Oehrle, Bach and Wheeler, eds, 1988 for a collection of "classic" and more recent papers, and Jacobson's paper in this volume for a current view.) Other frameworks have been suggested which combine some properties of categorial grammar with properties of X-bar syntax or other kinds of grammars; see Flynn (1981), Ross (1981), and HPSG (Pollard and Sag 1987), which basically combines GPSG with aspects of Bach's (1984) Extended Categorial Grammar.

In Section 4.2 below I mention more recent alternatives to the function-argument type structure of classical MG.

The other main topic that belongs in this section is the lambda-calculus. I have been quoted (accurately) in print as having remarked in a 1980 talk on "The First Decade of Montague Grammar" that "Lambdas changed my life". That is certainly true, and one can find many introductions to them and to their use in semantics (Partee 1973c, 1975a, Cresswell 1973, Dowty et al. 1981, Gamut 1991, Partee, ter Meulen and Wall 1990, and other introductions to formal semantics). Since it is particularly difficult for me to start discussing the importance of lambdas without exceeding the time or length limits I am supposed to observe, I will only reiterate the central point that lambdas provide a particularly perspicuous tool for representing and working with function-argument structures explicitly and compositionally.

3.4   *Compositionality and consequences for syntax*

I would suppose that the most important contribution of Montague's work to linguistics is attention to the importance of compositionality in the conception of the relation between semantics and syntax. This was something which some if not all linguists already accepted in some form as an important ideal, since something like compositionality has seemed necessary as part of an account of semantic competence. Probably the most explicitly compositional prior linguistic theories were those of Katz and Fodor (1963) and Katz and Postal (1964), which as noted earlier were really theories of translation into "Markerese" rather than "real semantics". But Montague's work gave a particularly clear and rigorous account of how such a principle might be made precise, and how a strong version of compositionality could be used in both directions to affect arguments about competing syntactic analyses as well as about semantic analyses.

With the rich tools that Montague's typed intensional logic (including lambdas!) provided, it was suddenly possible to provide semantic analyses that captured the kinds of generalizations the generative semanticists had called attention to and still work with a syntax that stayed remarkably close to surface structure, even less abstract in many respects than the relatively conservative grammars preferred among interpretive semanticists (e.g. infinitival complements were generated as VP complements rather than as sentential complements with subsequent Equi-NP deletion; phrasal conjunctions with "sentence-conjunction meanings" were generated directly rather than via Conjunction Reduction).[18] The real excitement of this was that natural language syntax suddenly looked much less crazy; instead of the great mystery of how English syntactic structure related to its putative logical form (which, as noted above, was generally assumed to resemble first-order logic plus some trimmings, an assumption we now can see as the myopia of only being acquainted with one logic, and one which was not invented for linguists' purposes), there suddenly arose the remarkable possibility that surface structure or something close to it – a reasonably motivated syntactic structure of the actual natural language, at least – might be very well designed as a logical form for expressing what natural languages express. This is the chief import of Montague's use of the expression, "English as a Formal Language", and the chief importance of his work for linguistics.

An immediate payoff of having an explicit compositional semantics for a natural language is that less burden needs to fall on the syntactic component; sameness of meaning does not require sameness of deep structure (cf. Thomason 1976) (or sameness at any other syntactic level, including "LF"). It was quickly noted that many of the arguments for syntactic relatedness that motivated various transformations were at least in part implicitly semantic; this realization then led to the new possibility of English as a context-free language (Gazdar 1982 and subsequent work in GPSG), and is probably the principal reason for the positive (although partial) correlation between preference for a nontransformational syntax (GPSG, HPSG, versions of categorial grammar, etc.) with work in formal semantics.

Compositionality and model-theoretic semantics together brought the responsibility for providing an explicit interpretation for whatever "operators" or functors one included in a semantic analysis, and this led to a flowering of research on topics such as tense and aspect, the semantics of determiners, modal verbs, conditionals, questions, plurals and mass nouns, and other such topics that had not been on center stage when semantics was approached principally in terms of configurational representations which were good for elucidating scope ambiguities and the like but silent on many other semantic issues. The substantive articles in parts VI and VIII of this volume concern the fruits of two decades or more of work on topics which were largely absent from the linguistics agenda before the advent of formal semantics.

3.5 Controversies and critiques

There have been many different sources of controversy within linguistics and philosophy concerning various aspects of the Montague grammar program, in addition to the expected continuing debates over the proper analysis of particular phenomena. Many linguists were unimpressed by Montague's syntax: while the rule-by-rule "bottom up" derivational approach offered an interesting and important perspective and constraint on possible ways to look at the syntax-semantics relation, the actual syntactic operations were unconstrained. Linguists would not consider Montague grammar a linguistic theory without an accompanying theory of constraints on the syntactic operations; diversity of opinions on the best way to go about this (among those who found the other aspects of Montague's program worth exploration) led to a distinction between "Montague semantics" (note the title of Dowty et al. 1981), which became the core of the foundation of formal semantics more generally, and "Montague Grammar", which has survived more as a collection of ideals and ideas and technical tools than as a specific linguistic theory of grammar per se; see Section 4.4 below.

Another perennial source of controversy has been the possible-worlds basis of the analysis of intensionality in Montague's semantics. Most, although not all, linguists and philosophers consider it an inadequacy that all logically equivalent sentences are treated as having the same semantic interpretation when propositions are analyzed as sets of possible worlds. This perceived inadequacy together with the insistence of philosophers like Montague and Lewis on distinguishing the description of a language from the description of the language-user's knowledge of the language (a principled stand which is markedly at odds with the Chomskyan program of equating grammar with what is in the head) has led some linguists and philosophers to dismiss the Montagovian program as foundationally unsuitable for a linguistic theory. This dismissal is not limited to linguists who prefer representational approaches, but also comes from the influential segment of the cognitive science community that models language processing and cognition in general in terms of formal processes on symbolic representations. The formal semantic response has been severalfold: (1) a critique of proffered representational theories of intensionality as even more inadequate;[19] (2) attempts to develop more adequate logics and model structures (see sections 4.2, 4.3); and (3) linguistic, philosophical, and psycholinguistic explorations of issues of "psychological reality" and the possibility or impossibility of reconciling the Chomskyan and the Montagovian views about the nature of grammar (Partee 1979a,b, 1982, 1989a, Johnson-Laird 1983, Stalnaker 1984, Soames 1987, Dowty et al. 1981, Chapter 6, sec.IV), some of which has suggested interesting differences between semantics and other aspects of grammar. (Note for instance the emergence of the idea that LF is basically another level of syntax, with "real semantics" something that goes beyond linguistics proper (Chomsky 1977).)

Another controversial issue, of course, is the principle of compositionality itself, as already noted in Section 2.3. Formal semanticists themselves have not been uniform in their attitudes toward the absoluteness of the compositionality principle, but internal disputes have been mild in comparison to such basic attacks as that in Chomsky (1975), where it is suggested that compositionality is in conflict with the principle of autonomy of syntax. Partee (1975b) argues that on the one hand, "descriptive" autonomy is part of Montague's program: the syntactic algebra is a separate subsystem, so syntactic rules do not appeal to or involve any semantic properties of expressions; and on the other hand, "explanatory" autonomy is methodologically a working hypothesis about which reasonable people can disagree. One can easily understand Chomsky's negativity towards Montague's remark that he failed to see any interest in syntax other than as a preliminary to semantics. On the other hand, it seems to me quite worthwhile that some linguists should pursue the task of seeing how much of syntax they can explain without any assumptions about semantics, and others see how much of syntax and semantics they can explain assuming a strong version of the compositionality principle. In addition to such critiques "from outside", there have been and still are controversies among formal semanticists concerning whether one or another theory is properly compositional, or how strong a version of compositionality is reasonably imputed to the structure of natural languages: see Janssen (1983), Partee (1984), Chierchia and Rooth (1984), and the recent debates between Groenendijk & Stokhof and Kamp concerning whether Kamp's DRT is or can be made to be compositional, and whether that is even a crucial desideratum. (See Gamut 1991, pp.285–96; Groenendijk and Stokhof 1991; Kamp 1990; van Eijck and Kamp, forthcoming.) As these debates make clear, determining the relevant formal properties of diversely presented semantic frameworks is often difficult, and respect for the letter of compositionality is not always at the top of everyone's priority list, with many semanticists content if their semantics is sufficiently explicit and systematically related in some way to their syntax.[20] Among formal semanticists, one can approximately categorize attitudes towards compositionality into three sorts: (1) empirical: compositionality represents a major claim about the architecture of grammar, and the formal semantics enterprise is in part an investigation of whether this claim can be maintained (e.g. Partee 1975a); (2) methodological: compositionality is adopted as a fundamental constraint on theories of grammar, so that, for instance, only grammars that include a disambiguated syntax count as well-formed grammars; the formal semantics enterprise is in part an exploration of the fruitfulness of this methodological principle (Janssen 1986; Gamut 1991, Section 6.5); (3) "mental hygiene": the principle of compositionality is not itself given any special status but only taken as one clear example of the more fundamental methodological principle that there must be a systematic relation of some sort between syntax and semantics (Kamp and Reyle 1993).

Other lines of controversy and critique relate to such matters as various properties of Montague's intensional logic and his type theory, the possible bias implicit in Montague's work (and others) toward English and other Indo-European languages (but see Stein 1981, Gil 1982, 1988, Bach 1993, Bach et al. (eds) 1995), and the method of fragments in the face of the Chomskyan shift toward principles and parameters instead of explicit rules. Not all linguists are convinced that truth-conditions should have the central place (or any place at all) in linguistic semantics that formal semantics gives them. And some, like Lakoff (see Lakoff and Johnson 1980), criticize formal semantics for its practitioners' nearly total absence of work on metaphor (but see Indurkhya 1992), arguably an extremely pervasive feature of natural language and one of central importance for cognitive science; Lakoff's contention that formal semantics is intrinsically unsuited to the investigation of metaphor is a challenge that has not yet been sufficiently addressed.

4   The Expansion, Naturalization, and Diversification of Formal Semantics

4.1   *Natural language metaphysics*

Bach (1986a) suggested the term "natural language metaphysics" to character-ize a linguistic concern which may or may not be distinct from metaphysics as a field of philosophy: that is a controversy among philosophers themselves. Metaphysics is concerned with what there is and the structure of what there is; natural language metaphysics, Bach proposes, is concerned not with those questions in their pure form, but with the question of what metaphysical assumptions, if any, are presupposed by the semantics of natural languages (individually and universally.) In the domain of time, one can ask whether a tense and aspect system requires any assumptions about whether time is dis-crete or continuous, whether instants, intervals, or events are basic, whether the same "time line" must exist in every possible world, etc.

Two prominent examples of such research which have had considerable repercussions on contemporary developments in semantics can be found in the semantics of mass and plural nouns and the area of tense, aspect, and the semantics of event sentences.

Link (1983) proposed a treatment of the semantics of mass and plural nouns whose principal innovations rest on enriching the structure of the model by treating the domain of entities as a set endowed with a particular algebraic structure. In the model Link proposes, the domain of entities is not simply an unstructured set but contains some subdomains which have the algebraic struc-ture of semilattices. A distinction is made between *atomic* and *non-atomic* semilattices. Intuitively, atomic lattices have small discrete elements (their atoms), while non-atomic ones (really "not necessarily atomic") may not.

These atomic and non-atomic join semilattice structures, when used to pro-vide structures for the domains of count and mass nouns respectively, give an excellent basis for showing both what properties mass and plurals share and how mass and count nouns differ, as well as for formally elucidating the parallelism between the mass/count distinction and the process/event dis-tinction (Bach 1986b.) Some brief introductions to the main ideas can be found in Bach (1986b), Partee (1992, 1993b) and in Landman's contribution to this volume; for more complete expositions, see Link (1983), Landman (1989, 1991).

A chief payoff is that these lattice structures also make it possible to give a unified interpretation for those determiners (and other expressions) that are insensitive to atomicity, i.e. which can be used with what is intuitively a com-mon interpretation for mass and count domains, such as *the*, *all*, *some*, and *no*. *The*, for instance, can be elegantly and simply defined as a "supremum" op-eration that can be applied uniformly to atomic and non-atomic structures. "Count-only" determiners such as *three* and *every* have interpretations that inherently require an atomic semilattice structure.

One of the most important features of this analysis is that the mass lattice structure emerges as unequivocally more general than the count noun structure, i.e. as the unmarked case. The domains of mass noun interpretations are simply join semilattices, unspecified as to atomicity. Atomic join semilattices are characterized as the same structures but with an added requirement, hence clearly a marked case. This means that languages without the mass/count distinction are describable as if all their nouns are *mass* nouns; we need not seek some alternative structure that is neutral between mass and count, since mass itself turns out to be the neutral case (see also Stein 1981).

Another area which has been fertile ground for hypotheses about natural language metaphysics has been tense and aspect, together with the study of event sentences, generic sentences, and modality. Researchers have argued from a variety of points of view for the addition of events as basic entities (Davidson 1967a, Parsons 1985, 1990, Bach 1986b, Kamp 1979, Higginbotham 1983, and others), and several have argued for an analogy between the structure of mass vs. count nouns and processes vs. events (Bach 1986b).

In early situation semantics as developed in Barwise (1981) and in Barwise and Perry (1983), the ontological status of situations and "situation types" was a matter of some controversy, especially with respect to those authors' avoidance of possible worlds or possible situations. Subsequent work by Kratzer and by some of her students has developed the possibility of letting situations, construed as parts of worlds, function both as individuals (analogous to events, playing a direct role in the interpretation of event nominals, for instance) and as "world-like" in that propositions are reinterpreted as sets of possible situations and expressions are evaluated at situations rather than at world-time pairs. (See e.g. Kratzer 1989a,b, Berman 1987, Portner 1991, Zucchi 1989.) The rich research opened up by this development may shed light not only on the linguistic constructions under study but on properties of cognitive structurings of ontological domains which play a central role in human thought and language.

4.2   Developing more adequate logics, semantic algebras, model structures

Of course much of the work in formal semantics over the last 25 years has been directed at the analysis of particular constructions and semantic phenomena in natural language; this work is well represented in other chapters in this handbook and is too extensive to begin to review here. In this section we very briefly review a small sample of work which has involved alternatives to or modifications of aspects of the formal framework – the choice of logic, type theory, model structures, etc. These developments have often involved the collaboration of linguists with logicians, philosophers, and mathematicians.

Just as Montague's work freed linguists from many of the constraints imposed by a rigid adherence to classical first-order predicate logic, so later developments have freed linguists from some of the constraints of Montague's particular choices in his intensional logic and the type theory of PTQ and opened up new perspectives on quantification, anaphora, context-dependence, intensionality, and many other fundamental semantic phenomena. Relatively few of these developments involve genuinely "new" logics or formal devices; most rather involve new ideas about the application of existing logical or algebraic tools to linguistic phenomena.

The work of Kamp and Heim beginning in the early eighties is one of the important recent developments. Kamp (1981) and Heim (1982) offer solutions to certain problems involving indefinite noun phrases and anaphora in multi-sentence discourses and in the famous "donkey-sentences" of Geach (1962) like (2) and (3):

(2)   Every farmer who owns a donkey beats it.
(3)   If a farmer owns a donkey, he beats it.

On their theories, indefinite and definite noun phrases are interpreted as variables (in the relevant argument position) plus open sentences, rather than as quantifier phrases. The puzzle about why an indefinite NP seems to be interpreted as existential in simple sentences but universal in the antecedents of conditionals stops being localized on the noun phrase itself; its apparently varying interpretations are explained in terms of the larger properties of the structures in which it occurs, which contribute explicit or implicit unselective binders which bind everything they find free within their scope.

From a broader perspective the Kamp–Heim theories have brought with them important fundamental innovations, most centrally in the intimate integration of context-dependence and context change in the recursive semantics of natural language. A related important innovation is Heim's successful formal integration of Stalnaker's (1978) context-change analysis of assertion with Karttunen's (1976) discourse-referent analysis of indefinite NPs.

Kamp's and Heim's work has led to a great deal of further research, applying it to other phenomena, extending and refining it in various directions, and challenging it. Heim herself has been one of the challengers, arguing for a revival of a modified version of Evans' (1980) "E-type pronouns" in Heim (1990). One interesting alternative that has been developed in part in connection with a claim that Kamp's Discourse Representation Theory is insufficiently compositional is "Dynamic Montague Grammar", developed by Groenendijk and Stokhof (1990, 1991) and extended by colleagues in Amsterdam and elsewhere (see Chierchia 1992).

One line of my own recent research also concerns the interaction of quantification of context-dependence, in a slightly different way, starting from the observation of Mitchell (1986) that open-class context-dependent predicates such as *local* and *enemy* behave like bound variables in that they can anchor not only to utterance contexts and constructed discourse contexts but also to "quantified contexts" as discussed in Partee (1989b).

An area in which there has been considerable diversification is in the type theory, which is central to what sorts of semantic categories a framework will have and what the basic semantic combining operations are like. Modifications can be relatively small as with Gallin's (1975) two-sorted type theory Ty2, which gives to possible worlds their own primitive type and constructs all complex types uniformly as functor types; this difference is formally rather small but can make a considerable difference to the form of linguistic analyses: see Gamut (1991, vol. 2, Section 5.8) for an introductory discussion. Other alternative type theories differ in such dimensions as choice of primitive types, choice of formation rules for complex types (Cartesian product types, recursive types, etc.), possibilities of polymorphic types and type-shifting mechanisms, etc. (see Turner, forthcoming.)

Montague required all functions to be total. There have been arguments from many different directions for allowing partial functions. Arguments for partiality are sometimes (not always, and not intrinsically) accompanied by arguments for relations rather than functions as the principal non-primitive types; these two changes correspond to two different ways one can loosen up the notion of functions. Partiality introduces some complexity in the formal apparatus (to cope with the consequences of undefinedness) but offers advantages in non-artificiality and in epistemological dimensions (see Landman 1991). Major advances in the incorporation of partiality into a Montague-style formal semantics were made in recent work of Muskens (Muskens 1989a, 1989b, 1989c).

It was mentioned in Section 3.5 that one criticism of Montague's semantics was that intensions analyzed as functions from possible worlds to extensions are not intensional enough: logically equivalent expressions of any category are then counted as semantically identical. Of the many responses to this problem, one that has a wide range of potential consequences is to replace the background metatheory, substituting a property theory for the normally presupposed set theory. (The principal feature which distinguishes all property theories from all set theories is the rejection of the axiom of extensionality.) The notion of "function" normally assumed in formal semantics, including when we speak of functions from possible worlds to something else, is the very extensional notion of function found in the Russell–Whitehead set-theoretic construction of mathematics, which identifies a function with the set of its argument-value pairs. The pretheoretic notion of function seems not to be so extensional, but rather somewhere in between the very procedural notion of algorithm and the very extensional standard notion: we can make intuitive sense both of two different algorithms producing the same function and of two different functions turning out to have the same input-output pairs. Property theory represents an attempt to provide an intrinsically intensional foundation for those domains for which the extensionality of set theory appears to have undesirable consequences. Different proposals for property theory have been advanced in recent years; none has yet succeeded in widely supplanting set theory, but their existence offers linguists new options for the analysis of intensionality. (See Chierchia and Turner 1988, Turner 1987, 1989 and Chierchia et al. eds, 1989.)

The work mentioned above is of course just a small sample of important current research; in many cases it is the analysis of subtle semantic phenomena such as anaphora and nominalization that has provided and continues to provide the impetus for important advances in theoretical frameworks.

4.3   *Developments in theories of grammar and lexicon*

This section is very brief; there are other chapters in this handbook devoted to the role of semantics in various theories of grammar, and here we confine ourselves to a few remarks relating the evolution of formal semantics with other developments in theories of grammar and of the lexicon.

In Section 3.4 we noted a number of effects of Montague Grammar on syntax. Both the availability of a powerful new semantic component and dissatisfaction with Montague's own unconstrained syntax contributed to efforts by a number of linguists to devise more constrained syntactic components that would be compatible with Montague's semantics while meeting linguistic criteria of syntactic adequacy. Cooper and Parsons (1976) showed how a Montague semantics could be incorporated into either a generative semantics or interpretive semantics sort of framework for a fragment that matched that of PTQ. The early attempts of Partee (1976b, 1979a), Bach (1976, 1979) and others to blend Montague Grammar with a constrained transformational grammar were soon supplanted by the introduction of theories which eliminated transformations altogether, as in the work of Gazdar (1982) and unpublished work by Bach and Saenz, leading to the rapid development of a variety of sorts of "monostratal" syntax as mentioned in Section 3.4. While the question of whether natural languages are context-free has remained controversial, research on "slightly context-sensitive" grammars has continued to progress, and both the formal semantics community and to an even greater degree the computational linguistics community have been hospitable and fertile environments for the exploration of varieties of non-transformational grammars, including unification grammars, various kinds of categorial grammars, GPSG, HPSG, and TAG grammars (see Joshi et al. 1975; Joshi 1985; for classic works on TAGs, Shieber 1986; Kay 1992 for unification grammars). Other linguists have developed the option of taking the GB level of LF as the input to compositional semantic rules, departing further from classical MG's approach to syntax but making use of many of the valuable ideas from Montague's semantics, and still paying attention to compositionality in the relation between LF and the model-theoretic interpretation. (See von Stechow 1991 and Heim and Kratzer, unpublished.) Bresnan's LFG was first given a model-theoretic semantic component by Halvorsen (1983), and LFG also figures in some of the computational approaches in Europe that incorporate aspects of formal semantics.

Other theoretical approaches should be mentioned because they represent in certain respects relevant alternatives to rather than "descendents" of Montague Grammar (although the family trees in these areas are never neat): One is game-theoretical semantics (see e.g. Hintikka and Kulas 1985), with its "inside-out" alternative version of compositionality and its emphasis on interpretation as a verification-falsification game between the language-user and "Nature", truth consisting in the existence of a winning strategy on the part of the language-user. Another is Situation Semantics (Barwise and Perry 1983; Cooper 1986, 1987; Halvorsen 1988; Cooper et al., eds, 1990), which is intended as an alternative to Montague's semantics and may itself be combined with various sorts of syntax, and which has emphasized the situatedness of language in context, partiality, extensionality, and indexicality, and has advocated replacing possible worlds with (actual) situations and situation types in various ways. (A very different development of the integration of (possible) situations into formal semantics, much more as a refinement of Montague's semantics than an alternative to it, can be found in the work of Kratzer (1989a, 1989b) and her colleagues and students (Diesing 1990, 1992; Portner 1992; Partee 1991)). A third approach which is on the borderline between "descendent" and "alternative" is Kamp's Discourse Representation Theory (Kamp 1981; Kamp and Reyle 1993). Note that the work of Heim (1982), which presents a very similar theory of indefinites, anaphora, context-sensitivity, context change, is formalized in a manner that is completely consistent with Montague's Universal Grammar, so the choice of departing from strict compositionality and claiming an indispensable role for the intermediate DRS "box-language" is a choice independent of those leading ideas of Kamp and Heim.

There are of course many more approaches to syntax (and semantics) than have been mentioned here; some are theoretically too clearly incompatible with formal semantics to have led to cooperative efforts, some perhaps only accidentally separated in time or space or attention from researchers in the formal semantics community (as was the case until recently, for instance, with the Prague School work on dependency grammar and theories of topic-focus structure as an integral part of grammar with semantic as well as pragmatic import; see Hajicova, Partee and Sgall (forthcoming)). Other approaches may not have been mentioned here because this author assumed, correctly or incorrectly, that they were similar enough to mentioned approaches, or for limitations of time and space, or by oversight or ignorance.

There have also been interesting developments in lexical semantics related to the issues and formal tools that have been brought into linguistics with the development of formal semantics. Before Montague Grammar, semantics was largely lexical semantics plus syntax-like investigations of relatedness between sentences. What issues in lexical semantics tended to preoccupy linguists? Well, linguists are always looking for ways of getting at "structure". In semantics this often led to proposals for decomposition into primitive concepts or "semantic features". Antonymy was once on the list of important semantic properties to be captured by a linguistic account (e.g. Katz and Fodor 1963);

it is no longer much mentioned, although the fact that "opposites" generally have the same meaning except for one salient "feature" renders them a rich area for uncovering sublexical structure (and, by the way, a stimulating domain for undergraduate research projects). One of the radical aspects in Montague's work was the relegation of most of lexical semantics to a separate "empirical" domain; the only aspects of lexical semantics that he included in grammar were what could be characterized in terms of type structure, explicit logical definition, or meaning postulates (a term from Carnap 1952 later applied to what Montague characterized as constraints on possible models). Meaning postulates (see Dowty 1979 for general discussion and important early applications in the domain of aspect and Aktionsart; but also see Zimmermann 1993 for some recent cautions) can be seen as ways of spelling out model-theoretic content of what linguists represent as semantic features.

One example of the kind of lexical semantics work that arose in the context of formal semantics starts from considering adjectives as functions that apply to nouns as arguments; adjectives are then naturally subclassified as intersective, subsective, and non-subsective, with the intersective ones corresponding to the first-order logic idea of adjectives as predicates that combine with their nouns via simple predicate conjunction. (See Kamp and Partee (forthcoming) for an introduction to adjective semantics, as well as some investigation of the possibility of melding some aspects of prototype theory with formal semantics in the analysis of vague concepts.) Another very rich example is the lexical classification of determiners in terms of properties like "monotone increasing/ decreasing on their first/second argument", "weak/strong" and the like; these investigations are a central part of generalized quantifier theory. Lexical semantics has been greatly enriched by the greater structure that has been imposed on the basic domains of entities and events by work such as Link's (1983) proposal for modelling atomic and non-atomic part-whole structures by appropriate semilattices, and proposals by Bach, Link, Dowty, Krifka and others of comparable structures for the domains of eventualities and situations. These structures allow much more to be said about the semantics of determiners, mass and count nouns, verbs and auxiliaries. Portner (1992) is a good illustration of the new possibilities that are available: Portner makes fine-grained semantic distinctions among kinds of nominalizations and the different verbs and constructions that embed them, in a way that wasn't possible with Montague's original model theory, but became possible with the advent of Kratzer's work on situations and Link's algebraic perspective on the structure of such domains.

The lexicon is one of many areas in which there is a great need for research on a typologically wider variety of languages, including polysynthetic languages where much more of the grammar takes place at the level of the word; see Bach (1993) for a start.

There are of course many approaches to lexical semantics that are more or less independent of formal semantics (see, for example, the article by Levin and Rappaport in this volume), and one may expect an increasingly fruitful interchange of ideas as model-theoretic approaches pay increasing attention to lexical as well as "structural" semantics.

5 Current Perspectives

Within and around the field of formal semantics, there is a great deal of diversity, as the foregoing discussion has tried to make clear. There does exist a (loose) "formal semantics community" across which discussion and debate is possible and fruitful, with Montague Grammar serving as a reference point in the background. No one of its properties is universally accepted by people who would be willing to identify themselves as doing formal semantics or model-theoretic semantics or "post-Montague" semantics, but there is a shared sense that Montague's work represented a positive contribution to ways to think about semantics in linguistics, and an introductory course or course sequence in formal semantics normally includes either an explicit "Montague Grammar" component or at least many of the formal tools and concepts that were central in Montague's work.

The relation of formal semantics to "generative grammar" is also diverse, as partially described in Section 4.3 above, and will undoubtedly continue to be so. For reasons that are undoubtedly more sociological than scientific, the formal semantics community has tended to be characterized by a spirit of openness to alternative theories and a recognition of the value of exploring a range of options deeply enough to begin to evaluate their relative merits and disadvantages in a substantive way. The present decade can be expected to be a period of continuing development of approaches that differ along many of the dimensions discussed above, with continuing interaction of linguists, logicians, philosophers, and researchers in computational linguistics and AI.

The connection between formal semantics and philosophy is weaker now than it was in the early years of MG, at least in the United States, where philosophical attention seems to have shifted away from the philosophy of language and in the direction of philosophy of mind and foundations of cognitive science. The situation in the Netherlands, however, is interestingly different: there the strong tradition of "Informatica" (roughly, information theory) has fostered a long-standing cooperation among mathematicians, logicians, philosophers, computer scientists, and (some) linguists, as evident in the co-authorship of Gamut (1991; original Dutch edition 1982)[21] and the founding in the late eighties of the interdisciplinary ITLI (Institute for Language, Logic, and Information) at the University of Amsterdam which led to the founding in 1990 of the European Foundation for Logic, Language, and Information which sponsors a new journal of the same name and annual summer schools that always include courses on the latest developments in formal semantics. The newest journal (first volume 1992) in formal semantics edited in the US, on the other hand, is one that specifically aims to integrate formal semantics more closely into linguistic theory, as suggested by its name, *Natural Language Semantics*. (The first journal, and still a central one, for the development of formal semantics has been *Linguistics and Philosophy*.) These developments point to an increasing specialization into more logical, computational, and linguistic aspects of formal semantics, but with continuing overlap and interaction.

Many of the most fundamental foundational issues in formal semantics (and in semantics as a whole) remain open questions, and there may be even less work going on on them now than there was in the seventies; perhaps this is because there is more work by linguists and less by philosophers, so the empirical linguistic questions get most of the attention now.

It would be foolhardy (as well as too lengthy) to try to summarize topical areas of current active investigation. The table of contents of this handbook represents one perspective on what topics are currently of central interest, although any such list is always an over-rigidification of constantly shifting boundaries, and one can never anticipate the next unexpected breakthrough that may open up some currently neglected domain or suggest brand new questions about old familiar subjects.

Since this article has been in large part a historical overview, it doesn't have a conclusion. It is possible in the nineties to have some historical perspective on the sixties and the seventies, and to some extent on the eighties, but the closer we come to the present, the more inconclusive any survey is bound to be. The only possible conclusion is wait – no, work! – and see.

NOTES

*   I am grateful first of all to Emmon Bach for reading and making valuable suggestions on initial drafts, and to several colleagues who responded to queries and helped me track down references, especially Theo Janssen and Ede Zimmermann; Theo also helped me get clearer about a couple of points. Many thanks to Kathleen A. Adamczyk, who managed to get the final manuscript into proper form while I was communicating from 3500 miles away. Time to work was made possible by a research leave from my department, and for the most pleasant imaginable working environment I am grateful to Emmon Bach, with thanks for inviting me to come away with him to northern British Columbia for a semester.
1   See for instance the references to Lewis (1968) in Lakoff (1968), to Geach (1962) in Karttunen (1969), and the evidence of awareness of logical and philosophical concerns in Keenan (1971a,b), Karttunen (1971), McCawley (1971), Bach (1968) and the volume Davidson and Harman (1972), in part a proceedings from one of the earliest linguistics and philosophy conferences (in 1969), one to which Montague was not invited.
2   See the rebuff by Chomsky (1955) of the exhortation to collaboration made by Bar-Hillel (1954).
3   Quine was evidently not satisfied by these advances; Quine (1970) expresses as much aversion to intensions as Quine (1961) and Quine (1960), although possible

worlds semanticists generally considered it one of their major accomplishments to have satisfactorily answered the important concerns Quine had raised concerning quantifying into modal contexts.

4 The variant type system Ty2 of Gallin (1975) is a possibly more perspicuous version of Montague's typed intensional logic, especially with respect to explicitly showing the ubiquity of function-argument structure in the analysis of intensions. See Turner (forthcoming) for fuller discussion of type theories, something which linguists in general were encountering for the first time in Montague's work.

5 I recall learning this from one of Montague's UCLA colleagues or former students, but I no longer recall who: probably David Lewis or David Kaplan or Michael Bennett or Hans Kamp, but my misty memory makes a proper acknowledgement impossible.

6 When I once mentioned to him the linguist's preferred conception of universal grammar as the characterization of all and only possible human languages, his reaction was to express surprise that linguists should wish to disqualify themselves on principle from being the relevant scientists to call on if some extraterrestrial beings turn out to have some kind of language.

7 Three good references include Halvorsen and Ladusaw (1979), Link (1979), Janssen (1983).

8 Actually, there is a way of respecting the homomorphism requirement while working with semantically ambiguous expressions, and that is to employ the strategy of Cooper (1975) of working with "sets of meanings" as the semantic objects, mapping each (possibly ambiguous) linguistic expression onto the semantic object which consists of all of its possible meanings; not all kinds of ambiguity are amenable in a natural way to this kind of treatment, but Cooper's device of "quantifier storage" for handling scope ambiguities for which there is no independent evidence of syntactic ambiguities is one of the serious options in this domain.

9 "It appears to me that the syntactical analyses of particular fragmentary languages that have been suggested by transformational grammarians, even if successful in correctly characterizing the declarative sentences of those languages, will prove to lack semantic relevance; and I fail to see any great interest in syntax except as a preliminary to semantics." (from the notorious footnote 2 of UG, p.223 in Montague 1974.) Footnote 2, which goes on to criticize other aspects of "existing syntactical efforts by Chomsky and his associates", was not designed to endear Montague to generative linguists, although in the beginning of the paper he does present himself as agreeing more with Chomsky than with many philosophers about the goals of formal theories of syntax and semantics.

10 but not indispensable; the lambda-calculus just gives one very good way to provide compositional names for functions, and function-argument structure was one of Montague's principal ways, following Frege, of providing a compositional interpretation of complex syntactic part-whole structures.

11 The use of individual concepts as central to the interpretation of nouns and noun phrases was mostly abandoned in later work, following the lead of Bennett (1975). See Dowty et al. (1981) for discussion, but also see Janssen (1983) for defense.

12 Although it was principally through PTQ that this analysis became influential in linguistics, this may be one of the ideas that Montague got from David Lewis, since it also appears in Lewis (1970), embedded in a theory which combined a categorial grammar phrase-structure with a transformational component.

13 There has not been much explicit discussion of pros and cons of the method of

fragments in theoretical linguistics, and the methodological gap is in principle even wider now that some theories don't believe in rules at all. In practice the gap is not always unbridgeable, since e.g. principles for interpreting LF tree structures can be comparable to descriptions of rules of a Montague Grammar whose analysis trees those LFs resemble.

14   See Bach's (1976, 1979b) re-examination of generalized transformations in this context.

15   The author sat in on some of Montague's seminars at UCLA along with David Lewis, who was very helpful in interpreting Montague to her. The 1970 two-part workshop at which Montague presented PTQ in September and Partee (1973a) was presented as commentary in December took place only months before Montague's untimely death in early 1971. Partee began teaching seminars on Montague Grammar in 1971 and 1972 at UCLA, Stanford, the Philosophy and Linguistics Institute organized by Donald Davidson and Gil Harman at UC Irvine (Summer 1971), and the 1972 California Linguistics Institute at UC Santa Cruz; and continued at the University of Massachusetts at Amherst from 1972 in courses and seminars and at the 1974 Linguistic Institute in Amherst. In the course of giving these seminars and various talks on Montague Grammar and transformational grammar, the author was greatly aided by colleagues and students, especially David Kaplan, David Lewis, Frank Heny, Michael Bennett, Donald Victery, Enrique Delacruz and Richmond Thomason at the beginning, and Terry Parsons and Ed Gettier at UMass.

16   The generation of a single syntactic tree structure requires Partee's (1973c) amendment to the effect that the syntactic rules generate trees rather than strings.

17   Linguists not bound by the commitment to making truth conditions and entailment relations central to semantic adequacy criteria have the possibility of not representing scope as a linguistic ambiguity at all. This was a possibility sometimes entertained in Chomsky's earlier work, allowed for in current Prague school work such as Hajičová and Sgall (1987), explored in the context of parsing by Hindle and Rooth (1993), and in the context of Discourse Representation Theory by Reyle (1993); see also Poesio (1991, 1994).

18   Earlier proposals for directly generated phrasal conjunction in the transformational literature, by Lakoff and Peters, by Schane, and by others, concerned "non-Boolean" *and*; "Boolean" *and* was quite uniformly believed to be syntactically derived from sentential conjunction.

19   Max Cresswell (personal communication) once remarked that theorists who say that their theories have no problem with propositional attitudes usually turn out not to have developed their theories as far as those theories for which one can identify what the problems are.

20   But see Janssen's (1983) cautionary advice that failures of compositionality are often symptoms of defects in analysis.

21   "L. T. F. Gamut" is a pseudonym for five co-authors: the philosophers Jeroen Groenendijk and Martin Stokhof, the logicians Johan van Benthem and Dick de Jongh, and the linguist Henk Verkuyl; the initials L. T. F. stand for the Dutch words for "logic, linguistics, philosophy", and "Gamut" is derived from the authors' (then) institutions, the Universities of Groningen, Amsterdam, and Utrecht.

II Generalized Quantifier Theory

2 The Semantics of Determiners

EDWARD L. KEENAN

The study of generalized quantifiers over the past 15 years has enriched enormously our understanding of natural language determiners (Dets). It has yielded answers to questions raised independently within generative grammar and it has provided us with new semantic generalizations, ones that were basically unformulable without the conceptual and technical apparatus of generalized quantifier theory. Here we overview results of both these types.

Historical Note

It was Montague (1969a) who first interpreted natural language NPs as generalized quantifiers (though this term was not used by him). But it was only in the early 1980s with the publication of B&C (Barwise and Cooper 1981) that the study of natural language Dets took on a life of its own. Also from this period are early versions of K&S (Keenan and Stavi 1986) and Higginbotham and May (1981). The former fed into subsequent formal studies such as van Benthem (1984, 1986) and Westerståhl (1985). The latter focussed on specific linguistic applications of binary quantifiers, a topic initiated in Altham and Tennant (1974), drawing on the mathematical work of Mostowski (1957), and pursued later in a more general linguistic setting in van Benthem (1989) and Keenan (1987b, 1992). Another precursor to the mathematical study of generalized quantifiers is Lindström (1966) who provides the type notation used to classify quantifiers in many later studies.

Since these beginnings, work on the semantics of Dets has proliferated, both empirically and mathematically. Westerståhl (1989) provides an historical overview up to 1987. Some important collections of articles are: van Benthem and ter Meulen (1985), Gärdenfors (1987), and van der Does and van Eijck (forthcoming). From a more linguistic perspective we note Lappin (ed., 1988b) and ter Meulen and Reuland (1987). K&W (Keenan and Westerståhl, forthcoming) is a recent overview relating the natural language studies and concurrent work in mathematical logic.

1   Background Notions and Terminology

Terminology first: In the S in (1), we call *work hard a (tensed) one place predicate* or P_1,

(1)   Most students work hard

most students is a *noun phrase* or NP, *student(s)* is a *(common) noun* or N, and *most* is a *(one place) Determiner* or $Det_{(1)}$. So we think of a Det_1 as combining with an N to make an NP, the latter combining with P_1s to make Ss.

Semantically we interpret Ss like (1) as true (**T**) or false (**F**) in a given situation (state of affairs). A situation s consists, in part, of a *universe* E_s, the set of (possibly abstract) objects under discussion in s; we think of tense marking on P_1s as giving us some information about the situation we are to interpret the sentence in. Given a situation s, we interpret P_1s as subsets (called *properties*) of E_s and we interpret NPs as *generalized quantifiers* (GQs), that is as functions from properties to truth values (possible sentence interpretations). Using upper case bold for interpretations (in a situation s), the truth value of (1) is given by:

(2)   (**MOST STUDENTS**)(**WORK HARD**)

That is, the truth value (**T** or **F**) which (1) is interpreted as in s is the one the function **MOST STUDENTS** maps the set **WORK HARD** to. (An equivalent formulation common in the literature: interpret *most students* as a set of properties and interpret (1) as **T** if the set **WORK HARD** is an element of that set).

Now the denotation of *most students* is built from those of *most* and *student*. And given a universe E, Ns like *student* (as well as *tall student*, *student who Mary likes*, etc.) are, like (tenseless) P_1s, interpreted as properties over E (= subsets of E). So Dets like *most* can be represented as functions from P_E, the set of properties over E, into GQ_E, the set of generalized quantifiers over E (We usually suppress the subscript E when no confusion results).

We illustrate the interpretation of some Dets. Let E be given and held constant throughout the discussion. Consider **EVERY**, the denotation of *every*. We want to say that *Every student is a vegetarian* is (interpreted as) true, **T**, iff each object in the set **STUDENT** is also in the set **VEGETARIAN**. Generalizing,

(3)   For all properties A, B **EVERY**$(A)(B) = $ **T** iff $A \subseteq B$

What (3) does is define the function **EVERY**. Its domain is the collection P_E of subsets of E and its value at any A in P_E is the GQ **EVERY** (A) – namely, that function from properties to truth values which maps an arbitrary property B to **T** if and only if A is a subset of B. Here are some other simple cases which employ some widely used notation:

(4) a. **NO**$(A)(B) = $ **T** iff $A \cap B = \emptyset$

Here $\emptyset$ is the empty set and (4a) says that *No A's are B's* is true iff the set of things which are members of both A and B is empty.

b. **(FEWER THAN FIVE)**$(A)(B) = $ **T** iff $|A \cap B| < 5$
c. **(ALL BUT TWO)**$(A)(B) = $ **T** iff $|A - B| = 2$

Here $A - B$ is the set of things in A which are not in B, and in general for C a set, $|C|$ is the cardinality of C that is, the number of elements of C. So (4b) says that *All but two A's are B's* is true iff the number of things in A which are not in B is exactly 2.

d. **(THE TEN)**$(A)(B) = $ **T** iff $|A| = 10$ and $A \subseteq B$

This says e.g. that *The ten children are asleep* is true iff the number of children in question is 10 and each one is asleep.

e. **NEITHER**$(A)(B) = $ **T** iff $|A| = 2$ & $A \cap B = \emptyset$
f. **MOST**$(A)(B) = $ **T** iff $|A \cap B| > |A - B|$

Here we have taken *most* in the sense of *more than half* □
To test that the definitions above have been properly understood the reader should try to fill in appropriately the blanks in (5).

(5) **(MORE THAN FOUR)**$(A)(B) = $ **T** iff ____
BOTH$(A)(B) = $ **T** iff ____
(EXACTLY TWO)$(A)(B) = $ **T** iff ____
(JUST TWO OF THE TEN)$(A)(B) = $ **T** iff ____
(LESS THAN HALF THE)$(A)(B) = $ **T** iff ____
(BETWEEN FIVE AND TEN)$(A)(B) = $ **T** iff ____

Finally, Keenan and Moss (1985) extend the class of Dets to include two place ones such as *more ... than ...* which they treat as combining with two Ns to form NPs like *more students than teachers*. Such expressions have the basic distribution of NPs: they occur as subjects (6a), objects (6b), objects of prepositions (6c); they occur in ECM = "raising to object" constructions (6d), and they move under passive (6d).

(6) a. More students than teachers came to the party
b. John knows exactly as many students as teachers
c. Mary has talked with fewer students than teachers
d. We believe more students than teachers to have signed the petition
e. More students than teachers are believed to have signed the petition

We may correctly interpret NPs like *more students than teachers* as the value of the Det$_2$ function (**MORE ... THAN ...**) at the pair ⟨**STUDENT, TEACHER**⟩ of properties given as follows (writing **MORE** *A* **THAN** *B* instead of (**MORE ... THAN ...**)(*A*)(*B*)):

(7)   For all properties *A, B, C* (**MORE** *A* **THAN** *B*)(*C*) = **T** iff |*A* ∩ *C*| > |*B* ∩ *C*|

Again on this pattern the reader should be able to define the functions in (8). See Beghelli (1992, 1993) for much more extensive discussion of cardinal comparatives.

(8)   **FEWER ... THAN ..., FIVE MORE ... THAN ..., EXACTLY AS MANY ... AS ..., MORE THAN TWICE AS MANY ... AS ..., THE SAME NUMBER OF ... AS ...**

2   Two Types of Generalizations

One type of generalization we will be concerned with involves characterizing linguistically significant classes of NPs in terms of the Dets used to build them. (So here semantic work converges with such syntactic work as Abney (1987), Stowell (1987, 1991) and Szabolcsi (1987b), which takes Dets as the "heads" of expressions of the form [Det + *N*]). For example, which NPs occur naturally in the post *of* position in partitives is significantly determined by the choice of Det:

(9)   a.   Two of the/these/John's cats
      b.   *Two of no/most/few cats

Changing the *N* from *cats* to *students* or *pictures that John took* does not change grammaticality in (9a) or (9b), but changing the Dets may. Similarly which NPs occur naturally in Existential There contexts, (10a,b), and which license negative polarity items in the predicate, (11a,b), are significantly determined by the choice of Det.

(10) a.   There aren't more than ten boys in the room
      b.   *There aren't most boys in the room

(11) a.   Fewer than five students here have ever been to Pinsk
      b.   *Some students here have ever been to Pinsk

Queries like those in (12) determine a second type of Det-based generalization:

(12) a. Are there constraints on which functions from properties to generalized quantifiers can be denoted by natural language Dets?

  b. Do lexical (= syntactically simple) Dets satisfy stronger constraints on their possible denotations than syntactically complex ones?

Questions like these arise naturally within generalized quantifier theory, but they also have a natural interpretation in a more classical linguistic setting. An affirmative answer to (12a) limits the task faced by the language learner and thus helps account for how the semantic system is learned with limited exposure to imperfect data. An affirmative answer to (12b) is even more interesting from the learning theory perspective. Modulo idioms, syntactically complex expressions are interpreted as a function of their parts. Thus if we know how a complex expression is built and we know what its parts mean, we can figure out what the entire expression means. So a significant part of the learning problem in semantics reduces to the learning of the meanings of lexical items (including grammatical morphology).

Both types of questions we raise push us to consider as large a class of Dets as possible. The more Dets we consider the more NPs we classify and the more significant are claims concerning constraints on Det denotations.

Let us first then overview the classes of Dets we consider. The classes overlap and are only informally given; later we provide several precisely defined subclasses of Dets. Our purpose is to make the reader aware of the diversity of NP and Det types we generalize over. Some linguists would prefer to analyze some of our complex Dets differently. But eliminating some of our examples preserves the generalizations we make, since they hold for the larger class. Delimiting the class too narrowly by contrast runs the risk that our generalizations will be vitiated when new examples are added. Our discussion of Det$_1$s draws extensively on K&S.

3 Some Types of Determiners in English

Lexical Dets
  every, each, all, some, a, no, several, neither, most, the, both, this, my, these, John's, ten, a few, a dozen, many, few
Cardinal Dets
  exactly/approximately/more than/fewer than/at most/only ten, infinitely many, two dozen, between five and ten, just finitely many, an even/odd number of, a large number of
Approximative Dets
  approximately/about/nearly/around fifty, almost all/no, hardly any, practically no
Definite Dets
  the, that, this, these, my, his, John's, the ten, these ten, John's ten

Exception Dets

all but ten, all but at most ten, every ... but John, no ... but Mary,

Bounding Dets

exactly ten, between five and ten, most but not all, exactly half the, (just) one ... in ten, only SOME (= some but not all; upper case = contrastive stress), just the LIBERAL, only JOHN's

Possessive Dets

my, John's, no student's, either John's or Mary's, neither John's nor Mary's

Value Judgment Dets

too many, a few too many, (not) enough, surprisingly few, ?many, ?few

Proportionality Dets

exactly half the/John's, two out of three, (not) one ... in ten, less than half the/John's, a third of the/John's, ten per cent of the/John's, not more than half the/John's

Partitive Dets

most/two/none/only some of the/John's, more of John's than of Mary's, not more than two of the ten

Negated Dets

not every, not all, not a (single), not more than ten, not more than half, not very many, not quite enough, not over a hundred, not one of John's

Conjoined Dets

at least two but not more than ten, most but not all, either fewer than ten or else more than a hundred, both John's and Mary's, at least a third and at most two thirds of the, neither fewer than ten nor more than a hundred

Adjectively Restricted Dets

John's biggest, more male than female, most male and all female, the last ... John visited, the first ... to set foot on the Moon, the easiest ... to clean, whatever ... are in the cupboard

The three dots in the expressions above indicate the locus of the *N* argument. E.g. in *not one student in ten* we treat *not one ... in ten* as a discontinuous Det. In general we have two *prima facie* reasons for positing discontinuous analyses:

One, often the *N* + postnominal material has by itself no reasonable interpretation and so is not naturally treated as a constituent. Thus if we analyzed *not one student in ten* as [*not one* [*student in ten*]] we should have to assign a meaning to *student in ten*, but this string seems meaningless. So does *student but John* in *no student but John* and *man to set foot on the Moon* in *the first man to set foot on the Moon*.

And two, often the presence of the postnominal material and the prenominal material are not independent. If the *N* + postnominal material, such as *student in ten* above, were a constituent it would have to be able to combine with Dets (e.g. *not one*) prenominally. But in fact the choice of Det is highly constrained. How would we block *the/this/John's student in ten* and *the/this/Mary's/one student but John*?

Our point here is simply that there are some sensible reasons (K&S) for treating the complex expressions above as Dets. Our analysis is certainly not without problems of its own (see Lappin (1988a) and Rothstein (1988)) and very possibly some of our cases will find a non-discontinuous analysis (see Moltmann, forthcoming, and von Fintel (1993b) on exception Dets).

Finally we note some further candidates for two (and $k > 2$) place Dets. The most natural cases are the cardinal comparatives like *more ... than ...* and *as many ... as ...* mentioned in (6) and (8). But Keenan & Moss (1985), the most extensive discussion of k-place Dets, suggest for example a 2 place analysis of *every ... and ...* in (13).

(13) a. every man and woman jumped overboard
      b. **(EVERY ... AND ...)(MAN,WOMAN)(JUMPED OVERBOARD)**
      c. **(EVERY ... AND ...)(A,B)(C) = T** iff **EVERY** (A)(C) = T and **EVERY** (B)(C) = T

On this analysis (13a) would be true iff every man jumped overboard and every woman jumped overboard, in fact the natural interpretation of (13a). Possibly (13a) has another interpretation on which it means that everyone who was both a man and a woman jumped overboard. This is accommodated by treating *man* and *woman* as conjoined Ns, combined then with the Det_1 *every*. Such an analysis is less implausible in *every author and critic*. One advantage of the 2 place analysis of *every ... and ...* is that it generalizes naturally to $k > 2$ place Dets. In *every man, woman and child* we allow that *every ... and ...* has combined directly with three Ns. So we might treat *every ... and ...* as a Det of variable arity, combining with $k \geq 1$ Ns to form an NP and taking the form *every* in the case $k = 1$.

Before turning to our promised generalizations we note first one restriction on the Dets we generalize about. Namely, we limit ourselves to Dets that are *extensional*, as defined by:

(14) A Det_1 D is *extensional* iff for all common noun phrases N, N' if N and N' are interpreted as the same set in a situation s then [D + N] and [D + N'] are interpreted as the same GQ in s.

One sees that *not enough* and *too many* are not extensional: we can imagine a situation in which the doctors and the lawyers are the same individuals but *Not enough doctors attended the meeting* is true and *Not enough lawyers attended the meeting* is false (say we need a hundred doctors for a quorum and just one lawyer for legal purposes, and just 95 doctor-lawyers show up). Judgments concerning the interpretation and extensionality of *many* and *few* are problematic in the literature. K&S argue that they are not extensional but B&C, Westerståhl (1985) and Lappin (1988a) attempt more extensional treatments, though their proposals are not identical. In this paper we shall largely exclude *many* and *few* from the generalizations we propose since our judgments regarding their interpretations are variable and often unclear. Comparable problems obtain for Det$_2$s when *many* modifies them, as in *many more students than teachers* [*came to the party*].

4   Generalizations about English Determiners

Let us write DNP (*Determined NPs*) for NPs built from a Det and an appropriate number of Ns. Some semantic properties of DNPs are determined by the semantic nature of their Ns and other of their properties are determined by the Det.

For example, whether a DNP is animate, human or female is determined by the nature of its Ns. More generally, whether a DNP satisfies the selectional restrictions of a predicate is determined by its Ns. Thus #*Every ceiling laughed* is bizarre (here noted #) since ceilings are not the kind of things that can laugh. And the judgment doesn't change if *every* is replaced by *most of John's* or *at least two but not more than ten*.

For DNPs built from Det$_2$s both Ns are relevant (Keenan, 1987c). Thus *Fewer girls than boys laughed at that joke* is natural, but **Fewer floors than ceilings laughed . . .*, **Fewer children than ceilings laughed . . .*, and **Fewer floors than children laughed . . .*

Here we are concerned with properties of DNPs that are due to their Dets rather than their Ns. As a first case, we consider several *monotonicity generalizations*, including the linguistic problem of characterizing the subject NPs which license negative polarity items, discussed in depth in Ladusaw (this volume). We shall later provide a general definition of monotonicity which will have (15) and (16) as special cases:

> (15)   A function F from properties to truth values is *increasing* if and only if for all properties A, B if $F(A) = \mathbf{T}$ and $A \subseteq B$ then $F(B) = \mathbf{T}$. An NP is said to be *increasing* if it always denotes an increasing function. One verifies that an NP X is increasing by checking that it satisfies **Test 1** below (making changes in number agreement where appropriate):

Test 1   If all A's are Bs and X is an A then X is a B

For example *more than six women* is increasing since if all A's are B's and the number of women with property A is more than six then all those women with property A are also ones with property B, so more than six women are B's. By contrast *fewer than six women* is not increasing: Imagine a situation in which exactly four women are A's, all A's are B's, and there are many B's who are not A's, including as it happens two women. Then *Fewer than six women are A's* is true but *Fewer than six women are B's* is false, so *fewer than six women* is not increasing. The same situation shows that *exactly four women* is also not increasing.

Whether a DNP is increasing is determined by the choice of Det and not the choice of N. If [D + *women*] is increasing then so is [D + *men*], [D + *students who John knows*], etc.

For the most part, syntactically simple (= *lexical*) NPs are increasing. Here is a snapshot of the lexical NPs of English: they include one productive subclass, the Proper Nouns: *John, Mary, . . . , Siddartha, Chou en Lai, . . .* ("productive" = new members may be added without changing the language significantly). They also include listable sprinklings of (i) personal pronouns – *he/him, . . .* and their plurals *they/them*; (ii) demonstratives – *this/that* and *these/those*; (iii) possessive pronouns – *his/hers . . . /theirs*; and (iv) possibly the "indefinite pronouns" *everyone, everybody*; *someone/body*; and *no one/body*, though these expressions appear to have meaningful parts. We might also include some uses of Dets, as *all* in *A good time was had by all*, *some* in *Some like it hot*, and *many* and *few* in *Many are called but few are chosen*, though the lexical status of these "NPs" is again doubtful as we are inclined to interpret them as having an understood N *people* to account for their +*human* interpretation (a requirement not imposed by the Dets themselves).

Now one verifies that except for *few* and the "*n*" words (*no one, nobody*) the lexical NPs above are increasing. Moreover the exceptions, while not increasing, have the dual property of being *decreasing*.

(16)   A function F from properties to truth values is *decreasing* iff for all properties A, B if $A \subseteq B$ and $F(B) = \mathbf{T}$ then $F(A) = \mathbf{T}$. To verify that an NP X is decreasing verify that it satisfies **Test 2**:

Test 2   If all A's are B's and X is a B then X is an A

Clearly if all A's are B's and the number of women who are B's is less than six then the number who are A's must be less than six (if it were six or greater then all those women would be B's, making the number of women who are B's greater than six, contrary to assumption). Thus *fewer than six women* is decreasing. So is *no woman* and so are *no one, nobody* and *few* (*people*). Now, calling a function *monotonic* if it is either increasing or decreasing and calling an NP *monotonic* if it always denotes a monotonic function we claim:

(17)   Lexical NPs are always monotonic, almost always monotonic increasing

(18)   Lexical Det$_1$s always form "continuous" NPs, usually monotonic (increasing)

(17) has already been supported, but we should note that many NPs are not monotonic at all (whence even the weak form of (17) is logically very

non-trivial). We have already seen that *exactly four women* is not increasing. But equally it is not decreasing: if all A's are B's and exactly four women are B's it might be that just two are A's, the other two being B's who are not A's. Thus *exactly four women* is neither increasing nor decreasing, hence not monotonic. Here are some other NPs that are not monotonic:

(19)   between five and ten students, about a hundred students, every/ no student but John, every student but not every teacher, both John and Bill but neither Sam nor Mary, most of the students but less than half the teachers, either fewer than five students or else more than a hundred students, more boys than girls, exactly as many boys as girls

Thus the kinds of functions denotable by the NPs in (19) are not available as denotations for lexical NPs in English. In fact K&S show that over a finite universe each GQ is denotable by some NP. So (17) is a strong semantic claim about natural language, one that restricts the hypotheses the language learner need consider in learning the meanings of NPs.

To support (18) observe that of the lexical Det_1s in Section 3, most clearly build increasing NPs: *each, every, all, some, my, the, this, these, several, . . . most*. But *no* and *neither* clearly build decreasing NPs. *many* and *few* we put aside for the reasons given earlier. The remaining case is bare numerals, like *two*, which are problematic since their interpretation seems to vary somewhat with the linguistic context. In environments like *Are there two free seats in the front row?*, we interpret *two free seats* as *at least two . . .* , which is clearly increasing. In contexts like *Two students stopped by while you were out* the speaker seems to be using *two students* to designate two people he could identify, and as far as he himself (but not the addressee) is concerned he could refer to them as *they* or *those two students*. So this usage also seems increasing. But in answer to a question *How many students came to the lecture? – Two* the sense is "exactly two (students)", which is non-monotonic. It is perhaps not unreasonable to think of the basic uses of bare numerals as increasing (B&C, K&S), and the non-monotonic uses as ones which draw on additional information from the context.

But even if we take as basic the non-monotonic sense of bare numerals, it remains true that the GQs denotable by NPs of the form [Det + N] with Det lexical are a proper subset of the set of denotable GQs. Reason: GQs denotable by NPs of the form *exactly n A's* are expressible as a conjunction of an increasing NP and a decreasing one: *Exactly n A's* denotes the same as *At least n A's and not more than n A's*, and Thysse (1983) has shown that meets of increasing and decreasing functions are just the continuous functions, defined by:

(20)   *A GQ F over E is continuous* iff $\forall A, B, C \subseteq E$, if $A \subseteq B \subseteq C$ and $F(A) = F(C) = \mathbf{T}$ then $F(B) = \mathbf{T}$.

So monotonic NPs are special cases of continuous ones. But many NPs are not continuous. Typical examples are disjunctions of increasing with decreasing NPs (*either fewer than six students or else more than ten students*) or disjunctions of properly continuous ones (*either exactly two dogs or exactly four cats*). Also NPs like *more male than female students* are not continuous. Thus by analogy with the distinction between lexical vs complex NPs we also see that there are functions denotable by complex Dets which are not denotable by lexical ones, examples being the functions denotable by *more male than female* and *either fewer than ten or else more than a hundred*.

Some further monotonicity generalizations are given by the ways the monotonicity of complex NPs and Dets depends on that of the expressions they are built from:

(21) a. Conjunctions and disjunctions of increasing (decreasing) NPs are increasing (decreasing). The corresponding claims hold for Dets. Thus *John and every student* is increasing since both conjuncts are. And *both John's and Bill's* builds increasing NPs (*both John's and Bill's cats*) since each conjunct builds increasing NPs.
   b. Negation reverses monotonicity. Thus *not [more than six cats]* is decreasing since the NP *more than six cats* is increasing. And *not more than six*, as in *at least two and not more than six*, builds decreasing NPs since *more than six* builds increasing ones.
   c. The monotonicity value of partitives is determined by the Det preceding *of*. Thus *less than five of the students* is decreasing since *less than five* builds decreasing NPs.
   d. Possessive Dets, e.g. [*X's*] in [*X's N*], build increasing NPs if X is increasing, decreasing NPs if X is decreasing, and non-monotonic ones if X is not monotonic. Thus *no student's* builds decreasing NPs (*no student's doctor*) since *no student* is decreasing.

A more surprising monotonicity generalization concerns **negative polarity items (npi's)**. To characterize the set of English expressions judged grammatical by native speakers, we must distinguish (22a) and (23a) from their ungrammatical counterparts (22b) and (23b).

(22) a. John hasn't ever been to Moscow
   b. *John has ever been to Moscow

(23) a. John didn't see any birds on the walk
   b. *John saw any birds on the walk

Npi's such as *ever* and *any* above, do not occur freely; classically (Klima 1964) they must be licensed by a "negative" expression, such as *n't* (= *not*). But observe:

(24) a. No student here has ever been to Moscow
      b. *Some student here has ever been to Moscow

(25) a. Neither John nor Mary saw any birds on the walk
      b. *Either John or Mary saw any birds on the walk

(26) a. None of John's students has ever been to Moscow
      b. *One of John's students has ever been to Moscow

The *a*-expressions here are grammatical, the *b*-ones are not. But the pairs differ with respect to their initial NPs, not the presence vs absence of *n't*. *The linguistic problem:* define the class of NPs which license the npi's, and state what, if anything, those NPs have in common with *n't*/*not*.

A syntactic attempt to kill both birds with one stone is to say that just as *n't* is a "reduced" form of *not* so *neither . . . nor . . .* is a reduced form of [*not (either . . . or . . .)*], *none* a reduction of *not one*, and *no* a reduction of *not a*. The presence of *n-* in the reduced forms is thus explained as a remnant of the original *not*. So on this view the licensing NPs above "really" have a *not* in their representation, and that is what such NPs have in common with *n't*. Moreover NPs built from *not* do license npi's:

(27) a. Not a single student here has ever been to Moscow
      b. Not more than five students here have ever been to Moscow

But this solution is insufficiently general (Ladusaw (1983)). The initial NPs in the *a*-sentences below license npi's; those in the *b*-sentences do not. But neither present reduced forms of *not*.

(28) a. Fewer than five students here have ever been to Moscow
      b. *More than five students here have ever been to Moscow
      a. At most four students here have ever been to Moscow
      b. *At least four students here have ever been to Moscow
      a. Less than half the students here have ever been to Moscow
      b. *More than half the students here have ever been to Moscow

A better hypothesis, discovered by Ladusaw (1983), building on the earlier work of Fauconnier (1975, 1979), (see also Zwarts (1981)) is given by:

(29) *The Ladusaw–Fauconnier Generalization (LFG)*
      Negative polarity items occur within arguments of monotonic decreasing functions but not within arguments of monotonic increasing functions

(The *LFG* assumes the properly general definition of *decreasing*; see (32)). Clearly the NPs in (24) – (28) which license npi's are decreasing, and those which do not are not. Also, drawing on (21d) and (21c), we see that the LFG yields correct results for (30) and (31), NP types not considered by Ladusaw or Fauconnier.

(30) No player's agent should ever act without his consent
*Every player's agent should ever act without his consent
Neither John's nor Mary's doctor has ever been to Moscow

(31) None of the teachers and not more than three of the students have ever been to Moscow

To see what property decreasing NPs have in common with negation we must give the properly general definition of *decreasing*.

(32) a. A *partial order* is a pair $(A,\leq)$, where A is a set, the *domain* of the partial order, and $\leq$ is a binary relation on A which satisfies, for all $a, b, d \in A$, $a \leq a$ (reflexivity), $a \leq b$ & $b \leq a \Rightarrow a = b$ (antisymmetry) and $a \leq b$ & $b \leq d \Rightarrow a \leq d$ (transitivity).
b. If A and B are domains of partial orders and F is a function from A into B,
i) F is *increasing* iff for all $x, y \in A$, if $x \leq y$ then $F(x) \leq F(y)$. (That is, if elements x, y of A stand in the order relation in A then their values $F(x)$ and $F(y)$ stand in the order relation in B. So F preserves the order.)
ii) F is *decreasing* iff whenever $x \leq y$ in A then $F(y) \leq F(x)$ in B. So decreasing functions are ones which reverse the order.

Now it is overwhelmingly the case that the sets in which expressions of an arbitrary category denote are domains of partial orders. P_1s denote elements of $P(E)$, the collection of subsets of E, and the ordering relation is just the subset relation, $\subseteq$. (One verifies that $\subseteq$ is reflexive, antisymmetric and transitive). As for Sentence denotations, the set $\{T,F\}$ carries the *implication* order, defined by: $\forall x, y \in \{T,F\}$, $x \leq y$ iff an arbitrary formula of the form "if P then Q" is true when P denotes x and Q denotes y. So the relation obtains in just the following cases: $T \leq T$, $F \leq T$ and $F \leq F$. Again one verifies directly that this relation is a partial order relation. And one sees from our earlier definition (15) that increasing NPs are just the ones which denote order preserving maps from the P_1 order into the implication order. And from (16) we see that decreasing NPs are just the ones that reverse the order relations.

But now we can observe that (ignoring tense) *didn't laugh* denotes $E -$ **LAUGH**, the set of objects under discussion that are not in the **LAUGH** set. So **not** (**n't**) maps each subset A of E to $E - A$. And clearly, if $A \subseteq B$ then $E - B \subseteq E - A$, that is, **not**$(B) \subseteq$ **not**(A), so **not** is decreasing. (So is classical logical negation which maps **T** to **F** and **F** to **T**).

In this way then we find a semantic property that "negative" NPs and negation have in common: They all denote decreasing functions. For more extended and refined discussion see Zwarts (forthcoming) and Nam (forthcoming). We turn now to a second type of generalization.

Constraints on Determiner Denotations

In the interpretation of *Ss* of the form $[[_{NP} \text{Det} + N] + P_1]$ the role of the noun argument is quite different from that of the P_1 argument. It serves to limit the domain of objects we use the predicate to say something about. This simple idea of *domain restriction* is captured in the literature with two independent constraints: *conservativity* and *extension*.

To say that a Det is conservative (CONS) is to say that we can decide whether Det *A*'s are *B*'s if we know which individuals are *A*'s and which of those *A*'s are *B*'s. So for *B* and *C* possibly quite different predicate denotations, if it happens that the *B*'s who are *A*'s are the same individuals as the *C*'s who are *A*'s then *Det A's are B's* and *Det A's are C's* must have the same truth value. Formally, we define:

(33)   A function *D* from P_E to GQs is *conservative* iff $\forall A, B, C \subseteq E$
      if $A \cap B = A \cap C$ then $D(A)(B) = D(A)(C)$

Note that if *D* is CONS as per (33), then for all properties *A,B* we have that $D(A)(B) = D(A)(A \cap B)$, since *B* has the same intersection with *A* as $A \cap B$ does. The converse holds as well. For suppose that for all X,Y $D(X)(Y) = D(X)(X \cap Y)$. We show that *D* satisfies the condition in (33). Let $A \cap B = A \cap C$. Then by the condition on *D*, $D(A)(B) = D(A)(A \cap B) = D(A)(A \cap C)$, by the assumption, $= D(A)(C)$, again by the condition on *D*. □

To check that Det is CONS check that (34a) and (34b) must always have the same truth value (= are logically equivalent), changing singulars to plurals where appropriate.

(34)   a. Det doctor is a vegetarian
      b. Det doctor is both a doctor and a vegetarian

So e.g. *John's* is CONS since *John's doctor is a vegetarian* is logically equivalent to *John's doctor is both a doctor and a vegetarian*.

The apparent triviality of such equivalences suggests, wrongly, that CONS is a very weak condition. K&S show that, for $|E| = n$, the number of conservative functions is 2^{3^n}, whereas the total number of functions from P_E to GQs is 2^{4^n}. Thus in a situation with just 2 individuals there are $2^{16} = 65,536$ functions from P_E to GQs, but only 512 of these are CONS. So conservativity rules out most ways we might associate properties with NP denotations. For example, the function *G* given by $G(A)(B) = 1$ iff $|A| = |B|$ is not CONS. Nonetheless,

(35)   With at most a few exceptions[1] English Dets denote conservative functions

We note finally here that the format in which Conservativity is stated, (33) or its equivalent, does not require that $D(A)(B)$ be a truth value; it just requires that $D(A)(B) = D(A)(C)$ (or $D(A)(A \cap B)$ in the equivalent formulation). Thus it makes sense to ask whether interrogative Dets such as *Which?* are CONS. An affirmative answer would imply that e.g. *Which students are vegetarians?* and *Which students are both students and vegetarians?* are logically the same question, that is, request the same information. And this seems to be the case – a true answer to either of these questions is a true answer to the other. So interrogative *Which?* is CONS.

Moreover (33) is actually just the special case of conservativity for Det_1 denotations. The general statement is: if D is a k-place Det denotation (that is a function from k-tuples of properties to GQs) then D is CONS iff for all k-tuples A and all properties B, C if $A_i \cap B = A_i \cap C$ then $D(A)(B) = D(A)(C)$. In other words if two predicate properties B and C have the same intersection with each noun property, then the Det takes the same value at the noun properties and the first predicate property as it does at the noun properties and the second predicate property. Usually for ease of reading in what follows we just give definitions for the case of Det_1 denotations, assuming the appropriate generalization to Det_k's.

A more subtle constraint satisfied by Det denotations is *Extension* (EXT), first noticed by van Benthem (1984). The intuition is that Dets cannot make crucial reference to objects which fail to have the property expressed by their noun arguments. So English could not have a Det *blik* such that *Blik A's are B's* would mean that there are exactly three things that aren't A's. One might have thought that this was covered by Conservativity but in fact it is not. E.g. given E, the function F defined by $F(A)(B) = \mathbf{T}$ iff $|E-A| = 3$ is CONS. The problem here is that once E is given a condition on $E-A$, the non-A's in E, can always be expressed as a condition on A's, and conservativity allows that we place conditions on the noun arguments A. (See K&W for worked out examples). To test whether crucial reference to non-A's is made we must hold A constant and vary the non-A's, $E-A$. So now we think of a Det denotation D as a function which chooses for each universe E a function D_E from P_E to the generalized quantifiers over E. Then,

(36) D satisfies *Extension*[2] iff $\forall E, E'$ with $A, B \subseteq E$ and $A, B \subseteq E'$, D_E $(A)(B) = D_{E'}(A)(B)$

Thus if D satisfies extension (EXT), then the truth of $D_E(A)(B)$ does not change if we change the non-A's in the universe (and we may continue to write simply $D(A)(B)$ instead of $D_E(A)(B)$ since the truth value does not vary with the choice of E). And we claim:

(37)   The denotations of natural language Dets always satisfy Extension

We note that CONS and EXT are independent: the functional D which maps each E to that function D_E which sends A, B to **T** iff $A = B$ satisfies EXT but D_E fails CONS in each (non-empty) E. By contrast the functional F which maps E to **EVERY**$_E$ if E is finite and **SOME**$_E$ if E is infinite fails to satisfy EXT but in each universe E, F_E is CONS.

The combined effect of CONS and EXT, namely Domain Restriction, is a kind of "logical topicality" condition. It says in effect that the head noun determines the relevant universe for purposes of the statement we are concerned with. Worth noting here is that mathematical languages such as those used in Elementary Arithmetic, Euclidean Geometry or Set Theory are special purpose in that the range of things we can talk about is fixed in advance (numbers, points and line, sets). But natural languages are general purpose – speakers use them to talk about anything they want, and common nouns in English provide the means to delimit "on line" what speakers talk about and quantify over.

Subclasses of Dets: Existential There Ss

So given a universe E, whether an arbitrary Det$_1$ denotation D holds of a pair A,B can only depend on which individuals are A's and which of those are B's. But Dets differ greatly among themselves with regard to how much of this information they use. Below we distinguish several subclasses together with linguistic generalizations based on these classes.

We call a Det denotation D *intersective* (INT) if we can determine the truth of $D(A)(B)$ just by checking which individuals lie in $A \cap B$. So $D(A)(B)$ depends just on $A \cap B$. For example, **MORE THAN TEN** is INT: to know if *More than ten students applauded* we only need to know about individuals in the intersection of **STUDENT** with **APPLAUD**. We need not concern ourselves with students who didn't applaud. Also **SOME** in the sense of *at least one* is INT. **SOME**$(A)(B) = $ **T** iff $A \cap B \neq \varnothing$, so we decide whether *Some A's are B's* just by checking the set of A's who are B's. Since **SOME** corresponds to the existential quantifier in logic we shall sometimes refer to intersective Dets as *generalized existential* Dets.

By contrast *co-intersective* (= CO-INT) Dets just depend on $A–B$, the complement of $A \cap B$ relative to A. For example, whether *All but ten A's are B's* is true is decided just by checking that $A–B$, the set of A's that are not B's, has cardinality 10. Similarly **EVERY** $(A)(B) = $ **T** iff $A - B = \varnothing$. (Note that $A - B = \varnothing$ iff $A \subseteq B$). Since such Dets include **EVERY** and **ALL BUT TEN** they will also be called *generalized universal*. We define:

(38)   a. D is *intersective* (INT) iff for all A, A', B, $B' \subseteq E$,
             if $A \cap B = A' \cap B'$ then $D(A)(B) = D(A')(B')$
       b. D is *co-intersective* (CO-INT) iff for all A, A', B, $B' \subseteq E$,
             if $A - B = A' - B'$ then $D(A)(B) = D(A')(B')$

(38a) for example says that an intersective D cannot tell the difference between arguments A,B and A',B' if they have the same intersection. That is, whether $D(A)(B)$ is true just depends on the intersection of A with B.

As we shall be primarily concerned with INT and CO-INT below, let us contrast them first with Dets that are neither. *Proportionality* Dets like *most, less than half the* and *over ten per cent* (*of the*) are an important case in point. To decide whether most students read the *Times*, we must be able to compare the students who do with those who don't. Just knowing which students read the *Times* is insufficient to decide whether most do; and just knowing which students don't is also insufficient. Formally,

(39) a. D is *basic proportional* iff for some $0 < n < m$
       $\forall A, B\ D(A)(B) = \mathbf{T}$ iff $|A \cap B| = (n/m)\cdot|A|$ or $\forall A, B\ D(A)(B) = \mathbf{T}$
       iff $|A \cap B| > (n/m)\cdot|A|$
      b. The *proportionality Ds* are the non-trivial boolean compounds of
       basic proportional ones.

From (39b) we see that *exactly a third* (*of the*) is proportional since it denotes the same function as *at least a third and not more than a third*. Equally (39b) covers *co-proportional* Dets like *all but a third* when the noun argument A is finite – the only case where proportions like $(n/m)\cdot|A|$ are intuitive. In such a case *All but a third of the A's are B's* must have the same value as *Exactly two thirds of the A's are B's*. The non-triviality condition rules out **ALL AND NO** (expressible for example as *more than half and less than half*).

Thus to decide whether a Det D relates A and B we must know more if D is a proportionality one than if D is merely INT or CO-INT. In fact B&C show that even if we restrict the universe E to be finite, *more than half* is not definable in first order logic. This claim extends (see K&W and references cited there) to the full class of basic proportional Dets. These results also imply that cardinal comparative Det$_2$s like **MORE ... THAN ...** are not definable in first order; if they were we could use them to define **MORE THAN HALF** in first order by: **MORE THAN HALF**$(A)(B) = $**MORE**$(A \cap B)$**THAN**$(A–B)(E)$. This just says that *more than half the A's are B's* means *more A's who are B's than A's who are not B's exist*. These remarks lay to rest the issue about whether natural language semantics can be represented in first order logic: it can't.

We consider now the (co-)intersective Dets in more detail. Observe first that the INT Dets considered so far satisfy a stronger condition than intersectivity: they are *cardinal* (CARD): the value of $D(A)(B)$ only depends on $|A \cap B|$, the cardinality of $A \cap B$. Dually the CO-INT Dets are *co-cardinal* (CO-CARD); their value just depends on $|A–B|$. The formal definitions of these notions follow those for INT and CO-INT, replacing everywhere $A \cap B$ with $|A \cap B|$, etc. Some examples:

SOME CARDINAL DETS: at least/more than/fewer than/exactly ten; between five and ten; not more than ten; either fewer than ten or else more than a hundred; just finitely many

SOME CO-CARDINAL DETS: all, almost all, not all, all but ten; all but at most ten; all but finitely many

Note that not all CARD (CO-CARD) Dets are first order definable: *just finitely many* (and its boolean complement *infinitely many*) is not; nor is *all but finitely many*. So the properly proportional Dets do not have a monopoly on being non-first order definable.

Note also that Det$_2$s like *more . . . than . . .* are INT and in fact CARD. To say that a Det$_2$ D is INT is to say that the value of $D(A_1, A_2)(B)$ depends just on the intersections $A_1 \cap B$ and $A_2 \cap B$. To say that it is CARD just says that it depends on the cardinalities of these intersections. And in fact we can decide the truth of *More A_1's than A_2's are B's* if we know $|A_1 \cap B|$ and $|A_2 \cap B|$ so **MORE . . . THAN . . .** is CARD and so *a fortiori* INT. For further discussion of such Det$_2$s see Keenan and Moss (1985) and Beghelli (1992, 1993).

Are there (co-)intersective Dets in English that are not (co-)cardinal? There seem to be no syntactically simple cases, but two candidates for somewhat complex ones are *Exceptive Dets* such as *no/every . . . but John* in NPs like *no student but John/every student but John* and *Cardinal Adjectival Comparative Dets* like *more male than female* in *more male than female students*. In both cases alternative analyses are certainly possible (see section 3). But interpreting them as Dets they clearly fall into the (co-)intersective class:

(40)   a.   (**NO** A **BUT JOHN**)(B) = **T** iff $A \cap B = \{$John$\}$
       b.   (**EVERY** A **BUT JOHN**)(B) = **T** iff $A{-}B = \{$John$\}$

(40a) says that *No student but John laughed* is true iff the set of students who laughed has only John as an element. So the value of **NO . . . BUT JOHN** at a pair A,B of properties is decided just by checking their intersection, so **NO . . . BUT JOHN** is intersective. Dually **EVERY . . . BUT JOHN**$(A)(B)$ just depends on $A{-}B$ so it is co-intersective. Equally taking adjectives like *male* and *female* as absolute, that is the male A's are just the A's who are male individuals, so **MALE**(A) = **MALE**$(E) \cap A$, the reader may check that *more male than female* defined in (41) is intersective but not cardinal.

(41)   **MORE MALE THAN FEMALE**$(A)(B)$ = **T** iff $|\textbf{MALE}(A) \cap B| > |\textbf{FEMALE}(A) \cap B|$

The notions of (co-)intersectivity play an important role in many linguistically revealing generalizations. Here is a first, non-obvious one. We have been interpreting Ss like *Some swans are black* directly as **SOME(SWAN)(BLACK)**. But in standard logic it is represented as $(\exists x)$ (Swan(x) & Black(x)), where the quantification is over all the objects in the model, not just the swans. In our variable free notation this would be **SOME**(E)(**SWAN** $\cap$ **BLACK**). This formulation eliminates the restriction to swans in favor of quantifying over all the objects in the universe, and it preserves logical equivalence with the original by replacing the original predicate property **BLACK** with an appropriate boolean compound of the noun property and the predicate property, **SWAN ∩ BLACK**. Thus *some* does not make essential use of the domain restriction imposed by the noun argument. The same equivalence obtains if we replace *some* by e.g. *exactly two*. *Exactly two swans are black* is logically equivalent to *Exactly two objects are both swans and are black*.

We shall say then that quantifiers like *some* and *exactly two* are *sortally reducible*, meaning that we can eliminate the restriction on the domain of quantification, compensating by building a new predicate property as some boolean compound (in our examples it was boolean compounds with *and*) of the original noun property and the original predicate property. Formally

(42)   For each E, a function D from P_E to GQs is *sortally reducible* iff there is a two place boolean function h such that for all $A, B \subseteq E$, $D(A)(B) = D(E)(h(A,B))$. D is called *inherently sortal* if there is no such h.

Query: Which English Dets are sortally reducible, and which are inherently sortal? One other reducible one comes to mind immediately, based on the standard logic translation *All swans are black*: $(\forall x)(\text{Swan}(x) \rightarrow \text{Black}(x))$. This just says that **ALL(SWAN)(BLACK) = ALL(E)(¬SWAN ∨ BLACK)**, where here the boolean compound has been built with complement and disjunction (drawing on the equivalence of $(P \rightarrow Q)$ and $(¬P \vee Q)$). Thus like *some*, *all* is sortally reducible. By contrast *most* is not. *Most swans are black* provably has no paraphrase of the form (For most x)(... Swan(x) ... Black(x) ...) where the expression following (*For most x*) is a formula built from the predicates *Swan* and *Black* (as many times as we like) using any combination of *and*, *or*, and *not*. Now in fact Keenan (1993) provides a complete answer to the query:

(43)   A conservative D from P_E to GQ_E is sortally reducible iff D is intersective or D is co-intersective

We turn now to the role of intersectivity in providing an answer to a problem which arises in the context of generative grammar. Consider:

(44)   There wasn't more than one student at the party
Are there more dogs than cats in the garden?
There was no one but John in the building at the time
Weren't there more male than female students at the party?

Such Ss, called Existential There (ET) sentences, are used to affirm, deny or query the existence of objects (e.g. students) with a specified property (e.g. being at the party). NPs like *more than one student* which naturally occur in such Ss will be called *existential NPs*. So the NPs italicized in (45) are not existential, as the Ss are either ungrammatical or assigned an unusual interpretation.

(45)   *There wasn't *John* at the party
      *There were *most students* on the lawn
      *Was there *every student* in the garden?
      *There wasn't every student but John in the garden
      *Were there two out of three students in the garden?
      *There weren't John's ten students at the party

The linguistic problem: define the set of existential NPs in English. B&C, drawing on Milsark (1977), were the first to propose a semantic solution to this problem, and they located the solution in the nature of the Dets rather than the NPs themselves. In (46) we present a somewhat different solution, one that draws on theirs and on Keenan (1987a). See ter Meulen and Reuland (1987) for extensive discussion of the empirically problematic issues here.

(46)   NPs which occur naturally in ET contexts are (boolean compounds of) ones built from intersective Dets

The data in (44) and (45) support (46). The clause on boolean compounds correctly predicts the acceptability of Ss like *There were about five dogs and more than ten cats in the kennel*. Equally one proves that boolean compounds of intersective Dets are intersective, whence (46) predicts *There were neither exactly two nor exactly four cats on the mat*.

Thus we have a linguistic property which correlates reasonably well with intersectivity. No corresponding property correlating with co-intersectivity is known. But there is a non-obvious semantic property determined jointly by the INT and CO-INT Dets. Namely, for each universe E, $CONS_E$ (the set of conservative functions over E) is exactly the functions which are buildable by boolean operations on the intersective and co-intersective functions. Here the negation of a Det, e.g. *not more than ten*, denotes the boolean complement of the Det denotation, $\neg(\textbf{MORE THAN TEN})$, where in general $\neg D$ is that function mapping A, B to $\neg(D(A)(B))$, where of course $\neg\textbf{T} = \textbf{F}$ and $\neg\textbf{F} = \textbf{T}$. Similarly $D_1 \wedge D_2$ is that map sending each A, B to $D_1(A)(B) \wedge D_2(A)(B)$. So *At least two and not more than ten A's are B's* is true iff at least two A's are B's and not more than ten A's are B's. And we claim (Keenan (1993)):

(47)   For each universe E, $CONS_E$ = the complete boolean closure of $INT_E \cup CO\text{-}INT_E$

In other words, modulo the boolean operations on Det denotations we can represent $CONS_E$, the possible Det denotations over E, by the generalized existential and generalized universal ones. This is a surprisingly large reduction. Most elements of $CONS_E$ are not intersective or co-intersective. E.g. in a universe of just 3 individuals there are more than 130 million conservative functions, only 510 of which are either intersective or co-intersective. The general figure:

(48)   For $|E| = n$, $|CONS_E| = 2^{3^n}$ and $|INT_E \cup CO\text{-}INT_E| = 2^{2^{n+1}} - 2$

A last property of intersective Dets concerns the role INT plays in yielding the cardinal Dets from the more general class of "logical" Dets. Alongside of such classical quantifiers as *some*, *every*, and *most* we have been treating as Dets "non-logical" expressions such as *John's* and *more male than female*. But for various purposes, such as mathematical or logical study, we want to distinguish these classes, and we can do so in terms of properties of their denotations. Informally first, the "logical" Dets are ones which cannot distinguish among properties according to which particular individuals have them. So such Dets do not themselves make any contingent (= empirical) claims about how the world is. Thus once we are given the set of cats and the set of black things in a situation the truth of *Some/All/Most cats are black* is determined, but that of *John's cats are black* is not. In this latter case we must still distinguish among the individual cats according to whether they are John's or not. Which cats John "owns" in a given situation is a contingent property of that situation and may be different in another situation (even with the same universe). (See K&S for more extensive discussion.) Formally the "logical" Dets are the isomorphism invariant ones:

(49) D is *isomorphism invariant* (ISOM) iff $\forall E$ and all bijections π with domain E, $\pi(D_E) = D_{\pi E}$

By πE is meant $\{\pi(x)|x \in E\}$ and similarly for πA and πB. So π is just a way of replacing the objects in E without omitting any or collapsing any (= mapping different ones to the same one). And by $\pi(D_E)$ is meant that map which sends each $\pi A, \pi B$ to whatever D_E send A, B to. So (49) says in effect that $D_E(A)(B) = D_E(\pi A)(\pi B)$, for all bijections π with domain E. And this just means that the value of $D(A)(B)$ doesn't change if we systematically replace some individuals by others.

One shows that all (co-)cardinal Dets are ISOM. So are the proportionality Dets like *half of the* (but not *half of John's*), and so are definite Dets like *the ten* (but not *John's ten*) which is neither proportional nor (co-)cardinal. And we observe that the cardinal Dets are just the ISOM intersective Dets.

(50)   If D satisfies Extension[2] then
    a. D is cardinal iff D is isomorphism invariant and intersective, and
    b. D is co-cardinal iff D is isomorphism invariant and co-intersective

Definite Dets and NPs

The last result we consider here is again based on B&C. We are concerned to define the set of NPs which occur grammatically following the *of* phrase in partitives such as *more than ten of John's cats*, *each of those students*, and *all but two of his ten children*. Linguists usually consider that such NPs have the form

[Det_1 of NP], one we generalize to [Det_k (of NP)^k] to account for such NPs as *more of John's cats than of Bill's dogs* of the form [Det_2 (of NP)^2].

Now it turns out that the acceptability of an NP in the post *of* position in partitives is significantly determined by its choice of Det (which is in part why, earlier, we treated *more than ten of John's, each of those*, etc. as complex Det_1s). Observe:

(51)   a.   [*at least two of* Det *cats*] is acceptable when Det = *the, the six, the six or more, John's (six (or more)), those(six(or more)), John's doctor's (six(or more))*

b.   [*at least two of* Det *cats*] is not acceptable when Det = *each, no, most, at least/exactly/less than nine, no children's (six)*

To characterize the Dets which build NPs acceptable in plural partitives we need two preliminary observations. First, given $A \subseteq E$, we say that a function G from properties to truth values is *the filter generated by* A iff for all B, $G(B) = \mathbf{T}$ iff $A \subseteq B$. So **EVERY**(A) is the filter generated by A and **THE SIX** (A) is the filter generated by A if $|A| = 6$, otherwise it is **0**, that GQ which sends each subset B of E to 0. And (**JOHN'S SIX**)(A) is the filter generated by (A **which John has**) if in fact John has exactly six A's, otherwise it is **0**.

Secondly, a point we have been ignoring for simplicity of presentation is that given a universe E, there are typically many acceptable ways of interpreting a non-logical Det such as *John's two*. These interpretations differ according to which individual *John* denotes and, for each such individual, which objects that individual stands in the **HAS** relation to. In the general case then, we should think of Dets D as functionals associating with each universe E a *set* D_E of functions from P_E to GQs over E. Our earlier definitions of notions like *cardinal* lift easily to the more general setting. E.g. D is CARD iff for each E, each $F \in D_E$ is CARD as defined earlier (viz., $F(A)(B) = F(A')(B')$ whenever $|A \cap B| = |A' \cap B'|$, for all subsets A,A',B,B' of E). We may now define:

(52) D is *definite* iff D is non-trivial and for all E, all $F \in D_E$, all $A \subseteq E$, $F(A) = 0$ or $F(A)$ is the filter generated by some non-empty $C \subseteq A$. If C always has at least two elements D is called *definite plural*.

The Dets in (51a) are definite plural and those in (51b) are not. And we propose:

(53)   NPs which occur in plural partitive contexts like [*two of* ___] are (conjunctions and disjunctions of) ones built from definite plural Det_1s.

Conclusion

These remarks cover several of the major applications of generalized quantifier theory to linguistic analysis. For each generalization we have made, we encourage the reader to consult the literature referred to. Of necessity an overview omits much fine grained linguistic analysis in favor of comprehensiveness.

NOTES

1   See for example K&S, Johnsen (1987), Westerståhl (1985) and Herburger (forthcoming). All putative counterexamples to Conservativity in the literature are ones in which a sentence of the form *Det A's are B's* is interpreted as $D(B)(A)$, where D is conservative. So the problem is not that the Det fails to be conservative, rather it lies with matching the Noun and Predicate properties with the arguments of the Det denotation. Thus Westerståhl points out that *Ss* with *many* as *Many Scandinavians have won the Nobel Prize* admit of an interpretation in which it means that many Nobel Prize winners have been Scandinavian. Herburger points out that this reversal of the domain restricting and predicate properties is not allowed by all Dets. E.g. *Most Scandinavians have won the Nobel Prize* does not allow such reversal. And the whiff of generality is in the air: Can we find a property of Dets which allows us to predict whether they allow the reversal of the Noun and Predicate properties?
2   See K&W for the appropriate generalization of "satisfies Extension" to the case of "non-logical" Dets, in which case a Det D associates with each non-empty universe E a set of functions from P_E to GQ_E.

3 The Role of Situations in Generalized Quantifiers*

ROBIN COOPER

1 Introduction

In this paper we will look at the role of situations in a situation theoretic treatment of generalized quantifiers.[1] We will use the notation and underlying situation theory of Barwise and Cooper (1991, 1993b), Cooper (1992), Cooper and Poesio (1994c) and the reader is referred to these papers for a more detailed introduction to the tools used here.

We will first introduce some tools needed for treating generalized quantifiers in situation theoretic terms (Section 2). We will then sketch the basic idea of a situation theoretic treatment of generalized quantifiers and its relationship to the traditional set theoretic approach (Section 3). We will isolate three points where situations play a role and discuss each of these roles in the remainder of the paper.

2 Some Tools

2.1 Types and properties

In classical generalized quantifier theory natural language determiners are considered to denote relations between sets. Here we will introduce QUANTIFIER RELATIONS corresponding to determiners. Following Gawron and Peters (1990) and Cooper and Poesio (1994a) we will treat quantifier relations as relations which have two argument roles for a TYPE and a PROPERTY (one-place relation) respectively. For the purposes at hand, the difference between a type and a property is that the first involves reference to a situation whereas the second does not. Thus we may talk of the *type* of "being a woman in situation *s* at time *t''* and the property of "running at time *t'''*". Suppose that an individual *a* has the type of "being a woman in situation *s* at time *t''*" then it will be the case that *s* supports the infon **woman**(*a,t*), i.e. *s* is a part of the world which contains that information. Thus whether an object is of a given type is a question to which there is a definite answer. In this case it depends on the nature of the situation *s*. Suppose now we ask the question whether *a* has the property "running at time *t'''*". In order to provide an answer we need to know which part of the world/situation is being referred to or construe the question as one which quantifies over situations: is there some situation *s* such that *s* supports **run**(*a,t'*)?

Let us now look in more detail at the structure of such types and properties. The type of "being a woman in situation *s* at time *t''*" can be viewed as an abstract which we can represent in the graphic notation EKN (Extended Kamp Notation) of Barwise and Cooper (1991, 1993) as (1a) and in linear notation as (1b).

(1)   a.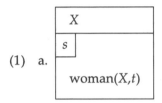

   b. $\lambda[X](s : woman(X,t))$

These notations reveal the structure of the objects. **woman**(*X,t*) is an infon, a certain kind of situation type, which is parametric (represented by the upper case parameter *X*). Thus it represents the "type of situation in which *X* is a woman at *t''*". (2) represents (in both EKN and linear notation) the proposition that *s* is of this type (which is another way of saying that *s* supports the infon).

(2)   a.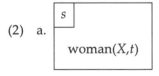

   b. $(s : woman(X,t))$

The expressions in (1) represent the result of abstracting over *X* in this parametric proposition.

An individual *a* will be of this type, just in case the result of applying the type to *a*, notated as in (3) is a true proposition.

(3)   a. 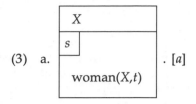 . [a]

b. $\lambda[X](s : \text{woman}(X,t))$. [a]

The proposition resulting from this application is (4). That is to say that (3) and (4) represent the same situation theoretic object.[2]

(4)   a.

s
woman(a,t)

b. $(s : \text{woman}(a,t))$

The proposition is true just in case the situation *s* really does support **woman**(a,t) and false otherwise. The truth or falsity of the proposition is not determined by situation theory but by the world, or, if you like, the model of the world you are working with.

The property of "running at time *t'"* is a one-place relation which can be viewed as an abstract constructed from a parametric infon. This is represented in (5).

(5)   a.

X
run(X,t')

b. $\lambda[X](\text{run}(X,t'))$

The result of applying this to an individual *a* is represented in (6).

(6)   a.

X
run(X,t')

. [a]

b. $\lambda[X](\text{run}(X,t'))$. [a]

(6) is identical to the infon in (7).

(7)   a. run(a,t')
      b. run(a,t')

An infon as such is not true or false. It is a type of situation. We can ask of a given situation whether it supports the infon, i.e. whether it is of that type. Or we can ask whether there is a situation of that type.

3   The basic idea

Following Gawron and Peters (1990), we will treat quantifier relations as relations between types and properties. This means that we will allow ourselves infons of the kind in (8).

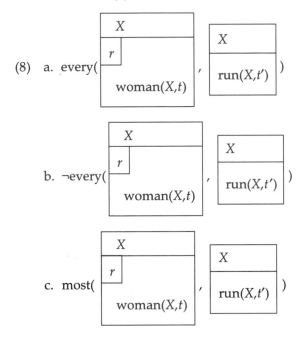

What follows if a situation supports such a QUANTIFICATIONAL INFON? In answering this question we connect the situation theoretic approach to generalized quantifiers to the classical set theoretic approach put forward, for example, in Barwise and Cooper (1981) and subsequent literature. For each determiner relation q there is a corresponding set theoretic relation between sets q^* of the familiar kind from generalized quantifier theory. The q and q^* relations obey the general constraints in (9).

(9)   a. $\exists s[s \models q(\tau,\rho)]$ iff q^* ($\{x \mid x : \tau\}$, $\{x \mid \exists s'\ s' \models \rho.[x]\}$)
      b. $\exists s[s \models \neg q(\tau,\rho)]$ iff $\neg q^*$ ($\{x \mid x : \tau\}$, $\{x \mid \exists s'\ s' \models \rho.[x]\}$)

Suppose that there is some situation *s* which supports the quantificational infon

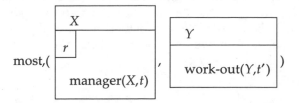

corresponding to *most managers* (in situation *r*) *work out*. This will be true just in case

$$\text{most}^*(\{x \mid r \models \text{manager } (x,t,)\}, \{x \mid \exists s' \models \text{work-out, } (x,t')\})$$

that is, **most*** holds between the set of managers in situation *r* at time *t* and the set of individuals who work out in some situation *s'* at time *t'*. In other words, most of the managers in the resource situation *r* at *t*, which identifies the range of the restricted quantification, work out in some situation *s'* at *t'*.[3]

There are then three points at which situations are entering into the situation-theoretic analysis of generalized quantifiers. This is represented schematically by the boxed letters in (10).

(10) $\boxed{s} \models q(\quad\quad , \boxed{\rho})$

The three situations are

the situation *s* that supports the quantificational infon. This is the situation DESCRIBED by an utterance of a simple quantificational sentence such as *most managers work out*. We will refer to it informally as the QUANTIFICATIONAL SITUATION.

the situation *r*, the RESOURCE SITUATION, which provides the background information to determine the range of the quantifier

and finally, the "hidden" situation which is introduced by the constraints on the generalized quantifiers which represents where the property ρ holds. This is the situation where individual events or states hold. We will refer to it informally as the INDIVIDUAL SITUATION.[4]

In the remainder of the paper we will discuss the roles played by these three situations and the relationships between them. There are a number of important questions to be asked such as: why they are situations and not worlds; whether there really needs to be three of them; whether they are all provided by context or can be quantified over. We begin with the resource situation.

4   Resource situations

4.1   *Why a situation and not a world?*

Barwise and Perry (1983) introduced the notion of resource situation in order to be able to treat definite descriptions. They wanted to preserve the intuition that definite descriptions have a uniqueness requirement, even though it is quite clear that a sentence like *the dog ran away* does not require that there only be one dog in the universe. We want to be able to preserve the basic intuition concerning uniqueness behind the Russellian treatment of definite descriptions and at the same time to show the context dependence of uses of definite descriptions. Hence the resource which we use to determine the referent of a definite description must be part of the world, i.e. a situation, rather than the whole world.

We are assuming here that *a* and *the* are treated as quantifier relations as in classical generalized quantifier theory in Montague (1973), Barwise and Cooper (1981), although this is not standard in situation semantics. Barwise and Perry (1983), like Kamp (1981) and Heim (1982), make a distinction between singular noun-phrases (i.e. indefinite and definite descriptions) which essentially pick out an individual and general noun-phrases such as "no fish" and "every man" which must be analysed as quantifiers. Gawron and Peters (1990) follow Barwise and Perry and make the distinction by analysing the singular noun-phrases in terms of restricted parameters and the general noun-phrases in terms of generalized quantifiers. Essentially, the points we are making here are independent of whether definite descriptions are treated as generalized quantifiers or not. The role of the resource situation on both analyses is to provide a part of the world small enough to allow the referent of the noun-phrase use to be uniquely identified by the property.[5]

A particular instantiation of the constraint on generalized quantifiers proposed above for *the dog barked* will look like (11).

Hence an equivalent way of expressing the set which is the first argument to **the*** is

$$\{x \mid r \models \text{dog}(x,t)\}$$

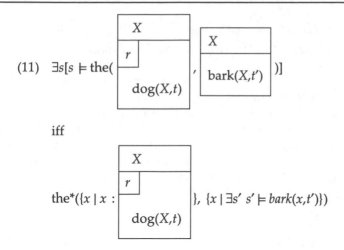

iff

$$the^*(\{x \mid x : \boxed{\begin{array}{l} X \\ \boxed{r} \\ dog(X,t) \end{array}} \}, \{x \mid \exists s' \ s' \models bark(x,t')\})$$

Now situation theory tells us that

$$x : \boxed{\begin{array}{l} X \\ \boxed{r} \\ dog(X,t) \end{array}} \quad \text{iff } r \models dog(x,t).$$

Standard generalized quantifier theory (e.g. Barwise and Cooper, 1981) will require that this is a singleton set in order for the relation **the*** to hold between the two sets.

Of course, one standard argument for the definite article as a generalized quantifier relation is that it allows a unified treatment of both quantified and non-quantified noun-phrases. The role of resource situations can be viewed as another component of this general treatment in that treating definite and indefinite descriptions as generalized quantifiers makes clear the contribution of the resource situation in both the quantified and non-quantified noun-phrases. It provides the informational resource which determines the restriction on the range of the quantifier.

Although resource situations were introduced by Barwise and Perry to account for definite descriptions and other noun-phrases that they called "singular" such as *a man* and *my wife*, our analysis of generalized quantifiers predicts that there might be a resource situation contributed by the context for any quantified noun-phrase. Consider, for example, the sentence *everybody came to the party*. It is a well-known fact that the quantification here is not over the entire universe of people, or even all the people in the domain of discourse. It is generally assumed that the range of quantification for any quantifier has to be limited in some way by the context of use. Resource situations provided by the type which is the first argument to the quantifier relation provide us with an obvious way to do this in situation semantics.

4.2   *Why are resource situations distinct from the quantificational and individual situations?*

Why is it not enough to think of the situation that supports the quantificational infon, i.e. the situation that is described by a use of a simple quantificational sentence, as providing the context which limits the range of the quantifier?

One might think that a situation semantics would analyze sentences such as *the dog barked* as describing situations which contain exactly one dog. However, other examples (due originally, I believe, to McCawley 1979, and further discussed by Lewis 1979) show that it cannot be the described situation in which there is a unique dog. Consider the discourse

(12)   We have a dog and a cat and I think we are going to have to keep them under better control. Yesterday the dog got into a fight with the neighbor's dog and bit it and the neighbor is thinking of reporting us to the police.

Here it is clear that the sentence

(13)   Yesterday the dog got into a fight with the neighbour's dog

describes a situation in which there are two dogs, and so there is no way that we could analyse the description as giving us a unique dog in that situation. McCawley makes an exactly similar argument with respect to the sentence (14).

(14)   The dog had a fight with another dog yesterday

In fact, McCawley's argument is parallel except that he does not talk in terms of situations but rather in terms of a contextual domain conceived of as a set. He makes the point that it is not sufficient to analyze such examples with reference to a domain of discourse for the whole sentence or discourse.

With examples like (13) and (14) one might argue that an approach involving incremental interpretation might equally serve to preserve the uniqueness of the dog referred to, since at the point that the NP *the dog* is encountered only one dog has been introduced into the discourse. So it could be argued that the described situation, as so far revealed, does indeed only contain one dog. At the point in the paper where he discusses (14), McCawley seems to be suggesting the analogue of exactly this view since he talks of the contextual domain as a set of "objects that have been 'identified' up to that point of the discourse". However, it seems that (15) is equally acceptable.

(15)   We have a dog and a cat and I think we are going to have to keep them under better control. They seem to work together defending

the territory around our house. Yesterday, a dog jumped over the wall into our front yard. The cat hissed at it and the dog chased it and bit it. The owner is thinking of reporting us to the police.

Here the NP *the dog* successfully refers after the second dog has been introduced into the discourse. In spoken discourse it even seems possible to begin the last sentence with *the owner of the dog*, i.e. with the second occurrence of *the dog* referring to the one that jumped over the wall. Later in his paper, McCawley makes a similar argument against his initial proposal that the contextual domain was built up in a way that we would now call incremental. He gives (16) as an example.

(16)   Yesterday the dog got into a fight with a dog. The dogs were snarling and snapping at each other for half an hour. I'll have to see to it that the dog doesn't get near that dog again.

McCawley's suggestion at this point is that there should be a hierarchy of contextual domains. In terms of situations, one might think of McCawley's proposal as suggesting that (16) is analysed in terms of a situation *s* which contains a unique dog referred to by *the dog* and a larger situation *s'* of which *s* is a part but which has both dogs as members. The singular definite description *the dog* successfully refers in *s* but not in *s'*, although the plural definite description *the dogs* does successfully refer in *s'*. (The demonstrative *that dog* presumably does not require uniqueness in the same way as the singular definite description.)

While such a hierarchical analysis might be successful for (16) it would not be successful for our example (15) if we modify the last sentence to be *the owner of the dog is thinking of reporting us to the police*. Lewis (1979) discusses a similar example.

(17)   The cat is in the carton. The cat will never meet our other cat, because our other cat lives in New Zealand. Our New Zealand cat lives with the Cresswells. And there he'll stay, because Miriam would be sad if the cat went away.

Lewis explains that the first occurrence of *the cat* refers to Bruce, who lives in the United States whereas the last occurrence refers to Albert, who lives in New Zealand. Lewis discusses the example not in terms of a hierarchy but in terms of salience. As the discourse progresses our attention is shifted from Bruce to Albert. If the discourse (which is uttered in the United States) now continues with *The cat is going to pounce on you!* this is either patently false or the hearer is required to accommodate by changing the relevant salience of Bruce and Albert.

Barwise and Perry (1983) suggested that each use of a definite description could, in principle, be related to a different resource situation in which there is exactly one dog. For them, this resource situation was used to determine the singular referent of the use of the definite description. Since resource situations are related to uses of definite descriptions, it could be the case that we could have two occurrences of the same definite description in the same sentence which nevertheless have different referents. Thus under certain circumstances the situation described above could be described by

(18)   the dog bit the dog

Admittedly two occurrences of the same definite description within the same clause are a bit difficult to understand in this way. However, I do not believe that it is impossible, given a rich enough context to allow us to distinguish the resource situations. The trouble is that the sentence on its own does not provide us with any clues which would establish which available resource situations would be associated with one noun-phrase use or the other.

Just as with definite descriptions, we can argue that the range of quantification is not determined by the described situation alone. Consider the following scenario. Suppose that we have a university department whose members consist of linguists and philosophers. On one particular year two people are coming up for tenure, a linguist and a philosopher, but the department is only allowed to recommend one of them. To the shame of this department

(19)   every linguist voted for the linguist and every philosopher voted
       for the philosopher

Now, if the resource situations were identical with the quantificational situation, this would seem to describe a situation in which the department had exactly two members, a linguist and a philosopher who voted for themselves. However, clearly the sentence can describe a more normal kind of scenario where there is a unique linguist and a unique philosopher coming up for tenure and it was the other linguists and philosophers in the department who were involved in the voting. One might still try to argue that this only shows that we need distinct resource situations for definites. However, if several linguists were coming up for tenure one might be able to say

(20)   every linguist voted for every linguist

although, as with the definite case, the repetition of exactly the same noun-phrase does seem to make processing harder. However, the following examples where we have two occurrences of quantified noun-phrases with different ranges seem to be natural and establish the point that the resource can be distinct from the described quantificational situation (as it is possible to assume that the voting linguists are disjoint from the linguists being voted for).

(21) a. every linguist voted for more linguists than philosophers
      b. every linguist voted for several linguists
      c. most linguists voted for every linguist (and no philosopher)

An apparently simpler example of the same phenomenon is (22).

(22) everything is on the table

The intuitive argument goes thus: This describes a situation in which there is a table and "everything" is on it. However, "everything" cannot include everything in the situation; since on the assumption that resource situations are not distinct from the described situations, the table is in the situation, and the sentence does not mean that the table is on itself. Hence we need a resource situation distinct from the described quantificational situation to determine the range of quantification for the use of "everything". However, the intuitive argument here, while, I believe, basically right, needs some further assumptions to be made clear before it goes through technically. The example is discussed in some detail in Cooper (1993a).

From the theoretical point of view, distinguishing between resource situations and described situations is important because it allows us to maintain the generalization that infons are persistent types of situations. This means that for any infon σ and situation s of type σ, for any s' of which s is a part, s' will also be of type σ. This assumption allows us to give a simple definition of what it means for one situation to be part of another.

(23) Situation s is part of situation s' ($s \trianglelefteq s'$) iff $\{\sigma \mid s \models \sigma\} \subseteq \{\sigma \mid s' \models \sigma\}$

Clearly, quantifiers like **the** and **every** are potential counter examples to persistence if the range of quantification grows with the situation, since we could always add in extra individuals in the larger situation which would falsify the quantification. However, if the range of the quantifier is determined separately by the resource situation, then no matter how much the quantificational situation grows, it will still support the quantification infon, since the range of the quantifier is held constant.

4.3 Why a situation and not a set?

Barwise and Perry (1983) suggested that the intuition that definite descriptions require uniqueness can be preserved if we introduce the notion of resource situation. Thus where McCawley introduces a set (his contextual domain), they introduce a situation which can be used to determine a set (the members of the situation in the sense discussed in Barwise and Cooper 1991). Given that we have argued that resource situations have to be distinct from the quantificational situation, we must now address the question of why the resource should be a situation at all rather than a set.

This question is hard to address in purely semantic terms (at least as traditionally conceived), since in a technical sense it is the sets that are necessary to obtain the correct truth-conditions. However, we are in addition interested in how it can be that certain sets become salient for an agent in a particular context. Why is it that an agent in a given context will group certain objects together and not others? Sets are rather abstract objects which codify the result of some kind of cognitive process or perception. The situation theorist would want to say that we group things together because we perceive relations holding between them in parts of the world, i.e. in situations. This seems like a useful beginning if we want to go beyond traditional formal semantics towards some explanation of how certain objects become salient for an individual at a certain point in a conversation. In particular if we are interested in computational applications where an artificial agent is to reason about salient objects, for example, on the basis of both linguistic and visual input, then it seems that it is important to reason about the properties of individuals and the relationships that hold between them in the part of the world that is in focus. Some concrete examples of this are discussed in connection with resource situations in Poesio (1993).

Here is an attempt to argue that it is intuitive to think of situations as being salient rather than sets of individuals (though of course the salient situations determine sets of individuals). Precisely because the situations determine sets and it is these sets which are the range of quantification, the argument is really not watertight as a narrow semantic argument. But it makes sense if semantics is to be interfaced to contextual reasoning.

Let us return to Lewis' example discussed earlier, but modify it slightly. Imagine that, in their US household, the Lewises have not only a cat but also a dog, both of whom have been dashing around the room, brushing past your teacup and causing you some apprehension. Eventually, the situation quiets down and David Lewis engages you in calming conversation. He starts to speak to you:

> (24)   The dog is under the piano and the cat is in the carton. The cat will never meet our other cat, because our other cat lives in New Zealand. Our New Zealand cat lives with the Cresswells and their dog. And there he'll stay, because the dog would be sad if the cat went away. ‖ The cat's going to pounce on you. And the dog's coming too.

At the point marked ‖ some kind of accommodation is necessary because it is no longer the conversationally salient New Zealand cat which is being referred to but rather the approaching US cat. One can imagine that this change is indicated in the actual spoken discourse by any of a number of techniques that speakers seem to use for this purpose – change in volume or a change in pitch or speech rate perhaps; perhaps Lewis begins to extend his hand in the direction of your teacup. On Lewis' account this corresponds to a change in focus from a more salient cat to a less salient cat. For Barwise and Perry, it represents a change from a resource situation supporting infons about a cat and a dog in New Zealand to one supporting infons about a cat and a dog in this room. For Lewis, the reference back to the US dog could require just as much accommodation as the reference back to the US cat, unless the US and New Zealand animals are bundled up in different context sets. For Barwise and Perry, the accommodation gives us back a whole previous resource situation. Thus on the Barwise and Perry view you would not expect a change to be signalled for the dog, provided you had divided up the resource situations in an intuitive way. Similarly, if Lewis were to continue the conversation about the New Zealand dog, for example, replacing the last sentence with *It's amazing how much affection the dog shows for other animals in the house*, one has the feeling that the reference to the cat pouncing would have to be clearly marked off as parenthetical in some way. What is switching here is whole situations, not just individuals or arbitrary sets of individuals determined independently from the situations that are being talked about.

4.4 Where do resource situations come from?

Resource situations can be any situation which is available to a dialogue participant. Situation semantics as such places no constraints on what resource situations might be available. Indeed, we should not expect a theory that predicts the resources available to a given agent on a given occasion any more than we should expect a theory that predicts the total knowledge state of an agent at a given point in her life. However, this is not to say that there are not generalizations to be made and heuristics to be formulated that could usefully be used to partially predict the behavior of agents at a given point in the processing of a text or dialogue. It seems like the most useful way to approach such heuristics is to look at restricted tasks such as the processing of text with respect to no general context. In this case one would need to give heuristics for creating resource situations on the basis of the situation(s) described by the text so far and also to make predictions about the salience of given resource situations at certain points in the text. A slightly more complex case would be the processing of a text under the assumption that there is some fixed general knowledge base which provides resource situations. This would mean that we would have to give an account of how the resource situations constructed from the text interact with those from the general knowledge base. Restricted tasks that are of considerable interest are those which involve agents taking part in a conversation where a restricted visual situation is available to provide resource situations, e.g. a map as in the Map Task (Anderson et al. 1991). Poesio (1993) presents some important work relating to visual situations in the TRAINS task, where dialogue participants are discussing a schematic map of a small railway and formulating plans to transport goods from one depot to another. This work also raises the important issue of how resource situations can be related to plans which have not yet been carried out. A great deal more work in this area is urgently needed.

4.5   *Quantifying over resource situations*

We have been talking so far as if resource situations are always fixed by context. However, many things that can be fixed by context can also be quantified over, as is, for example, well established in the case of tense and pronouns (e.g. Partee 1973b). We might therefore expect that resource situations could be quantified over. In fact, I think that potentially the strongest arguments for resource situations as opposed to context sets may derive from cases where the resource situations need to be quantified over. Quantifying over sets does not seem to provide us with the right kind of information content. Unfortunately, this is an area of situation semantics that has not been developed. Below I will indicate some suggestive examples and indicate why I think quantifying over resource situations would be appropriate, and why it might be difficult to analyze these examples in terms of straightforward quantification over context sets.

The most obvious cases of quantification over resource situations is where the quantification is explicit in the sentence, as in (25).

> (25)   a. At John's parties, everybody gets drunk
> b. Whatever office you go to, the supervisor is always unavailable
> c. Whatever John does, most people turn up late for the experiment

In (25a–b) one might think of alternative ways of handling the quantification than by quantifying over situations. One might say that in (25a) *at John's parties* contributes a restricting predicate to *everybody*. In (25b) one might treat *supervisor* as a relational noun with an argument which is bound by the quantification over offices. But in (25c) neither of these options seems to be available. A rough stab at an appropriate paraphrase for (25c) would be (26).

> (26) $\forall r \; r \models$ John does something $\rightarrow$ most people in r turn up late for the experiment in r

Clearly the interpretation of the *whatever* clause is more refined by context than what we have represented here; since it seems pretty clear that we are not quantifying over arbitrary situations where John does something, but rather where John does something related to the experiment, or to stopping people turning up late for the experiment. What is important here, though, is that there is a reading for the sentence in which for each case of John's action *most people* has a different range and indeed the experiment might be different in each case as well. If this example needs to be handled by quantification over situations, then I tend to think that the others should be too for the sake of a general treatment. It is not clear how quantifying over context sets restricting the range of *most* would get you the right result. Just saying that there is some set which could be used to restrict the range of the quantifier and make the sentence true does not place appropriate restrictions on the information expressed. Clearly there is always a way of finding a small enough set as the range of the quantifier so that quantification with *most* comes out true.

Now let us consider another kind of case as in (27).

(27)   Few passengers have a bus pass which is valid for the whole year

There is a strong intuition here that the predicate *passengers* is not necessarily limited to one particular resource situation (or time), but rather that there is a reading for this sentence which makes a statement about "passengers in general" (or at least "bus passengers in general"). So far we have talked about the meaning of *passengers* as if it is dependent on context for providing both a resource situation and a time. In the compositional treatment provided by Cooper and Poesio (1994a) this context dependence is treated by having an additional level of abstraction where parameters for the time and resource situation are abstracted over.[6] A slightly simplified version of what is needed is presented in (28).

(28)
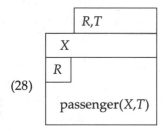

What is needed for the "passengers in general" reading is a modification of this (which can be easily obtained by routine λ-calculus style manipulations) as in (29).

(29)
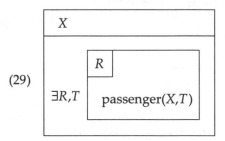

This is the type of individual X for which there is a situation and a time such that the situation supports the fact that X is a passenger at that time. It seems that some determiners have a strong preference for these general types which

are not context dependent, among them *few* and *most*, unless there is explicit
indication to the contrary as in (25c). This might explain why in many cases
it feels wrong to utter noun-phrases such as *most passengers*, but instead *most
of the passengers* seems more appropriate. We need the definite description to
introduce the resource situation since *most* does not provide it. Thus (30a)
sounds strange if we are describing some particular event of a school trip (i.e.
we are not talking about students in general, but students taking part in a
particular event, the resource situation); whereas (30b) sounds fine, since the
definite description provides the hook for the resource situation.

> (30)   a. Most students arrived late for the bus[7]
>   b. Most of the students arrived late for the bus

This should be contrasted with the examples in (31), conceived of as describing the same situation of the school trip, where the determiners *every* and
three seem to easily provide the contextual hook for the resource situation
themselves.

> (31)   a. Every student arrived late for the bus
>   b. Three students arrived late for the bus

Note that (31b) is ok despite the fact that we also have the possibility of saying
(32).

> (32)   Three of the students arrived late for the bus

It is not clear to me what the difference between these examples is except that
(32) seems to require a contextually determined resource situation, whereas
without the definite description the "students in general" reading is also available; that is, you have no prior way of limiting the range of students being
quantified over.

It seems to me that some determiners could differ just in terms of whether
they allow contextually determined resources or not. This seems to be a candidate analysis for the difference between the indefinite article *a* and singular
some. Consider the difference between (33a) and (33b).

> (33)   a. (We were late because) a student arrived late for the bus
>   b. (We were late because) some student arrived late for the bus

(33b) seems to disavow previous knowledge of the student and gives the
impression of "she wasn't one of us", which seems inappropriate given standard assumptions about the school trip we are describing. The use of *some*
would be more appropriate in a case where you could imagine that the individual introduced wasn't previously known (i.e. there was no contextually
determined resource), as in (34).

(34)   (We were late because) some policeman insisted on inspecting the
       bus

There seems to be a similar difference between *many* and *lots of*. (35a) sounds
rather stilted or foreign,[8] whereas (35b) quite happily allows the context dependent resource.

(35)   a. (We were late because) many students were late for the bus[9]
       b. (We were late because) lots of students were late for the bus

Presence or absence of a contextually determined resource could be handled
perhaps by the presence or absence of a context set rather than quantification
over resources within the scope of the determiner. At this point, it is not clear
what would choose between these analyses in this kind of case except that the
resource situation is more explanatory in the sense that it involves the properties and relations holding of the individuals being quantified over, and
allows for explicit references to resources such as the school-trip rather than
an arbitrary set of students.

In Cooper (1993a) an argument is made that we can get generic-like readings by quantifying over resource situations. This is a case where you need
generic or universal quantification over resource situations and therefore seems
less susceptible to an analysis involving quantification over context sets. (It's
not the case that sets usually, generally, or by default, have the kinds of properties that are important for understanding generic-like sentences.) There is
much that I would now want to change in the proposal presented in Cooper
(1993a). Here I will discuss some generic-like readings for indefinite and definite determiners. I say "generic-like" because they may not coincide with what
is normally understood as generic readings. I am interested in the natural
readings one gets for sentences like those in (36).

(36)   a. A man snores
       b. (It used to be that) the man went to work and the woman stayed
          at home

I am interested in trying to explain why in language after language the articles
used for indefinite and definite quantification also have readings which appear to involve generic quantification. I am interested in explaining this without abandoning the original quantificational force associated with the article
since I think that it plays a role in the meaning of these sentences. This is
perhaps more clearly the case in (36b). Note that the reading here is not the
generic involving quantification over kinds as in (37).

(37)   The giraffe has a long neck

Rather it seems to be talking about situations (in particular marriages) where
there is a unique man and a unique woman. The analysis that I now want to

propose for these examples involves something like generic quantification over resources and existential quantification over quantificational situations. Informally, the analysis for *a man snores* goes like this: "if *r* is a resource for some quantificational statement saying there's a man, then this indicates that there is some situation which supports 'a man snores' using the same resource for *man*". The word "indicates" is used here in the sense of channel theory (Barwise and Seligman, 1994, Seligman and Barwise, in preparation), that is, it represents a defeasible inference. The intuition is basically that given a situation with a man in it, you can lay reasonable bets that there's some situation in which he snores, unless you have evidence to the contrary. More formally we can represent the indication using ⇒ as holding between types of resource situation, as in (38).

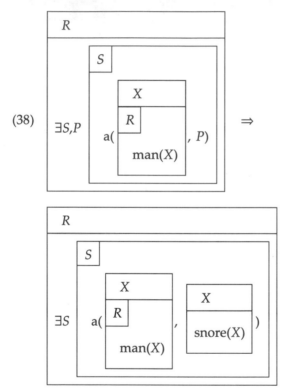

(38)

The indication here should be taken as reflexive; that is, a resource situation of the first type is indicated to be of the second type.[10] I would propose an exactly similar analysis of *the man went to work* except with **the** instead of **a** as the determiner relation. This would then say something like: "a situation in which there is a unique man is indicated to be one which is a resource for some situation where the man works". It seems to me that an analysis along these lines would be quite difficult to recreate using context sets instead of resource situations.

5   Quantificational situations

5.1   *Why a situation and not a world?*

So far the examples of quantificational situations we have discussed have been related to sentences where we would want to say that the quantificational situation is the described situation. It is not obvious in this case that what is described needs to be a situation as opposed to a world, i.e. a complete and coherent situation that for each relation and appropriate assignment to that relation supports either the positive or negative basic infon with that relation and assignment. The argument for quantificational situations being situations rather than worlds involves perception complements. Let us consider the two sentences with perception complements in (39).

> (39)   a. John saw every person in the room leave
> b. John saw each person in the room leave

It seems to me that the first sentence could report that John saw a situation in which everybody rushed out of the room, perhaps in the case of a fire alarm going off. It may well be that he saw a room full of people, followed by a mad scramble to get to the door and then an empty room, and that he need not have seen each individual person leave the room. The second sentence, on the other hand, does not allow this general reading. It requires that John saw each person leave the room individually.[11]

We analyze (39a) as in (40).

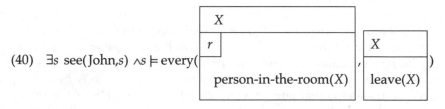

$$(40) \quad \exists s \; \text{see}(\text{John},s) \; \wedge s \models \text{every}(\quad,\quad)$$

While our constraint on **every** requires that individual "leaving infons" for each of the people in the room be supported somewhere, it does not require that they be supported by *s* (though, of course, it does not exclude this possibility). If we are to allow for the possibility that *s* supports the quantificational infon without supporting the individual infons we must consider *s* to be a situation rather than a world, since the world would support all the infons that are supported anywhere.

This claim that situations can support quantificational infons without supporting the individual infons that follow from them is not limited to *every*. Suppose you see 150,000 people make their way into the stadium and Tom is among those that you saw. You still may not want to conclude that you saw

Tom, individually, enter the stadium. He may have been hidden from sight within a large group. Nevertheless, you were watching the entrance all the time, and what you saw was a scene of 150,000 people entering the stadium.

5.2   *Why distinct from the individual situation?*

The argument presented in the previous section is, of course, also an argument that the quantificational situation can be distinct from any "individual" situations associated with the second argument of the generalized quantifier. According to the constraint on generalized quantifiers we have proposed the fact that s supports the infon "every person in r leave" only requires that there be some situation s' which supports for each x who is a person in r the infon leave (x). Hence the quantificational and the individual situation may be distinct (although they are not required to be).

I would like to treat quantification with *each* as a case where the quantificational and individual situations are required to be the same. This is implemented by requiring *each* to obey another constraint given in (41) in addition to the general ones which we proposed in (9).

(41) $s \models \text{each}(\tau,\rho)$ iff $\text{each}^*(\{x \mid x : \tau\}, \{x \mid s \models \rho.[x]\})$

This requires that any situation that supports the quantificational infon also itself supports the individual infons that follow from it. It would be natural to suppose that this is the only difference between *every* and *each*, and that the set-theoretic quantifier relations **every**∗ and **each**∗ are identical, i.e. the subset relation as standardly assumed.

There is an alternative view of the distinction between *each* and *every* which suggests that *each* requires a quantification over situations. The intuition in this case is that if John saw each person leave the room, then he saw a number of different situations each one of which supported the information that a person left the room. It has been suggested to me (separately by Hans Kamp and Karen Brown) that such a view might be preferable to the one above. More work needs to be done on this approach, and also on other alternatives to my analysis and problems that might arise when it is applied to different examples. At this point I will just say that while the Brown/Kamp suggestion might be made to work well for these examples, it is more difficult to see how it would predict a difference between the simple sentences.

(42)   a. Every person left
        b. Each person left

The analysis I am suggesting makes clear predictions about the type of situation that can be described by utterances of these sentences. Note that there is no "truth-conditional" difference between the sentences, since they both require that the same infons be supported in the world at large. But nevertheless the information supported by the described situations can be different in that example (42a) need not describe a situation that supports the individual infons. This accords with our intuition that example (42b) focusses on the information about the individuals.

6 Conclusion

In this paper we have looked at a situation theoretic treatment of generalized quantifiers which builds directly on the traditional set theoretic analysis but which allows situations to enter into the picture at three points in the analysis. We placed a good deal of emphasis on the notion of resource situation as separate from the quantification situation described by simple quantified sentences, emphasizing that there can be potentially as many resource situations as there are noun-phrase uses. We also allowed situations to support infons whose relation is a generalized quantifier relation and we suggested that these "quantificational" situations could support just the quantified infons without the "individual" infons that follow from them. Distinguishing quantificational from individual situations allows us to make a distinction between *every* and *each*, in that *each* is treated the same as *every* except that a situation which supports a quantified infon with the quantifier relation **each** must in addition support the individual infons that follow from the quantification. While this is just a difference in information structure and not truth-conditions in simple sentences, in the case of perception complements it appears to make a difference in truth-conditions as well. Thus what might appear in root sentences to be a matter of "pragmatics" shows up as a semantic truth-conditional distinction in embedded sentences.

NOTES

*   This work was supported by DYANA, ESPRIT Basic Research Action project 3175 and FraCaS, LRE project 62–051. I am grateful to the STaGr group at Edinburgh, the STASS group at CSLI and particularly Jon Barwise for help with various aspects of the research that is reported here. Conversations with Hans Kamp have also contributed to this research. This paper contains revised material from Cooper (1991) and Cooper (1993).

1   For an illuminating discussion of a number of alternatives for treating generalized quantifiers in situation theory see Richard Cooper (1990, 1991).

2   This, of course, is the familiar rule of β-conversion from the λ-calculus.

3   Actually, a more likely reading for this sentence is one where t' is existentially quantified within the scope of *most*. In this paper we will concentrate on situations and ignore fine points about tense.

4   Note that in a sentence with more than one quantifier, this "individual" situation may itself support a quantified infon, i.e. it may be a quantificational situation in its own right.

5   For a treatment of non-quantified noun-phrases as restricted parameters embedded in generalized quantifiers – along the line of Montague's original treatment of pronouns – see Cooper and Poesio (1994a).

6   This is, of course, related to Montague's technical notion of meaning in "Universal Grammar" (Montague 1973) and Kaplan's notion of character (Kaplan 1979).

7   Sheila Glasbey (personal communication) points out that it seems to be much harder to get a reading with a contextually determined resource when *most* is not in subject position. Compare (i) The bus nearly left behind *most* students. (ii) The bus nearly left behind *most* of the students.

8   In many languages, even closely related to English, the translation of *many* does not have this preference for general types but freely allows contextually determined resource situations.

9   Again Sheila Glasbey (personal communication) points out to me that (35a) may sound fine, but putting *many* in object position sounds odd. (i) We interviewed many students. (ii) We interviewed lots of students.

10   The alternative in channel theory is that it indicates that there is a situation of the second type.

11   This observation concerning (39a) may seem to fly in the face of the majority of the literature on perception complements, recently summarized on this point by Hendriks (1993, p.180f). Nevertheless, it seems that for some speakers at least, the distinction I have drawn holds. The issue is somewhat vexed because it has been discussed in terms of exportation of quantifiers and intensionality. Intensionality is not the issue here. The construction is extensional whether the quantifier is exported or not.

III The Interface between Syntax and Semantics

4 The Syntax/Semantics Interface in Categorial Grammar

PAULINE JACOBSON

1 Introduction

While research in the tradition of Categorial Grammar (hereafter, CG) dates back to Ajdukiewicz (1935), Bar-Hillel (1953), and Lambek (1958), much of its current interest arguably stems primarily from its account of the syntax/semantics interface of natural language. The elegance of this account centers on the fact that CG contains the necessary tools for an explicit and transparent correspondence between the syntactic and the semantic combinatorics – indeed, this fact was exploited in Montague (1973), whose adoption of a categorial syntax was driven by his hypothesis that the (surface) syntactic combinatorics of natural language accurately reflect how meanings are also put together.

There are, then, two claims which are either implicit or explicit in almost all work in CG:

(1) Each (surface) linguistic expression is (directly) assigned a model-theoretic interpretation as a function of the meaning of its parts. Thus the syntactic system can be seen as a recursive specification of the well-formedness of certain linguistic expressions (the base step being the lexicon), and as the syntax "builds" larger expressions from smaller ones the semantics assigns each expression a model-theoretic interpretation. Of course all explicit theories of semantics adopt some kind of compositional view of the semantics – but the concern here centers on what level of representation is interpreted by the compositional semantics. In many theories surface structures are not directly interpreted; rather these are mapped into (or, derived from), some mediating level such as Logical Form, and meaning is assigned to that level. The interesting hypothesis of CG, then, is what we will call the *hypothesis of direct surface compositionality*: as the syntax directly builds surface expressions, the compositional semantics assigns each such expression a model-theoretic interpretation, and no mediating level is needed.

(2)   The particular combinatorics used by the semantics at any point is a mirror of the syntactic combinatorics; given the syntax one can "read off" the semantics. (The reverse is not the case because the syntactic system is somewhat richer than the semantic system – for example, word order plays a role in syntax with, presumably, no semantic correlate.) This article, then, will first develop some tools of CG (Sections 2 and 3), and in Sections 4 and 5 we show how these tools allow for direct surface compositionality in a number of cases which are often thought to challenge this hypothesis.

2   CG syntax and the syntax/semantics map

2.1   *Syntactic categories*

We begin with the uncontroversial premise that a linguistic expression is (at least) a triple ⟨phonology, syntactic category, meaning⟩. Given some expression α, the notation [α] will indicate the phonological form of α,[1] and α' will indicate its meaning (which we assume to be some model-theoretic object). We turn first to the set of syntactic categories.[2] In CG, the syntactic category of an expression is a statement of its syntactic distribution. Consider, for example, an ordinary transitive verb like *loves*. This is something which combines with an NP to its right to give a VP; using the notation of CG we can write such a category as VP/$_R$NP. But note further that "VP" itself need not be seen as a primitive category – any expression which is a VP is something which combines with an NP to its left to give a S.[3] Thus "VP" could be taken as an abbreviation for S/$_L$NP;[4] this in turn means that a transitive verb like *loves* actually has the category (S/$_L$NP)/$_R$NP. Similarly, a determiner such as *the* can be viewed as being of category NP/$_R$N.

More generally, then, we will assume a small set of basic syntactic categories and a recursive definition of other categories as follows:

(1)   If A is a category and B is a category, then $A/_R B$ is a category, and $A/_L B$ is a category.

For the present purposes, we can take the basic categories to be S, NP, and N, but there may well be others. In fact, following ideas developed most explicitly within GPSG (Gazdar, Klein, Pullum, and Sag, 1985) it may be that the primitives are not unanalyzed categories like S and NP but rather a set of features which combine to give the set of "basic categories".[5] Moreover, assume that the syntactic component of at least English but probably of all languages contains the following rule schemata (we return to the semantics of these below):

(2)   a.   Given an expression α with phonology [α] and category $A/_R B$ and an expression β with phonology [β] and category B, then there is an expression γ with phonology [$\alpha\beta$] of category A.

      b. Given an expression α with phonology [α] and category $A/_L B$
        and an expression β with phonology [β] and category B, then
        there is an expression γ with phonology [$\beta\alpha$] of category A.

There are several points to make about the mini-grammar developed here. First, note that the syntactic component contains only two extremely general rule schemata. As will be discussed below, most versions of CG incorporate rule schemata in addition to these, but almost all current versions do adopt the view that the syntax contains just a few very general schemata like these. (This is quite similar to the view taken in GPSG, except that the schemata in CG tend to be even more general.) Just how few and how general these should be varies according to the particular researcher – some specific questions which arise are whether or not there are rule schemata which refer to specific categories (rather than having the full generality of schemata like those in (2)), and whether or not there are language-particular rule schemata. Nonetheless, most versions of CG agree that the syntax contains relatively few and relatively general schemata.

Second, we have adopted here a view in which syntactic categories encode their word order possibilities; ultimately, then, word order facts are built into the categorial specification of each word. But this does not mean that each word must be listed in the lexicon complete with a directional feature (L or R) on each of its "slashes". Indeed, such a system would be forced to simply list word order possibilities on a case-by-case basis, missing various obvious generalizations such as, for example, the fact that in English all subjects go to the left of the VP. Instead, lexical items are listed in some sort of underspecified category (for example, intransitive verbs in English are listed as just S/NP), and the directional features (and possibly other information) are filled out by general rules.

Finally, note that the two rule schemata in (2) only concatenate two expressions. Indeed, the categories allowed for in (1) contain only slashes whose interpretation is to place one expression to the left or to the right of the other. In fact, though, other syntactic operations besides just concatenation have been discussed in the literature. In particular, it has often been proposed that certain expressions combine with others by taking the latter as infixes; the operation which combines these has come to be known as Wrap (Bach, 1979a). Consider, for example, the underlined material in the VPs in (3):

    (3)   a. John <u>told</u> the children <u>a story</u>.
        b. Mary <u>persuaded</u> John <u>to leave</u>.
        c. Mary <u>told</u> a story <u>to the children</u>.

It has often been argued that this actually forms a "discontinuous constituent" (a proposal essentially due to Chomsky (1957)). We will not pursue the motivation for this claim within CG (see Bach 1979a, Dowty 1982a, Jacobson 1992c, among others), but will simply point out that beginning with Bach

(1979a), many researchers in CG have assumed that (3) requires a Wrap operation. Hence a ditransitive verb such as *tell* in (4a)[6] first combines with the second object to give *tell a story* and then combines with *the children* – the mode of combination used at that point is such that *the children* is infixed into the string. We leave it open as to how exactly to formalize this infixation operation (see Bach (1979a), Pollard (1984), Moortgat (1988), Jacobson (1992c) for relevant discussion), but we can note here simply that this means that the category of *tell* in (4a) must be $((S/_L NP)/_w NP)/_R NP$, where an expression of the form $A/_w B$ combines with a B by taking the latter as an infix. For the remainder of this article we will not deal with any 3-place verbs and thus will ignore cases involving Wrap.

2.2   *Semantic types and semantic composition*

The interest of a categorial syntax for the syntax/semantics interface lies in its ability to build up the semantic composition in tandem with – and in a way transparently related to – the syntactic composition. What allows for this simple map from the syntax to the semantics is two hypotheses made (in modified form) in most work within CG:

(1)   Each basic syntactic category corresponds to one (and only one) semantic type. In other words, all expressions of category A (for A any basic category) have the same kind of meaning.

(2)   Moreover, let us use the symbol a to stand for the semantic type corresponding to any syntactic category A (i.e. an expression of category A denotes a member of set a). Then for any expression of category A/B, its meaning is a function in bXa, which, following standard practice, we notate as a function of type $\langle b,a \rangle$. It should be noted that we have made one rather large simplification for expository purposes: here and throughout this article we ignore intensions altogether, and deal with a completely extensional semantics. Obviously this is inadequate, but the syntax/semantics interface developed below could be elaborated in systematic ways to fold in intensionality (see, e.g. Montague 1973). It follows from these two requirements that all expressions of a given syntactic category C have the same type of meaning. (However, the reverse does not hold; the mapping from syntactic category to semantic type could be many-to-one, see fn. 7.)

   To flesh this out, we begin with two basic types of model theoretic objects; the set of truth values (t) and the set of individuals (e). The semantic type of S, then, is t, and (departing from Montague 1973) we will take the semantic type of NP to be e. Further, we take common nouns (N) to have denotations of type $\langle e,t \rangle$. Notice that an intransitive verb, then, is also of type $\langle e,t \rangle$, and so both common nouns and intransitive verbs denote functions which characterize a set of individuals.[7] A determiner such as *the* is of category $NP/_R N$ and so must be of type $\langle\langle e,t\rangle,e\rangle$. Following Partee (1987) we take it to be the *ι*-operator – it is defined only for singleton sets, and it maps such a set into its unique member. The meaning of a transitive verb such as *love* is of type $\langle e,\langle e,t\rangle\rangle$ – it maps an individual into a (function characterizing a) set of individuals. We return to quantified NPs such as *every man* in Section 3.

At this point, the semantics associated with each rule schema in (2) is obvious; the meaning of the newly composed expression is the meaning of α (which is a function of type $\langle b,a\rangle$) applied to the meaning of β. Accordingly, we can complete (2a) as in (4a) ((2b) is just the obvious inverse):

(4)   a. Let α be an expression: $\langle[\alpha],A/_RB,\alpha'\rangle$, and β be an expression: $\langle[\beta],B,\beta'\rangle$. Then there is an expression γ as follows: $\langle[\alpha\beta]; A,\alpha'(\beta')\rangle$.

We will refer to (4a) (and its inverse) as the functional application schema.

2.3   Conjunction

Before turning to an elaboration on this system, let us first illustrate the general CG program by a consideration of conjunction, since its analysis has been quite central in the development of CG. Consider (5):

(5)   Mary sees John and walks.

In much of classical transformational grammar, it is assumed that (5) cannot directly be assigned a meaning, but rather must be mapped into (or derived from) the bisentential structure (6):

(6)   Mary sees John and Mary walks.

The reason for this is the assumption that the meaning of *and* is defined only for propositions (as it is in first order logic). But one of the leading ideas in the syntax/semantic interface since Montague (1973) is that surface compositionality can be maintained by simply allowing lexical items to have "fancier" meanings than one might at first glance assume, and the case of *and* provides a good illustration. Thus (5) can easily be directly assigned a meaning by first recursively defining a generalized "meet" operation, notated $\sqcap$ (versions of this are given in Gazdar, (1980); Partee & Rooth, (1983); Keenan & Faltz, (1985)):

(7)   a. Let α' and β' be meanings of type t. Then $\alpha' \sqcap \beta' = \alpha' \wedge \beta'$.
       b. Let α' and β' be functions of type $\langle a,b\rangle$. Then $\alpha' \sqcap \beta' = \lambda X[\alpha'(X) \sqcap \beta'(X)]$ (for X a variable of type a)

This means that $\sqcap$ is defined for any two functions of the same semantic type, provided that the ultimate result of each such function is t. (Note that in the case of two functions α' and β' which each characterize sets, then $\alpha' \sqcap \beta'$ characterizes their intersection.) Given this, we can now simply assume that *and* is listed in the lexicon as follows:

(8) $\langle$[and],$(A/_LA)/_RA;\lambda Y[\lambda X[X \sqcap Y]]$, for A a variable over any syntactic category$\rangle$.[8]

We thus predict that any two items of the same category can conjoin (see also Gazdar, Klein, Pullum, and Sag 1985).[9] Hence *sees John and walks* can be directly composed and interpreted – this expression is an $S/_LNP$ with meaning loves'$(j) \sqcap$ walks' which is equivalent to $\underline{\lambda x[\text{loves}'(j)(x) \wedge \text{walks}'(x)]}$.

3   Elaborations

Much of the research in CG within the last decade has centered on an elaboration of the simple system developed above. This work has been driven by the convergence of ideas from research concerned largely with the syntactic combinatorics (such as Steedman 1987b; Moortgat 1988, etc.) with ideas on "type shifting" in the semantics put forth in particular in Partee and Rooth (1983) and Partee (1987).

3.1   *NP meanings and type lifting*

3.1.1   *NPs as generalized quantifiers*

Consider quantified NPs like *every man, no man,* etc. There are two important observations to be made about their syntactic distribution: (a) the syntax of English treats such expressions as syntactic constituents, and (b) they have (at least roughly) the same syntactic distribution as ordinary (individual-denoting) NPs like *John, the man who came to the party,* etc. It is in part these observations – combined with the premise that the syntactic and semantic combinatorics go hand-in-hand – which led to Montague's (1973) famous treatment of NP meanings as generalized quantifiers. Thus the assumption that each expression which is built in the syntax is assigned a meaning by the semantics leads to the conclusion that *every man* must have some kind of meaning. Montague thus proposed that these have denotations of type $\langle\langle e,t\rangle,t\rangle$; each such expression characterizes a set of sets of individuals (see Keenan, this volume). *Every man,* for example, characterizes the set of sets of individuals which contain the man'-set as a subset, while *no man* characterizes the set of sets of individuals whose intersection with the man'-set is null. This means that when quantified NPs occur in subject position, as in (9), they are actually semantically the function which takes the meaning of the VP as argument –

the semantic composition is such that it asserts that the set characterized by *walk'* is in the set of sets characterized by *every-man'*.

(9) Every man walked.

Furthermore, given the premise that the syntactic combinatorics directly encode the semantic combinatorics, and given the functional application schema (4), it follows that quantified expressions must also syntactically be the function and not the argument of a VP. In other words, the category of *every man* must be $S/_R(S/_LNP)$, and not the basic category NP.

But now consider ordinary noun phrases like *John*. As noted above, these have the same syntactic distribution as quantified noun phrases like *every woman*. Moreover, these two expressions can conjoin:

(10) John and every woman walked.

Given the assumption that *and* only conjoins expressions of the same category and that its semantics is defined only for meanings of the same type, this leads to the conclusion that *John* and *every woman* are of the same syntactic category and the same semantic type. Montague's solution was thus to take all of the expressions which we have been calling "NP" to denote generalized quantifiers. That is, these have meanings of type $\langle\langle e,t\rangle,t\rangle$ – they denote sets of properties. Thus if *j* is an individual, the (lexical) meaning of *John* is not *j* but rather $\lambda P[P(j)]$ – which is the characteristic function of the set of sets containing *j* as a member. In terms of the syntax, we would thus also take *John* to be listed in the lexicon not as an NP, but rather as being of category $S/_R(S/_LNP)$. Hence the noun phrases in subject position actually take the VP meaning as argument. Similarly, *every* and *the* are both of category $(S/_R(S/_LNP))/_RN$. (The meaning of *the* would thus be $\lambda P[\lambda Q[Q(\iota x[P(x)])]]$ and not simply the ι-operator as discussed earlier.) It is worth pointing out that Montague's strategy of "raising" the type of meaning of an ordinary NP like *John* embodies one of the main insights which has proven quite useful in maintaining the hypothesis of direct surface compositionality. This insight is that natural language expressions might have more complex meanings than might at first glance be apparent, but these more complex meanings are often just more complex "packagings" of the simple (and obvious) meanings, and these more complex "packages" relate to the simple meanings in systematic ways.

Given this account, it also becomes necessary to revise the category of transitive verbs so that they take as objects not NP but rather S/(S/NP) (we will henceforth omit the directional features on slashes when not relevant). Thus the syntactic category of a verb like *read* must be (S/NP)/(S/(S/NP)). Moreover, *read'* is not of type $\langle e,\langle e,t\rangle\rangle$ but of the more complex type $\langle\langle\langle e,t\rangle,t\rangle,\langle e,t\rangle\rangle$. As to its actual meaning, one can think of this as follows. Imagine that the world contains the ordinary "read" relation – a function of type $\langle e,\langle e,t\rangle\rangle$ – which we will notate as *read$_*$*. The claim, then, is that while such a function does indeed exist, the English word *read* denotes not this function but rather a more complex "packaging" of this. Thus the actual meaning of the English word *read* is:

(11) $read' = \lambda \mathcal{P}[\lambda x[\mathcal{P}(\lambda y[read_*(y)(x)])]]$

3.1.2   *Lifting and argument lift*

There is, however, one peculiar aspect to the system of syntactic categories and semantic types developed above. Although the primitive semantic types include *e* (the set of individuals) there are no linguistic expressions which denote individuals. Similarly, there are no actual expressions of category NP in the syntax, although it is one of the basic categories. One solution to this anomaly was proposed in Partee and Rooth (1983) and Partee (1985, 1987). Since these particular papers did not assume a categorial syntax, we will not develop exactly those proposals here, but will rather consider a modification which is in keeping with a categorial syntax.

Thus, let us modify the above system as follows. First, as with Montague (1973), we let *every man* be of category S/(S/NP) with meaning of type $\langle \langle e,t \rangle, t \rangle$. This means that *every* is of category (S/(S/NP))/N. However, we will take *John* to be listed in the lexicon as an NP with a meaning of type *e* – in particular, its denotation is simply the individual *j*. Similarly, as in Section 2.2, we take *the* to be of category NP/N (hence it is not of the same category as *every*) – it maps an N into an NP with an individual type meaning, and is the *ι*-operator. Moreover, we will take a transitive verb to be the type that one might naively expect it to be: *read* is of category (S/NP)/NP with meaning $read_*$. (Since we are now claiming that $read_*$ is the meaning of *read*, we will henceforth just refer to this as *read'*.)

This solves the above-mentioned anomaly: there are indeed linguistic expressions of type *e* and of category NP. What it does not account for, however, is the fact that ordinary (individual-denoting) NPs have the same syntactic distribution as quantified expressions like *every woman* – which fact led Montague (1973) to assume the more complex type for the lexical meaning of *John*. Moreover – as noted above – *John* and *every woman* can conjoin.

But rather than raising the types in the lexicon, one can instead accommodate these distributional facts by assuming that expressions are listed in the lexicon "in their lowest type" (hence *John* is an NP with meaning of type *e*, etc.) and by simply adding some additional rule schemata to the mini-grammar developed in Section 2. In particular, we add a unary operation which takes NPs as input and yields as output expressions with a more complex meaning and a more complex syntactic category, as follows:

(12)   Let α be an expression as follows: $\langle [\alpha];NP;\alpha' \rangle$. Then there is a linguistic expression β as follows: $\langle [\alpha];S/_R(S/_LNP);\lambda P[P(\alpha')] \rangle$.

This means that any NP can "lift" into a higher type and higher category.[10] Thus *John* is listed in the lexicon as an NP whose denotation is just j, but this can be mapped into a homophonous expression of category $S/_R(S/_LNP)$ and with meaning $\lambda P[P(j)]$. It follows, then, that this new expression can conjoin with a quantified NP. Similar remarks hold for *the man*. Let *the* be of category $NP/_RN$ and have as its meaning the ι-operator. *The man* is therefore an NP with meaning $\iota x[man'(x)]$. But this expression can also lift to an $S/_R(S/_LNP)$ with meaning $\lambda P[P(\iota x[man'(x)]]$.

Operations like this are often referred to as type-shifting and/or category-changing operations. It is worth noting, however, that these are quite analogous to the rules discussed in (4) – they map ⟨phonology, syntax, semantics⟩ triples into other such triples. The main difference is that (12) is a unary rather than a binary operation; moreover, it has no phonological effect (although one might well find operations like this which do indeed have a morphological and/or phonological effect).

A similar strategy can be taken for verb meanings. Again suppose that *read* is listed in the lexicon as an $(S/NP)/NP$ with a denotation of type $\langle e, \langle e, t \rangle \rangle$. Suppose further that there is a type shift operation – which we will refer to as "argument lift" – which allows it to shift in such a way that it takes generalized quantifiers in object position:

(13)   Let α be an expression $\langle [\alpha], (S/_LNP)/_RNP, \alpha' \rangle$. Then there is an expression β of the form: $\langle [\alpha], (S/_LNP)/_R(S/_R(S/_LNP)),$ $\lambda P[\lambda x[\mathcal{P}(\lambda y[\alpha'(y)(x)])]] \rangle$

This will let an ordinary transitive verb like *read* shift into the category and meaning that Montague assigned to such verbs in the lexicon. (An alternative strategy is to dispense with (13) and instead have a rule by which generalized quantifiers can shift so that they take transitive verbs as arguments to yield intransitive verbs. We will not explore this here.) Note that (13) is defined only for 2-place verbs, and it "lifts" only on the outermost argument position (i.e. the object position); this will be generalized slightly below.

First, however, let us return to (12), which is also stated in a very ungeneral way: it lifts only NPs, and lifts them only to the category of $S/_R(S/_LNP)$. But it is perfectly possible to derive the rule in (12) as a special case of a far more general operation – and, in fact, recasting (12) more generally has proven quite useful (see, e.g. Section 4.4). In order to do this, we first give a general definition of the semantics of the lift operation. Consider any x which is a member of set a, and consider the set of functions from a to another set b. Then we can define an operation on x which we will call *lift over aXb* and which we notate as $\text{lift}_{\langle a,b \rangle}$ as follows:

(14)   Let x be a member of set a. Then $\text{lift}_{\langle a,b \rangle}$ is that function from aXb to b such that for all f in aXb, $\text{lift}_{\langle a,b \rangle}(x)(f) = f(x)$.

(We will omit the subscripts on the lift operation when not needed.) In the case of NPs lifted over meanings of type $\langle e,t \rangle$, the result is just the generalized quantifier meaning. With this apparatus, then, we can now give a perfectly general lifting operation as follows; we refer to this as *lifting α over B/A*:

(15) Let α be an expression: $\langle [\alpha], A, \alpha' \rangle$. Then, for any category B, there is an expression γ of the form: $\langle [\alpha], B/_R(B/_LA)$ or $B/_L(B/_RA)$, $\text{lift}_{\langle a,b \rangle}(\alpha') \rangle$.[11]

It is worth pointing out that a consequence of (15) is that a linguistic expression such as *John walks* has an infinite number of analyses which yield the same meaning. The simplest is the one in which *walks* is the function taking *John* as argument. However, *John* can lift over *walks* such that it is the function and *walks* is the argument (in which case its meaning is of type $\langle \langle e,t \rangle, t \rangle$). But yet another lift can apply, lifting *walks* over generalized quantifiers, and so on. These different analyses, however, all yield the same meaning – indeed, this fact follows directly from the definition of lift.

The question remains as to whether or not the argument-lift rule in (13) should also be generalized and if so, in what ways. It could be generalized to lift the outermost NP argument slot of any expression (thus, for example, it would lift the subject position of a VP as well as the outermost position of a 3-place verb); it could also be generalized to lift on any NP argument position (thus, for a verb of category $(S/_LNP)/_RNP$ it could lift on the subject position); and it could even be generalized so as to lift other argument positions besides NP. For the present purposes we will generalize only in the first way. To this end, we adopt the notational convention $V \to$ to indicate a (possibly null) sequence of categories, $\lambda v \to$ to indicate a (possibly null) sequence of λ's each followed by a variable of the appropriate type, and $v \to$ to indicate a (possibly null) sequence of appropriate variables. (13) can thus be generalized as follows:

(16) Let α be an expression of the form $\langle [\alpha]; (S/V \to)/NP; \alpha' \rangle$. Then there is an expression β of the form: $\langle [\alpha]; (S/V \to)/(S/(S/NP))$; $\lambda P[\lambda v \to [P(\lambda x[\alpha'(x)(v \to)])]] \rangle$.

(This rule allows for any directional features on the slashes, although these could be further specified if needed.)[12]

3.2   *Function composition*

The strategy of adopting rule schemata in addition to the functional application schema in (4) has proven quite useful in the analysis of a range of natural language constructions. Before turning to this strategy, we consider one additional schema which has been explored quite widely in the CG literature (see especially Steedman, 1985, 1987b). This is the function composition schema specified as follows:

(17) a. Let α be an expression of the form $\langle[\alpha],A/_RB,\alpha'\rangle$ and β be an expression of the form $\langle[\beta],B/_RC,\beta'\rangle$. Then there is an expression γ of the form: $\langle[\alpha\beta],A/_RC,\alpha' \circ \beta'\rangle$.

  b. Let α be an expression of the form $\langle[\alpha],A/_LB,\alpha'\rangle$ and β be an expression of the form $\langle[\beta],B/_LC,\beta'\rangle$. Then there is an expression γ of the form: $\langle[\beta\alpha],A/_LC,\alpha' \circ \beta'\rangle$.

Notice that these two schemata only allow function composition when the expressions which are composing both have the same directional feature on their "slash". Other kinds have, in fact, been proposed. Thus Steedman (1987b) proposes that, for example, there are cases where an expression of category $A/_RB$ may take to its right a $B/_LC$ to yield an $A/_LC$ (where the semantics remains function composition). Steedman further argues that this does not happen generally but only with expressions of certain categories and that the particular categories allowed are subject to language-particular variation. If, for example, this kind of mixed composition were allowed to occur with all categories in English, then it would be possible to derive *John every man believed died* (with the meaning "John believed every man died.") This is because "believed" is an $(S/_LNP)/_RS$ and "died" is an $S/_LNP$. The two could compose by free mixed composition to yield "believed died" of category $(S/_LNP)/_LNP$. Whether or not such cases of mixed composition do occur is a matter which we leave open here.

Notice that allowing function composition schemata as in (17) again means that certain strings can have more than one analysis but with the same meaning. Consider, for example, (18):

(18) Every woman saw Bill.

This can be derived in the "normal" way; by combining *saw* of category $(S/_LNP)/_RNP$ with *Bill* of category NP and then having *saw Bill* be the argument of the subject. Alternatively, the subject – which is of category $S/_R(S/_LNP)$ can first function compose with the verb to give the expression $\langle[\text{every woman saw}]; S/_RNP; \lambda x[\text{every-woman}'(\text{saw}'(x))]\rangle$ where this then takes *Bill* as its argument. By the definition of function composition, the two analyses yield the same meaning. (Thus *every-woman*'(*saw*'(*Bill*')) is equivalent to *every-woman*' $\circ$ *saw*'(*Bill*') since, by definition, $g(f(x)) = g{\circ}f(x)$.) The reader may wonder, then, what could possibly be the rationale for adopting the function composition schema. The answer will be detailed in Section 4 but, in a nutshell, the idea is that this allows *every woman saw* to be a syntactic expression (and have a meaning). The advantage of this is that this expression in turn can be the argument of other expressions. We will see such cases below.

Finally, note that (17) is given as a binary rule – it takes as input two expressions and concatenates them. But another possibility is to break this down into a unary operation followed by functional application; the relevant unary operation is often known as the "Geach rule" (Geach 1971). Thus instead of (17a) one could replace this with (19) (similarly for (17b), which we will not spell out here):

> (19)   Let α be an expression of the form $\langle[\alpha],A/_RB,\alpha'\rangle$. Then there is an expression γ of the form $\langle[\alpha],(A/_RC)/_R(B/_RC),\lambda f[\lambda x[\alpha'(f(x))]]\rangle$ (for f a variable of type $\langle c,b\rangle$ and for x a variable of type c).

Notice that if some expression α first undergoes (19) and then the result combines with an expression β, of category $B/_RC$, by the functional application schema in (4) the result is the same (phonologically, syntactically, and semantically) as combining α with β by the function composition schema in (17). For expository purposes, the ensuing discussion will for the most part use the binary function composition schemata in (17), but this can be taken simply as an abbreviation for (19) followed by (4). One potential advantage of breaking composition down into this two-step process will emerge in Section 4.3.

4   Applications

We turn now to some applications of the general program sketched above. Our primary concern is to show how apparatus of this type can be used to carry out the program of direct model-theoretic interpretation of surface structures: the syntax builds (surface) expressions and the semantic combinatorics work in tandem with this to assign a meaning to each expression. To this end, we will consider some cases which are often claimed to necessitate abstract levels of representation (such as LF) and/or abstract elements in the syntax (such as traces). Before turning to these, one caveat is in order. For almost all of the cases to be discussed below, there are competing analyses within the CG literature, and so the particular analyses chosen here should not be taken as agreed upon by all categorial grammarians. Our purpose is simply to quickly sketch a few analyses as representative of the types of analyses available within this general program; space will preclude a thorough discussion of many of the details and alternatives.

4.1   *Quantifier scopes*

No discussion of how to dispense with LF would be complete without at least a brief mention of quantifier scope ambiguities, as in (20):

> (20)   Every man read some book.

Since at least as early as the work in Generative Semantics (McCawley 1970; Lakoff 1971; see also May 1977) such ambiguities have often been thought to necessitate a level of LF. The received wisdom is based (albeit often implicitly) on two assumptions:

(1) There is some level of representation which is assigned a model-theoretic interpretation by the semantics, and each constituent at this level is assigned only one meaning.

(2) (20) has only one surface constituent structure and, moreover, it contains no lexical ambiguity.

Therefore, since (20) is ambiguous, these two assumptions taken together entail that surface structure cannot be the level which inputs the model-theoretic interpretation. Rather, it must be mapped into (or, in Generative Semantics, derived from) a disambiguated level of LF, and this is the level which receives the model-theoretic interpretation. In (20), of course, the idea is that there are two distinct LFs for the different scope possibilities.

Obviously, though, the hypothesis of surface compositionality could be maintained by abandoning either of the above assumptions. Indeed, Cooper (1983) explores an approach to surface compositionality which abandons (1). However, given the sorts of tools sketched above, another quite natural tack to take is to abandon (2). Note, for example, that if the grammar contains function composition, then (20) does have two (surface) structures; this was shown above with respect to (18). Now this in itself is not sufficient to assign two different meanings to (20). Suppose that in both cases we are dealing with the argument-lifted version of *read* – call it **AL**(read). Then *every-man'*(**AL**(*read'*) (*some-book'*)) is equivalent to *every-man'* o **AL**(*read'*)(*some-book'*) by definition of function composition. But notice that there can also be lexical ambiguity here – since we have at least two homophonous items "read". This fact – combined with the use of function composition – allows for the two different scope possibilities, as shown in (21):[13]

(21) a. subject wide scope reading = every-man'(**AL**(read')(some-book'))
        (the same meaning results from the derivation every-man' first
        function composes with **AL**(read')
        read; $(S/_LNP)/_RNP$;read'$\rightarrow$ $_{AL}$ read; $(S/_LNP)/_R(S/_R(S/_LNP))$;
        $\lambda P[\lambda x[P(\lambda y[read'(y)(x)])]]$
        read some book; $S/_LNP$; $\lambda x[some\text{-}book'(\lambda y[read'(y)(x)])]$
        every man read some book; S; every-man'$(\lambda x[some\text{-}book'(\lambda y$
        $[read'(y)(x)])]) = \lambda P[\forall z[man'(z) \rightarrow P(z)]](\lambda x[\lambda Q[\exists w[book'(w) \wedge$
        $Q(w)]](\lambda y[read'(y)(x)])]) = \forall z[man'(z) \rightarrow \exists w[book'(w) \wedge$
        $read'(w)(z)]]$
     b. object wide scope reading: **AL**(every-man' o read')(some-book')
        every man read; $S/_RNP$; $\lambda x[every\text{-}man'(read'(x))]$ (by 17a) $\rightarrow$ **AL**
        (as in (16)):

every man read; $S/_R(S/_R(S/_LNP))$; $\lambda P[P(\lambda y[\lambda x[\text{every-man}'$
$(\text{read}'(x))](y)])] = \lambda P[P(\lambda y[\text{every-man}'(\text{read}'(y))])]$
every man read some book; S; $\text{some-book}'(\lambda y[\text{every-man}'$
$(\text{read}'(y))]) = \lambda Q[\exists w[\text{book}'(w) \wedge Q(w)]](\lambda y[\lambda P[\forall z[\text{man}'(z) \rightarrow$
$P(z)]](\text{read}'(y))]) =$
$\exists w[\text{book}'(w) \wedge \forall z[\text{man}'(z) \rightarrow \text{read}'(w)(z)]]$

A different approach is proposed in Hendriks (1987). He suggests general-izing Argument Lift in such a way that any argument position may be lifted and notes that different scope possibilities will be a consequence of the order in which the various argument positions undergo the lift operation. He also extends this to *de re* readings of certain embedded NPs by positing an opera-tion which lifts on result positions. We will not pursue these various alterna-tives here; the point is simply that the kinds of type shift operations explored in Section 3 may well allow for scope ambiguities without the use of LF.

4.2   Unbounded "extraction" constructions

One of the most widely discussed uses of the above apparatus centers on the analysis of unbounded "extraction" constructions, as in (22):[14]

(22)   every man who Mary said Bill invited

Much work in generative grammar assumes that unbounded "extraction" con-structions such as (22) involve movement of the *wh* word in such a way that this leaves a trace in the object position after *invited*. This trace translates as a variable, and hence the entire constituent *Mary said that Bill invited* translates as the open proposition:

(23) $\text{said}'(\text{invite}'(x)(b))(m)$

The details of the rest of the semantic composition vary from account to account. To the extent that the semantics is made explicit, however, most accounts assume that somehow the $\underline{x}$ variable is eventually λ-abstracted over so that the meaning in (23) is mapped into the property in $\lambda x[\text{said}'(\text{invite}'(\underline{x})(b))(m)]$. What is crucial here is the assumption that the meaning of a subconstituent such as *Bill invited* contains an (as yet) unbound variable in object position which is only later λ-abstracted over. This variable in turn must somehow be "supplied" during the semantic composition, and so there must (at some level) be some linguistic expression (perhaps a trace) in object position whose translation is this variable.

But as shown in Steedman (1987b), the above apparatus provides an elegant account of both the syntax and the semantics of this construction – this ac-count rests on the observation that there is no need for any variable or trace in object position and hence no need for movement or traces. With the use of type lifting and function composition, the expression *Mary said that Bill invited* can be directly put together as follows:

(24)

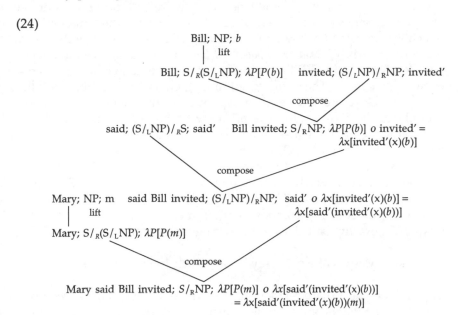

The rest of the semantic and syntactic composition is straightforward. Assume that *who* is of category $(N/_LN)/_R(S/_RNP)$ with meaning $\lambda P[\lambda Q[\lambda x[Q(x) \wedge P(x)]]]$. Thus it wants to combine to its right with a sentence that contains a gap in its rightmost position,[15] and the result is a common noun modifier. Semantically, *who'* applies to two sets (one the denotation of the $S/_RNP$ and the other the denotation of the common noun) and returns their intersection. This illustrates a point hinted at above: we allow for the composition of meaningful expressions like *Mary said Bill invited* which can occur as arguments of something else (in this case, of the relative pronoun). Thus *who Mary said Bill invited* is a common noun modifier (of category $N/_RN$) with meaning $\lambda Q[\lambda x[said'(invited'(x)(b))(m) \wedge P(x)]]$, and *man who Mary said Bill invited* is of category N with meaning $\lambda x[said'(invited'(x)(b))(m) \wedge man'(x)]$.[16] This then occurs as argument of the determiner, exactly as any other common noun can.

4.3   Antecedent-Contained Deletion

One of the classic arguments in the literature for a level of Logical Form concerns the phenomenon of Antecedent Contained Deletion (Bouton, 1970; Sag, 1976), exemplified in (25):

(25)   Mary read every book that John will.

The conventional wisdom here is as follows: a "missing" VP must be understood as some property. Moreover, this property must, in general, be the meaning of some actual linguistic expression in the discourse context (Hankamer and Sag 1976) – it cannot generally be just any salient property (but see, e.g. Dalrymple, Shieber, and Periera 1991). Now consider the "missing" meaning which is understood as the complement of *will*. This cannot be the meaning of the entire matrix VP *read every book that John will* since this would engender an infinite regress – this VP has no meaning until some meaning is fixed for the complement of *will*. The standard solution, then, involves pulling out the object at LF, so that there is a level of representation at which the matrix VP is roughly of the form *read t*. The meaning of this LF VP is thus supplied as complement of *will'*. Hence, while there is no surface VP which can supply a meaning, there is an LF VP which can.

However, as detailed in Cormack (1985) and Jacobson (1992a), the approach to relative clauses sketched above obviates the need for an LF VP here. In a nutshell, the idea is that *will'* need not apply to a VP meaning (i.e. a property). Rather, it can function compose with a meaning of type $\langle e,\langle e,t\rangle\rangle$ (a 2-place relation) – exactly as it does in an analogous non-elliptical case like (26):

(26)   Mary will read every book which John will read.

In (25), then, the 2-place relation that is ultimately picked up as "complement" of *will'* is just the meaning of the transitive verb *read* rather than the meaning of the matrix VP.

To flesh this out, let us first return to VP Ellipsis in general. Assume that there is a rule allowing auxiliaries to shift in such a way that they are missing one argument position. Roughly, the idea is that an auxiliary – which is of syntactic category $(S/_L NP)/_R(S/_L NP)$ with meaning of type $\langle\langle e,t\rangle,\langle e,t\rangle\rangle$ shifts into one of category $S/_L NP$ and applies to some free variable P over properties. Thus the "VP Deletion" version of *will* will have as its meaning $will'(P)$. For reasons which remain mysterious, the value of P in general must be supplied by the meaning of an overt linguistic expression in the discourse context.

Second, suppose that instead of adopting the function composition rule in (17) we break this down into the Geach rule (19) plus application. This means that the ordinary auxiliary *will* can shift by (19) into the expression: $\langle$[will]; $((S/_L NP)/_R NP)/_R((S/_L NP)/_R NP)$; $\lambda R[\lambda x[will'(R(x))]]$ (for R a variable of type $\langle e,\langle e,t\rangle\rangle$)$\rangle$. Finally, we need only generalize the argument drop process discussed immediately above in such a way that the "Geach'ed" version of *will* can also lose an argument place and apply to a free variable of the appropriate type (in this case, of type $\langle e,\langle e,t\rangle\rangle$). Our new item, then, is as follows: $\langle$[will]; $(S/_L NP)/_R NP$; $\lambda x[will'(S(x))]\rangle$ where S is now a free variable over 2-place relations whose value is ultimately supplied by the meaning of some other linguistic expression. (In the case at hand, this is the meaning of *read*.) Note then that this item can now function compose with the type-lifted subject in exactly the same way that an ordinary transitive verb can. (Of course we have broken function composition down into (19) plus application. Strictly speaking, then, the lifted subject undergoes the Geach rule and then applies to the auxiliary.) Thus *John will* is of category $S/_R$NP and means $\lambda P[P(j) \circ \lambda x[\text{will}'(S(x))]]$ which is equivalent to $\lambda x[\text{will}'(S(x))(j)]$. This then occurs as argument of the relative pronoun. Cormack (1985) and Jacobson (1992a) also show that with the kind of approach to scope ambiguities sketched in Section 4.1, some facts elucidated in Sag (1976) centering on the interaction of *de re* readings and Antecedent Contained Deletion are straightforwardly accounted for.[17]

4.4 Right Node Raising

We turn now to another – and quite striking – illustration of this general program. This centers on a phenomenon which has been extremely recalcitrant for most theories within generative grammar – so-called Right Node Raising and/or Non-Constituent Conjunction. Consider first a Right Node Raising sentence such as (27):

(27) Mary loves and John hates model-theoretic semantics.

The traditional view of (27) is that it must be derived from or mapped into a bisentential representation as in (28). Again this view stems (in part) from the assumption that *Mary loves* is not a meaningful expression combined with the assumption that the meaning of *and* is defined only for propositions:

(28) Mary loves model-theoretic semantics and John hates model-theoretic semantics.

But Dowty (1987) shows how the CG apparatus provides all the pieces for the syntax to directly build a Right Node Raising sentence like (27) (without making use of any transformational devices) and for the semantics to interpret it. As shown above, *Mary loves* can be composed in the syntax, and it denotes the (characteristic function of the) set of individuals that Mary loves. Similar remarks apply to *John hates*. Since these are both of category $S/_R$NP they can conjoin to give a constituent of category $S/_R$NP; the meaning of *Mary loves and John hates* is the intersection of the set of individuals that Mary loves and the set of individuals that John hates. These can then combine with the "right node raised" object by functional application. This is detailed in (29):

(29) Mary; NP;$m \rightarrow_{\text{lift}}$ Mary; $S/_R(S/_L$NP$)$; $\lambda P[P(m)]$
loves; $(S/_L$NP$)/_R$NP; loves$'$
Mary loves; $S/_R$NP; $\lambda P[P(m)] \circ$ loves$' = \lambda x[\text{loves}'(x)(m)]$ (by composition)
John hates; $S/_R$NP; $\lambda y[\text{hates}'(y)(j)]$ (analogous to above derivation)
and; $(A/_LA)/_RA$; $\lambda Y[\lambda X[X \sqcap Y]]$

and John hates; $(S/_RNP)/_L(S/_RNP)$; $\lambda P[P \sqcap \lambda y[\text{hates}'(y)(j)]]$
Mary loves and John hates; $S/_RNP$; $\lambda x[\text{loves}'(x)(m)] \sqcap \lambda y[\text{hates}'(y)(j)]$
    $= \lambda x[\text{loves}'(x)(m) \wedge \text{hates}'(x)(j)]$
Mary loves and John hates model-theoretic semantics; S;
    $\text{loves}'(m\text{-}t\text{-}s)(m) \wedge \text{hates}'(m\text{-}t\text{-}s)(j)$

Dowty (1987) further provides an account of even more recalcitrant cases of "non-constituent conjunction" such as (30), whose analysis is given in (31). Notice that the key insight in the analysis of both (27) and (30) is that these simply reduce to "constituent conjunction". By adopting additional combinatory operations we allow for meaningful expressions like *Mary loves* (in (27)) or *Mary today* (in (30)) and these in turn can occur as arguments of *and*.

(30)   John saw Mary yesterday and Bill today.

(31)   (we use the notation VP here as an abbreviation for $S/_LNP$, and the
          notation TV as an abbreviation for $VP/_RNP$)
        Mary;NP;$m \rightarrow$ lift over TV: Mary; $VP/_L(VP/_RNP)$; $\lambda R[R(m)]$ (for R
          a variable of type $\langle e,\langle e,t\rangle\rangle$)
        yesterday; $VP/_LVP$; yesterday$'$
        Mary yesterday; $VP/_L(VP/_RNP)$; yesterday$'$ $\circ$ $\lambda R[R(m)]$ =
          $\lambda R[\text{yesterday}'(R(m))]$ (by composition rule 17b)
        Bill today; $VP/_L(VP/_RNP)$; $\lambda S[\text{today}'(S(b))]$ (analogous to above)
        Mary yesterday and Bill today; $VP/_L(VP/_RNP)$; $\lambda R[\text{yesterday}'$
          $(R(m))] \sqcap \lambda S[\text{today}'(S(b))] =$ (by def of $\sqcap$) $\lambda R[\text{yesterday}'(R(m)) \sqcap$
          $\text{today}'(R(b))]$
        saw Mary yesterday and Bill today; VP; yesterday$'$(saw$'$(m)) $\sqcap$
          today$'$(saw$'$(b)) = (by def of $\sqcap$) $\lambda x[\text{yesterday}'(\text{saw}'(m))(x) \wedge$
          today$'$(saw$'$(b))(x)]

5   Binding and Variable-Free Semantics

The remainder of this article focusses on an account of variable-binding phenomenon which is inspired by work in Combinatory Logic (Curry and Feys, 1958) and by Quine (1966) and which is explored in recent CG works such as Szabolcsi (1987a, 1992); Hepple (1990); Jacobson (1992b, 1992c, 1994); Dowty (1992). While these works represent a variety of implementations, they are all in much the same spirit. Here we follow the implementation in Jacobson (1994).

5.1   *Binding with and without variables*

By way of background, consider first the standard approach to binding in a sentence such as:

(32)   Every man$_i$ thinks that he$_i$ lost.

The usual assumptions are: (1) A pronoun translates as a variable in the semantics; thus let *he* in (32) translate as x. (2) The embedded S in (32) therefore
translates as lost'(x) and the matrix VP as think'(lost'(x)). (3) The above translations are, of course, only representations. We can thus ask what sort of
model-theoretic objects these represent. Take, for example, the meaning of the
embedded S whose representation is lost'(x). This represents a function from
the set of assignment functions (G) to propositions, where each assignment
function in G is a function from variables to objects. This means that the
assignment functions – and, in turn, the variables themselves – are model-
theoretic objects, or are at least key parts of the semantic machinery.

   Moreover, the standard approach takes all expressions to correspond to
functions from G to something else. In the case of a "closed" expression such
as the embedded S in (33) this is simply a constant function into propositions:

(33)   Every man thinks that Mary lost.

Notice, though, that if all expressions were "closed" then the assignment functions would do no actual work and could as easily be stripped away. (Indeed,
this is the move which will be made momentarily.) The rationale, then, for
assignment functions is to provide a way to assign a meaning to a constituent
which contains a pronoun which is unbound within that constituent (such as
the embedded S in (32)). Before continuing, then, there is one point which
should be clarified. In the discussion in Section 4 we took an expression like
$\lambda x[$eats'$(x)(j)]$ to be the representation of a function from individuals to propositions. But under the standard view of variable-binding, this is actually an
oversimplification: since all expressions have meanings which are functions
from G to something else, this formula (if intended as the representation for
some linguistic expression) is actually a constant function from G to functions
from individuals to propositions. In all cases that we were concerned with
earlier, there were no unbound variables and so the oversimplification made
no difference.

   Consider now the question of how a pronoun eventually gets bound under
the standard approach. (We consider only binding by subjects here.) While
there is more than one possible answer, a representative one assumes that the
meaning of the matrix VP in (32) is think'(lost'(x)) (which represents a function
from G to properties), and that this type-shifts into the "closed" property
$\lambda x[$think'(lost'(x))$(x)]$. This then occurs as argument of the subject.[18]

   However, given the kinds of tools for semantic and syntactic composition
discussed earlier, it becomes natural to look at binding and at pronouns in a
very different way. As noted above, if all expressions are "closed" then one
could strip away the variables. In fact, we have already made one move in this
direction – this concerns the meaning of relative clauses, as in (34):

(34)   the man who <u>Mary thinks Bill invited</u>

In the account sketched in Section 4, no crucial use was made of variables (except in the representations); the meaning of *Bill invited* is not <u>invite'$(x)(b)$</u> which contains an unbound variable, but is, rather $\lambda x[$invite'$(x)(b)]$. The strategy which we will thus pursue is to say that pronouns are similar to gaps in their semantic contribution: all expressions containing a pronoun denote not functions from G to something else, but rather functions from individuals to something else. In other words, we will dispense altogether with the notion of variables as part of the model-theoretic apparatus and will dispense with the set of assignment functions. Variables are thus only a part of the language used to represent meanings.

   To flesh this out, suppose that any constituent containing a pronoun which is not bound within that constituent denotes a function from individuals to whatever kind of meaning the constituent would have if it did not contain the pronoun. For example, the embedded *S he lost* in (32) is a function from individuals to propositions – in particular, it is simply the function <u>lost'</u>. Or, consider:

(35)   Every man$_i$ loves his$_i$ mother.

We will not provide a semantics for genitives here, but will simply assume that an NP such as *John's mother* has as its meaning the individual <u>$\iota x[$mother-of'$(j)(x)]$</u>, which we can also represent as <u>the-mother-of'(j)</u>. Then *his mother* denotes a function of type $\langle e,e \rangle$. This function is $\lambda x[$the-mother-of'$(x)]$, which is simply the-mother-of function. Moreover, we let a pronoun like *him* denote not an individual (nor a function from assignment functions to individuals) but rather just the identity function on individuals.

   Before turning to the question of how to set up the semantic combinatorics, let us first consider the implications for the syntax. Given the program of having a tight fit between the syntactic category and the semantic type, we would expect the semantic type to be recorded in the syntactic category. We of course do not want the syntactic category of *he lost* in (32) to be an S/NP since this expression never combines in the syntax with an NP to give an S. However, we can record the semantic type by allowing any expression which contains (or is) a pronoun to be marked with a superscript of the appropriate type. Thus an expression containing a pronoun is of category A^{NP}, where the superscript can be seen as a feature. A pronoun itself is of category NP^{NP}.

   As to how the superscript feature is "passed up" to an expression containing a pronoun, let us adopt the following rule whose semantics will be given directly:

(36)   Let α be an expression of category A/B. Then there is an expression β with phonology $[\alpha]$ of category A^C/B^C.

Thus when an expression of category B^C is taken as argument, the information that it contains a proform is inherited as a feature on the result. ((36) only allows proform features to pass from arguments and not from functions, but this is no problem. If there is free type-lifting one can always "flip-flop" the function/argument structure such that the would-be function is instead the argument and so a proform feature could pass from either (or both) constituents.) Note that (36) is reminiscent of feature passing conventions within GPSG.

There is, moreover, a perfectly natural semantics to hook into (36) – this is the semantics of the Geach rule. Thus (36) can be completed as in (37). We will refer to the operation of this on some expression α as $g_c[\alpha]$ (but we will generally ignore the subscript c):

(37) Let α be an expression of the form $\langle[\alpha]; A/B; \alpha'\rangle$. Then there is an expression β of the form $\langle[\alpha], A^C/B^C; \lambda V[\lambda c[\alpha'(B(c))]]$ (for V a variable of type $\langle c,b\rangle$ and c a variable of type c)$\rangle$.

With this apparatus, it follows that *he lost* in (32) is of category S^{NP} with meaning *lost'*; this is shown in (38):

(38) lost; $S/_L NP$; lost' $\rightarrow_g$ lost; $S^{NP}/_L NP^{NP}$; $\lambda f[\lambda x[\text{lost}'(f(x))]]$ (for f a variable of type $\langle e,e\rangle$)
   he; NP^{NP}; $\lambda y[y]$
   he lost; S^{NP}; $\lambda f[\lambda x[\text{lost}'(f(x))]](\lambda y[y]) = \lambda x[\text{lost}'(\lambda y[y](x))] = \lambda x[\text{lost}'(x)]$
   $= \text{lost}'$

It remains only to say how binding occurs. To this end, we first define a semantic operation **z** as follows:

(39) Let f be a function of type $\langle a,\langle b,c\rangle\rangle$. Then $\mathbf{z}(f)$ is a function of type $\langle\langle b,a\rangle,\langle b,c\rangle\rangle$ such that $\mathbf{z}(f) = \lambda g[\lambda x[f(g(x))(x)]]$ (for g of type $\langle b,a\rangle$ and x of type b).

The effect of **z** is easiest to illustrate by example. Consider love' – which is a function of type $\langle e,\langle e,t\rangle\rangle$. Then $\mathbf{z}(\text{love}')$ is a function of type $\langle\langle e,e\rangle,\langle e,t\rangle\rangle$ (i.e. a relation between individuals and functions from individuals to individuals) such that to $\mathbf{z}(\text{love}')$ some function f is to be an x who stands in the ordinary love' relation to $f(x)$. Similarly, think' is a relation between individuals and propositions – thus of type $\langle t,\langle e,t\rangle\rangle$. $\mathbf{z}(\text{think}')$ is that relation between individuals and properties such that to $\mathbf{z}(\text{think}')$ a property P is to be an x who thinks' $P(x)$.

We can now account for binding by adopting the rule schema in (40):

(40) Let α be an expression of the form $\langle[\alpha];(C/B)/A;\alpha'\rangle$. Then there is an expression β of the form $\langle[\alpha],(C/B)/A^B;\mathbf{z}(\alpha')\rangle$.

In (32), then, *thinks* undergoes (40) – it maps from an (S/NP)/S with meaning think' to an (S/NP)/S^{NP} with meaning z(think'). This, then, takes as argument the expression *he lost* which is an S^{NP} and means *lost'*. Hence the meaning of *thinks he lost* is **z**(think')(lost') which is equivalent to $\lambda x[\text{think}'(\text{lost}'(x))(x)]$. This then occurs as argument of the subject. Similar remarks apply to (35). Here *loves* undergoes **z** and takes *his mother* as object. Hence the meaning of *loves his mother* is **z**(loves')(his-mother'). Recall that <u>his-mother'</u> is just the-mother-of function; thus this VP characterizes the set of x's who stand in the **z**(love') relation to the-mother-of function, and this is the set $\lambda x[\text{love}'(\text{the-mother-of}'(x))(x)]$. Again, then, this occurs as argument of the subject.

Although this account of binding relies on the addition of the rule in (40), it is worth noting that the standard account also makes use of a type-shift rule. The difference is just that in the standard account what shifts is the meaning of the entire VP (*thinks he lost*, or *loves his mother*) while here binding is accomplished via a rule which shifts only the meaning of *thinks* or *loves*. One further interesting point to note is that we have formulated (40) in full generality, but in fact – at least in English – the only clear instances of binding are those where a pro-NP is bound. But this fact (if correct) can be reduced to a fact about the lexicon. We can assume that the only lexical items of category A^A in English are those of category NP^{NP}.

5.2   Applications

We now turn to two applications of this view of binding.[19] Our concern again is to show how these tools allow for a simple account of the syntax / semantics interface which is consistent with the hypothesis of surface compositionality.

5.2.1   Functional questions without traces

Consider first a so-called "functional question" such as (41). The reading of concern here is one in which *his mother* is an appropriate answer:

(41)   Who does every Englishman love? (His mother.)

Groenendijk and Stokhof (1983) and Engdahl (1986) propose that this reading can be accounted for by allowing (41) to ask for the identity of a function from individuals to individuals. Its meaning is thus (roughly) as given in (42):

(42)   what is the function f (of type $\langle e,e \rangle$) such that: every-Englishman' $(\lambda x[\text{love}'(f(x))(x)])$?

We will assume that this basic analysis is correct, and so our concern centers on how the meanings of the parts are put together to yield this.

In Groenendijk and Stokhof (1983) and Engdahl (1986), the basic idea is that there is some NP or trace in object position, where the translation of this object is the complex variable <u>$f(x)$</u>. f here is a variable over functions of type $\langle e,e \rangle$

while $\underline{x}$ is a variable over individuals. $\underline{x}$ is later λ-abstracted over and bound by the subject (this would be accomplished by the rule for variable-binding in general), while $\underline{f}$ is presumably also eventually λ-abstracted over. Thus the meaning of *(does) every Englishman love* would be λf[every-Englishman' $(\lambda x$[love'$(f(x))(x)]$, and this then occurs as argument of the question pronoun. (The full details depend on a full analysis of the semantics of questions, which is orthogonal to the points at hand.)

But now consider the implications of this for the analysis of extraction sketched in Section 4.2[20] – the analysis sketched there for relative clauses should extend to questions in general. Thus, take an ordinary question like (43) under the reading which simply asks for the identity of an individual:

(43)   Who does Mary love? (John.)

Again, *Mary love* can be put together in the syntax by type-lifting *Mary* and function composing it with *love* in such a way that this is an expression of category $S/_RNP$ with meaning λx[love'$(x)(m)$]. This then presumably occurs as argument of the question pronoun *who*. But note that at first glance this analysis does not appear to extend to the case of a functional question like (41). The problem is that the "missing" object appears to have the complex meaning $f(x)$ – yet if there is no actual NP or trace in object position there is nothing to assign this complex meaning to.

In fact, though, given the account of binding sketched above, (41) is unproblematic, and its analysis is exactly analogous to an ordinary question like (43). The only difference is that here *loves* has undergone the z-rule. Informally, then, the question asks for the identity of a function f (from individuals to individuals) such that every Englishman z-loves f. Put differently, *loves* shifts by z, and so it is expecting an argument of type $\langle e,e \rangle$ rather than an argument of type e. It can thus function-compose with *every Englishman* in exactly the same way as (ordinary) *loves* does in the ordinary, individual question. The full details are shown in (44):

(44)   loves; $(S/_LNP)/_RNP$; loves'$\rightarrow z$ loves; $(S/_LNP)/_RNP^{NP}$; z(loves') = $\lambda f[\lambda x$[loves'$(f(x))(x)]]$
every Englishman; $S/_R(S/_LNP)$; every-Englishman'
every Englishman loves; $S/_RNP^{NP}$; every-Englishman' $\circ$ z(loves') = λf[every-Englishman'$(\lambda x$[loves'$(f(x))(x)])]$

This then occurs as argument of the question pronoun *who*.[21] Thus, there is a straightforward analysis of functional questions under the hypothesis of direct interpretation and under the hypothesis that there is no NP or trace in the object position.

Incidentally, functional questions provide another very strong piece of motivation for the variable-free account developed above. This centers on the fact that an NP like *his mother* is an appropriate answer to a functional question.

Notice that under the standard approach to binding, *his mother* denotes an individual (or, a function from assignment functions to individuals). But the question does not ask for the identity of an individual, but rather for the identity of a function of type $\langle e,e \rangle$. Under the approach to binding sketched above, however, *his mother* does indeed denote a function of the appropriate sort – its meaning is just the-mother-of function.

5.2.2   *Right Node Raising and across the board binding*

In Sec. 4.4 we showed how the tools of Categorial Grammar lead to an elegant account of Right Node Raising cases like (27) under the hypothesis of direct interpretation. There is, however, one apparent complication. This is that two different quantified NPs may bind "across-the-board" in a Right Node Raising construction, as in (45):

(45)   Every man$_i$ loves and no man$_j$ marries his$_{i/j}$ mother.

The reading we are concerned with is the one which is paraphrased by (46):

(46)   Every man$_i$ loves his$_i$ mother and no man$_j$ marries his$_j$ mother.

Under the standard approach to binding – combined with the CG approach to RNR outlined above – there is no (obvious) way to get the relevant reading. Space precludes a full demonstration of this, but it can be elucidated informally by the following considerations. Consider again how binding works in an ordinary case, such as in the case of the first conjunct in (46). As discussed above, one way to effect binding is to map the meaning of the VP *loves his mother* – which is the open property loves'(the-mother-of'(x)) into the closed property λx[loves'(the-mother-of'(x))(x)], and then have this occur as argument of the subject. (There are other ways to effect binding, but similar remarks will apply to these as well.) In other words, binding is the result of a type-shift rule which applies to an expression containing a pronoun just before that expression combines with the binder – in this case the type-shift rule applies to the meaning of the VP *loves his mother*. But in the case of a Right Node Raising sentence like (45) there in fact is no such surface VP. In fact, there is no surface expression which contains the pronoun and which then combines with the subject. It is unclear, then, wherein to locate a type-shift rule which will effect binding. Thus *his mother* has as its meaning the (open) individual the-mother-of'(x) and the pronoun should remain free. This might, then, appear to be a strong argument for a bisentential analysis of Right Node Raising constructions whereby (45) is actually mapped into (or derived from) a structure like that in (46) and where binding applies to this structure (and hence there are two pronouns which can be bound separately).

In fact, though, (45) does not threaten the hypothesis of surface compositionality if this is combined with the approach to binding developed in Section 5.1. (45) will receive the across-the-board binding reading under an analysis in which *love* and *marry* undergo the z-rule.[22] Thus the first conjunct *every man loves* will characterize the set of functions f (of type $\langle e,e \rangle$) such that every man z-loves f, and the second conjunct *no man marries* will characterize the set of functions g such that no man z-marries g. These two may then conjoin such that *every man loves and no man marries* characterizes the intersection of these two sets of functions. Moreover, as noted above, the "Right Node Raised" constituent *his mother* does not denote an "open" individual but rather the-mother-of function, which is of type $\langle e,e \rangle$. The entire sentence, then, says that this function is in the set characterized by *every man loves and no man marries*. This is shown formally in (47):

(47) every man loves; $S/_R NP^{NP}$; $\lambda f[\text{every-man}'(\lambda x[\text{loves}'(f(x))(x)])]$ (as given in (44))

no man marries; $S/_R NP^{NP}$; $\lambda g[\text{no-man}'(\lambda x[\text{marries}'(g(x))(x)])]$ (analogously)

and; $(A/_L A)/_R A$; $\lambda Y[\lambda X[X \sqcap Y]]$

and no man marries; $(S/_R NP^{NP})/_L(S/_R NP^{NP})$; $\lambda X[X \sqcap \lambda g[\text{no-man}'(\lambda x[\text{marries}'(g(x))(x)])]]$ (for X a variable of type $\langle\langle e,e \rangle,t \rangle$)

every man loves and no man marries; $S/_R NP^{NP}$;
$\lambda f[\text{every-man}'(\lambda x[\text{loves}'(f(x))(x)])] \sqcap \lambda g[\text{no-man}'(\lambda x[\text{marries}'(g(x))(x)])] = \lambda f[\text{every-man}'(\lambda x[\text{loves}'(f(x))(x)]) \wedge \text{no-man}'(\lambda x[\text{marries}'(f(x))(x)])]$

his mother; NP^{NP}; the-mother-of'

every man loves and no man marries his mother; S;
$\text{every-man}'(\lambda x[\text{loves}'(\text{the-mother-of}'(x))(x)]) \wedge \text{no-man}'(\lambda x[\text{marries}'(\text{the-mother-of}'(x))(x)])$

6 Conclusion

This article has centered on the hypothesis of surface compositionality which is maintained in most versions of CG: the syntax (directly) builds expressions and the semantic combinatorics work in tandem with (and in a way transparently related to) the syntax so as to assign each surface expression a model-theoretic interpretation. We have thus sketched some of the combinatory tools explored within the CG literature, and have briefly shown how these tools allow for surface compositionality in several cases which are traditionally thought to necessitate a mediating level such as LF. Of course there is far more to say about each of the cases above, but this brief exploration will hopefully give a sense of the usefulness of the CG tools and their "tight fit" between the syntactic and semantic combinatorics.

NOTES

1   We are using the term "phonological form" in a somewhat loose sense. The rules to be discussed below which manipulate or combine linguistic expressions may well be sensitive to phonological strings with a certain amount of structure encoded in them. For example – as will be discussed below – it has often been proposed that two expressions may combine in such a way that one is infixed into the other (Bach 1979a). The input expressions, then, must contain at least enough structure as to indicate the point relevant for infixation.

2   The details of this set actually vary under different versions of CG. For example, here we adopt a version of CG in which word order facts are built into the syntactic categories, but other views are possible; for some discussion, see Flynn, (1981).

3   This is an oversimplification since other categories besides NP can serve as subject.

4   Hence we distinguish "leftward looking" expressions (like VP) from "rightward looking" expressions by a subscript on the slash. In a number of works, this is instead encoded by the notation A/B vs. $A\backslash B$. However, a word of caution. While all authors who employ this notational distinction use A/B to mean an expression which takes a B to its right to give an A, the notation $A\backslash B$ has two different interpretations. In Dowty (1987), Steedman (1987b) and others, $A\backslash B$ indicates an expression which takes a B to its left to give an A, while Lambek (1958), Moortgat (1987) and others use $A\backslash B$ to mean an expression which takes an A to its left to give a B.

5   Note, though, that the CG slash is not a feature, at least not one with the same logic as in GPSG. First, it has a somewhat different interpretation: the CG slash encodes a verb's subcategorization while the GPSG one does not. Second, GPSG does not allow its SLASH feature to occur recursively, while CG quite crucially does.

6   This discussion assumes that the "dative shifted" verb *tell* in (3a) and the verb *tell* in (3c) are actually different verbs, related by a lexical rule. See Dowty (1982a) for discussion.

7   If this type theory is correct, then this is a case where two distinct syntactic categories have the same semantic type. Note further that we have treated N as a basic category, even though semantically it denotes a function. Assuming that common nouns do have denotations of type $\langle e,t\rangle$, we might expect "N" to actually be an abbreviation for a more complex syntactic category – something with the general form X/NP. (See Jacobson (1994)). In fact, this is exactly the move made in Montague (1973). There are, however, reasons for rejecting the assumption that common nouns syntactically are functions; see Jacobson (1994) for discussion.

8   Thus *and'* is simply the "Curry'd" version of the generalized $\sqcap$ operator defined above – that is, it takes its arguments one at a time rather than being a binary operation. It should also be noted that there are other ways available to treat *and*. For example, rather than having it be listed in the lexicon, it could be introduced syncategorematically by either of the following rules:

   (i)   Given an expression of the form $\langle[\alpha],A,\alpha'\rangle$, there is also an expression of the form $\langle[\text{and }\alpha],A/{}_LA,\lambda X[\alpha' \sqcap X]\rangle$.

or

(ii)   Given two expressions $\langle[\alpha], A, \alpha'\rangle$ and $\langle[\beta], A, \beta'\rangle$, there is also an expression of the form $\langle[\alpha$ and $\beta], A, \alpha' \sqcap \beta']\rangle$.

There are actually some interesting differences between (8) and (i) on the one hand vs. (ii) on the other with respect to Coordinate Structure Constraint effects, as the interested reader can verify.

9   Actually, this holds only for categories whose meanings are of a type for which $\sqcap$ is defined – these are the categories corresponding to functions whose final result is *t*. Notice that given the treatment of NPs above (in which they have meanings of type *e*) there is no way to assign a meaning to ordinary NP conjunction as in *Mary and John*. This will be remedied in the next section (although there may well be a second *and* which applies to individuals to form a plural individual in the sense of Link (1983); see Partee and Rooth (1983)).

10   The difference between this and the proposal in Partee (1987) is that her rule performed only the semantic operation without a corresponding change in syntactic category.

11   In this formulation, it appears to be purely stipulative that the directional features on the slashes of the lifted category "balance" in such a way that lifting does not change word order possibilities (that is, for example, applying a subject generalized quantifier to a VP yields exactly the same order as does applying the VP to an ordinary NP subject). However, this need not be built in as a stipulation. There is considerable work done within the tradition of the Lambek Calculus (Lambek, 1958) in which the particular additional combinatorics which are possible are derived as theorems from more general principles, and their order-preserving possibilities thus follow from that. See also Jacobson (1992c) for discussion.

12   It is interesting to note that the result of argument-lifting on the subject position of an expression α of category $S/_L NP$ yields exactly the same meaning as would result from ordinary type-lifting of α over $S/(S/NP)$. We leave this for the interested reader to verify. The syntax, however, is not quite the same: ordinary type-lifting of an $S/_L NP$ can yield either an $S/_L(S/_R(S/_L NP))$ or an $S/_R(S/_L(S/_L NP))$, while (16) can also yield an expression of category $S/_R(S/_R(S/_L NP))$. The usefulness of allowing expressions in this latter category will become apparent in Section 4.1. Note that independent of the need to lift on subject position, a rule at least as general as that in (16) is motivated since it allows for lifting the outermost argument of ditransitive verbs.

13   Hendriks (1987) notes that this kind of approach to quantifier scope ambiguities appears not to generalize to cases where the two quantifiers are on the same side of the verb. However, he was working in a system without any kind of Wrap operation – it is not clear that his remarks would hold in a system incorporating Wrap.

14   There is actually considerable debate in the CG literature as to the treatment of unbounded extraction gaps. Here we follow Steedman (1987b), but Moortgat (1988), Oehrle (1991) and others have proposed an approach which is closer to that taken in GPSG.

15   Notice that the formulation of function composition in (17) combined with this account of relative clauses only allows for relative clauses in which the gap is in rightmost position rather than allowing for clauses with internal gaps. For discussion, see Steedman (1987b), Moortgat (1988), Jacobson (1992c).

16   This assumes a "Det-Nom" analysis of relative clauses rather than an "NP-S" analysis (Stockwell, Schachter, and Partee 1973). It could, however, be recast into the latter.

17   It would appear that this does not cover all cases of Antecedent Contained Deletion, for it appears not to generalize to:

(i)   John introduced every girl who asked him to.

However, given the approach to variables discussed in Section 5, the above account does in fact generalize to this case; see Jacobson (1992a).

18   This is not, strictly speaking, correct. The addition of the extra "layer" of the assignment functions means that the types are not right for the meaning of the VP to be the argument of the meaning of the subject. Rather, the meaning of the entire S is that function from G to propositions such that for all g in G, $S'(g) = every\text{-}man'\ (g)$ $(VP'(g))$.

19   For additional applications, see Jacobson (1992a, 1992b, 1994).

20   As noted earlier, there are competing accounts of extraction within the CG literature, but all have in common the property that a "gap" is not a trace but is, rather, simply the failure of some expected argument to be introduced in the normal way. The remarks below, then, hold equally well for these other accounts.

21   There is one slight complication here, which is that this account requires *who* to be polymorphic: it can combine not only with an $S/_RNP$ but also with an $S/_RNP^{NP}$. Moreover, its meaning is such that it can combine not only with an expression of type $\langle e,t \rangle$ but also with one of type $\langle\langle e,e \rangle,t \rangle$. However, the same sort of polymorphicity (at least in the semantics) is also required under the Groenendijk and Stokhof/ Engdahl account and is independent of the question at issue here, which concerns how it is that the subject NP *every Englishman* binds the argument of the function f.

22   Not only can one account for (45) under the hypothesis of surface compositionality, but this analysis actually has some advantages over a bisentential analysis in which there are two pronouns, each of which is bound separately. Space precludes a discussion of this point here, but see Jacobson (forthcoming).

5 Anaphora and Identity

ROBERT FIENGO and ROBERT MAY

In constructing a theory of meaning for a natural language, there are two general characteristics of natural language that the theory must accommodate, and which make natural language unlike formal languages such as the propositional or predicate calculi. First is that speakers use such languages to express their communicative intentions – they normally wish to say something by the utterances which they make. Second is that the sentences of such languages may contain open indexical expressions, whose values can only be determined contextually. To cite an example of David Kaplan's, "I am here now" (or "He was there then") makes no particular statement in and of itself, as the who, when and where are left open by language. A theory of meaning for a natural language therefore must contain not only a semantics – a recursive characterization of truth – but also a theory of use, so as to determine how sentences may be used by speakers to make statements, given the material conditions for their truth, speakers' intentions and context.

Part of the characterization of the theory of meaning, therefore, will be what speakers of a language may state (or propose, question, order, etc.) through their use of the language they speak, *relative to particular contexts*. The semantics respects this relativization, so that the semantic predicate will not be *is true*, but rather *is true, relative to a context and an occasion of use*, where contexts "fix" or "anchor" the open indexical points in sentences. Thus, for natural languages, the semantics can take the form of a truth theory, an algorithm which, given that sentences are grammatical structures as determined by syntactic theory, and contexts are sequences of (at least) persons, places and times, specifies for each s in L a T-sentence of the form $\ulcorner s$ is true relative to c iff $s^* \urcorner$, where s^* is a "disquotation" of s which has a value from c specified for every indexical in s. The semantics for a natural language understood this way is thus a function $\sigma(s,c) = s^*$, where s^* is closed everywhere s is open. Now given that properly using a natural language entails knowing this function, the semantics will then underlie the following use principle: If an utterer $\cup$ says s in context c, then $\cup$ utters s under the truth-conditions as given by s^*.

If ∪ makes a statement, he then believes he has said what he intends to say by uttering a truth.[1]

On this view, that which is not determined by the grammar, that which is left open, has its value specified from context. Conversely, that which is non-contextual is what is determined in virtue of language. While this relation of sentences and contexts seems relatively straightforward, its precise formulation is central to the subject matter of semantics. The balance of the contextual and the grammatical is a delicate one, since it is sensitive to the increasing sophistication in our concepts of both context and grammar. For instance, in addition to persons, places and times, our notions of context may be extended to include such things as events, properties, frequencies, quantities, etc. (We will have more to say about one of this list – properties – below.) These additions may very well lead us to areas of indexicality in language other than the referential, locative and temporal indexicals. On the other hand, our developing conceptions of syntax may lead to results in the opposite direction, allowing us to see as grammatically determined what otherwise might appear to be indexical. Determining the correct relation between these areas is an empirical matter.

A sense of the sort of issues which arise can be gathered from considering the pronoun in *He left*. This string, while syntactically a sentence, cannot be used as it is to make a statement, since it contains an open indexical term. Hence, whatever statement(s) it may be used to make is underdetermined by its linguistic form. In order for this sentence to be used to make a statement, the indexical term must be closed; some value must be fixed for it. This is the role of context – it must provide closure for what is open in sentences. Thus, fixing the value of the pronoun to be Oscar, the sentence *He left* will say, *relative to context*, what the sentence *Oscar left* says. Any adequate theory of meaning for natural language must entail such relations.[2]

Now consider the pronoun in *Oscar kissed his mother*. One way to proceed would be to treat the pronoun in this sentence just like the pronoun in *He left*, as an open indexical. The pronoun would then be evaluated relative to context; this sentence may be used to state, for instance, that Oscar kissed Max's mother or that Oscar kissed Harry's mother. It may also state that Oscar kissed Oscar's mother, Oscar being a likely candidate as the value of the pronoun, given the salience of the NP *Oscar* in the immediate (linguistic) surrounds. Prior use of a name is one of a variety of means, both linguistic and non-linguistic, at the disposal of a speaker to bring some individual to prominence in context. Such use, however, does not depend on the name holding some privileged linguistic relation to the pronoun; it would be improper to speak of it as the antecedent of the pronoun. For this would be to claim there is an ambiguity, where on this view there is none, between whether the pronoun in *Oscar kissed his mother* is anaphoric, and hence linguistically closed, or indexical, and hence linguistically open. Rather all that would be at stake would be relative prominence.

The view just described entered the linguistics literature with Howard

Lasnik's paper "Remarks on Coreference" (1976). Lasnik observed that whatever the virtues of the pragmatic theory just described, it is not fully adequate, as it would allow coreference in *He kissed Oscar's mother* just as it does (properly) in *Oscar kissed his mother*. That theory, therefore, had to be supplemented with a *non-coreference* (or disjoint reference) rule which proscribed the pronoun from having the same value as the name in the former sentence. It was central to Lasnik's approach that this be a *grammatical* rule of non-coreference, and that non-coreference stand in opposition to coreference, which is always contextual, and never grammatical.[3]

Gareth Evans, in his paper "Pronouns" (1980), observed that assuming a grammatical non-coreference rule undermines Lasnik's theory because it is stated in terms of reference extensionally characterized. Evans developed a number of arguments in support of this observation; perhaps the most devastating being that true identity statements will be ungrammatical. Thus, for *He is Oscar* to be grammatical, the name and the pronoun must be non-coreferential, by grammatical rule; however, if the sentence is to be true, then, to the contrary, they must be coreferential. Additionally, we can observe that negative identity statements will be trivial. Since non-coreference would be determined by grammar, in *He isn't Oscar* the name and the pronoun would be non-coreferential by linguistic rule, so that what the sentence asserts would be part of its meaning as a matter of language.

A second sort of problem, developing an observation of James Higginbotham's, arises with cases like the following. Suppose that Max sees a man leaving the room but cannot see his face. Max asks the person next to him who that person is, and she replies "He put on Oscar's coat; you figure it out." Here the speaker seeks to implicate that the person who left is Oscar, based on the tacit assumption that people put on their own coats. But if the grammar required that the name and the pronoun not corefer, then no such implication could follow.

Yet a third problem is found with what is known as the "masked ball" circumstance. An attendee at a masked ball hears someone claim that Oscar is crazy. The attendee reports this by uttering "He thinks Oscar is crazy." It turns out, upon unmasking, that the person who claimed Oscar was crazy was Oscar himself. Nevertheless, what the attendee said was true, clearly not false, and certainly not ungrammatical, which it would be if the grammar required that *he* and *Oscar* be non-coreferential on this (and any other) occasion of use of this sentence.

There are two ways to avoid these problems. The first is to shift the locus of the non-coreference rule from grammar to speakers' intentions: Speakers, in uttering certain sentences with pronouns on given occasions, *intend* that the pronouns are non-coreferential with some other expression(s). This drops the claim that the applicable notion of reference is extensional, adopting in its place one which is intentional. What is grammatically determined is that speakers, in their use of certain sentences, will intend that there is non-coreference. A speaker who utters the sentence *He is Oscar* would now be taken only to utter this sentence with the intention that the noun phrases do not corefer. Taken this way, coreference is not precluded; only precluded is that coreference comports with the speaker's intentions in uttering that sentence.

But while it would certainly no longer be the case that *He is Oscar* is ungrammatical, there would seem to be little advance here, since as Evans observes, by sincerely uttering an identity statement, a speaker's intention is just that there is coreference of the phrases flanking the copula. This is a consequence of the speaker intending that his statement be true. In the circumstance with Oscar's coat, the speaker knows and intends that the pronoun and the name corefer; what she wants is for her interlocutor to figure this out on his own. Similarly, in the masked ball case, the speaker may be quite unsurprised to discover that behind the mask is Oscar, if, for instance, the speaker were acquainted with Oscar's evaluation of his own mental well-being. (The speaker's utterance is also consistent with her remaining utterly uncommitted as to whether the pronoun and the name corefer.) Indeed, in none of these cases does it seem appropriate to describe the speaker as intending *non*-coreference by his or her utterance.

One might try to refine this position by distinguishing a speaker's *primary* intention of non-coreference, from his *secondary* intention. The account of the cases at hand would then go something like the following. Since what the speaker wants to communicate is her secondary, and not her primary, intention, in order to avoid confusing the hearer, she will have to choose carefully those contexts which will supply enough information to the hearer so that he will bypass taking the sentence with the primary intention in favor of the secondary. Implicit in this view is that primary intentions are determined by grammar – a speaker who seeks to use a sentence such as *He kissed Oscar's mother* will primarily intend disjoint reference, in virtue of the form of this sentence. Secondary intentions are not constrained in this manner. But however the theory of referential intentions is to be elaborated to accommodate this two-tiered system, distinctions would have to be quite finely made, so as to avoid the obvious contradiction in the speaker's intentions.

The alternative response is just to drop the claim that there is any grammatically based non-coreference condition at all, extensional or intentional. The grammar by this view would not be determinative of non-coreference, so the cases at hand would no longer be problematic, as the coreferential status of the expressions would be left open to the speaker, relative to what he intends to communicate. Thus, a speaker of *He kissed Oscar's mother*, rather than being committed to non-coreference by his utterance, would *not* be committed to non-coreference, (nor, for that matter, to coreference). But if we reject that grammar is determinative of non-coreference, should we also reject that it is determinative of coreference, and maintain that all pronouns are indexical, as above? This view would be radically non-grammatical; how speakers seek to make references and cross-references through their linguistic acts would be completely independent of the grammatical structure of the sentences they utter (aside from how that structure interacts with saliency effects). The difficulty with this view is that it would not appear to capture the apparent intuitive difference which remains between *Oscar kissed his mother* and *He kissed Oscar's mother*. With respect to grammar they would be just the same – for both, the grammar would be mum with respect to the values of the pronouns. Somewhere, it would seem, a distinction needs to be made.

The line of reasoning we have been following started from the assumption that all pronouns are indexical. In particular, anaphoric uses of pronouns are not to be taken as a separate reading, but rather to result from a saliency effect, and hence not a matter of grammar. Evans, however, urges us to reject this view, and take seriously the idea that there is indeed an ambiguity between the anaphoric and non-anaphoric (indexical), and that anaphora is to be linguistically characterized. What we then arrive at is a view of pronouns which is just the opposite of that which we initially described. Whereas previously non-coreference was grammatically determined but not coreference, now coreference is grammatically determined but not non-coreference. Let us consider the consequences of this approach to anaphora.

First off, how are we to structurally represent anaphora, that is, grammatical coreference? The way that suggests itself is through a system of indexing – what we want to say is roughly that expressions which bear occurrences of the same index, that is, those which are coindexed, are coreferential. Numerals provide us with a convenient representational device for indices, so that we can represent *Oscar kissed his mother* as follows:

(1)   Oscar$_1$ kissed his$_1$ mother

We have chosen the numeral "1" here, but this is of no syntactic importance. The value of using numerals to represent indices is that they directly provide for an appropriate notion of *indexical identity*. It does so by giving clear means for distinguishing occurrences of the same index, as in (1), from occurrences of distinct indices, as in (2):[4]

(2)   He$_1$ kissed Oscar$_2$'s mother

What the *syntax* provides is a theory of the distribution of indexical occurrences in phrase structures, where indices are understood as part of categorial structure (comparable to a category label). We refer to this theory as the *Binding Theory*. Standard formulations of Binding Theory, as originating in the work of Chomsky (1981, 1986b), include the following three principles:[5]

(3)   a. Reflexive pronouns are locally bound.
      b. Personal pronouns are locally free.
      c. All other NPs (including names) are globally free.

It is a consequence of the Binding Theory that coindexing is possible in (1), but not in (2). (1) follows from Principle B, which restricts coindexing of pronouns only in local syntactic domains, while (2) follows from Principle C, which restricts coindexing of names in global syntactic domains.

Semantically, indexing relates expressions to assignments in context, so that the value assigned to an NP bearing an occurrence of index i will be $c(i)$, the ith-individual of the context.[6] Since this relation holds for any expression bearing an occurrence of i in a discourse, a simple relation links coindexing to coreference: if two NPs are coindexed, they are coreferential. Let us elaborate a bit. Because indexing is part of linguistic structure, insofar as coindexing determines coreference, it does so grammatically. Hence, it is appropriate to speak of "grammatically determined coreference," linguistically represented by coindexing. Put somewhat differently, in virtue of the coindexing in (1), it is part of that sentence's linguistic meaning that the name and the pronoun corefer, and this will be so for any utterance of that sentence. A speaker who utters a sentence with coindexing as in (1) is committed to coreference simply in virtue of the form of the sentence itself he or she uses to make his or her statement. Thus, the sort of reading represented by coindexing is an *anaphoric reading*, as opposed to a contextual reading of the sort associated with indexicals. Anaphoric pronouns therefore are *closed* expressions, in the sense of not being dependent on context, as indexicals are.

Coindexing determines coreference, as it were, by linguistic rule. Thus, by using a sentence with coindexing, a speaker cannot mean to express anything but that the coindexed expressions corefer. This is not at the discretion of the speaker. A speaker who utters a sentence such as (1), therefore, would intend by his utterance to make a statement in which the name and the pronoun corefer, but only in a trivial sense, since their coreference is a matter of grammar. What other intention could comport with his utterance? A speaker who utters a sentence containing such coindexing would therefore be making an utterance which would, *ipso facto*, comport with his communicative intentions.

One might object at this point that if non-coreference is not to be determined by linguistic rule, then neither should coreference. Rather, coindexing would represent something weaker, namely that a speaker who utters a sentence with an anaphoric expression only intends coreference, and it is just this which he intends to convey by his utterance. The coindexing simply indicates that the speaker stands in this particular intentional state towards his utterance. This sense of intended coreference would be non-trivial, and distinct from that described above, as it would not preclude that (1), for instance, could be grammatical and true if the name and the pronoun are non-coreferential (just as it would not be precluded that the name and the pronoun in (2) corefer, as a speaker would only intend non-coreference).

This view of anaphora is based on a particular assumption. That assumption is that there can be constituent intentions of a speaker's intention to make a statement by uttering a sentence. That is, a speaker who intends to state that Oscar kissed Oscar's mother by uttering (1), is also in an intentional state with regard to relations among components of that sentence; he intends coreference between the name and the pronoun. Not only then would the language be compositional, but so would be, in a sense, our communicative intentions in using that language. There seems to us good reason to doubt this picture of communicative intention.

Suppose a speaker intends to communicate something, and accordingly selects a sentence which he sincerely believes that, when uttered, will express what he intends. For example, suppose that the speaker wishes to inform you that you should move your leg, by way of a warning against an impending accident. He might say any of the following:

> You should move your leg.
> Run!
> Come over here!

Any of these might equally well fulfill the speaker's communicative intention; the choice between them, and presumably scores of others, will result from many factors, including what the speaker wishes to assert or implicate. Suppose the speaker chooses the first sentence; by doing so he utters a sentence in which there is coreference, between *you* and *your*. Does the presence of this property follow from the speaker's communicative intention to issue a warning? Clearly not, since a number of other sentences might have been chosen to express the same communicative intention in which coreference does not figure. Granting that the presence of coreference does not follow from the speaker's communicative intention, is it not still at least possible to say that, given his communicative intention, the speaker chooses a sentence each of whose properties is intended? That is, given that he may choose from a variety of expressive tools, isn't it true that each property of the tool chosen is one that is intended?

Consider an analogy. Suppose we tell someone to utter the word *cat*, and suppose that person complies. It seems correct to say of that person that he or she intended to utter the word *cat*. Part of that performance is the velar closure associated with the initial stop. Did the speaker intend velar closure? Presumably not. True, one can intend to close one's velum, and saying the word *cat* is one way to carry that intention through. But, unless one *knows* that velar closure is associated with the initial stop of *cat*, one cannot rightly be said to have intended velar closure when uttering the word *cat*. The point is that there are limitations on the extent to which one's intentions distribute down to the tools which one uses to express them. If someone intends to fire a revolver, it does not follow that he or she intends that the cylinder revolve. So too, we think, with language. If one intends to use a sentence to express some particular communicative intention, it does not follow that each property of the sentence chosen is intended by the speaker (except in the trivial sense). Can speakers, then, intend coreference? Of course. One can, for example, comply with the instruction to utter a sentence in which there is coreference by uttering a sentence in which there is coreference. But from this it does not follow that a speaker making a "normal" utterance of *You should move your leg* in a conversation intends coreference (in the non-trivial sense) any more than a speaker intends velar closure in making a "normal" utterance of *cat*.

Let us be clear here about what we are saying: anaphoric coreference is determined by grammar, as a matter of linguistic rule. The speaker does not use a sentence with coindexing because he intends coreference, but only because such a sentence allows him to state what he wants to state. Speakers' intentions do not enter into determining such coreference; intentions only enter in to the extent that stating *s* satisfies *U*'s communicative intentions (in the case above, to issue a particular warning). What fact about speakers' use of sentences with anaphoric pronouns is being missed by this non-intentional account? It obviously can't be that speakers use such sentences because they intend coreference, as this would only beg the question. What reason is there to assume that speakers intend coreference (or non-coreference) in any sense other than the trivial sense which arises from them using sentences in accordance with the properties which the grammar assigns to them?

If coindexing determines coreference, then what does non-coindexing signify, as in (2), if it is neither non-coreference or intended non-coreference, as we have argued? It is, rather, the absence of grammatically determined coreference – that is, where there is no coindexing, there is no grammatical indication of coreference. What the grammar says is nothing. This leaves it open, as far as the grammar is concerned, whether there is coreference or non-coreference in a sentence with the indexing in (4):

(4)   He$_1$ thinks Oscar$_2$ is crazy

Speakers, however, want to say *something* by the use of their language, and the sentences they utter must allow for the expression of their communicative intentions. Now, the primary circumstance in which a speaker might choose to use a sentence in which there are non-coindexed NPs is one in which fulfillment of his communicative intentions demands that the NPs not be taken as coreferent. This circumstance is by far the most common, since typically speakers' communicative intentions are not consistent with leaving the reference of an NP open. Speakers normally know to what they wish to refer, and accordingly will utter sentences consistent with this knowledge. The operative principle is: Don't leave referential options open. Thus, speakers will normally exclude coreference in the face of non-coindexing in favor of structures which grammatically determine coreference; that is, those with coindexing. This leaves non-coreference as the normal *assumption* when a structure in which there is non-coindexing (as determined by the Binding Theory) is encountered. It now follows that if a sentence with non-coindexed expressions is stated by the speaker with just its normal implicatures, it will be taken that there is non-coreference.

Given that sentences with non-coindexed expressions yield a non-coreference implicature, what is the status of this implicature on occasions of use of such sentences? One possibility is that it just stands as an implicature. Suppose A walks up to B and utters out of the blue "He admires Oscar"; A will have implicated that the name and the pronoun do not corefer. How do we know this is an implicature? Suppose that A continues on by uttering "In fact, he is Oscar, that arrogant SOB". A is not taken as having said anything contradictory; only as canceling the implicature that the name and pronoun do not corefer. (Perhaps the most common "out of the blue" cases arise when linguists discuss the anaphoric status of sentences like (4).) Now suppose that Max is not Oscar, and A walks up to B and Max, and pointing to Max, utters "He admires Oscar". Through the ostension, the pronoun becomes publicly grounded, its reference unmistakably known to all. This utterance now *entails* non-coreference.[7] If A had continued as before, he would be taken at least as having spoken falsely, since entailments cannot be canceled in the manner of implicatures. This strengthening to an entailment also holds for the second sentence in (5), (uttered in the same context as the first sentence):

(5) Max_1 left. He_1 admires $Oscar_2$

Here coreference of the pronoun and the NP *Max* is grammatically determined. Since anaphora is a matter of grammar, the pronoun refers to Max and not Oscar, and this is just as much publicly grounded as it would be if the pronoun were accompanied by a demonstration as above.

The non-coreference implicature, observe, is an implicature which appears to have characteristics of both conventional and conversational implicature. On the one hand, it falls in with conventional implicature in its relation to grammatical structure. On the other hand, it can be canceled like a conversational implicature. There are various ways it can be canceled; we observed one above. Another arises from the fact that speakers don't always know who the person they are speaking of is. In such situations, such as the masked ball, it comports with their communicative intentions to precisely leave coreference or non-coreference as an open matter. But while (4), uttered in the masked ball situation, will be true if the man behind the mask is Oscar, so that the pronoun and the name corefer, it remains the case that the speaker has declined to make a statement in which coreference is part of his assertion; to wit, by utterance of *Oscar thinks he is crazy*. He has declined precisely because he is not in an intentional state appropriate to support the use of a sentence in which coreference is grammatically determined. For instance, he may have not been sufficiently certain it was Oscar declaiming on his mental health, or he may have had no beliefs whatsoever that it was Oscar or, for that matter, any other person. Because of this lack of knowledge, the normal implicature of non-coreference will not arise, (and, indeed, if he lacks this knowledge, the speaker, while making a statement, as he does successfully refer by his use of the pronoun in (4), will not know what statement he makes at the moment of utterance). It may turn out, however, that the speaker of (4) sincerely and firmly believed that the masked person was not Oscar. He would then speak in a way that would give rise to the normal implicature of non-coreference. While in these circumstances the speaker's utterance of (4) is grammatically impeccable and indeed true, it is nevertheless of a different status than an utterance made by a speaker who wishes to leave open of whom he speaks, since the implicature has turned out to be false, based as it is on mistaken beliefs. In this case, there is a sense in which we can regard coreference as "accidental" on the part of the speaker; he did not "mean" to implicate this, but yet it is so. On the other hand, where the speaker has no relevant beliefs regarding the identity of the masked person, coreference would not be accidental, as there is no failing implicature.

The non-coreference implicature arises fundamentally from the way grammar represents anaphora; since the speaker did not choose to use a sentence in which anaphora is expressed (i.e. with coindexing), then it ought to be non-coreference which comports with his communicative intentions, given that he knows of whom he speaks. For a speaker who asserts an identity statement such as *He is Oscar* the situation is different however, since in virtue of the meaning of *be*, this sentence entails that the expressions flanking *be* corefer, so it will of course comport with his communicative intentions that there is coreference. This entailment will supersede any implicature of non-coreference, since, again, implicatures, but not entailments, can be canceled. (Identity statements differ from the cancellation case mentioned above in that both the canceling entailment and the canceled implicature are found in a single sentence.) Non-coreference never enters into the picture with identity statements, not even as an implicature; it is certainly not required by the grammar. Structurally the name and the pronoun in *He is Oscar* will not be coindexed; this follows from Binding Theory. But this is no bar to their coreferring; when spoken truthfully, the (indexically) distinct NPs will corefer. This coreference in identity statements is not, however, indexically determined coreference, which it would be if the expressions flanking *be* were coindexed. But then identity statements would be tautologous, as identity of reference would follow as a matter of linguistic rule. Correctly, such an indexing is not one permitted by grammar.

Now what of the case of Oscar's coat? Here, the speaker's goal by uttering "He put on Oscar's coat; you figure it out" is to give the first premise of an inference which will lead to "That person was Oscar" as the answer to the question "Who was that person?" If the speaker had made his utterance so that it carried the normal implicature of non-coreference, then, in conjunction with the (unsaid) premise that people put on their own coats, it would lead only to the conclusion that that person was *not* Oscar, and that would only obliquely, and unsatisfactorily, answer the questioner. This would lead the hearer to assume that the normal implicature was not in place, and that the speaker wished to implicate that there is coreference, which would be grammatically consistent with the sentence uttered. This would lead to the proper conclusion. Notice that the speaker would not be well-served in his communicative intentions if he had uttered "Oscar put on his (own) coat; you figure it out", in which the pronoun can be anaphoric (i.e. coindexed with the name), since then what he wishes to be inferred would follow trivially, leaving the hearer to wonder why he didn't simply give a direct answer to the question.

Implicature cancellation is also at play in (6), an example of Gareth Evans':

(6)   If everyone admires Oscar, then he admires Oscar

It is a consequence of the antecedent clause that the pronoun *he* can refer to anybody; from the antecedent it follows that no one can be excluded from those who admire Oscar. The non-coreference implicature must therefore be canceled in the consequent, since it would say that there is someone who couldn't be referred to, namely Oscar. (7), on the other hand, appears to contrast with (6), in that the non-coreference implicature is in effect, short of an overt demonstration of Oscar by the speaker:

(7)   If Max admires Oscar, then he admires Oscar

But suppose that the speaker and hearer share the tacit premise that Max is the pickiest person there is; if he admires someone, then everyone does. Then as with (6) the non-coreference implicature will be canceled, since all (relevant) values must be available as values of the pronoun.

Two options exist for speakers for coreference: Use a sentence in which it is grammatically determined, or cancel implicatures of sentences in which it is not so determined. Otherwise, the non-coreference implicature will stand in the presence of non-coindexing. Note that determining such implicatures will be based on the indexing of the sentence a speaker actually uses; the possible meanings of any other sentences of the language will be immaterial. A non-coreference implicature arises because the speaker uses a sentence with non-coindexing; if it were coreference which comported with his communicative intentions, then he would have used a sentence in which coreference is grammatically indicated by coindexing, (modulo the cancellation conditions). In the case of non-coreference implicature, it may very well be part of the reasoning of the hearer that the speaker did not use a sentence in which there is coindexing; but from this it does not follow that the hearer has, or needs to have, any access whatsoever to the identity of any particular sentence that the speaker didn't say. The proposals of Tanya Reinhart, as found in her book *Anaphora and Semantic Interpretation* (1983b) – especially Chapter Seven – have precisely this latter characteristic. By her view, a hearer will take a speaker of an utterance U to not intend coreference in his utterance of U – for example an utterance of *He saw Oscar's mother* – because the speaker did not use some other *particular* sentence which could grammatically express the coreference the speaker would have intended – in this case, *Oscar saw his mother*. For a hearer to evaluate an utterance U of a sentence s, he must have access to at least one other sentence s^1 (known to be of an appropriate sort) in order to determine whether s can grammatically express coreference.[8] s itself does not contain enough information for the hearer to evaluate it anaphorically. The speaker for his part normally will use a sentence which grammatically expresses coreference if it is coreference which he intends, although he may have "good reasons" to express coreference otherwise (and the hearer knows this).[9] What count as good reasons? Here is an example Reinhart provides. The identity statement *He is Zelda's husband* allows coreference because the alternative in which coreference is grammatically expressed, *Zelda's husband is himself*, is a tautology. Hence, the alternative would not express what the speaker intends to say, which is something non-tautological and informative. Since an appropriate alternative is not provided for the speaker by the grammar, (and the hearer knows this), identity statements can be uttered backed by the speaker's coreferential intentions.

It seems to us that there are fundamental objections to be made to both of the central assumptions on which this picture rests. Our objections to the first assumption – that speakers intend coreference, and their seeking to communicate this intention to their interlocutors through their utterances is part of the linguistic account of the relevant phenomena – we have already made clear. Our objections to the second – that speakers' and hearers' access to the grammatical meanings of particular alternative sentences of the language is essential for the hearer's computation of what the speaker intends – can be garnered from the following *gedanken* experiment. Suppose there was a language just like English except that the sentence *Oscar saw himself* was ungrammatical (or otherwise unavailable in the language, say because there were no reflexive pronouns). Would there still be non-coreference with *He saw Oscar*? On Reinhart's theory, the answer is no; because there is no alternative to which the speaker has access, coreference would have to be possible. But this does not seem right, as nothing about the sentence *He saw Oscar* is any different in the two languages; they are certainly not indexed any differently.[10] Since it is the same sentence in both languages, the uses to which it could be put by speakers of each would appear to be precisely the same, so that in either case the non-coreference implicature would arise with normal use.

Now suppose that natural languages are used in the way described by Reinhart; that is, with the access requirement. If natural languages are Reinhart languages, they would have some very curious properties. One such property is that they would not be very suitable for logical discourse, as speakers could not express simple tautologies or contradictions by their use. Consider the sentence *Zelda's husband is Zelda's husband*, which a speaker utters as a tautology. This should not be possible in a Reinhart language, because the speaker has avoided using (without good reason) the sentence *Zelda's husband is himself*, also a tautology, in which coreference is grammatically indicated.[11] Rather, *Zelda's husband is Zelda's husband* should only be understandable with non-coreference; the hearer, therefore, would take the speaker as intending to say something which is necessarily false, that two different people are the same. On the other hand, the sentence *Zelda's husband isn't Zelda's husband* should not be usable as a contradiction in a Reinhart language, since the speaker would have done so in avoidance of the contradictory *Zelda's husband isn't himself*. Hence, *Zelda's husband isn't Zelda's husband* should also only be understandable with non-coreference, and in this case the hearer would take the speaker as intending to say something which is necessarily true, that two different people are different. Clearly these are unacceptable results.

Setting aside Reinhart's account, what then is the correct analysis of identity statements such as *Zelda's husband is Zelda's husband*? Given the indexing resources provided by the grammar of English as we have described them, it certainly follows as a matter of grammar that sentences of this form could be true, since for identity statements non-coindexing is consistent with coreference. Such sentences would be perfectly usable in appropriate circumstances. Suppose that Max knows that Paderewski is a virtuoso pianist and that Paderewski is a great statesman, but doesn't know that the pianist and the statesman are one and the same. Someone could seek to relieve Max of his ignorance by uttering "But Max, Paderewski is Paderewski", which Max, taking the point, would find sufficiently informative so as to revise his beliefs, (or, if he found such revision unbearable, have a nervous breakdown). If such circumstances of ignorance were lacking, for instance if Max were knowledgeable about Paderewski's achievements, then Max obviously would not find this utterance informative. Rather than taking the point, Max's reaction would presumably be one of puzzlement, (which would persist if "Paderewski is himself" had been uttered instead).

Now there is something of a puzzle which would seem to arise with the use of *Paderewski is Paderewski* as just described. The speaker in this case is fully informed (or at least sufficiently informed) about Paderewski, so that he knows factually that the pianist and the statesman are one and the same. So for him there is only one name *Paderewski*, used twice in the sentence above, which then ought to be the utterance of a tautologous sentence, of the form $\ulcorner a = a \urcorner$. Yet the speaker's utterance is informative in the circumstance described, and thus must be of the form $\ulcorner a = b \urcorner$, and not tautologous. How can this be?

The point to observe is that an utterance of "Paderewski is Paderewski" will be informative only to someone who holds the mistaken assumption that there are two different names "Paderewski" when there is only one. That is, what Max, ignorant of the facts about Paderewski, holds is that the sentence *Paderewski isn't Paderewski* is true, and hence of the form $\ulcorner a \neq b \urcorner$, with a and b different names. For him, the occurrences of *Paderewski* must be names of different people, since otherwise he could not take this sentence to be true. More precisely, what Max takes to be true is the sentence *Paderewski$_1$ isn't Paderewski$_2$*, the occurrences of *Paderewski* not being coindexed being sufficient to indicate that they are different names. (If they were coindexed, then Max would hold a sentence of the form $\ulcorner a \neq a \urcorner$ to be true, which obviously he does not.) Now, in the service of dissuading Max of this belief, and hence in relief of his ignorance, the speaker, based on what he knows, will deny what Max believes to be true, by asserting its negation. This denial must be in terms that make sense to Max; accordingly, what he will return to Max is Max's sentence, *with its indices intact*, negated. What the speaker will then utter is *Paderewski*₁ is *Paderewski*₂, of the form $\ulcorner a = b \urcorner$, saying to Max, in effect: Your two names *Paderewski* corefer. Max will then draw the conclusion that the two people he calls *Paderewski* are in fact one. Thus, the reason that the speaker's utterance of *Paderewski is Paderewski* is informative is because as a discourse unfolds in conversation, what a speaker utters need not be his own sentences, but may be modifications or reports of the utterances of others. In this case, what the speaker utters is Max's sentence negated, for if it were his own sentence, then what he said would be tautologous, as the speaker has only one name *Paderewski* which would be used twice, and hence *Paderewski is Paderewski* would not be informative.

In presenting this account, we have assumed that speakers normally hold, for any pair of distinct names a and b, that $a \neq b$, and that they will fix and maintain their beliefs accordingly. Speakers, of course, may wish to be more cautious at times, and ask whether $a = b$ before initially settling on their beliefs, or when contemplating revising their beliefs from their settled steady state. So, suppose Max develops an inkling of the truth about Paderewski, and contemplating revising his beliefs asks "Is Paderewski Paderewski"? If the reply is "Yes, Paderewski is Paderewski", then Max's beliefs will be revised to a new steady state; if it is "No, Paderewski isn't Paderewski", they will remain in their previous state. (The situation here differs from that described above only in that the latter lacks Max's crisis of belief, and the overt request for information (a question) that it triggers.) Now, it might be thought that speakers, as a normal state of affairs, leave open for distinct names a and b whether $a = b$ or $a \neq b$, hence holding something weaker than what we have maintained. But, if this were the case, it would seem that one would be constantly questioning one's beliefs – were but the man on the street so philosophically inclined! Even so, what if the weak state were the normal state? Suppose that *Cicero* and *Tully* denote two different people; then being told "Cicero isn't Tully" should be informative and relieve ignorance in just the same way as being told "Cicero is Tully" when they denote the same person. But this does not seem right; rather, the utterance seems merely redundant, which it would be if the hearer assumed already that *Cicero isn't Tully* is true. Further, observe that in the case of the two names *Paderewski* it is not even possible to hold $a = b$, since to hold this is true is to hold that there is only one person Paderewski, and hence only one name *Paderewski*, so that what one would hold would be $a = a$. But this is not to hold open the options above, but only to have one of them; hence, someone who holds that there are two names *Paderewski* holds only that *Paderewski isn't Paderewski* is true.

In general, where distinct names are otherwise indistinguishable as linguistic forms, their linguistic distinctiveness in sentences is established via their bearing distinct indices. This means that a sentence such as *Paderewski is Paderewski*, appearances notwithstanding, can be of the form $\ulcorner a = b \urcorner$, and hence can be informative, as described above. The formal difference which makes this so is the difference in the indices the NPs bear. On the other hand, if there is only one name, then there is no linguistic distinction to be drawn, so that *Paderewski is Paderewski* will be of the form $\ulcorner a = a \urcorner$. While such sentences are not informative in the sense of relieving ignorance, there is at least one area of English where such sentences are appropriately usable, namely when English is used as a medium of logical discourse. So consider (8):

(8)   If everyone is himself, then Oscar is Oscar,

used by a logic teacher to illustrate the inference in (9):

(9) $\forall x (x = x) \rightarrow a = a$

How might we represent *Oscar is Oscar*, as it appears in (8)? The way that recommends itself is to coindex the NPs, as there is just one name employed twice. Then, as desired, the sentence is tautologous, since it will follow as a matter of grammar that the NPs corefer. It might be argued, however, that coindexing is unnecessary to obtain this result, since in (8), *Oscar* is being employed as a logically proper name (individual constant), and hence independently has a value which is invariant over occurrences. What need would there be for the grammar to additionally stipulate that there is coreference? The need arises from the fact that it is the linguistic resources of English which are being used to express logic. Since there are many different names *Oscar* in English, how are we to insure that we have used a sentence which expresses (9), and not (10)?

(10) $\forall x (x = x) \rightarrow a = b$

That is, what gives it to us that (8) is not comparable to (11)?

(11)   If everyone is himself, then Oscar is Max

What gives it is the coindexing of the NPs. Thus, just as ambiguous names are distinguished in sentences in which they are employed by bearing distinct indices, coindexing the names in (8) indicates they are syntactically identical, and hence occurrences of the same "logically proper" name.

The use of natural language for logical discourse is part of a more general phenomenon in which theoretical discourse masquerades in the guise of sentence forms of natural language. Such masquerades are common; for example, besides logical discourse, we have arithmetic discourse, as in (12):

(12)   Three plus one equals two plus two

Sylvain Bromberger has called terms such as the number words in (12) *nomenclature terms*. Nomenclature terms are terms which take advantage of the syntactic resources of language, allowing us to "speak" arithmetic or logic or whatever. They may be interspersed with sentences of "ordinary" English, and may occur mixed in as terms of such ordinary sentences. Bromberger observes that characteristic of such terms is that they are understood against a background of scientific or logical theories which fix their denotations – they (rigidly) designate whatever the theory in which they are embedded stipulates they designate. They amount, in certain cases, to linguistic renderings of the iconography of the theory. For example, the number word *two* can be replaced graphically by the numeral "2". But perhaps the most important property of nomenclature terms for our concerns is that their indexing is not constrained by the Binding Theory. (In particular, such terms are not subject to Principle C.) We have tacitly assumed this for (8) and (12); it also holds for the cases in (13):

(13)   a. If every number is greater than two, then two is greater than two
       b. If everyone admires Oscar, then Oscar admires Oscar

Why should Binding Theory be inapplicable? In part, it must be so as to allow discourse in linguistic theory. Suppose I wish to report my judgment about the anaphora found in the sentence of English *Oscar saw his mother*. I do so by the sentence in (14):

(14)   Oscar saw Oscar's mother

If English forms are to be able to report on pronominal anaphora in this way – that is, to indicate that there is coindexing of the name and pronoun in *Oscar saw his mother* – there must be some way of expressing grammatically determined coreference other than by use of the pronoun whose anaphoric status is being reported. This will be so just in case Binding Theory does not regulate the indexing of the occurrences of *Oscar* in (14), hence allowing for coindexing.

By our reckoning, then, there are three sorts of identity statements – (i) *Cicero$_1$ is Cicero$_1$*; (ii) *Cicero$_1$ is Tully$_2$*; and (iii) *Cicero$_1$ is Cicero$_2$* – all of which are true in the same material conditions (since, as a matter of fact, Cicero *is* Tully). The truth of (i), however, is trivial, since it is tautologous in virtue of the indices, and while it cannot be informative so as to relieve ignorance, it can be used in logical contexts. (ii), on the other hand, is not tautologous, and can be informative, as can (iii), which like (ii), contains two names asserted to corefer. Of course the ignorance they can relieve is not the same. If Oscar were ignorant about the poet and orator in the way that Max is about the pianist and the statesman – he believes that there are two people each named *Cicero* – (iii) would be efficacious for the reasons described above, but (ii) would not be. Being told (ii) would only bring up a query as to *which* Cicero is Tully; it will not inform him that the person he knows as the orator and the person he knows as the poet are one and the same. On the other hand, uttering (i) in this circumstance would be like uttering *Smith is Smith*; it would be taken as just an irrelevant verbal ejaculation (Gricean considerations aside), although given the logical role of (i), it could be replaced by *Smith is Smith* as an instance of $\ulcorner a = a \urcorner$.

Let us take stock. We undertook this look at pronouns as a way of clarifying the picture of the relation of form and context in semantic analysis. Our starting point was that all pronouns are indexical pronouns. Our finishing point is that some pronouns are not indexical; some are anaphoric. What we have ascertained is that there is a *formal structure of anaphora*; for anaphoric elements, the grammar determines coreference in virtue of *identity* of this formal structure. Thus, just as coreference in *Oscar loves Sally because Oscar is a good son* is assuredly just a consequence of using words over again, so too are we saying for the name and pronoun in *Oscar loves Sally because he is a good son*. But the intuitive conditions which might lead one to identify two occurrences of the word *Oscar* in the former sentence do not obviously secure this result in the latter sentence, as the name and pronoun are in some sense *different* words. Some more sophisticated notion is needed, one which isolates a more abstract notion of formal linguistic structure. This is provided by indexing. Indices, we take it, are part of the syntactic structure of linguistic expressions, (in more technical parlance, part of the feature content of categories). The formal identity appropriate to anaphora is then captured by coindexing; intuitively, expressions are the "same" if they bear occurrences of the same index, "different" if they bear occurrences of different indices. Now, since expressions which are coindexed are in the defined sense formally the same, that a name and an anaphoric pronoun corefer is a phenomenon of the same order as two occurrences of a given name coreferring.

With pronouns, identity of indices, we are saying, is sufficient for anaphoric identity. It is this relationship which fixes which expression a pronoun stands in for; it is needed because pronouns are bereft of the sort of lexical content which could otherwise distinguish one name from another, *Oscar* from *Max*. For a sentence such as *Oscar saw his mother* coindexing will thus determine that it has the following T-sentence, with two occurrences of "Oscar" on the right-hand side:

(15)   "Oscar$_1$ saw his$_1$ mother" is true iff Oscar saw Oscar's mother

On the other hand, in *He saw Oscar's mother* or *He is Oscar*, where the pronoun and name will not be coindexed, there are anaphorically distinct expressions, so all that can be concluded on the basis of sentential form is a necessary condition:

(16)   "He$_1$ saw Oscar$_2$'s mother" is true only if He saw Oscar's mother

Sufficiency obtains only relative to context, including contexts in which the pronoun refers to Oscar. In that case *Oscar saw his mother* and *He saw Oscar's mother* will have the same truth-conditions, although the circumstances for appropriate use of these sentences will differ, since in the former coreference is grammatically determined, but not in the latter.[12]

It should be apparent at this point that insofar as we have spoken of coindexing as *being* or *representing* coreference, we have misspoken somewhat. This is because coindexing could not represent coreference as such, as co-reference is not itself a property of phrase structure. Rather, coindexing is a basic notion of phrase structure, as it enters into characterizing syntactic identity; it is, by hypothesis, part of the characterization of what are occurrences of the "same" phrase in a structure, of occurrences of expressions. Now, because coindexing grammatically determines a syntactic identity, it *entails* coreference, given that the coindexed expressions are occurrences of a word which is referential. The rider is all important, as this entailment has apparent failures, as Geach in *Reference and Generality* has instructed; *A man loves Sally because he is a good son* is not the same as *A man loves Sally because a man is a good son*, as the latter, but not the former, is compatible with Oscar loving Sally because Max is a good son. This is not to say, however, that the pronoun in this case is not anaphoric, only that the indexical identity which underlies anaphora is not manifest in the structure as depicted. It is not manifest because the relevant coindexing holds not between *he* and *a man*, but between *he* and *a variable* bound by *a man* in this sentence's logical form. The pronoun is another occurrence of this variable, and in this sense anaphoric; but the syntactic identity which makes this so does not entail coreference in the sense that this term is applicable to names and pronouns anaphoric to them. Thus, we can clearly speak of coindexing as representing or determining anaphora, in virtue of syntactic identity, but not of coindexing as representing or determining coreference (or, for that matter, variable binding).[13]

The central semantic question which now emerges is this. Under what conditions does the grammar determine that there are multiple occurrences of expressions in sentences where superficially it would appear that there are not? This question defines a class of identity problems in syntactic theory known as *reconstruction* problems. Reconstruction problems draw the border-line between language and context; they are problems as to how the form of sentences constrains what can be stated, independently of the contribution of context. Anaphora is a reconstruction problem. The issue in this problem re-volves around whether there is a formal identity condition which can distin-guish pronouns which are anaphoric from those which are indexical. We have argued that there is, and that this identity condition arises from the characteri-zation of identity of indices, which are taken as aspects of syntactic structure. This syntactic structure, moreover, must have the property of embedding a representation of the form of the logical terms, inclusive of the representation of quantification; the intimacy of reconstruction and logical form is Geach's lesson. We call that linguistic level which encodes a logical form LF. It is a characteristic of reconstruction problems that they have their solution in terms of the structure of LF. In the case at hand, this entails that indices are part of the formal structure of LF.[14]

What sorts of conditions govern reconstruction, and hence the contribution of structure to what is said? Here is a more or less plausible one: *The only syntactic structure which contributes to what is said is that which is projected from what is uttered*. The intent of this "utterance condition" is to limit, so to speak, the search space in which structure determining identical occurrences can be located. It thus partially determines the domain of reconstruction problems. At first glance this condition might seem almost trivial, but it does make certain distinctions. For instance, anaphora falls under this condition as a reconstruction problem – the coindexing of the name and pronoun in *Oscar saw his mother* is between parts of the syntactic structure projected from the words the speaker uses in his utterance. On the other hand, ellipsis, such as the verb phrase ellipsis in (17), apparently does not fall under reconstruction:

(17)   Oscar collects antiques, and Max does, too

Here the missing verb phrase means "collect antiques", just as the overt verb phrase does. The utterance condition tells us that this understanding cannot be a matter of language, since there is no utterance from which the identical structure can be projected. Rather, our understanding of the missing verb phrase must be a matter of context.

On the approach being described, elided verb phrases "denote" elements in context. What verb phrases denote are properties; in the case at hand, this will be the property of collecting antiques.[15] The choice of the appropriate property in context will be governed by saliency conditions. For (17), the prior occurrence of the VP *collects antiques* in the immediate linguistic context will raise to salience the property it denotes. This immediate saliency context need not be in the speaker's utterance itself. It may extend to utterances of others: One speaker may utter "Oscar collects antiques" and another "Max does, too". Nor, for that matter, need the raising of properties to saliency be linguistically based. Consider an utterance of "Please do", said to someone as they walk into an office, the speaker wishing to politely indicate that the standing visitor take a seat. Since this is the initial utterance of the conversation, there are no prior utterances to set linguistic context. Yet, the speaker's utterance is understood as meaning please sit down, appropriately, given the salience of the property of sitting down in the conversational context.[16]

The approach to ellipsis just sketched is of course highly reminiscent of the contextual approach to pronouns described above, the difference consisting in pronouns denoting individuals in context, rather than properties. While for pronouns we had to abandon this sort of approach, the argument for ellipsis would appear to be stronger, since understanding elided VPs in an utterance appears not to be based on any occurrent piece of syntactic structure; the elided verb phrase, after all, is not uttered. Hence the utterance condition apparently mandates, on principled grounds, that ellipsis depends on context. Ellipsis, so to speak, is indexical, rather than anaphoric; as such, elided verb phrases denote properties as elements of context, elements which exist independently of language.

This conclusion about the contextual nature of ellipsis follows from the utterance condition given a certain assumption. This assumption is that an *utterance* is defined in terms of its verbal (or graphical) form, and that there is a one-to-one correspondence between such utterance formatives and sentential formatives. Hence, in (17) there is no syntactic verb phrase in the second clause since there is no corresponding utterance of a verb phrase. The notion of utterance which underlies this conclusion strikes us as plainly implausible. If one asks what speakers utter – what they do by their verbal acts – the answer is that they utter, on occasions of use, *sentences* in contexts, so as to make statements. What is important here is that *what* is uttered is independent of the physical medium utilized to make the utterance. Assuredly, our capacities to form linguistic representations do not depend on our capacities to externally realize those representations; after all, don't the sentences "in our heads" have linguistic structure, too? Consequently, there is nothing which requires that an utterance of a sentence must phonetically or otherwise realize each lexical formative of that sentence. There may be silent parts of utterances; the spoken (or written) parts may be truncated forms of the sentences we speak. All that is required is that a speaker's verbal act be sufficient to give rise in the hearer to the sentence which the speaker wishes to communicate.

The distinction which must be borne in mind is between what speakers utter and what speakers verbalize (or write or sign). What is uttered on an occasion of use is a function of the representation of the language spoken, while what is verbalized is a matter of phonetic realization of those representations in a sonic (or other) medium. In the line of reasoning above, ellipsis was forced to be contextual because of a confusion of utterance with verbalization. Once this confusion is eliminated, however, ellipsis can be treated as a reconstruction problem falling under the utterance condition. Suppose a speaker verbalizes (17); the question is then what sentence has been uttered? The answer we give is that he has uttered the same sentence as if he had verbalized (18):

(18)   Oscar collects antiques, and Max collects antiques, too

In (18), there obviously are two syntactic occurrences of the verb phrase *collect antiques*. (18), *qua* sentence, therefore contains a structural redundancy, in virtue of the identity of the verb phrases. Such redundancy allows a speaker who utters this sentence two verbal options – either to verbalize (18) with all the formatives intact, or, taking advantage of the redundancy, to economize on his words and verbalize the form in (17) instead, with the second occurrence of the verb phrase unpronounced. Since this ellipsis is governed by syntactic identity, the hearer will be able to "reconstruct" the sentence the speaker wishes to communicate through his utterance; that is, determine that it contains a verb phrase which is identical to some other verb phrase. Thus, regardless of whether the speaker chooses to verbalize the verb phrase or not, the sentence which he utters is the same.[17]

The solution to the reconstruction problem for ellipsis then is that ellipses have structure, and the way that ellipses are understood is a result of this structure. This understanding arises in virtue of identity of *syntactic* structure, so that in the case at hand there are multiple syntactic occurrences of a verb phrase, the elided and unelided being equally well there in the sentence represented, and hence uttered, by the language user. What the ellipsis is not is verbalized, but this is not necessary for the recognition of the appropriate structural representation. Now given that central to understanding ellipsis is that the same syntactic structure is present with or without ellipsis, a certain expectation arises: If there is identical structure, then the effects of syntactic constraints should be found with or without ellipsis. This is indeed the case; an illustration can be found by considering the pair in (19):

(19) a. I know which book Max read, and which book Oscar thinks that Sally read
      b. *I know which book Max read, and which book Oscar wonders why Sally read

The contrast here just reflects the contrast between the sentences *I know which book Oscar thinks that Sally read* and **I know which book Oscar wonders why Sally read*. In linguistic terms, the problem with the latter sentence is that there has been an illicit extraction of a *wh*-phrase from an embedded question, leaving a trace as the object of *read* which is free in a *wh*-island. In (19), the sentences have been placed in a discourse context which permits the final verb phrase to be elided, so that we also have the pair in (20):

(20) a. I know which book Max read, and which book Oscar thinks that Sally did
      b. *I know which book Max read, and which book Oscar wonders why Sally did

That there is no difference between (19) and (20) is hardly surprising, given that they are in their syntactic structure identical. They would not be identical, however, if ellipsis were contextual; while (19b) might be ill-formed for syntactic reasons, the reasons would not carry over to (20b), since the relevant syntactic structure would not be present. Rather, (20b) should be of the same status as (20a), as the ellipsis in each would denote the same property in context.[18]

Ellipsis, as a reconstruction problem, thus has a solution of the same general sort as anaphora, as both cases turn on formal identity of syntactic structures. Each involves a certain abstraction in order to obtain this identity, and these are different. For anaphora, it is from lack of morphophonemic identity, which can be set aside in favor of identity of indices, while for ellipsis, it is from lack of identical verbalization. In the case of ellipsis, there are, by hypothesis, linguistic expressions which simply have not been spoken, the identity of elided and non-elided forms then being one of strict replication, right down to the fine grain of syntactic structure. As noted, in *Oscar collects antiques, and Max does, too*, there are literally two occurrences of the verb phrase *collect antiques*. These two ways of expressing structural identity, that found with anaphora and that found with ellipsis, can be embedded, as in (21):

(21)   Mary thinks Oscar is smart, and he does, too

There is a way of understanding (21) so that the second clause is taken as an utterance of *He thinks that Oscar is smart*; this is, of course, no different from the previous cases. There is also, however, a way of understanding (21) so that the second clause is comparable to an utterance of *Oscar thinks that he is smart*, with an anaphoric pronoun. In this case, the (unelided) name *Oscar* is matched, in the elided material, with a pronoun, albeit one with the same reference. This alteration in linguistic "vehicle" is possible because it does not distort syntactic identity relations; thus observe (22), what is uttered by a speaker who verbalizes (21), on the intended reading:

(22)   Mary thinks Oscar$_1$ is smart, and he$_1$ thinks he$_1$ is smart, too

The only difference between the verb phrases here is the alternation of the name and the pronoun. But since there remains coindexing, syntactic identity is maintained, just as it would be if the verbalization of (22) contained no ellipsis at all.[19]

It might be thought that there is a closer kinship between anaphora and ellipsis than we have made out; it is not merely that they are both reconstruction problems, but that they are the same reconstruction problem. This would be revealed by taking ellipsis on the order of the pro-form in (23), ellipsis just being the unspoken counterpart:[20]

(23)   Oscar collects antiques, and Max does it, too

The mechanisms we have developed to analyze the statements made when pronominal anaphora is employed could then be carried over to the analysis of ellipsis. Taking ellipses as pro-forms would receive support from the properties mentioned above which appear to be shared by ellipses and pronouns. Thus, like pronouns, ellipses may apparently be indexical, as in the case of the polite *Please do*, where there is seemingly no prior utterance of the verb phrase *sit down*, or anaphoric, as in the cases we have been otherwise discussing. When anaphoric, ellipses and their antecedents may be found spread among the various sentences that make up a discourse, as well as among various verbalizations of these sentences, spread among many speakers, or they may all be located in the verbalizations of a single speaker.[21] Again, this is just as with pronouns, supporting the suggested unification of nominal and verbal pro-forms.

These correlations seem striking, but they are not telling, as further observation sheds doubt on the hypothesis that ellipses are null allomorphs of pro-forms. This hypothesis would lead us to expect that as a rule sentences which differ only with respect to having the null or non-null forms would be of the same status. But we find points of divergence, as in the contrast in (24):[22]

> (24) a. I know which book Max read, and which book Oscar didn't
>   b. *I know which book Max read, and which book Oscar didn't do it

This contrast follows, however, if we make the following assumptions. (i) In (24a) the ellipsis is unverbalized structure, and (ii) in (24b) the pro-form structurally exhausts the verb phrase. Then, just like in *I know which book Max read, and which book Oscar didn't read*, the *wh*-phrase in the second clause of (24a) will properly bind a trace. But since (24b) is not like this sentence – by (ii), there is no internal VP structure – such trace binding will not be found for the comparable *wh*-phrase, and this will be the cause of its ill-formedness. (Compare (24b) to *I know that Max will read* The Stones of Venice, *but that Oscar won't do it*, where no trace binding is called for.) What is significant here is that the analysis of (24) rests on the presumption that verb phrase ellipsis and verb phrase anaphora are not the same thing, but that the former is structured in a way that the latter is not. Hence it argues against the hypothesized reduction of ellipsis to a type of anaphora comparable to pronominal anaphora.

The other observations cited in support of the unitary hypothesis show not so much anything about correlations of nominal and verbal pro-forms, but rather something more interesting about the relations of sentences, utterances and their verbalizations. Consider first that antecedent and elliptical occurrences may be found spread out among various verbalizations. So suppose what comes out of one speaker's mouth is "Oscar collects antiques", and a second speaker chimes in "and Max does, too." What utterance has the second speaker made? The answer is that he must have made the same utterance as a single speaker who utters "Oscar collects antiques, and Max does, too". Both have the same representation; they differ only in their choice of verbalization. The second speaker must have a representation of what she has heard, since without it, how would she know what to say, or what would count as a sensible utterance? The legitimacy of her elliptical production is based on this representation, itself partly derived from her perception. The speaker need not, however, repeat (that is, reverbalize) that part of her utterance which has already been entered into the conversation, at pain of prolixity, although for certain rhetorical purposes she may wish to do so. Thus, suppose she wished to voice her agreement with what the first speaker had said; then she could quite appropriately have said "Yes indeed Oscar collects antiques, and Max does, too". The point here is that verbalization is only tangentially related to the representations which underlie speakers' utterances. Indeed, it is not even required that verbalizations correspond to utterances of complete sentences; they may be arbitrary fragments. Suppose the first speaker said "Oscar collects antiques, and Max", the second speaker can finish it up by saying "does, too". The second speaker's representation in this case is no different than in the other cases mentioned. At any given point in a conversation, the sentences a speaker represents will include those which have already been uttered (if there are any), the one being uttered, and perhaps some which will be uttered. Prior verbalizations will be the proximate cause for much of this representation, the result of aural (or visual) perception. Such perception is not causal for all of the speaker's representation, however; it is not of the sentence being currently uttered in the conversation, or of any future sentences the speaker may represent. Rather, these representations were "thought up" by the speaker with the intent to communicate them to the hearer, (perhaps under the distal influence of his perception of prior verbalizations). Such intention to communicate, however, is not necessary for formation of representations; representations may be formed because participants in a conversation just believe they are part of the conversation. Typically, speakers make verbal utterances if they believe that the hearer does not already represent the corresponding sentence; if the speaker wishes that the hearer represent some sentence, this can be insured (if not guaranteed) by making an appropriate verbalization. If, however, the speaker believes a sentence is already represented by the hearer, he may refrain from verbalizing it, and continue on with the conversation. This belief may be based on the speaker's belief that the hearer was perceptually present at a prior verbalization, but it need not be.

These considerations weigh on the "indexical" occurrences of ellipsis, ones in which there is seemingly no prior utterance of the elided verb phrase – the case of *Please do*. Care is required here in analyzing "prior utterance," since as we have seen what is verbalized is not the same as what is uttered. What we observe is that uttering *Please do* makes sense only if there is a *question* as to whether the person who walked into the room should sit down. Conventions of etiquette being what they are, the person entering may very well represent the question *Should I sit down?*, and the person in the room may believe that he does, but it may be inappropriate to actually ask to do so. But if the etiquette were different, or the person entering were uncertain about what the person in the room believed about his representations, the exchange in (25) would have worked just as well:

(25)   *Question*: Should I sit down?
       Answer: Please do

Whether the verbal conversation consists of just the simple utterance of *Please do*, or of the two utterances in (25), is thus a function of what sentences the speaker and hearer think they share. But regardless of which form of verbal conversation the interlocutors engage in, their sentential discourse is invariant; predictably, the constraints on such discourses will emerge either way. Thus, the simple utterance **Please do, too* is not a possible politeness, either when verbalized alone, or when accompanied by a prior verbalization of *Should I sit down*? The conclusion then is that even with *Please do*, the elided verb phrase is an occurrence of a verb phrase which has a prior occurrence in discourse, and is not indexical. This in turn reinforces the view that pronouns and ellipses are distinct, although pronominal anaphora and ellipsis fall together as types of reconstruction problems.

To conclude, our remarks in this paper have been in the service of illuminating a correspondence principle for a theory of meaning: If expressions are identical in sentences, then they are identical in their corresponding semantics. The carry-over of syntactic identity into the semantics will fix aspects of meaning which result from linguistic form per se, and hence will determine in part the statements sentences can be used to make. On the face of it this principle seems plain enough, but in practice its application may be complicated by the correspondence being partially or wholly masked so as to obscure the syntactic identity of expressions. We have looked at two forms of such masking arising from the use of anaphoric pro-forms and elliptical silence. In these cases we have asked whether grammar provides rules in order to reconstruct the identity, or does analysis require that linguistic form be augmented by context? The answer we have given is that in both cases there are such rules, although in other cases, such as indexicals, there are not. Exactly how these "reconstruction rules" for sentences are to be formulated, and how they interact with semantic computation of statements, including any notions of identity which this algorithm itself might impose, forms one of the core parts of the semantics of natural language. When taken along with the roles of context and use, our understanding of reconstruction problems will isolate in a theory of meaning for natural language the role of linguistic form, including logical form, and hence will contribute to answering the overall semiotic question of how natural languages may be used by speakers and hearers in the service of their communicative intentions.[23]

NOTES

1   We give a strong form of the use principle in the text, but since, for instance, it may be appropriate to speak irrelevantly or falsely in the service of giving rise to conversational implicature, the principle would need to be weakened, so as to allow utterers to "make as if to say." See Grice (1989) and Neale (1992) for discussion of this point.
2   The semantics could entail this in a number of ways. For instance, there could be an objectual fixation of reference, giving some sort of Russellian propositions; see Kaplan (1989). An alternative would be a substitutional approach, in which an expression which names the referent metalinguistically replaces the pronoun; see Evans (1977).

3   Technically, the rule states that an expression such as a name (that is, one which is neither a personal nor reflexive pronoun) cannot be coreferential with any NPs which c-command it. Also, bear in mind that the comments in the text only apply to personal pronouns, and not to reflexive pronouns, for which coreference is (at least usually) grammatical determined.

4   Bear in mind that *Oscar kissed his mother* is only indexically ambiguous between two conditions: coindexing and non-coindexing. It is not in any sense infinitely ambiguous; to take it as such would be to confuse a superfluous numerical property of the notation with the linguistic distinctions it is being used to represent.

5   An expression is *locally bound* iff within the minimal clause or noun phrase dominating it, there is some coindexed c-commanding expression; it is *locally free* iff it is not locally bound. It is *globally free* iff it is not c-commanded by a coindexed phrase in any dominating category. We purposely leave vague the notion "anaphorically local domain;" glossing it for the purposes at hand as the minimal noun phrase or clause. The precise formulation of such domains has been widely discussed in the literature. For some recent representative discussion, see the contributions in Koster and Reuland (1991).

6   For discussion of the relation of indices and context, see Fiengo and May (1994), chapter 2.

7   This distinction between implicature and entailment corresponds to a distinction between whether distinct assignments corresponding to distinct indices is just assumed in context, subject to revision in the course of the discourse, or whether this is fixed in context. For discussion of the relation of indices and context, see Fiengo and May (1994), chapter 2.

8   Note that it is far from clear how to exactly characterize the access relation. Presumably, speakers and hearers must be in some sort of epistemic relation to a linguistic structure, the identity of which is determined by some computation over the structure of the actual utterance made. But neither the character of this epistemic relation, nor the computations which generate the alternative sentence has ever been spelled out with any satisfactory precision.

9   Strictly speaking, for Reinhart grammatically expressed coreference is only to be found if there is "bound anaphora," by which she means that the pronoun is c-commanded by its antecedent. The c-command requirement is too strong, however, precluding cases sharing the properties of grammatical coreference, but in which c-command is lacking. See discussion in Fiengo and May (1994), chapters 2 and 3.

10   So we are not considering a perfectly imaginable language, which because there are no reflexives in the language, would have a different binding theory than English. E. Keenan and U. Lahiri have brought to our attention Fijian and Sinhala as languages which have no reflexives, but sentences comparable to *He saw Oscar* have the same status as in English. It is not entirely clear that these are actual cases of the *gedanken* experiment, as the counterparts to *Oscar saw him* in these languages can be understood as reflexive. It might just be that they have personal and reflexive pronouns which are homophonic.

11   Depending on how the access relation is defined, we might also allow *Zelda's husband is identical to himself* or *Zelda's husband is self-identical* as the tautological alternatives to *Zelda's husband is Zelda's husband*.

12   We can also have sentences like *He saw his mother* in which coindexing would determine that there are two occurrences of an indexical pronoun whose value is

fixed relative to context. For an explicit presentation of a semantics incorporating indexed expressions, see Fiengo and May (1994), chapter 2.

13 There are at least two other uses of pronouns which we categorize as anaphoric, in the sense that their interpretation is a matter of linguistic rule, which we will not otherwise discuss here. One is Evans' eponymous E-type pronouns (Evans 1977, 1980), as these are found in the context of Geach's "donkey" anaphora; cf. *Everyone who owns a donkey beats it.* To these, there are two broad classes of approaches. (i) The pronoun is identified with a variable, with concomitant adjustment of the quantificational structure of the antecedent (Haïk 1984, Heim 1982, Kamp 1981); (ii) The pronoun is identified with a description which is recovered from its antecedent as it occurs in its linguistic surroundings (Evans 1977, Neale 1990 in somewhat different versions). The second type is what Geach (1976) called "pure pronouns of laziness," where a pronoun has an antecedent which itself contains a pronoun. Geach remarks that these are a "repetition or near-repetition of an antecedent for which a pronoun goes proxy", but that they do not "repeat or continue the reference of the antecedent as its original occurrence". An example of a pure pronoun of laziness is in the sentence *Max, who sometimes ignores his boss, has more sense than Oscar, who always gives in to him,* where the pronoun *him* goes proxy for *his boss,* that is, Oscar's boss. We have analyzed the basic effect here, which falls under the phenomenon of sloppy identity, in Fiengo and May (1994) chapters 3, 4 and 5. Also, see comment in note 20.

14 For discussion of the syntax and semantics of LF we presuppose, see May (1985, 1989, 1991a, 1991b). There are a number of issues engendered by this view of logical form and LF. Syntactically, a question arises as to the applicability of the Binding Theory; we assume that it is part of the theory of the structure of LF. See Fiengo and May (1994), chapters 2 and 6.

15 In this line of thinking, which originates with the work of Sag (1976) and Williams (1977), properties are taken as characteristic functions of sets, represented as λ-expressions. The discussion which follows is to be taken against a general background of skepticism, empirical and conceptual, on the need to encompass such a notion of property in the semantic analysis of natural language. Empirical shortcomings of approaches to ellipsis based on property identity are discussed in Fiengo and May (1994), chapter 4 under the rubric of the "eliminative puzzles of ellipsis."

16 For a recent presentation of this perspective on ellipsis, see Hardt (1991, 1992). Notice that more than one property can be raised to salience. For example, in *I swim and I play tennis, and Max does, too,* an example of a sort due to Webber (1978), the VPs will raise to salience the properties they each denote, with the ellipsis understood as the conjunction of these properties.

17 These comments carry over to ellipsis of multiple phrases, provided that the syntactic identity condition is satisfied for each. Thus, recall from note 16 the example *I swim and I play tennis, and Max does, too*; this is an alternative to *I swim and I play tennis, and Max swims and plays tennis, too.* Notice that nothing requires that the elided VPs, which are conjoined, have a conjoined antecedent. See discussion in Fiengo and May (1994), chapter 5.

18 The initial observation that syntactic constraints carry over to ellipsis is due to Isabelle Haïk (Haïk 1987). The observations are extended in Fiengo and May (1994), chapter 6; see also Lappin (1993a). Notice that the contextual analysis would face difficulties in analyzing the well-formed (20a), including how to legitimize the

occurrence of the *wh*-phrase in (20a), and the proper way to formulate the appropriate property as a λ-expression, which turns out to be non-trivial. On the latter, see Larson (1986), Fiengo and May (1994), chapter 6, Dalrymple, Shieber and Pereira, (1991).

19   As a generalization, vehicle change is possible up to non-distinctness of syntactic feature paradigms; in the case above this is with respect to the feature [±pronoun]. We also find fluctuation in realization of pronominal agreement features. Cf. *I turned in my assignment, and you did, too*, in which the elided verb phrase can be *turned in your assignment*. In part, the limits of vehicle change are given by Binding Theory; vehicle change will be apparent to the extent that it allows an elliptical structure to have a well-formed indexing. For the theory of vehicle change, see Fiengo and May (1994), chapters 5 and 6.

20   Notice that the pro-form in (23) can be a pronoun of laziness, as its antecedent can contain a pronoun; cf. *Oscar sold his antiques, and Max did it, too*, which shows the sloppy identity effect mentioned in note 13 and the references cited there.

21   Or they may be within a single sentence of a discourse, as for example in antecedent contained deletion sentences like *Oscar collects everything that Max does* or when ellipsis is into a sentential subject; cf. *That Oscar could surprised everyone else who had climbed Kilimanjaro.*

22   These examples are based on an original observation of Greg Carlson (Carlson, 1977a). Consequences of it are developed in Fiengo and May (1994), chapter 6.

23   We would like to thank Kent Bach, Utpal Lahiri, Peter Ludlow and Gila Sher for helpful comments. We would also like to thank audiences at UCLA, University of Venice, University of Padua, University of Milan, CREA, Paris and at the Workshop on Identity Through Time at the University of Geneva, to which portions of this material were presented.

6 The Interpretation of Ellipsis[1]

SHALOM LAPPIN

1 Introduction

The interpretation of elided structures and incomplete constituents raises an important question for linguistic theory. What are the procedures by which speakers of a language are able to systematically generate appropriate meanings for these fragments? More specifically, what is the nature of the formal representations which speakers assign to different sorts of incomplete constituents in order to arrive at their interpretation? Consider the three sorts of incomplete structure illustrated in (1).

(1) a. John read the paper before Bill did.
    b. Max gave flowers to Lucy, and chocolates too.
    c. No student arrived, except John.

(1a) is a case of VP ellipsis, where the VP of the PP adjunct phrase *Bill did* is missing. (1b) is an instance of bare argument ellipsis in which the second conjunct of the sentence, *chocolates*, consists only of an NP corresponding to the object of the verb in the first conjunct. (1c) is an example of an exception phrase fragment. It appears, at first glance, to be similar to bare argument ellipsis in that the fragment consists of an NP which corresponds to an argument (the subject) of the preceding clause.

Arriving at a proper characterization of the procedures through which interpretations are assigned to the incomplete constituents in (1) will provide insight into the interaction of syntactic structure and semantic interpretation. In particular, it will give us a clearer sense of the extent to which syntactic structure constrains interpretation in cases where a phrase is only partially realized by lexical elements.

One possibility worth considering is that the same set of procedures are involved in interpreting the three types of incomplete constituents exemplified in (1). In particular, one might suggest that meanings are constructed for these constituents by recovering predicative structures at the same level of representation in each case. There are two variants of this unified approach to the interpretation of the incomplete structures in (1). On the semantic version, the non-elided clause provides the source for the recovery of a property expression which is applied to the argument of the incomplete constituent to yield a complete predication. The syntactic variant of the approach assigns missing syntactic structure to the incomplete constituent, or establishes a syntactic relation between this constituent and the non-elided clause. A semantic procedure for interpreting elided constituents and phrasal fragments involves identifying a property which is applied directly to the denotation of an argument (or set of argument terms). By contrast, a syntactic approach mediates the interpretation of incomplete constituents through syntactic structures which are restored by reconstruction.

An example of a semantic procedure for ellipsis resolution through property recovery is the higher-order unification account of ellipsis proposed in Dalrymple et al. (1991). This account can be briefly characterized as follows. For any i ($1 \leq i$) let a_i be a phrase in an antecedent expression and b_i be the parallel phrase in an expression containing an ellipsis. S_1 and S_2 are interpretations of the antecedent clause and the clause containing the ellipsis site, respectively. Ellipsis resolution consists in finding a property (relation) which unifies with the property (relation) variable P to solve the equations in 2.

(2) $P(a_1, \ldots, a_n) = S_1$ & $P(b_1, \ldots, b_n) = S_2$

If we take *John* and *Bill* to be the parallel elements in (1a), then higher order unification will solve the equations as indicated in (3). The value which unifies with the property variable P is given in (3c). This property term applies to the denotation of *Bill* to yield the interpretation of the elided VP expressed by (3d).[2]

(3)   a. $a_1 = $ john & $b_1 = $ bill
       b. $S_1 = $ (read the paper)(john)
       c. $P = \lambda x[x$ read the paper]
       d. $\lambda x[x$ read the paper] (john) before $\lambda x[x$ read the paper](bill)

When *flowers* and *chocolates* are taken as parallel arguments in (1b), higher-order unification gives the values in (4a–c) to generate (4d) as the interpretation of the bare argument ellipsis in (1b).

(4)   a. $a_1 = $ flowers & $b_1 = $ chocolates
       b. $S_1 = $ (gave flowers to lucy)(max)
       c. $P = \lambda x[$max gave x to lucy]
       d. flowers($\lambda x[$max gave x to lucy]) and chocolates ($\lambda x[$max gave x to lucy])

Dalrymple et al. do not discuss exception phrase fragments. If we take these as instances of ellipsis, then higher-order unification will provide the interpretation in (5d) for (1c), through the unifications of (5a–c).

(5)   a. a_1 = no student & b_1 = John
      b. S_1 = no student(arrived)
      c. $P = \lambda x[x$ arrived]
      d. (no student)($\lambda x[x$ arrived]) except John($\lambda x[x$ arrived])

Let us briefly consider how a reconstruction based approach could deal with the fragments in (1). May (1985) and Fiengo and May (1994) (F&M) propose an analysis of VP ellipsis resolution on which the elided VP is an empty category which is associated with the syntactic structure and lexical content of an antecedent VP.[3] This association has the effect of copying the antecedent into the elided VP. Thus, the syntactic structure of (1a) is (6a), and reconstruction yields (6b).

(6)   a. John [$_{VP}$[$_V$ read] [$_{NP}$ the paper]] before Bill did [$_{VP}$]
      b. John [$_{VP}$[$_V$ read] [$_{NP}$ the paper]] before Bill [$_{VP}$[$_V$ *read*] [$_{NP}$ *the paper*]]

In bare argument cases like (1b) the missing material required to obtain a predicate for the argument fragment does not correspond to a constituent in the antecedent clause, and so reconstruction through copying (association of an empty constituent with a lexically realized antecedent) is not possible.[4] Reinhart (1991) suggests that a predicate is recovered from the antecedent clause by applying LF movement to the NP argument in the clause which corresponds to the fragment. This NP is adjoined to the bare argument in order to create a coordinate NP which binds a variable in the clause at LF, as in (7a). The clause is taken to denote a property which applies to the coordinate NP, as in (7b).

(7)   a. [$_{IP'}$[$_{IP}$ Max gave t_1 to Lucy] [$_{NP}$[$_{NP}$ flowers)$_1$ [$_{NP}$ and [$_{NP}$ chocolates]$_2$]$_2$]]
      b. (flowers and chocolates)(λx[max gave x to lucy])

In principle, either copying of a VP or reconstruction of a coordinate NP argument and a predicate through LF movement could be used to interpret the exception fragment in (1c). Copying yields (8a), while LF adjunction of the subject NP in the antecedent clause gives (8b), with the interpretation specified in (8c).

(8)   a. No student [$_{VP}$ arrived], except John [$_{VP}$ *arrived*]
      b. [$_{IP'}$[$_{IP}$ t_1 arrived] [$_{NP}$[$_{NP}$ no student]$_1$ [$_{NP}$ except [$_{NP}$ John]$_2$]$_2$]]
      c. (no student except John)($\lambda x[x$ arrived])

Reinhart observes that if we understand *except* in (8a) to imply conjunction and we take John to be a student (which (1a) entails), then (8a) is a contradiction (as is (5d), the interpretation generated by higher-order unification). She concludes that only reconstruction through NP movement at LF yields the correct representation of (1a).

In this paper I will argue that in fact neither a semantic procedure of property identification nor syntactic operations of reconstruction will cover all three types of incomplete structure considered here. Each fragment type requires a different procedure for generating an appropriate interpretation. In Section 2 I provide motivation for the claim that syntactic reconstruction is required for VP ellipsis resolution. I argue (contrary to May (1985) and F&M) that S-structure rather than LF is the level of representation at which VP ellipsis resolution is achieved. In Section 3 I cite evidence to support a higher-order unification account of bare argument ellipsis. Finally, in Section 4, I argue that a third kind of interpretive process, NP storage, is required to establish the connection between an exception phrase fragment and an NP in the antecedent clause. This argument is based upon a syntactic and semantic analysis of exception phrases as NP modifiers (functions from NP's to NP's).

The general view which emerges from these analyses of the cases in (1) is that both VP ellipsis and bare argument ellipsis are genuine cases of elided predicates. However, while VP ellipsis resolution requires interpretation through the reconstruction of a VP, bare argument ellipsis resolution involves the identification and direct assignment of a property (or relation) to the denotation of the bare argument (set of bare arguments). Exception phrase fragments, on the other hand, are not interpreted by recovering elided predicates. They are displaced NP modifiers which are connected to their arguments by a semantic operation of storage.

2   VP Ellipsis

2.1   *Antecedent contained ellipsis*

Haïk (1987) observes that antecedent contained VP ellipsis (ACE) structures are subject to barrier conditions, like subjacency, as the comparison between the ACE cases in 10 with their non-elided counterparts in 9 illustrates.

(9)   a. John read everything which$_1$ Mary believes that he read t_1
       b. *John read everything which$_1$ Mary believes the report that he read t_1
       c. *John read everything which$_1$ Mary wonders why he read t_1

(10) a. John read everything which Mary believes that he did.
       b. *John read everything which Mary believes the claim that he did.
       c. *John read everything which Mary wonders why he did.

The fact that ACE structures exhibit barrier effects indicates that operator-trace chains are present in the ellipsis site. This is incompatible with the view that ellipsis resolution in these cases consists in associating the elided VP directly with the representation of a property. Subjacency is a constraint on syntactic A' chains, and there would seem to be no basis for applying it to semantic representations.[5] Therefore, it is unclear how a semantic approach to ellipsis, like higher-order unification, can deal with this fact.

2.2 Ellipsis in parasitic gap constructions

Contreras (1984 and 1993), and Chomsky (1986a) note that parasitic gaps obey subjacency, as the examples in (11) show.

(11) a. This is the book which$_1$ Max read t_1 before knowing that Lucy read e_1
     b. *This is the book which$_1$ Max read t_1 before hearing the claim that Lucy read e_1
     c. *This is the book which$_1$ Max read t_1 before knowing why Lucy read e_1

As F&M point out, parasitic gap constructions continue to exhibit subjacency effects under ellipsis in ACE structures.[6]

(12) a. This is the book which$_1$ Max read t_1 before knowing that Lucy did.
     b. ??This is the book which$_1$ Max read t_1 before hearing the claim that Lucy did.
     c. ??This is the book which$_1$ Max read t_1 before knowing why Lucy did.

This fact is particularly problematic for a semantic view of ellipsis. When a resumptive pronoun is substituted for the parasitic gaps in (11b,c), the resulting sentences are fully acceptable.

(13) a. This is the book which$_1$ Max read t_1 before hearing the claim that Lucy read it$_1$
     b. This is the book which$_1$ Max read t_1 before knowing why Lucy read it$_1$

Therefore, the contrast between (12a) and (12b,c) provides strong evidence for the claim that the interpretation of the elided VP in these sentences involves the representation of an operator-bound empty category within the VP.

Contreras and Chomsky propose that the subjacency effects in parasitic gap structures can be explained by positing a second A' chain in which the gap is a syntactic variable bound by an empty operator. On this analysis, the S-structure of (11a) is (14).[7]

(14)   This is the book which$_1$ Max [$_{VP}$ read t_1 [$_{PP}$ before [$_{CP}$ O_1 PRO knowing that Lucy read e_1]]]

They observe that the relation between the chain containing the *wh*-trace and the chain containing the second gap is governed by a locality condition which requires that the empty operator heading the second chain be (at least) subjacent to the initial trace in the first chain.[8] This condition is satisfied in (15a) where only one barrier, the PP in which the second chain is contained, intervenes between the empty operator and the *wh*-trace. By contrast, in (15b) the empty operator is separated from the *wh*-trace by two PP's, each of which is a barrier. As (15c) illustrates, the locality condition does not apply when a resumptive pronoun is substituted for a parasitic gap.

(15)   a.   This is the performance which$_1$ John [$_{VP}$ attended t_1 [$_{PP}$ in order [$_{CP}$ O_1 PRO to review e_1]]]
       b.   *This is the performance which$_1$ John [$_{VP}$ attended t_1 [$_{PP}$ after [$_{CP}$ PRO coming [$_{PP}$ in order [$_{CP}$ O_1 PRO to review e_1]]]]]
       c.   This is the performance which$_1$ John attended t_1 after coming in order to review it$_1$

The contrast between (16a) and (16b) (where the intended interpretation of the elided VP in these sentences is *see e_1*) indicates that the locality condition on parasitic gap chains remains in effect under ellipsis.

(16)   a.   This is the play which$_1$ John saw t_1 because Bill wanted to
       b.   *This is the play which$_1$ John saw t_1 before Bill went because he wanted to

The fact that the locality condition for parasitic gap chains continues to apply under ellipsis gives additional support to the claim that an A'-bound empty category is represented within the elided VP of this construction. It would seem, then, that reconstruction is required in order to generate appropriate representations of elided VP's, at least for ACE structures and elided parasitic gap constructions.

2.3   *Reconstruction at S-structure vs reconstruction at LF*

We can characterize reconstruction in the context of VP ellipsis as follows. Reconstruction is a relation between an elided VP and an equivalence class of lexically anchored syntactic structures which correspond to an antecedent VP. All elements of the equivalence class exhibit the same syntactic structure, but variation among corresponding lexical anchors with respect to a restricted set of specified features is possible. In (6), the relation of reconstruction between the antecedent and the elided VP involves identity of corresponding lexical anchors, as well as identity of syntactic structure.

(6) a. John [vp[v read] [NP the paper]] before Bill did [vp]
     b. John [vp[v read] [NP the paper]] before Bill [vp[v *read*] [NP *the paper*]]

F&M suggest that one of the features with respect to which corresponding lexical items in an equivalence class for reconstruction can vary is [+/-pronoun]. Specifically, they allow referring NP's to correspond to pronominal counterparts under reconstruction. They refer to this correspondence as *vehicle change*. If reconstruction of the elided VP in (17a) is specified in terms of lexical identity with the antecedent, as in (17b), the result is a violation of condition C of the binding conditions. However, if vehicle change is invoked, as in (17c), the result is a reconstruction which satisfies the binding conditions.

(17) a. Mary spoke to John₁, and he₁ hopes that Lucy will too.
      b. *Mary spoke to John₁, and he₁ hopes that Lucy will [vp *speak to John₁*]
      c. Mary spoke to John₁, and he₁ hopes that Lucy will [vp *speak to him₁*]

An important question which arises for a reconstruction based approach to VP ellipsis resolution is at what level of syntactic representation the reconstruction relation is specified. May (1985) and F&M claim that reconstruction takes place at LF. They assume that the elided VP in an ACE structure like (10a) is an empty category, and that the S-structure of (10a) is (18).

(10) a. John read everything which Mary believes that he did.
(18)   John [vp read everything which Mary believes that he did [vp]]

They argue that if reconstruction holds of the elided VP and its antecedent in (18), then an interpretive regress arises, as the lexically anchored VP structure which is associated with the empty VP in (18) will itself contain an elided VP that must be resolved through reconstruction. The solution which they propose to this problem is to require that reconstruction apply to the output of the rule of quantifier raising, QR, which adjoins the quantified NP object of *read* to the matrix IP, in order to derive the LF in (19a).⁹ The elided VP in (19a) is no longer antecedent-contained, and so reconstruction can apply to yield (19b).¹⁰

(19) a. [IP[everything which₁ Mary believes that he did [vp]]₁ [John read t₁]]
      b. [IP[everything which₁ Mary believes that he [vp *read t₁*]]₁ [John read t₁]]

In fact, an alternative analysis of ACE structures is possible on which reconstruction applies at S-structure rather than at LF.[11] On this view, the elided VP
of (10a) is not a syntactically unstructured empty category at S-structure, but
a structured partially empty category in which the trace of the *wh*-phrase is,
in fact, present. Therefore, the S-structure of (10a) is not (18) but (20a). Ellipsis
resolution is achieved by identifying the head verb *read* of the antecedent VP
as the lexical anchor of the partially elided VP in (20a), which generates the
reconstruction in (20b).

(20)   a. John [$_{VP}$ read everything which$_1$ Mary believes that he did [$_{VP}$[$_V$]
           t_1]]
       b. John [$_{VP}$ read everything which$_1$ Mary believes that he [$_{VP}$[$_V$ read]
           t_1]]

As reconstruction in (20a) involves only the head of the elided VP and the
head of the antecedent VP, it is not necessary to remove the (partially) elided
VP from the antecedent VP in which it is contained.[12]

More generally, on the S-structure based approach to VP ellipsis resolution,
reconstruction consists in specifying a correspondence between the head of an
elided (or partially elided) VP and its arguments and adjuncts on one hand,
and the head of a non-elided VP antecedent and its arguments and adjuncts
on the other. This analysis reduces VP ellipsis to pseudo-gapping, where a
fully elided VP, like the one in (21a), is the limit case in which all arguments
and adjuncts of the elided verb are missing.[13] (21b–d) illustrate pseudo-gapping
structures where selected complements and modifiers of the elided head are
realized.

(21)   a. John sent flowers to Lucy before Max did.
       b. John sent flowers to Lucy before Max did chocolates.
       c. John sent flowers to Lucy before Max did to Mary.
       d. John sent flowers to Lucy before Max did chocolates to Mary.

F&M point out that pseudo-gapping is subject to a locality condition which
requires that the arguments and adjuncts which appear in a pseudo-gapped
structure be complements and modifiers of the elided verb. Thus, for example,
the elided material in (22) must be understood as *gave Lucy* rather than *claimed
that he gave Lucy*.

(22)   Max claimed that he gave Lucy flowers before John did chocolates.

This would appear to create problems for the S-structure analysis of VP ellipsis. In (23), both the complement verb *read* and the matrix verb *promised* can
be taken as the antecedent of the elided verb.

(23)   John promised to read everything which Rosa did.

If the trace of the *wh*-phrase is realized in the elided VP of the relative clause in (23), it can only be an argument of *read*. This would appear to incorrectly rule out the interpretation of the sentence on which *promised to read* is understood as the antecedent of the elided VP.

In fact, the locality condition on pseudo-gapping is not as strict as F&M suggest. Cases of pseudo-gapping in which a matrix verb takes a non-tensed complement do allow both the matrix verb and the lexically realized complement verb to serve as the antecedent of the elided verb in these structures. The matrix verbs in the sentences of (24) are possible (and in (24b–d), the preferred) antecedents for the heads of the pseudo-gapped VP's. In (24c), for example, *wants to gain admission* is the preferred interpretation of the elided material in the pseudo-gapped VP.

(24) a. John will agree to complete his paper before Bill will his book.
   b. Mary hoped to win the race more fervently than John did the baseball game.
   c. Lucy wants to gain admission to Harvard as much as Sue does to MIT.
   d. Max insists on visiting London more adamantly than Bill does Paris.

What may be happening in these cases is that the matrix verb and the verbal head of its complement are re-analyzed as a complex verb. Such a re-analysis would yield *want to gain* as a complex verb that takes *admission* as its argument in (24c), and *insist on visiting* as a complex verb with *London* as its object in (24d). Similarly, re-analysis will give *promise to read* in (23), which provides a suitable antecedent for the head of the partially elided VP in the relative clause. The object trace of the elided verb in (23) would then be the complement of the complex verb under reconstruction. As the contrast between (22) and the sentences in (24) indicates, tensed complements are barriers to the formation of complex verbs from matrix and complement verbs.

The analysis of ACE structures as instances of pseudo-gapping, taken together with the assumption that tense is a barrier to complex verb formation, predicts that only the complement verb can be taken as the antecedent of the elided verb in both the ACE sentence in (25a) and the overt instance of pseudo-gapping in (25b).

(25) a. John promised that he read everything which Rosa did.
   b. John agreed that he completed his paper before Bill did his book.

The judgements of most speakers who I have consulted confirm this prediction. A minority can interpret the elided verb as dependent upon the matrix verb in both these sentences. For these speakers, tense is not a barrier to complex verb formation, and so the locality condition on pseudo-gapping does not apply. The general prediction of the proposed analysis of ACE structures is that ACE and overt pseudo-gapping will exhibit the same range of possibilities for matrix and complement verb antecedents. This does, in fact, seem to be the case.

Ellipsis in parasitic gaps provides motivation for the view that reconstruction in the case of VP ellipsis occurs at S-structure rather than LF. Consider the elided parasitic gap structure in (26).

> (26)   This is the book which Mary thinks she reviewed before she could have.

On the LF account, the non-contradictory reading of (26) is obtained by applying QR to the PP adjunct clause and adjoining it either to the matrix VP headed by *thinks*, or the matrix IP.[14] Reconstruction then applies to the elided VP, producing the post-LF structures in (27a,b).

> (27)   a.   This is the book $[_{CP}$ which$_1$ $[_{IP}$ Mary $[_{VP}[_{PP}$ before O_1 she could have $[_{VP}$ *reviewed* $e_1]]]_2$ $[_{VP}$ thinks $[_{CP}$ she $[_{VP}$ reviewed t_1 $t_2]]]]]]]$
>   b.   This is the book $[_{CP}$ which$_1$ $[_{IP'}[_{PP}$ before O_1 she could have $[_{VP}$ *reviewed* $e_1]]]_2$ $[_{IP}$ Mary $[_{VP}$ thinks $[_{CP}$ she $[_{VP}$ reviewed t_1 $t_2]]]]]]]$

The problem with this analysis is that both (27a) and (27b) violate the locality condition on parasitic gap chains which requires that the empty operator binding the gap be subjacent to the initial trace in the chain headed by the *wh*-phrase that licenses the empty operator. The empty operator is separated from the *wh*-trace t_1 by a PP and a VP in (27a), and a PP and two VP's in (27b).

One might suggest that (27b) does, in fact, satisfy the locality condition by virtue of the fact that the empty operator in this structure is subjacent to the *wh*-phrase *which*$_1$. This phrase can then be taken as its local binder in the sense of Contreras (1993). The problem with this suggestion is that if *which*$_1$ is the local binder for the empty operator, then it heads a *wh*-chain in which the empty operator is, in effect, an intermediate trace, and the parasitic gap is a *wh*-trace in argument position. But this analysis incorrectly predicts that (28a) should be grammatical. Given that (28b) is a possible LF representation for (28a), the *wh*-phrase heads a well formed A' chain which satisfies subjacency at LF.

> (28)   a.   *This is the paper which John revised the book after submitting.
>   b.   This is the paper $[_{CP}$ which$_1$ $[_{IP}[_{PP}$ after O_1 PRO submitting $e_1]_2$ $[_{IP}$ John revised the book $t_2]]]$

It should also be pointed out that it is not possible to escape the problem which (26) poses for the LF account of VP ellipsis resolution by claiming that parasitic gaps are reconstructed under vehicle change as pronominal correlates of the *wh*-traces which license them, and so they are exempt from locality conditions.[15] This implies that parasitic gaps in elided VP's are reconstructed as resumptive pronouns. But this view fails to account for the fact that subjacency and the locality condition on the empty operator of a parasitic gap chain hold under ellipsis, as illustrated by the contrasts in (12) and (16), respectively.

None of these problems arises on the S-structure account of VP ellipsis resolution. The analysis of ACE structures like (10a) applies directly to (26). The S-structure of (26) is (29a), where the partially elided VP contains a realized parasitic gap bound by the empty operator. Reconstruction applies only to the elided head of this VP to yield (29b).

(29) a. This is the book $[_{CP}$ which$_1$ $[_{IP}$ Mary $[_{VP}$ thinks$]$ $[_{CP}$ she $[_{VP}[_{V'}$ reviewed $t_1]$ $[_{PP}$ before O_1 she could have $[_{VP}[_V$ $]e_1]]]]]]]$

b. This is the book $[_{CP}$ which$_1$ $[_{IP}$ Mary $[_{VP}$ thinks $[_{CP}$ she $[_{VP}[_{V'}$ reviewed $t_1]$ $[_{PP}$ before O_1 she could have $[_{VP}[_V$ *reviewed*$]$ $e_1]]]]]]]$

As the parasitic gap chain is present at S-structure, this analysis accounts for the fact that parasitic gap chains are sensitive to subjacency and the locality condition on the empty operator under ellipsis.

2.4 Ellipsis and non-restrictive relative clauses

VP ellipsis in non-restrictive relative clauses also provides motivation for the pseudo-gapping analysis of ACE structures.[16] Consider the examples in (30).

(30) a. Max trusts Rosa, who Bill does too.
     b. John kissed Lucy, who Bill didn't.

If we assume that QR does not apply to non-quantified NP's, then the elided VP in these sentences must be reconstructed in antecedent-contained position. F&M claim that the name which occurs as the object of the matrix verb in (30a,b) is reconstructed as a trace under vehicle change, yielding, for example, (31) as the interpretation of (30a).

(31) Max trusts Rosa$_1$, [who$_1$ Bill $[_{vp}$ *trusts* $t_1]]$ too

This analysis gives the wrong results for cases with several non-restrictive relatives containing elided VP's that take the same verb as their antecedent but modify distinct NP's, as in (32a). Similarly, it will not work for (32b), where an elided VP in a non-restrictive relative is dependent upon a non-elided VP in another non-restrictive relative.

(32)   a. John trusts Rosa, who Bill does too, and even Lucy, who Bill
          doesn't.
       b. John kissed Rosa, who Bill likes, and he kissed Lucy, who Bill
          doesn't.

On the F&M analysis, reconstruction assigns (32a,b) the representations in
(33a,b), respectively.

(33)   a. *John trusts Rosa$_1$, [who$_1$ Bill [$_{VP}$ *trusts* t_1]] too, and even Lucy$_2$,
          [$_{VP}$ who$_2$ Bill doesn't [$_{VP}$ *trust* t_1]]
       b. *John kissed Rosa$_1$, [who$_1$ Bill [$_{VP}$ *likes* t_1]], and he kissed Lucy$_2$,
          [who$_2$ Bill doesn't [$_{VP}$ *like* t_1]]

The second elided VP in (33a) takes either the non-elided matrix VP or the
reconstructed VP of the first elided VP as its antecedent. In either case, the
index of the reconstructed trace in the second non-restrictive relative is inherited from the object NP of its antecedent.[17] As the index of the *wh*-phrase in
a non-restrictive relative clause is identical to the index of the NP which it
modifies, the index of the reconstructed trace in the second relative does not
match the index of the *wh*-phrase in its clause. Therefore, this trace is unbound,
and the *wh*-phrase is a vacuous operator. The reconstructed trace in (33b)
bears the wrong index for the same reason.

  This problem does not arise on the pseudo-gapping account. The S-structures
of (32a,b) contain appropriately indexed traces in partially elided VP's. Reconstruction involves lexical anchoring of the empty head of the VP in the lexically
realized (or previously anchored) head of the antecedent VP. Therefore, the
result of reconstruction in (32a,b), is (34a,b) respectively.

(34)   a. John trusts Rosa$_1$, [who$_1$ Bill [$_{VP}$[$_V$ *trusts*] t_1]] too, and even Lucy$_2$,
          [who$_2$ he doesn't [$_{VP}$[$_V$ *trust*] t_2]]
       b. John kissed Rosa$_1$, [who$_1$ Bill [$_{VP}$[$_V$ *likes*] t_1]], and he kissed Lucy$_2$,
          [who$_2$ Bill doesn't [$_{VP}$[$_V$ *like*] t_2]]

The pseudo-gapping analysis of ACE structures applies uniformly to VP ellipsis in both restrictive and non-restrictive relative clauses.

2.5   *VP ellipsis without syntactically matched antecedents*

Advocates of the semantic approach to VP ellipsis resolution have pointed
to cases in which elided VP's are interpreted relative to syntactically non-
matching antecedents as evidence for the claim that ellipsis resolution consists
in the direct assignment of a property to an empty VP.[18] The sentences in 35
are examples of this kind.[19]

(35) a. A lot of this material can be presented in a fairly informal and
          accessible fashion, and often I do.
      b. Wendy is eager to sail around the world and Bruce is eager to
          climb Kilimanjaro, but neither of them can because money is too
          tight.
      c. China is a country that Joe wants to visit, and he will too, if he
          gets enough money.

In light of the evidence for syntactic reconstruction which the appearance of
A′ chains in elided structures provides on one hand, and the apparent support
which cases like those in (35) give for direct semantic interpretation on the
other, Chao (1988) and Kehler (1993) propose mixed models of ellipsis resolution. In these models reconstruction applies to elided VP's satisfying certain
parallelism conditions; specifically, those where barrier effects are observed.
When these conditions are not satisfied, semantic representations of properties
are directly assigned.[20]

F&M argue that the sentences in (35) can be handled through reconstruction. They point out that an A-chain headed by a lexically realized NP and
containing an NP trace constitutes a single argument marked for one theta-
role and one Case position. Therefore, the A-chain in the first conjunct of (35a)
is a single argument containing the lexically realized NP *This material* in the
Case position of the subject and an NP trace in the theta-marked object position of the passive verb *presented*. F&M claim that, for purposes of reconstruction, the identification of an argument in an antecedent with its reconstructed
appearance in an elided VP is not sensitive to whether the Case and theta-role
components of the argument occupy the same position. Therefore, the two-
element A-chain in the antecedent of (35a) can be identified with a single
element A-chain under reconstruction, and so (36) is a possible reconstruction
of (35a).

(36) [$_{NP}$ a lot of this material]$_1$ can be [$_{VP}$ presented t_1 in a fairly informal
      and accessible fashion], and often I do [$_{VP}$ *present* [$_{NP}$ *a lot of this*
      material]$_1$ *in a fairly informal and accessible fashion*]

F&M also claim that when an elided VP corresponds to a co-ordinate structure, each of the conjuncts (disjuncts) of this structure can be reconstructed
from independent non-co-ordinate antecedents. This assumption permits them
to reconstruct the elided VP in (35b) as in (37).

(37) Wendy is eager to [$_{VP}$ sail around the world] and Bruce is eager to
      [$_{VP}$ climb Kilimanjaro], but neither of them can [$_{VP}$ [$_{VP}$ *sail around the*
      world] *or* [$_{VP}$ *climb Kilimanjaro*]] because money is too tight

Finally, if we apply vehicle change to the trace of the relative clause operator in the antecedent VP of (35c), we obtain (38) as the reconstruction of (35c).

(38)   China is [$_{NP}$ a country [that O_1 Joe wants to visit t_1]]$_1$, and he will
[$_{VP}$ *visit it*$_1$] too, if he gets enough money.

By accepting the assumptions which F&M make to deal with the examples
in 35, it may be possible to handle a significant number of cases in which
elided VP's apparently lack syntactically matching antecedents. However, there
are at least some instances of ellipsis for which this approach will not go
through. Consider the sentences in 39.

(39)   a. Irv and Mary want to go out but Mary can't, because her father
disapproves of Irv. (based on an example in Webber (1979))
b. Harry used to be a great speaker, but he can't any more, because he lost his voice. (from Hardt (1993))

The elided VP in (39a) is understood as *go out with Irv*. Given that the antecedent VP *go out* is intransitive and the adjunct *with each other* (or *together*) is only
pragmatically implied in the antecedent clause, *go out with Irv* is not available
as an antecedent, even within the extended notion of reconstruction which
F&M invoke to deal with the examples in (35). The elided VP in (39b) is
interpreted as *speak*, which is obtained from the predicate nominal *speaker* in
the antecedent clause. It is unclear how the identification of a verb with an NP
or N' antecedent could be accommodated as a case of reconstruction. It would
seem that ellipsis resolution in (39) is mediated by inference of a sentence
containing an appropriate antecedent VP. Specifically, it is necessary to infer
(40a,b) from the antecedent clauses of (39a,b), respectively, in order to obtain
antecedents for the elided VP's in the second conjuncts of the latter sentences.[21]

(40)   a. Mary wants to go out with Irv.
b. Harry used to speak.

However, it is important to recognize that the fact that inference is required
in order to interpret the elided VP's in (39) does not, in itself, provide motivation for the semantic approach to ellipsis resolution. The semantic representations of (40a,b) are not directly obtained from the semantic representations
of (39a,b), respectively. The inference from (39a) to (40a) depends, in part, on
pragmatic factors, and (40b) follows from (39b) only on the assumption of at
least two meaning postulates. One of these postulates licenses inferences from
sentences of the form *NP V's Adv* to sentences of the form *NP V's* for the class
of extensional adverbs. The other specifies that *NP is an N* implies that *NP V's*,
where *N* is a deverbal noun and *V* is the verb which corresponds to *N*. Therefore, the semantic account of ellipsis resolution must invoke inference in order
to deal with (39a,b). However, we can also handle (39a,b) within the framework of a reconstruction based account if we assume that ellipsis resolution in
these cases involves inferring (40a,b) as lexically anchored syntactic structures
whose VP's provide the antecedents for the elided VP's in the former sentences.

But if both the semantic approach and the reconstruction based view require inference, the formal nature of the representations between which relations of inference hold in ellipsis resolution remains open. On the semantic approach, inference is a relation between semantic representations. For the reconstruction based view, it is a relation between lexically anchored syntactic structures (which are, of course, semantically interpreted). How do we decide between these alternatives? The existence of elided VP's without syntactically matched antecedents cannot be used here as support for the semantic approach, as it is precisely these sorts of cases which require inference, and it is the nature of the relevant relation of inference which is in question. ACE structures and the behavior of parasitic gaps in elided VP's provide independent motivation for syntactic reconstruction in VP ellipsis resolution. If we adopt the semantic characterization of inference for (39), it will be necessary to recognize two distinct procedures of VP ellipsis resolution. We will have to permit reconstruction for the ACE and parasitic gap cases, and direct assignment of property representations through inference for (39a,b). We can sustain a fully uniform account of VP ellipsis if we take the reconstruction based view of inference and ellipsis resolution here. In the absence of independent evidence to the contrary, a uniform account of VP ellipsis resolution is to be preferred to one which posits two distinct procedures for interpreting elided VP's.

3 Bare Argument Ellipsis

3.1 *LF movement and higher-order unification*

As we saw in Section 1, on Reinhart's LF movement analysis of bare argument ellipsis, the NP in the antecedent clause which corresponds to the bare argument is adjoined to this argument at LF to create a coordinate NP operator which binds a trace in the original position of the raised NP. The interpretation of the bare argument structure is obtained by applying lambda abstraction to the trace in the antecedent clause. The coordinate NP is taken as a subject function which applies to the property term denoted by this lambda expression. Thus, (7a) is the LF of (1b), and (7b) is the interpretation induced by this LF.

(1) b. Max gave flowers to Lucy, and chocolates too.

(7) a. $[_{IP}[_{IP}$ Max gave t_1 to Lucy$]$ $[_{NP}[_{NP}$ flowers$]_1$ $[_{NP}$ and $[_{NP}$ chocolates$]_2]_2]]$
     b. (flowers and chocolates)(λx[max gave x to lucy])

As Chao (1988), and Kempson and Gabbay (1993) point out, ellipsis with bare adjuncts is also possible, as in (41).

(41)   John sings, and well too.

(41) would seem to be an instance of the same sort of bare ellipsis phenomenon as bare argument ellipsis, but it is unclear how Reinhart's LF movement account could handle structures of this kind.

Also, when adjuncts are combined with bare arguments, Reinhart's analysis yields the wrong results. It assigns (42a) the LF in (42b) and the incorrect interpretation in (42c).[22]

(42)   a. Max gave flowers to Lucy yesterday, and flowers today too.
       b. $[_{IP}[_{IP}$ Max gave t_1 to Lucy yesterday$]$ $[_{NP}[_{NP}$ flowers$]_1$ $[_{NP}$ and $[_{NP}$ flowers today$]_2]_2]]$
       c. (flowers and flowers today) (λx [max gave x to lucy yesterday])

The higher-order unification account of bare argument ellipsis can generate the correct representations for (41) and (42a). Let us assume that semantic representations of action verbs contain manner adverb functions of the form *in the manner*( ). If this function is not lexically realized by an adverb or implied by the verb, then the argument of the modifier is *unspecified*. We can then take the argument *unspecified* of the manner adverb in the representation of *sing* and the argument *well* of the manner adverb which is the bare adjunct as parallel arguments in (41), and resolve the relevant equations as in (43a–c). These equations yield (43d), which provides the desired interpretation of (41).

(43)   a. a_1 = the manner (unspecified) & b_1 = the manner(well)
       b. S_1 = ((in (the manner(unspecified))))(sings))(john)
       c. $P = \lambda x[((\text{in } (x))(\text{sings}))(\text{john})]$
       d. (the manner(unspecified))$\lambda x[((\text{in } (x))(\text{sings}))(\text{john})]$ and (the manner(well))$\lambda x[((\text{in } (x))(\text{sings}))(\text{john})]$

(43d) is equivalent to the assertion that John sings (in some manner or other) and John sings well.

If we take the NP-adjunct pair ⟨*flowers,yesterday*⟩ in the antecedent clause and the bare argument-adjunct pair ⟨*flowers,today*⟩ as the parallel elements ⟨a_1,a_2⟩ and ⟨b_1,b_2⟩, respectively, then it is necessary to apply lambda abstraction to the designated pair ⟨*flowers,yesterday*⟩ in the interpretation of the antecedent clause when determining a value for the relation variable R. This selection of parallel elements permits us to obtain the solutions indicated for the equations in (44a–c).[23] These equations generate (44d) which is the desired interpretation of (42a).

(44)   a. ⟨a_1,a_2⟩ = ⟨flowers,yesterday⟩ & ⟨b_1,b_2⟩ = ⟨flowers,today⟩
       b. S_1 = (gave flowers to lucy (at) yesterday)(max)
       c. $R = \lambda x\lambda y[\text{max gave } x \text{ to lucy (at) } y]$
       d. (flowers)($\lambda x[(\text{yesterday})(\lambda y[\text{max gave } x \text{ to lucy (at) } y])])$) and (flowers)($\lambda x[(\text{today})(\lambda y[\text{max gave } x \text{ to lucy (at) } y])])$)

A reconstruction based account of bare ellipsis, like Reinhart's LF adjunction treatment of bare arguments, must derive a suitable predication structure for the bare fragment through syntactic operations on the antecedent clause and the fragment. The syntactic structures of the antecedent clauses in (41) and (42a) do not seem to provide appropriate representations for reconstructing the predication which interprets these sentences. By contrast, higher-order unification derives the property term to be applied to the bare fragment directly from the semantic interpretation of the antecedent clause. Given the interpretations specified as the value of this clause in (43b) and (44b), it is possible to unify the property variable P and the relation variable R with the lambda expressions given in (43c) and (44c), respectively.

3.2 Bare argument ellipsis and subjacency

Reinhart claims that the relation between a bare argument and the argument to which it corresponds in the antecedent clause is constrained by subjacency. Thus, for example, the fragment in (45a) cannot be understood as asserting that we have not interrogated the burglar who stole the diamonds. Similarly, (45b) cannot be interpreted as stating that a musician who loved Bach arrived, and a musician who loved Mozart arrived.

(45)   a. *We have interrogated the burglar who stole the car already, but not the diamonds.
       b. *A musician who loved Bach arrived, and Mozart too.

These readings are excluded on Reinhart's analysis, as adjunction of the relevant NP to the bare argument at LF involves movement out of a relative clause, and so violates subjacency.

In fact, it is not at all clear that bare argument ellipsis is sensitive to subjacency. Consider the sentences in (46).

(46)   a. John enjoyed reading the articles which appeared in the *New York Times* last week, but not the *Daily Telegraph*.
       b. Dancing with Mary in the garden is a pleasure, but not the park.
       c. John agreed to the request that he submit articles to the journal, but not book reviews.

In each of these cases it is possible to interpret the negated fragment as outside of the scope of the syntactic island containing its corresponding NP in the antecedent. The most natural reading of (46a), for example, is that John enjoyed reading the articles which appeared in the *New York Times* last week, but he did not enjoy reading the articles which appeared in the *Daily Telegraph* last week. While examples like those in (45) suggest that some sort of locality condition may govern the connection between a bare fragment and the constituent to which it corresponds in the antecedent clause, the sentences in (46) indicate that this condition is not subjacency. Therefore, it is not possible to use subjacency as an argument for an LF movement treatment of bare argument ellipsis.

I conclude that higher-order unification provides a more adequate account of the general class of bare ellipsis phenomena than a reconstruction based analysis.

4   Displaced Exception Phrases

4.1   *The interpretation of exception phrases*

We observed in Section 1 that Reinhart applies the LF movement account of bare argument ellipsis to displaced exception phrases, like the one in (1c), in order to derive the LF representation in (8b) and the predicative structure in (8c).

(1)   c. No student arrived except John.
(8)   b. $[_{IP}[_{IP} t_1 \text{ arrived}] [_{NP} [_{NP} \text{ no student}]_1 [_{NP} \text{ except } [_{NP} \text{ John}]_2]_2]]$
      c. (no student except John)($\lambda x[x \text{ arrived}]$)

The primary motivation which she offers for this account is that it sustains the analysis of exception phrases proposed in Keenan and Stavi (1986) (K&S). According to K&S, *no ... except John* and *every ... except John* are complex one-place determiners which receive the interpretations in (47a) and (47b), respectively.

(47)   a. $B \in \|\text{no } A \text{ except John}\|$ iff $A \cap B = \{\text{john}\}$
       b. $B \in \|\text{every } A \text{ except John}\|$ iff $A \cap B' = \{\text{john}\}$

Reinhart's analysis of (1c) reconstructs the NP consisting of the determiner *no ... except John* and the N' *student* at LF by adjoining the NP *no student* to the exception phrase.

The K&S treatment of exception phrases as components of a lexically complex determiner is inadequate in that it does not provide a unified compositional representation of the role which these phrases make to the interpretation of the NP's in which they occur. Specifically, it does not indicate how (47a) and (47b) follow from a general rule for computing the meaning of an NP in terms of the meanings of its N', determiner, and exception phrase. In fact, exception phrases can also appear with the determiners *each, all, any,* and *none of the,* as the sentences in (48) illustrate.

(48) a. Each/any/all student(s) except John can take the course.
      b. None of the students except John can take the course.

Similarly, the K&S account does not exhibit the general contribution of the NP argument of *except* to the meaning of the containing NP. As the cases in (49) show, a wide range of NP's can occur in the argument position of an exception phrase.

(49) Every student except five law students/John and three physics students/five computer science students and at most two logic students participated.

Let us assume that NP's are generalized quantifiers, which denote sets of sets.[24] It is possible to construct a general compositional analysis of exception phrases if we take them to be syntactic functions from NP's to NP's, and to denote functions from NP denotations to NP denotations. On this view, exception phrases are NP modifiers, and ||*except*|| is a function from an NP denotation to an NP modifier function. In order to specify the function which phrases of the form *except* (*NP*) denote, it will be necessary to state several definitions.[25]

Following Barwise and Cooper (1981) (B&C), van Benthem (1983), and K&S, we will say that a generalized quantifier ||NP|| is conservative for the set A if (50) holds.[26]

(50) ||NP|| is conservative for the set A iff for every $X \in$ ||NP||, $X \cap A \in$ ||NP||.

B&C define a witness set for a generalized quantifier ||NP|| and a set A for which ||NP|| is conservative as in (51).

(51) If ||NP|| is conservative for A, then W is a witness set for ||NP||, relative to A, iff $W \subseteq A$ and $W \in$ ||NP||.

Moltmann (forthcoming) modifies (51) to obtain (52), which we will adopt as our definition of a witness set for a generalized quantifier.

(52) If A is the smallest set for which ||NP|| is conservative, then W is a witness set for ||NP|| iff $W \subseteq A$ and $W \in$ ||NP||.

Thus, for example, given (52), any set of five students is a witness set for ||five students||, {john} is the only witness set for ||John||, and any set containing John and three physics students is a witness set for ||John and three physics students||. For any generalized quantifier ||NP||, let w(||NP||) = the set of witness sets for ||NP||.

We define a *total* relation R between two sets as in (53).

(53) R is total iff (i) $R = \subseteq$, or (ii) for any two sets A,B, $R(A,B)$ iff $A \cap B = \varnothing$.

According to (53), R is total iff it is either inclusion or exclusion.

Let NP_2 be the NP to which the exception phrase $except(NP_1)$ applies, and let X' be the complement of X. Assume that $\|NP_2\| = \{X \subseteq E: R(A,X)\}$. We can specify the interpretation of exception phrases by means of the rule given in (54).[27]

(54) $(\|except\|(\|NP_1\|))(\|NP_2\|) = \{X \subseteq E: R(A^{rem},X)\}$, where $\|NP_2\| = \{X \subseteq E: R(A,X)\}$, R is total, and $\exists S(S \in w(\|NP_1\|)$ & $S \subseteq A$ & $A^{rem} = A - S$ & $R(S,X'))$.

If we apply (54) to *every student except five law students*, we obtain (55a). The interpretation of (49), with the selection of *except five law students* as the exception phrase modifying the subject NP, is given in (55b).

(55)   a. $(\|except\|(\{X \subseteq E: |\text{Law\_Students} \cap X| \geq 5\})(\{X \subseteq E: \text{Students} \subseteq X\}) = \{X \subseteq E: \text{Students}^{rem} \subseteq X\}$, where $\exists S(S \in w(\{X \subseteq E: |\text{Law\_Students} \cap X| \geq 5\})$ & $S \subseteq \text{Students}$ & $\text{Students}^{rem} = \text{Students} - S$ & $S \subseteq X'))$.

   b. $\|$every student except five law students participated$\| = t$ iff $\text{Students}^{rem} \subseteq \{a: a \text{ participated}\}$, where
   $\exists S(S \in w(\{X \subseteq E: |\text{Law\_Students} \cap X| \geq 5\})$ & $S \subseteq \text{Students}$ & $\text{Students}^{rem} = \text{Students} - S$ & $S \subseteq \{a: a \text{ participated}\}'))$.

(54) captures three central properties of exception phrases. First, given this definition, both (1c) and (48a,b) imply that John is a student. This implication holds by virtue of the fact that the witness sets for $\|NP_1\|$, the argument of the exception phrase, which render the existential assertion in (54) true must be subsets of the N′ set of the NP to which the exception phrase applies.

Second, it sustains the inference from (1c) to the assertion that John did arrive, and the inference from (49) to the statement that five law students (/John and three physics students/five computer science students and at most two logic students) did not participate. These inferences hold because of the requirement that the same total relation R which holds between the remnant set A^{rem} and the VP set, also hold for the witness set S for $\|NP_1\|$ in terms of which A^{rem} is defined and the complement of the VP set.

Finally, (54) restricts the domain of exception phrase functions to generalized quantifiers whose determiners denote total relations between their N′ sets and the VP sets of the predicate. Therefore, it correctly excludes the application of exception phrases to NP's whose determiners are not universal, like those in (56).

(56) a. *Five students except John arrived.
      b. *Most MPs except the Tories supported the bill.
      c. *Mary spoke to many people except John.
      d. *Not many students except five law students participated.

Moltmann (forthcoming) points out that exception phrases can also apply to certain coordinate NP's. In (57), for example, *except the teachers* can be understood as modifying the conjoined NP *every mother and every father*.

(57) Every mother and every father except the teachers joined the PTA.

It seems that when exception phrases modify coordinate NP's, they are restricted to conjunctions of positive or negative universally quantified NP's.[28]

(58) a. *Every mother and no/several/most fathers except the teachers joined the PTA.
      b. *Every mother or every father except the teachers joined the PTA.
      c. No mother and no father except the teachers attended the meeting.
      d. *No mother and every/several/most fathers except the teachers attended the meeting.
      e. *No mother or no father except the teachers attended the meeting.

The denotation of an NP of the form $every(A_1), \ldots, and\ every(A_k)$ $(1 \leq k)$ is $\cap_{i=1}^{k}\|every(A_i)\|$ (the intersection of the denotations of each of the NP conjuncts). Similarly, the denotation of an NP of the form $no(A_1), \ldots, and\ no(A_k)$ $(1 \leq k)$ is $\cap_{i=1}^{k}\|no(A_i)\|$. For example, $\|every\ mother\ and\ every\ father\|$ is the intersection of the set of sets containing all mothers and the set of sets containing all fathers. But this set is identical to the set of all sets containing the union of the set of mothers and the set of fathers. Similarly, the denotation of *no mother and no father* is the set of all sets whose intersection with the union of the set of mothers and the set of fathers is empty. Therefore, the identities in (59) hold.

(59) a. $\|every(A_1), \ldots, and\ every(A_k)\| = \{X \subseteq E: (A_1 \cup \ldots \cup A_k) \subseteq X\}$
      b. $\|no(A_1), \ldots, and\ no(A_k)\| = \{X \subseteq E: (A_1 \cup \ldots \cup A_k) \cap X = \varnothing\}$

Given (59), the interpretation of exception phrases specified in (54) covers (57) and (58c), while excluding the ill formed cases of (58).

It is important to note that the fact that exception phrases can apply to conjoined NP's provides strong motivation for treating them as modifiers of NP rather than as constituents of complex determiners.

4.2 *LF movement vs NP storage*

The interpretation of exception phrases as NP modifiers removes the primary motivation for Reinhart's syntactic reconstruction account of displaced exception phrases. If such a phrase is not a component of a complex determiner, then it is not necessary to express its relation to the NP with which it is connected through the reconstruction of a syntactic constituent. The semantic operation of NP storage, as characterized in Cooper (1983) and Pereira (1990), provides an alternative to syntactic movement.[29] Storage involves substituting a variable v for the denotation $\|NP\|$ of an NP in the semantic representation of an expression A, and constructing a stored assumption, which is the pair $\langle\|NP\|,v\rangle$. The interpretation of A, containing v, is combined with the denotations of progressively larger constituents. When the assumption is released from storage, v is bound by a set abstraction operator to yield a set to which the generalized quantifier assumption is applied. As an example, consider the derivation of the interpretation for *John read every paper* in (60), where *every paper* is placed in storage in (60b), and released in (60e).

(60) a. John read every paper.
    b. $\langle$every paper,$x\rangle$ |- x
    c. $\langle$every paper,$x\rangle$ |- $\{a: a$ read $x\}$
    d. $\langle$every paper,$x\rangle$ |- j read x
    e. |- (every paper)$(\{x: j$ read $x\})$
    f. |- Papers $\subseteq \{x: j$ read $x\}$

If storage is applied to the NP subject *No student of* (1c), the function denoted by the displaced exception phrase can apply to the stored assumption to yield a new NP denotation in storage. The correct interpretation of the sentence will result when this new assumption is released. (61) gives this derivation for (1c).

(61) a. No student arrived, except John.
    b. $\{a: a$ arrived$\}$
    c. $\langle$no student,$x\rangle$ |- $x(\{a: a$ arrived$\})$
    d. $\langle$(except(John))(no student),$x\rangle$ |- $x(\{a: a$ arrived$\})$
    e. |- (except(John))(no student)$(\{x: x(\{a: a$ arrived$\})\})$
    f. |- (except(John))(no student)$(\{a: a$ arrived$\})$
    g. Students$^{rem} \cap \{a: a$ arrived$\} = \phi$, where $(\exists S)(S \in w(\|$John$\|)$ & $S \subseteq$ Students & Students$^{rem} =$ Students $- S$ & $S \cap \{a: a$ arrived$\}' = \emptyset)$

At this point, it seems that both LF movement and NP storage can handle displaced exception phrases. However, consider (62), from Hoeksema (1991).

(62) Everyone was pleased and no one complained, except John.

As Hoeksema observes, the exception phrase can be taken as modifying both *everyone* and *no one*. But it is not possible to adjoin these NP's to the exception phrase, as they are contained in a conjoined sentence. Nor, as Hoeksema notes, can they be extracted by across-the-board movement (in the sense of Williams (1978)), given that they are NP's of different types. Therefore, Reinhart's LF movement account does not extend to (62).

Unlike QR, NP storage is a semantic operation, and so it is not constrained by syntactic locality conditions. Therefore, it can apply to (the denotations of) each of the NP subjects in (62) to generate a store containing two NP assumptions. The function denoted by *except John* can apply to each of these assumptions separately, and each new assumption will be released to a set corresponding to the VP of the appropriate conjunct of the sentence. Simplifying somewhat, the derivation of the interpretation for (62) proceeds as in (63).

(63)   a.   {⟨(except(John))(everyone),x⟩,⟨(except(John))(no one),y⟩}|-
 x({a: a was happy)}) & y({b: b complained})

 b.   (except(John))(everyone)({a: a was pleased}) &
 (except(John))(no one)({b: b complained})

 c.   (Persons$_1^{rem}$ ⊆ {a: a was pleased}, where (∃S)(S ∈ w(‖John‖) & S
 ⊆ Persons & Persons$_1^{rem}$ = Persons − S & S ⊆ {a: a was_pleased}'))
 & (Persons$_2^{rem}$ ∩ {b: b complained} = ∅, where (∃S)(S ∈ w(‖John‖)
 & S ⊆ Persons & Persons$_2^{rem}$ = Persons − S & S ∩ {b: b complained}' = ϕ))

(62) provides evidence for using NP storage rather than LF movement to express the relation between a displaced exception phrase and the NP which it modifies.

5   Conclusion

I have considered three types of phrasal fragments with a view to identifying the level of representation at which each one is interpreted and the nature of the process that generates its interpretation. Initially, a unified approach to all of the fragment types seems to offer the most attractive way of handling these structures. However, an examination of two plausible proposals for implementing such an approach indicates that neither is able to provide an adequate analysis for all three constructions considered here.

Higher-order unification is an instance of a semantic view of ellipsis. On this account, the fragment phrase is matched with a phrase in an antecedent clause, and a property (relation) term which applies to both phrases is then extracted from the semantic interpretation of the antecedent. While higher-order unification does seem to provide a viable analysis of bare ellipsis, it does not give the right results for either ACE cases of VP ellipsis or displaced exception phrases. Moreover, it is not clear how any other semantic theory of ellipsis could deal with these two fragment types. ACE structures exhibit sensitivity to constraints which indicate the presence of syntactic structure in the elided VP, while exception phrases are not instances of ellipsis at all.

Syntactic reconstruction offers an alternative, syntactically based model of fragment interpretation. It takes the fragment as the argument of a predicate which is generated through syntactic reconstruction. If ACE structures are taken as instances of pseudo-gapping, then a version of a reconstruction based analysis yields a reasonable treatment of VP ellipsis. However, reconstruction cannot deal adequately with either bare ellipsis or exception phrases, as there are cases of both types of fragment which it does not cover.

It is possible to construct an appropriate compositional semantic representation of exception phrases if they are characterized as NP modifiers. Given this analysis, the semantic operation of NP storage (but not LF movement) offers a suitable procedure for representing the relation between displaced exception phrases and the NP's which they modify.

If these arguments are correct, then the interpretation of incomplete phrases does not involve only one level of representation, nor is it achieved through the application of a single repertoire of formal operations. VP ellipsis is resolved through syntactic reconstruction, bare ellipsis involves the direct assignment of a property (relation) to the denotation of a fragment phrase, and displaced exception phrases are connected to the NP's they modify by the application of storage to these NP's. The interpretation of each fragment type is achieved at a distinct level of representation and through a different set of procedures.

NOTES

1   Earlier versions of this paper were presented at the SOAS Workshop on Deduction in Natural Language in March, 1994, and at the Tenth Annual Conference of the Israel Association for Theoretical Linguistics, University of Haifa, in June, 1994. I am grateful to the participants of these forums for their comments. I presented the material on VP ellipsis which appears in Section 3 in my advanced syntax seminar at SOAS, which I taught together with Ruth Kempson in the second term of 1994. I am grateful to the students who took part in this seminar for helpful comments and criticisms. I would also like to thank Ruth Kempson with whom I have had extensive discussions on ellipsis, and whose remarks have had a significant impact on my thinking concerning the problems I deal with here. Finally, I am grateful to Michael Brody, Jaap van der Does, Robert May, and Friederike Moltmann for useful discussion of some of the ideas proposed in this paper.
2   For other semantic accounts of VP ellipsis resolution see Lappin (1984), Gawron and Peters (1990), and Hardt (1993). Lappin (1993a) and Fiengo and May (1994) provide detailed critical treatments of the semantic approach to VP ellipsis.

3   As we will see in Section 2, the analyses given in May (1985) and F&M crucially assume that copying occurs at LF. Haïk (1987) and Kitagawa (1991) also suggest LF copying approaches to VP ellipsis resolution. Sag (1976) and Williams (1977) propose a treatment of VP ellipsis which combines aspects of the semantic approach and LF reconstruction (in the case of Sag, LF deletion). They invoke a syntactic operation, the Derived VP Rule, to convert the antecedent VP into a lambda expression which denotes a property. However, the lambda term is not a pure semantic representation, but an LF expression which is subject to syntactic constraints. Ellipsis resolution consists in identifying an antecedent lambda term which satisfies certain correspondence conditions relative to the elided VP (or, in the case of Sag, finding an appropriate antecedent lambda term to license deletion of the lambda expression in the elided VP). For critical discussions of Sag and Williams see Lappin (1984), Dalrymple et al. (1991), Hardt (1993), and F&M. See Lappin (1991) for discussions of May (1985) and Haïk (1987). Lappin (1993a) and (1993b) provide detailed comments on some of the proposals in F&M.

4   This conclusion should be taken as tentative. In Lappin (1995a) I explore the possibility of extending the S-structure reconstruction account to bare argument/ adjunct ellipsis.

5   Kempson and Gabbay (1993) and Kempson (this volume) develop a categorially driven system of interpretation through natural deduction. In this framework, the *wh*-phrase which introduces a relative clause defines a locality domain within which the gap associated with the head of the relative clause must be discharged in an appropriate argument position. This requirement prevents binding of the gap from outside of the relative clause. When combined with the procedure for recovering elided predicates which Kempson and Gabbay, and Kempson (this volume) propose, this locality condition will rule out ACE cases involving extraction out of a relative clause, like (i).

> (i)   *John discussed every issue that Mary recommended the book which also did.

However, this condition does not capture the full range of subjacency effects, and so does not exclude cases like (9b,c) and their elided counterparts in (10b,c), respectively.

6   Some speakers find (12b,c) relatively acceptable. However, while many speakers agree that these sentences are somewhat improved relative to their non-elided counterparts in (11b,c), most informants that I have consulted find (12a) considerably better than (12b,c).

7   See Kayne (1984), Postal (1994), and Manzini (1994) for alternative accounts of subjacency and locality effects in parasitic gap dependencies. I will adopt the Contreras–Chomsky analysis in my discussion of ellipsis in parasitic gap structures.

8   Chomsky (1986a) proposes that the two chains in a parasitic gap construction are composed into a single chain. He requires that the empty operator in the chain containing the gap be O-subjacent to the final trace in the *wh*-trace chain. He permits the empty operator to adjoin to the PP phrase in which it is immediately contained in order to satisfy this condition. Contreras (1993) assumes that the empty operator has the features [-anaphor] and [-pronominal], and he derives the locality condition on the relation between the two chains from the general principle that an empty category which has these features (this set of empty categories includes

syntactic variables) must be subjacent to its local binder. In parasitic gap structures, the closest local binder of the empty operator heading the second chain is the initial trace in the *wh*-trace chain. As Contreras points out, his analysis permits him to derive the locality condition on parasitic gap chains from general locality principles governing empty categories. Therefore, he can dispense with the otherwise unmotivated notions of chain composition and O-subjacency.

9   Hornstein (1994) suggests an alternative analysis of ACE structures within the framework of Chomsky's (1993) minimalist model of syntax. On Chomsky's account, object NP's are moved into Spec of AgrO position (the specifier of an object agreement phrase), where they are checked for Case agreement with the head of AgrO. Spec of AgrO is external to the VP out of which the object NP is moved. Therefore, if the object NP contains an ACE structure, the elided VP is no longer antecedent contained when the NP has been moved into Spec of AgrO, and reconstruction through copying of the matrix verb can proceed without QR. Cases of ACE in PP complements ((i)a) and PP adjuncts ((i)b) pose a difficulty for Hornstein's analysis.

(i)   a. John spoke to everyone who Mary did.
      b. Max performed in every city which Lucy expects to.

On Chomsky's account of Case assignment (checking), the PP's in (i)a,b are not moved to the specifier of an agreement phrase external to the matrix VP. Hornstein attempts to solve the problem which (i)a raises by suggesting that indirect PP complements are, in fact, moved to a Spec of Agr position external to the matrix VP for Case checking. He deals with (i)b by claiming that PP adjuncts are generated outside of the core matrix VP (or V'), and so the elided VP which appears within the PP adjunct is not antecedent-contained. He cites the contrast in the interpretations of (ii)a and (ii)b as support for these claims.

(ii)   a. John wanted to talk to everyone that Bill did.
       b. John wanted to word every question as I did.

The elided VP in (ii)a can be understood as either *wanted to talk to t* or *talked to t*, while only the embedded VP *word t* can serve as the antecedent of the elided VP in (ii)b. According to Hornstein, the ambiguity in (ii)a follows if the PP complement in (ii)a is moved to a Spec of AgrIO position outside of the matrix VP, from where either the matrix or the embedded VP can be used to reconstruct the elided VP. By contrast, the existence of the single available reading for (ii)b is predicted if the PP adjunct *as I did* appears outside of the core VP headed by *word* (which it modifies) but within the matrix VP headed by *wanted*, and it is not moved to a Spec of Agr position for Case checking. In this configuration, only the embedded VP is available for ellipsis resolution. In fact, this contrast between ACE structures in PP complements and in PP adjuncts is not general or systematic. The elided VP in the PP adjuncts of (iii)a,b can take the matrix as well as the embedded VP as its antecedent.

(iii)   a. John applied to study at every university that Bill did.
        b. Mary intends to travel through every city which Lucy does.

It would seem, then, that there is no independent empirical support for Hornstein's treatment of ACE structures in PP complements and adjuncts. Therefore, the fact that such structures occur freely in PP's remains unexplained on Hornstein's analysis.

10   Diesing (1992) (following Carlson (1977a)) claims that ACE structures in NP's with strong determiners are more acceptable than in NP's with weak determiners (see Milsark (1977), Barwise and Cooper (1981), and Lappin and Reinhart (1988) for discussions of the distinction between strong and weak determiners). She also maintains that, to the extent that ACE in NP's with weak determiners is possible, these NP's require a presuppositional interpretation, which she identifies with a partitive reading. She argues that while the cases of ACE in (i)a are unproblematic, those in (i)b require a partitive reading of the object NP.

(i)   a.   John read every/each/most book(s) which Mary did.
        b.   John read five/some/many/books which Mary did.

Thus, for example, with the determiner *five*, (i)b cannot be understood to mean that the number of books which John and Mary read is five. It can only be taken as asserting that John read five of the books which Mary read. According to Diesing, NP's with weak determiners are ambiguous between a non-presuppositional cardinal reading and a presuppositional partitive reading. Only on the latter is the NP interpreted as a restricted quantifier and subject to QR. On the cardinal reading it is interpreted *in situ*. Diesing argues that the fact that (i)b is only acceptable on a partitive reading indicates that ACE structures are reconstructed through QR, as weak NP's are only subject to QR on the partitive interpretation.

In fact, this argument for a QR account of ACE does not go through. As the cases in (ii) illustrate, the non-elided counterparts of (i)b also require a partitive reading.

(ii)   John read five/some/many/books which Mary read.

Taking the determiner in (ii) as *five*, for example, the sentence can only be understood as specifying that John read five of the books which Mary read. Therefore, the requirement that the object NP in (i)b receive a partitive reading is independent of the fact that it contains an ACE structure.

11   See Lappin (1993a) and (1993b) for more detailed presentations of this analysis of VP ellipsis. Lappin and McCord (1990) present an implemented algorithm for VP ellipsis resolution based on this analysis.

The account of VP ellipsis proposed here has consequences for Chomsky's (1993) and (1995) minimalist program for syntax. If S-structure rather than LF (as defined by QR) is required for VP ellipsis, then it is not dispensable as a level of representation. Alternatively, one could argue that QR is not part of the grammar, and what I am referring to as S-structure is really LF in the sense that it is the syntactic representation which provides the interface with semantic (and other principles of) interpretation. The latter view is presented in Lappin (1991). The problem here is that Chomsky also postulates non-QR LF movement of NP's into Spec of AgrO and Spec of AgrS for Case and agreement checking, and LF head movement of verbs. However, it may be possible for the proposed pseudo-gapping account of ACE to apply to the structures created by such non-QR LF movement. I leave this issue open.

12   The account of ACE structures proposed here has certain points of analogy with the analysis which Jacobson (this volume) suggests within the framework of

categorial grammar. On the latter analysis the auxiliary of an ACE construction is a function which applies to a relational property variable having the semantic type of a transitive verb. The variable is assigned an interpretation through identification with the meaning of a lexically realized verb in the discourse context. The result of applying the auxiliary to this variable is an expression which combines with the subject NP of the relative clause to yield an appropriate argument for the relative pronoun. As on the account proposed here, ellipsis resolution in an ACE structure like (10a) involves retrieving an object corresponding to the head verb of the antecedent VP rather than the entire antecedent VP. However, unlike the proposed reconstruction account, Jacobson's analysis relies on a semantic object and does not posit a trace (or variable) in the ellipsis site. Therefore, it is not immediately clear how this approach can capture the subjacency and locality effects which ACE structures exhibit.

13 Brody (forthcoming) proposes an alternative analysis of ACE structures on which reconstruction applies prior to QR. He suggests that vehicle change applies to the entire NP which contains the ellipsis site to yield a trace as the object of the reconstructed matrix VP. Therefore, the result of reconstructing the antecedent-contained elided VP in (18) is (i).

(i)   John [$_{VP}$ read [everything which$_1$ Mary believes that he [$_{VP}$ *read* t_1]]]$_1$

F&M apply a similar analysis to elided VP's in non-restrictive relative clauses. I argue in Section 2.4, that examples like (32a,b) indicate that this analysis is problematic if one adopts F&M's assumption that A'-bound traces are α expressions, and so do not change their indexical values under reconstruction.

(32)   a. John trusts Rosa, who Bill does too, and even Lucy, who Bill doesn't.
       b. John kissed Rosa, who Bill likes, and he kissed Lucy, who Bill doesn't.

The trace which will be reconstructed in the elided VP of the second conjunct of each sentence will have the same index as *Rosa* rather than the index of *Lucy*, and so it will not be locally bound by the *wh*-operator of the non-restrictive relative clause where it appears (the latter phrase is coindexed with *Lucy*, which it modifies). Brody (personal communication) suggests that we can avoid this problem by allowing A'-bound traces to be either α or β terms (the indexical value of a beta expression can change under reconstruction). This would render them analogous to pronouns in F&M's system. However, this proposal raises a serious difficulty. The status of a pronoun as an α or a β expression depends upon whether it is interpreted as an independently referring term (an α expression) or through anaphoric dependence upon an antecedent (a β expression). Unlike pronouns, an A'-bound trace receives a uniform interpretation for all its occurrences. It is a bound variable ranging over the elements in the domain of the operator which binds it. It is not clear how its indexical status as an α or a β term can be variable while its semantic (specifically its referential) status is constant.

14 See Larson (1987) for an analysis of VP ellipsis where reconstruction applies to an elided VP in a PP adjunct clause after QR has adjoined the PP to IP.

15 F&M propose taking parasitic gaps in ACE structures as pronominal correlates of *wh*-traces.

16 May (1985) observes that elided non-restrictives like the one in (i) is ill-formed.

    (i)   *John trusts Rosa, who Bill does.

He argues that this is due to the fact that QR does not apply to proper names, and so the non-restrictive relative in (i) is not moved out of its antecedent to a position at LF where reconstruction can apply. Clark (1992) suggests that QR can apply to any constituent, but that a modifier of an expression subject to QR can only be moved along with it if it serves to restrict the quantificational scope of the expression at LF. While a restrictive relative which applies to a quantified NP satisfies this condition, a non-restrictive relative on a name generally does not. On Clark's account, (i) is ill-formed because even if QR applies to *Rosa*, the non-restrictive relative cannot move with it, and so the elided VP remains antecedent-contained at LF. He also suggests that when negation occurs in a non-restrictive relative, it contributes an independent scope element, and so the clause can be moved along with the name which it modifies (hence the acceptability of (30b)). Clark's analysis incorrectly predicts that (30a) should be ungrammatical. As F&M point out, the ill-formedness of (i) is due to the fact that *too* (or *also*) does not appear as a modifier on the elided VP, rather than the fact that the restrictive relative contains an elided VP. This modifier expresses identity between the predicates which the elided VP and its antecedent represent. Its absence is also responsible for the unacceptability of (ii)

    (ii)   *John sang, and Rosa did.

When the modifier is added, VP ellipsis is possible in the non-restrictive relative in (i), as (30a) indicates.

17 Note that according to F&M, both proper names and A'-bound traces are referentially independent NP's (in their terms α *occurrences* of terms), whose indices remain constant under reconstruction.

18 See particularly Dalrymple (1991) and Hardt (1993) for this line of argument.

19 (35a) appears in Chomsky et al. 1982, and is cited by Dalrymple (1991). (35b) and (35c) are from Webber (1979).

20 Hardt (1993) also invokes a mixed model in that he adopts the pseudo-gapping account of ACE proposed in Lappin and McCord (1990), and Lappin (1993a) and (1993b), while adopting a purely semantic treatment of non-ACE cases of ellipsis.

21 Webber (1979) claims that inference is also involved in the interpretation of the sentences in (35). See F&M for a discussion of this view.

    In general, it seems that cases of VP ellipsis which are resolved through inference are more marked than those in which a syntactically matched antecedent is available. Thus, (39a,b) are less natural than (i)a,b.

    (i)   a. Mary wants to go out, but her father won't let her, because he disapproves of her coming home late.
         b. John used to speak well, but he can't any more, because he lost his voice.

    (ii)   a–c also seem less marked than the corresponding sentences in (35a–c).

(iii) a. A lot of this material can be presented in a fairly informal and accessible fashion, and often it is.
   b. Wendy and Bruce are eager to sail around the world and climb Kilimanjaro, but neither of them can because money is tight.
   c. Joe wants to visit China, and he will too, if he gets enough money.

This could be taken as indicating that inference is also involved in the interpretation of the elided VP's in (35).

22   One might suggest that LF movement applies to the temporal adverb *yesterday* as well as the NP *flowers* in the antecedent clause of (42a) to create a structure like (i).

(i) $[_{IP'}[_{IP}$ Max gave t_1 to Lucy $t_2]$
   $[_{NP}[_{NP}$ [flowers]$_1[_{ADV}$ yesterday]$_2]_2[_{NP}$ and $[_{NP}$ flowers today]$_3]_3]]$

Leaving aside the problem of determining how the traces in (i) can be properly bound, there are at least two difficulties with this proposal. First, it is not clear how (i) will produce the desired interpretation of (42a). Presumably, on Reinhart's approach (i) will yield the representation (ii), which is not well-formed.

(ii) ((flowers yesterday) and (flowers today))$(\lambda x \lambda y[$max gave x to lucy $y])$.

The second problem is that there is no obvious syntactic motivation for applying QR to temporal adverbs like *yesterday*.

23   For purposes of simplicity and clarity, in (44) I have omitted the explicit representation of the temporal adverbs *yesterday* and *today* as constituents of functions on the property *gave flowers to Lucy*.

24   See, for example, Barwise and Cooper (1981), van Benthem (1983), K&S, Keenan and Moss (1985), and Keenan (this volume) for the basic concepts of generalized quantifier theory.

25   For a detailed presentation of this analysis of exception phrases and a discussion of some of its major formal and linguistic consequences see Lappin (1995b).

26   B&C characterize this relation as one in which *A lives on* ||NP||.

27   The account proposed here is similar in spirit to the one given in Moltmann (1993) and (forthcoming). It also bears a certain resemblance to an interpretation considered in Hoeksema (1991) (specifically, his definition for what he terms *connected* exception phrases). However, there is at least one important difference between the proposed account and the other two analyses. The interpretation specified in (54) excludes the application of an exception phrase to NP's of the form *neither N'*, *both N'*, and *all n N'*, and so correctly rules out the sentences in (i).

(i) a. *Neither boy except Max arrived.
   b. *Both girls except Mary sing.
   c. *All five professors except Rosa attended the meeting.

This is due to the fact that the determiners in the subject NP's in (i) denote a relation between the N' and predicate sets which is not a total relation, but the conjunction of a total relation and a cardinality condition on the N' set. The analyses which Moltmann and Hoeksema present require additional assumptions to rule out the cases in (i). For discussions of these analyses, see Lappin (1995b). For additional discussion of Hoeksema (1991) and a critical review of the treatment of exception phrases given in Von Fintel (1993b), see Moltmann (1993).

28 The indicated grammaticality judgements in the sentences of (58) are for the reading on which the exception phrase applies to the entire conjoined NP rather than only to one of its conjuncts.

29 See Dalrymple et al. (1991), Lappin (1991), and Pereira and Pollack (1991) for applications of NP storage. Lappin (1991) presents arguments for employing storage rather than QR to represent a variety of scope phenomena.

IV Anaphora, Discourse and Modality

7 Coreference and Modality

JEROEN GROENENDIJK,
MARTIN STOKHOF and
FRANK VELTMAN

1 Static and Dynamic Interpretation

1.1 *Towards dynamic interpretation*

The prevailing view on meaning in logical semantics from its inception at the end of the nineteenth century until the beginning of the eighties has been one which is aptly summarized in the slogan "meaning equals truth conditions". This view on meaning is one which can rightly be labeled static: it describes the meaning relation between linguistic expressions and the world as a static relation, one which may itself change through time, but which does not bring about any change itself. For non-sentential expressions (nouns, verbs, modifiers, etc.) the same goes through: in accordance with the principle of compositionality of meaning, their meaning resides in their contribution to the truth-conditions of the sentences in which they occur. In most cases this contribution consists in what they denote (refer to), hence the slogan can be extended to "meaning equals denotation conditions".

Of course, although this view on meaning was the prevailing one for almost a century, many of the people who initiated the enterprise of logical semantics, including people like Frege and Wittgenstein, had an open eye for all that it did not catch. However, the logical means which Frege, Wittgenstein, Russell, and the generation that succeeded them, had at their disposal were those of classical mathematical logic and set-theory, and these indeed are not very suited for an analysis of other aspects of meaning than those which the slogan covers. A real change in view then had to await the emergence of other concepts, which in due course became available mainly under the influence of developments in computer science and cognate disciplines such as artificial intelligence. And this is one of the reasons why it took almost a century before any serious and successful challenge to the view that meaning equals truth-conditions from within logical semantics could emerge.

The static view on meaning was, of course, already challenged from the outside, but in most cases such attacks started from premises which are quite alien to the logical semantics enterprise as such, and hence failed to bring about any radical changes.

An important development has been that of speech act theory, originating from the work of Austin, and worked out systematically by Searle and others, which has proposed a radical shift from the proposition with its cognate truth conditions as the principal unit of analysis, to the speech act that is performed with an utterance. Here a move is made from the essentially static relationship between a sentence and the situation it depicts, which underlies the view that meaning equals truth-conditions, to a much more dynamically oriented relationship between what a speaker does with an utterance and his environment. This is especially clear from the emphasis that is laid on the performative aspects of speech acts.

This development, however, did not succeed in overthrowing the static logical view, mainly because it turned out not to be a rival, but a companion: the speech act theory of Searle actually presupposes some kind of denotational theory of meaning as one of its components. Nevertheless, speech act theory has been a major influence on work in the logical tradition.

In a similar vein the emergence of the artificial intelligence paradigm only indirectly exercised some influence on the logical tradition. When people working in this area began to think about natural language processing they quite naturally thought of meaning in procedural terms, since, certainly before the development of so-called declarative ("logic") programming languages, the notion of a procedure (or process) was at the heart of that paradigm. This line of thinking, too, may be dubbed dynamic rather than static, since a procedure is essentially something that through its execution brings about a change in the state of a system. However, although this approach has a straightforward appeal, it failed to overthrow the static view, mainly because the way it was worked out failed to address the issues that are central to the logical semantics approach (viz., the analysis of truth and in particular entailment), and also because it lacked the systematic nature that characterizes logical semantics.

The real challenge to the static view on meaning in logical semantics has come from within, from work on recalcitrant problems in logical semantics whose solution required a step beyond the static view on meaning.

Already in the seventies several people had begun to explore a conception of meaning which involved the notion of change. Trying to deal with the many intricacies of context-dependence (such as are involved in presuppositions) Stalnaker (1974) suggested that in studying the meaning of an utterance what must be taken into account is the change it brings about in the hearer, more specifically in the information she has at her disposal.

Although Stalnaker's conception of meaning does indeed have a dynamic, rather than a static flavor, it cannot quite count as a really dynamic notion of meaning after all, for Stalnaker's way of dealing with the dynamic aspect essentially leans on the static conception. He describes the change brought about by the utterance of a sentence in terms of the addition of the proposition the sentence expresses to the set of propositions that constitutes the (assumed) common information of speaker and hearer. But this uses the static notion of a proposition as the basic unit for the analysis of sentence meaning.

In a different setting, that of philosophy of science, Gärdenfors (1984) developed dynamic tools for modeling the structure and change of belief, in particular the process of belief revision.

The real breakthrough, at least within logical semantics, occurred at the beginning of the eighties when, at the same time but independently of each other, Kamp (1981) and Heim (1982) developed an approach that has become known as "discourse representation theory". Earlier, similar ideas had been put forward within different traditions, such as the work on discourse semantics of Seuren (1985) within the framework of semantic syntax, and the work of Hintikka (1983) on game-theoretical semantics. In his original paper, Kamp describes his work explicitly as an attempt to marry the static view on meaning of the logical tradition with its emphasis on truth-conditions and logical consequence, with the procedural view emerging from the artificial intelligence paradigm with its appeal of dynamics. Instead of giving it up, both Kamp and Heim stay within the logical tradition in that they want to extend its results, rather than re-do them.

1.2   Dynamic semantics

One particular way of formalizing the idea of dynamic interpretation is the following. It is called "dynamic semantics" to distinguish it from other approaches, since, as will become clear shortly, it places the dynamics of interpretation in the semantics proper. Unlike other approaches, such as discourse representation theory, which makes essential use of representational structures in the process of dynamic interpretation, dynamic semantics locates the dynamics of interpretation in the very heart of the interpretation process, viz., within the core notions of meaning and entailment.

Very generally, the dynamic view on meaning comes to this: the meaning of a sentence is the change that an utterance of it brings about, and the meanings of non-sentential expressions consist in their contributions to this change. This description is general in at least two ways: it does not say what it is that gets changed, and it does not say how such changes are brought about. As in the traditional view, most dynamic approaches start from the underlying assumption that the main function of language is to convey information. Hence, a slightly more concrete formulation can be obtained by replacing "change" in the slogan above by "change in information". But this still leaves a lot undecided: what is this information about, and whose information is it? Here, the empirical domain that one is concerned with gets to play a role. For example, when one analyzes anaphoric relations between noun phrases and pronominal anaphors, the relevant information is that of the hearer about individuals that

have been introduced in the domain and about the binding and scope relations that obtain between them. When analyzing temporal relations in discourse, information concerns events, points in time, and such relations between
them as precedence, overlap, and so on. In other cases, for example when
describing information exchanges such as question–answer dialogues, the information that is relevant is about the world, and one has to keep track of both
the information of the questioner and that of the addressee. When analyzing the way presuppositions function in a discourse, another aspect is introduced: the information which the speech participants have about each other's
information.

Leaving these distinctions and refinements aside, and restricting ourselves
to sentences, the dynamic view can be paraphrased as follows: "meaning is
information change potential". Per contrast, the static view can be characterized as: "meaning is truth-conditional content".

In line with this difference, it must be observed that in a static semantics the
basic notion that occurs in the definition of interpretation is that of information *content*, whereas in a dynamic system it is the notion of information *change*
that is defined recursively. As is to be expected, different views on meaning
lead to different views on entailment. In a static system entailment is meaning
inclusion. In a dynamic system there are several options. One that is rather
natural is the following: a premise entails a conclusion iff updating any information state with the premise leads to an information state in which the
conclusion has to be accepted.

The remainder of this paper is devoted to an analysis of a specific problem
area, which is not only of interest descriptively, but which also presents an
interesting theoretical challenge.

The descriptive area is that of the interaction between indefinites, pronouns,
and epistemic modalities, a subject renowned for the many puzzles it creates,
including questions concerning identity of individuals, specificity of reference,
and rigidity of names. Obviously, not all of these long-standing problems can
be studied in depth within the span of a single paper. The aim is merely to
show that the dynamic perspective suggests interesting new solutions to some
of them.

The paper provides a dynamic semantics for a language of first order modal
predicate logic. This system is meant to combine the dynamic semantics for
predicate logic developed in Groenendijk and Stokhof (1991) with the update
semantics for modal expressions of Veltman (forthcoming). This combination
is not a straightforward fusion of two distinct systems, but poses some interesting technical problems. Various people have studied this issue (see van
Eijck and Cepparello, forthcoming; Dekker 1992), and the present paper builds
on their work. It tries to solve the problems in a different way, by slightly
adapting the original definition of existential quantification in dynamic predicate logic, and making use of the notion of a referent system, originally developed in Vermeulen (forthcoming b).

Natural language is not the primary target of the analyses provided below.

However, it is a main source of inspiration, and the paper claims that the dynamic approach which is exemplified here using a logical language, can be applied fruitfully to natural language, too. The long-term aim is to come up with a logical system which may function as a tool in the analysis of natural language meaning in much the same way as Montague's IL. The present paper is meant as a step towards that goal.

2   Information

In dynamic semantics the meaning of a sentence is equated with its potential to change information states. An implementation of this idea requires, among other things, a specification of the nature of information states. One general conception of an information state is that of a set of possibilities, consisting of the alternatives which are open according to the information. The nature of the possibilities that make up information states depends on what the information is about.

2.1   Two kinds of information

Not all discourse serves the same purpose. Here, the focus is on one such purpose: that of information exchange. Within this (limited) perspective, two kinds of information need to be distinguished.

First, there is factual information, i.e. *information about the world*. In the end, that is what counts: to get as good an answer as possible to the question *what the world is like* is the prime purpose of this type of discourse.

There are many ways in which information about the world can be gathered: through perception, reasoning, recollection. One particular way is by the use of language: linguistic communication. And this is what is at stake here: the interpretation of informative language use. This type of discourse is primarily focussed on answering questions about the world. But the interpretation process brings along its own questions.

When one is engaged in a linguistic information exchange, one also has to store *discourse information*. For example, there are questions about anaphoric relations that need to be resolved. This requires a mechanism to keep track of the objects talked about and the information gathered about them; a model of the information of other speech participants has to be maintained, and so on.

In the present paper the focus will be on discourse information of the first kind. Discourse information of this type looks more like a book-keeping device, than like real information. Yet, it is a kind of information which is essential for the interpretation of discourse, and since the latter is an important source of information about the world, discourse information indirectly also provides information about the world.

2.1.1   Information about the world

Information about the world is represented as a set of possible worlds, those worlds that, given the information that is available, still might be the real one. Worlds are identified with complete first order models. Such models consist of a set of objects, the domain of discourse, and an interpretation function. Relative to the domain of discourse, the interpretation function assigns a denotation to the non-logical vocabulary of the language, individual constants and predicates.

In this paper it is assumed that language users know which objects constitute the domain of discourse (although they may not know their names). Consequently, all possible worlds share one domain.[1] Hence, a possible world can be identified with the interpretation function of a first order model.

Since they are identified with (interpretation functions of) complete first order models, worlds are "total" objects. Information of language users about the world is characteristically partial. Partiality of information about the world is accounted for by representing it as a set of alternative possibilities. Extending this kind of information amounts to eliminating worlds which were still considered possible.

Even taking into account the restriction to a first order language, this picture of information is very simple, and in many ways not "realistic". An obvious alternative is to look upon information as a partial model of the world which is gradually extended as information grows. Or one might combine this more constructive approach with the eliminative approach as it was sketched above. Such more constructive approaches, however, are technically more complicated. For the purpose of the present paper, it suffices to explore the simplest, the eliminative approach.

2.1.2   Discourse information

As was said above, discourse information keeps track of what has been talked about. In the logical language at hand, it is the use of an existential quantifier that introduces a new item of conversation, a new *peg*. Pegs are formal objects. One can think of them as addresses in memory, for example. But it does not really matter what pegs are. The only thing that counts is that they can be kept apart, and that there are enough of them, no matter how many things are introduced in a discourse. In what follows, natural numbers will be used as pegs. Pegs are introduced one by one in consecutive order, starting from 0.

Variables are the anaphoric expressions of the logical language. To enable the resolution of anaphoric relations, discourse information also keeps track of the variables which are in use, and the pegs with which they are associated. The use of a quantifier $\exists x$ adds the variable x to the variables that are in active use; it introduces the next peg, and associates the variable x with that peg. This is how discourse information grows: extending discourse information is adding variables and pegs, and adjusting the association between them.

2.1.3 Linking the two kinds of information

Gathering discourse information is not an aim in itself. It is to serve the purpose of gathering information about the world. To achieve this, discourse information is connected to information about the world. The two kinds of information are linked *via* possible assignments of objects from the domain of discourse to the pegs (and hence, indirectly, to the variables associated with these pegs). In general, not every assignment of an object to a peg is possible – both the discourse and the information that is available may provide restrictions – , but usually, more than one is.

Becoming better informed on this score is eliminating possible assignments. Suppose a certain assignment is the only one left with respect to some world which is still considered possible. In that case, elimination of the assignment brings along the elimination of the world. This is how discourse information may provide information about the world.

2.2 Information states

2.2.1 Referent systems

In the possibilities that make up an information state, the discourse information is encoded in a *referent system*,[2] which tells which variables are in use, and with which pegs they are associated:

Definition 2.1 A *referent system* is a function r, which has as its domain a finite set of variables v, and as its range a number of pegs.

If the number of pegs in a referent system is n, then the numbers $m < n$ are its pegs.

The use of a quantifier $\exists x$ adds the variable x to the variables that are in use. It introduces the next peg, and associates the variable x with that peg. The corresponding update of a referent system is defined as follows:

Definition 2.2 Let r be a referent system with domain v and range n. $r[x/n]$ is the referent system r' which is like r, except that its domain is $v \cup \{x\}$, its range is $n + 1$, and $r'(x) = n$.

Note that it is not excluded that x is already present in v. This situation occurs if the quantifier $\exists x$ has been used before. In that case, even though the variable x was already in use, it will be associated with a new peg. The peg that x was connected with before remains, but is no longer associated with a variable. This means that a referent system r is an injection.

The main reason to allow for the possibility of re-using a quantifier, is that this is usual logical practice. But a case can be made that in natural language things work in a similar way. A noun phrase such as "a man" introduces a new peg associated with that noun phrase. A subsequent anaphoric pronoun "he" would be linked to that same peg. If later on in the discourse the noun phrase "a man" is used again, it should introduce a new peg and associate it with this occurrence of the noun phrase, and a subsequent anaphoric pronoun "he" would naturally be linked to this new peg. One could still refer back to the first man, not by using a pronoun, but rather by means of a definite description, such as "the man I talked about earlier".

Associating a variable with a new peg is the prototypical way in which the discourse information encoded in a referent system is extended:

Definition 2.3   Let r and r' be two referent systems with domain v and v', and range n and n', respectively.
r' is an *extension* of r, $r \leq r'$, iff $v \subseteq v'$; $n \leq n'$; if $x \in v$ then $r(x) = r'(x)$ or $n \leq r'(x)$; if $x \notin v$ and $x \in v'$ then $n \leq r'(x)$.

A referent system r' is an extension of r iff (i) the variables which were in use in r are still in use in r', but new variables may have been added to r'; (ii) r' has as least as many pegs as r; (iii) the variables that were in use already in r either remain associated with the same pegs in r', or are associated with new pegs, just as (iv) the variables in r' which were not already in use in r are associated with new pegs.

Note that a referent system $r[x/n]$, as defined above, is always a *real* extension of r.

2.2.2   Possibilities

A distinction was made above between discourse information, information about the world, and a link between the two. These three ingredients are present in the *possibilities*, which in turn make up information states.

Definition 2.4   Let D, the *domain of discourse*, and W, the set of *possible worlds*, be two disjoint non-empty sets.
The *possibilities* based on D and W are the set I of triples $\langle r,g,w \rangle$, where r is a referent system; g is a function from the range of r into D; $w \in W$.

The function g assigns an object from the domain of discourse to each peg in the referent system. The composition of g and r indirectly assigns values to the variables that are in use: $g(r(x)) \in D$.

The possibilities contain all that is needed for the interpretation of the basic expressions of the language: individual constants, variables, and n-place predicates.

Definition 2.5   Let α be a basic expression, $i = \langle r,g,w \rangle \in I$, with v the domain of r, and I based upon W and D.

The *denotation of* α *in* i, $i(\alpha)$, is defined as:

    i.   If α is an individual constant, then $i(\alpha) = w(\alpha) \in D$.

    ii. If α is an n-place predicate, then $i(\alpha) = w(\alpha) \subseteq D^n$.

    iii. If α is a variable such that $\alpha \in v$, then $i(\alpha) = g(r(\alpha)) \in D$, else $i(\alpha)$ is not defined.

The first two clauses exploit the identification of possible worlds with interpretation functions of first order models. If $i(c) = w(c) = d$, this means that in world w in the possibility i, the denotation of the name c is the object d. Similarly for predicates.

The value of a variable is determined by the referent system and the assignment. It is the object assigned by g to the peg that is associated with x by the referent system r. Recall that variables are anaphors, hence they need antecedents: a variable will only be assigned a value if it has already been introduced in the domain of the referent system.

2.2.3 *Information states*

Information states are subsets of the set of possibilities:

Definition 2.6 Let I be the set of possibilities based on D and W.
The set of *information states* based on I is the set S such that $s \in S$ iff $s \subseteq I$, and $\forall i, i' \in s$: i and i' have the same referent system.

Variables and pegs are introduced globally with respect to information states. That is why an information state has a unique referent system. Instead of putting a copy of this single referent system in each possibility, it could also be introduced as a separate component. However, the present set-up makes the definitions run more smoothly, and for the language of modal predicate logic there is no difference.[3]

An information state encodes information about the possible denotations of the expressions of the language. For example, the question who c is, what the denotation of the name c is, is settled in an information state if in all worlds in the information state the denotation of c is the same. And, similarly, the question which objects have the property P is answered if in all worlds the denotation of P is the same. Note that in order to have the information that c has the property P, the questions who c is and which objects have P, need not be settled. It suffices that in each world in each possibility the denotation of c in that world is in the denotation of P in that world.

An information state also encodes information about the possible values of variables. This information, too, is relative to possible worlds. Consider the existentially quantified formula $\exists x P x$. This conveys the information that there is an object which has the property P. Updating an information state with this formula results in a state s in which the following holds: in every possibility $i = \langle r,g,w \rangle$ in s, the assignment g will assign to the peg associated with x by r

an object which in w has the property P. If there is more than one object in w with the property P, then there will be several alternative possibilities i' with the same world w, assigning different objects in the denotation of P in w to the peg associated with x.

Thus, the typical situation is one in which the same world appears in several possibilities, which differ in the assignments of objects to the pegs. With respect to the same world there may be different possible assignments of objects to the pegs.

2.3   *Information growth*

In dynamic semantics information states are used to define the information change potential of expressions. The change brought about by (the utterance of) a sentence defines a relation between information states. Among the various relations between such states, the relation of *extension* (or strengthening) is of primary importance.

2.3.1   *Assignment*

One way in which information states can be extended is by adding variables and pegs to the referent system, while assigning some object to them:

Definition 2.7   Let $i = \langle r,g,w \rangle \in I$; n the range of r; $d \in D$, $s \in S$.
   i. $i[x/d] = \langle r[x/n],g[n/d],w \rangle$.
   ii. $s[x/d] = \{i[x/d] \mid i \in s\}$.

According to the second clause, assigning some object d in the domain of discourse to a variable x in an information state s is a pointwise operation on the possibilities i in s. Given definition 2.2, the first clause boils down to this: the next peg is added to the referent system r of i, the variable x is associated with this peg, and the object d is assigned to it.

It will appear that this assignment procedure plays an important role in the interpretation of existential quantification.

2.3.2   *Extension*

Information can grow in two ways: by adding discourse information, and by eliminating possibilities. Both are captured in the following definition:

Definition 2.8   Let $i, i' \in I$, $i = \langle r,g,w \rangle$ and $i' = \langle r',g',w' \rangle$, and $s, s' \in S$.
   i. i' is an *extension* of i, $i \leq i'$ iff $r \leq r'$, $g \subseteq g'$, and $w = w'$.
   ii. s' is an *extension* of s, $s \leq s'$ iff $\forall i' \in s'$: $\exists i \in s$: $i \leq i'$.

An information state s' is an extension of state s if every possibility in s' is an extension of some possibility in s. This means that in the new state some of the possibilities of the original state may have disappeared. These are properly eliminated. Other possibilities, or one or more extensions of them, may re-occur.[4]

A possibility i' is an extension of a possibility i if i' differs from i at most in that in i' variables have been added and associated with newly introduced pegs, that have been assigned some object.

A simple example: Suppose an information state s is updated with the sentence $\exists x Px$. Possibilities in s in which no object has the property P will be eliminated. The referent system of the remaining possibilities will be extended with a new peg, which is associated with x. And for each old possibility i in s, there will be just as many extensions $i[x/d]$ in the new state s', as there are objects d which in the possible world of i have the property P. So, it may very well happen that even though some possibilities are eliminated, the number of possibilities in s' is larger than in s. Still, each possibility in s', will be an extension of some possibility in s. Actually, every i' in s' will be a real extension of some i in s, hence s' will be a real extension of s.

If the resulting state s' is subsequently updated with the atomic formula Qx, then all possibilities in s' will be eliminated in which the object assigned to the peg associated with x does not have the property Q. So, in this case, the resulting state s'' is just a subset of s': there is only elimination of possibilities, no extension of them.

The extension relation is a partial order. There is a unique minimal information state, the *state of ignorance*, in which all worlds are still possible and no discourse information is available yet. This state, $\{\langle \emptyset, \emptyset, w \rangle | w \in W\}$, is referred as **0**. Subsets of the state of ignorance are called *initial states*. In such states there may be some information about the world (some possible worlds are eliminated), but there is no discourse information yet. The maximal element in the extension ordering, **1** $= \emptyset$, is called the *absurd state*. It is the state in which no possibility is left. Less maximal, but more fortunate, are states of *total information*, consisting of just one possibility.

2.3.3 Subsistence

Some auxiliary notions, which will prove useful later on, are the following:

Definition 2.9   Let $s, s' \in S$, $s \leq s'$, $i \in s$, $i' \in s'$.
  i. i' is *a descendant* of i in s' iff $i \leq i'$.
  ii. i *subsists in* s' iff i has one or more descendants in s'.
  iii. s *subsists in* s' iff all $i \in s$ subsist in s'.

It follows from the definition that if s subsists in s', then s' is an extension of s. This means that every possibility in s' is an extension of some possibility in s. But if s subsists in s', it also holds that no possibility in s is eliminated. The state s' may contain more information than s, but only in the sense that variables and pegs may have been added and have been assigned some object.

That is to say, whatever new information s' contains is discourse information, not information about the world. If two states have the same referent system, then the one can only subsist in the other if they are identical.

By way of illustration, consider again the update of s with $\exists x P x$. The original state s subsists in the resulting state s' if there are no possibilities in s in which no object has the property P. In that case every i in s subsists in s', and there will be as many descendants $i[x/d]$ of i in s' as there are objects d in $i(P)$.

3   Updating Information States

Information states being defined, they can be put to use in providing a dynamic interpretation for the language of modal predicate logic.

A formula ϕ of this language is interpreted as a (partial) function, $[\phi]$, from information states to information states. Postfix notation is used: $s[\phi]$ is the result of updating s with ϕ, $s[\phi][\psi]$ is the result of first updating s with ϕ, and next updating $s[\phi]$ with ψ. Whether s can be updated with ϕ may depend on the fulfillment of certain constraints. If a state s does not meet them, then $s[\phi]$ does not exist, and the interpretation process comes to a halt.

Definition 3.1   Let $s \in S$ be an information state, and ϕ a formula of the language. The *update of s with ϕ* is recursively defined as follows:

  i. $s[Rt_1 \ldots t_n] = \{i \in s \mid \langle i(t_1), \ldots, i(t_n) \rangle \in i(R)\}$.
  ii. $s[t_1 = t_2] = \{i \in s \mid i(t_1) = i(t_2)\}$.
  iii. $s[\neg \phi] = \{i \in s \mid i \text{ does not subsist in } s[\phi]\}$.
  iv. $s[\phi \wedge \psi] = s[\phi][\psi]$.
  v. $s[\exists x \phi] = \bigcup_{d \in D}(s[x/d][\phi])$.
  vi. $s[\Diamond \phi] = \{i \in s \mid s[\phi] \neq \emptyset\}$.

The update of an information state with an atomic formula eliminates those possibilities in which the objects denoted by the arguments do not stand in the relation expressed by the predicate. The same holds for identity statements: those possibilities are eliminated in which the two terms do not denote the same object.

The update expressed by an atomic formula may be partial. If one of the argument terms of the formula is a variable that is not present in the referent system of the information state to which the update is to be applied, then its denotation is not defined, and hence the update does not exist. This source of undefinedness percolates up to all the other update clauses. If somewhere in the interpretation process a variable occurs that at that point has not been introduced, then the whole process comes to a halt.[5]

In calculating the effect of updating a state s with $\neg \phi$, s is updated hypothetically with ϕ. Those possibilities that subsist after this hypothetical update are eliminated from the original state s.

Updating a state with a conjunction is a sequential operation: the state is updated with the first conjunct, and next the result is updated with the second conjunct. The update expressed by a conjunction is the composition of the updates associated with its conjuncts.

If a state s is updated with $\exists x \phi$, its referent system is extended with a new peg, and the variable x is associated with that peg. An object d is selected from the domain and assigned to the newly introduced peg. Then the state $s[x/d]$ is updated with ϕ. This procedure is repeated for every object d. The results are collected, and together make up the state $s[\exists x \phi]$.

The operator $\Diamond$ corresponds to the epistemic modality *might*. Updating a state s with $\Diamond \phi$ amounts to testing whether s can be consistently updated with ϕ. If the test succeeds, the resulting state is s again. If the test fails because updating s with ϕ results in the absurd state, then $s[\Diamond \phi]$ is the absurd state.

The semantics just presented defines the interpretation of the formulae of the language in terms of their information change potential. Actually, they change information states in a particular way:

Fact 3.1 For every formula ϕ and information state s: $s \leq s[\phi]$.

In view of this observation the semantics defined above can properly be called an *update semantics*. The interpretation process always leads to an information state that is an extension of the original state.

Other logical constants can be introduced in the usual way. Calculation of the definitions results in:

Fact 3.2
   i. $s[\phi \to \psi] = \{i \in s \mid \text{if } i \text{ subsists in } s[\phi], \text{ then all descendants of } i \text{ in } s[\phi]$ subsist in $s[\phi][\psi]\}$.
   ii. $s[\phi \vee \psi] = \{i \in s \mid i \text{ subsists in } s[\phi] \text{ or } i \text{ subsists in } s[\neg\phi][\psi]\}$.
   iii. $s[\forall x \phi] = \{i \in s \mid \text{for all } d \in D: i \text{ subsists in } s[x/d][\phi]\}$.
   iv. $s[\Box \phi] = \{i \in s \mid s \text{ subsist in } s[\phi]\}$.

It is not possible to make a different choice of basic and defined constants which leads to the same overall results. This can be seen as follows. From the definitions of negation and the existential quantifier it follows that an existential quantifier which occurs inside the scope of a negation cannot bind variables outside its scope.

Consider $\neg \exists x P x$. The negation eliminates all possibilities in which the denotation of P is non-empty. The change in the referent system of an information state s that takes place inside the hypothetical update of s with $\exists x P x$ which is performed in calculating the update of s with $\neg \exists x P x$ is not inherited by the resulting state $s[\neg \exists x P x]$. Hence, the existential quantifier no longer acts dynamically. This means that in general $\exists x \phi$ cannot be defined as $\neg \forall x \neg \phi$. For similar reasons conjunction cannot be defined in terms of negation and disjunction, or negation and implication.[6]

3.1   Consistency, support, and entailment

Truth and falsity concern the relation between language and the world. In dynamic semantics it is information about the world rather than the world itself that language is related to. Hence, the notions of truth and falsity cannot be expected to occupy the same central position as they do in standard semantics. More suited to the information oriented approach are the notions of *consistency* and *support*.

Two very simple observations concerning information exchange illustrate this. No hearer will be prepared to update his information state with a sentence if the result would be the absurd state. And a speaker can only assert a sentence correctly if it does not constitute a "real" update in her information state.

Definition 3.2   Let s be an information state.
  i. ϕ is *consistent* with s iff $s[\phi]$ exists and $s[\phi] \neq \emptyset$.
  ii. ϕ is *supported* by s iff $s[\phi]$ exists and s subsists in $s[\phi]$.

ϕ is *consistent* with s is often expressed by saying that s *allows* ϕ. The notion of support is defined in terms of subsistence, and not, as one might perhaps expect, in terms of identity. If $s = s[\phi]$ then s supports ϕ, but the converse does not hold.

Consider a (non-absurd) information state s such that there is no possibility in s containing a world in which the denotation of P is empty. Intuitively, such an information state should count as one which supports the sentence $\exists x P x$. Nevertheless, as was indicated already above, in such a state s it will never be the case that $s = s[\exists x P x]$. It will always hold that $s[\exists x P x]$ is a *real* extension of s. However, the information added to such a state s is purely discourse information. In updating such a state s with $\exists x P x$ no possibility, no possible world or possible assignment of objects to the pegs already present in s is eliminated. This is precisely what is captured in the notion of subsistence, and hence in the notion of support.

3.1.1   Consistency and coherence

The observations about information exchange made above can be generalized as follows. A sentence is unacceptable if there is not at least *some* state with which it is consistent. And if a sentence is not supported by *any* non-absurd state, which means that no speaker could ever sincerely utter it, then that sentence is judged unacceptable, too.

Definition 3.3
  i. ϕ is *consistent* iff there is some information state with which ϕ is consistent.
  ii. ϕ is *coherent* iff there is some non-absurd state by which ϕ is supported.

Note that coherence implies consistency. Concerning the acceptability of a single sentence, it would suffice to require coherence. Still, it is important to distinguish between these two notions if not just the acceptability of single sentences is at stake, but the acceptability of a discourse, which may consist of a sequence of sentences possibly uttered by different speakers in different information states.

The acceptability of such a discourse minimally requires that one by one the sentences which make it up are coherent. But it would be wrong to require that the discourse as a whole can be supported by a single information state.

For example, one speaker might start a discourse uttering the sentence "It might be raining outside". And a hearer may be able to happily confirm this. Another speaker, or even the same one after having opened the blinds, can continue the discourse with "It isn't raining". And the same hearer could easily be able to consistently update his state with this information. So, the discourse as a whole is consistent. And each of its two sentences taken separately is coherent. Yet, without an intermediate change in information state, as can be caused by opening the blinds and looking outside, no single speaker can coherently utter the discourse as a whole.

3.1.2   Entailment

The properties of consistency and coherence present criteria for testing the adequacy of a proposed semantics. For the same purpose, the notion of entailment is important, too. Entailment is not defined in the usual way in terms of truth, but in terms of sequential update and support:[7]

Definition 3.4 $\phi_1, \ldots, \phi_n \models \psi$ iff for all information states s such that $s[\phi_1] \ldots [\phi_n][\psi]$ exists, it holds that $s[\phi_1] \ldots [\phi_n]$ supports ψ.

A sequence of sentences $\phi_1, \ldots, \phi_n$ entails a sentence ψ if whenever an information state is sequentially updated with $\phi_1, \ldots, \phi_n$, the resulting state is one which supports ψ, provided that along the way no free variables occur that at that point have not been introduced in the referent system.

3.2   Equivalence

A suitable notion of equivalence may be expected to tell when two expressions can be substituted for each other in a meaning preserving way. Within update semantics, meaning is preserved if the update effects are preserved. This being so, the usual definition of equivalence in terms of mutual entailment cannot be used.

For example, $\exists x P x$ and $\exists y P y$ mutually entail each other. Whenever a state s has been updated with $\exists x P x$, there will be no possibilities left containing a world in which there are no objects that have the property P. Any such state will support $\exists y P y$. But, obviously, $\exists x P x$ and $\exists y P y$ cannot be substituted for each other in all contexts, because although they always contribute the same information about the world, they make different contributions to the discourse information.

Likewise, a characteristic feature of the dynamic entailment relation is that it allows for binding relations between quantifiers in the premises and variables in the conclusion. For example, $\exists x P x \models P x$. And it also holds that $P x \models \exists x P x$, because in any state s such that $s[P x]$ exists, it will hold that after updating s with $P x$, the resulting state will support $\exists x P x$. Nevertheless, the two formulae are not equivalent. Whereas an update with $\exists x \neg P x \wedge P x$ will always lead to the absurd state, replacing the second conjunct $P x$ by $\exists x P x$ yields a consistent sequence of sentences.

On the other hand, the requirement that ϕ and ψ always have the same update effects, i.e. that $[\phi] = [\psi]$, would be too strong. Under such a definition, $\exists x \exists y R x y$ and $\exists y \exists x R x y$ would not be equivalent. The reason for this is that the referent system of an information state not only keeps track of which variables and pegs are present, but also of the order in which they were introduced. After updating an initial state with $\exists x \exists y R x y$, the first peg will be associated with x, and the second with y, and only possibilities are left in which the first peg stands in the relation R to the second. In case that same state is updated with $\exists y \exists x R x y$, things are the other way around. Still, in terms of the possible values of the variables x and y, things are exactly the same in both cases. Although $s[\exists x \exists y R x y]$ and $s[\exists y \exists x R x y]$ are not the same, both states will allow and support exactly the same formulae.

Similarly, updating a state with $\exists x P x$ and with $\exists x P x \wedge \exists x P x$ does not result in the same state. Consider the minimal state. After updating it with $\exists x P x$ there will be only one peg present, associated with the variable x. If it is updated with $\exists x P x \wedge \exists x P x$, there will be two pegs, and only the second is associated with the variable x, the first is no longer associated with a variable anymore. But, again, in terms of the possible values of the variable x, things are the same, and both resulting states allow and support the same formulae.

In view of this, in order for two formulae to be equivalent, it is not required that an update with either one of them always leads to exactly the *same* result, but that the results are *similar*, where the notion of similarity is defined in such a way that it ignores differences between information states which are irrelevant with regard to which formulae they allow and support.

Definition 3.5   Let $i, i' \in I$, $i = \langle r,g,w \rangle$, $i' = \langle r',g',w' \rangle$, with v and v' the domain of r and r', respectively; and let $s,s' \in S$.

  i.   *i is similar to i'* iff $v = v'$, $w = w'$, and $\forall x \in v$: $g(r(x)) = g'(r'(x))$.
 ii.   *s is similar to s'* iff $\forall i \in s$: $\exists i' \in s'$: *i is similar to i'*, and $\forall i' \in s'$: $\exists i \in s$: *i' is similar to i*.

The notion of similarity robs the pegs of their identity. It does not matter what they are. The only thing that matters is what hangs on them: the variables they are associated with, and the values these variables are assigned through their mediation.

Why then have pegs to begin with? The question allows for several answers. In the present context the short answer is that they are useful. Pegs make it possible to use an existential quantifier more than once, and still formulate the semantics as an *update* semantics. Without pegs, a proper dynamic semantics for the existential quantifier involves an operation of downdate, which throws away any information about possible values of the variable involved. The introduction of such downdates complicates the formulation of the basic semantic notions. Another answer is the following. Consider a language (natural language?) without variables, or just a very limited amount of them. Then an account of anaphora demands a device like that of pegs. Moreover, if a language has other means than pronouns to establish anaphoric links (such as anaphoric definite descriptions), pegs are very useful, too.[8]

Similarity is an equivalence relation.

Definition 3.6 $\phi \equiv \psi$ iff for all information states s: $s[\phi]$ is similar to $s[\psi]$.

Under this notion of equivalence, $\exists x \exists y Rxy$ and $\exists y \exists x Rxy$ are equivalent, and so are $\exists x Px$ and $\exists x Px \wedge \exists x Px$. And $\exists x Px$ and $\exists y Py$ are not equivalent, and neither are $\exists x Px$ and Px.

4 Illustrations

4.1 Modality

4.1.1 Order matters

A characteristic feature of dynamic semantics, is that it can account for the fact that order matters in discourse. Consider:

(1) It might be raining outside. [. . .] It isn't raining outside.
(2) It isn't raining outside. [. . .] *It might be raining outside.

Given the sequential interpretation of conjunction and the interpretation of the *might*-operator as a consistency test, the unacceptability of (2) is readily explained. After an information state has been updated with the information that it is not raining, it is no longer consistent with the information that it might be raining. If, as in (1), things are presented in the opposite order, there is no problem.

So, the difference between (1) and (2) is explained by the following fact:[9]

Fact 4.1 Whereas $\Diamond p \wedge \neg p$ is consistent, $\neg p \wedge \Diamond p$ is inconsistent.

Note that the dots in example (1) are important. If they are left out, or replaced by "and", one is more or less forced to look upon (1) as a single utterance, of a single speaker, on a single occasion. But in that case, (1) intuitively is no longer acceptable. The following fact explains this:

Fact 4.2   Although consistent, $\Diamond p \wedge \neg p$ is incoherent.

An utterance of a sentence is incoherent if no *single* information state can support it. Even though multi-speaker discourses are not explicitly introduced, the semantics explains that a discourse like (1) is only acceptable if the two sentences are uttered by different speakers in different information states, or by one and the same speaker who has gained additional information in between uttering the two sentences. Only when the two sentences are taken separately can each of them be coherent. And when the order in which they are presented is as in (1), the sequence of the two sentences is also consistent, whereas in the order presented in (2) it is not.

4.1.2   Idempotency

Another way to look at the consistency and incoherence of $\Diamond p \wedge \neg p$ is as follows. Since $\Diamond p \wedge \neg p$ is consistent, there are states that can be updated with it. But once a hearer has updated his/her information state with $\Diamond p \wedge \neg p$, s/he cannot confirm what was said. For any non-absurd state s, $s[\Diamond p \wedge \neg p]$ does not support $\Diamond p \wedge \neg p$. This means that $\Diamond p \wedge \neg p$ is not idempotent:

Fact 4.3 $\Diamond p \wedge \neg p \not\models \Diamond p \wedge \neg p$.

And this, in turn, means that dynamic entailment does not have the property of idempotency.

The reason behind this is the *non-persistence* of formulae of the form $\Diamond \phi$: a state s may support $\Diamond \phi$, whereas a more informative state s' may be inconsistent with it. If the consistency test $\Diamond p$ succeeds in a situation s, and a subsequent update with $\neg p$ succeeds too, the state $s[\Diamond p \wedge \neg p]$ is a real extension of s. The information that $s[\Diamond p \wedge \neg p]$ contains in addition to the information contained by s is the reason why $\Diamond p$ is no longer consistent with $s[\Diamond p \wedge \neg p]$.

The non-persistence of modal formulae also causes non-monotonicity of entailment:

Fact 4.4 $\Diamond p \models \Diamond p$ but $\Diamond p, \neg p \not\models \Diamond p$.

Commutativity, idempotency, and monotonicity also fail for reasons having to do with coreference rather than with modality. For example, whereas $\neg Px \wedge \exists x Px$ is consistent, $\exists x Px \wedge \neg Px$ is not. And notice that $\neg Px \wedge \exists x Px$ is not idempotent. Finally, although $\exists x Px \models Px$, it holds that $\exists x Px, \exists x \neg Px \not\models Px$.

4.1.3   Modality and information

If one is told that it might be raining, this may very well constitute *real* information, on the basis of which one could decide, for example, to take an umbrella when going out. In many cases, a sentence of the form *might-ϕ* will have the effect that one becomes aware of the possibility of *ϕ*. The present framework is one in which possible worlds are total objects, and in which growth of information about the world is explicated in terms of elimination of possibilities. Becoming aware of a possibility cannot be accounted for in a natural fashion in such an eliminative approach. It would amount to extending *partial* possibilities, rather than eliminating total ones. To account for that aspect of the meaning of *might*, a constructive approach seems to be called for.

The present semantics merely takes into account that upon hearing *might-ϕ*, one checks whether one's information allows for the possibility that *ϕ*. This does explain the following observation. Suppose again that one is told that it might be raining. And suppose furthermore that the information one has indicates that this is not so. Then, in all likelihood, one will not accept the remark just like that. One will start arguing. ("No! Look outside! The sun is shining!"). It is this aspect of the meaning of *might* that is accounted for by the semantics that was given above.

If *ϕ* is inconsistent with an information state *s*, updating *s* with $\Diamond \phi$ would result in ∅. But one does not want to end up in the absurd state. Hence, if that threatens to happen, one does *not* just update one's information state, but one will start arguing with whoever tries to tell one that $\Diamond \phi$.

One way to look upon this, is that epistemic modal statements such as *might-ϕ* are not primarily meant as providing information about the world as such; rather they provide information about the information of the speaker. If a speaker utters *might-ϕ*, the hearer may infer, on the assumption that the speaker's utterance is correct, that his/her information is consistent with *ϕ*. Since this type of higher-order information is left out of consideration here, this kind of update effect is not accounted for.

Another possible update aspect of epistemic modal statements is the following: In some situations *might-ϕ* draws attention to a hypothetical possible extension of one's information. Often this is done with the intention of saying something more about "what if". An example is the following sequence of sentences:

(3)   It might rain. It would ruin your blue suede shoes.[10]

The effect of updating one's information state with this sequence of sentences should roughly be that it is extended with the conditional that if it rains, the blue suede shoes one is wearing will be ruined, which could be a real update, and not just a consistency test.

This phenomenon, which is known under the name of *modal subordination*, is a central feature of the meaning of natural language modalities. (And, actually, it can be used as a first rate argument in favor of a dynamic treatment of it.) Nevertheless, except for a slightly more elaborated discussion at the end of the next section, we largely ignore it in the present paper.

For the moment it suffices to indicate that there is more to *might* than the semantics presented in this paper for the modal operator ◊ covers. On the other hand, the observations made above may have made clear that consistency testing is indeed an essential ingredient of its meaning.[11]

4.2   *Coreference and modality*

4.2.1   *Coreference*

It is a characteristic feature of dynamic semantics that an existential quantifier can bind variables outside its scope. The variable in the second conjunct of (4) is bound by the quantifier in the first conjunct:

> (4) $\exists x Px \wedge Qx$
> A man is walking in the rain. He wears blue suede shoes.

Let n be the number of pegs in an information state s. First, s is updated with $\exists x Px$. Each possibility $\langle r, g, w \rangle \in s$ will have as many possibilities $\langle r[x/n], g[n/d], w \rangle$ as its descendants in $s[\exists x Px]$, as there are objects $d \in D$ such that $d \in w(P)$. From those, the update with Qx eliminates the possibilities i in which $i(x) \notin i(Q)$.

Exactly the same result is obtained when s is updated with:

> (5) $\exists x(Px \wedge Qx)$
> There is a man walking in the rain who wears blue suede shoes.

This equivalence is a basic fact of dynamic predicate logic:

Fact 4.5 $\exists x Px \wedge Qx \equiv \exists x(Px \wedge Qx)$.

With the aid of the extended binding power of the existential quantifier, a compositional and incremental account of cross-sentential anaphora can be given, and the same holds for donkey-anaphora, as is guaranteed by the following equivalence:

Fact 4.6 $\exists x Px \rightarrow Qx \equiv \forall x(Px \rightarrow Qx)$.

These equivalences are the trade mark of dynamic predicate logic. They make it possible to translate the sentences in (6) and (7) into logical formulae which reflect the structure of these sentences more transparently than their usual logical translation (8)

(6) If a farmer owns a donkey he beats it.
$(\exists x Px \wedge \exists y (Qy \wedge Rxy)) \rightarrow Sxy$
(7) Every farmer who owns a donkey beats it.
$\forall x (Px \wedge \exists y (Qy \wedge Rxy) \rightarrow Sxy)$
(8) $\forall x \forall y ((Px \wedge Qy \wedge Rxy) \rightarrow Sxy)$

The equivalences stated above guarantee that the formulae in (6), (7), and (8) are logically equivalent.[12]

4.2.2 Modality and coreference

Modal operators are transparent to the extended binding force of existential quantifiers. In (9), the occurrence of the variable within the scope of the *might*-operator is bound by the quantifier in the first conjunct:

(9) $\exists x Px \wedge \Diamond Qx$

In this case, the second conjunct only tests whether there is at least one possibility $i \in s[\exists x Px]$, such that $i(x) \in i(Q)$. If so, the test returns the state that resulted from updating with $\exists x Px$. If not, it gives the absurd state. In particular, this means that there may be possibilities $i \in s[\exists x Px \wedge \Diamond Qx]$ such that for no $i' \in s[\exists x Px \wedge \Diamond Qx]$ it holds that $i(x) \in i'(Q)$. In other words, among the possible values for x there may be objects d that do not have the property Q in any of the worlds compatible with the information.

As is to be expected, both (10) and (11) are inconsistent:

(10) $\exists x Px \wedge \Diamond \neg Px$
(11) $\exists x Px \wedge \Diamond \forall y \neg Px$

This corresponds to the problematic nature of the following discourses:

(12) There is someone hiding in the closet. [. . .] He might not be hiding in the closet.
(13) There is someone hiding in the closet. [. . .] It might be that no-one is hiding in the closet.

The first discourse is unacceptable if the pronoun in the second sentence is interpreted as anaphorically linked to the indefinite in the first. The second discourse is unacceptable unless the second sentence is looked upon as a revision or a correction of the information provided by the first sentence.

Unlike (10) and (11) the following formula is *not* inconsistent:

(14) $\exists x Px \wedge \forall y \Diamond \neg Py$

The typical situation in which an information state supports (14), is where it is known that someone is hiding in the closet, but where any information on

the person's identity is lacking. That means that for any of the persons involved, it is consistent with the information that it is not that person who is
hiding in the closet.

More formally, suppose the domain consists of just two objects, and that
according to some information state, just one of them has the property P, but
that it does not decide which one it is. Then for each of these objects it holds
that it might not have the property P.

Unlike (14), (15) *is* inconsistent:

(15) $\exists x(Px \wedge \forall y \Diamond \neg Py)$

The brackets make a difference. In updating a state s with (15), some object
d is chosen, and $s[x/d][Px \wedge \forall y \Diamond \neg Py]$ is performed. In all possibilities that
remain after updating $s[x/d]$ with Px, d has the property P. But then $\forall y \Diamond \neg Py$
will be inconsistent with $s[x/d][Px]$. And this holds for each choice of d. Hence
(15) is inconsistent.

The fact that (14) is consistent, whereas (15) is not, means that dynamic
modal predicate logic lacks some features which characterize dynamic predi-
cate logic. It is no longer the case that $\exists x \phi \wedge \psi$ and $\exists x(\phi \wedge \psi)$ are always
equivalent. This point may be elaborated.

4.2.3   The case of the broken vase

Imagine the following situation. You and your spouse have three sons. One of
them broke a vase. Your spouse is very anxious to find out who did it. Both
you and your spouse know that your eldest didn't do it as he was playing
outside when it happened. Actually, you are not interested in the question
who broke the vase. But you are looking for your eldest son to help you do
the dishes. He might be hiding somewhere.

In search for the culprit, your spouse has gone upstairs. Suppose your spouse
hears a noise coming from the closet. If it is the shuffling of feet, your spouse
will know that someone is hiding in there, but will not be able to exclude any
of your three sons. In that case your spouse could utter:

(16)   There is someone hiding in the closet. He might be guilty.
       $\exists x Qx \wedge \Diamond Px)$

But the information state of your spouse would not support:[13]

(17)   There is someone hiding in the closet who might be guilty.
       $\exists x(Qx \wedge \Diamond Px)$

If the situation is slightly changed, and it is imagined that the noise your
spouse hears is a high-pitched voice, things are different. Now, your spouse

knows it cannot be your eldest. He already has a frog in his throat. In that case your spouse *can* say (17).

This also means that if your spouse yells (17) from upstairs, you can stay were you are, but if it is (16), you might run upstairs to check whether it is perhaps your helper that is hiding there.

So, there is a difference between (16) and (17),[14] and the semantics accounts for it:

Fact 4.7 $\exists x Px \wedge \Diamond Qx \neq \exists x(Px \wedge \Diamond Qx)$.

For $\exists x Px \wedge \Diamond Qx$ to be supported by an information state s, it is sufficient that in any possibility in s the denotation of P is not empty, and that there is at least one possibility in which an object which has the property P also has the property Q. In particular, this leaves open the option that there is some possibility such that the object(s) satisfying P in that possibility fail to have the property Q in any possibility. This is why in the example, your spouse can correctly utter (16) in case it is possible according to the information of your spouse that your eldest is hiding there, whereas your spouse knows that he cannot be guilty of breaking the vase.

If a state s supports $\exists x(Px \wedge \Diamond Qx)$, the following holds. In any possibility in s the denotation of P is not empty. Moreover, at least one of the objects which in a possibility satisfies P must satisfy Q in some possibility. This excludes the option that there is some possibility such that the object(s) satisfying P in that possibility fail to have the property Q in any possibility. This is why your spouse can only correctly utter (17) in case the information state of your spouse does not allow for the possibility that your eldest is hiding in the closet.

A similar observation applies to the following pair of examples.

(18) If there is someone hiding in the closet, he might be guilty.
      $\exists x Qx \rightarrow \Diamond Px$
(19) Whoever is hiding in the closet might be guilty.
      $\forall x(Qx \rightarrow \Diamond Px)$

Take the same situation again. Only in case your spouse heard some high-pitched voice is (19) a correct utterance. In the other case, (19) is not supported by the information state of your spouse, and only (18) is left.

Fact 4.8 $\exists x Qx \rightarrow \Diamond Px \neq \forall x(Qx \rightarrow \Diamond Px)$.

These facts are significant for at least two reasons. First, unlike in the predicate logical fragment of the language, in the full language it makes a difference whether a bound variable is inside or outside the scope of the quantifier that binds it. Second, since in any static semantics a variable can only be bound by a quantifier if it is inside its scope, it can never account for such differences.

4.2.4   Two features

There are two features of the proposed semantics which together are responsible for this result. The first is that the consistency test performed by the *might*-operator not only checks whether after an update with the formula following the *might*-operator there will be any worlds left, but also whether there will be any assignments left. Thus, even in a situation in which knowledge of the world is complete (or irrelevant), epistemic qualification of a statement may still make sense. Example:

(20) $\exists x (x^2 > 4) \wedge \Diamond(x > 2) \wedge \Diamond(x < -2)$

Consider the world that results when the operations and relations mentioned in (20) are given their standard interpretation in the domain of real numbers. In that case (20) will be supported by any state consisting of possibilities in which only this world figures.

The second feature is that existential quantification is *not* interpreted in terms of *global* (re-)assignment. Global reassignment, which would give wrong results, reads as follows:

$s[\exists x \phi] = (\cup_{d \in D} s[x/d])[\phi]$

Updating with $\exists x \Diamond Px$ would output *every* $d \in D$ as a possible value for x, as long as there is *some* d that, in some world compatible with the information, has the property P. The present definition reads:

$s[\exists x \phi] = \cup_{d \in D} (s[x/d][\phi])$

Updating with $\exists x \Diamond Px$ outputs as possible values of x only those d such that in some w compatible with the information in s, d has the property P in w. If $\Diamond Px$ is within the scope of $\exists x$, the consistency test is performed one by one for each $d \in D$, and those d are eliminated as possible values for x for which the test fails.[15]

4.2.5   Modalities de dicto *and* de re

Note that there is a difference between $\exists x \Diamond Px$ and $\Diamond \exists x Px$. Like negation, modal operators block the binding of quantifiers inside their scope. An update of a state s with $\Diamond \exists x Px$ only tests whether there is some possibility in s in which the denotation of P is non-empty. If so, $s[\Diamond \exists x Px] = s$, if not $s[\Diamond \exists x Px] = \emptyset$. In calculating $s[\Diamond \exists x Px]$, a hypothetical update of s with $\exists x Px$ is performed. But apart from the question whether $s[\exists x Px]$ leads to the absurd state or not, the effects of this hypothetical update are ignored. In particular, the extension of the referent system of s with a new peg associated with x is not inherited by the update of s with $\Diamond \exists x Px$ as a whole. This is why the quantifier inside the scope of the modal operator has no binding force outside the scope of that operator.

In case the consistency test $\Diamond\exists x Px$ fails, not only $\Diamond\exists x Px$, but also $\exists x\Diamond Px$ leads to the absurd state. In case the test $\Diamond\exists x Px$ succeeds in a state s, $s[\exists x\Diamond Px]$ is a real extension of $s[\Diamond\exists x Px] = s$. But the additional information only concerns discourse information: s subsists in $s[\exists x\Diamond\phi]$. Although $\Diamond\exists x Px$ and $\exists x\Diamond Px$ are not equivalent, they do entail each other.[16]

The unacceptability of the discourse in (21) squares with the fact that the existential quantifier inside the scope of $\Diamond$ in the first conjunct of the formula in (21), does not bind the variable in the second conjunct:

> (21)   It might be the case that someone is hiding in the closet. *He broke the vase.
>
> $\Diamond\exists x Px \wedge Qx$

However, there are also cases that seem to point in a different direction:

> (22)   It might be the case that someone is hiding in the closet. It might be that he broke the vase.
>
> $\Diamond\exists x Px \wedge \Diamond Qx$

Here, it seems, the pronoun in the second sentence can be interpreted as anaphorically linked with the indefinite in the first sentence. However, in the present semantics, the variable in the second conjunct is not bound by the quantifier in the first.

4.2.6   Modal subordination

There is a notable difference between the discourses in (21) and (22): whereas the second sentence in (21) is in the indicative mood, the second sentence in (22), like the first, is a modal statement. The discourse in (22) is a typical example of what Roberts called "modal subordination".[17] The possibility of anaphoric linking between an indefinite embedded in a modal statement and a pronoun in a subsequent sentence, seems to be restricted to cases where the latter has a similar modal force.

As it stands, the analysis of modality and coreference presented here, does not account for the phenomenon of modal subordination. But it is not too difficult to see in which way the framework could be extended to be able to deal with it. Consider the well-known example:

> (23)   A wolf might come in. It would eat you first.

Intuitively, what this little horror story tries to tell the hearer is, first of all, that there are possibilities in which a wolf comes in; and, secondly, that in every such possibility she is the first to be consumed by the ferocious animal. In effect, the second sentence provides the information also conveyed by "If a wolf comes in, it will eat you first".

The first sentence is of the form $\Diamond\exists xPx$. What is needed to interpret the second sentence is to keep track of the hypothetical update of the original state s with $\exists xPx$, which is involved in the consistency test constituted by the first sentence. The second sentence is of the form *would Qx*, where its mood indicates that, in addition to the original state s, the hypothetical state $s[\exists xPx]$ must be taken into consideration. Updating with the second sentence involves a further hypothetical update of $s[\exists xPx]$ with Qx. Finally, the interpretation of the modal operator *would* effectuates the elimination of those possibilities in s which subsist in $s[\exists xPx]$ but the descendants of which do not subsist in $s[\exists xPx][Qx]$. So, the end result can be a real update of the original state, in which the less frightening possibilities where a wolf comes in and eats someone else first, or even better, eats no one at all, are eliminated. (But look at it from the bright side: the best of all possible worlds in which no wolf comes in are not eliminated!)

To make an analysis like this work, the framework needs to be extended in such a way that within the update procedures intermediate hypothetical states are remembered, rather than immediately forgotten.[18] Roughly speaking, if the next sentence is in the indicative mood, such hypothetical states can be removed from memory. If the next sentence is a modal statement, this signals that if such hypothetical states are in memory, they can be put to use, where the particular modality involved, determines the way in which they should be used.

Once the framework has been extended along these lines, not only can the discourse in (23) be handled, but also the earlier example (22) poses no problem anymore. In interpreting $\Diamond\exists xPx \wedge \Diamond Qx$ in a state s, the consistency test $\Diamond Qx$ could be performed with respect to the hypothetical state $s[\exists xPx]$. The overall effect would be the same as in case of performing the single consistency test $\Diamond(\exists xPx \wedge Qx)$. (Of course, $\Diamond\phi \wedge \Diamond\psi$ in general would still not be equivalent to $\Diamond(\phi \wedge \psi)$.)

Note that once modal subordination has been accommodated, the difference between $\Diamond\exists xPx$ and $\exists x\Diamond Px$ becomes even more apparent. Consider the following examples:

(24)   It might be the case that there is someone hiding in the closet. *But he might also not be hiding in the closet.
$\Diamond\exists xPx \wedge \Diamond\neg Px$

(25)   There is someone who might be hiding in the closet. But he might also not be hiding in the closet.
$\exists x\Diamond Px \wedge \Diamond\neg Px$

In the case of (24), the pronoun in the second sentence can only be interpreted as anaphorically linked to the indefinite under the scope of *might* in the first sentence, if one interprets the second sentence as modally subordinated to the first. But as was pointed out above, under such an interpretation $\Diamond \exists x P x \wedge$ $\Diamond \neg P x$ means the same as $\Diamond (\exists x P x \wedge \neg P x)$. The obvious inconsistency of the latter explains the unacceptability of the discourse in (24).

As for (25), since the indefinite has scope over *might*, the pronoun can be anaphorically linked to it without recourse to modal subordination. (In fact, because the modal operator is inside the scope of the existential quantifier, it seems that the first sentence of (25) does not count as a modal statement; and hence, the possibility of modal subordination does not even arise.) And, to be sure, the semantics as it is presented here renders (25) coherent and consistent, thus explaining the acceptability of the discourse in (25). Any state in which there is at least one possibility in which there is some object d that has the property P and some possibility in which this object d does not have the property P supports $\exists x \Diamond P x \wedge \Diamond \neg P x$.

5 Identity and Identification

Consider the following example:

> (26) Someone has done it. It might be Alfred. It might not be Alfred.
> $\exists! x P x \wedge \Diamond (x = a) \wedge \Diamond (x \neq a)$

$\exists x! P x$ is used as an abbreviation for $\exists x P x \wedge \forall y (P y \rightarrow y = x)$. $\exists x! P x$ expresses that there is precisely one object with the property P.

The sequence of sentences in (26) is coherent, and hence consistent. If it is continued with (27), everything remains consistent. But viewed as a single utterance, (26) followed by (27) would be incoherent.

> (27) It is not Alfred. It is Bill.
> $(x \neq a) \wedge (x = b)$

There are several situations in which (26) can be coherently asserted. One is the situation in which the speaker is acquainted with the person who did it, but does not know his name – his name might be Alfred, his name might not be Alfred. In this case the question who did it is decided in the information state of the speaker: in every possibility, the denotation of the predicate P is the same single object from the domain of discourse. What is not decided in the information state of the speaker is the denotation of the name a. But if the information state supports (26), then in at least one possibility the denotation of a is the object that according to the information of the speaker constitutes the denotation of P.

However, also the opposite case, in which the speaker does know perfectly well who is called Alfred, is possible. In that case the sentence reports that the question is still open whether or not this person did it. A typical example of a situation like this, not involving a name but a deictic pronoun, is this:

(28) Someone has done it. It might be you. But it might also not be you.
$\exists!xPx \land \Diamond(x = you) \land \Diamond(x \neq you)$

This is consistent and coherent, as the hearer probably would like it to be.

In ordinary modal predicate logic, the means for an adequate representation of the discourse in (26) or (28) are lacking. In ordinary (modal) predicate logic variables can not be bound unless they are in the scope of a quantifier. So, one would have to add brackets to achieve the required binding:

(29) $\exists x(Px \land \Diamond(x = a) \land \Diamond(x \neq a))$

But in case a denotes the same object in every possible world, (29) is rendered inconsistent by any modal system, including the present one.

The examples (26) and (29) show once more that whether a bound variable occurs inside or outside the syntactic scope of the quantifier that binds it can make a crucial difference. The latter type of binding is a typical feature of dynamic semantics. So, it seems that an account of the consistency of (28) calls for a dynamic set-up.[19]

5.1   *Identification and identifiers*

Consider the following example:

(30) $\exists!xPx \land \forall y\Diamond(x = y)$
Someone has done it. It might be anyone.

Intuitively, (30) is an acceptable discourse. Formally, (30) is coherent and consistent. An information state supports (30), if it is known that just one object has the property P, but one has no idea which object it is.

Actually, under the assumption that the domain consists of more than one object, (30) entails $\forall y\Diamond(x \neq y)$. There is no static system in which $\forall y\Diamond(x \neq y)$ is consistent. In the present dynamic system it is.

Like (30), (31) expresses an ultimate form of non-identification:

(31) $\forall x\Diamond(x = a) \lor \forall x\Diamond(x \neq a)$
Anyone might be Alfred. Anyone might not be Alfred.

If an information state supports (31), it is not known of which object a is the name.

Sometimes more information is available.

Definition 5.1 Let α be a term, $s \in S$.
    i. α is an *identifier* in s iff $\forall i, i' \in s$: $i(\alpha) = i'(\alpha)$.
   ii. α is an *identifier* iff $\forall s$: α is an identifier in s.

If a term α is an identifier in an information state s, then s contains the information which object α denotes (or, who α is, in at least some sense of "knowing who"[20]). If α is not an identifier in s, then there is at least some doubt about which object α refers to.

A term is an identifier *per se* if no matter what the information state is, it cannot fail to decide what the denotation of the term is.

Whether or not a term is an identifier in an information state can be tested:

Fact 5.1 Let α be a term which differs from x.
   i. α is an identifier in s iff s supports $\forall x(\Diamond(x = \alpha) \to (x = \alpha))$.
   ii. α is an identifier iff $\models \forall x(\Diamond(x = \alpha) \to (x = \alpha))$.

Identifiers are epistemically rigid designators:

Fact 5.2 Let α and β be identifiers.
   i. $\models \Diamond(\alpha = \beta) \to (\alpha = \beta)$.
   ii. $\models (\alpha = \beta) \to \Box(\alpha = \beta)$.

5.1.1 Leibniz' law

One more aspect in which the present dynamic modal logic differs from standard ones appears if one takes a look at what happens with Leibniz' law:

Fact 5.3 If s supports $a = b$, then $s[\phi(a/x)] = s[\phi(b/x)]$

(Here, $\phi(a/x)$ is the formula which is obtained from ϕ by substituting a for free occurrences of x in ϕ.)

What this observation expresses is that as soon as one knows that $a = b$, $\phi(a/x)$ and $\phi(b/x)$ get the same meaning. In particular, it holds that:

$$\phi_1, \ldots, a = b, \ldots, \phi_n \models \psi(a/x) \text{ iff } \phi_1, \ldots, a = b, \ldots, \phi_n \models \psi(b/x)$$

In a standard modal semantics this holds only if a and b are rigid. In the present system it holds for all names, whether they are identifiers or not. However, since it does not generally hold that $\Diamond(a = b) \models a = b$, it does not follow that:

$$\phi_1, \ldots, \Diamond(a = b), \ldots, \phi_n \models \psi(a/x) \text{ iff } \phi_1, \ldots, \Diamond(a = b), \ldots, \phi_n \models \psi(b/x)$$

Counterexample:

$$\Diamond(a = b), \Diamond(a \neq b \not\models \Diamond(b \neq b)$$

5.2   Why identifiers are needed

Identifiers are needed. Otherwise, if one starts from a state of ignorance, one can never really find out who is who, in the sense of coming to know the names of the objects one is talking about.

Suppose one starts out in a state of ignorance. Consider a situation with a domain of discourse consisting of just two individuals. Let a and b be names for them. Further, let there be any number of predicates. Being ignorant, one has no idea about who a is and who b is, but assume that one has learned already that $a \neq b$. Furthermore, assume that one has no idea about the denotations of the predicates.

What can one learn? A lot. For example, one can learn that Pa and $\neg Pb$; that Qa and Qb; that Rab and $\neg Rba$ and Raa and $\neg Rbb$; and so on. After having learned all this, one seems to know who has the property P: a, and no-one else. About the property Q one knows that it applies both to a and to b. Further, one has the information that a stands to both himself and to b in the relation R. Imagine that one has gained such information about all the predicates.

One's knowledge is not confined to the denotations of the predicates, one also seems to know a lot about a and b. One knows that a has the property P and the property Q, and that he stands in the relation R to himself and to b. And likewise one has learned a lot about b. Lots and lots of possibilities that one's initial state of ignorance allowed, have been eliminated. Imagine that, with respect to some fixed set of predicates and constants, one has learned anything that there is to learn in this way.

But even in that case, there are still two basic things one does not know. And because of that, there are lots of other things one does not know either. One's information still supports both $\forall x \Diamond (x = a)$, and $\forall x \Diamond (x = b)$. And that leads to a certain type of uncertainty about the predicates, too. Of the predicate P one knows that one individual has that property, but one has no idea who this is. With respect to Q things are different: since one knows that both a and b have Q, one is certain as to who is Q: everyone. As for R, there is again uncertainty. One knows which pairs form its extension, but since these are not all pairs, and since one does not know who a and b are, there is a sense in which one does not know between which individuals the relation holds.

So, although one has learned all there is to learn in this way, one has not, and will not, come to know who is a and who is b. This predicament can be formulated as follows.

Definition 5.2   Let $\langle r, g, w \rangle \in I$, $\langle r, g', w' \rangle \in I$.
$\langle r, g, w \rangle \simeq \langle r, g', w' \rangle$ iff there exists a bijection f from D onto D such that:

    i.   For every peg m in the domain of g: $g'(m) = f(g(m))$.

    ii. For every individual constant a: $w'(a) = f(w(a))$.

    iii. For every n-place predicate P: $\langle d_1 \ldots , d_n \rangle \in w(P)$ iff $\langle f(d_1), \ldots , f(d_n) \rangle \in w'(P)$.

Fact 5.4 Let **0** be the minimal information state.
If $i \in \mathbf{0}[\phi_1] \ldots [\phi_n]$, then for every $i' \simeq i$, $i' \in \mathbf{0}[\phi_1] \ldots [\phi_n]$.

What this observation says is this. If one starts out from a state of ignorance – in which names are not identifiers – then, no matter how much information one gains by purely verbal means, one will never get to know to which particular object a given name refers, or which particular objects have which properties. To get this kind of information about the world, purely linguistic means are not sufficient. For identification one needs in addition non-linguistic sources of information, such as observation.

To satisfy this need, deictic demonstratives are added to the inventory of the language. It is assumed (rather naively) that if a demonstrative is used, an object is observably present in the discourse situation which can unambiguously be pointed out to the hearer by the speaker.

Definition 5.3
    i. Let $d \in D$. Then $this_d$ is a term.
   ii. Let $i \in I$. Then $i(this_d) = d$.

By definition, demonstratives are identifiers. Once they are added to the language, fact 5.4 no longer holds. Expressions such as $this_d = a$ are now available, which can tell one which object a refers to.

5.2.1 *Instantiation and generalization*

Identifiers have a special logical role, which, among others, becomes clear from their behavior with regard to instantiation and generalization.

Suppose the domain consists of two distinct individuals d and d'. The state of total ignorance is updated with the following sentence.

    (32) $a \neq b$

The resulting information state, s, supports

    (33) $\Diamond(this_d = a) \wedge \Diamond(this_d = b)$

But s does not support:

    (34) $\forall x \Diamond(this_d = x)$

Actually, s does not even allow (34), despite the fact that s supports the two instantiations with a and b – and these are the names of all the objects around!
The state s does support (35) and (36):

    (35) $\Diamond(this_d = a) \wedge \Diamond(this_{d'} = a)$
    (36) $\forall x \Diamond(x = a)$

However, at the same time the state s is inconsistent with:

(37) $\Diamond(b = a)$

which can be straightforwardly derived from (36) by universal instantiation –
or so it would seem. In other words, universal instantiation is not always
valid. In particular, things may go wrong if one instantiates with a term which
is not known to be an identifier. Likewise, existential generalization sometimes fails:

(38) $\forall y \Diamond(y \neq a) \not\models \exists x \forall y \Diamond(y \neq x)$

Here, too, generalization is not allowed because the constant a is not an
identifier.

6   Concluding Remarks

The aim of the present paper was to present an introduction to dynamic semantics, and to show that it can be fruitfully applied. Rather than by giving
a bird's eye view, and advocating the approach by displaying a wide range of
empirical applications, we have focussed on a more detailed analysis of a
particular set of problems, using a particular logical language.

However, the research that has been carried out in the framework of dynamic semantics comprises both empirical studies and more theoretical research on a great variety of topics. In what follows, a very brief overview is
given, along with some references to readily accessible sources.

On the empirical side, the main focus of attention has been the analysis of
pronominal coreference, in particular donkey anaphora and intersentential
anaphora of various kinds, and related problems, such as the proportion problem, modal subordination, symmetric and asymmetric quantification. Such
topics are treated in Groenendijk and Stokhof (1991); Groenendijk and Stokhof
(1990a); Dekker (1993b); Pagin and Westerståhl (1993); Muskens (1991). A characteristic feature of the dynamic approach is that it vindicates the traditional
quantificational analysis of indefinites. This makes it possible to extend the
dynamic view to a theory of dynamic generalized quantifiers (van Eijck 1993;
Chierchia 1992; Blutner 1993; Kanazawa 1994). A dynamic treatment of
anaphora and plurals is a closely related topic.

Other empirical phenomena that have been studied in a dynamic framework include: implicit information and scripts (Bartsch 1987); verb phrase
ellipsis (Gardent 1991; van Eijck and Francez 1994); relational nouns and implicit arguments (Dekker 1993a); temporal expressions (Muskens, forthcoming); existential sentences (Blutner 1993); epistemic modalities (Veltman,
forthcoming; Veltman et al. 1990); questions.

Other important areas of application are presuppositions (Zeevat 1992), and the analysis of default reasoning (Veltman, forthcoming; Veltman et al. 1990).

Theoretically oriented, logical studies within the field of dynamic semantics are concerned with the formal properties of various dynamic systems. Some such studies deal with completeness, expressive power, and related topics (van Eijck and de Vries 1992; van Eijck and de Vries, forthcoming). An algebraic view on dynamic semantics is explored in among others van Benthem (1991b); van Benthem (1991a); Visser (1994).

Other theoretical studies are directed towards: a comparison of various systems (Vermeulen 1993; Groenendijk and Stokhof 1988; Groenendijk and Stokhof 1990b; van Eijck and Cepparello, forthcoming); a study of incrementality of contexts (Vermeulen, forthcoming a; Vermeulen 1994b); various strategies for dealing with variables (Vermeulen, forthcoming b)); the relationship between dynamic semantics and various proof systems.

An example of a philosophical application is the analysis of the Liar paradox in a dynamic framework in Groeneveld (1994).

ACKNOWLEDGMENTS

We owe special thanks to Paul Dekker. The present paper builds heavily on the last chapter of his thesis. His comments on various stages of the work reported here have prevented us from making many mistakes. For the remaining ones we take the blame. Maria Aloni and Jelle Gerbrandy also provided useful feed-back. Earlier versions of the paper were presented on various occasions. The first of these was the Workshop on Tense and Modality (Columbus, Ohio, July 1993). For their helpful comments, we thank the participants of that workshop, and of other events where we talked about this material. Preparation of this paper was part of the Esprit Basic Research Project Dyana (6852).

NOTES

1 In due course, this is an assumption one would like to drop. For normally, one is only partially informed about what there is. No deep technical issues are involved. The reason for the choice made here is convenience. As a matter of fact, the system outlined in the present paper deals with one particular way in which information is partial. There are many others, which are equally interesting, but not all of the same nature. Some of these will be pointed out along the way. However, it will not do to try to deal with them all at once in the scope of a single paper.

2 The use of referent systems was inspired by the work of Kees Vermeulen. See Vermeulen forthcoming, Vermeulen (1994a, chapter 3).

3 It could turn out to be the case that for a proper account of phenomena such as

ambiguity, different alternatives regarding discourse information need to be distinguished, which would surface as different referent systems in distinct possibilities.

4   It is worth noting that the definition of the extension relation between information states is largely independent of the particular contents of what constitutes the set of possibilities. For example, whether worlds are taken to be total objects, as is the case here, or partial ones, does not make a difference. Also, incorporating "higher-order" information as such does not necessitate a change in the definition of extension. Generally speaking, what counts is that possibilities are constructed from sets of objects which are (partially) ordered.

5   This source of undefinedness is a kind of presupposition failure. The presupposition is of a particular nature: the condition that a variable be introduced cannot be expressed in the object language. It is a "meta"-presupposition concerning discourse information. Also, it cannot be accommodated.

6   In some contexts, negation in natural language does not block anaphoric reference. See Groenendijk and Stokhof (1991, pp. 89–92), Groenendijk and Stokhof (1990a, pp. 37–47), Dekker (1993b, chapter 2) for discussion.

7   See van Benthem (1991a), Groenendijk and Stokhof (1991), Groenendijk and Stokhof (1990c), Veltman (forthcoming), for some discussion of other options.

8   See Groenendijk et al. (forthcoming). See also Vermeulen (1994a, chapter 3) for a discussion of the syntactic and semantic roles of variables.

9   Propositional variables are zero-place predicates. Definition 2.5 guarantees that if p is a zero-place predicate: $w(p) \in \{0, 1\}$.

10   Just like stepping on them would.

11   Consistency testing is an essential ingredient of *might* as an *epistemic* modality. In the present paper only epistemic modalities are treated. Although the information-based nature of dynamic semantics may suggest otherwise, this is not a principled limitation. Alethic modalities can be added, making it possible to implement the Kripkean distinction between metaphysical and epistemic necessity. For this purpose a set of metaphysically possible worlds must be added to each possibility. Different possibilities may contain different alternative sets of such worlds. In this way, one can account for the learnability of what is metaphysically possible, necessary, and impossible.

12   For an extensive discussion of the analysis of donkey-anaphora in a dynamic setting, and a comparison with their treatment in the framework of discourse representation theory, see Groenendijk and Stokhof 1991.

13   Note that the interpretation of (17) that is relevant here, is marked by a specific intonation contour, which has stress on "closet". If the stress is on "might", a different interpretation results, which is the same as that of (16), or so it seems.

14   Thanks to David Beaver for pointing this out.

15   It is these two features which distinguish the present system from the one defined in van Eijck and Cepparello (forthcoming).

16   Of course, when the assumption that the language users know which objects constitute the domain of discourse is dropped, $\lozenge \exists x Px$ and $\exists x \lozenge Px$ are not only non-equivalent, but it also does not hold anymore that $\lozenge \exists x Px$ entails $\exists x \lozenge Px$.

17   See Roberts 1987; Roberts 1989; Roberts (this volume) for extensive discussion.

18   An extension along these lines is presented in Zeevat 1992, where it is applied in an analysis of presupposition accommodation. Non-local accommodation of presuppositions also requires keeping track of (part of) the update history. Furthermore, it seems worthwhile to investigate whether, as an alternative to the analyses

provided in Groenendijk and Stokhof 1990a; Dekker 1993b, anaphoric binding across negation and other "externally static" operators, can be accounted for in this manner as well.

19 But note that such a set-up is at best necessary, but not sufficient. For example, the system of dynamic modal predicate logic proposed in van Eijck and Cepparello (forthcoming) renders (28) inconsistent.

20 There are many. Cf. Boër and Lycan 1985; Hintikka and Hintikka 1989.

8 Anaphora in Intensional Contexts

CRAIGE ROBERTS

Introduction[1]

In the semantic literature, there is a class of examples involving anaphora in intensional contexts, i.e. under the scope of modal operators or propositional attitude predicates, which display anaphoric relations that appear at first glance to violate otherwise well-supported generalizations about operator scope and anaphoric potential. In Section 1, I will illustrate this phenomenon, which, for reasons that should become clear below, I call **modal subordination**; I will develop a general schema for its identification, and show how it poses problems for most theories of scope and anaphoric relations. In Section 2, I will review the main approaches which have been considered in attempting to account for modal subordination and argue that only an approach involving accommodation can account for the full range of examples. The notion of **accommodation** is due to Lewis, who defines it as follows:

> If at time t something is said that requires presupposition P to be acceptable, and if P is not presupposed just before t, then – *ceteris paribus* and within certain limits – presupposition P comes into existence at t. (Lewis 1979: 340)

The interesting question, of course, is what the limits on accommodation might be. I believe that the proper account of modal subordination has something to say about this. I will argue this briefly in section 3, where I draw some conclusions and also sketch some problems for further research.

1 The Phenomenon of Modal Subordination

We have come to understand quite a bit about the way that anaphora works in discourse and about its relationship to semantic phenomena such as the scopes of quantificational elements. Consider the relation of **anaphoric accessibility** between NPs, where NP x is anaphorically accessible to a definite NP y (e.g. a pronoun) iff x is a potential antecedent for y in the discourse in question. The following descriptive generalizations seem quite robust:

Scope constraint on anaphoric relations: If NP x is anaphorically accessible to NP y, then any quantificational elements which have scope over x have scope over y as well.

Sentential scope constraint: The maximal scope of a quantificational element is the sentence in which it occurs.

If we ignore definite and indefinite NPs,[2] these generalizations follow straightforwardly from several formal theories of discourse interpretation developed recently (e.g. those of Kamp (1981), Heim (1982), Barwise (1987), Rooth (1987), and Groenendijk & Stokhof (1990a) – see references and relevant articles in this volume), under fairly standard assumptions about the relationship between anaphora and binding, and between binding and scope. Their combined effects are illustrated by (1)–(3), with anaphoric relations indicated by underlining:

    (1) **Every** frog that saw <u>an insect</u> ate <u>it</u>.
           #<u>It</u> was a fly.
    (2) **Usually** Fred buys <u>a muffin</u> every morning and eats <u>it</u> at the office.
           #<u>It</u>'s being baked.
    (3) You **should** buy <u>a lottery ticket</u> and put <u>it</u> in a safe place.
           #<u>It</u>'s worth a million dollars.

In each, there is an indefinite NP with scope under a quantificational element (the quantificational determiner, adverb of quantification, or modal in bold face). The NP is anaphorically accessible only to the first of two pronouns, the one which is also under the scope of the quantificational element, and not to the second pronoun, which is outside that scope under the assumption that quantifier scope is sentence-bounded. Because the second sentence in each discourse contains a pronoun with no potential antecedent, the sentence is uninterpretable and hence infelicitous, as indicated by the "#" sign.

    Often in natural language discourse, however, we find *prima facie* counterexamples to the scope constraint, as illustrated by (1′)–(3′):

    (1′) **Every** frog that saw <u>an insect</u> ate <u>it</u>.
           <u>It</u> disappeared forever.
    (2′) **Usually** Fred buys <u>a muffin</u> every morning and eats <u>it</u> at the office.
           <u>It</u>'s **always** oat bran.
    (3′) You **should** buy <u>a lottery ticket</u> and put <u>it</u> in a safe place.
           <u>It</u> **might** be worth a million dollars (if you were lucky).

These discourses and many others like them are perfectly acceptable to most speakers, despite the apparent anaphoric relation between a pronoun in the second sentence and an indefinite NP which is under the scope of the boldface quantificational element in the first. One might attempt to account for their acceptability, while retaining classical assumptions about anaphora and binding, by revising the assumption that scope is sentence-bound (see Groenendijk & Stokhof (1990a), Dekker (1993b)). This would be compatible with the observation that in (1')–(3'), each of the second sentences itself seems to be a generalization – over frog-eaten insects, occasions when Fred buys a muffin, or possible lottery tickets, whereas in (1)–(3), the infelicitous second sentences appear to give information about specific entities on specific occasions. But there are two problems with this approach. First, this would leave us without an account of the unacceptability of (1)–(3); from the perspective of the generative tradition, which aims to generate all and *only* the acceptable structures at some level of linguistic analysis, this would be unacceptable. Second, this would yield incorrect truth conditions for many of the relevant examples. E.g. for (2'), we want to derive a reading where on most relevant occasions Fred buys a muffin and on every occasion where Fred buys a muffin, it's oat bran; i.e. the scopes of the two adverbs of quantification are independent of each other. Merely extending the scope of the first adverb of quantification would lead instead to a reading where *always* would have narrow scope with respect to *usually*, resulting in weaker truth conditions than desired and leaving it unclear how to restrict the domain of *always*. Similarly, in (3'), we get a reading where the hearer is instructed that ideally he would buy a lottery ticket and that if he bought one (and was lucky), there's a possibility that it would be valuable. Again, merely extending the scope of *should* would yield a strange reading where it takes wide scope over *might*, so that the possibility would be part of what was claimed to be deontically ideal.

There is a closely related phenomenon involving propositional attitude verbs and "world-creating" predicates more generally (see Baker (1966), Lakoff (1972), Jackendoff (1972), Montague (1973), Morgan (1973), Karttunen (1974), McCawley (1981), and Heim (1992) for earlier discussions of relevant examples). Consider the following:

(4) Jan **expect**ed to get <u>a new puppy</u> soon.
   She **intend**ed to keep <u>it</u> in her back yard.
(5) John **want**s to catch <u>a fish</u>.
   He **plan**s to eat <u>it</u> for supper.
(6) Alice **fear**s there's <u>a squirrel</u> in her kitchen cabinets.
   She **hope**s to trap <u>it</u> alive and turn <u>it</u> loose outside.

In these examples, on the readings of interest, the indefinite NP which is the apparent antecedent of the pronoun has a *de dicto* reading; e.g. in (5) there is no specific fish that John wants to catch. Hence, as in (1')–(3'), we need to explain how the indefinite can both have narrow scope with respect to the intensional predicate in its main clause, and yet apparently serve as antecedent for a pronoun in subsequent discourse. This is obviously facilitated in (4)–(6) by the presence of another intensional predicate in the second sentence. But note that not all pairs of sentences with predicates that take sentential complements license the anaphoric phenomenon in question. Montague (1973) noted that unlike (7a), which has a *de dicto* reading, (7b) does not:

(7a)　John **tries** to find <u>a unicorn</u> and **wish**es to eat <u>it</u>.
(7b)　#John **wish**es to find <u>a unicorn</u> and **tries** to eat <u>it</u>.

And Lakoff (1972) notes the following pair:

(8a)　You are **require**d to find <u>a bear</u> and **permit**ted to take <u>its</u> picture.
(8b)　#You are **permit**ted to find <u>a bear</u> and **require**d to take <u>its</u> picture.

As in (7b) and (8b), all the following examples are infelicitous on the *de dicto* readings of the underlined indefinites:

(9)　Jan **expect**ed to get <u>a puppy</u>.
　　?#She **managed** to housebreak <u>it</u> quickly.
(10)　Alice **denies** that there's <u>a squirrel</u> in her kitchen cabinets.
　　#She **hopes** to trap <u>it</u> alive and turn <u>it</u> loose outside.

Finally, as McCawley (1981) points out, the problem with these examples is related to that found in Geach's (1967) statements of "intentional identity", such as:

(11)　Hob **thinks** <u>a witch</u> has blighted Bob's mare, and Nob **wonders** whether <u>she</u> (<u>the same witch</u>) killed Cob's sow.

Again, the interpretation of interest here is one where the speaker does not commit his/herself to the existence of a witch; both the indefinite and the pronoun/definite description are interpreted *de dicto*, as in the cases we've already examined. Since the definite NP and its antecedent do not occur under the scope of the same opacifying predicate, the latter cannot bind the former. Further, as Edelberg (1986) points out, in order for (11) to be true, Nob needn't know anything about Hob or about Bob's mare; e.g. they might both reside in a community whose newspaper has reported the presence of a witch on a destructive rampage. Hence, the example can't be readily explained by treating *she* in the second conjunct as a pronoun of laziness meaning something like *the witch that blighted Bob's mare,* or *the witch that Hob thinks blighted Bob's mare.*[3]

It should now be clear why this problem is framed as a question about anaphora in intensional contexts. All the felicitous examples except (1') involve either a modal, an opacifying predicate, or an adverb of quantification in the second sentence. Following Kripke (1959), Hintikka (1969), and Montague (1973), both modality and opacifying predicates are analyzed semantically as involving quantification over possible worlds. More recently (following Barwise & Perry (1983), Kratzer (1989)) they have been analyzed as quantifying over possible situations, with situations viewed either as concrete entities replacing possible worlds (Barwise & Perry (1983)), or as partial possible worlds (Kratzer (1989b)). Also in recent literature (see the line of development from Lewis (1975) through Barwise & Perry (1983), Kratzer (1989b), Berman (1987), and de Swart (1991)), quantificational adverbs have been analyzed involving quantification over situations, effecting a unification with the semantics of modals and propositional attitudes. Example (1'), illustrating what I elsewhere (Roberts 1987, 1989) called *telescoping,* may be amenable to a similar treatment, where we analyze the second sentence as containing an implicit adverb of quantification with universal force, ranging over the relevant minimal situations, each one containing a single frog and the insect it ate. (But see Poesio & Zucchi (1992) for another view of this phenomenon.)

Roberts (1987) called the phenomenon illustrated by examples like (3') and (13) "modal subordination" because the material under the scope of the modal in the second sentence is semantically subordinate to irrealis propositions considered in previous discourse.

Here I will generalize the term to cover the cases involving intensional predicates, as well. I retain the term *modal subordination* under the common assumption that intensional phenomena in natural language generally involve modality at some level of analysis. Should that prove to be problematic, one might re-name the phenomenon which is illustrated by the examples above *intensional subordination.*

Modal subordination arises not only with anaphora, but with various presuppositional elements, as well:

(12) **Usually** Fred buys a muffin every morning and eats it at the office. He buys [a cup of coffee]$_F$, too.
(13) Maxine **should** become a carpenter. Her friends **would** discover she could build things, and she'd be very popular on weekends.
(14) Mary is **consider**ing getting her Ph.D. in linguistics. She **would**n't regret attending graduate school.

In each of these examples, the underlined constituent in the second sentence carries a presupposition which, in the discourses in question, is only satisfied by material which is under the scope of the quantificational element or predicate in boldface in the first sentence. Following Heim (1992), in (12) *too* presupposes that it is known by the interlocutors that there is some salient entity which could replace the property denoted by the focused constituent *a cup of coffee* while preserving truth, i.e. there is something else which the interlocutors already know that Fred buys. Further, the bare present tense with a non-stative verb is interpreted as the generic mood, in recent literature often formalized with an adverbial operator (see Carlson (1977), Wilkinson (1991)). In (13), *discover* presupposes the truth of its complement. But, under the assumption that Maxine isn't already skilled as a carpenter, this presupposition is only satisfied in those deontically ideal worlds where she becomes one, verifying the proposition introduced under the scope of *should* in the previous sentence. The modal auxiliary *would* will have to range over such worlds in which that proposition, that Maxine is a carpenter, is true, in order to satisfy the factive presupposition of *discover*. *Regret* is similarly factive; in (14) it is under the scope of a modal, but (assuming Mary hasn't yet gone to graduate school) its presupposition is only satisfied in those worlds which realize what she is considering, introduced by the previous sentence. Such examples could be multiplied indefinitely, with various combinations of modal auxiliaries and intensional verbs. These presuppositional parallels with the earlier anaphoric examples support the analysis of anaphora as essentially presuppositional, as argued e.g. by Heim (1982).[4] Hence, a more appropriate title for this paper might be "Presupposition satisfaction in intensional contexts". But for simplicity I will focus on the examples involving anaphora.

The schema in (15) captures the general logical form of examples displaying modal subordination, while that in (16) gives the anaphoric sub-type:

(15)   **operator**$[_s \ldots \pi \ldots]$
       operator$_{\text{intensional}}[_s \ldots \text{presupposition of } \pi \ldots]$

(16)   **operator**$[_s \ldots \text{NP}_x \ldots]$
               [-def]
       operator$_{\text{intensional}}[_s \ldots \text{NP}_x \ldots]$
                  [+def]

In each discourse there are two sentences, each containing a wide scope operator. In the second sentence, the operator is intensional – the operator logically associated with a propositional attitude predicate, a modal auxiliary, or an adverb of quantification, ranging over situations – though this operator is sometimes implicit, as in (1') and (12). In the general case, some element π under the scope of the operator in the first sentence is presupposed by an element which has narrow scope under the intensional operator in the second sentence. In the sub-case of interest, the presupposition is one of the familiarity of some entity introduced by an indefinite NP_x in the first sentence; i.e. there is an anaphoric relationship to an NP which is inaccessible under the scope constraint on anaphoric relations and the sentential scope constraint.

Note that the operator in the first sentence needn't be intensional, as we see in (17), where it is an auxiliary negation:

(17)   John doesn't have <u>a car</u>.
       <u>It</u> would be in the garage.

The felicitous reading of the second sentence of (17) might be paraphrased "if John had a car, it would be in the garage."

Finally, note that the schemas in (15) and (16) are logical forms – it is the indicated interpretation which characterizes modal subordination, and not mere surface form. Consider (18):

(18) Since he saved his money last summer, John could buy a car.
He should sell it, if he needs money now.

(18) is superficially similar to the examples in (3') and (13). However, the interpretation which most speakers appear to get for the second sentence presupposes that John did, in fact, buy a car. That is, (18) means "John could buy a car, and hence he did, and now if he needs money he should sell the car he bought", instead of the modally subordinate "John could by a car; if he did buy a car and he needs money now, he should sell it", where the purchase is purely hypothetical.[5]

Modal subordination forces us to reconsider the otherwise robust scope principles – the scope constraint on anaphoric relations and the sentential scope constraint. Either these must be revised to permit binding across sentences, or if they are to be maintained, an account must be developed for the anaphora in modal subordination which does not involve a direct anaphoric relation between the apparent antecedent and the pronoun or other definite. Merely extending the scope of the first operator in the schema in (16) does not yield the correct truth conditions in all examples, as in (2') above. So the challenge is to find some other way of accounting for the anaphoric relations in question.

2   Analysis of the Phenomenon

The foundation of the account I will give here is an account of the semantics of modality which follows from the work of Kratzer (1977, 1981) and Veltman (1984). Modal elements are notoriously vague semantically, and seem to admit a variety of kinds of interpretations – e.g. epistemic, deontic, alethic, dynamic, etc. The latter has often led to the assumption that modals are multiply ambiguous, leading to a rather large number of lexical entries for a given modal, with the intuitive relations between them left unexplained. Kratzer and Veltman explain the variety without lexical ambiguity, while accounting for vagueness, by assuming that in any given context the domain of a modal operator is pragmatically restricted by a set of "premises" – contextually relevant and salient propositions. For example, the interpretation of *must* which is traditionally called epistemic would be relative to the set of propositions which some salient person, perhaps the speaker, believed to be true; whereas the deontic interpretation would be constrained by propositions reflecting the actual circumstances (see Thomason (1981)) as well as those reflecting what some authority decrees should be the case given those circumstances.

Kratzer (1981) calls the function which pragmatically retrieves these sets of premises for a given modal in a given context of utterance its **modal base**.[6] The modal base is a function from worlds (or situations) to sets of propositions, where a proposition is a set of worlds (or situations). We can relate the premises given by the modal base for a given world of evaluation to the modal accessibility relations of modal logic, which determine which worlds or situations a modal operator will range over. Given a modal accessibility relation R, the truth of *must* ϕ depends on the truth of ϕ in all those worlds accessible to the world of evaluation under R. Since *must* has universal force, *must* ϕ is true in w relative to R iff for all w' such that $\langle w,w' \rangle \in R$, ϕ is true in w'. A modal base f is a function from worlds to sets of propositions. We can characterize R as relating any world w to a set of worlds where the premises assigned to w by its (contextually-given) modal base f are all true: $R \subseteq WxW$ such that for all $w, w' \in W$, $\langle w,w' \rangle \in R$ iff $w' \in \cap f(w)$. Since a proposition is a set of worlds, those where the proposition is true, the intersection of a set of propositions is itself a set of worlds – all those worlds where all the propositions in the set are true; so $\cap f(w)$ is the set of worlds where all the propositions assigned to w by the modal base f are true. Given these definitions, modal bases, like accessibility relations, effectively restrict the domain of a modal operator. Different contexts in which a modal is used yield different modal bases, and the different ways in which different modal bases restrict the domain of the operator yield different "readings" of the modal, which itself, however, is unambiguous. Now we can capture the notion of a "deontic" reading of a given modal in terms of a certain class of modal bases which may be used to restrict it – those which yield, for any world w, the set of propositions which characterize what an individual is obligated or permitted to do in w, according to some authority. Similarly, there are no "epistemic" modals, but only epistemic modal bases – those which characterize what some individual or group of individuals believe in any given world. And we can put constraints on the type of modal bases compatible with a given modal auxiliary, as a way of capturing the types of "readings" (deontic, epistemic, etc.) which that auxiliary can have.

Modal bases are given pragmatically, retrieved by hearers on the basis of contextual clues and knowledge of the world. Technically, they are accommodated. The speaker, in uttering a sentence containing a modal, presupposes a certain modal base – deontic, epistemic, etc. – and assumes that s/he has given the hearer adequate clues to retrieve it.

In order to correctly interpret the utterance, the hearer must accommodate the speaker by assuming the modal base which is presumably intended.

Roberts (1987, 1989) argued that in modal subordination, with reference to a logical form like (16) above, a proposition suggested by the first sentence (specifically, by all or part of the material under the scope of the first operator in (16)) serves as at least one of the premises which restrict the domain of the intensional operator in the second sentence, i.e. is in the set of propositions given by the modal base for the world of evaluation. Consider again (3'):

> (3') You should buy <u>a lottery ticket</u> and put it in a safe place.
> <u>It</u> might be worth a million dollars.

It is intuitively obvious that the modal *might* is restricted by the proposition that the hearer buys a lottery ticket. Kratzer (1981) argues that a conditional *if*-clause specifies one of the premises used to relativize the domain of a modal in the main clause which it modifies, i.e. one of the propositions in the set $f(w)$, f the modal base for the world of interpretation w. This predicts that we can paraphrase the obvious interpretation of (3') as (3"), which seems correct:

> (3") You should buy a lottery ticket and put it in a safe place.
> If you bought a lottery ticket, it might be worth a million dollars.

Since *might* only ranges over worlds (or situations) in which the restricting proposition "you buy a lottery ticket" is true, i.e. worlds where the interlocutors know that there is a lottery ticket purchased by the hearer, the familiarity presupposition associated with the pronoun *it* in the second sentence, is satisfied. But the relation between the underlined indefinite NP and pronoun in (3') and other examples of modal subordination is only indirect – it is the proposition which restricts the domain of the modal that satisfies the familiarity presupposition of the pronoun, and not directly the indefinite NP or the proposition to which it contributes.

This illustrates another sense in which assumption of a modal base involves accommodation: Given a world (or situation) of interpretation w, the modal base applied to w yields a set of propositions, say $\{p, q, \dots\}$. Each of those propositions restricts the domain of the relevant modal. We can say, then, that each of these propositions has been *locally accommodated*, in the sense defined by Heim (1983), i.e. it hasn't been accommodated as an asserted proposition, but only under the scope of an operator, here the modal. So in (3'), we can say that the proposition 'the hearer buys a lottery ticket' is locally accommodated to serve as part of the domain restriction on the modal *might*.

Along the lines just sketched for (3') and (3"), we might readily paraphrase the most likely reading of (2') as (2"), and that of (6) as (6'):

> (2') Usually Fred buys a muffin every morning and eats it at the office. It's always oat bran.
> (2") Usually Fred buys a muffin every morning and eats it at the office. When he buys a muffin, it's always oat bran.
>
> (6) Alice fears there's a squirrel in her kitchen cabinets. She hopes to trap it alive and turn it loose outside.
> (6') Alice fears there's a squirrel in her kitchen cabinets.

Assuming there is a squirrel in her kitchen cabinets, she hopes to trap it alive and turn it loose outside.

On independent grounds, temporal adverbial clauses like that in (2″) and free adjuncts like that in (6′) have been argued to serve as domain restrictions on operators in the main clause to which they adjoin (e.g. see Stump (1985)). The fact that these paraphrases seem to adequately capture the most obvious interpretations of (2′) and (6) supports a domain restriction account of modal subordination.

Given the basic plausibility of such an account, the question which arises is what factors govern this relativization of the domain of the second intensional operator to a proposition suggested by the first sentence. We argued in Section 1 that it cannot in general be a question of extending the scope of the operator in the first sentence. Further, adjacency of the sentences containing these operators isn't necessary, as illustrated by (19) (due to Louise McNally (personal communication)):

(19a)   You should buy a lottery ticket and put it in a safe place.
(19b)   You're a person with good luck.
(19c)   It might be worth a million dollars.

(19c) is modally subordinate to (19a); this corresponds to the intuitively correct paraphrase in (19c′):

(19c′)   If you buy a lottery ticket, it might be worth a million dollars.

But (19b) is factual, so that there is no local adjacency in the irrealis mood associated with the general phenomenon of modal subordination schematized in (15). Hence, the explanation doesn't seem to lie in facts about the local structure of discourse, e.g. licensing a local extension of irrealis mood.

Two types of accounts appear to have the greatest explanatory potential, an entailment-based, and hence semantic account, and one which crucially incorporates pragmatic processes, specifically accommodation. Semantic accounts for some of the types of examples outlined above have been offered by Lakoff (1972), Karttunen (1974), McCawley (1981), and Heim (1992), while Roberts (1987, 1989) offered an account which essentially involves accommodation.[7] I will argue that a purely semantic account is inadequate. However, the two types of accounts aren't really incompatible; assuming that entailment plays a role in licensing the anaphora in some examples does not preclude the necessity of using accommodation in many others. And in fact both have something to offer to our understanding of modal subordination; the lexical entailments of predicates naturally interact with other, contextual factors to constrain the accommodation that is possible in a given example.

The semantic accounts involve explaining both felicitous and infelicitous examples in terms of entailments. For example, Lakoff (1972) and McCawley

(1981) argue that in examples along the lines of (8a) and (4), repeated below, there are logical relations between the two intensional predicates in question (in boldface) which entail the possibility of the highlighted anaphoric relations (underlined NPs). They argue that cases where there is no such entailment fail to support the anaphoric relation, as in (8b). Or there may even be some aspect of the meaning of one of the predicates which precludes the necessary accessibility relation, as in (9) or (10).

(8a) You are **required** to find <u>a bear</u> and **permit**ted to take <u>its</u> picture.
(8b) #You are **permit**ted to find <u>a bear</u> and **required** to take <u>its</u> picture.
(4)   Jan **expec**ted to get <u>a new puppy</u> soon.
      She **intend**ed to keep <u>it</u> in her back yard.
(9)   Jan **expec**ted to get <u>a puppy</u>.
      ?#She **managed** to housebreak <u>it</u> quickly.
(10) Alice **denies** that there's <u>a squirrel</u> in her kitchen cabinets.
      #She **hopes** to trap <u>it</u> alive and turn <u>it</u> loose outside.

According to Lakoff, if x requires y to S, this entails that x permits y to S, but the converse does not hold. Hence, in a possible worlds semantics, anything which the speaker requires the hearer to do, such as find a bear, will be true in any world realizing the speaker's permissions to the hearer, but not vice versa. In (8a), this means that in all the speaker's permission worlds, there will be a bear that the hearer found, which then becomes the permitted object of a photo. But in (8b), it is not the case that all the worlds realizing the speaker's requirements are entailed to contain a bear; hence, the example is infelicitous.[8] With respect to (4), note that our intentions are generally contingent on our expectations about how things will be in the future. Hence, that Jan expects to get a new puppy entails that in all worlds which realize her expectations there is a puppy that Jan owns. These are the worlds which are accessible to her intentions, so that the guarantee of the existence of the puppy licenses the anaphora – i.e. the latter relation is based on a semantic relation of entailment between the embedding predicates.

McCawley bases his account of examples like (9) on the fact that the predicate *manage* is implicative, in the sense of Karttunen (1971). I believe the following retains the basic form of McCawley's argument, while assuming the terminology and assumptions about anaphora of Karttunen (1973), Stalnaker (1979) and Heim (1982, 1983). Among other things, *manage* entails the truth of its complement sentence, and is a hole to presuppositions. Hence, in a theory of presuppositions along the lines of Stalnaker and Karttunen as extended by Heim, its felicitous use requires the satisfaction of the presuppositions of its complement in the common ground of the interlocutors of the conversation. But the first sentence in (9) does not entail that there is a puppy, or that the interlocutors expected a puppy, only that Jan did, and hence does not satisfy the anaphoric presupposition of the pronoun.

With repect to (10), the accessibility relation for the second predicate, *hope*, is given by the beliefs of the subject, Alice. But, per McCawley's (1981:337) discussion of these verbs, the first sentence entails that Alice does not believe in the existence of a squirrel in her kitchen cabinets.[9] So instead of an entailment relation to license the anaphoric relation to the pronouns in the complement of *hope*, there is one which precludes it. This contrasts with (6), where one's fears entail one's near-belief, which appears to be sufficient grounds for hope.

(6)   Alice **fears** there's <u>a squirrel</u> in her kitchen cabinets.
         She **hopes** to trap <u>it</u> alive and turn <u>it</u> loose outside.

Karttunen (1974) grounds his account of examples involving propositional attitudes in a generalization which Heim (1992) paraphrases as follows:

(20)   If ζ is a verb of propositional attitude, then a context c satisfies the presuppositions of "$\alpha \ \zeta \ \phi$" only if $B_\alpha(c)$ satisfies the presuppositions of ϕ; where "$B_\alpha(c)$" stands for the set of beliefs attributed to α in c.

Given that a set of (believed) propositions satisfies the presuppostion of a proposition π iff the set entails π, then this is an entailment-based account of examples involving the attitudes. In a refinement of Karttunen's approach, Heim (1992) presents a detailed examination of examples involving a small set of propositional attitude verbs: *believe, want, wish, intend,* and *be glad that.* Given the presupposition projection properties of these predicates, she develops an account within the framework of context change semantics of how in examples like (21) the presupposition in the second conjunct is filtered by entailments of the first conjunct:

(21)   John believes that Mary is coming, and he wants Susan to come too.

She makes the assumption that, like modals, intensional predicates have modal bases conventionally given as part of their lexical meaning. E.g. consider the meaning of *want*. Let us call the set of all worlds where all the propositions that some individual α believes to be true are true, α's **doxastic alternatives**. If we relativize belief to a world of evaluation w (under the reasonable assumption that someone might have different beliefs in different worlds), then α's doxastic alternatives relative to w are the set of propositions given by a doxastic modal base for α for the argument w. The meaning of *want* is a relation between individuals (possible denotations of the subject) and propositions (possible denotations of the sentential complement) which holds (in a given world w) just in case all the subject's doxastic alternatives (relative to w) where the complement is true are more desirable to the subject than those doxastic alternatives where the complement is false. The doxastic alternatives in effect provide a local context for the interpretation of *want*, and hence the presuppositions of the complement of *want* must be entailed by the doxastic alternatives. In an example like (21), the first conjunct tells the interlocutors that in all of John's doxastic alternatives Mary is coming. These alternatives then entail the presupposition of the *want* complement, which is that someone besides Susan is coming. Hence, via the lexical semantics of *want*, the first conjunct entails the presuppositions of the second conjunct, satisfying Karttunen's generalization. Though Heim does not adopt Karttunen's (20) for all propositional attitude predicates, her account of the other predicates she considers is also entailment-based, and like Lakoff and McCawley, she assumes that lack of entailment generally leads to infelicity. E.g. along with Karttunen, she predicts that it isn't felicitous to interchange the order of *believe* and *want* in examples like (21). Consider (21'), where the order has been changed, as well as (22)/(22'), which are anaphoric counterparts of (21)/(21'):

(21')   #John wants Mary to come, although he believes that Susan is going to come too.

(22)   Patrick believes I'm going to buy him a cello, and he wants to take his cello to France.

(22')   #Patrick wants me to buy him a cello, although he believes that his cello is going to take up a lot of space.

The second conjunct of (21') presupposes that John believes that someone besides Susan is going to come, but this is not entailed by the first conjunct, given the semantics for *want* outlined above. Though in (22) Patrick's beliefs are taken into consideration in calculating what he wants, as in (21), in (22') what he wants does not play a semantic role in the determination of what he believes, since most people realize that what they want may not be realized. Hence, the first conjunct in (22') doesn't filter out the (familiarity) presuppositions of the second.

Though entailments clearly play a role in many examples displaying modal subordination, there are at least three arguments that entailment is not a necessary condition for modal subordination, even in those examples where the intensional operator is an opaque verb. First, many of the examples which an entailment-based account would predict to be bad seem to be less than fully infelicitous. Judgments tend to vary from informant to informant, variation which is typical of accommodation-based felicity (indeed predictable, given its nature), but not of entailment. Second, there are a number of types of examples which cannot be accounted for by entailment alone, and must involve the accommodation of the presuppositions in question; this accommodation is local in Heim's sense – it is not accommodation of the relevant propositions to the common ground of the interlocutors, but only as hypothetical premises to restrict the domain of an intensional operator (in the schema for modal subordination in (15), the operator in the second sentence). And third, an alternative explanation of the infelicitous examples can be given within the context of an account involving accommodation.

We see the first problem, variation in acceptability, in a number of examples. As reported by Heim, (21′) and (22′) above are acceptable to some speakers under the interpretations in (21″) and (22″). And Cresswell (1988) and Asher (1987) claim that (23) and (24), respectively, can have the readings suggested by (23′) and (24′) (again, we're interested in *de dicto* readings of the indefinites):

(21″)   John wants Mary to come, although he believes that if she does, Susan is going to come too.

(22″)   Patrick wants me to buy him a cello, although he believes that if I buy him a cello, it is going to take up a lot of space.

(23)   Susan wants a pet. She believes she will look after it.

(23′)   Susan wants a pet. She believes that if she gets a pet she will look after it.

(24)   John wants a woman to marry him. He believes he can make her happy.

(24′)   John wants a woman to marry him. He believes if a woman marries him he can make her happy.

Technically, in order to generate these interpretations, we modify the modal base for *believe* in each case so that the set of premises which determine Susan's or John's doxastic set includes the proposition indicated by the *if*-clause. This is local accommodation – we do not assume once and for all that Susan believes she'll get a pet or that John believes that a woman will marry him. A similar strategy would suffice to explain the felicity of (5), on at least one reading:

(5)   John wants to catch a fish.
       He plans to eat it for supper.

One's plans are arguably dependent on what one believes. Hence, in order to satisfy the familiarity presupposition associated with the pronoun, one may assume that John's plans are contingent on the fulfilment of his desires – "he plans, if he catches a fish, to eat it for supper", so that again, local accommodation makes the example felicitous.

Of course, accommodation, whether local or global, requires both cooperation and imagination, either of which may be lacking to some degree in our interlocutors. So it shouldn't surprise us that not all speakers are willing or able to derive a felicitous interpretation of such examples. I myself find it more natural to make (21′) and (5) felicitous with global accommodation (which is not, then, modal subordination) than with local (modal subordination); e.g. in (21′), to globally accommodate that John believes he can get Mary to come, which then entails the presupposition of the second clause.[10]

The second problem, the existence of examples which entailment alone cannot account for, is pointed out by Heim herself, who notes that her entailment-based proposal cannot account for the felicity of examples like (25), which have the same status in her theory as examples like (26):

(25)   John wants Fred to come, and he wants Jim to come too.
(26)   If Mary comes, we'll have a quorum. If Susan comes too, we'll have a majority.

Further, the entailment-based approach cannot, so far as I can see, generalize over the cases involving adverbs of quantification, such as (2′) and (12); over many examples of modal subordination involving mixed operators, e.g. (3′) and (13), which involve mixed types of modals (the first a deontic, the second epistemic or counterfactual), and (14), with a propositional attitude predicate in the first sentence and a counterfactual modal auxiliary in the second; over examples where the operator in the first sentence is negation, as in (17); or over the Hob/Nob examples, to which I return below. In none of these is there evidence that an entailment of the first clause interacts with the modal base for the second intensional operator to satisfy the presupposition in the second, modally subordinate clause. All appear to be amenable to a treatment involving local accommodation. As Heim notes, "Once this mechanism is invoked, of course, the question arises to what extent it could also have been employed to yield some of the predictions that I took pains to make follow directly from the CCP [Context Change Potential] definitions," i.e. from facts about the lexical semantics of the propositional attitude predicates under investigation. The evident parallels among all these types of examples would appear to weigh in favor of an account involving accommodation, i.e. a partly pragmatic account, where modal subordination often requires the local accommodation of the salient premises to restrict the domain of the intensional operator in the final clause of (15). Of course that does not preclude the possibility that entailments often do license modal subordination, via lexical presuppositions about modal bases, as in Heim's account. Entailment is still a sufficient, though not a necessary condition for modal subordination.

But we need to say more than this to explain the distribution of cases where accommodation cannot take place. How can an accommodation-based account match the correct predications of infelicity made by the entailment-based accounts, as in examples (8b), (9), and (10) above? The crucial thing to note in these examples is that in each, the accommodation which would be necessary in order to plausibly satisfy the presupposition at issue would contradict information in the common ground at the time of processing the second clause, information given as entailments or implicatures of the first sentence or clause. If we assume, as I believe most authors do, that accommodated material must be logically compatible with the local context to which it is accommodated, we can explain the infelicity of these examples in terms of contextual incompatibility. This amounts to a weaker claim than the entailment-based theories.

The latter claim that examples of the sort under consideration are only acceptable when the presupposition of the second clause is entailed by the first. But the accommodation approach predicts that these examples are only unacceptable when there is some incompatibility between the presupposition of the second clause and the information in the common ground of the interlocutors. If this is not the case, then an example could, in principle, be acceptable, so long as the hearers feel that they are licensed to accommodate the relevant proposition(s) by their relevance and salience in prior discourse.

Consider again the examples in (7):

(7a)   John tries to find a unicorn and wishes to eat it.
(7b)   #John wishes to find a unicorn and tries to eat it.

Try presupposes that what the referent of its subject believes entails any presuppositions of its complement. Hence, if the unicorn from the first conjunct of (7b) were to serve felicitously as the antecedent of *it*, John would have to actually believe there is a unicorn he'll catch. But since *wish* is a counterfactual-like propositional attitude (see Heim 1992), and does not project its complement's presuppositions onto the belief-worlds of its subject, John's wishing to find a unicorn doesn't entail that John believes he'll find a unicorn, and strongly implicates, at least, that he has some misgivings about it. Further, *wish* is future-oriented: we can only wish for something that isn't, so far as we know, yet true. Hence the first conjunct of (7b) has a negative presupposition, that John mustn't, so far as he knows, have already found a unicorn. But the verb in the second conjunct is also in the present tense, requiring the present truth of its complement's presupposition of the existence of a unicorn John has found. So there are two contradictions here: one between the counterfactual-induced implication of the first conjunct and the presuppositions of the second, the other between the future-oriented presupposition of *wish*, of the form $\neg believes(j,p,t)$, t the utterance time, and the present presupposition of *try*, i.e. $believes(j,p,t)$. These combine to yield the infelicity of the example.

On close inspection, even (7a) is a problem for an entailment-based account: The felicity of the example still cannot be reduced to entailments between *try* and *wish*, for trying to achieve ϕ doesn't entail wishing for ϕ: I might be forced by a villain to try to rob a bank, even though I myself don't wish to rob a bank.[11] In order to satisfy the familiarity requirement of the pronoun, we must accommodate that John wishes to find a unicorn (which is arguably the default explanation for why he's trying to find one).

Some of the other examples we have considered involve a contradiction between an implicature generated by the first clause and a presupposition of the second. Consider again (8b):

(8b)   #You are permitted to find a bear and required to take its picture.

According to an entailment-based account, this example is unacceptable because the first clause doesn't entail that the hearer is required to find a bear.

But I think something more is involved. Giving someone permission to do ϕ also implicates that they are permitted not to do ϕ. This is a scalar implicature: if one were required to do ϕ, then the speaker should have said so, since this would entail its permissibility. Hence, the speaker of (8b) implicates that the hearer is permitted to not find a bear; i.e. there are permission worlds where the hearer does not find one. On the other hand, a prerequisite for taking a bear's picture is to first find one; the second VP presupposes that the hearer finds a bear in all her obligation worlds. But there is a relationship between one's permissions and obligations (relative to the same authority): the permission worlds must be a subset of the obligation worlds. This leads to a contradiction. We cannot accommodate that the hearer finds a bear in all her obligation worlds without contradicting the strong implication that there are obligation worlds where she doesn't find a bear. So, though the entailment does license (8a), what explains the infelicity of (8b) is the pragmatic contradiction: It is pragmatically quite odd to REQUIRE taking the picture but only PERMIT finding the bear, even though there is no direct truth conditional contradiction.

When a presupposition is not satisfied, there are two ways to repair the situation – globally, adding the presupposition to the common ground, or locally, adding it only as a hypothetical premise. On the account of (8b) I just gave, the global accommodation is blocked because of a contradiction with the scalar implicature generated by *permit*. But this leaves open the possibility of a local repair strategy. This reading doesn't come across too readily in the rather outlandish (8b), but seems more readily available in the structurally parallel (27), with the interpretation paraphrased in (27'):

(27) To a new Ph.D. candidate, just finished with her qualifying examination:
You are now permitted to write a dissertation, but required to finish it by the end of next year.

(27') ... but you are required, if you write a dissertation, to finish it ...

Example (28) displays the same pattern, where the predicate in the second sentence requires a stronger commitment on the part of the subject to the truth of the presuppositions of its complement than is entailed by the first sentence.

(28) Ram is **consider**ing getting <u>a cat</u>.
?#He **intends** to have <u>it</u> declawed.

If Ram planned to get a cat, which he'd have to do in order to felicitously intend to do something to it, then the speaker in (28) should have said so. Instead, s/he suggested by the weaker assertion that Ram's intent wasn't yet firm. The global repair strategy would require that the hearer assume that in uttering the second sentence the speaker presupposes the Ram believes he'll get a cat. But this would contradict the implicature which the speaker induced by using *consider* in the first clause, and hence is not available. However, the example improves considerably if the two sentences are spoken by two different speakers. The hearer would then take the second speaker to presuppose that Ram intends to get a cat.[12] This would be a global repair strategy, since if the hearer does not protest, the felicity of the utterance requires adding the proposition to the common ground. The local repair strategy would yield the conditional interpretation of the second sentence, paraphrased in (28′):[13]

(28′)   If Ram gets a cat, he intends to have it declawed.

Another way of talking about the failed presupposition of *intend* in (28) is to say that the predicate's modal base must reflect the actual beliefs of the subject, so far as the interlocutors know. This is a type of limited factivity. (9) illustrates the more classical type of factive verb:

(9)   Jan expected to get a puppy.
      ?#She managed to housebreak it quickly.

In terms of the Kratzer/Heim theory of intensional predicates, factive *manage* takes a totally realistic modal base; that is, for each world in the domain of the modal base – the worlds in the interlocutors' common ground – the set of premises which the function yields is just those propositions which are true in that world. In order to relevantly satisfy the familiarity presupposition of *it*, the hearer would have to globally accommodate the proposition that Jan got a puppy. Hence, we might expect this example to be comparable in acceptability to (21′), repeated below, on the interpretation where the hearer globally accommodates the proposition that John believes that Mary will, in fact, come:

(21′)   #John wants Mary to come, although he believes that Susan is
        going to come too.
(21″)   John wants Mary to come, although he believes that if she does,
        Susan is going to come too.

In fact, I think (9b) is somewhat more amenable to global repair than (21′), because expectations are more likely than mere desires to come true. This is perhaps easier to see if we compare (21′) with the present tense version of (9), in (9′):[14]

(9′)   Jan expects to get a puppy.
       She will manage to housebreak it quickly, I'm sure.

The past tense in (9) tends to more strongly implicate that Jan didn't get a puppy – we might be expected to know by now if she did get one, and to make the stronger claim if possible. Hence the tendency to avoid global accommodation in (9). And because of the factive presupposition of *manage*, there is no purely local accommodation possible, unlike the possible interpretation of (21′) in (21″). Factivity in (9) forces the presupposition to "percolate" to the global level, via requiring that the modal base be totally realistic.

The contradiction which explains the infelicity of (10) arises in a different fashion than in the other examples we have considered:

(10) Alice denies that there's a squirrel in her kitchen cabinets.
#She hopes to trap it alive and turn it loose outside.

As noted above, the contradiction doesn't follow directly from the lexical semantics of *deny* and *hope*, but only from the additional assumption that Alice's denial is an honest one, based on her belief. This is probably the default assumption in a context in which the speaker doesn't give any reason to doubt Alice. But default assumptions don't arise in all contexts. Assuming that the default assumption in (10) is crucial to generating the contradiction which results in its infelicity, we might expect that it could be contextually overridden, and this seems to be the case in the acceptable (10′), where accommodation of Alice's belief that there's a squirrel in her kitchen cabinets is clearly crucial to its felicity:

(10′) Alice loves wildlife and dislikes her landlord because he thinks a good wild animal is a dead wild animal.
So, she **denies** that there's a squirrel in her kitchen cabinets.
But really, she **hope**s to trap it alive and turn it loose outside.

But this raises a question about the examples involving scalar implicatures, such as (8b), (27), (9) and (21). If default assumptions can be overridden, as in (10)/(10′), why can't the offending implicatures be cancelled in these examples, so that the contradiction doesn't arise under global accommodation? A proper answer to this question would take us well beyond the focus of this paper, into a careful examination of conversational implicature.[15] Suffice it to say that I do not believe that implicatures are truly cancelled. Instead, in the classical examples of implicature "cancellation", the hearer comes to understand that s/he originally misunderstood the context of utterance, including the purposes which the speaker intended to address by her utterance.

In a relevant passage, Grice (1989:17) points out that in certain contexts it is difficult to see how the utterance of *x tried to VP* could fail to generate an implicature that *x* failed to VP. The point, though Grice did not make it directly, is that use of a given expression in a certain type of context is both necessary and sufficient to generate a given implicature. The account of implicature in Welker (1994) is intended to be generative in just this sense. On such an account, so-called implicature "cancellation" is really context revision. It is thus the discourse equivalent of the garden-path sentences from psycholinguistics (Ferreira & Clifton 1986), the latter requiring a re-parsing of the sentence in question up to the point of a misleading turn, while implicature "cancellation" requires a re-construction of the intended context of interpretation, stemming from an improved appreciation on the part of the hearer of the speaker's intentions (or plan). But there is nothing in the examples in question here to suggest that the speaker did not intend the crucial scalar implicatures. E.g. with *permit*, when it is the speaker who is granting permission as in (8), it is difficult to see how to avoid generating the scalar implicature that there is no requirement: If the hearer is REQUIRED to find a bear in (8b), why not just say so? So the implicatures are strong ones, I think unavoidable in the contexts given, and their existence precludes global accommodation of the missing familiarity presuppositions, on pain of contradiction.

Now note that the propositional attitude examples in (8) are analogous to those in (29), with deontic modal auxiliaries replacing the embedding predicates:

(29) You **must** find <u>a bear</u>. [Then] you **may** take <u>its</u> picture.
(29′) #You **may** find <u>a bear</u>. [Then] you **must** take <u>its</u> picture.

The indicated judgements will follow if we assume that there are restrictions on the deontic modal bases of the auxiliaries *must* and *may* which reflect the relations between one's obligation worlds and permission worlds, so that, relative to a single authority, the worlds which reflect what a subject must do are a subset of the worlds which reflect what she may do. Again, there is a contradiction involved in asserting that one must do something which presupposes something that one needn't do.

The examples in (29) and in (30)–(32) below illustrate how lexical restrictions on the modal bases suitable for particular modal auxiliaries, just as in the case of the propositional attitude verbs, constrain the possibility of modal subordination. The infelicities noted arise because there is a contradiction between the modal base required by the modal and a premise which would have to be locally accommodated in order to satisfy the familiarity presupposition of a pronoun in the context provided:

(30) John would have bought a car if he'd saved enough money.
      #He must have parked it in the garage.
(31) John would have bought a car if he'd saved enough money.
      #He must insure it before he drives it to work.
(32) Because public transportation is unreliable, John should buy a car to commute to work.
      #He would have enjoyed it in the bad weather last winter.
(32′) Because public transportation is unreliable, John should buy a car to commute to work.
      He would enjoy it on the weekends, too.

In (30), we are interested in the reading where we have a counterfactual *would* followed by an epistemic *must*. Infelicity follows from the fact that an epistemic takes an epistemic modal base, which would have to include the proposition that John bought a car in order for this utterance to be felicitous in this context. But without previous context, the counterfactual conversationally implicates that the speaker believes that John didn't buy a car. Again, the required accommodation would lead to contradiction (pragmatic, since this is only a contextual implication).

In (31), the same first sentence is followed by a deontic *must*. But as mentioned above, alluding to Thomason (1981), deontics presupposes a modal base which reflects the subject's circumstances in all relevant respects: one that yields, for any world, a set of propositions which includes those propositions corresponding to the subject's circumstances. This is because, intuitively, our obligations must correspond to real possibilities open to us under the circumstances in which we find ourselves. The first sentence in (31) leads one to understand that the proposition that John saved enough money to buy a car is counterfactual, and hence that John couldn't and didn't actually buy a car. Then, the presumed counterfactual proposition that John bought a car isn't compatible with the modal base of *must*, which must include the relevant available information about John's circumstances, including the fact that he didn't buy a car. This example contrasts neatly with (18), where the proposition that John bought a car is compatible with what the interlocutors know about John, and hence is globally accommodable.

> (18)   Since he saved his money last summer, John could buy a car.
> He should sell it, if he needs money now.

In (32), a counterfactual *would* is preceded by the deontic modal *should*. Deontics has a future-orientation, analogous to that of *wish* (as discussed above in connection with (7)): it is about what John is to do in the future. But *would* in the second sentence is combined with a perfect auxiliary to yield a (presumed) counterfactual claim about the past, presupposing that John had the use of the intended referent of the pronoun at some time in the past. In order to relevantly satisfy the familiarity presupposition of the pronoun, we must accommodate that he bought a car in the past, but this interpretation, "if John had bought a car, he would have enjoyed it on the weekends", would make the utterance irrelevant to John's present obligation, and hence to the first sentence, and that in turn undercuts the assumption that the accommodated premise was relevant. This is another type of infelicity, more subtle than contradiction of an entailment or implication, involving relevance and temporal as well as modal factors. (32'), with non-past *would* is considerably more felicitous.[16]

A thorough investigation of how the lexical presuppositions of modals constrain the possibility of modal subordination would take us too far afield.[17] The point here is to see the evident parallels with the examples involving propositional attitude verbs. In both cases, semantic entailments alone are not sufficient to explain all the felicitous examples involving modal subordination, but they do enter into the explanation of infelicitous examples, along with implicatures and other pragmatic aspects of interpretation. Accommodation must be invoked to account for many examples of modal subordination, and the pragmatic factors discussed then serve as constraints on accommodation, which must always result in a consistent (local) context of interpretation.

There remains one further possible avenue for explanation of modal subordination, by appeal to pronouns of laziness or "E-type" pronouns (see Cooper (1979), Evans (1977, 1980), and Chierchia (1992)). I argue in detail against one account of this type in Roberts (1995). Briefly, in the simplest type of E-type account, there are no built-in constraints on when modal subordination can occur, and in fact, there is no inherent expectation that the pronoun (or other presupposition) will occur in an intensional context, even though its apparent antecedent NP has a *de dicto* interpretation. It might be possible to construct a more sophisticated E-type account which somehow included such constraints, e.g. using modal accessibility relations. But then it seems to me that the resulting account would be very much like that in Roberts (1989), modulo the question of whether definites and indefinites are variables or disguised definite descriptions, an issue which appears to be orthogonal to the question of how to treat modal subordination.

I would argue that we should approach Geach's intentional identity problem, exemplified by (11), as a special case of modal subordination involving accommodation about beliefs. This seems to be basically the view of McCawley (1981: 336–7). He considers examples like (33) (his 11.2.20) and compares them with parallel examples involving "the conduct of normal science", such as (34) (his 11.2.21):

(11)   Hob thinks <u>a witch</u> has blighted Bob's mare, and Nob wonders whether <u>she</u> killed Cob's sow.

(33)   Jake believes that <u>a witch</u> has ruined his crops, and Zeke is convinced that <u>she</u> (the selfsame witch) has cursed his cows.

(34)   Halle believes that English has a productive rule of trisyllable laxing and that that rule is responsible for the vowel alternation in *divine/divinity*, and Keyser is convinced that the same rule is the reason for the shortness of the vowel in such words as *develop*; but Stampe has pretty convincingly demonstrated that English has no such rule.

About these, McCawley says:

> The plausibility of these examples depends on the ease with which we can imagine the beliefs of the one person being communicated to and accepted by the other. For example, [(33)] becomes quite strange if one inserts *secretly* before *believes*. It is indeed such migration of beliefs and supposed objects from one person's belief world to those of others that makes it possible for scientific communities to exist. The acceptability of [(33)] reflects not merely the scheme of

worlds and contexts developed here but also knowledge on the part of those accepting [(33)] and [(34)] of a basic mechanism in the sociology of science.

He then acknowledges that the felicity of such examples requires something more than entailment:

> [T]his principle of the sociology of science only tells one that the witch and the proposition that she ruined Jake's crops CAN migrate to Zeke's belief world: nothing in that principle or in the first conjunct of [(33)] tells us that they HAVE migrated there.

But this is just where a plausible and natural accommodation comes in. The very names *Hob* and *Nob*, or *Jake* and *Zeke*, are chosen to suggest similarity, to imply that these are members of the same community, as we happen to know of the real-life Halle and Keyser. We know that it is quite common that the same beliefs, be they scientific or superstitious, tend to be held throughout a given community, whether they are spread via journal publication, newspaper article, or gossip. We say this even when we know that not all members of such a community know each other. As noted by Edelberg, Hob and Nob needn't know of each others' beliefs in order for such examples to be felicitous. In fact, I imagine that they needn't know of each others' existence, if the community is large enough. But in order for the example to be felicitous, there must be some ground for claiming that they share beliefs about the same, though perhaps non-existent, witch. We only need accommodate the proposition that, as suggested by their names, Hob and Nob participate in a community whose common ground includes the existence of a witch in the vicinity. It is this assumed community common ground which warrants the identification of the two witches: The rumor about the witch which reached Hob's ears has spread to Nob as well, yielding a reading of the second conjunct something like "Nob wonders whether the witch that his community (including Hob) believes in killed Cob's sow."

The witch in Hob's belief worlds must share certain properties with that in Nob's world, but their beliefs about this witch needn't be identical, as in the case where Hob and Nob don't know of each other's beliefs about her relations to Bob's mare and Cob's sow. This is no different in principle than beliefs about actual persons: I may believe that Mozart died of poisoning, while you believe that he died of a hematoma of the brain, and you and I may not even have met. But should we meet, we would have no problem agreeing that it is the same Mozart about whom we hold these contradictory beliefs – the Mozart in my belief worlds and that in yours are in some sense counterparts. Hence, the problem of intentional identity in examples like (11) reduces to the more general problem of intensional identity, i.e. identity across possible worlds. Such an approach, of course, encounters difficult problems in attempting to specify what it is for two individuals to believe in the existence of the same, possibly mythical entity (see Lewis (1986) and references therein). But as these problems are not unique to examples like (11), I do not believe that they undermine the basic approach suggested by McCawley. In order to understand examples like (11), both complement clauses must be modally subordinate to assumptions about the community of believers in which Hob and Nob participate. This involves accommodation in the same basic fashion as we saw in examples considered above.

In summary, I have argued in this section that an adequate theory of modal subordination must involve the selection of an appropriate modal base for an intensional operator, and hence of propositions restricting the domain of that operator. In the cases of interest, those propositions will locally satisfy the presuppositions, familiarity or otherwise, of material in the nuclear scope of the operator. While the truth conditions of earlier material may in some cases entail the appropriate modal base for an operator or intensional predicate, explaining the possibility of modal subordination semantically in those cases, in the general case we must admit of the possibility that modal base selection is pragmatically directed, technically involving accommodation. Finally, note that the proposal offered here has the advantage of not requiring the extension of scope beyond the sentence, while respecting the relationship between scope and anaphoric accessibility. Hence, we can maintain the scope principles from Section 1, while providing an account for the whole range of examples involving modal subordination.

3   Conclusions and Remaining Questions

The most obvious conclusions which can be drawn from what we know about modal subordination, as reviewed in Sections 1 and 2, pertain to the nature of anaphora.[18] The clear parallels between anaphora and presupposition projection in modal subordination support the view of anaphora as a presuppositional phenomenon (e.g. as in chapter three of Heim (1982)). Perhaps more controversial, the theory promoted here entails that not all apparent anaphoric relations between two NPs are real, or at least direct. Recall the schema in (16):

(16)   **operator**[$_s$ ... NP$_x$ ...]
            [−def]
        operator$_{intensional}$ [$_s$ ... NP$_x$ ...]
                [+def]

In cases of modal subordination, the first, indefinite NP is not anaphorically accessible to the later pronoun (or other definite NP). Instead, the occurrence of the apparent antecedent only serves to pragmatically license the accommodation of appropriate material restricting the domain of the intensional operator over the second clause, material which includes a discourse referent that is asserted to have properties corresponding to the descriptive content of the indefinite NP. The moral is that when we see apparent anaphora in discourse, we should not jump to the conclusion that it is direct. Rather, there may be a more indirect relation between the NPs in question. And in fact, I would claim that the existence of such only apparent anaphoric pairs in discourse is wide-spread, quite apart from examples of modal subordination. So far as I can see, any attempt to reduce all apparent anaphora to binding will ultimately run afoul of the scope constraint on anaphoric relations and / or the sentential scope constraint, and end up overgenerating wildly.

Further evidence of the indirectness of the anaphoric relations involved in modal subordination comes from the role in felicity of the grammatical feature of number. Compare the felicitous (17), repeated from above, with (35):[19]

> (17) John doesn't have <u>a car</u>.
>   <u>It</u> would be in the garage.
> (35) No student has <u>a car</u>.
>   <u>It</u> would be in the garage.

The difference in the expression of negation in these examples – the auxiliary negation in (17) vs. the wide-scope negative quantificational determiner in (35) – leads indirectly to their differential acceptability. The first sentence in (17) is about the proposition that John has a car, denying its truth. The relevance of this proposition, and therefore of the car whose existence it pertains to, are what suggest the appropriate understanding of the second sentence, involving accommodation of the counterfactual proposition "John has a car" to restrict the domain of counterfactual *would*. The pronoun in the second sentence is singular in number because there is but a single car in question. The singular pronoun is unacceptable in (35). But a plural *they* improves the felicity of the example, as in (35′):

> (35′) No student has <u>a car</u>.
>   <u>They</u> would be in the garage.

Because of the quantificational determiner in *no student* (which happens to be downward entailing), there is no single student whose ownership of a single car is being denied; rather, the first sentence in (35)/(35′) yields a generalization about students and cars.[19] One reading of (35′) involves an implicit restriction of the domain of *would* by the relevant counterfactual proposition that some unspecified number of students have cars. It is the discourse referent corresponding to this set of cars which then satisfies the familiarity presupposition of the pronoun; since the set is likely non-singleton, the discourse referent is plural. Then if we assume that a pronoun must agree in number with the discourse referent which satisfies its familiarity presupposition, we can explain (35)/(35′). Assume that a pair of NPs in a true antecedent/anaphor relation must agree in number; call this the **Principle of Anaphoric Agreement**. Then, though the singular *a car* plays an important role in licensing the use of *they* in the second sentence, their relationship must be indirect, not a direct anaphoric relation. I would say that the apparent antecedent only **licenses** the occurrence of the pronoun, since it is part of what licenses the crucial accommodation. There is much more to be said about this subject. For example, not everyone assumes the Principle of Anaphoric Agreement, a difference which leads to quite differrent analyses of anaphora in discourse.[20] And it remains to be clarified in what sense a discourse referent is "plural." But this topic is too complex to permit fuller discussion here.

Modal subordination can also give us some insight into the nature and function of the common ground between interlocutors in a discourse and of the role of accommodation. It has been claimed (Heim (1983), van der Sandt (1990), Beaver (1992)) that there is a default preference for global accommodation, that is, accommodation of otherwise failed presuppositions to the common ground, rather than local accommodation, where the presupposed material is satisfied by the restriction on an operator's domain. If this generalization is correct, we might reasonably ask why this should be the case. But further, when modal subordination involves accommodation, it is, by the nature of modal subordination, local accommodation restricting the domain of an intensional operator, as described in §2. We have also seen that in some cases, such as (18), repeated here, the resolution of the familiarity presupposition of a pronoun in a discourse with the relevant surface structure is accomplished via global accommodation of the relevant material.

> (18)   Since he saved his money last summer, John could buy a car.
> He should sell it, if he needs money now.

Why then do we not find global accommodation in all or most examples of the general surface form of interest? Here again, a suggestion by McCawley (1981, §11.2, p.331) points toward an answer to the first question, why global accommodation seems to be the default. He considers examples (36) and (37):

> (36)   Tom thinks Alice doesn't know her house is on fire.
> (37)   Betty: Tom thinks Alice's house is on fire.
> Marvin: How on earth could he think that? Surely if Alice's house was on fire, she wouldn't just be sitting in the next room doing a crossword puzzle – she'd be trying to save her collection of James Joyce manuscripts from the fire.
> Betty: Tom thinks Alice doesn't know her house is on fire.

McCawley says:

> Example [(36)] clearly does not semantically presuppose that Alice's house is on fire.... Any presupposition embodied in [(36)] is a pragmatic presupposition, that is, a demand that the sentence makes on its context.... [I]t is not so much

that the presupposition of the complement clause [in (36)] is passed on to the whole sentence as that, without additional context as in [(37)], the world of the main clause (or better, the 'context' of the main clause, in the sense of [Karttunen (1973)]) is the only available source of information about Tom's belief world.

This suggests to me that global accommodation appears to be the default not because of any inherent preference for global over local accommodation *per se*. Rather, I will argue, it follows from practical principles for the maintenance of the common ground of the interlocutors, plus the function of accommodation.

It has been extensively argued in the literature on counterfactuals that we make the default assumption that counterfactual contexts are as much like the actual world as is compatible with what's explicitly said about them (e.g., see Lewis (1973)). Call this the **principle of optimal realism**. I would argue that we can generalize this claim about counterfactuals to the claim that all hypothetical contexts are assumed to be optimally realistic, whether they are counterfactual or merely characterized by non-asserted propositions. I speculate that the principle of optimal realism is motivated by the need to assure that all interlocutors' assumptions are as similar as possible, whether these are assumptions about the actual world – for which the common ground defines the candidate set – or about hypothetical or counterfactual contexts under discussion. Those aspects of hypothetical or counterfactual contexts which aren't spelled out by the speaker are assumed to be identical with what we know about actuality, as reflected in the common ground, at least insofar as this doesn't lead to contradictions with what's explicitly spelled out. This enables us to avoid misunderstanding, while minimizing the need for detailed (and often redundant) description of hypothetical contexts.

Technically, in order for accommodation to satisfy a presupposition, it must take place at the most local level, at least. From the perspective just offered, the question is not whether or why there is a default to global accommodation, but how far "up" the accommodation will percolate from the most local level. For simplicity, let's assume only one level of hypotheticality, which is the local context at which some presupposition ϕ must be accommodated. If we accommodate ϕ at the local level and we also assume the principle of optimal realism, then we will accommodate ϕ to the global level as well unless ϕ is counterfactual or we have some other reason to think that (the speaker thinks that) ϕ may not be actually true. This would explain both why there is a tendency to global accommodation, all things being equal, and also why examples involving modal subordination form a systematic exception to that rule, with no hint of infelicity or difficulty in processing.

When we've already been talking about a counterfactual or hypothetical circumstance with certain properties, so long as that information is relevant and plausibly true in the present hypothetical context as well,[22] then we may take it that that prior information is accommodable locally, to enrich the present hypothetical context. But the fact that the information was only discussed hypothetically at least implicates that it is not in the common ground, so far

as the speaker is concerned. In order to avoid any conflict with that implication, the accommodation doesn't percolate to the global level. In cases where
local accommodation would conflict with presuppositions about the modal
base of the modal or intensional predicate, we can only achieve felicity via
global accommodation of the otherwise unsatisfied presuppositions. We see
this in (18), repeated just above. Here, the circumstantial modal base of deontics
like *should* (as discussed in Section 2) would be incompatible with the purely
local accommodation of the proposition that John bought a car, a proposition
only hypothetically entertained in the preceding utterance. So, in order to
make the example felicitous, we must globally accommodate the proposition,
an accommodation which is plausible if we know that owning a car is generally considered desirable, that John had enough money to buy a car, and that
people generally do what they want when they can. And we saw forced per-
colation of accommodated material to the global level in (9), as well, where the
factivity of the intensional predicate was reflected in the requirement of a
totally realistic modal base.

Behind all this is the assumption that when accommodation is required, the
material to be accommodated is both maximally relevant and salient, again
in the interest of the maintenance of the common ground. This is especially
important in the examples involving pronominal anaphora, since otherwise
the descriptive content of pronouns is so impoverished as to make the recovery and accommodation of an intended antecedent impossible.[23]

Of course, this approach to explaining the default preference for global
accommodation, as well as the systematic class of exceptions involving modal
subordination, all hinges on the idea that the purpose of conversation is to
build, extend, and maintain a common ground. Insofar as it is a plausible
explanation, we might take it to underline the central importance of the common ground in human discourse.[24] I think as we begin to appreciate that more
fully, and to investigate the types of constraints and strategies which we employ
to guarantee the maintenance of the common ground, we will come to understand that accommodation actually is very constrained, and the suspicion that
accommodation is too powerful a mechanism to play a part in a falsifiable
theory will lose its force.

Finally, I will briefly mention some remaining questions about modal
subordination:

The class of examples displaying telescoping, like (1), remains ill-under-
stood, though they obviously involve a natural language counterpart to universal instantiation in logic. See Roberts (1989), Poesio & Zucchi (1992).

Farkas (1993) discusses what she calls "modal anchoring" of NPs in non-
intensional contexts, illustrated by her examples (38) and (39):

(38)   Mary thought that there was a castle behind the trees.
       The castle turned out to be a huge oak tree.
(39)   Mary believes that there is a castle in the park.
       John believes that the castle is a figment of Mary's imagination.

She describes (38) as a case where "a noun phrase is modally subordinated to a constituent occurring in previous discourse, while the sentence the noun phrase is part of is not modally subordinated," leading to her conclusion that (p.8), "the modal anchoring of the descriptive content of noun phrases is independent of the modal anchoring of the sentence the noun phrase occurs in." This is strongly reminiscent of Enç's (1981) discussion of the temporal anchoring of NPs independently of the tense of the clause in which they occur. It would appear promising to explore this parallel.

Examples like (40), originally due to Partee, are often cited in discussions of anaphora in discourse (see, for example, Heim (1982), Roberts (1987, 1989), Groenendijk & Stokhof (1990a), Dekker (1993b), van der Sandt (1992), Beaver (1992)):

(40) Either there's no bathroom in this house or it's in a funny place.

Generally, a quantificational NP which occurs in one disjunct of a sentence with *or* cannot serve as antecedent to pronouns outside the disjunct, in keeping with the scope constraint. There is no modal or other intensional operator in (40), so it doesn't obviously involve modal subordination. Yet I argued in Roberts (1987, 1989) that there is a relationship to the latter phenomenon, in that the anaphora in (40) also involves accommodation of a presupposition. On the analysis proposed there, disjunctions may be taken to provide alternative answers to a single topic of discussion, here the question of whether there is a bathroom in the house. The first disjunct of (40) asserts a negative answer, while the second disjunct presupposes a positive answer. It is this presupposition which is accommodated, yielding an interpretation like "or there is a bathroom in this house and it's in a funny place". Alternative accounts have been proposed, notably those of Groenendijk & Stokhof and Dekker. But none of these proposals is well-grounded in an independent exploration of the general semantics and pragmatics of disjunctive assertions, and I take it that the problem posed by (40) will remain unresolved until such an exploration is undertaken.

Possibly relevant in this regard is recent work by Portner, in which he has explored in some detail the technical realization of the notion of *mood*, both in complement clauses (Portner 1992) and in matrix clauses (Portner 1993). He proposes that rather than assuming an implicit operator in just those cases, such as (12), in which one is needed to match the schema for modal subordination in (15)/(16), we generalize to assume that all utterances, even indicatives, have what he calls a *modal force*, either universal or existential, and a *modal context*, which determines the domain of the modal force. In modal subordination, the modal context would be influenced by previous irrealis contexts, which I take it would be compatible with the accommodation approach argued for here. This way of treating mood would appear to be particularly promising in accounting for examples such as (41):

(41)   Lisa **dream**ed she was talking to <u>a racoon</u>.
<u>It</u> was telling her how <u>it</u> broke into her garbage can.

Here, the default interpretation of the second sentence does not involve the assumption that there is a real raccoon in question, but instead continues the discussion of the dream raccoon. Though there is no explicit intensional operator with scope over the second sentence, Roberts (1987, 1989) claimed that such examples involve an implicit operator. But, unlike the implicit modals in bare indicative conditionals (Kratzer 1981) or the generic operator in examples with bare present tense (Carlson 1977b, Wilkinson 1991), this is not a kind of operator whose existence has been independently argued for in the literature. Though technically we want a universal quantification over Lisa's dream worlds, grammatically we have a simple indicative utterance, so that the stipulated implicit operator seems to be *ad hoc*. Perhaps Portner's work, exploring the relation between mood in such examples and that in complement clauses, will shed more light on their proper analysis. In disjunctions like (40), neither disjunct is asserted; then mood in Portner's sense, and hence ultimately modality, may prove relevant to its analysis after all, making all such examples cases of modal subordination.

NOTES

1   Thanks to Shalom Lappin for suggesting that I write this article. Thanks also to Louise McNally and to Kate Welker for insightful comments on an earlier draft and to Fred Landman, for valuable discussions on several occasions.
2   I don't want to take a stand here about whether definite and indefinite NPs are quantificational or are unselectively bound variables. So far as I can see, this problem is tangential to the problem I describe here. On either type of theory, these NPs display a different anaphoric potential than other types of NPs. Unlike NPs with determiners like *every* or *no*, definite and indefinite NPs may be anaphorically accessible across discourse. But unlike proper names, the anaphoric accessibility of definite and indefinite NPs is subject to the scope constraint on anaphoric relations, as we see in the examples below. My point is that apart from definite and indefinite NPs, all the theories cited agree in entailing the sentential scope constraint for quantificational elements.
3   See Edelberg for a more detailed description of the problem, and an extended argument against a quantificational analysis of intentional identity.
4   I assume Heim's account of the presuppositional character of anaphora, where pronouns and other definites presuppose the familiarity of a discourse referent, introduced by an antecedent NP or a deictic act, in the common ground of the interlocutors. The notion of *common ground* is due to Stalnaker (1979), and roughly includes the (maximal) set of propositions held true in common by the interlocutors in a conversation. Technically, Heim extends the common ground to include not only a set of propositions, but also a set of discourse referents (abstract entities

under discussion – see Karttunen (1976)). Satisfaction of the familiarity presupposition introduced by a definite NP requires the existence of a discourse referent in the common ground which is coindexed with the definite. For simplicity here, I will talk of familiarity presuppositions as if they were propositional, specifically as presuppositions of the existence of some entity.

5 The interpretation in question is one which arguably involves accommodation. That is, the hearer assumes the truth of the proposition that John did buy a car, and hence assumes the existence and familiarity of a car that John bought. This assumption is triggered by the apparent assumption on the part of the speaker, in the second sentence, that John has something familiar to sell; see the discussion in Section 2 of possible modal bases for deontic *should* for an indication of how the speaker's assumption is communicated in this example.

6 Actually, there are two functions involved, the modal base and the ordering source, the latter crucially involved in the interpretation of deontics and counterfactuals. See Kratzer (1981) for general discussion, Roberts (1989) for application to the theory of modal subordination. Here I will only talk about the modal base, for simplicity.

7 According to Heim (1992), Cresswell (1988) also offers an account based on accommodation. However, I have been unable to locate the discussion she alludes to from that volume.

8 Some speakers find the example acceptable with local accommodation of the proposition that the hearer finds a bear in the second conjunct. But here, for the sake of argument, I'll assume McCawley's judgment.

9 McCawley assumes that denying *p* entails that one doesn't believe that *p*. However, this is arguable, since in denying, one might lie. Hence, the relationship between the complements of *deny* and *hope* is less direct than McCawley would have it.

10 I return briefly to consider this tendency to global accommodation in Section 3. Deriving the reading in (21″) is easier for me when the complement clause itself has a modal, as in (i):

  (i) John wants Mary to come, although he believes that Susan <u>would</u> come too.

Here's one possible explanation for this: Auxiliary *would* tends to suggest some unwillingness on the part of the speaker (in a main clause) or superordinate subject (in an attitude context such as (i)) to directly assert the proposition in question. Since *want* tends to conversationally implicate a lack of belief, using auxiliary *would* for the modally subordinate interpretation in (21″) may be more compatible with the conditional hedging than using the indicative in (21′). The lack of modally subordinate interpretation for the indicative (21′) might then be at least partly the result of an implicature based on the availability of the more suitable (i).

11 There are some subtle questions here, since one's wishes needn't all be compatible (see Heim for some discussion), so that one might consistently both wish to rob a bank and not wish to rob a bank. That is, it is important to keep constant the other factors which play a part in determining one's wishes in order to check the sort of entailments at issue here. However, my intuition is that having to do something doesn't entail desiring it. Hence one might try to do something one doesn't wish for, even relative to the same assumptions, because one has to.

12 Again, I don't think a conditional interpretation of the second sentence, as in (27'), is readily available:

    (27')   If Ram gets a cat, he intends to have it declawed.
    (27")   Ram is considering getting a cat.
             He would have it declawed.

This is because there is no hint of irrealis mood in the second clause of (27). But (27') is the preferred interpretation of (27"). There, the modal *would* both introduces the irrealis mood required for the modally subordinate interpretation, and conveys Ram's intent, his will, in keeping with the etymology of the auxiliary (hence, adding *intend* to this clause would be redundant for me).

13 For reasons that are not entirely clear, I find this less successful than the local repair for (27) given in (27'). But other speakers appear to find local repair equally possible in the two examples.

14 This comparison was suggested by Louise McNally (personal communication), who gets a conditional interpretation for the second sentence of (9'). I more readily get the global accommodation suggested in the text. This is the kind of difference in interpretation which we expect with accommodation.

15 See Welker (1994) for such a careful study, based on the way in which interlocutors' publically evident intentions (or *plans*) play a role in generating implicatures.

16 Though *should* is in some respects similar in meaning to the semi-modal *have to*, the following is infelicitous, unlike (32'):

    (i)   John has to buy a car to drive to work.
        *He would enjoy it on the weekends, too.

I suspect that *have to* has factive entailments: If John has to buy a car, he will. The strong likelihood that he will do what he has to do is incompatible with the hedge associated with the counterfactual *would*.

17 For some discussion of lexical constraints on modal bases, see Kratzer (1981). See Roberts (1994) for discussion and a new proposal about how to capture these constraints.

18 On the analysis suggested in Section 2, modal subordination also helps to explain certain apparent contradictions which arise within the theory of presupposition of Stalnaker (1974) see Landman (1986a) for examples and discussion.

19 This comparison was suggested by Louise McNally (personal communication), who, however, might not agree with the conclusions I draw from it.

20 At least, not in a model with more than one student. And many have argued that use of a quantificational NP in such a context presupposes the existence of multiple entities in the denotation of the CN.

21 See, e.g. Groenendijk & Stokhof (1990a) and Dekker (1993b), who do not, though they do not explicitly discuss this principle or its rejection.

22 I take plausible truth of a proposition with respect to a set of worlds to entail compatibility with them, i.e. non-empty intersection of those sets of worlds. But there may be other criteria for plausibility, as well.

23 See Roberts (1993) for extensive discussion of distinctions between the presuppositions associated with pronouns and those of definite descriptions.

24 E.g. contra the arguments of Sperber & Wilson (1986) that there is no utility to such a notion, indeed that one cannot even make sense of it.

9 Quantification, Quantificational Domains, and Dynamic Logic

JEAN MARK GAWRON

1 Introduction

The prototypical example of quantification is an English noun phrase like *every boy*. In standard accounts it is assumed that the domain of quantification, the set of boys, is determined by the syntax, roughly, by the material in the noun phrase excluding the determiner. But it is well known that in general the domain of quantification can be affected by various other factors. The domain can, of course, be constrained pragmatically; the set of boys actually relevant in the discourse may be the set involved in some event or at some location. In some cases, as in some adverbial quantifications, the domain may be unconstrained by the syntax and left to discourse control. The domain may also be affected by focus or by quantificational subordination. This paper collects some of the relevant phenomena, tries to show why a "dynamic" account might be desirable, and presents a brief sketch of a promising approach in the form of a logical fragment based on a revised notion of discourse context.

In Rooth (1985), Rooth (this volume), a technical notion of *alternatives under consideration* is proposed to account for a variety of focus-related phenomena. One way of explaining the intuition behind this technical notion is to identify it with a dynamic property of real discourses: A discourse tracks not just what is known or established as common ground, but also what is merely under discussion. In this paper, in order to explore various non-local ways of affecting quantificational domains, I want to explore two related ideas:

1. The alternatives under discussion should be built into the context in the sense used in dynamic frameworks.
2. Sets of things quantified over should be treated as alternatives under consideration, persisting through the discourse even outside the scope of the quantification.

One benefit of 2. will be a natural treatment of the interaction of quantification and focus. Another will be to provide the beginnings of an account of how quantifications can be "anaphoric" or "parasitic" on other quantifications.

If one takes seriously the idea of building quantificational alternatives in as a fundamental part of a dynamic discourse, one would expect each quantification to potentially affect subsequent quantification as the discourse goes on; in fact, anaphoric quantification is the rule rather than the exception. Quantifications have a tendency to be over "familiar sets" and keeping quantifications familiar is a fundamental part of how discourse stays coherent. Consider:

(1) a. Few harbor seals in California live long. Most pups die in the first few weeks of life.
 b. ? A harbor seal in California died last week. Most pups die in the first few weeks of life.

Here, in (a) the pups we are talking about can clearly be the pups within the set of harbor seals in California; the discourse in (b), however, is much less natural, and it is difficult to interpret the second sentence as a claim specifically about *California* seals. Quantificational NPs seem to be natural devices for introducing quantificational domains that may be exploited by later quantifications; indefinite NPs do not. This observation will play a central role in the account sketched below.

The dynamic behavior of quantificational domains is very nicely illustrated through an example in Partee (1993):

(2) a. Henrik likes to travel. He goes to France in the summer and he usually travels by car. He goes to England for the spring holidays and he usually travels by ferry.
 b. Henrik likes to travel. He usually travels by car and he goes to France in the summer and he usually travels by ferry and he goes to England for the spring holidays.

In discourse (a), the domain of the quantifier *usually* is first restricted to trips to France and then to trips to England. Discourse (b) because of the reordering is hard to interpret with those restrictions. The result is that it sounds contradictory.

The contrast in (2) illustrates a general problem. Domains of quantification are constructed by combining constraints that arise from different sources. In (2a), a quantification over traveling events is naturally restricted to be over the sorts of traveling events under discussion. What is going on here is no less a part of discourse coherence than anaphoric relations between pronouns and NPs (for an extensive discussion of quantificational domains, see von Fintel (1993)). Some constraints on quantificational domains are contributed in syntactically determined ways, as in the case of the common noun phrases of quantified NPs like *every man who owns a Subaru*. But even in those cases the discourse in which the quantification is embedded may make contributions in a variety of other ways.

Indeed the problem of domain of quantification can interact with the problem of anaphora, because material determining the domain of quantification may provide the antecedents for pronouns:

(3) a. Every summer Henrik rents a car to go France. He usually takes it on the ferry.
     b. Usually *e*, Henrik rents a car *x* to go to France in summer in *e*, Henrik takes *x* on the ferry in *e*.

Here the set of events which *usually* quantifies over is events in which Henry rents a car to go to France. The quantified over cars can then be a "donkey-antecedent" for a pronoun. This phenomenon, known as quantificational subordination, is a clear instance of a pronoun finding an antecedent whose scope it lies outside of, but our chief interest in it here is the non-local determination of the domain of quantification. The domain of quantification of the operator *usually* is clearly affected by the operator *every* in a previous sentence.

The idea that discourse needs to keep track of alternatives under consideration as well as what is common ground was suggested by phenomena like questions, discussed by Rooth as one of a class of focus-related phenomena:

(4) a. Who did Mary introduce John to?
     b. No one.
     c. Mary only introduced John to BILL.

In the case of the discourse given in (a) and (b), although the identity of who Mary introduced John to is under discussion, the facts as ultimately established are that she introduced John to no one. Rooth argues that uses of *only* invoke the same notion of alternatives under discussion. Following Jackendoff, he also argues persuasively against an account that appeals to an existential presupposition.

But the chief subject of this paper is what all this has to do with quantification. Building in a close relationship between Rooth's notion of alternatives under discussion and the treatment of quantification is best motivated with an example of the interaction of focus and quantification.

The clearest examples of such interactions involve adverbial quantification:

(5) Mary always took John to the movies.

Again different readings are possible, depending on the focus:

(6) a. always *e*[if there exists *x* such that Mary takes *x* to the movies at *e*, then Mary takes John to the movies at *e*.]
     b. always *e*[if there exists *x* such that *x* takes John to the movies at *e*, then Mary takes John to the movies at *e*.]

The account we will pursue will cash out the presuppositional requirements of focus as requirements on the quantificational domains of the discourse.

2   A Logic for Quantificational Domains

2.1   *Information states, update functions, and denotation*

Because there are so many variant approaches that are all called dynamic in one way or another, I will introduce this approach with a small unadorned fragment of a logic first, which I will call DLF (for Dynamic Logic Fragment). That is, I will begin by introducing and defining the basic notions of information state, update function, and denotation in a dynamic fragment that attempts no innovations regarding quantificational domain. This logic will be dynamic in the sense that it builds in a notion of sentence meanings as update functions from states to states. It will also introduce dynamic binders and thus the kind of work the systems of Kamp (1981), Heim (1982), Groenendijk and Stokhof (1990a), Groenendijk, Stokhof and Veltman (this volume), and Chierchia (1988a) do, though it will do that work in a somewhat different way.

We begin with the notion of an information state. In this preliminary extensional treatment we will define a state as in File Change Semantics, as a set of assignments. An information state can be thought of as a set of different ways the world might be to make what is known thus far be true.

To define different ways things might be we use partial assignments, all with the same domain, which we call the domain of the state. It would appear that everything proposed here extends naturally to a system in which worlds and assignments are paired, but I have left that extension for future work.

2.1.1   *Types of DLF*

We assume a set of syntactic types T, defined as the smallest set *PreT* such that:

1. $e, t \in PreT$;
2. If $a_1, \ldots a_n, b \in PreT$; then $\langle a_1, \ldots a_n, b \rangle \in PreT$, with $n \geq 1$.

We define the set of syntactic types T as $PreT \cup \{i, det\}$ (i will be the syntactic type for variables, *det* the type for determiners).

We designate the set of meaningful expressions of type a with ME_a. The syntax of our preliminary fragment will be as follows.

2.1.2 Syntax of DLF

1. We assume an infinite stock of expressions of type ME_i called variables (written in italics x, y, z ..);
2. We assume an infinite stock of expressions of type ME_e called constants (written in roman a, b, c ..);
3. {walk, man, boy, donkey, farmer, Hardy-boy-mystery} $\subseteq ME_{\langle e,t\rangle}$;
4. {no, most, $\forall$} $\subseteq \text{ME}_{det}$;
5. {like, read, beat, own} $\subseteq \text{ME}_{\langle e,e,t\rangle}$;
6. If $\alpha \in \text{ME}_{\langle e,t\rangle}$ and $\beta \in \text{ME}_e \cup \text{ME}_i$, then $\alpha(\beta) \in \text{ME}_t$;
7. If $\alpha \in \text{ME}_{\langle e,e,t\rangle}$ and β, $\gamma \in ME_e \cup \text{ME}_i$, then $\alpha(\beta,\gamma) \in \text{ME}_t$;
8. If $\phi \in \text{ME}_t$, and $\psi \in \text{ME}_t$, then $\phi; (\psi) \in \text{ME}_t$;
9. If $\phi \in \text{ME}_t$, and $\beta \in \text{ME}_i$, then $\exists\beta(\psi) \in \text{ME}_t$;
10. If $\alpha \in \text{ME}_{det}$, ϕ, $\psi \in \text{ME}_t$, and $\beta \in \text{ME}_i$, then $\alpha\beta(\phi,\psi) \in \text{ME}_t$.

This syntax allows, for example:

(7) a. $\exists x$ (man(x)); $\exists y$ (book(y)); read(x,y)
    b. $\forall x$ (man(x), $\exists y$ book(y); (read(x,y)))

We let a model be a triple $\langle D,F,I\rangle$, where D is the usual domain of individuals, F is an interpretation function from ME_a to D_a (the domain corresponding to type a), and I is a set of indeterminates (place-holders, variable slots).

Note that a set of indeterminates replaces what Groendendijk and Stokhof (1990a) call a set of states. Since states, in their simple fragment, do the work of assignments here, the choice they have made is to introduce assignment-like entities into the model in place of variable-like entities. This requires that some structure be postulated (their Distinctness and Update postulates) in order to be able to individuate these assignment-primitives in assignment-like ways. Rather than take assignments as primitive model theoretic objects, and impose a structure on them, I have assumed indeterminates as primitive,[1] and will take assignments to be partial functions from indeterminates to individuals in D. If assignments are less objectionable model-theoretic primitives than indeterminates, everything here could be reformulated for models with an appropriately structured set of assignments replacing the set of indeterminates.

We write D_a for the semantic domain corresponding to the type a. Denotations of particular expressions will be elements of the appropriate domain. The domains are:

2.1.3 Denotation domains of DLF

1. $D_e = D$
2. $D_i = I$
3. $D_{\langle a_1,\ldots a_n,b\rangle} = D_b^{D_{a_1} \times \ldots D_{a_n}}$
4. Let

$$D_S = \{S \mid S \in \wp(D^1) \text{ and for all } f, g \in S, \text{Dom}(f) = \text{Dom}(g)\}$$

We define an information-state as a set of assignments. In addition, however, we require of a state S that the (possibly partial) assignments in it all have the same domain, which we write as $\text{Dom}(S)$. Then

$$D_t = D_S^{D_S}$$

The two "surprises" here are that variables denote indeterminates, and that the denotation of a sentence will be a function from a state to a state. As we will see shortly, partial functions will be allowed.

If ϕ is a sentence, we let $[\![\phi]\!]^{\mathcal{M}}$ denote the function from states to states assigned by model $\mathcal{M}$. Expressions denoting states will not be part of the logic proper but they will be part of the metalanguage; by convention we use capitalized roman letters like S, S', T, T', for states. We write the result of applying a meaning to a state using postfix notation.

$$S[\![\phi]\!]^{\mathcal{M}}$$

We turn to the semantics of our logic fragment. As is usual in dynamic logic fragments, we need to specify both the update functions for a sentence ϕ, which we give simply as its *denotation* with respect to the model, written $[\![\phi]\!]^{\mathcal{M}}$, and its truth conditions. To this end, we build in a distinction between the *denotation* of an expression and its *interpretation*. We will get at the truth of a sentence ϕ through the *interpretation* of ϕ with respect to a model and an assignment, written $[\![\phi]\!]^{\mathcal{M},f}$. We define $[\![\alpha]\!]^{\mathcal{M},f}$ for other types of α as well. Except in the case of expressions of type t and type i (variables), interpretation with respect to an assignment will simply equal the denotation with respect to the model.

2.1.4 Semantics of DLF

1. a. If $\alpha \in \text{ME}_i \cup \text{ME}_e \cup \text{ME}_{\langle e,t \rangle} \cup \text{ME}_{\langle e,e,t \rangle}$ then $[\![\alpha]\!]^{\mathcal{M}} = F(\alpha)$.
   b. If $\alpha \in \text{ME}_e \cup \text{ME}_{\langle e,t \rangle} \cup \text{ME}_{\langle e,e,t \rangle}$ then $[\![\alpha]\!]^{\mathcal{M},f} = [\![\alpha]\!]^{\mathcal{M}}$.
   c. If $\alpha \in \text{ME}_i$ then $[\![\alpha]\!]^{\mathcal{M},f} = f([\![\alpha]\!]^{\mathcal{M}})$.
2. If $\alpha \in \text{ME}_{\langle e,t \rangle}$ and $\beta \in \text{ME}_e \cup \text{ME}_i$, then $[\![\alpha(\beta)]\!]^{\mathcal{M}}$ is that function in D_t such that

$$S[\![\alpha(\beta)]\!]^{\mathcal{M}} = \{f \mid f \in S \text{ and } [\![\beta]\!]^{\mathcal{M},f} \in [\![\alpha]\!]^{\mathcal{M}}\}$$
if and only if
if $\beta \in \text{ME}_i$, then $[\![\beta]\!]^{\mathcal{M}} \in \text{Dom}(S)$;
else undefined.

Thus, the denotation of a sentence is a partial function from states to states, undefined for states that do not have the necessary variable in their domain.

3. If $\alpha \in \mathrm{ME}_{\langle e,e,t\rangle}$ $\beta \in \mathrm{ME}_e \cup \mathrm{ME}_i$, and $\gamma \in \mathrm{ME}_e \cup \mathrm{ME}_i$, then $[\![\alpha(\beta,\gamma)]\!]^{\mathcal{M}}$ is that function in D_t such that

$$S[\![\alpha(\beta,\gamma)]\!]^{\mathcal{M}} = \{f \mid f \in S \text{ and } \langle [\![\beta]\!]^{\mathcal{M},f}, [\![\gamma]\!]^{\mathcal{M},f}\rangle \in [\![\alpha]\!]^{\mathcal{M}}\}$$
if and only if
if $\beta \in \mathrm{ME}_i$, then $[\![\beta]\!]^{\mathcal{M}} \in \mathrm{Dom}(S)$;
if $\gamma \in \mathrm{ME}_i$, then $[\![\gamma]\!]^{\mathcal{M}} \in \mathrm{Dom}(S)$;
else undefined.

4. If ϕ, $\psi \in \mathrm{ME}_t$ then $[\![\phi;\psi]\!]^{\mathcal{M}}$ is $[\![\psi]\!]^{\mathcal{M}} o [\![\phi]\!]^{\mathcal{M}.2}$
5. If $\phi \in \mathrm{ME}_t$ and $\beta \in \mathrm{ME}_i$, then $[\![\exists\beta(\phi)]\!]^{\mathcal{M}}$ is that function in D_t such that

$$S[\![\exists\beta(\phi)]\!]^{\mathcal{M}} = \{f \mid f \in S^{+[\![\beta]\!]^{\mathcal{M}}}[\![\phi]\!]^{\mathcal{M}}\}$$

Here $S^{+[\![\beta]\!]^{\mathcal{M}}}$ is simply S with $[\![\beta]\!]^{\mathcal{M}}$ added with no constraining information:

$$S^{+[\![\beta]\!]^{\mathcal{M}}} = \{g \mid$$
There exists $g' \in S$, $g \geq g'$, and $\mathrm{Dom}(g) = \mathrm{Dom}(S) \cup \{[\![\beta]\!]^{\mathcal{M}}\}\}$

6. a. If ϕ, $\psi \in \mathrm{ME}_t$ and $\beta \in \mathrm{ME}_i$, then $[\![\forall\beta(\phi,\psi)]\!]^{\mathcal{M}}$ is that function in D_t such that $S[\![\forall\beta(\phi,\psi)]\!]^{\mathcal{M}} =$

$\{f \mid f \in S$ and every assignment g such that $g = \setminus_{[\![\beta]\!]^{\mathcal{M}}}f$ and such that there exists $g' \geq g$, $g' \in S[\![\phi]\!]^{\mathcal{M}}$ is such that for every assignment $h \geq g$, if $h \in S[\![\phi]\!]^{\mathcal{M}}$, then there exists $h' \geq h$ such that $h' \in S[\![\phi]\!]^{\mathcal{M}}[\![\psi]\!]^{\mathcal{M}}\}$

This gives the so-called strong reading. The other determiners will work similarly to $\forall$ except that the first "every" will be replaced by "most" and "no" respectively, and for "no", we will choose the weak reading.

b. If ϕ, $\psi \in \mathrm{ME}_t$ and $\beta \in \mathrm{ME}_i$, then $[\![\text{no } \beta(\phi,\psi)]\!]^{\mathcal{M}}$ is that function in D_t such that $S[\![\text{no } \beta(\phi,\psi)]\!]^{\mathcal{M}} =$

$\{f \mid f \in S$ and no assignment g such that $g = \setminus_{[\![\beta]\!]^{\mathcal{M}}}f^3$ and such that there exists $g' \geq g$, $g' \in S[\![\phi]\!]^{\mathcal{M}}$ is such that there exists an assignment $h \geq g$ such that $h \in S[\![\phi]\!]^{\mathcal{M}}[\![\psi]\!]^{\mathcal{M}}\}$

c. If ϕ, $\psi \in \mathrm{ME}_t$ and $\beta \in \mathrm{ME}_i$, then $[\![\text{most } \beta(\phi,\psi)]\!]^{\mathcal{M}}$ is that function in D_t such that $S[\![\text{most } \beta(\phi,\psi)]\!]^{\mathcal{M}} =$

$\{f \mid f \in S$ and most assignments g such that $g = \setminus_{[\![\beta]\!]^{\mathcal{M}}}f$ and such that there exists $g' \geq g$, $g' \in S[\![\phi]\!]^{\mathcal{M}}$ are such that for every assignment $h \geq g$, if $h \in S[\![\phi]\!]^{\mathcal{M}}$, then there exists $h' \geq h$ such that $h' \in S[\![\phi]\!]^{\mathcal{M}}[\![\psi]\!]^{\mathcal{M}}\}$

7. If $\alpha \in \mathrm{ME}_t$, then $[\![\alpha]\!]^{\mathcal{M},f}$ is defined if and only if there is an S such that $f \in S$ and $S[\![\alpha]\!]^{\mathcal{M}}$ is defined. If $[\![\alpha]\!]^{\mathcal{M},f}$ is defined, then $[\![\alpha]\!]^{\mathcal{M},f} = 1$, if and only if there is an S such that $f \in S[\![\alpha]\!]^{\mathcal{M}}$; otherwise $[\![\alpha]\!]^{\mathcal{M},f} = 0$.

2.2 Sketch of restriction logic

I have suggested that quantificational domains be assimilated to alternatives under discussion. The basic idea I want to explore involves separating the introduction of a quantificational operator into a discourse from the introduction of the quantificational domain, thus allowing the domain to be fixed nonlocally. To help sketch out the proposal I will present a logic which syntacticizes some of the distinctions I want the semantics to make. But the real work lies in making semantically precise a notion of context which separates alternatives under consideration from informational state.

To illustrate the novel syntactic feature of the new logic, which I will call RL (for Restriction Logic), consider a candidate sentence:

(8) $x \mid (\mathrm{boy}(x))$; $y \mid (\mathrm{Hardy\text{-}boy\text{-}mystery}(y))$; most $x[\exists y\ \mathrm{read}(x,y)]$

This gives a rough representation for something like *most boys have read a Hardy boy mystery*. It can be glossed roughly as follows: in the environment in which x is restricted to range over boys and y is restricted to range over Hardy boy mysteries, assert

most $x\ [\exists y\ \mathrm{read}(x,y)]$

For the moment, $x \mid \phi$ may be read as meaning, "Change the alternatives under consideration to those in which x satisfies ϕ."

With respect to the analysis of English, the general idea is that each noun phrase will be split into a restrictor component and an operator. This includes indefinites. Thus, the intended representation of *A boy walks*, for example, is:

(9) $y \mid \mathrm{boy}(y)$; $\exists y[\mathrm{walk}(y)]$

Note that this separation of operator and restrictor is standard for adverbial quantification:

(10)   When Mary goes to the movies, she   always   takes John.
                                          usually

This syntactic separation even occurs for noun phrases in the case of some phenomena like quantifier-float, which is far more robust in a language like Japanese than English.

The notation above will be familiar to some readers. This proposal resurrects the notion of restricted variable explored in Gawron and Peters (1990), but RL departs syntactically in allowing restrictions to restrict more than one variable at a time. As we will see, this is because a variable restriction is intended to capture the general notion of alternatives under discussion. Because of the interactions of focus and quantification and phenomena like multiple foci, restrictions might need to be polyadic.

RL will require a context with two pieces. The piece incorporating alternatives under discussion I will call the environment, because it will resemble a variable environment. The piece incorporating what is known I will call the information-state, because it is an information-state as defined in Section 2.1. The intention is that a restricted variable updates the environment part of the context and has no effect on the information-state.

In RL, sentences will denote functions from contexts to contexts, and a context will be a pair $\langle E, S \rangle$ consisting of an environment E and an information state S. The first step in moving from DLF to RL, then, is redefining D_t, using a new domain D_E (the set of environments) and D_S (the same set of states as before).

2.2.1 New D_t for RL

Let

$$D_E = D_S^I$$

Then

$$D_t = (D_E \times D_S)^{(D_E \times D_S)}$$

In Restriction Logic, environments will be functions from variables to information states. The main reason is that environments are going to keep track of what information functions as a restrictor on a variable, but *no other information about that variable*. The following sentences will involve the same variables with the same conditions placed on them:

(11) a. Every farmer beats a donkey who hates him.
      b. Every farmer who is hated by a donkey beats it.

Yet the sentences have different domains of quantification, and different truth-conditions. The difference will be due to the fact that the quantificational environments are different.

So we need a notion of environment which has enough structure to keep track of which conditions restrict the set of alternatives being considered for each variable and which are simply other conditions on them.

An important point is that being incorporated into the environment has no existential import. To give an example:

(12) $x \mid \text{boy}(x); y \mid \text{Hardy-boy-mystery}(y); \text{no } y \; [\forall \; x \; \text{read}(x,y)]$

This might be the most natural reading for *No Hardy boy mystery was read by every boy*. Notice that this sentence ought to come out true in a world in which there are no books. When a restricted variable such as $x \mid \text{boy}(x)$ is evaluated in a context, the correct interpretation is simply that alternative boys are under discussion. But there may be actually no boys allowed by the information-state when the dust has settled.

A related point is that the fact that a variable is restricted in the environment will not in itself license anaphoric uses of that variable. This is how variables have scope in RL. Even if a variable is defined in the environment, a quantificational operator on that variable is still required to "activate" the alternatives in which that variable is instantiated. Thus, under the semantics given in the next section

(13) $y \mid \text{boy}(y)$; walk(y)

will denote a context-change function that is undefined for any context in which y is not in the domain of the *information-state*. The intended representation for *A boy walks* is not (13) but (9).

Domain of quantification relations differ from anaphoric relations and may extend beyond the scope of an operator (as the effect of the quantification *Few Harbor seal in California* persists beyond the scope of *few* in (1)). Thus, variables will remain in the environment even after they have been captured by quantifiers, and even when those operators fall under the scope of other operators. The chief effect of variables in the environment will be to affect future quantifications. This is another reason why being an environment variable can have no existential import.

In effect, variables in the environment can be understood as variables pending quantification. The main point of this syntactic change is to make it possible to restrict a variable in more than one way. The plan for the rest of this paper is to sketch the technical details of a proposal in Section 2.3 and then to return to the examples of Section 1 in Sections 3 and 3.3.

2.3   *Syntax and semantics of restriction logic*

We need to make two revisions to the syntax of DLF to give us the sentences we need in Restriction Logic (RL). First we need to change the syntax of determiners. Next, we need to license restricted variables as expressions of type *t*. The rest of the syntax can remain as before. We present the revised and new rules, numbering so as to be consistent with the numbering of Section 2.1.

2.3.1   *Syntax of RL (Revised Rules Only)*

10. If $\alpha \in \text{ME}_{det}$, $\psi \in \text{ME}_t$, and $\beta \in \text{ME}_i$, then $\alpha\beta(\psi) \in \text{ME}_i$;
11. If $\phi \in \text{ME}_t$, and $\beta_1, \ldots \beta_n \in \text{ME}_i$, then $\beta_1, \ldots \beta_n \mid (\psi) \in \text{ME}_t$.

We are now ready to provide the semantics for RL. As noted above, in RL, the denotations of expressions of type t are functions from contexts to contexts, where contexts are pairs of environments and information-states. The interpretation will, as in DLF, be a truth value, but interpretations in RL will be relative to environments and assignments.

We will define two new concepts to give the semantics of RL, a relation on assignments $\odot$ (read as "is compatible with"), and $\wedge$, an operation on states (read as "greatest lower bound of"):

1. $f \odot g$ if and only if there exists h such that $h \geq f$ and $h \geq g$.
2. $S_1 \wedge S_2 = \{f \mid \text{Dom}(f) = \text{Dom}(S_1) \cup \text{Dom}(S_2)$ and there exists $g \in S_1$, $g' \in S_2$ and $f \geq g$ and $f \geq g'.\}$

We present versions of the revised rules, with appropriate numbering.

2.3.2 Semantics of RL (Revised Rules)

1. a. If $\alpha \in \text{ME}_i \cup \text{ME}_e \cup \text{ME}_{\langle e,t \rangle} \cup \text{ME}_{\langle e,e,t \rangle}$ then $[\![\alpha]\!]^M = F(\alpha)$.
   b. If $\alpha \in \text{ME}_e \cup \text{ME}_{\langle e,t \rangle} \cup \text{ME}_{\langle e,e,t \rangle}$ then $[\![\alpha]\!]^{M,f,E} = [\![\alpha]\!]^M$.
   c. If $\alpha \in \text{ME}_i$ then $[\![\alpha]\!]^{M,f,E} = f([\![\alpha]\!])$.

2. If $\alpha \in \text{ME}_{\langle e,t \rangle}$ and $\beta \in \text{ME}_e \cup \text{ME}_i$, then $[\![\alpha(\beta)]\!]^M$ is that function in D_t such that

$$\langle E,S \rangle [\![\alpha(\beta)]\!]^M = \langle E,S' \rangle$$
$$S' = \{f \mid f \in S \text{ and } [\![\beta]\!]^{M,f,E} \in [\![\alpha]\!]^M\}$$
if and only if
if $\beta \in \text{ME}_i$, then $[\![\beta]\!]^M \in \text{Dom}(S)$;
else undefined.

3. If $\alpha \in \text{ME}_{\langle e,e,t \rangle}$ and $\beta \in \text{ME}_e \cup \text{ME}_i$, and $\gamma \in \text{ME}_e \cup \text{ME}_i$, then $[\![\alpha(\beta,\gamma)]\!]^M$ is that function in D_t such that

$$\langle E,S \rangle [\![\alpha(\beta,\gamma)]\!]^M = \langle E,S' \rangle$$
$$S' = \{f \mid f \in S \text{ and } \langle [\![\beta]\!]^{M,f,E}, [\![\gamma]\!]^{M,f,E} \rangle \in [\![\alpha]\!]^M\}$$
if and only if
if $\beta \in \text{ME}_i$, then $[\![\beta]\!]^M \in \text{Dom}(S)$;
if $\gamma \in \text{ME}_i$, then $[\![\gamma]\!]^M \in \text{Dom}(S)$;
else undefined.

4. If $\phi, \psi \in \text{ME}_t$ then $[\![\phi;\psi]\!]^M$ is $[\![\psi]\!]^M \circ [\![\phi]\!]^M$.
5. If $\phi \in \text{ME}_t$ and $\beta \in \text{ME}_i$, then $[\![\exists\beta(\phi)]\!]^M$ is that function in D_t such that

$$\langle E,S \rangle [\![\exists\beta(\phi)]\!]^M = \langle E,S' \rangle$$
$$S' = S'' \wedge E([\![\beta]\!]^M) \text{ and } S'' = S^{+[\![\beta]\!]^M}[\![\phi]\!]^M$$

if and only if $[\![\beta]\!]^{\mathcal{M}} \in \mathrm{Dom}(E)$ and $[\![\beta]\!]^{\mathcal{M}} \notin \mathrm{Dom}(S)$;
else undefined.

Note that we have revised existentials to require that they be defined in the environment and revised the semantics to incorporate the information from the environment.

The well-definedness or felicity requirements are of interest. In RL, all quantification is required to be over variables in the environment; that is, a quantificational domain must be defined. This is the $[\![\beta]\!]^{\mathcal{M}} \in \mathrm{Dom}(E)$ requirement. In general in RL, one quantification can reuse the variable of another quantification, acquiring its restrictions (see Sections 3.1 and 3.3). Since indefinites update the domain of the information-state, the requirement that $[\![\beta]\!]^{\mathcal{M}} \notin \mathrm{Dom}(S)$ prevents the re-use of indefinite variables, or loosely speaking, referential variables, for quantification. This requirement is what captures the contrast between the discourses in example (1).

6. a. If $\psi \in \mathrm{ME}_t$ and $\beta \in \mathrm{ME}_i$, then $[\![\forall \beta(\psi)]\!]$ is that function in D_t such that

$\langle E,S \rangle \ [\![\forall \beta(\psi)]\!]^{\mathcal{M}} = \langle E,S' \rangle$
$S' = \{f \mid f \in S$ and every assignment g such that $g = \backslash_{[\![\beta]\!]^{\mathcal{M}}} f$ and such that there exists $g' \odot g$, $g' \in E([\![\beta]\!]^{\mathcal{M}})$, is such that for every assignment $h \odot g$, if $h \in E([\![\beta]\!]^{\mathcal{M}})$, then there exists $h' \geq h$ such that $h' \in$ Info-State $(\langle E,E([\![\beta]\!]^{\mathcal{M}}) \wedge S \rangle [\![\psi]\!]^{\mathcal{M}})\}$
if and only if $[\![\beta]\!]^{\mathcal{M}} \in \mathrm{Dom}(E)$ and $[\![\beta]\!]^{\mathcal{M}} \notin \mathrm{Dom}(S)$;
else undefined.

Here $E([\![\beta]\!]^{\mathcal{M}})$ retrieves the state containing the domain information on the indeterminate $[\![\beta]\!]^{\mathcal{M}}$; modulo the fact that the variable restrictions on β have potentially been collected at different points in the discourse, it returns essentially the same information as $S[\![\phi]\!]^{\mathcal{M}}$ in the semantic definition for $\forall$ in DLF. Similarly, given that the function Info-State retrieves the information-state from the environment/information-state pair,

Info-State$(\langle E,E([\![\beta]\!]^{\mathcal{M}}) \wedge S \rangle [\![\psi]\!]^{\mathcal{M}})$

returns essentially the same information as

$S[\![\phi]\!]^{\mathcal{M}}[\![\psi]\!]^{\mathcal{M}}$

in the semantics for $\forall$ in DLF.

  b. If $\psi \in \mathrm{ME}_t$ and $\beta \in \mathrm{ME}_i$, then $[\![\mathrm{no}\ \beta(\psi)]\!]$ is that function in D_t such that

$\langle E,S \rangle [\![\mathrm{no}\ \beta(\psi)]\!]^{\mathcal{M}} = \langle E,S' \rangle$
$S' = \{f \mid f \in S$ and no assignment g such that $g = \backslash_{[\![\beta]\!]^{\mathcal{M}}} f$ and

such that there exists $g' \odot g$, $g' \in E([\![\beta]\!]^{\mathcal{M}})$, is such that there exists an assignment $h' \geq g$ such that $h \in$ Info-State($\langle E, E([\![\beta]\!]^{\mathcal{M}}) \wedge S\rangle [\![\psi]\!]^{\mathcal{M}}$}

if and only if $[\![\beta]\!]^{\mathcal{M}} \in \text{Dom}(E)$ and $[\![\beta]\!]^{\mathcal{M}} \notin \text{Dom}(S)$;
else undefined.

c. If $\psi \in ME_t$ and $\beta \in ME_{i}$, then $[\![\text{most } \beta(\psi)]\!]$ is that function in D_t such that

$$\langle E, S\rangle [\![\text{most } \beta(\psi)]\!]^{\mathcal{M}} = \langle E, S'\rangle$$

$S' = \{f \mid f \in S$ and most assignments g such that $g = \backslash_{[\![\beta]\!]^{\mathcal{M}}} f$ and such that there exists $g' \odot g$, $g' \in E([\![\beta]\!]^{\mathcal{M}})$ are such that for every assignment $h \odot g$, if $h \in E([\![\beta]\!]^{\mathcal{M}})$, then there exists $h' \geq h$ such that $h' \in$ Info-State($\langle E, E([\![\beta]\!]^{\mathcal{M}}) \wedge S\rangle [\![\psi]\!]^{\mathcal{M}}$)}

if and only if $[\![\beta]\!]^{\mathcal{M}} \in \text{Dom}(E)$ and $[\![\beta]\!]^{\mathcal{M}} \notin \text{Dom}(S)$;
else undefined.

7. If $\alpha \in ME_t$, then $[\![\alpha]\!]^{\mathcal{M},f,E}$ is defined if and only if there is an S such that $f \in S$ and $S[\![\alpha]\!]^{\mathcal{M}}$ is defined. If $[\![\alpha]\!]^{\mathcal{M},f,E}$ is defined, then $[\![\alpha]\!]^{\mathcal{M},f,E} = 1$ if and only if there is an S such that $f \in \langle E, S\rangle [\![\alpha]\!]^{\mathcal{M}}$; otherwise $[\![\alpha]\!]^{\mathcal{M},f,E} = 0$.

8. If $\phi \in ME_t$ and $\beta_1 \ldots \beta_n \in ME_{i}$, then $[\![\beta_1 \ldots \beta_n \mid (\phi)]\!]^{\mathcal{M}}$ is that function in D_t such that $\langle E, S\rangle [\![\beta_1 \ldots \beta_n \mid (\phi)]\!]^{\mathcal{M}} = \langle E', S\rangle$, where

E' is that function in D_E such that $\text{Dom}(E') = \text{Dom}(E) \cup \{[\![\beta_1]\!]^{\mathcal{M}} \ldots [\![\beta_n]\!]^{\mathcal{M}}\}$ and such that for all indeterminates i, if $i \in \{[\![\beta_1]\!]^{\mathcal{M}} \ldots [\![\beta_n]\!]^{\mathcal{M}}\}$, and if

$$S^{\text{rest}} = \text{Info-State}(\langle E, S^{+[\![\beta_1]\!]^{\mathcal{M}} \ldots [\![\beta_n]\!]^{\mathcal{M}}}\rangle [\![\phi]\!]^{\mathcal{M}}),$$

then

$E'(i) = \{f \mid$ There exists g, $f \geq g$, $g \in S^{\text{rest}}$. If $i \in \text{Dom}(E)$, then there exists g', $f \geq g'$, $g' \in E(i)$ and $\text{Dom}(f) = \text{Dom}(S^{\text{rest}}) \cup \text{Dom}(E(i))$. Otherwise $\text{Dom}(f) = \text{Dom}(S^{\text{rest}})\}$.

If $i \notin \{[\![\beta_1]\!]^{\mathcal{M}} \ldots [\![\beta_n]\!]^{\mathcal{M}}\}$, then $E'(i) = E(i)$. If E' is undefined for any element in $\{[\![\beta_1]\!]^{\mathcal{M}} \ldots [\![\beta_n]\!]^{\mathcal{M}}\}$, then $\langle E, S\rangle [\![\beta_i \ldots \beta_n \mid (\phi)]\!]^{\mathcal{M}}$ is undefined.

It is instructive to compare Semantic clause 6 for RL directly with semantic clause 6 for DLF to see that as far as the semantics of operators goes, the move to Restriction Logic is not very profound technically. Instead of giving the semantics for $\forall \beta(\phi, \psi)$, we give the semantics for $\forall \beta(\psi)$. Since all the information that used to be in the restrictor ϕ is now in the environment E, we just replace each reference to $S[\![\phi]\!]^{\mathcal{M}}$ in the old semantics with a slightly more verbose reference to $E([\![\beta]\!]^{\mathcal{M}})$ in the new semantics. In Section 3.3, we will revise the semantics of quantificational operators so as to handle a wider range of phenomena, but the basic task of making quantificational domains dynamic is accomplished through the changes above.

The real action in RL is Clause 8, the definition of how an environment is updated by a restricted variable. The key point to note there is that a restriction just *updates* the information on a variable x. Any previous information placed there by a previous restriction on x is conserved. This is what will allow for non-local effects on quantificational domains.

3 Dynamic Domains of Quantification

We now turn to exploring the treatment of the examples in Section 1 in RL.

3.1 *Dependent domains of quantification*

The effect of the semantics of RL is that any number of restrictions may be placed on a variable at any point in an ongoing discourse. When that variable is quantified away by an operator, all the restrictions taken together define the quantificational domain.

To illustrate the central feature of Restriction Logic that plays a role in accounting for the examples of Section 1, we turn first to (1a) repeated here as (14).

> (14) Few harbor seals in California live long. Most pups die in the first few weeks of life.

> (15) $x \mid (\text{harbor-seal}(x); \text{in } (x, \text{california}))$; few x [live-long(x)];
> $y \leftarrow x$;
> $y \mid (\text{pup}(y))$; most y [die-in-first-month(y)];

A new operator is introduced into (15). This operator needs to update the environment as follows:

> (16) $\langle E_I, S_I \rangle [\![\beta_1 \leftarrow \beta_2]\!]^{\mathcal{M}} = \langle E, S_I \rangle$
> where
> E is that function in D^E such that $\text{Dom}(E) = \text{Dom}(E_I) \cup \{[\![\beta_1]\!]^{\mathcal{M}}\}$ and
> for all indeterminates i, if $i = [\![\beta_1]\!]^{\mathcal{M}}$, then
> $E(i) = \{f \mid \exists g \in E_I([\![\beta_2]\!]^{\mathcal{M}})$ and $f = \backslash [\![\beta_2]\!]^{\mathcal{M}} g$ and $[\![\beta_2]\!]^{\mathcal{M},g,E} = [\![\beta_1]\!]^{\mathcal{M},f,E}\}$;
> and if $i \neq [\![\beta_1]\!]$, then $E(i) = E_I(i)$. If $[\![\beta_2]\!]^{\mathcal{M}} \notin \text{Dom}(E_I)$, then $\langle E_I, S_I \rangle$
> $[\![\beta_1 \leftarrow \beta_2]\!]^{\mathcal{M}}$ is undefined.

The $\leftarrow$ operator is essentially a copying operator that adds a new variable y with all the restrictions of x. The variable y may now be restricted in turn to subsets of the restrictions on x. In this case y is restricted to pups.

The treatment of this discourse dependency is *indirect* rather than *direct*. That is, rather than re-using an old variable, a new variable is related to an old variable. Thus, the dependency is treated more like the dependency of the definite in:

(17)   The performance was a complete disaster. The audience was leaving by the end of the first act.

Here *the first act* in question is the first act of the performance. A new variable is related to an old variable by a pragmatically inferred relation.

I think it makes sense to regard the ← -operator as pragmatic glue. That is, the meaning of the second sentence of (14) is:

(18) $y \,|\, (\text{pup}(y))$; most y [die-in-first-month(y)];

Whether y is understood as dependent on another quantifier depends on whether (18) is evaluated in a context that sets up that dependency.

One might think that it would make sense to treat (14) directly, to re-use x and dispense with the ← -operator. In fact, nothing in RL prevents such a re-use; but this is not what is going on in general in quantificational dependency:

(19)   Few Harbor Seals in California live long. Most males die in their first year. Most females die before the end of their second.

Clearly the same variable couldn't be used to handle both the second and third sentences in a linear discourse, since disjoint subsets are invoked.

Example (19) is a good illustration of how quantificational domains may not be monotonically narrowed as one proceeds through a discourse. Constraints such as maleness may be added, then lifted. Such cases can be handled with the ← -operator, as long as there is a point in the discourse to which one can back up where all the constraints to be kept in force are in force and none of the constraints to be dropped are yet in force. But this is not always the case. Sometimes, in conversation, certain domain constraints are dropped while others are simultaneously preserved:

(20)   Show me night-time flights from Boston to Denver. [After some more conversation]. Show me daytime flights.

Here, the intended interpretation of *daytime flights* is *daytime flights from Boston to Denver*. Thus this domain of quantification is still parasitic on previous discourse. The night-time constraint has been over-ruled, but others have been retained. At no point in the discourse is there an NP that introduces exactly the set of constraints that stay in effect throughout the dialogue (flights from Boston to Denver), so the ← -operator can't help here. What's going on is something apparently nonmonotonic: domain constraints are in effect unless they are explicitly over-ruled. Night-time is inconsistent with daytime, so it counts as over-ruling it.

For cases like these, some form of accommodation of a quantificational domain via minimal revision of an existing one is required. However, this does not necessarily mean that a monotonic account of discourse processing needs to be abandoned. A reasonable guess is that some sort of focusing of properties is at issue in (20). If the property *night time* is focused in the first sentence of (20), yielding a range of properties of flights from Boston to Denver at different times of day, then the property *daytime* may function as a contrast to it, and select the daytime property from that range. I leave this as topic for future research.

3.2 Focus

In what follows we will assume, with Rooth, that the effect of focus is primarily presuppositional. There are a variety of ways one might implement this idea, but given that we are illustrating some semantic ideas here through a logical notation, the easiest way is to introduce presupposition into our dynamic system through a logical operator. To this end, we borrow ∂, the presupposition operator of Beaver (1992). The semantics of ∂ is quite simple; it is a "test" operator which tests whether the information of its operand is already available in context.

> If $\phi \in ME_t$, then $[\![\partial\phi]\!]^M$ is that function in D_t such that $\langle E,S\rangle[\![\partial\phi]\!]^M = \langle E,S\rangle$ if and only if $\langle E,S\rangle[\![\phi]\!]^M = \langle E,S\rangle$. Otherwise, $\langle E,S\rangle[\![\partial\phi]\!]^M$ is undefined.

To illustrate how this would work, we begin with a case of focus without quantification, as in say, *Tom loves Jane*, on readings on which *Tom* and *Jane*, respectively, are focus. Along with Rooth (1992), we assume an anaphoric account, on which each occurrence of focus introduces some specific pragmatically bound variable into discourse. Unlike Rooth, for an individual level focus, we assume an individual level variable, x in (21):

(21)   (a) *Tom* as Focus: $\partial(x \mid \text{love}(x,j))$; love$(t,j)$
       (b) *Jane* as Focus: $\partial(x \mid \text{love}(t,x))$; love$(t,j)$

What is asserted is the same in both cases. The difference lies only in the presupposition. In each case, what Partee (1991b) calls the focus frame is in the environment, restricting a variable about which no assertion is made.[4]

The expression in (21a) is only well-defined if evaluated against an environment in which x is already constrained to range over entities that love Jane. The expression in (21b) is only well-defined if evaluated against an environment in which x is already constrained to range over entities that Tom loves. The presupposition is not existential; it is merely a presupposition about the environment of "alternatives under consideration" in the discourse.

As an example of the interaction of focus and quantification, we return to an example taken from Rooth (1985).

(22) Mary always took John to the movies.

The semantics of the sentence involves quantifying over something like events or situations in the sentence. We will use the second term, which is usually taken to have a broader sense, but we will take a very simple, Davidsonian-style implementation of situations, since this will suffice for our purposes. Thus, as in event quantifications like (23), we will introduce situations as extra arguments of lexical relations. On this picture, the rough semantics for the two readings is:

(23) a. $\partial(x \mid \text{take-to-movie}(m,x,e))$; $\forall e[\text{take-to-movie}(m,j,e)]$
      b. $\partial(x \mid \text{take-to-movie}(x,j,e))$; $\forall e[\text{take-to-movie}(m,j,e)]$

In (a), the alternatives under consideration in the discourse must constrain x to be an entity that Mary takes to the movies in e; in (b), x must be an entity that takes John to the movies.

What kind of discourses will satisfy the presuppositional requirements of (23)? The simplest cases are those in which the following variable restrictions have been introduced:

(24) a. $x, e \mid \text{take-to-movie}(m,x,e)$
      b. $x, e \mid \text{take-to movie}(x,j,e)$

Restriction (a) will give the reading on which we are quantifying over events in which there is some x that Mary takes to the movies; restriction (b), the reading on which we are quantifying over events in which there is some x that takes John to the movies. The presuppositional requirements of the two focus possibilities can also be satisfied by *stronger* restrictions, as illustrated in the following sentences, in which the event restrictions are overt:

(25) a. Whenever Mary took someone to the movies in Boston, she always took JOHN to the movies.
      b. Whenever someone took John to the movies in Boston, MARY always took him to the movies.

Assuming the main clauses receive the semantics in (23) in these two cases, the stronger restrictions of (25a) and (25b) will pass the presuppositional test imposed by ∂.

In sum, the presuppositional requirements of focus are always analyzed as requirements on the quantificational environment of a discourse. In the case in which focus interacts with an overt quantification, as in (22), that requirement can be satisfied either overtly as in (25), or by accommodation of restrictions like those in (24).

3.3   *Quantificational subordination*

We turn now to the treatment of quantificational subordination, using (26), a simplified version of (3):

(26)   a. Every fall Henrik rents a car. He usually takes it on the ferry.
       b. Usually *e*, Henrik rents a car *x* in fall in *e*, Henrik takes *x* on the ferry in *e*.

In (26b), we see a rough representation of the relevant reading of the second sentence in this discourse: the quantification is over events of the type introduced in the first sentence, events in which Henrik rents a car in fall. The most straightforward RL representation of the two sentences in (26a) is:

(27)   a. f | (fall(f)); c | (car(c)); $\forall f$ [$\exists c(\exists_2 s$ rent(h,c,s); in (s,f))]
       b. most s[take-on-ferry(h,c,s)]

Note that we have employed a new operator, $\exists_2$ here. We need to guarantee that

$\exists_2 s$[rent(h,c,s)]

will be well defined even in a context in which s is not in the environment. Thus, $\exists_2$ is just a version of $\exists$ which doesn't presuppose its variable is in the environment:

If $\phi \in ME_t$ and $\beta \in ME_i$, then $[\![\exists_2\beta(\phi)]\!]^{\mathcal{M}}$ is that function in D_t such that $\langle E,S\rangle[\![\exists_2\beta(\psi)]\!]^{\mathcal{M}} = \langle E',S'\rangle$

$E' = \text{Environment}(\langle E,S\rangle[\![\beta \mid \phi]\!]^{\mathcal{M}})$
$S' = S'' \wedge E([\![\beta]\!]^{\mathcal{M}})$ and $S'' = S^{+[\![\beta]\!]^{\mathcal{M}}}[\![\phi]\!]^{\mathcal{M}}$

Here Environment is just the companion function to Info-State, a function which returns the first or environment member of a context pair.

However, even with $\exists_2$, (27) won't do. The problem with (27a) is that even though $\exists_2$ updates the environment, there is no possibility that it can have any effect on the outermost environment, and thus there is no way s can help provide a quantificational domain for the quantification in (26b). This is because $\exists_2$ in (27a) is under the scope $\forall$ and $\exists$. Note how the semantics for $\forall$ is defined in RL:

If $\psi \in ME_t$ and $\beta \in ME_i$, then $[\![\forall\beta(\psi)]\!]$ is that function in D_t such that $\langle E,S\rangle[\![\forall\beta(\psi)]\!]^{\mathcal{M}} = \langle E,S'\rangle$, where

$S' = \{f \mid \text{and etcetera} \ldots\}$

Note that while S is updated to S', E is left unchanged; therefore, according to this semantics, nothing inside the scope of a universal can have any effect on the environment outside the scope.

One of the interesting possibilities opened up by RL is that it makes sense to experiment with changing this. Therefore let us propose a second version of RL, RL', in which $\exists_2$ is included and the following is the semantics for the universal:

(28) If $\psi \in ME_t$ and $\beta \in ME_i$, then $[\![\forall\beta(\psi)]\!]$ is that function in D_t such that $\langle E,S\rangle[\![\forall\beta(\psi)]\!]^{\mathcal{M}} = \langle E',S'\rangle$, where

> $E' = \text{Environment } (\langle E,S''\rangle[\![\psi]\!]^{\mathcal{M}})$, where
> $S'' = S \wedge E \,([\![\beta]\!]^{\mathcal{M}})$ and
> $S' = \{\, f \mid f \in S \text{ and every assignment } g \text{ such that } g = \backslash {}_{[\beta]^{\mathcal{M}}} f \text{ and }$
> such that there exists $g' \odot g$, $g' \in E([\![\beta]\!]^{\mathcal{M}})$ is such that
> for every assignment $h \geq g$, if $h \in S''$, then there exists
> $h' \geq h$ such that $h' \in \text{Info-State}(\langle E,S''\rangle[\![\psi]\!]^{\mathcal{M}})\}$
> if and only if $[\![\beta]\!]^{\mathcal{M}} \in \text{Dom}(E)$ and $[\![\beta]\!]^{\mathcal{M}} \notin \text{Dom}(S)$;
> else undefined.

Thus, we propose to update the environment of a universal quantification with whatever updates its scope makes relative to an information-state, S'', which is just like the input information-state S, except that it incorporates the information of the restriction on the quantified variable, β. We do likewise for the other determiners and for $\exists$ as well. The net result is that each quantification can greatly expand the set of quantificational alternatives available to the discourse; how greatly will depend on what happens in its scope. But none of those alternatives are realized in the information-state until some other operator (like the "most" in (27)) comes along to activate them.

Since the semantics of $\exists$ is directly involved in (27), we present the revised clause for that operator as well:

(29) If $\psi \in ME_t$ and $\beta \in ME_i$, then $[\![\exists\beta(\psi)]\!]^{\mathcal{M}}$ is that function in D_t such that $\langle E,S\rangle[\![\exists\beta(\psi)]\!]^{\mathcal{M}} = \langle E',S'\rangle$, where

> $E' = \text{Environment}(\langle E,S''\rangle[\![\psi]\!]^{\mathcal{M}})$, where
> $S'' = S \wedge E([\![\beta]\!]^{\mathcal{M}})$ and
> $S' = \text{Info-State}(\langle E,S''\rangle[\![\psi]\!]^{\mathcal{M}})$
> if and only if $[\![\beta]\!]^{\mathcal{M}} \in \text{Dom}(E)$ and $[\![\beta]\!]^{\mathcal{M}} \notin \text{Dom}(S)$;
> else undefined.

The effect of these two changes is that (27a) now does what we would like to the environment which follows. It updates the environment with a restriction on s that it be an event in which Henrik rents a car in some fall. If we interpret a subsequent event quantification, such as that in (26b), as a quantification over the same s, we are now restricted to s's in which Henrik rents some car c; since we also reuse c in the scope of the quantification of (26b), that c is restricted to be a car rented by Henrik in some fall.

RL' would seem to be the opening of a Pandora's box. Now quantificational domains set within the scope of other quantifications are freed to roam through the discourse. But it is not quite as unconstrained as one might think. Consider:

> (30)   a. Henrik rented a car. He usually takes it on the ferry.
>   b. $c \mid (\text{car}(c)); [\exists c \, \exists_2 s \, \text{rent}(h,c,s)]; \text{most } s \, (\text{take-on-ferry}(h,c,s))$

The indicated semantics is apparently what would be required for an interpretation on which most of Henrik's car-rentings involve a car involved in instances of Henrik's ferry-taking, that is a reading quantifying over renting-occasions in which different cars could be taken on the ferry on different renting-occasions. But this interpretation is not possible for the discourse in (30). As has often been observed, quantificational subordination seems to require two quantifications operating in concert, as the $\forall$ and the *most*-determiner do in (27). It turns out that (30b) is not well-defined in RL'. This is because of the felicity requirement on all quantifications that $\beta \notin S$. That is, quantification over variables introduced by previous existentials is out. Thus, the quantification of the *most*-operator ranging over s in (30b) is precluded. The reason the analogue in (27b) is not precluded is that the existential introducing the situation variable s in (27a) is under the scope of a universal; thus $s \notin S$ is not in the information-state when the *most*-determiner is evaluated against $\langle E,S \rangle$.

4   Conclusion

We have explored a proposal in which quantificational operators are separated from quantificational domain setters in a dynamic system. The main idea was to let quantificational domains for the same variable be set more than once so that non-local domain effects could be given a dynamic treatment. We have tried to show that this idea offers illuminating ways of looking at pragmatic quantificational domain effects, interactions of focus and quantification, and quantificational subordination.

NOTES

1   The use of the term "indeterminate" in this connection is Barwise's. He suggests in Chapter 12 of Barwise (1989b) that indeterminates be thought of as unknown objects, and draws an analogy with the adjunction of a set of indeterminates to the real numbers in giving an algebraic account of the theory of equations.

2 $f \circ g$ is the function composition of f and g:

$$f \circ g(x) = f(g(x)).$$

3 We use $g = \backslash_x f$, to mean that g is exactly like f except possibly in the assignment to x.

4 I will have nothing to say about how such a focus frame could be produced compositionally, but in dealing with the semantics of focus, (Rooth 1985) and (Krifka 1991a) both give fairly concrete proposals which involve arranging the compositional semantics so as to get hold of something similar at some stage of interpretation. Gawron (1992) and Pulman (1992) take a somewhat different line, using higher-order unification.

V Focus, Presupposition and Negation

10 Focus

MATS ROOTH

1 Phenomena

The term *focus* is used here to describe prosodic prominences serving pragmatic and semantic functions such as those surveyed below.[1] Following Jackendoff (1972) and most studies on focus in generative grammar, I will assume that focus is marked as a feature on phrases in a syntactic description, a feature which is to have both a semantic/pragmatic and phonological/phonetic interpretation. In most examples discussed below, the focus correlates with a prominent and readily perceptible pitch accent within the focused phrase. However, I wish to leave open the possibility that focus may have other phonological and/or phonetic correlates, perhaps sometimes in the absence of pitch accent.

1.1 Question-answer congruence

The position of focus in an answer correlates with the questioned position in *wh*-questions, and the position of disjoined alternatives in alternative questions. In the following diagram, the solid lines link appropriate question-answer pairs; the diagonal pairings are inappropriate.

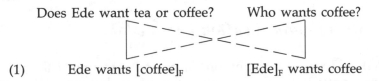

Does Ede want tea or coffee?   Who wants coffee?

(1)   Ede wants [coffee]$_F$ [Ede]$_F$ wants coffee

In the answers, the feature F indicates which phrase is focused. The feature is syntactic rather than phonological or phonetic. Thus while (2b) and (2d) have different syntactic representations – since the F feature is in different places –

I leave open the question whether their phonological representations need be different.

(2)   a. What is Ede doing?
    b. He's [buying coffee]$_F$.
    c. What is Ede buying?
    d. He's buying [coffee]$_F$.

1.2   Focusing adverbs

John introduced Bill and Tom to Sue, and there were no other introductions. In these circumstances, the first sentence below is false, and the second one true.

(3)   a. John only introduced [Bill]$_F$ to Sue.
    b. John only introduced Bill to [Sue]$_F$.

Since the variants differ only in the location of focus, focus has a truth-conditional effect in the context of *only*. In a situation where John introduced Bill to Sue and Jane and there were no other introductions, the truth values are reversed, so that the first sentence is true, and the second false.

With other focusing adverbs, the effect is presuppositional. In the examples below, the focusing adverbs, in combination with the focus on [$_{NP}$Bill], introduce a presupposition that a proposition of the form "John introduced x to Sue", where x is not Bill, is true. Or equivalently, John introduced someone other than Bill to Sue.

(4)   a. John also introduced [Bill]$_F$ to Sue.
    b. John introduced [Bill]$_F$ to Sue, too.
    c. John even introduced [Bill]$_F$ to Sue.

With *even*, there is an additional presupposition along the lines of John introducing Bill to Sue being less likely than his introducing other people to Sue.

1.3   Adverbs of quantification and modals

A bank clerk escorting a ballerina (in the Saint Petersburg of the relevant period) runs counter to the first generalization below, but not the second.

(5)   a. In Saint Petersburg, [officers]$_F$ always escorted ballerinas.
    b. In Saint Petersburg, officers always escorted [ballerinas]$_F$.

Similarly, a bank clerk escorting a ballerina would violate the first rule of etiquette below, but not the second, and an officer escorting a journalist would violate the second rule but not the first.

(6) a. Officers$_F$ must escort ballerinas.
     b. Officers must escort ballerinas$_F$.

Along similar lines, Halliday (1967) noted the rather different impact of the following regulations imposed on passengers in the London underground:

(7) a. Shóes must be worn.
     b. Dógs must be cárried.

If you bring along no dog at all, you obey the second regulation, but if you bring no shoes at all, you violate the first. If you carry one dog and bring another one on a leash, you violate the second regulation. But if you wear one pair of shoes and carry another pair in a shopping bag, you obey the first.

The proper assignment of focus features in Halliday's examples is not entirely clear; one idea is that (7b) has a focus on the verb phrase [$_{VP}$ carried], while (7a) has no focus at all, or focus on the entire clause inside the scope of the modal.

1.4   *Reasons and counterfactuals*

In a modified version of a scenario from Dretske (1972), Clyde has been carrying on an intermittent affair with Bertha, an archeologist who is out of the country most of the time, something he is quite satisfied with. But since he finds out that he will inherit a lot of money if he weds before the age of 30, he arranges to marry her, with the view of carrying on their relations as before. Marrying someone else would have involved too much of a commitment. Under these circumstances, the sentences in (8) are true – or at least might well be true. The sentences in (9) are false.

(8) a. The reason Clyde [married]$_F$ Bertha was to qualify for the inheritance.
     b. The reason Clyde married [Bertha]$_F$ was to avoid making too much of a commitment.

(9) a. The reason Clyde married [Bertha]$_F$ was to qualify for the inheritance.
     b. The reason Clyde [married]$_F$ Bertha was to avoid making too much of a commitment.

Similarly, (10a) strikes me as false, while (10b) strikes me as true, though the intuition is a volatile one.

(10)   a. If he hadn't married [Bertha]$_F$, he would not have been eligible
          for the inheritance.
       b. If he hadn't [married]$_F$ Bertha, he would not have been eligible
          for the inheritance.

Dretske discusses a number of other constructions, perhaps all involving underlying counterfactual reasoning.

1.5   *Conversational implicature*

After my roommates Steve and Paul and I took a calculus quiz (which was
graded on the spot), George asked me how it went. In answering with the first
variant below, I suggested that I did no better than passing. In answering with
the second, I would have suggested that Steve and Paul did not pass.

(11)   a. Well, I [passed]$_F$.
       b. Well, [I]$_F$ passed.

The focus-conditioned suggested inferences have the logic of Gricean quantity
implicatures, so-called scalar implicatures: they are derived by comparing what
I actually said to logically stronger things I might have said (that I did very
well, or that Steve and I both passed). For instance, George's reasoning in (11a)
would be that if Mats had done very well on the exam, he would have said
so, and therefore he must have done no better than passing.
   In a modified plot of the film *The Conversation* (Coppola 1973), a private
investigator has been hired by a businessman to eavesdrop on his wife and a
male friend. A conversation is recorded in a noisy park, and in the course of
analyzing the recording, the detective uncovers the sentence:

(12)   He'd kill us if he got the chance.

After delivering the recording to his employer, the detective becomes morti-
fied at the prospect of being responsible for a murder of the young pair by the
businessman. But instead, the businessman is killed. The detective subjects the
recording to some further analysis, uncovering the prosody:

(13)   [He]$_F$'d kill [us]$_F$ if he got the chance.

And so, the intonation suggests, the lovers are justified in killing the businessman. The focus either communicates a conversational implicature on the part
of the speaker (though not a scalar one), or indicates discourse structure in a
way which gives information about other parts of the conversation – parts the
detective was not able to make intelligible.[2]

2 Semantics

> ... contrastive differences ... however one may choose to classify them, are significantly involved in determining the meaning (hence, semantics) of a variety of larger expressions in which they are embedded. If $C(U)$ is a linguistic expression in which U is embedded, and U can be given different contrastive foci (say U_1 and U_2), then it often makes a difference to the meaning of C(U) whether we embed U_1 or U_2. Linguistically, this is important because it means that any adequate semantical theory, one that is capable of exhibiting the semantical differences between complex expressions, between $C(U_1)$ and $C(U_2)$, will have to be provided with resources for distinguishing between U_1 and U_2. (Dretske 1972)

This suggests the following project. We somehow modify our way of modeling the semantics of phrases so that phrases differing in the location of focus have different semantic values. We then state semantic and pragmatic rules for focus-sensitive constructions and discourse configurations in terms of such focus-influenced semantic values.

In the 1980s this program, which amounts to a hypothesis of semantic mediation of focus effects, was developed in proposals which have come to be called the structured meaning semantics and the alternative semantics for focus. In the structured meaning approach, focus has the effect of structuring the propositions denoted by sentences: the focus-influenced semantic value of a clause with a single focus is a pair consisting of (i) a property obtained by abstracting the focused position, and (ii) the semantics of the focused phrase. The semantic values of (14a) and (14b) are (15a) and (15b) respectively.

(14)   a. John introduced [Bill]$_F$ to Sue.
      b. John introduced Bill to [Sue]$_F$.

(15)   a. $\langle \lambda x \ [\textbf{introduce}(j,x,s)], \textbf{b} \rangle$
      b. $\langle \lambda y \ [\textbf{introduce}(j,b,y)], \textbf{s} \rangle$

The property in (15a) is the property of being introduced by John to Sue, and **b** is the individual denoted by *Bill*. The property in (15b) is the property of being a y such that John introduced Bill to y, while **s** is the individual denoted by *Sue*.

In the tradition of generative grammar, structuring as a semantics for focus was first proposed in Jackendoff (1972: 245), but it can be viewed as reconstruction of the notion that intonation can have the effect of dividing a sentence into a psychological predicate and psychological subject (Paul 1880, Wegener 1885) or a theme and rheme (e.g. Daneš 1957).[3]

The utility of structuring in stating semantic and pragmatic rules for focus-sensitive constructions was hinted at by Jackendoff and developed in much more detail in a number of semantically oriented studies, starting with Jacobs (1983) and von Stechow (1985/89). To illustrate how such rules are stated, let us consider the focusing adverb *only*. For simplicity, I will assume that when it is syntactically in auxiliary position, a focusing adverb combines with a structured meaning contributed by the rest of the sentence. Horn's (1969) semantics for *only* dictates the following rule:

(16) *only* combining with the structured meaning $\langle R, \alpha_1 \ldots \alpha_k \rangle$ yields the assertion $\forall x_1 \ldots \forall x_k [R(x_1 \ldots x_k) \rightarrow \langle x_1 \ldots x_k \rangle = \langle \alpha_1 \ldots \alpha_k \rangle]$ together with the presupposition $R(\alpha_1 \ldots \alpha_k)$.

(17) a. $\langle \lambda x\ [\textbf{introduce}(\textbf{j},x,\textbf{s})], \textbf{b} \rangle$
      b. $\forall x\ [\textbf{introduce}(\textbf{j},x,\textbf{s}) \rightarrow x = \textbf{b}]$
      c. $\textbf{introduce}(\textbf{j},\textbf{b},\textbf{s})$

Thus (3a) asserts that John introduced nobody other than Bill to Sue, and presupposes that John introduced Bill to Sue. ((17b) is the assertion, and (17c) is the presupposition.) In this case, there is just one focused phrase, and the left-hand part of the structured meaning in (17a) is a one-place relation.

The rule (16) is stated in terms of a general version of structured meanings which allows for more than one focused phrase: $\alpha_1 \ldots \alpha_k$ is a tuple of one or more semantic values of focused phrases, and R is a relation with a corresponding number of arguments of appropriate semantic type. This allows for several focused phrases associated with a single focusing adverb:

(18) a. John only introduced Bill$_F$ to Sue$_F$
      b. $\langle \lambda x \lambda y\ [\textbf{introduce}(\textbf{j},x,y)], \textbf{b}, \textbf{s} \rangle$
      c. $\forall x_1 \forall x_2\ [\textbf{introduce}(\textbf{j},x_1,x_2) \rightarrow \langle x_1, x_2 \rangle = \langle b, s \rangle]$

A wealth of phenomena have been analyzed in the structured meaning framework; for discussion, see Jacobs (1988), von Stechow (1991), and Krifka (1991a).

2.1 *Alternative semantics*

The basic idea of alternative semantics can be illustrated with the question – answer paradigm. The question [does Ede want tea or coffee] determines the basic answers "Ede wants tea" and "Ede wants coffee".[4] Similarly, focus in the answer [Ede wants [coffee]$_F$] indicates that propositions obtained by making substitutions in the position of the focused phrase – propositions of the form "Ede wants *y*" – are alternatives to the actual answer. Congruence is simply a matter of the question and answer characterizing the answer set consistently.

According to Rooth (1985), evoking alternatives is the general function of focus. Semantically, focus determines an additional focus semantic value, written $[\![\alpha]\!]^f$, where α is a syntactic phrase.

[[Ede wants [coffee]$_F$]^f = the set of propositions of the form "Ede wants
 y"
[[Ede]$_F$ wants coffee]^f = the set of propositions of the form "*x* wants
 coffee"

Ordinary semantic values are not directly affected by focus: the two variants
contribute the same proposition as an ordinary semantic value [[α]]^o. Here is a
semantic rule for *only* stated in terms of alternative semantics:[5]

> *only* combining with a clause ϕ yields the assertion $\forall p[p \in [\![p]\!]^f \wedge {}^\vee p \to p$
> $= [\![\phi]\!]^o]$ and the presupposition *p*.

The rule differs from the earlier one in that the quantification is at the level of
propositions: no alternative to [[ϕ]]^o is both distinct from [[ϕ]]^o and true. As
applied to the introduction scenario, the formulation explains why (3a) is
false. The relevant semantic values are as follows:

> [[John introduced [Bill]$_F$ to Sue]]^f = the set of propositions of the form
> "John introduced *x* to Sue"
> [[John introduced [Bill]$_F$ to Sue]]^o = the proposition "John introduced Bill
> to Sue"

Given the described course of events, "John introduced Tom to Sue" is a true
proposition distinct from "John introduced Bill to Sue". Furthermore, it is an
element of the focus semantic value of the argument of *only*, namely the set of
propositions of the form "John introduced *x* to Sue".

On the other hand, the variant with focus on [$_{NP}$Sue] is predicted to be true.
The relevant semantic values are as follows:

> [[John introduced Bill to [Sue]$_F$]]^f = the set of propositions of the form
> "John introduced Bill to *z*"
> [[John introduced Bill to [Sue]$_F$]]^o = the proposition "John introduced Bill
> to Sue"

Given the described course of events, there is no true proposition of the form
"John introduced Bill to *z*" except for "John introduced Bill to Sue".

3   A Problem of Restrictiveness

Structured meanings and alternative semantics are, minimally, tools for at-
tacking the descriptive problem posed by focus-sensitive constructions and
discourse configurations. They give us semantic objects in terms of which we
can state rules, and thus define the contribution of focus to the semantics or

pragmatics of a given construction. A theory of focus should do more, though: it should tell us what focus-sensitive constructions have in common, characterizing a notion of possible focus-sensitive construction. As a consequence, it should tell us what pragmatic and semantic functions focus could not serve. An analysis which fails to address this requirement might be saying a lot about specific constructions, but it says nothing about focus in general. By omission, it maintains that there is no uniform semantic or pragmatic phenomenon of focus.

The problem is severe for the structured meaning semantics, since it gives access to so much information. It seems only a slight exaggeration to say that it gives access to all the information which could possibly be relevant, namely the semantics of the focused phrase and the semantics of the rest of the sentence. Using this information, it is possible to define quite implausible operators. Consider the following paradigm, involving a hypothetical verb *tolfed*, a focus-sensitive version of *told*.

(19) a. I tolfed [that [he]$_F$ resembles her] ≡ I told him that he resembles her.
   b. I tolfed [that he resembles [her]$_F$] ≡ I told her that he resembles her.
   c. I tolfed [that [he]$_F$ resembles [her]$_F$] ≡ I told him and her that he resembles her.

That is, *tolfed* ϕ amounts to *told the focus* (or *foci*) *of* ϕ *that* ϕ. It is trivial to define *tolfed* as a focus-sensitive operator in the structured meaning semantics. If we use the structured meaning semantics as our theory of focus, and say no more, we are claiming that there could be such a lexical item.

Alternative semantics may not be subject to the restrictiveness objection to the same extent. But if we maintain that grammars contain construction-specific rules stated in terms of alternative semantics, we are making a weak claim. A symptom of this is that one of the rules could be dropped, without affecting anything else. At an extreme of implausibility, by removing a pragmatic rule we could obtain a language with no phenomenon of question-answer congruence, but otherwise just like English.

A hint to what is missing in alternative semantics is that, at least in some cases, it is clear that the alternative set has a different status from the ordinary semantic value: it has an independent semantic origin or pragmatic motivation. In question-answer congruence, the ultimate source of the alternative set is the semantics and/or pragmatics of questions: questions determine sets of possible answers. Focus seems to evoke this alternative set in a presuppositional way, indicating that it is present for independent reasons. In Rooth (1992) this idea is used to simplify the architecture of alternative semantics. The interface between focus-sensitive constructions and the focus feature is handled by a single operator which introduces a presupposed alternative set:

(20) Where ϕ is a syntactic phrase and C is a syntactically covert semantic variable, $\phi \sim C$ introduces the presupposition that C is a subset
of $[\![\phi]\!]^f$ containing $[\![\phi]\!]^o$ and at least one other element.

The operator being defined is "$\sim$", the focus interpretation operator. In the
question-answer paradigm, it would have scope over the answer:

(21)

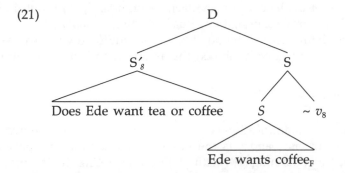

The variable C in (20), or v_8 in the representation above, denotes an alternative
set. Focus interpretation contributes a constraint on this variable, though it
does not fix its reference uniquely. In each specific case, the variable is identified with some semantic or pragmatic object present for an independent
reason. In the question-answer paradigm the antecedent for the variable introduced by focus interpretation can be taken to be the ordinary semantic value
of the question itself, given an appropriate semantics for questions. In a semantics in the style of Hamblin (1973), the semantic value for a question is a
set of propositions corresponding to potential answers, both true and false
ones. In the present case, the ordinary semantic value of the question is a set
containing just the propositions "Ede wants tea" and "Ede wants coffee". The
constraint introduced by $\sim$ in this case is that v_8 be a set of propositions of the
form "Ede wants y" containing "Ede wants coffee" and something else. Thus
the question and answer contribute consistent characterizations of the set of
propositions v_8. If the answer instead had focus on [$_{NP}$Ede], focus interpretation would dictate a set of propositions of the form "x wants coffee", which
would be inconsistent with the information contributed by the question, since
"Ede wants tea" is not of the required form.

The advantage of casting this analysis of question-answer congruence in
terms of the $\sim$ operator is that we do not need to state a rule or constraint
specific to the question-answer configuration. Rather, focus interpretation introduces a variable which, like other free variables, needs to find an antecedent
or be given a pragmatically constructed value. Identifying the variable with
the semantic value of the question is simply a matter of anaphora resolution.

To apply this analysis to focusing adverbs, we need to restate their lexical
semantics in a way which does not refer directly to focus semantic values. We
retain the idea that *only* quantifies propositions, but assume that the domain

of quantification is an implicit free variable, the reference of which is to be fixed by context. Writing this variable over sets of propositions as C in the notation $only(C)$, we can then assume the following representation:

(22)   [$_S$ only(C) [$_S$[$_S$ John introduced Bill$_F$ to Sue] ~ C]]

Focus interpretation at the level of the syntactic argument of *only* contributes a constraint on C, the implicit domain of quantification for *only*.

The appropriate definition for the adverb is now the following, where to sidestep technical issues I have combined the assertion and presupposition.

(23) $\lambda C \lambda p \forall q[q \in C \wedge {}^\vee q \leftrightarrow q = p]$

The implicit domain of quantification is C, p is the proposition contributed by the overt argument of *only*, and q is the universally quantified proposition variable. The effect of combining (20) with (23) in interpreting the representation (22) is as before, except that instead of identifying the domain of quantification with the focus semantic value of [$_S$ John introduced Bill$_F$ to Sue], focus interpretation simply requires C to be some subset of this focus semantic value containing "John introduced Bill to Sue" and something else. Furthermore, in the representation (22), C remains a free variable. This is understood to mean that its reference is to be fixed pragmatically, subject to the constraint introduced by focus interpretation. This is a welcome change, since in the sentence below, the domain of quantification is understood as consisting of just three propositions, rather than the full set of propositions of the form "John introduced y to Sue".

(24)   John brought Tom, Bill, and Harry to the party, but he only introduced Bill$_F$ to Sue.

4   Compositional Issues

One might think that the theory just sketched (provided that it could be shown to be successful in a broad variety of empirical domains) would resolve the debate between structured meanings and alternative semantics in favor of an improved version of the latter. This is not completely true, though. While the structured meaning theory as construed above is an unacceptably weak theory of focusing operators, structured meanings – or something a lot like them – may be the right solution to another problem. So far, I have simply assumed that focus-sensitive operators have access to focus-determined semantic values of their arguments, without saying where such focus-determined semantic objects come from. If focus is marked as a feature in syntactic trees, the problem is to formulate semantic and/or syntactic rules ensuring that the required semantic objects are available at the required syntactic level. In the example below, a structured semantic object or alternative set should be available at the S level, in order to interact with the semantics of *too*.

(25) [$_S$ John introduced Bill$_F$ to Sue], too.

In both the structured meaning semantics and non-restricted alternative semantics, *too* is treated as a focus-sensitive operator, the semantics of which is defined in terms of focus-determined semantic values. So these semantic objects have to be made available at the level of the adverb. In restricted alternative semantics, we employ the representation (26), where focus interpretation is handled by the operator ~, and *too* has a covert domain-of-quantification variable C.

(26) [$_S$[$_S$[$_S$ John introduced Bill$_F$ to Sue] ~ C] too(C)]

In order to define the semantics of ~, we need access to focus-determined semantic objects at the level of the minimal S node.

A straightforward approach to the compositional semantics of focus is suggested by the discussion in Chomsky (1976): focused phrases are assigned scope, as if they were quantifiers:[6]

(27) [$_S$[$_S$ Bill$_F$ λe_2[$_S$ John introduced e_2 to Sue]], too]

In the standard formulation of the semantics for quantifier scope, a variable in the surface position of the quantifier is bound by a lambda operator, as indicated in the representation above. If we treat the focus feature as the principal operator in this structure, taking the scoped phrase and the abstract as arguments, we can produce the required focus-determined semantic objects by choosing an appropriate semantics for the focus feature. The definition required for structured semantics is the trivial pair-forming operator $\lambda x[\lambda P[\langle P,x\rangle]]$. The semantics appropriate for alternative semantics is an operator which forms the set of propositions obtainable by applying the abstract to some individual matching the focused phrase in type. And in general, it seems that any desired semantics for focus could be encoded by choosing an appropriate function as the semantics for the focus feature in the quantificational representation.

There is a close similarity between this approach to the logical form of focus and the structured meaning semantics for focus, since the scoped representation for focus could be considered a syntactic representation of a structured proposition. Indeed, von Stechow (1985/1989) introduced structured propositions in this way. But the criticism of the structured semantics discussed in the previous section – that it is not a sufficiently constrained theory of focus-sensitive operators – does not apply in the present context, since a solution to the compositional problem does not aim to provide a theory of focus-sensitive operators. In particular, if we adopt restricted alternative semantics, we have a constrained theory of focus-sensitive operators and constructions, and there is no need to look for further constraints in the compositional mechanism.

4.1   *Recursive definition of focus*

A competitor to scoping – and more generally, to compositional mechanisms involving variable binding – is the recursive definition of focus semantic values proposed in (Rooth 1985). The idea is that focus semantic values are present not only at the level where they are used by the semantic rule for a focus-sensitive operator, but also at more embedded levels. That is, in the representation (26) or (27), focus semantic values are present not only at the level of *too* or ~, where they are used by semantic rules for these operators, but also at more embedded levels. Here are the focus semantic values in question:

(28)

$[\![Bill_F]\!]^f = E$, the set of individuals
$[\![John]\!]^f = \{j\}$, the unit set $[\![John]\!]^o$
$[\![Sue]\!]^f = \{s\}$, the unit set of $[\![Sue]\!]^o$
$[\![introduced]\!]^f = \{\mathbf{introduce}\}$,
    the unit set of $[\![introduced]\!]^o$
$[\![_{VP}introduced\ Bill_F\ to\ Sue]\!]^f = \{\lambda x \mathbf{introduce}(x,y,s)|y \in E\}$
    the set of properties of the form "introducing y to Sue"
$[\![_S John\ introduced\ Bill_F\ to\ Sue]\!]^f = \{\mathbf{introduce}(j,y,s)\ |y \in E\}$
    the set of propositions of the form "John introducing y to Sue"

The focus semantic values are derived compositionally by means of a definition along the following lines:[7]

(29)   a.   The focus semantic value of a focused phrase of semantic type τ is the set of possible denotations of type τ.
     b.   The focus semantic value of a non-focused lexical item is the unit set of its ordinary semantic value.
     c.   Let α be a non-focused complex phrase with component phrases $\alpha_1, \ldots, \alpha_k$, and let Φ be the semantic rule for α, e.g. function application. The focus semantic value of α is the set things obtainable as $\Phi(x_1, \ldots, x_k)$, where $x_1 \in [\![\alpha_1]\!]^f \wedge \ldots \wedge x_k \in [\![\alpha_k]\!]^f$.

In the following subsections, I will review several phenomena which bear on the compositional semantics of focus.

4.2   Scope islands

A quantificational representation suggests the possibility of sensitivity to structural constraints on the scope of operators. Using the term "scope" as a partly theory-neutral term for the level at which focus is interpreted, we can ask whether there are any constraints on the scope of focus, and if so whether they are parallel to constraints on other linguistic elements for which a notion of scope can be defined, such as quantifiers and *wh*-phrases. Consider operators taking scope from the subject position of relative clauses. As exemplified in (30a,b), an occurrence of *only* outside the NP modified by the relative clause can readily associate with a focus in this position. This appears to distinguish focus from quantifiers, in that the quantifiers in (30c,d,e) cannot take scope outside their embedding noun phrases.

(30)   a. Dr. Svenson only rejected the proposal that [John]$_F$ submitted.
       b. Dr. Svenson rejected only the proposal that [John]$_F$ submitted.
       c. Dr. Svenson rejected the proposal that no student submitted.
       d. Dr. Svenson rejected the proposal that exactly one student submitted.
       e. Dr. Svenson rejected the proposal that almost every student submitted.

A similar contrast can be observed for operators originating in adverbial clauses:

(31)   a. Dr. Svenson will only complain if [Bill]$_F$ doesn't finish his job.
       b. Dr. Svenson only complains when [Bill]$_F$ leaves the lights on.
       c. Dr. Svenson will complain if exactly one lab assistant doesn't finish his job.
       d. Dr. Svenson complains when almost every lab assistant leaves the light on.

Association with focus is possible into the *if*- and *when*-clauses, meaning that focus can (descriptively) take scope outside an adverbial clause. The corresponding scope for the quantifiers seems impossible.

On the surface, these data refute the scoping approach to the logical form of focus, since that approach requires logical forms where the focused phrase has been moved out of an island. In contrast, the recursive definition of alternatives allows us to assume non-scoped representations where the required information is available. In evaluating this argument, we have to keep in mind that there are quantifier scope mechanisms on the market which do not assume LF movement, such as quantifier storage (Cooper 1975) and type raising (Hendriks 1993). But these are variant mechanisms for achieving the same semantic end – binding of a variable by lambda. In the context of such theories, we could continue to maintain that there is something essentially different about the semantics of focus which explains island insensitivity. In several respects, the recursive definition of alternatives seems to embody a weakened notion of variable. First, while it allows for variation in the position of the focused phrase, there is no provision for co-variation: there is no issue as to whether two focus features correspond to the same variable or different ones.[8] Second, no operation corresponding to substitution for a variable can be defined, at least directly.

Since the form of the recursive definition of alternatives appears to be more than accidentally related to the weakened notion of variable, there may be some truth to the notion that the recursive definition of alternatives derives the island-insensitivity of focus in an interesting and explanatory way. However, as an argument against a semantics for focus involving lambda binding, the scope-island argument ignores the fact that the island-sensitivity of scope-bearing operators is quite diverse. Similar insensitivity to scope islands can be observed for indefinites, and for *in-situ wh*. (On the latter, see Huang (1982), and Lasnik and Saito (1992) for a more recent discussion. On the former, see Abusch (1994).) Island insensitivity is illustrated for relative clauses in (32). The generic indefinite *a student* has scope outside the containing noun phrase, at the level of the operator *usually*. Similarly, in (32b) the second occurrence of *who* is structurally the subject of the relative clause, but semantically has scope at the level of the *wh*-complement of *tell*.

(32) a. Dr. Svenson usually rejects the first three proposals that a student submits.
      b. Tell me who rejected the proposal that who submitted.

The group of island-escaping operators does not appear to be an arbitrary one. As mentioned in section 2, there is a connection between the semantics of focus and the semantics of questions. Several existing theories of *wh* semantics (e.g. Karttunen 1977) make a different connection with indefinites, in that *wh* phrases themselves (as opposed to the question clauses they are embedded in) are given an existential semantics. This semantic similarity, together with the common insensitivity to scope islands, suggest that we should not be satisfied with a theory which treats focus as *sui generis*. We would like to replace the focus-specific definition with a theory in which focus is one of a family of island-insensitive operators which, roughly, use restricted variables to name families of propositions, open propositions, and/or their existential closures. It is not at all clear to me how this should be done.[9]

The above discussion assumes that the superficial insensitivity of focus to scope islands is genuine. Steedman (1991) takes a different tack, proposing that the grammatical representation of such examples contains no operators escaping islands. Instead, nested focus is involved. This idea can be rendered in restricted alternative semantics by extending the semantic representation to include a representation of the alternatives to the focused element itself. That is, instead of considering anything of appropriate type an alternative, we include an explicit specification of alternatives. Let us understand *A* in the notation $\alpha_{F(A...)}$ as naming the set of alternatives to $[\![\alpha]\!]^0$. The notation is convenient, in that it allows understood restricted alternative sets to be annotated. A focused occurrence of *think*, understood as contrasting with *know*, would be written:

(33) I think$_{F(\{think,know\},...)}$ she has a chance.

To interpret these representations in a direct way, let us fold the meaning formerly assigned to ~ into the semantics of the focus feature. We adopt a scoped logical form:

(34) [$_S$ think$_{F(\{think,know\},C)}$ [$_S$ λe_4 [$_S$ I e_4 she has a chance]]]

The focus feature is the main function, and to give the right characterization of *C*, we define $F(A,C)(x)(P)$ as adding the presupposition that *C* is the set of propositions of the form $P(y)$, where *y* is an element of *A*. The assertion of $F(A,C)(x)(P)$ is simply $P(x)$. In the case of (34), *A* has just two elements, and *C* consists of the the propositions "I think she has a chance" and "I know she has a chance".

This definition has a curious consequence: the focus feature itself becomes a focus-sensitive operator in the sense of restricted alternative semantics, assuming that we allow nested focus structures. The reason is that an embedded focus can restrict the *A* argument of a higher one. In (35b) below, the embedded focused phrase [$_{NP}$ Bill]$_F$ takes scope at the level of [$_S$ *e* left]$_F$, which in turn takes scope at the maximal level.

(35) a. [$_S$ I said [$_S$ Bill$_F$ left]$_F$]
      b. [$_S$[$_S$[$_S$[$_{NP}$Bill$_{F(\{b,d,h\}, D)}$] [λe_2 [$_S$ e_2 left]]]$_{F(D,C)}$] [λe_3 [$_S$ I said e_3]]]

We take *A* to be a set of three elements *b* (Bill), *d* (Dick), and *h* (Harry). The focus on *Bill* constrains *D* to be the set containing the three propositions "Bill left", "Dick left", and "Harry left". This set is then used as an explicit set of alternatives to the other focused phrase, and *C* is constrained to be the set of propositions obtainable by substituting elements of *D* into the frame "Mats said *p*". The resulting value for *C* is the set containing the propositions "Mats said Bill left", "Mats said Dick left", and "Mats said Harry left". This is the same as the one obtained in the simpler non-nested structure below, which has just one focus and one focus interpretation operator.

(36) [$_S$[$_{NP}$Bill$_{F(\{b,d,h\},C)}$] [λe_2 [$_S$ I said [$_S$ e_2 left]]]]

While this example involves no scope island, a similar nested analysis of scope island examples might succeed in building a bridge to the island. Suppose that the scope of the focus on [$_{NP}$ John] in (30a) is the relative clause, and that the relative clause bears an additional focus feature. This would dictate the representation:

(37)   [$_S$ only(C) [$_S$ [$_{S'}$[$_{S'}$[$_{NP}$[$_{NP}$ John]$_F$(A,D)] [λe$_2$ [$_{S'}$that e$_2$ submitted]]] F(D,C)]
       [λe$_3$ [$_S$ Dr Svensen rejected [$_{NP}$ the proposal e$_3$]]]]]

Here e$_3$ is the trace of the scoped relative clause, and e$_2$ is the trace of [$_{NP}$ John]$_F$, which takes scope inside the relative clause. Just as above, we obtain equivalence with a simpler non-nested representation where [$_{NP}$ John]$_F$ has been moved out of the relative clause:

(38)   [$_S$ only (C) [$_S$ [$_{S'}$[$_{S'}$[$_{NP}$[$_{NP}$ John]$_F$(A,C)] [λe$_3$ [$_S$ Dr Svensen rejected [$_{NP}$the proposal [$_{S'}$that e$_3$ submitted]]]]]]]

Depending on one's theory of constraints on movement, (37) or a similar representation with nested focus and nested movement might successfully bridge the scope island.

4.3   *Multiple focus and multiple focus operators*

As mentioned above, two distinct foci may be associated with a single operator:

(39)   John only introduced [$_{NP}$ Bill]$_F$ to [$_{NP}$ Sue]$_F$

Alternately, they may associate with distinct operators:

(40)   John only introduced [$_{NP}$ Bill]$_F$ to Mary.
       He also only introduced [$_{NP}$ Bill]$_F$ to [$_{NP}$ Sue]$_F$

The adverb *also* has maximal scope, and the second sentence may be read as presupposing that for some z distinct from Sue, John introduced only Bill to z. Similarly, in (39), *Bill* can be associated with *only*, and the focus on *Sue* can be read as having a discourse function, for instance suggesting that the question "To whom did John introduce only Bill?" is being answered.

Depending on one's approach to the compositional problem, representing these readings may or may not pose a problem. Krifka (1991a) proposes a solution within the structured meaning framework, which in addition to possibilities such as those above, treats nested focus structures. Consider the reading of (41b) which presupposes that there were past occasions when John only drank x, where x is distinct from wine.

(41)   a. Last month John only drank beer.
       b. He has also only drunk WINE.

Krifka proposes a recursive focus structure [$_{NP}$[$_{NP}$ wine]$_F$]$_F$, where the outer focus is associated with *only*, and the inner one with *also*. Derivationally, we think of the focused phrase [$_{NP}$[$_{NP}$ wine]$_F$]$_F$ being scoped to a level where it interacts with *only*. Further, the interior focused phrase [$_{NP}$ wine]$_F$ is scoped to a level where it interacts with also:

(42)   also [$_S$[wine]$_F$ λe_2 [$_S$ have [$_S$ only [$_S$[e_2]$_F$ λe_1 [$_S$ John drunk e_1]]]]]

In the second movement, [$_{NP}$ wine]$_F$ is moved out of the phrase [$_{NP}$[$_{NP}$ wine]$_F$]$_F$, leaving a trace e_2. Thus the phrase interacting with only is the focused trace [$_{NP}$ e_2]$_F$, the focus feature which corresponds to the outside focus in the nested-focus representation. Rather than working with logical forms, Krifka uses an extended type system to achieve similar ends within an *in situ* interpretation strategy.

An approach to the compositional problem using the recursive definition of alternatives entails that all foci are bound by the first focus-interpretation operator they meet. This does not have an impact in simple examples, because of the possibility of scoping a focused phrase to a level where it escapes one focus operator, in order to be captured by the next. The logical form for (40) would be:

(43)

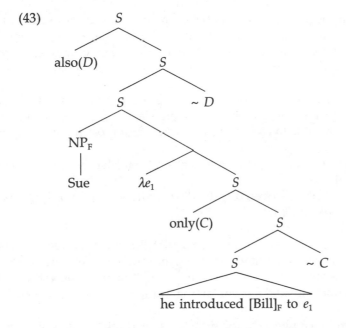

Examples such as (41b) can be represented by means of Krifka's nested focus proposal, combined with scoping of the inside focus to a level outside the first focus-sensitive operator:

(44)

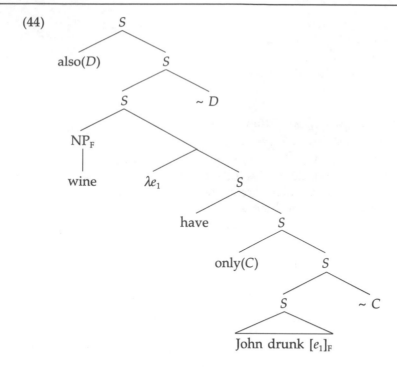

While there is an appearance of conflict between such logical forms and an *in situ* approach to focus interpretation, the opposite is true: once we have a theory which allows for scoping (which we do, motivated by quantifier scope), we would be hard put to keep focused phrases from being optionally assigned scope.

Genuine problem cases can be constructed by putting the focus which associates with the top focus-sensitive operator in an island, so that we would not expect that focus to be able to escape the lower operator by structural scoping.

(45)   We only$_3$ recovered [$_{NP}$the diary entries [that Marylyn$_{F3}$ made about John]]
        We also$_1$ only$_2$ recovered [$_{NP}$the diary entries [that Marylyn$_{F2}$ made about [Bobby]$_{F1}$]]

While the example is complex, I find it clear that *Bobby* can be read as associated with *also*, as informally indicated by the numerals on the focusing adverbs and focus features. In order to escape being bound by *only*, [Bobby]$_{F1}$ would have to scope outside the containing complex nominal, which is a scope island.

Unless this example can be accounted for by something like a nested focus analysis, its theoretical impact is quite dramatic: the recursive definition of alternatives has no advantage over the scoping approach to the logical form of focus.

4.4   *Bound variables*

Chomsky (1976) discussed a bound variable reading of (46), one which suggests alternatives of the form "x was betrayed by the woman x loved".

(46) $[_{NP}$ John$]_{1,F}$ was betrayed by the woman he$_1$ loved.

This reading is predicted fairly immediately by a quantificational representation, since the lambda operator produced by scoping a quantifier has the opportunity of binding a pronoun. Chomsky further pointed out that the variant (47a) does not have the bound reading suggesting alternatives of the form "the woman x loved betrayed x".

(47)   a. The woman he$_1$ loved betrayed $[_{NP}$ John$]_{1,F}$.
       b. Tell me who the woman he$_1$ loved betrayed.
       c. The woman he$_1$ loved betrayed $[_{NP}$ at most one man$]_1$.

Since this is parallel to weak crossover effects for overt *wh*-movement (47b) and quantifiers (47c), a quantificational analysis of focus can reduce the crossover effect for focus to crossover effects for quantification. This argument is not as strong as one might think, though. It provides reason to assume that bound variable readings for pronouns with focused antecedents involve representations where the antecedent is scoped, but does not bear on the general interpretation strategy for focus. As shown in Rooth (1985:76), the most straightforward combination of the *in-situ* interpretation strategy with the standard semantics for variable binding entails that the logical form for a bound variable reading of (46) is (48a), rather than the non-scoped structure (48b).

(48)   a. $[_S[_{NP}$ John$]_{1,F}$ $[_S$ e_1 was betrayed by the woman he$_1$ loved$]]$
       b. $[_S[_{NP}$ John$]_{1,F}$ was betrayed by the woman he$_1$ loved$]$

(48b) is a representation of a distinct reading suggesting alternatives of the form "x was betrayed by the woman John loved".

Turning to the logical form of (47a), in order to generate a bound variable reading, the focused phrase would have to be scoped, and so parallelism with quantifiers and moved or *in situ wh* is accounted for.

According to this analysis, quantifier-type scoping of focused phrases is needed in order to generate bound variable readings for pronouns, but is not required in order to interpret focus. This makes an interesting prediction: configurations where focus descriptively takes scope through a scope island should not be consistent with a bound variable reading for a pronoun outside the island. For instance, (49a) should not have the reading 'John is the only x such that we discussed the proposal x made with x's advisor.

(49)   a. We only discussed the proposal [NP John]$_{1,F}$ made with his$_1$ advisor.
       b. [S[NP John]F [S λe_1 [S we only discussed the proposal e_1 made with his$_1$ advisor]]]

The prepositional phrase [with his$_1$ advisor] is outside the relative clause island. A bound variable reading requires scoping [NPJohn] to the level where the resulting lambda operator can bind the pronoun [NPhis]. That is, it requires the representation (49b), where the focused phrase has scoped outside the island configuration. An *in-situ* representation would not preclude association of *only* with focus, but would not represent a bound variable reading. I think the prediction that (49a) does not have a bound variable reading might be right, though the intuition is quite delicate.

For further discussion of bound variable readings for pronouns with focused antecedents, see Kratzer (1991).

4.5   Conclusion on compositional issues

Alternative semantics as originally conceived is a theory of focus-sensitive operators which simultaneously explains the island-insensitivity of focus, based on the recursive definition of alternatives. I have reviewed several arguments which, although they are not entirely conclusive, justify skepticism about the second part of the package. Given standard assumptions about scope, the theory breaks down in configurations combining multiple focus operators with islands. This seems to show that, contrary to initial impressions, the recursive definition of alternatives has no advantage over the scoping approach to the syntax/semantics interface for focus. Independently, and in part undermining the first point, we should not necessarily expect focused phrases to be sensitive to islands if they were quantifier-like, since not all scope-bearing operators are island-sensitive.

As a working hypothesis, I think we might as well adopt scoping or some other compositional mechanism with a semantics of lambda binding as our compositional semantics for focus. This leaves us without an explanation for island-insensitivity. But unless we are arguing in terms of a systematic account of why some scope-bearing operators are island sensitive and others not, this is not exactly a defect in the theory of focus, just a sub-case of a general problem. If focus were instead island-sensitive, we would be in an entirely equivalent position of needing to explain why.

None of this affects the conclusion from the previous section that the theory of focus must be constrained in a way which prevents focus semantic values from being manipulated in arbitrary ways. As proposed above, in restricted alternative semantics one can adopt logical forms for focus interpretation of the following kind:

(50)   [$_S$[$_{NP}$ Bill]$_{F(A,C)}$ [$_S$ λe_2 [$_S$ John introduced e_2 to Sue]]]

The elements of meaning formerly introduced by ~ are encoded in the meaning of the focus feature. That is, $F(A,C)(x)(P)$, where x corresponds to the focused phrase and P corresponds to the abstract, introduces a presupposition that A contains x and something else, and that C is the set of propositions obtainable as $P(y)$, where y is an element of A.[10] This strategy eliminates the focus-semantic-value component of semantic interpretation in favor of a compositional mechanism of scoping. As to external behavior, though, the logical form (50) is equivalent to the following logical form of the other version of restricted alternative semantics.

(51)   [$_S$[$_S$ John introduced [$_{NP}$ Bill]$_F$ to Sue] ~ C]

That is, modulo the difference having to do with the explicit representation of A (which could be incorporated in (51) as well, or removed from (50)), the logical forms are semantically equivalent – they have the same assertions and presuppositions.

5   Alternatives versus Existential Presupposition

In restricted alternative semantics, the focus interpretation operator introduces an alternative set characterized by a presuppositional constraint. It can be emphasized that this theory does not equate the semantics of focus with existential presupposition. That is, in the example below, focus does not introduce a presupposition that someone is going to dinner with the speaker.

(52)   John$_F$ is going to dinner with the speaker.

Assuming that the focus is interpreted at the clause level, a set of alternatives of the form "x is going to dinner with the speaker" is introduced. This is weaker than an existential presupposition because such alternatives can be relevant without any of them necessarily being true.

In the above example, it is in fact hard to determine whether the weak semantics of introducing alternatives is to be preferred, since in many contexts an existential presupposition would be satisfied. For instance, in the question context below, the questioner might well be understood as taking for granted that someone is going to dinner with the speaker.

(53)   A: Who is going to dinner with the speaker?
       B: John$_F$ is going.

For comparison, consider an answer with a cleft instead of just intonational focus:

(54)   It's John who is going.

The cleft sentence is an appropriate answer to A's question in (53). According to standard assumptions, a cleft does introduce an existential presupposition (see e.g. Karttunen and Peters 1979). So there would be no problem with assuming that the intonational focus in (53) introduced an existential presupposition, perhaps in addition to introducing alternatives.

A standard way of diagnosing the presence of presupposition is a projection test. According to most authors, the presupposition of the complement of *unlikely* projects to the global environment (e.g. Karttunen and Peters 1979: 7). The clause (55a) carries a presupposition that Mary is away. In the syntactic context (55b), this presupposition is projected.

(55)   a. John knows that Mary is away.
       b. It's unlikely that John knows that Mary is away.

The pragmatic consequence is that someone using sentence (55b) will typically be perceived as taking for granted that Mary is away. This indeed seems correct; working backward, we can use our intuitions about the presupposition of the complex sentence (55b) as a diagnostic for determining the presupposition of (55a).

Let us apply this diagnostic to intonational focus and clefts. In my department, a football pool is held every week. Participants place bets by predicting the precise score of games. The contest is set up so that at most one person can win in a given week. If nobody makes a correct prediction, nobody wins, and the jackpot is carried over to the next week. Consider the following conversation:

(56)   A: Did anyone win the football pool this week?
       B: I doubt it, because it's unlikely that Mary$_F$ won it, and I know that nobody else did.

To make sense of the dialogue, suppose that B knew that Mary had made a silly bet, and so was unlikely to have won. He further knew that nobody else won, and therefore doubted that there was any winner at all.

I assume that in B's response, the focus on [$_{NP}$Mary] has scope over the clause [$_S$ Mary won it]. That is, we have the following representation:

(57)   it's unlikely that [[Mary$_F$ won it]~ C], and I know that nobody else did.

The alternative set C consists of propositions of the form "x won the football pool", where x ranges over the people in the department who participate: "Mary won the football pool", "Sue won the football pool", and so forth. The question we want to consider is whether it would be possible to assume that

the focus interpretation operator contributes, in combination with a characterization of the alternative set, a presupposition that some alternative is true. In
this case, this would amount to the presupposition that someone won the pool
this week. It is clear that this existential presupposition would be unwelcome:
it would project to the global context, and at this level it would be incompatible with the rest of what B was saying. Under normal circumstances, B could
not be taking for granted that someone had won at the same time as he was
saying that he doubted that anyone had won.

For comparison, consider a cleft variant:

(58) A: Did anyone win the football pool this week?
     B: I doubt it, because it's unlikely that it's Mary$_F$ who won it, and
        I know that nobody else did.

Again, I am assuming that clefts do introduce an existential presupposition.
This presupposition is expected to project, resulting in a conflict between the
projected presupposition that someone won, and the rest of what B said. Indeed, this cleft version of B's response seems quite incoherent and contradictory. This tends to confirm the conclusion that if focus in (56) introduced an
existential presupposition, the presupposition would project, resulting in perceptible contradiction or incoherence.

I conclude that we should not give focus a semantics of existential presupposition. Assuming that we settle on the weaker semantics of evoking alternatives, there is some work to do in explaining how the alternatives "x won the
football pool" are licensed by the discourse context in (56). Since A asked a
yes-no question rather than a wh-question, we can not directly identify C with
the semantic value of the question. The same problem arises in simpler dialogues, where both the yes-no question (59a) and the wh-question (59b) license
an answer with a focus appropriate for the the wh-question.

(59) a. Did anyone win the football pool this week?
     b. Who won the football pool this week?
     c. Mary$_F$ won it.

For present purposes, it is sufficient to observe that the pragmatics of questions and answers is complicated, involving such things as implicated questions and over-informative answers. An account of the pragmatics of evoked
alternatives in question-answer dialogues will have to take this into account.

5.1 Association with negation

Jackendoff (1972) treated negation as an operator associating with focus.
Naively, the focus effect can be described in the following way. In saying
the sentence (60), I am not using the negation to deny the content of the whole

sentence. Instead, the negation has a more limited scope – only the *car* part is negated. The remainder of the sentence is not negated, in the sense that I am granting that I took something of yours.

(60)   I didn't take your [car]$_F$

For somebody familiar with the Boolean semantics for negation, this sounds like a confused way of talking. But this simply means that we have to modify this semantics. A rule quite similar to the one for *also* can be given in alternative semantics:

> When combined with the clause ϕ, *not* yields the assertion that the proposition $[\![\phi]\!]^o$ is false, and the further assertion or presupposition that some proposition in $[\![\phi]\!]^f$ is true.

That is, ϕ is false but some alternative (in the example above, something of the form "I took your Q") is true.

In restricted alternative semantics, we would assume logical forms with the following geometry:

(61) $[\text{not}(C)[[\ldots \ldots [\ldots]_F \ldots] \sim C]]$

Just as with focusing adverbs, *not* has an implicit argument C, interpreted as a set of alternatives to its overt argument. The semantics of *not* would entail that some alternative is true.

Since such an analysis simply puts *not* into the class of focusing adverbs, it is innocuous from the point of view of the general theory of focus. I think putting this much into the semantics of *not* is misconceived, though, because the effect disappears in certain contexts. In the discourse below, speaker B is certainly not using focus to convey an assertion or presupposition that someone is going to dinner with the speaker, since this is inconsistent with the first thing he said.

(62)   A: Is anyone going to dinner with the colloquium speaker?
       B: I don't know. I$_F$ 'm not going

Just as in example (56) above, focus is presumably being used to evoke alternatives, without any commitment to any alternative being true. By analogy with the logical form (57), this suggests a representation in which negation has scope over the focus interpretation operator:

(63) $[\text{not} [[I_F \text{ 'm going}] \sim C]]$

The set C is constrained to be a set of propositions of the form "x is going", which should somehow be licensed by the discourse context. Details aside, this seems like a plausible analysis. Another possibility, suggested to me by Regine Eckhard, is that the context licenses negative alternatives of the form "x is not going" in addition to positive ones. In this case, we can assume the opposite scope:

(64)   [[not [I$_F$ 'm going]] ~ C]

In either case, we are dealing not with association of negation with focus, but with ordinary boolean negation, combined with a focus with a discourse motivation.

Once we acknowledge that representations of this kind are required, assuming in addition a special lexical negation with an argument position for implicit alternatives becomes dubious. In contexts where we propose a logical form involving the focus-sensitive negation, another representation along the lines of (63) or (64) would also be possible, since these representations have the effect of weakening the constraints on context. So while there is no formal objection to focus-sensitive negation, it is redundant. This presumably makes it unlearnable for a language-learner who has mastered the general semantics of focus.

Further, if in the face of this objection we propose a lexical focus-sensitive negation, we are on a slippery slope. Intuitions of existential presupposition appear to be comparable for a variety of propositional operators, such as modals and sentence adverbs, and for sentence-embedding verbs:

(65)   a. John$_F$ might be going.
       b. John$_F$ is probably doing it.
       c. Mary said that [John$_F$ is going]

At the limit, we would have distinct lexical focus-sensitive versions of all words of the language, surely an absurd conclusion.

Jackendoff (1972) realized that existential presupposition was too strong as a semantics for focus-sensitive negation. He proposed a weaker semantics rather similar to the notion of alternatives being relevant in the discourse. Translating this into my notation, we assume (61) as a logical form for focus-sensitive negation, but drop the assumption that the semantics of *not* adds a presupposition that some element of C is true. We replace the existential presupposition with something along the lines of the alternatives in C being relevant in the discourse. In other words, the semantics of focus-sensitive negation is: "the overt argument is false, and elements of C are relevant", rather than "the overt argument is false, and some element of C is true". This is so weak that there is no reason to adopt a logical form where the negation has access to C as an argument. Instead, we can assume an LF with the geometry of (63), where focus is interpreted at the same level as in (61), but does not interact with the negation.

6   Focus in General

I have argued that intonational focus in English has a weak semantics of evoking alternatives. This conclusion has no immediate bearing on the semantics of other constructions in English and other languages which we choose to describe as focusing constructions. For instance, a cleft has a strengthened semantics of existential presupposition and exhaustive listing. According to the analysis of Szabolcsi (1981), the semantics of focus movement in Hungarian is similar to this cleft semantics, or perhaps even stronger.

Does it follow that we should drop any broad notion of focus from our theoretical vocabulary, replacing a discussion of the semantics of focus with e.g. "the semantics of the prominence feature in English" and "the semantics of such-and-such movement in Hungarian"? In the medium term, I think this might be a good idea. The right kind of question to ask at this point is not "is construction X in language Y a focusing construction", but rather "what is the semantics of X in Y, and how does this explain the properties of X in Y". In pursuing the second question, it is a handy research strategy to check whether the analogues of English prominence-feature-sensitive constructions are X-sensitive in language Y. This does not mean that we are using these constructions as diagnostics for an abstract formative with a universal semantics.

Still, it would be surprising if at least many of the things in the world's languages that we call focus did not turn out to have a common semantic and/or pragmatic core. Until we have done more work, we have little basis for speculating about this. Conceivably, though, the common core might turn out to be the weak semantics of the prominence feature in English, with some constructions and morphemes expressing additional semantic content – such as existential presupposition or exhaustive listing – in addition to and in terms of the basic semantics.

NOTES

* I thank Barbara Partee, Dorit Abusch and Shalom Lappin for their very helpful comments and corrections.
1 In this section, I have not attempted to say where in the linguistic literature various focus-sensitive phenomena were first identified. For discussion and references on this point, I recommend chapter 4 of Sgall, Hajičová and Panevová (1986) and von Stechow (1991). Several specific examples which are not attributed in the text stem from Rooth (1985) or Rooth (1992).
2 The situation in the film is more subtle. The recorded utterance has a pitch accent on *kill*. Much of the film consists of the detective (played by Gene Hackman) listening to the recorded sentence. The final version on the soundtrack has an accent on *us* rather than *kill*; there seems to be no accent on the subject. This might

reflect a focus with VP scope on the NP *us*, expressing a contrast between killing the couple and killing the businessman being at issue. It is unclear whether we are to understand this version as representing the recording, or the detective's mental repetition of it as modified by his present understanding. Since the versions are acoustically distinct, the latter option seems more satisfactory.

3   See again Sgall, Hajičová and Panevová (1986: Ch. 4).

4   On the analysis of alternative questions and the approach to question-answer congruence sketched here, see von Stechow (1985/1989), from whom I also borrowed example (1).

5   The conjunct "$^\vee p$" is understood as meaning that p is true; in Montague's intensional logic, "$^\vee$" evaluates a proposition at the current index. I use English phrases enclosed in single quotes, sometimes mixed with logical notation, as a deliberately informal way of naming propositions and other semantic objects. For a more formal development of alternative semantics, see the cited sources. Natural language syntactic objects are named with expressions enclosed in square brackets, without any additional quotational device, and isolated word forms are italicized.

6   Though Chomsky did not employ a representation as abstract as this, his point was to argue that the logical form of focus involves a bound variable in the position of the focused phrase. Chomsky assumed that focus has the force of an equality expressed in terms of a definite description, e.g. "the x such that John introduced x to Sue is Bill". As argued below, this is probably too strong as a semantics for focus in English.

7   Technical complexities arise in connection with the intension operator; see Rooth (1985) for a better definition.

8   In this respect focus in natural language is similar to variables in simple string pattern matching languages with wildcard variables. In such languages, a pattern "a?c?" matches the string "abcd" as well as the string "abcb".

9   I will only point out that the definition (29) is not sufficient as it stands, since it provides no way of dealing with the content of the properties restricting an indefinite or a *wh*-phrase, i.e. with the property denoted by *student* in (32). See Abusch (1994) for an argument that the restrictions of indefinites in such examples have wide semantic scope. Abusch reduces the island-insensitivity of indefinites to the hypothesis that they are quantified by external operators, rather than by an operator originating in the indefinite NP. While this is suggestively reminiscent of logical forms involving ~, it is not clear to me whether this idea could be applied in the semantics of focus.

10   It remains to be sorted out whether multiple focus examples such as (39) involve a single operator combining with two scoped arguments, or whether a representation involving nested operators is possible.

11 Presupposition and Implicature

LAURENCE R. HORN

> To say, "The king of France is wise" is, in some sense of "imply" to *imply* that there is a king of France. But this is a very special and odd sense of "imply". "Implies" in this sense is certainly not equivalent to "entails" (or "logically implies"). (Strawson 1950: III)

> If someone says "My wife is either in the kitchen or in the bedroom" it would normally be implied that he did not know in *which* of the two rooms she was. (Grice 1961: 130)

When first (re)introduced into the philosophical literature, and thence into the consciousness of linguists, presupposition and implicature each appeared in turn as the meaning relation that dare not speak its name, as The Other: that inference licensed in a given context which cannot be identified with logical implication or entailment. Further, both presupposition (on Stalnaker's pragmatic account) and implicature operate through the mechanism of exploitation. Unlike syntactic and semantic rules, pragmatic principles and conventions do as much work when they are apparently violated – when speaker S counts on hearer H to recognize the apparent violation and to perform the appropriate contextual adjustment – as when they are observed. This essay will trace the evolution of thought on these elusive yet crucial meaning relations, considering not just what presupposition and implicature are but what they are not.

1 Presupposition

The linguistic literature has tended to confine the presuppositional universe to one class of presupposing statements, those involving singular referring expressions as discussed by Frege (1892a), Strawson (1950), and more recently

Burton-Roberts (1989).[1] History does not support this move: presupposition first emerged in the Western tradition among *exponibilia*, syncategorematic terms that can be decomposed into two or more meaning components combining to yield the meaning contribution of the term in question. On Peter of Spain's thirteenth-century investigation of "reduplicative" expressions like *inquantum* "insofar as", such a particle presupposes (*præsupponit*) that a given predicate inheres in the subject and denotes (*denotat*) that the term to which it is attached causes that inherence (Mullally 1945: 112).[2]

The distinction between an expression *præsupponit* and what it *denotat*, while not formalized by the scholastics, contains the ungerminated seeds of what would later blossom as the Fregean doctrine of presupposition. When the case of the empty (non-denoting) singular term was reopened a century ago, the prevailing wisdom was Aristotle's: every proposition is of subject-predicate form and is either true or false. A given predicate may be affirmed or denied of its subject, and there are no external (propositional) connectives. For a singular affirmation like (1) to hold,

(1)   Socrates is ill.
(2)   Socrates is not ill.

the subject referent must exist and the predicate must be predicable of it. A predicate may be truly denied of its subject as in (2) because the subject fails to exist, because the predicate fails to apply naturally to it,[3] or because the predicate expresses a property the subject happens not to possess (in this case, if Socrates is well).[4]

For Sigwart, this truth-functional, entailment-based analysis yields an account building on the somewhat inchoate notion of presupposition:

> As a rule, the judgement *A is not B* presupposes the existence of *A* in all cases when it would be presupposed in the judgement *A is B* . . . "Socrates is not ill" presupposes in the first place the existence of Socrates, because only on the presupposition of his existence can there be any question of his being ill. (Sigwart [1889] 1895: 122)

Sigwart offers an ordinary-language argument for rejecting the Aristotelian position on which (2) is merely the semantic contradictory of (1), based on the observation that (2) is "commonly understood" to signify "Socrates does live but is well".

> If we answer the question "Is Socrates ill?" by yes or no, then – according to our usual way of speaking – we accept the presupposition upon which alone the question is possible; and if we say of a dead man that he is not ill, we are guilty of using our words ambiguously. (Sigwart [1889] 1895: 152)

Technically, however, Aristotle is correct: "We must admit . . . that formally, the truth of [(2)] is incontestable" if Socrates is not alive. Sigwart's conclusion that a presuppositionally unsatisfied statement is misleading or inappropriate though true foreshadows the pragmatic turn to come.

The first incorporation of a presuppositional account of singular terms into a formal semantic model is due to Frege (1892a). In his classic paper on sense and reference, Frege argues that both (3) and its contradictory (4) presuppose (*voraussetzen*) that the name *Kepler* denotes something.[5]

(3) Kepler died in misery.
(4) Kepler did not die in misery.

Every sentence (affirmative or negative) with a singular subject (name or description) presupposes the existence of a presumably unique referent for that subject. But this presupposition is not part of the content of the expressions in question, and hence (3) does not entail the existence of Kepler – else the negation of (3) would not be (4), which preserves the presupposition, but rather the disjunction in (5):

(5) Kepler did not die in misery, or the name Kepler has no reference.

While Frege seems to have taken this outcome as a *prima facie* absurdity, it prefigures the later emergence of a presupposition-canceling external negation operator with truth conditions equivalent to those of disjunctions like (5).

Unwilling to accept Frege's conclusion, Russell tries another approach to what he acknowledges to be a significant logical puzzle:

> By the law of the excluded middle, either "*A* is *B*" or "*A* is not *B*" must be true. Hence either "the present king of France is bald" or "the present king of France is not bald" must be true. Yet if we enumerated the things that are bald and the things that are not bald, we should not find the king of France on either list. Hegelians, who love a synthesis, will probably conclude that he wears a wig. (Russell 1905: 485)

To solve this puzzle while preserving a classical logic in which every meaningful sentence is true or false, Russell banishes descriptions like *the king of France* from logical form. Once this exorcism is performed, sentences like (6) and (7) no longer have subject-predicate form, their surface syntax notwithstanding.

(6) The king of France is bald.
(7) The king of France is not bald.

(6) emerges instead as the (false) proposition that there is a unique entity with the property of being king of France and that this entity is bald, i.e. as an existentially quantified conjunction:

(6') $\exists x(Kx \ \& \ \forall y(Ky \rightarrow y = x) \ \& \ Bx)$

But Russell acknowledges two distinct ways to unpack its negative counterpart (7). If the description *the king of France* has a wide scope over an internal negation, we get the proposition that there is a unique and hirsute king of France,

(7') $\exists x(Kx \ \& \ \forall y(Ky \rightarrow y = x) \ \& \ \sim Bx)$

a proposition "simply false" in the absence (or oversupply) of male French monarchs. But Russell admits a second reading of (7) with the description falling within the scope of external negation:

(7") $\sim \exists x(Kx \ \& \ \forall y(Ky \rightarrow y = x) \ \& \ Bx)$

This reading, which results in a true proposition when France is a republic, is favored with the appropriate fall-rise intonation contour and rectification (cf. Horn 1985):

(7''')   The king of France isn't ˅BALD – there ISN'T any king of France!

Notice that (7"), unlike (7'), fails to entail (8).

(8)   There is a king of France.

Indeed, the falsity of (8) guarantees the truth of (7").

Russell's theory of descriptions held sway for a half century (despite the development of non-standard logics motivated on other grounds) until it crashed against the ordinary-language intuitions of Strawson (1950, 1952) and his Oxonian colleagues. For Strawson, as for Russell, (6) is meaningful, but meaningfulness and meaninglessness are crucially properties of sentences, while reference and truth value are properties of the statement the sentence is used to make.

Strawson's celebrated attack on Russell's theory of descriptions is premised on the assumption that negation normally or invariably leaves the subject "unimpaired". Strawson tacitly lines up with Frege, and against Russell (and Aristotle), in regarding negative singular statements like (7) as essentially unambiguous. For Russell (as for Aristotle), (7) – on its "primary" reading, (7') – comes out false in the absence of a French king; for Frege, the utterance of the analogous (4) makes no assertion if there was no Kepler. For Strawson, someone who utters (7) does commit herself to the existence of a king of France but, contra Russell, she does not thereby assert (nor does her statement entail) the corresponding existential proposition (8). Rather, (7) – along with its positive counterpart (6) – implies ("in some sense of *imply*") or (Strawson 1952) presupposes (8). If this presupposition is not satisfied, a statement is indeed made, but the question of the truth value of (6) or (7) fails to arise.

Is this intuition captured by the formal device of assigning a third truth value, distinct from the classical two values of the Aristotelian and Russellian programs? Or is there simply a gap, a truth-functional black hole, at the point where truth values are normally assigned? Are statements with vacuous subject terms collapsible in some sense with meaningless or ungrammatical sentences and perhaps with future contingents (cf. Horn 1989: 2:1), given that in these cases the question of truth or falsity also arguably fails to arise? The quarter century following the publication of "On Referring" witnessed a rapid proliferation of three(plus)-valued logics in which truth-value gaps or non-classical values are admitted, i.e. in which meaningful declarative statements are in at least some contexts assigned neither of the two classical values. Ironically, these neo-Strawsonian formal accounts of presupposition consistently assume an ambiguity for negation to deal with non-presupposing negations like that in (7″), a position advocated by the arch-classicists Aristotle and Russell but never explicitly endorsed by the presuppositionalists Frege or Strawson themselves.

One approach distinguishes two propositional negation operators: an internal ("choice") negation that preserves presuppositions and a presupposition-canceling external ("exclusion") negation. Just in case a given affirmative proposition lacks a classical value, its internal negation lacks one as well; the external negation is always true or false. This is shown in (9), where # denotes the third or undesignated value.

(9)			
		INTERNAL	EXTERNAL
		NEGATION	NEGATION
	P	**¬P**	**-P**
	T	F	F
	F	T	T
	#	#	T

Within multi-valued logic it is clear that true and false must be taken as contraries rather than contradictories: if – but not only if – a proposition is false, it is not true.

Now a Strawsonian notion of presupposition can be defined in terms of (internal) negation and an inference rule identified as semantic entailment (Smiley 1960) or necessitation (van Fraassen 1968):

(9′)   (i) $A \parallel\!\!- B$ ("A necessitates B" or "A semantically entails B") if and only if whenever A is true, B is also true.

(ii) A presupposes B if and only if $A \parallel\!\!- B$ and $\neg A \parallel\!\!- B$.

Any coherent multi-valued or truth-gapped logic will capture the standard assumptions: a proposition and its (internal) negation share the same presupposition set, the presupposition of ϕ is a necessary condition for ϕ to be either true or false, and so on. Within such a formal system, necessitation – unlike classical entailment – does not allow contraposition. Similarly, while *modus ponens* is retained (from $A \parallel\!\!- B$ and A, we can infer B), *modus tollens* is not: Let A be any presupposing sentence (e.g. (6)) and B one of its presuppositions (e.g. (8)); then A (and likewise $\neg A$) necessitates / semantically entails – and indeed presupposes – B, but all we can infer from $\neg B$ is that A (and likewise $\neg A$) is not true, not that it is false.

Unfortunately, the doctrine of semantic presupposition thus defined is beset with significant conceptual and empirical problems.[6] Nor is it clear that the quest is worth undertaking: given the existence of sentences like (7″) and the undemonstrability of a true semantic ambiguity for natural language negation (see Atlas 1975, Kempson 1975, Gazdar 1979), presuppositionality does not readily accept truth-conditional modeling. Strawson himself, ever skeptical that any system of formal logic could do justice to his intuitions about truth and meaning in ordinary language, would discount the attempts to devise a formal presuppositional logic to represent his observations: "Neither Aristotelian nor Russellian rules give the exact logic for any expression of ordinary language; for ordinary language has no exact logic" (Strawson 1950: 344).

Kempson (1975: 86) has noted the irony of this concluding sentence from the presuppositionalist manifesto, containing as it does a definite description (*the exact logic . . .*) which evidently does not induce an existence presupposition. In fact this apparent inconsistency is consistent with the revisionist position of Strawson's later work (1964: 95ff.), where truth-value gaps arise only when non-denoting singular terms occur in referential positions (typically, as surface subject and / or topic). While we may "feel squeamish" about assigning a truth value to (10a,b), Strawson reports no such qualms in the assessment of (11a,b) as false and true, respectively.

(10)   a. The king of France visited the exhibition.
       b. The king of France didn't visit the exhibition.

(11)   a. The exhibition was visited by the king of France.
       b. The exhibition wasn't visited by the king of France.

While (10a,b) are about the king of France, whence the induced presupposition and truth-value gap, (11a,b) are about the exhibition, so that the expression which would be "guilty of reference failure" is absorbed harmlessly into the predicate and no existence presupposition is triggered.[7]

Even the classic gap-inducing (6) may be simply false, Strawson concedes, if it is taken not as a description of the king of France (*Does M. le roi have need of a royal barber? – No, the king of France is bald*) but as a statement about the class of hairless entities (*What bald notables are there? Well, let's see, the king of ᵛFrance is bald*), in which case the subject is not functioning as the sentence topic, as the prosody indicates.[8]

But how can this observation be reconciled with semantic theories of presupposition failure? And whatever we do with these cases, what move can be made for (12), where failure of the existential presupposition again intuitively results in simple falsity?

(12)   The king of France is standing next to me.

As discussed by Fodor (1979), Horn (1989, 1990a), and Lasersohn (1993), such sentences do not seem to differ from the standard (6)-type examples in topichood or aboutness, rendering Strawson's ploy inapplicable.

The analysis of sentences like (12) turns on the distinction between truth and verification. While (6) and (12) are equally false, they differ in that it can be straightforwardly determined that the king of France is not standing next to me (since whoever is in fact standing next to me, if anyone is, does not have the property of being identical to the king of France, whether or not there is one), while (6) can only be falsified indirectly, by determining that France has no king. Whether a given speaker takes the existence of the referent of a given singular term for granted (or at least as noncontroversially accommodable) is a matter of pragmatics, not semantics.[9]

This approach extends naturally to other familiar cases of sentences that must be either true or false but cannot be felicitously uttered (in a given context), including future contingent statements (e.g. Aristotle's *There will be a sea-battle tomorrow*), past "unknowables" (e.g. *There was an odd number of blades of grass in Harvard Yard at the dawn of Commencement Day, 1903*, from Quine 1981: 91) or unverifiable and unfalsifiable claims about the present (e.g. the medievals' *The number of stars is even*). A theory which severs questions of truth conditions from those of verification can account for such cases without sacrificing either classical bivalence or our intuitions of conditions on (un)assertability.

But if presuppositions are not truth-conditions and if their failure does not lead to truth-value gaps, presuppositional phenomena require a pragmatic rather than a semantic account. Such a theory has been urged since the mid-1970s, the seminal proposals being those of Stalnaker (1974, 1978) and Karttunen (1974). In presupposing ϕ, S treats ϕ as a non-controversial element in the context of utterance: "To presuppose something is to take it for granted in a way that contrasts with asserting it" (Soames 1989: 553). To assert ϕ is to propose adding the propositional content of ϕ to the common ground, the working set of propositions that constitute the current context. Equivalently, this assertion is a proposal to discard $\sim\phi$ from the set of live options, to winnow down the context set (those possible worlds consistent with the shared beliefs of S and H) by jettisoning the worlds in which ϕ does not hold. A proposition is presupposed if and only if it is (treated as) non-controversially true in every world within the working context set.[10]

To get specific, (13a,b) entail and indeed truth-conditionally equate to (13c); a speaker asserting either (13a) or (13b) is proposing to increment the common ground with (13c).

(13)   a. Even Peewee lifted the rock.
       b. Peewee managed to lift the rock.
       c. Peewee lifted the rock.

What *even* and *manage to* contribute to the context are presuppositions that *S* treats as noncontroversial: in the former case that others (in the context set) lifted the rock and that Peewee was the least likely member of this set to have done so, and in the latter that it was relatively difficult for him to lift the rock.

The notion of context operative here, as elsewhere, is crucially not a static construct but a dynamic model of the collaborative construction of a conversation. Appreciation of this point forestalls misunderstanding of the nature of pragmatic presupposition (and of implicature: see Green 1990). Thus, the neo-Strawsonian Burton-Roberts points out that a pragmatic theory of presupposition framed "in terms of assumption-sharing between speaker and hearer" is "quite simply wrong":

> If I were to say to you, "My sister is coming to lunch tomorrow", I do presuppose that I have a sister but in presupposing it I do not necessarily assume that you have a prior assumption or belief that I have a sister. (Burton-Roberts 1989: 26)

Thus, he concludes, presupposition cannot be defined directly in terms of mutual knowledge. But nobody ever said it could. For Stalnaker (1974), pragmatic presuppositions are "propositions whose truth [*S*] takes for granted, or seems to take for granted, in making his statement" (1974: 198); presupposed material can be communicated as new information by a speaker who "tells his auditor something . . . by pretending that his auditor already knows it":[11]

> I am asked by someone whom I have just met, "Are you going to lunch?" I reply, "NO, I've got to pick up my sister." Here I seem to presuppose that I have a sister even though I do not assume that the speaker knows this. (Stalnaker 1974: 202, citing Sadock (personal communication))

Or more dramatically, after *A* has danced with a handsome stranger with whom her friend *B* happens to be acquainted, *B* gently exploits the presuppositional semantics of the possessive to force *A* to accommodate the existence of the referent in her model.

(14)   *A*: John is very attractive:
       B: Yes, and his wife is lovely too.

The idea that *S* can act as if a proposition is part of the common ground, and thereby force *H* to adjust his map of the common ground to encompass it, is codified in Lewis's rule of accommodation for presupposition:

> If at time *t* something is said that requires presupposition *P* to be acceptable, and if *P* is not presupposed just before *t*, then – *ceteris paribus* and within certain limits – presupposition *P* comes into existence at *t*. (Lewis 1979: 340)

Accommodation, which Lewis generalizes to permission statements, descriptions, vagueness, relative modalities, performatives, and planning, is itself – as Stalnaker points out – a special case of Gricean exploitation, a connection forged by Grice himself:

> It is quite natural to say to somebody . . . *My aunt's cousin went to that concert,* when one knows perfectly well that the person one is talking to is very likely not even to know that one had an aunt, let alone know that one's aunt had a cousin. So the supposition must be not that it is common knowledge but rather that it is noncontroversial, in the sense that it is something that you would expect the hearer to take from you (if he does not already know). (Grice ([1970] 1981: 190)

Within the pragmatic approach, presuppositions are restrictions on the common ground, rather than conditions on truth and falsity; their failure or nonsatisfaction results not in truth-value gaps or the assignment of non-classical values but in the anomaly or inappropriateness of a given utterance in a given context. But any comprehensive theory of presupposition must resolve the projection problem: how are the presuppositions of a larger expression determined compositionally as a function from those of its subexpressions? One proposed solution to the projection problem (see especially Karttunen 1974, Karttunen & Peters 1979) involves the partition of operators into sub-classes of plugs, holes, and filters, according to their effect on presupposition inheritance. The fact that ordinary negation is transparent to presuppositions – that both (13b) and its negation *Peewee didn't manage to lift the rock* presuppose that it was relatively difficult for Peewee to lift the rock – is accounted for by treating negation as a hole to presuppositions. Factive predicates (*realize, regret*) are also holes, letting presuppositions percolate up to a higher level. Verbs of communication, on the other hand, are in principle plugs, blocking the transmission of presuppositions (though see Levinson 1983: 195–6 for a contrary view). Thus (15a) but not (15b) presupposes existence of a largest prime.

(15) a. John regrets that Mary is thinking about the largest prime.
       b. John said that Mary is thinking about the largest prime.

Another plug is the presupposition-canceling "contradiction" negation of (7").

Two-place logical connectives are neither plugs nor holes, but filters, letting some but not all presuppositions percolate through, depending on properties of the content and context of the utterance. Thus in (16a,b) the presupposition that would have been induced by the second clause – that Al has a cat – is entailed by the first clause and thus filtered out, while in (16'a,b) this same presupposition is not filtered out and survives to become a presupposition of the entire sentence. In both cases, the presupposition of the first clause (that Al exists) percolates up unfiltered.

(16)   a. Al has a cat, and his cat is jealous.
       b. If Al has a cat, his cat is jealous.

(16′) a. Al has a dog, and his cat is jealous.
       b. If Al has a dog, his cat is jealous.

Note the parallel projection of conditionals and conjunctions: in both *if p then q* and *p and q*, the presuppositions of the sentence as a whole will consist of the union of the presuppositions of *p* and of *q*, minus those presuppositions of *q* that are contextually entailed by the common ground incremented by *p*. On this account, the presuppositional behavior of conjunctions is just as asymmetric as that of conditionals, whence the irreversibility of (16a).

Gazdar (1979) identifies empirical problems for the Karttunen–Peters theory (focusing especially on a class of incorrect predictions for conditional sentences) and proposes an alternative projection mechanism in which subexpressions induce potential presuppositions that are automatically inherited as a default unless they clash with propositions already entailed or implicated by the utterance or the prior discourse context, in which case they are canceled.

Subsequent work (cf. Soames (1979), Landman (1981), Heim (1983, 1992)) identifies empirical and conceptual problems for both Karttunen–Peters and Gazdar models. Heim, seeking to synthesize the strengths of the preceding models, identifies an operator's projection properties in terms of its context-change potential. Presuppositions can be unpacked as invariant pragmatic inferences: If Σ is a sentence, Σ presupposes ϕ just in case every context admitting Σ entails ϕ. The connection between truth-conditions and context-change – between Strawsonian and Stalnakerian conceptions of presupposition – is elucidated as follows: If a context c (taken to be a set of propositions or the conjunction of the members of that set) is true and c admits a sentence Σ, then Σ is true with respect to c if $c + \Sigma$ (the context incremented by Σ) is true. But if Σ is uttered in a context c which fails to admit it, the addressee will adjust c to c', a context close to c but consistent with Σ. Heim's projection theory (1983: 117–19) thus incorporates the Stalnaker–Lewis process of accommodation, which appeals in turn to the Gricean model of a cooperative conversational strategy dynamically exploited to generate pragmatic inferences. At the same time, this line responds to the demand (voiced by Gazdar's critique of the Karttunen–Peters system) for an explanatory theory in which projection properties of "filters" follow directly from the meaning of the logical connectives.

Following Heim (1983, 1992) and Soames (1989: 577–9), the notion of presupposition accommodation can be related to presupposition cancellation, in which the specific utterance context makes it clear to H that the apparent violation of presuppositional requirements must be resolved not by altering the context to entail the presupposing statement but by reinterpreting the statement itself, "adjusting the requirements to fit the facts" (Soames 1989: 578). Heim distinguishes these processes as global vs. local accommodation, Soames as de facto vs. de jure accommodation. This permits an explanation of the surprising result in Gazdar (1979) that potential presuppositions can be canceled by implicatures.

The study of presupposition continues to play a major role in the evolution of current semantic theory. In the light of recent developments in formal pragmatics, we can see (following van der Sandt & Zeevat 1992) how Karttunen's contextual satisfaction-based approach to the projection problem anticipates today's dynamic theories of context change, while Gazdar's cancellation-based account prefigures current work on non-monotonic logics. Van der Sandt (1992), meanwhile, has been pursuing an anaphoric account of presupposition, projection, and accommodation formulated within discourse representation theory. For over a century, since Frege blazed the way, the analysis of presuppositional phenomena has served as a crucible in which semantic theories of natural language semantics have been tested; those theories incapable of providing a successful model of the generation and projection of presuppositions are destined to suffer the fate of the unfortunate King of France.

2 Implicature

Like pragmatic presupposition, the notion of implicature constitutes a non-truth-conditional aspect of speaker meaning, part of what is meant when S utters ϕ within context c without being part of what is said by S in that utterance. This contrast between the said and the meant, and thus between the said and the implicated (the meant-but-unsaid), dates back at least to the fourth-century rhetoricians Servius and Donatus who characterized litotes, the figure of pragmatic understatement, as a figure in which we say less but mean more ("minus dicimus et plus significamus"; see Horn 1991 for discussion).

Grice's contribution was to offer an explicit and general account of what he termed

> ... a distinction ... within the total signification of a remark ... between what the speaker has said (in a certain favored and maybe in some degree artificial, sense of "said"), and what he has implicated (e.g. implied, indicated, suggested, etc.), taking into account the fact that what he has implicated may be either conventionally implicated (implicated by virtue of the meaning of some word or phrase which he has used) or non-conventionally implicated (in which case the specification of implicature falls outside the specification of the conventional meaning of the words used). (Grice [1967] [1989a]: 118)

In his earliest published work on the then unnamed doctrine of implicature, Grice (1961: 3) distinguishes several separate species within the genus of non-entailment relations, as exhibited in the pairs in (17):

(17) a. Smith has left off beating his wife.
      a'. Smith has been beating his wife.

        b. She is poor but honest.
           b'. There is some contrast between her poverty and her honesty.
        c. Jones has beautiful handwriting and his English is grammatical.
            (in letter of evaluation of Jones for a faculty position in
            philosophy)
           c'. Jones is no good at philosophy.
        d. My wife is either in the kitchen or in the bathroom.
           d'. I don't know for a fact that my wife is in the kitchen.

Grice, taking (17a') as a (semantic) presupposition of (17a) (with the truth of the former thus a necessary condition for the truth or falsity of the latter), observes that this inference is neither cancelable (*Smith has left off beating his wife, but then he never beat her in the first place*) nor detachable, in the sense that any other means of asserting what (17a) asserts induces the same presupposition: *He has stopped/ceased beating her, He no longer beats her* . . . The inference in (17b,b'), on the other hand, while still non-cancelable, is detachable, since the same truth-conditional content we can express in a way that removes (detaches) the inference: *She is poor and honest.* This implication also differs from that of (17a) in its irrelevance to truth-conditional considerations: (17b) is true if the referent is both poor and honest and false otherwise. In later work (Grice 1975, Karttunen & Peters 1979), such detachable but non-cancelable inferences which are neither part of what is said (part of truth-conditional meaning) nor calculable in any general way from what is said are termed CONVENTIONAL implicata, corresponding essentially to the Stalnaker–Karttunen notion of pragmatic presupposition. Indeed, along with *but*, the now classic instances of conventional implicature involve precisely those particles traditionally analyzed as instances of pragmatic presupposition: adverbial particles like *even* and *too*, truth-conditionally transparent verbs like *manage to* and *bother to*, and syntactic constructions like clefts.[12]

But whereas these inferences are non-truth-conditional components of an expression's <u>conventional</u> lexical meaning, the inferences associated with (17c,d) are <u>non</u>-conventional in that they can be calculated from the utterance of such sentences in a particular context given the view of conversation as a shared goal-oriented enterprise of speaker and hearer. In each case, the inference of the corresponding primed proposition is cancelable (either explicitly by appending material inconsistent with it – "*but I don't mean to suggest that . . .*" – or by altering the context of utterance) but non-detachable (given that any other way of expressing the literal content of (17c,d) in the same context would license the same inference). Where (17c) differs from (17d) is in the fact that the utterance of the former "does not standardly involve the implication . . . attributed to it; it requires a special context to attach the implication to its utterance" (Grice 1961: 130), while the inference in the latter case that S did not know in which of the two rooms his wife was located, is induced in the <u>absence</u> of a special or marked context (e.g. that of a game of hide and seek). (17c) exemplifies particularized conversational implicature, while (17d) represents the more linguistically significant concept of generalized conversational implicature (Grice 1975). But in both cases, it is crucially not the proposition or sentence, but the speaker or utterance, that induces the relevant implicatum in the appropriate context.

Grice seeks to show how participants in a conversational exchange can compute what was meant (by S's utterance at a given point in the interaction) from what was said. The governing dictum is the Cooperative Principle (Grice 1975: 45): "Make your conversational contribution such as is required, at the stage at which it occurs." This rule in turn is analyzed into the four general and presumably universal maxims of conversation on which all rational interchange is grounded:

(18)   The Maxims of Conversation (Grice 1975: 45–6):
      QUALITY: Try to make your contribution one that is true.
        1. Do not say what you believe to be false.
        2. Do not say that for which you lack evidence.
      QUANTITY:
        1. Make your contribution as informative as is required
           (for the current purposes of the exchange).
        2. Do not make your contribution more informative than is
           required.
      RELATION: Be relevant.
      MANNER: Be perspicuous.
        1. Avoid obscurity of expression.
        2. Avoid ambiguity.
        3. Be brief. (Avoid unnecessary prolixity.)
        4. Be orderly.

There is, *a priori*, no privileged status to this classification, and neo- and post-Gricean pragmaticists have entertained a variety of reductionist efforts. In the first place, all maxims are not necessarily created equal. Grice and others have assigned a privileged status to Quality (though see Sperber & Wilson 1986 for a dissenting view):

> The maxims do not seem to be coordinate. The maxim of Quality, enjoining the provision of contributions which are genuine rather than spurious (truthful rather than mendacious), does not seem to be just one among a number of recipes for producing contributions; it seems rather to spell out the difference between something's being, and (strictly speaking) failing to be, any kind of contribution at all. False information is not an inferior kind of information; it just is not information . . . Indeed, it might be felt that the importance of at least the first maxim of Quality is such that it should not be included in a scheme of the kind I am constructing; other maxims come into operation only on the assumption that this maxim of Quality is satisfied. (Grice 1989: 371; Grice 1975: 46)

Of those "other maxims", the most linguistic mileage has been obtained from the first quantity maxim, which is systematically exploited to yield upper-bounding generalized conversational implicatures associated with scalar operators (Horn 1972, 1989; Gazdar 1979; Hirschberg 1985). This submaxim (under a variety of formulations) and its explanatory potential have long been recognized. Thus Sir William Hamilton (1860: 254) distinguishes two senses of *some*, the indefinite (*at least some*) and the semi-definite (*some but not all*), taking the latter as basic: "Some, if not otherwise qualified, means some only – this by presumption." While acknowledging the existence of this presumption in "common language", De Morgan (1847) and Mill (1867) marshal proto-Gricean reasoning to reject Hamilton's thesis in favor of the standard practice of relegating the *some* → *not all* inference to an extra-logical domain:

> No shadow of justification is shown . . . for adopting into logic a mere sousentendu of common conversation in its most unprecise form. If I say to any one, "I saw some of your children today", he might be justified in inferring that I did not see them all, not because the words mean it, but because, if I had seen them all, it is most likely that I should have said so: even though this cannot be presumed unless it is presupposed that I must have known whether the children I saw were all or not. (Mill 1867: 501)

Notice especially Mill's epistemic rider on quantity-based inference: the use of a weaker operator implicates that for all *S* knows the stronger operator on the same scale could not have been substituted *salva veritate*.

The tacit principle Mill alludes to, requiring *S* to use the stronger *all* in place of the weaker *some* when possible and licensing *H* to draw the corresponding inference when the stronger term is not used, is independently formulated by Strawson (1952: 178–9), who credits Mr H. P. Grice for this "general rule of linguistic conduct": "One should not make the (logically) lesser, when one could truthfully (and with greater or equal clarity) make the greater claim." Grice (1961: 132) later takes his own "first shot" at the relevant rule – "One should not make a weaker statement rather than a stronger one unless there is a good reason for so doing" – which has appeared on the market in different packaging.[13]

For Grice, the methods of radical pragmatics are enlisted in the defense of a conservative bivalent semantics, with the gap between what that logic gives us and what we seem to need bridged by the assumption that *S* and *H* are in business together under the banner of the Cooperative Principle and the attendant maxims. Quantity-based scalar implicature – my inviting you to infer from my use of *some* . . . that for all I know *not all* . . . – is driven in particular by your knowing (and my knowing your knowing) that I expressed a weaker proposition in lieu of an equally unmarked utterance that would have expressed a stronger proposition, one unilaterally entailing the one I did express. Thus, what is <u>said</u> in the use of a weak scalar value like those in boldface in the sentences of (19) is the lower bound (. . . *at least n* . . .), with the upper bound (. . . *at most n* . . .) <u>implicated</u> as a cancelable inference generated by (some version of) the first maxim of quantity.

(19)

		1-SIDED READING	→	2-SIDED READING
a.	Max has 3 children.	"... at least 3 ..."		"... exactly 3 ..."
b.	You ate **some** of the cookies.	"... some if not all ..."		"... some but not all ..."
c.	It's **possible** she'll win.	"... at least ◇ ..."		"... ◇ but not certain ..."
d.	Maggie is patriotic **or** quixotic.	"... and perhaps both"		"... but not both"
e.	It's **warm** out.	"... at least warm ..."		"... but not hot ..."

Negating such predications denies the lower bound: to say that something is not possible is to say that it's impossible, i.e. <u>less than</u> possible. When the upper bound is apparently negated (*It's not possible, it's <u>necessary</u>*), a range of syntactic and phonological evidence suggests that this is an instance of the metalinguistic use of negation, in which the negative particle is used to object to any aspect of a mentioned utterance, including its conventional and conversational implicata, register, morphosyntactic form or pronunciation (Horn 1989: Chapter 6).[14]

Setting Quality aside, we can collapse the remaining maxims and submaxims into two fundamental principles regulating the economy of linguistic information (Horn 1984, 1989, 1993). The **Q** Principle is a lower-bounding hearer-based guarantee of the sufficiency of informative content ("Say as much as you can, modulo Quality and **R**"); it collects the first Quantity maxim and the first two submaxims of Manner, and is systematically exploited (as in the scalar cases just discussed) to generate upper-bounding implicata. The **R** Principle is an upper-bounding correlate of the Law of Least Effort dictating minimization of form ("Say no more than you must, modulo **Q**"); it collects the Relation maxim, the second Quantity maxim, and the last two submaxims of Manner, and is exploited to induce strengthening or lower-bounding implicata. **Q**-based implicature is typically negative in that its calculation refers crucially to what could have been said but wasn't: *H* infers from *S*'s failure to use a more informative and/or briefer form that *S* was not in a position to do so. **R**-based implicature typically involves social rather than purely linguistic motivation and is exemplified by indirect speech acts (in particular, euphemism) and negative strengthening (including so-called neg-raising, the tendency for *I don't think that φ* to implicate *(I think that) not-φ*).[15]

The functional tension between these principles motivates and governs not just implicature but a wide range of linguistic phenomena from politeness strategies to the interpretation of pronouns and gaps, from lexical and semantic change to the analysis of conversational interaction (cf. Horn 1984, 1993; Brown & Levinson 1987; Levinson 1987a,b, 1991). Crucially, the two antinomic forces are not in simple opposition, but interact dialectically, each appealing to and constraining the other. Thus Grice incorporates **R** in defining the primary

Q maxim ("Make your contribution as informative as is required"), while Quantity$_2$ is constrained by Quantity$_1$ and essentially incorporates Relation: what would make a contribution more informative than is required, except the inclusion of contextually irrelevant material?[16]

The opposition of the two forces may result in maxim clash. Thus an utterance of *I broke a finger yesterday* **R**-implicates that it was one of my fingers I broke, unless the common ground entails or accommodates the proposition that I am enforcer for the mob, in which case the opposite, **Q**-based implicature is derived. Notice too that the use of *finger* here conveys ~[THUMB]. Truth-conditionally, a thumb is a finger: I have ten fingers, not eight. But if I tell my doctor I broke a finger, she will infer that the maimed digit wasn't a thumb, or I would have said so. (Saying so would be more informative and no less brief.) Thus *finger* **Q**-implicates *non-thumb*, just as *rectangle* is typically used so as to exclude squares.

Related to these cases of **Q**-based narrowing[17] is the division of pragmatic labor. Given two co-extensive expressions, the more specialized form – briefer and/or more lexicalized – will tend to become **R**-associated with a particular unmarked, stereotypical meaning, use, or situation, while the use of the periphrastic or less lexicalized expression, typically (but not always) linguistically more complex or prolix, will tend to be **Q**-restricted to those situations outside the stereotype, for which the unmarked expression could not have been used appropriately. Thus consider the following pairs, abstracting away from issues of conventionalization:

(20)   a. Black Bart caused the sheriff to die.
       Black Bart killed the sheriff.
    b. I'd like to see something in pale red.
       I'd like to see something in pink.
    c. He wants him to win.
       He wants PRO to win.
    d. I am going to marry you.
       I will marry you.
    e. It's not impossible that you will solve the problem.
       It's possible that you will solve the problem.
    f. I need a new driller./cooker.
       I need a new drill. /cook.

The use of a periphrastic causative suggests that the agent acted indirectly (cf. McCawley 1978: 250), *pale red* implicates a tint not pre-empted by pink (Householder 1971: 75), the selection of a full pronoun over a null PRO (or pro) signals the absence of the coreferential reading associated with the reduced syntax (Chomsky 1981, Levinson 1987a, 1991), the periphrastic blocks the indirect speech act function of promising conveyed by the modal (Searle 1975), a double contradictory negation signals a rhetorical effect absent from the direct positive (Horn 1991), and agentive *-er* nominals are excluded from meanings pre-empted by the more lexicalized zero-derived deverbals: a driller can only be an agent, given that drills are instruments, but a cooker can only be an instrument, given that cooks are agents (Kiparsky 1983 on avoid synonymy, Aronoff 1976 on blocking, Clark & Clark 1979 on pre-emption by synonymy). Whenever a speaker opts for a more complex or less fully lexicalized expression over a simpler alternative, there is always a sufficient reason, but the particular motivation depends on the particular context.

While the model described above retains two antinomic principles along with an unreduced maxim of quality or convention of truthfulness, a more radical simplification has been urged in the Relevance Theory of Deirdre Wilson, Dan Sperber, and their associates. For Sperber & Wilson (1986), a suitably refashioned Principle of Relevance is the only begetter of the bridgework connecting linguistic meaning to utterance interpretation.

Even for Grice, propositional content is not fully fleshed out until reference, tense, and other deictic elements are fixed. But Relevance theorists, expanding on earlier observations of Atlas (1979), recognize that the same pragmatic reasoning used to compute implicated meaning must also be invoked to fill out underspecified propositions where the semantic meaning contributed by the linguistic expression itself is insufficient to yield a proper accounting of truth-conditional content. Thus Carston (1985: 6) argues that what is said in the natural use of sentences like those in (21),

(21) a. The park is some distance from where I live.
     b. It'll take us some time to get there.

must be computed via the Principle of Relevance. The distance or time communicated by S is not simply an implicatum read off the underspecified content contributed by linguistic meaning alone, i.e. a trivially true existential proposition. Instead, the pragmatically recoverable strengthened communication comprises the explicature or truth-conditional content. Pragmatically derived aspects of meaning are not necessarily implicatures: "There is massive pragmatic penetration of explicit content" (ibid.). Nor does the acceptance of widespread pragmatic intrusion into propositional content result in an erosion of the boundary between semantics and pragmatics: "Linguistic semantics is autonomous with respect to pragmatics; it provides the input to pragmatic processes and the two together make propositional forms which are the input to a truth-conditional semantics" (Carston 1988: 176).

Thus, both one-sided and two-sided understandings of the scalar predications of (19) are directly represented at the level of logical content: "The conclusion that there is a lot more truth-conditional ambiguity than is contributed by the language in question is unavoidable" (Kempson 1986: 88). But while the scalar predications of (19) are now all taken to be ambiguous, the ambiguity is no longer situated at the lexical level but has been relocated to the propositional level: what is said in an utterance is systematically under-determined by what is uttered.

Other work has challenged some of these results. Thus, while a strong case can be made for an enrichment analysis of the meaning contribution of the cardinals, it does not generalize straightforwardly to "inexact" scalar values (Horn 1992). Evidence for this conclusion comes from the contextual reversibility of cardinal scales and the non-implicating ("exactly n") reading of cardinals in mathematical, collective, and elliptical contexts, none of which applies to the scalar operators in e.g. (19b–e). Thus contrast the exchanges below:

(22)   A: Do you have two children?
       B₁: No, three.
       B₂: ?Yes, (in fact) three.

(22′) A: Are many of your friends linguists?
       B₁: ?No, all of them.
       B₂: Yes, (in fact) all of them.

Further, notice that a bare *"No"* answer is compatible with a non-monotone ("exactly n") reading in (22) in an appropriate context, but never in (22′), where an unadorned negative response can only be understood as conveying "less than many". Similarly, if (19e) were truly propositionally ambiguous, there is no obvious reason why a *"No"* response to the question *"Is it warm?"* should not be interpretable as a denial of the enriched, two-sided content and thus as asserting that it's either chilly or hot, or why the comparative in *"It's getting warmer"* cannot denote "less hot" instead of "less cold". Nor could we explain the contrast in (23):

(23)   a. #Neither of us liked the movie – she hated it and I absolutely loved it.
       b. Neither of us has three kids – she has two and I have four.

Such paradigms support a mixed theory in which sentences with cardinals may well demand a pragmatic enrichment analysis of what is said, while other scalar predications continue to submit happily to a minimalist treatment on which they are lower-bounded by their literal content and upper-bounded, in default contexts, by quantity implicature.

Relevance Theory has proved a powerful construct for rethinking the role of pragmatic inference in utterance interpretation and its relation to other aspects of cognitive structure. It is also worth noting that the contrast between the dualistic **Q/R** model and the monistic approach of Relevance Theory is somewhat misleading in that Relevance for Sperber and Wilson is itself a two-sided coin. Both frameworks are predicated on a minimax or cost/benefit relation which takes the goal of communication as maximizing contextual effects while minimizing processing effort, and the Principle of Relevance is itself couched in terms of this trade-off of effort and effect.[18]

The explanatory scope of implicature may have been reduced from the heyday of the Gricean program, as that of presupposition was in previous work, but in each case the pragmatic principles underlying these constructs – accommodation, exploitation, common ground, and the distinction of implicit vs. explicit components of utterance meaning – continue to play a vital role in the elaboration of dynamic models of context and communication.

NOTES

1   Keenan (1971), Levinson (1983: 181–4), and the articles in Oh & Dinneen (1979) provide useful surveys of presuppositional phenomena. For an historically important treatment of non-existential presuppositions within early generative grammar, see Kiparsky & Kiparsky (1971).

2   The relation can be detected as well in the presupposition-dependent *sophisma* of choice for the medievals, *Do you still beat your ass?* which is in turn a lineal descendant of the 3rd century B.C. Megarians' *Have you stopped beating your father? Answer yes or no* (cf. Wheeler 1983: 290–1). The development from the father-beating of the ancients through the ass-beating of the medievals to the wife-beating of the moderns provides an eloquent commentary on 23 centuries of social progress.

3   This is the CATEGORY MISTAKE, e.g. *The number 7 is red* (cf. Horn 1989; see Section 2.2 for elaboration). Thus vacuous singular expressions and category mistakes are automatically false, and their denials automatically true.

4   In addition to predicate denial, which determines contradictory opposition via the law of excluded middle, Aristotle admits narrow scope, non-middle-excluding predicate term negation. Where predicate denial (*Socrates is not well*) denies a positive term of the subject, predicate term negation (*Socrates is not-well*) affirms a negative term of the subject; if Socrates does not exist, the former is true and the latter false.

5   At least three different relations are collapsed under Frege's *Voraussetzung*: sentences may have presuppositions, uses of sentences (i.e. assertions) may involve presuppositions, and speakers may make presuppositions (cf. Atlas 1975, Soames 1989). This ambiguity resurfaces within the generative semantics tradition, where (as in Kiparsky & Kiparsky 1971) *x* in the formula *x presupposes y* may range over sentences, sets of sentences, propositions, speech acts, speakers, utterances, or verbs, and *y* over sentences, propositions, or truth values.

6   For some discussion, see Rescher (1969: 160ff), Horn (1989: Section 2.4).

7   Within presuppositional semantics, the alternative to Strawson's concession that not all singular terms are equally presuppositional is the acceptance, with Burton-Roberts (1989: Chapter 9), of a "loosening of the tie between presupposition and lack of truth value": a sentence with a failed presupposition may nevertheless, in the right circumstances, be true or false. For other approaches, see McCawley (1979) and Lappin & Reinhart (1988).

8   The Strawsonian notions of topic and aboutness, discussed insightfully by Reinhart (1981), are related to pragmatic presupposition and to given/old information in Horn (1986, 1989).

9 Compare the moral drawn by Mates (1973: 417–18) from the contrast between (10a) and (11a):

> To make the truth-value of what is said fluctuate with these differences of situation and purpose is only to lose the difficulties in a haze of confusion. Far better, it seems to me, is to draw the semantics-pragmatics line in such a way that questions like "what topic is he talking about?" and "Was that an odd thing to say?" are classified as pragmatic, while "Is what he said *true*?" is semantic.

10 This formulation follows the exposition of Stalnaker 1978: 321ff.
11 A parallel process of exploitation is involved in (i) and (ii), where the presupposition lexically associated with factive *regret* must be noncontroversially accommodated:

> (i) We regret that children under the age of 12 cannot attend the exercises.
>   [from an MIT commencement brochure, cited by Karttunen]
> (ii) I regret to inform you that your insurance policy is hereby cancelled.

12 Following Gazdar (1979), we can say that (17a) <u>entails</u> (17a′) as well as (pragmatically) presupposing or conventionally implicating it; it is the entailment that is truth-conditionally relevant. Since the existential premise associated with clefts is also entailed in the positive – as is existence with singular expressions – it will function as part of what is said in the context but only as part of what is (conventionally) implicated in negatives or questions. Hence the parallel below:

> (i)   It's Kim who ate the pizza.   The King of France is bald.
> (ii)   It isn't Kim who ate the pizza.   The King of France isn't bald.
> (iii) Someone ate the pizza.   There is a King of France.

In each set, the statement in (i) but not that in (ii) entails the corresponding (iii) proposition, but in addition (the utterer of) both (i, ii) pragmatically presupposes or conventionally implicates (iii). With *even* or *manage to*, on the other hand, the non-truth-conditional component involving unlikelihood or effort is entailed by neither positive nor negative statement.

13 See *inter alia* the corresponding principles of Fogelin, O'Hair, and Harnish discussed in Horn 1990b.
14 Thus if it's hot, it is *a fortiori* warm, but if I know it's hot I can echo and reject the assertion that it's warm as (not false but) insufficiently informative:

> (i)   It's not <u>warm</u>, it's <u>hot</u>!
> (ii) You're right, it's not warm. It's <u>hot</u>!

As seen in (ii), the effect is often that of an ironic unsaying or retroactive accommodation: The metalinguistic understanding typically requires a second pass, after the descriptive reading self-destructs. It should be noted that the set of metalinguistic negations inducing double processing is not truth-conditionally homogeneous. When the focus of negation involves a truth condition for the corresponding affirmative (e.g. *The king of France is not bald: there is no king of France*), the metalinguistic negation suffices to render the sentence true as a descriptive negation. Thus, even though such a denial is most naturally uttered as an echoic objection to an earlier positive assertion, no truth-conditional contradiction arises in the processing of the negative utterance. When the objection focuses on an aspect of meaning that is <u>not</u> a truth condition of the affirmative, the use of metalinguistic negation fails to guarantee the truth of the corresponding descriptive negation. Hence the contrast in (iii):

(iii) a. The king of France isn't bald, (because) there is no king of France.
 b. It's not warm, (#because) it's hot.
 c. I didn't trap two monGEESE, (#because) I trapped two monGOOSES.
 d. Grandpa isn't 'feeling lousy', (#because) he's just indisposed.

Cf. Horn 1990a for related discussion.

15 R-based implicata, while calculable, are often not calculated on-line when conventions of use are involved; a specific form of expression may be associated with a given pragmatic effect while an apparently synonymous form is not. Thus *Can you close the window?* is standardly used for indirect requests while *Are you able to* is not; *I don't guess that* ϕ allows a strengthening "neg-raised" understanding in only a subset of the dialects for which *I don't think that* ϕ does. These are instances of standardized nonliterality (Bach & Harnish 1979: 192–219) or short-circuited conversational implicature (Morgan 1978, Horn 1989: Section 5.3).

16 For detailed discussion of the issues involved in the definition and interaction of the maxims, see Martinich (1980), Wilson & Sperber (1986), Levinson (1987a), Neale (1992).

17 Compare R-based narrowing, in which the restriction of e.g. *poison, liquor, drink, undertaker* to a particularly salient subset or exemplar of the original denotation is not prompted by the existence of a specific word pre-empting that portion of semantic space. Cf. Horn (1984) for discussion.

18 Compare Searle's acknowledgement (1965: 235) of "a principle of maximum illocutionary ends with minimum phonetic effort" or the minimax principle of Carroll & Tanenhaus (1975: 51), "The speaker always tries to optimally minimize the surface complexity of his utterances while maximizing the amount of information he effectively communicates to the listener", or various precursors of these formulations by Paul, Zipf, and Martinet (Horn 1993).

12 Negation and Polarity Items

WILLIAM A. LADUSAW

1 Introduction

My goal here is to survey some recent proposals and results in the analysis of natural language negation within the assumptions of generative grammar and the project of applying formal semantic techniques to the interpretation of natural language structures. I have focussed on three areas: the semantics of clausal descriptive negation, the analysis of the limitations on the distribution of so-called negative polarity items, and the interpretation of negative concord structures.

2 The Semantics of Negation

Fundamental to the semantics of negation is a notion of inconsistency. Negation is always rooted in an opposition between two elements which are inconsistent with each other. In terms of simple propositional logic, where formulas are assigned truth-values, this inconsistency is represented by the fact that a formula p and its negation $\neg p$ cannot both be true. The essence of this weak sense of negation is expressed in the Law of Contradiction ($\neg(p \& \neg p)$). Though this truth-value based notion of negation is archetypal, the opposition of inconsistent elements is relevant to other domains as well. For example, properties may be opposed in this way, as nothing may be both possible and impossible, or both hot and cold. The same opposition may be given a pragmatic construal in terms of the felicitous assertability of a sentence and two sentences may be negatively opposed because they cannot both be felicitously asserted in a given context. This weakest notion of negative opposition is termed *contrary* negation.

A stronger notion of negation, which naturally concentrates on binary oppositions, is derived when one of the opposed elements is applicable to every item in a relevant domain. This yields an opposition of *contradictory* negation. For example, the assumption that every model will satisfy (make true) either p or $\neg p$ shows that the truth-value based negation is a contradictory opposition, subject to the Law of the Excluded Middle. The opposition between the possible and impossible is likewise contradictory, but because one can easily imagine that something to which the properties hot and cold might apply might be neither hot nor cold, that opposition is seen as merely contrary and not contradictory.

Returning to pragmatic opposition based upon felicitous assertability in a given context, the "excluded middle" assumption would require that exactly one of two sentences in contradictory opposition would be assertable in every context. The fact that natural language sentences are routinely associated with presuppositions about the contexts in which they may be used means that negation is generally not contradictory with respect to the full domain of contexts but at best contradictory only with respect to the range of contexts in which the presuppositions of the sentence are satisfied.

These issues are surveyed broadly and in detail in Horn (1989). My purpose in beginning with them is first to address some points which are obscured when linguistic analysis is carried out using the simple notion of negation from standard propositional logic as the archetypal understanding of negation.

2.1   The multi-domain nature of negation

If negation is based upon an opposition of elements within a certain domain, we can recognize what is logically the same negative opposition in different semantic and pragmatic domains.

A good example of this is the boolean semantics of Keenan and Faltz (1985), which argues that the denotational domains for linguistic expressions of a wide variety of categories show a common algebraic structure within which boolean meet, join, and complementary negation operations can be defined. Contradictorily opposed linguistic expressions can be found in every category whose interpretations are complementary within their semantic type. This gives a well-defined sense in which the determiner phrases *no dogs* and *some dogs* are negations of each other and similarly for *every cat* and *not every cat* when interpreted as generalized quantifiers. Similarly, the pairs *few* / *many* and *sometimes* / *never* are negations of each other in terms of the denotation algebras appropriate for these categories. Given the homomorphic nature of many denotation functions, the boolean relations are preserved in semantic composition in such a way that sentences containing these phrases are correctly predicted to have contradictory truth-conditions without formal decompositions which would assimilate each to analysis in terms of propositional negation. There is no formal necessity of giving propositional negation primacy in linguistic analysis.

Another illustration of this point is provided by Horn's (1989, Chapter 6) distinction between descriptive and metalinguistic negation. The morphology of negation in natural languages does not generally explicitly differentiate between negation within the theory of semantic content and oppositions which are created in the pragmatic aspects of utterance interpretation. Sometimes negative morphology in a sentence should be interpreted as determining the content of an assertion, and sometimes it is the indication that the conversational function of an utterance is as a denial of some previous assertion or implication. Horn's analysis of the "pragmatic ambiguity" of negation builds on the view that the domains of negative opposition extend beyond the theory of semantic content.

2.2 Intra-domain and inter-domain negation

It is common to identify the negative morphology of a language as expressing the complement operation that relates two contradictorily opposed meanings. Though complement operations can be defined in many different domains, they are of necessity defined within a particular domain. That is, the opposition is always between elements drawn from the same domain. Contradictory opposition is symmetric; the proposition represented by p has as good a claim to being "the (contradictory) negation of" $\neg p$ as the reverse. Representationally, however, the latter is marked as "a negation" because it contains an expression whose interpretation is a unary operator which determines its interpretation as a function of the interpretation of the former. In a formal logic containing a negation operator, that operator is taken typically as directly expressing the complement operation, a function whose domain and range are identical. While in the language we may distinguish certain formulas as negative or not depending upon whether the negation operator is the superior operator, this asymmetry is not reflected in the semantics. For example, in systems where propositions are modeled as sets of possible worlds, it is impossible to distinguish any proposition as semantically negative; one may only discern pairs of contradictorily opposed propositions.

In natural languages, negation is taken as representationally marked; negative sentences are generally distinguished by the presence of certain morphology missing from affirmative sentences. Given the morphological asymmetry between negation and affirmation, it might seem that the tradition of formal logic, with a negation operator but no affirmation operator, is in harmony with a typological generalization about natural language.

But the standard view of negation as directly expressing a complement operation is in conflict with another typological generalization about natural language negation: negative morphology does not naturally directly iterate. That is, the direct analog of $\neg\neg p$ in natural language is generally not well-formed. The view of negative morphology as directly expressing a semantic complement operation, an intra-domain operation, makes this a semantic mystery. A function which has the same domain and range can always apply iteratively to its output.

At issue here is the relation between negation and affirmation. Should negation have a twin operator which forms affirmatives? The traditional dialogue on this subject is discussed in Horn (1989) under the rubric of the symmetrist vs. the asymmetrist view of negation. Traditional propositional logic treats the relation between negation and affirmation asymmetrically. A symmetrical treatment would not form a negative proposition from an affirmative one, but would rather create contradictorily opposed propositions by combining some semantic base with either a negation operator or an affirmation operator. We might therefore raise the question of whether natural language negation is better treated as symmetrically opposed to affirmation.

Construed in this way, the operations expressed by negation and affirmation would not be intra-domain operations, but rather inter-domain operations, relating some non-propositional basis for a proposition to a proposition. As an operator with a range different from its domain, it would follow that it could not naturally iterate directly.

2.3   *A hierarchy of strengths of negation*

It is possible to distinguish independent properties that are joined together in classical negation to create a family of operators which have claim to being negations of varying strengths. For example, contrary negation obeys the Law of Contradiction, but not the Law of the Excluded Middle. Similarly, the law of double negation has two halves: one which introduces double negation ($p \Rightarrow \neg\neg p$) and one which eliminates double negations ($\neg\neg p \Rightarrow p$). Only the former is valid if p and $\neg p$ are merely contrarily opposed; the latter is valid only for a contradictory opposition.[1]

The decomposition of the properties of classical negation into logically independent properties yields distinctions which have been claimed to be relevant for linguistic analysis. One example is the property defined in (1):

> (1)   If A and B are two boolean algebras, the function f from A into B is
> *polarity reversing* iff for any $a_1, a_2 \in A$, if $a_1 \leq a_2$ then $f(a_2) \leq f(a_1)$.

This is the property which Barwise and Cooper (1981) call *anti-persistent* for determiners and *monotone decreasing* for generalized quantifiers and which Ladusaw (1979, 1980) called *downward entailing*. It is a property of negation in the sense that the negation operation in any boolean domain will have the effect of inverting the ordering relation between its arguments, but other expressions, among them the determiners *few*, *at most n* and the adverb *rarely*, can be shown to have denotation functions which share this property, though they do not have the full range of semantic properties that classical negation has. In this sense, the definition provides a way of defining a broad class of "weakly negative" expressions.

Frans Zwarts (1993) (see also van der Wouden (1994b)) has proposed a finer-grained classification by decomposing the interaction of negation with boolean meet and join, creating a hierarchy of negative expressions with the polarity reversing ones properly including the stronger class of anti-additive operators as defined in (2), which in turn properly include the anti-morphic operators, as defined in (3).

(2)   A functor f is *anti-additive* iff $f(X \vee Y) = f(X) \wedge f(Y)$.
(3)   A functor f is *antimorphic* iff f is anti-additive and additionally $f(X \wedge Y) = f(X) \vee f(Y)$.

Classical propositional negation is an antimorphic operator, but the generalized quantifier *no dogs* is anti-additive but not antimorphic. The polarity reversing quantifier *at most 3 dogs* is not anti-additive, but it is polarity reversing. We will return to claims about the relevance of these semantic properties for linguistic analysis below, but the important point is that the semantics of negation has a richer structure than is evident when attention is restricted to classical propositional negation.

3   Negative Polarity Items

Viewed from the perspective of generative grammar, negative polarity items pose a semantic licensing problem. That is, a negative polarity item carries conventionalized requirements that limit its distribution to a proper subset of the grammatical contexts in which it would otherwise be expected to occur. Consider as representative the cases of negative polarity items in (4)–(8):

(4)   The dean **didn't** sign *any* of the letters before she left.
(5)   I **don't** *ever* take the train to work.
(6)   They **haven't** found a reliable contractor *yet*.
(7)   Mark **didn't** contribute *a red cent* to the relief fund.
(8)   I'm **not** *all that* anxious to visit them.

In each of these well-formed sentences, the italicized expression is a negative polarity item whose occurrence is dependent upon the presence of the negative expression in bold-face. That is, if the bold-faced expression were removed or replaced by a nonnegated auxiliary, the sentence would be ill-formed, because the occurrence of the negative polarity item would not be properly licensed. In general, it is true that a structure containing a negative polarity item will be well-formed only if the negative polarity item is interpreted as falling in the scope of a negative licensor. The fundamental problem for a theory of polarity items at a descriptive level is to find the appropriate theoretical assumptions under which this generalization may be entailed. My discussion of results in this area is organized by the following questions.

The Licensor Question: How can the class of licenses for a polarity item be delimited? Is the class of licenses for a particular polarity item subject to arbitrary variation or is the class of licenses determined by the explanation of the item's status as a polarity item?

The Licensee Marking Question: How are negative polarity items to be distinguished from polarity insensitive items of similar syntactic category? Is polarity sensitivity an arbitrarily conventionalized property of an expression or does its status follow from its meaning?

The Licensing Relation Question: What is the required relation between the licensor and the licensee? Taking the general view that the licensee must be interpreted in the semantic scope of the licensor and given that surface structural relations underdetermine semantic scope relations, is licensing dependent only upon the semantic notion of scope or are surface structural relations also relevant?

The Status Question: Finally, what is the theoretical status of a structure containing an unlicensed polarity item? Are such ill-formed strings syntactically well-formed but uninterpretable or do they have well-defined interpretations which make them pragmatically unusable?

I think it is fair to say that in none of these cases are fully satisfying explanatory answers available. Here I will survey some telling results from work in the area, though this survey will of necessity be incomplete. Before doing so I issue two caveats about the choice of concentrating on licensing negative polarity items.

The first may be termed the problem of the fine structure of polarity licensing. It seems clear that there is no uniform class of "negative polarity items". The range of licenses for some polarity items is larger than for others. Some polarity items are licensed by weak negatives as defined above, while others are licensed only by stronger negations. This suggests that there must be different ways of answering the licensee marking question and further that there should be a connection between the property that makes a particular item polarity sensitive and the class of licensors for it. The theory of polarity item licensing must be rich enough to explain this fine structure while still being general enough to account for the family resemblance among the items which are termed negative polarity items.

The second caveat is that negative polarity items are only a very salient and populous family of items which are subject to restrictions on their distribution. From the earliest work on these items in generative grammar (Klima (1964), Baker (1970)), it was recognized that there were parallel affirmative polarity items, items which could not be interpreted in the scope of negation. Among the affirmative polarity items of English are *some*, *already*, and *would rather*, illustrated in (9)–(11).

(9)   ?The dean didn't sign *some* of the letters before she left.
(10) ?They haven't *already* found a reliable contractor.
(11) ?I *would*n't *rather* go to a movie.

Though many affirmative polarity items have a close semantic relation to negative polarity items (such as *some* and *already* to *any* and *yet*), others like *would rather* do not. Nonetheless the fact that some affirmative polarity items fit in paradigmatic complementary distribution with negative polarity items suggests that their analysis should be related to the theory of negative polarity licensing.

However it also seems clear that rather than being subject to a requirement that they be interpreted in the scope of a negative expression, they are subject to a ban on interpretation in the scope of a negation. This kind of "anti-licensing" condition is the converse of the condition on negative polarity items in the way in which Principle B of the Chomskian binding theory is the inverse of Principle A, a position explored in detail in Progovac (1993, 1994).

The "violations" of (9–11) are also different in status from those involving unlicensed negative polarity items. What is to be explained about them is not that they are ill-formed simpliciter, but that the negation in them cannot be read as a clausal descriptive negation in the sense of Horn. Rather they can readily be used only as direct denials, presumably involving metalinguistic negation, or occur as well-formed substrings embedded in the larger structures termed "double negative contexts" by Baker (1970). Hence the interpretation of whatever licensing conditions are involved must involve pragmatic issues of conditions on use.[2]

3.1   The licensor question

It has been clear since Klima (1964) that the range of expressions which can license negative polarity items like *any* and *ever* is beyond syntactic characterization. In addition to morphologically transparently negative terms like *not, nobody,* and *never,* "covert negations" like *few* and *rarely* do as well as predicates like *unlikely* and *doubt.*

(12)   The dean **rarely** signs *any* of the letters before she eats lunch.
(13)   **Few** commuters *ever* take the train to work.
(14)   I **doubt** that they have found a reliable contractor *yet*.
(15)   Mark is **unlikely** to contribute *a red cent* to the relief fund.

In addition, some polarity items appear quite freely in the antecedent (*if*) clause of a conditional. Polar (*yes/no*) questions are polarity neutral environments, allowing both affirmative and negative polarity items to mix freely.

(16)   If *anyone* notices *anything* unusual, it should be reported to the campus police.
(17)   Has *anyone already* figured out the answer?

A particularly telling case is the determiner *every*, which licenses some polarity items in its restriction, but not in its nuclear scope.

(18)   **Every** customer who had *ever* purchased *anything* in the store was contacted.

(19)   *Everyone who was contacted had *ever* purchased *anything* in the store.

On the basis of such data, Ladusaw (1979) proposed that the class of licenses for negative polarity items be defined in semantic terms, as the class of expressions whose meanings were "downward entailing" (polarity reversing as in (1)). In this way, the syntactic heterogeneity of the class of licensing expressions is explained and the property of being a license is connected to the theory of inference and the traditional observation that the effect of many negative polarity items of the minimal value sort (*lift a finger, drink a drop, budge an inch*) is to strengthen a negative statement. The connection to monotonicity inferences if discussed in Hoeksema (1986) and Sánchez Valencia (1991). On this view, the property of being a polarity item licensor is predicted from independent semantic properties of an expression.

As a definition of *the* class of licensors of negative polarity items, the proposal of Ladusaw (1979) has a number of problems.

First, it does not take into account the "fine structure" of polarity licensing. Not all negative polarity items are licensed by all polarity reversing expressions; some require stronger negations to license them. The approach taken by Zwarts (1993) takes the hierarchy of negative expressions defined above as a family of possible licenses of which polarity reversing expressions are the weakest class. Hoeksema (1983) discusses the case of the Dutch item *ook maar* in the comparative licensing environment. Van der Wouden (1994a,b) elaborates a theory of polarity licensing in which different polarity items are associated with different strengths of licenses: some licensed by the polarity reversing expressions, some requiring anti-additive licenses and others requiring the strongest, antimorphic licenses. This places the burden of accounting for the fine-structure of licensing on licensee marking while maintaining that the property of being a license is defined in logico-semantic terms. In this way it seems to inherit another problem with the Ladusaw (1979) account: its context independence.

By treating the issue of polarity item licensing as a matter of grammatical well-formedness in the broadest sense and defining licensors in terms of properties of their logical denotations, Ladusaw (1979) predicts that polarity licensing should not be sensitive to inferential properties in context. This prediction is not borne out.

Heim (1984) discusses the problem of considering all antecedents of conditionals as being downward-entailing environments. She shows that antecedents of conditionals containing licensed negative polarity items can be seen as downward-entailing in only a limited way, when background assumptions are taken into account. In this way, the polarity licensing must be relativized to a context of use in a way that supports the general connection to inference but does not allow well-formedness to be decided in a context independent way. This point is in keeping with the approach of Fauconnier (1975), which stressed the role of pragmatic assumptions in determining the inferences from *any* and quantificational superlatives. Krifka (1991b) formalizes a theory of this type.

The context-dependence of polarity licensing and the status of sentences containing unlicensed polarity items is a main theme of the proposal by Linebarger (1980, 1987, 1991) that weak negative expressions do not directly license polarity items but do so only in virtue of negative implicatures that they make available in the communicative context. This point can be illustrated with (20–21):

(20) Exactly four people in the whole room *budged an inch* when I asked for help.

(21) He kept writing novels long after he had *any* reason to believe that they would sell.

Ladusaw's account predicts these examples to be ill-formed because no expression in them is polarity reversing. However they can easily be imagined as usable to convey that very few people budged an inch or that he kept writing even though there wasn't any reason to believe that they would sell. On Linebarger's view, the license for the polarity item is not anywhere in the sentence but is rather the negative implicatum. We will return to this theory below in the discussion of the licensing relation, but it illustrates the need for a theory of indirect licensing and poses problems for all accounts which interpret the conditions on polarity licensing as grammatical well-formedness conditions.

3.2 *Licensee marking*

Construed as a simple problem of marking expressions as subject to a licensing condition, marking negative polarity items as such poses the same problems that the general theory of idioms does: how are phrasal and sometimes non-constituent expressions marked as carrying some conventional property. How are *lift a finger, budge (an inch), so much as a* and *a red cent* to be associated with a polarity requirement? How are thin dimes distinguished from silver dimes so that mentioning the former is subject to licensing while mentioning the latter is not?

Though conventionalization is involved, there are clear semantic generalizations about which expressions are candidates for becoming negative polarity items. The most obvious generalization is that "minimum value" items are prone to become polarity items.

Viewed as a matter of determining well-formedness through enforcement of a licensing condition, the licensee marking question asks how the negative polarity items can be matched to the relevant licensing condition. The fine structure of negative polarity licensing suggests that this marking must be parameterized to indicate the relevant class of licenses. Some of this parameterization may be predicted from the meaning of the polarity item.

Linebarger contrasts the following two cases with the negative polarity item *so much as* in the restriction of *every*, which suggest that the polarity item is well-formed only if the sentence is used to express a necessary, rather than an accidental, generalization.

> (22)   Every restaurant that charges so much as a dime for iceberg lettuce ought to be closed down.
>
> (23)   ??Every restaurant that charges so much as a dime for iceberg lettuce actually has four stars in the handbook.

Heim (1984) notes that this is not true of *any* and *ever* and suggests that the additional requirement holds only of a proper subset of polarity items: the minimal value items, which she proposes carry conventional implicatures similar to those carried by *even*.

By contrast, Linebarger's (1980, 1991) pragmatic approach to polarity item licensing gives a different kind of answer. On her account, negative polarity items are marked by association with a conventional implicature that a complex condition hold of the context in which the sentences containing them are used. The core of the proposal is given in (24):

> (24)   A negative polarity item N contributes to a sentence S expressing a proposition P the conventional implicature that the following condition will be satisfied in the context of the utterance of S: P entails or implicates some proposition NI, which may be identical to P. In the LF (logical form) of some sentence S' expressing this negative implicatum, N occurs in the immediate scope of negation.

The licensor of the negative polarity item is in the logical form of the negative implicature, which is subject to three additional requirements: (i) that it be available, in the sense that the speaker must be actively attempting to convey it by utterance of the sentence; (ii) that the truth of the negative implicatum itself virtually guarantee the truth of the proposition expressed by the sentence, and (iii) that the negative implicatum count as foreground information, in the sense that it is conveyed as novel in the context or at least not required to be background information for the utterance.

This approach to the licensing of negative polarity items is inconsistent with the idea that sentences containing unlicensed polarity items are uninterpretable, as the licensing condition itself requires that the sentence express a proposition so that it can be compared with the potential negative implicatum.

Linebarger's approach has the advantage of making "licensing" of polarity items a context-dependent operation. Hence the sensitivity to background assumptions noted above in connection with Heim (1984) is no surprise.

A further advantage is that it gives a natural mechanism for the polarity item itself to prompt the creation of the conditions under which it is licensed. This can be seen in connection with the problem for a direct licensing account posed by (20–21) above. For Linebarger, it is the presence of the negative polarity item itself which creates the requirement that use of the sentence conveys the negative implicature. It is not necessary to analyze *exactly four* as being ambiguous between a reading on which it means simply exactly four and a reading in which it asserts exactly four and implicates only four even in cases where there is no negative polarity item to license.

These are advantages of the account, though as Linebarger (1991) concedes, it needs a theory of how appropriate negative implicatures are calculated, and how the question of which sentences that express the implicature are being alluded to by the use of the negative polarity item, particularly given that the entire burden of accounting for the fine-structure of licensing must be due to the calculation of potential negative implicatures and judging them as properly available. Nevertheless this approach represents an attempt at providing a connection between context-dependent inferencing and the presence of negative polarity items.

However it does not abandon entirely the view that fundamentally the problem is one of enforcing a licensing condition in a theory of structural well-formedness. The condition ultimately reduces all questions of polarity licensing to one of well-formedness of a logical form. Negative polarity items must occur in the immediate scope (see below) of a "negative" in some logical form. In the core cases, the logical form at issue is simply the logical form of the sentence itself. In the derivative licensing cases, the logical form at issue is the logical form of some sentence which expresses a strong, foreground, available negative conventional implicature. But in either case, it comes down to enforcing a licensing condition, which requires that the licensees be marked, that a class of licenses be delimited, and a relation which must hold between the licensor and the licensee. Linebarger's proposal differs from the preceding ones in what the appropriate class of licensors is.

Though it is the intent of Linebarger (1980) to defend the idea that the licensor can be reduced to a single abstract element appearing in logical forms (NOT, the only true negation), the theory could easily take advantage of the hierarchy of negative expressions defined above and propose, for example, that only anti-additive or anti-morphic operators license negative polarity items directly. Reinterpreted in this way, Linebarger's proposal can be viewed as assuming that ultimately all negative polarity items require a strong negative license; the apparent licensing ability of weakly negative items is due to their ability to invite indirect, context-dependent calculation of negative implicatures. Empirical evaluation of that correlation would require a more detailed procedure for calculating the negative implicatures.

A recent attempt to derive the distribution of a polarity item from an assumption of what conditions mark it as requiring licensing is the account of the distribution of *any* in Kadmon and Landman (1993). They propose to account for the distribution of the English determiner *any* in both its polarity sensitive and free-choice uses by assuming that it is simply an indefinite determiner phrase distinct from one headed by the indefinite article *a* by having an additional semantic aspect (widening) and being subject to a pragmatic licensing condition (strengthening). Although the proposal concentrates only on this one item, its architecture is a good illustration of how substantive assumptions about what the individual polarity items mean might in fact entail what expressions appear to license them and their paper provides detailed comparison between their account, Ladusaw's, and Linebarger's.

Under Kadmon and Landman's analysis, all occurrences of the item *any* are analyzed as indefinite, for concreteness let us assume as a restricted free variable in the sense of Heim (1982). Hence the sentences in (25)–(26) are analyzed as expressing substantially the same meaning, with the indefinites construed as existentially closed in the scope of the negation.

(25)   Mike didn't find a shirt in the closet.
(26)   Mike didn't find any shirts in the closet.

They assume however that *any* is distinct from *a* in that the former forms indefinites which have a wider domain than those formed by the latter. The domain of items which might count as *a shirt* may be restricted by certain reasonableness assumptions associated with the context. In this example, it might be a shirt which is appropriate for the purpose that took Mike to the closet in the first place. Kadmon and Landman assume that such reasonableness assumptions are called off in the case of *any*, so that even shirts unreasonable for the purpose at hand would have to count as potential referents for the *any* phrase.

They further assume that *any* is distinct from *a* in being subject to a licensing condition, but not one which directly mentions the class of expressions which license it, but rather a condition that requires that the domain widening contributed by the use of *any* actually results in a stronger proposition being expressed, that is one which (asymmetrically) entails the proposition formulated with the unwidened domain. The claim is that *any* will appear to be licensed in a sentence where and only where these conditions are met.[3]

It is an effect of this strengthening requirement that gives an account of the ill-formedness of unlicensed *any*. *Any* is licensed in (26) because the claim that Mike didn't find any shirts from domain S is a stronger claim than that he didn't find any shirts from the domain S', a proper subset of S. In affirmative, upward-entailing contexts, the strengthening requirement will not be met.

(27)   Mike found a shirt in the closet.
(28)   *Mike found any shirts in the closet.

Under the analysis, (28) expresses not a stronger proposition, but a weaker proposition than that expressed by (27). The polarity reversing property of negation is crucially involved in making the distinction, so there is a clear relation between this proposal and the assumption that the licensing condition on *any* mentions this class of operators. However the analysis succeeds in making something like the structural licensing condition a theorem of their account,[4] providing a principled reduction of the class of licenses for this item to the answer to the question of how to indicate that *any* is a polarity item.

3.3 *Licensing relation*

Returning to the view of polarity licensing as enforcing a condition between the licensor and the licensee in a logical form which makes semantic scope relations explicit, we now consider results involving the required relation between the licensee and the licensor.

Ladusaw (1979) imposes the requirement that the polarity item simply be somewhere within the logical scope of the licensing expression by requiring that it be within the constituent whose interpretation forms the argument to a downward-entailing expression. This requirement alone is too generous in two ways.

First, because nominal quantifiers can take scope over the entire clause in which they occur, this would predict that polarity sensitive items could be licensed anywhere within a clause containing a negative nominal quantifier. Similarly, because subject position can be interpreted in the scope of negative expressions associated with the tensed verb of the clause, one would expect that polarity items could appear in the subject position of a negated clause. However, this is not possible:

(29) *He read any of the stories to none of the children.
(30) *Any of the teachers didn't attend the meeting.

Consequently, Ladusaw (1979) imposes an additional surface structure condition on the relation between the licensor and the licensee: that licensors must precede clausemate licensees.[5] Given the right-branching character of English, much of the work of this condition would be done by a constraint requiring that the licensor c-command the licensee in surface structure.

By requiring that licensees be merely in the scope of the licensor, however, Ladusaw (1979) predicts that licensing is in effect unbounded. This is desirable for cases like (31), but Linebarger (1980) points out that this is too lax.

(31) Martha **didn't** say that *anyone* had *ever* found counterexamples to this claim.

Linebarger proposes that the core licensing condition on the relation between a polarity item and a licensing negation be the more restricted relation 'immediate scope'. In effect, she motivates a minimality requirement on polarity licensing that insures that no other logical operator can intervene between the polarity item and its licensor. This requirement can be illustrated by the following examples.

(32)   He didn't move because he was scared.
(33)   He didn't budge an inch because he was scared.

Though (32) is ambiguous, because the negation may be interpreted either as taking scope over the *because* clause or as part of the proposition modified by the *because* clause, (33) is unambiguous. It can be interpreted only by giving the negation narrow scope with respect to *because*. This follows on Linebarger's account assuming that *because* counts as an intervening nonlicensing operator.

(34)   Sam didn't read every child a story.
(35)   Sam didn't read every child any stories.

Similarly, while (34) can conceivably be interpreted as expressing the claim that not every child was read a story by Sam, (35) cannot be given that construal. The reading on which *every child* is construed as having *any stories* in its scope but within the scope of the negation is missing, despite the fact that this is the reading that would be in harmony with the surface structure c-command relations.

These effects are predicted by Linebarger's immediate scope requirement. Her original formalization required adjacency to NOT in LF and must be supplemented by some stipulated relaxations of adjacency for licensing multiple negative polarity items and also requires that all negative polarity items be moveable in logical form.

As her definition also requires a characterization of allowable and disallowable intervenors, an attractive reinterpretation of the evidence for the immediacy requirement is that the licensing relation is subject to a species of relativized minimality requirement in the sense of Rizzi (1990). That is, the class of licensors and intervenors (expressions of quantification, *because*) could be construed as potential licensors (governors, in a broad sense) and then the licensing condition would simply require minimality to be respected in licensing. This is the view taken in Ladusaw (1992) for the licensing of those negative polarity items which can be construed as Heimian indefinites. The licensing effect is there enforced as a condition on the operator which forces existential closure on the negative polarity indefinite and the minimality effect follows from the assumption that existential closure in the scope of an operator is exhaustively unselective.

In Linebarger's account of indirect licensing, the polarity items in sentences admitted through negative implicatures have no licensor in them, and hence the question of the licensing relation is not relevant for them. The licensor in these cases is a negation in a sentence which the speaker alludes to via a negative implicature. To the extent that something like a minimal scope requirement seems to hold in the sentence itself between the polarity items and the items which make manifest the negative implicature, it must result from assumptions about the formulation of the licensing implicatures.

Similarly, the approach of Kadmon and Landman does not need to characterize a licensing relation directly; rather the identification of a particular expression as a license and a relation between it and the polarity item is a product of the strengthening requirement and the general principles which determine the propositional content of the sentence.

3.4 Status question

Finally let us consider briefly the range of views with respect to the status of sentences containing unlicensed polarity items; in particular, what is the theoretical status of the star on the two strings below?

(36) *Meg ate any fruitcake.
(37) *Mark lifted a finger to help.

Ladusaw (1979) treated the polarity licensing requirement as one which simply disallowed interpretations which were the result of compositional interpretation when polarity items were not licensed at the top level of analysis, after all potential interpretations had been determined. Though compositional interpretation predicted that the former would express the claim that Meg ate some fruitcake and the latter that Mark did the minimal amount to help, these propositions are disqualified as interpretations by the stipulated polarity licensing requirement. So technically, these sentences were deemed uninterpretable. Approaches like that of Progovac (1993) and others who interpret the condition as deeming logical forms ill-formed give similar answers to the status question.

In searching beyond this stipulation for a way of deriving the result, one must be careful to realize that the requirement applies to these examples *qua* whole sentences rather than to their clausal structure. That is, it would be wrong to attempt to develop an explanation which entailed that the clauses in (36)–(37) had no meaning at all, because these same clauses occur as meaningful subparts of larger constructions:

(38) I doubt that Meg ate any fruitcake.
(39) I was surprised that Mark lifted a finger to help.

In these cases, the embedded complement has to be assigned an interpretation by the compositional semantics to be a meaningful part of the whole and the polarity item in them must be licensed by the embedding context. All of the approaches considered here are consistent with the enforcement of the polarity licensing requirements as a property of sentences as a whole.

Kadmon and Landman's proposed strengthening requirement on *any* and its natural extention to minimal value polarity items like *lift a finger* gives a different view of the status of these violations. The requirement that the widening contributed by the polarity item be a strengthening is attached to the polarity items. To test whether the requirement is met, the "ill-formed" sentences in (36)–(37) must have well-defined propositional interpretations. So they are not ill-formed because they have no meaning but rather their meaning is ill-suited to accomplish the conventionally required goal of strengthening the statement.

The whole-sentence character of polarity licensing and the context-sensitivity of inference and implicature discussed by Heim, Linebarger and Krifka suggest that the domain of pragmatics is the place to look for the explanation for the anomaly of (36)–(37). It is a theme running through the history of the investigation of this topic that negative polarity items strengthen negative statements, that they are useable precisely where they make strong statements, and hence when the polarity items are not licensed, the sentence makes such a weak statement that it is in effect unuseable. On this view, the anomalous sentences (36)–(37) are not syntactically ill-formed in any way. They are completely interpretable by compositional semantic interpretations, but because of what they mean they are unuseable for certain tasks. In particular, these are simply unassertable.

This approach is attractive as an explanation for effects that have not entered into the discussion so far. These show cases where the presence of negative polarity items influences the type of speech act the sentence can be used to perform. Lakoff (1969) provides a more complete discussion.

An explicit proposal for the interaction of the semantic issues with the pragmatic issues is by Krifka (1990, 1991b). His account retains the use of the polarity reversing property of weak and strong negations to account for the different inferential effects of licensing and non-licensing contexts. In a formal reconstruction of the scalar notions central to the accounts of Horn (1972) and Fauconnier (1975), Krifka defines polarity lattices whose minimum and maximum items are polarity items. The lattice of alternatives to the polarity item interpretation is associated with the interpretation of every sentence containing a polarity item. As a consequence, use of the polarity item generates implications associated with its alternatives.

On Krifka's account, the ill-formedness of (36)–(37) is completely uninformative and a violation of conditions on assertability. As Krifka notes, mere uninformativeness is not a prediction of anomaly; what is needed is a theory which makes these *conventionally* uninformative in some way. Krifka proposes that the use of polarity items generally is governed by a general pragmatic principle which states that for a speaker to use a negative polarity item in a sentence which is associated with a propositional lattice, in which the polarity item determines the minimal element, is to reveal that the speaker has reasons for not asserting any alternative proposition in the lattice. In effect, to use the negative polarity item is to deny the assertability of all the alternatives.

Krifka extends the approach to directives and questions as well, where there are important results to be derived. For example, the presence of negative polarity items in imperatives affects their utility as commands vs. requests vs. offers, and the differential effect of certain polarity items in questions as a whole category has a fine structure which must be related to pragmatic issues.

As Krifka notes (1991b: 181), the explanation of the pragmatic ill-formedness works better with items like *lift a finger*, which can be used ironically, than with *any*. This may well be an indication that what is needed is a theory which involves both a pragmatic explanation of the need for polarity items to be licensed and a theory of well-formedness conditions as well which apply to structures containing certain polarity items, such as the indefinites *any* and *ever*.

4 Negative Concord

Negative concord is the multiple occurrence within a sentence of apparent expressors of negation which express only a single semantic negation. Negative concord is a widely attested phenomenon, illustrated by the sentences in (40) from nonstandard English and three Romance languages.

(40)   a. **Nobody** said **nothing** (to **nobody**).
          "Nobody said anything (to anybody)."
     b. Mark **didn't** say **nothing** (to **nobody**).
          Mark didn't say anything (to anybody).
     c. Mario **non** ha parlato con **nessuno** (di **niente**)
          Mario neg has spoken with nobody (about nothing)
          Mario hasn't spoken with anybody (about anything). [*Italian*]

     d. **Nadie (*no)** ha venido.
          Nobody has arrived. [*Spanish*]

     e. **Non** ha telefonato **nessuno**.
          Nobody telephoned.

     f. **No** m'ha   telefonat   **ningú**
          neg me-has telephoned nobody
          Nobody has telephoned me. [*Catalan*]

     g. **Ningú (no)** ha arribat.
          Nobody has arrived. [*Catalan*]

The interpretation of negative concord structures poses a puzzle for compositional semantic interpretation, which has sometimes led people to call it "illogical" negation, based upon a (misguided) attempt to apply the logical laws of double negation cancellation to natural language. Rather than illogical, it is a very interesting probe on assumptions about semantic interpretation and the syntax-semantics interface.

In the past few years a good deal of work has been done on the formal syntactic description of negative concord constructions in many languages. Zanuttini (1991) and Laka (1990) are seminal works in this area. In this discussion I will restrict myself to discussing what I believe are the important semantic issues associated with this construction, at the expense of omitting interesting issues of structural description. The view presented here is substantially that of Ladusaw (1992).

Let us consider why negative concord should appear at first view to be a difficult construction to interpret. Consider the sentences in (41) interpreted as standard English sentences.

(41)   a. John **hasn't** seen that movie.
       b. **Nobody** has seen that movie.
       c. **Nobody hasn't** seen that movie.
       d. John **hasn't** seen **nobody.**
       e. **Nobody** has seen **nobody.**

If we take the auxiliary in (41a) to express clausal descriptive negation, then this sentence expresses a proposition which denies that John has seen that movie. In (41b), there is no visible marker of clausal negation on the finite head of the clause, but the sentence expresses a proposition that denies that anyone has seen the movie. Following the tradition of Montague grammar, however, this fact is completely expected if the determiner phrase *nobody* is interpreted as expressing the generalized quantifier which accepts properties just in case their intersection with the set of persons is null, i.e. the function denoted by the logical expressions in (42).

(42) $\lambda P[\neg \exists x[person'(x) \wedge P(x)]$, $\lambda P[person' \cap P = \phi]$

These assumptions make the prediction that (41c) should express the proposition that the intersection between the class of persons and the property of not having seen the movie is null; that is, it will require that everyone has seen the movie. That is the logical double negation interpretation. Similarly, these assumptions will predict that (41d) will deny that John has the property of not having seen anybody, committing the speaker to the existence of someone whom John has seen. In (41e), there are two tokens of the word *nobody*, both of which will express the negative quantificational meaning, so it should entail that someone has seen someone.

However these are not readings that these sentences would have in a negative concord language. (41c) is parallel to one of the Catalan sentences represented in (40g). There are dialects of English in which the sentences in (41) would all be interpreted as if they contained only one expression of negation. Hence the puzzle about the interpretation of negative concord. How could results which work so well for one version of English be avoided for the negative concord languages?

The multiple logical negation results derive from a minimal assumption of compositionality and very few additional assumptions about the syntax-semantics interface:

I. The expressions which are assigned lexical denotations are constituents of surface structure.

II. Expressions are assigned lexical denotations as expression types not occurrence tokens. That is, specification of lexical meaning is context free.

III. The assumption that *nobody* and *didn't* are interpreted as expressions of negation; that is, their denotation functions are (at least) anti-additive.

Hence the analysis of negative concord languages must abandon one of these assumptions. Approaches to negative concord interpretation, whether formal or informal, can be classified according to which of these assumptions are abandoned.

The problem of negative concord is most acute for "surface compositional" approaches to semantic interpretation in the spirit of Montague grammar (e.g. Ladusaw (1979)). Assuming that semantic interpretation principles apply to a distinct representation of logical form which is constructed from surface structures allows the puzzle of negative concord to be eliminated by the changes effected in the derivation of a logical form.

Among these accounts, we can distinguish three approaches to negative concord.

Absorption and resumption

If the first assumption is abandoned the multiple occurrences of the apparent expressors of negation (hereafter, *n-words*) can be merged into a single constituent of logical form to be assigned an interpretation. Though not proposed for negative concord *per se*, this is the concern of May (1989, 403) about the interpretation of (41e). This is the basis for the proposal of Haegeman and Zanuttini (1990) for interpreting their proposed logical forms for negative concord constructions.

Context-sensitive meaning assignment

One can also derive correct interpretations by assigning differential interpretations to the occurrences of the n-words. The approach of Rizzi (1982) can be seen as advocating this line. A version of this kind of account is one which proposes to treat n-words as systematically ambiguous between negative and non-negative meanings and then imposing licensing requirements which have the effect of restricting the negatively and nonnegatively interpreted occurrences of n-words into just the right environments. This view suggests a parallel between the licensing of negative polarity items and enforcement of the relations among n-words in the negative concord clauses. Such proposals are discussed and critiqued in Zanuttini (1991), Laka (1990), and Ladusaw (1992).

Van der Wouden and Zwarts (1993) advocate an approach to negative concord which makes meaning assignment context-sensitive. An analysis within a categorial syntax which connects the assignment of negative meanings in negative concord structures to the theory of monotonicity inferences is presented in Dowty (1994).

Configurational expression of negation

The other alternative is to abandon the assumption that any of the n-words in these sentences directly express negation. Rather the expression of negation is associated with an abstract element of clause structure associated with the head of the clause and unique within the clause. On this approach, the argument n-words are treated as non-negative indefinites which are obligatorily to be associated with this abstract expressor of clausal negation and whose syntactic configuration determines whether the negation is expressed. This is the proposal of Ladusaw (1992), intended as a semantic foundation for the syntactic proposals of Zanuttini and Laka.

The study of negative concord is currently a very active area. There is disagreement within and between languages about the status of certain crucial data. However it seems clear that the analysis of negative concord cannot be reduced to the theory of the licensing of negative polarity items by assuming that all or some of the negative concord terms are 'polarity items'. Negative concord systematically shows more sensitivity to syntactic constraints and more apparently arbitrary variation in the well-formedness conditions on n-word occurrences. The class of licensing negations for negative concord is different from negative polarity items.

5   Conclusion

Because of its universal occurrence in languages, its direct connection to the core of logical analysis, and the wide-spread related phenomena of negative polarity sensitivity and negative concord, analysis in the area of negation can yield results which bear on fundamental questions of semantics and its relation to syntax. Achieving results, however, requires going beyond the simplistic view of negation as a propositional operator inherited from "baby logic", to examining the multiple notions of negation in algebras of interpretation. A truly explanatory theory of negative polarity licensing must involve careful attention to the semantic contribution, but also involve enough formalized pragmatic theory to account for the context-sensitivity of the inferences supported by the use of negative polarity items and the resulting affects on conditions of use. Finally negative concord is a widespread construction which, when understood thoroughly in a number of different languages, should provide telling evaluation of some basic assumptions about the syntax-semantics interface.

NOTES

* The author gratefully acknowledges the support of National Science Foundation grant BNS-9021398 and the support of the Dutch Organization for Scientific Research (NWO) through its PIONIER-programme "Reflections of Logical Patterns in Language Structure and Language Use" at the University of Groningen.
1   This is an issue in the difference between classical and so-called intuitionistic logic. Cf. e.g. Dummett 1977. Dunn (forthcoming) surveys a detailed dissection of negations in formal systems.
2   There are other items of limited distribution which could be seen as "polarity items" sensitive to semantic properties other than negation that could deserve treatment from the general theory of such restrictions. Examples of these are the scalar endpoint polarity items of Horn (1972). For example, *absolutely* and *practically*, co-occur with e.g. *everyone* and *no one* but not weak quantifiers like *someone* and with verbal predicates involving telicity but not atelic ones.
3   I omit here discussion of their locality requirement on the proposition which is the source of the strengthening.
4   There are empirical differences, however, and crucially the proposal is intended to unify the account of polarity and free-choice *any*.
5   The statement involves the clausemate relation to account for examples like *That anyone had ever proposed such a constraint surprised me.*

VI Tense

13   Tense and Modality

MÜRVET ENÇ

1   Introduction

If a language allows the speaker to talk about past, present, and future times, can we conclude that the language has a past tense, a present tense, and a future tense? Clearly not. As has often been pointed out (cf. Comrie (1985)), natural languages have expressions belonging to a number of different categories that wholly or partially determine temporal interpretation. Adverbs such as *yesterday* and *next week*, and adjectives such as *former* are examples of expressions that fix a time and yet do not belong to the syntactic category tense. Similarly, it is generally accepted that the perfect and the progressive are aspects and not tenses, although their meanings have temporal content. It follows that the semantic property of affecting temporal interpretation is not sufficient for identifying an expression as a tense. It is also the case that in some languages like Chinese, it is possible to utter sentences which express propositions with specific temporal content even though there is no overt temporal expression in the sentence. This further indicates that tenses are not necessary for temporal interpretation. There are theories of temporal interpretation which are not sensitive to categorial differences between the temporal expressions. Hornstein (1990), for instance, treats tenses, modals and the perfect as having the same temporal organization. I have a narrower concern here. I believe there are properties shared only by elements which are morphologically, syntactically, and semantically identified as belonging to a particular category. For example, although the perfect *have* in English requires making reference to a situation which is in the past of a point of evaluation, it clearly behaves differently from the past tense in a number of ways. It can be in the scope of *will* whereas the past tense cannot, as (1) and (2) show.

(1)   Mary will have finished the book.
(2)   *Mary will finished the book.

A sentence initial adverb fixing the time of the event is possible with the past tense, but not with the perfect.

(3) Yesterday, Lucy met my mother.
(4) *Yesterday, Lucy has met my mother.

The difference between (3) and (4) stems from the fact that the perfect is formally in the present, although it refers to a past event. Given that interpretations must be assumed to be compositional and therefore a function of the interpretation of their constituents plus the syntactic structure, the fact that the perfect *have* is an auxiliary that can co-occur with tenses but that the past is a tense and cannot occur with, say, another past tense cannot be ignored. Such syntactic differences result in semantic differences and are therefore of theoretical interest. This paper is intended to contribute to an understanding of the different temporal categories and their behavior, in particular to an understanding of the category tense.

How are we to identify tenses? The tenses that have been proposed for natural languages are generally the past, the present and the future. These seem reasonable since they correspond to the basic broad divisions that humans seem to make in the way they view time.[1] Let us adopt the working hypothesis that these are indeed the tenses possible in natural languages. It does not follow from the universal availability of these tenses that every language will instantiate any or all of them, since there does not seem to be anything in the grammar that forces tenses. We could then say that Chinese, for example, does not have any tenses.[2] However, determining whether or not a tense exists in a particular language is not always as straightforward as in Chinese. There may be a morpheme in a language whose lexical meaning requires that a proposition be evaluated in the past or in the future, yet there may be questions about whether that morpheme is a tense. This is the case with the English *will*, as will be discussed below.

Suppose we assume that an expression is a tense if it has one and only one semantic contribution which is to specify whether the proposition expressed by the sentence is evaluated in the past, the present, or the future. Then we would be forced to conclude that English has no tenses, because all three morphemes that have been called tenses in English can have interpretations which are different from their usual tense interpretation. Consider (5) and (6).

(5) Sarah likes lobster.
(6) Sarah talks with her mouth full.

According to (5), Sarah's liking a lobster holds at the time of speech, i.e. at the present. This is the straightforward interpretation of the present tense. Yet the present tense in (6) does not yield a reading where the talking is going on at the time of utterance; instead, (6) has only a generic reading.

(7) If his father were more considerate, Tom wouldn't be so unhappy.

(7) is an example of a counterfactual sentence, which characteristically contains the past tense morpheme without a past interpretation.[3]

(8) Pat will be sleeping now.

(8) expresses a belief about the present, made explicit by the occurrence of the adverb *now*, yet contains *will* which is used to talk about the future.

If the strong definition of tense suggested above is adopted, one may conclude that these morphemes in English are ambiguous between a tense and something else, or that English does not have any tenses. However, the phenomena illustrated here are not particular to English. For example in Turkish, the counterfactuals also contain the past tense morpheme. The non-future modal interpretation of the future morpheme, as in (8), is also observable in other languages (cf. Yavaş (1982)). It is unlikely that such cross-linguistic generalities are random coincidences. It may be that, for reasons we do not yet understand, tense morphemes are in general capable of expressing these other notions. Until these issues become clarified, it seems advisable to abandon the strong definition of tense as a morpheme that only refers to a particular time segment. This still leaves us without a criterion for identifying tenses.

Comrie (1985) distinguishes between basic meaning and secondary or peripheral meaning. He suggests that a morpheme is identifiable as a tense if its basic meaning is temporal, even though it may have other secondary meanings. This seems intuitively attractive, yet there are no criteria for determining which meaning of a morpheme is basic. And until such criteria are formulated, this method of identifying tenses cannot be successful.

Even if we cannot give the defining characteristics of tenses, we may be able to advance our understanding by showing that certain elements usually assumed to be tenses are in fact something else. We can then assume that when we eliminate from the list of temporal expressions those which belong to other categories, we will be left with tenses. We already do this, for example, with the PP *in the past*. Semantically it seems no different from the past tense, yet we know that syntactically it is a prepositional phrase and not a tense. In recent work, I have argued that English does not have a present tense, and that the morphology we see on the verb in (5) and (6) is subject agreement (Enç (1990)).[4] If this view is correct, then we have eliminated one possible tense from the inventory of tenses in English, leaving the past and the future. I cannot construct arguments to show that -*ed* in English belongs to a category other than tense, and I will therefore assume that it is a true tense, the past tense. I already mentioned that *will* has undeniably non-future modal uses (cf. (8)). Some linguists assume that this morpheme is ambiguous between a tense and a modal (e.g. Hornstein (1977, 1990)), others assume that all occurrences of *will* are modal, i.e. that it is never a tense (e.g. Jespersen (1924), Smith (1978), Yavaş (1982)), and still others find the evidence inconclusive (e.g. Comrie (1985)). In this paper, I will address the question of which category *will* belongs to.

The non-future uses of *will* are intensional, and express a number of different modalities. For example in (8), repeated here, *will* expresses epistemic necessity.

(8)   Pat will be sleeping now.

(8) is true if in all possible worlds consistent with an actual plan or a schedule, Pat is sleeping. It differs from the epistemic *must* in that it requires a prior plan.

In (9), *will* expresses dispositional necessity.

(9)   Sarah will sometimes play loud music to annoy her mother.

(9) is true if in all possible worlds consistent with Sarah's general disposition there are times when she plays loud music to annoy her mother.

These are examples of clearly modal occurrences of *will*. The question is whether the occurrences of *will* where it seems to simply supply a future time, as in (10), can also be analyzed as modals.

(10)   Jim will give Tom his keys.

Jespersen (1924) claims that we know less about the future and that therefore we talk about it in a more vague way. That is to say, claims about the future are always weak as compared to claims about the past. Comrie (1985) also states that talk about the future is more speculative since our predictions and expectations about the future can be changed by intervening events. A similar point is made in Ultan (1972), where uncertainty is recognized as an inherent property of the future. Yavaş (1982) argues that this ontological difference between the past and the future justifies treating *will* as a modal even when its function seems to be to specify a future time. Comrie (1985) comments that future sentences such as (10) make a definite statement about a future time, and do not make reference to alternative worlds (where reference to alternative worlds is indicative of modality). He concludes that it is possible to have future time reference without modality. However, we must note that definiteness is indeed compatible with modality. Both (11) and (12) express propositions with a high degree of certainty, yet the words *certain* and *definite* are modal.

(11)   It is certain that Susan is the winner.
(12)   Susan is definitely the winner.

Thus definiteness does not preclude modality.[5] Yavaş characterizes the future use of *will* in English and of *-ecek* in Turkish as involving the modality of prediction. We may account for the meaning of (10) by stipulating that it is true if in every possible world consistent with current predictions, Jim gives

Tom his keys at some future time.[6] This characterization of *will* has the virtue of simplicity since it posits only one meaning for the morpheme. The fact that *will* can express different modalities is not surprising since, as Kratzer (1981) shows, modals commonly can be interpreted with respect to different conversational backgrounds (for example *must* can be either deontic or epistemic). One could argue that the view that *will* is always a modal is counterintuitive, even though it may be theoretically elegant. The evidence I discuss below provides empirical support for the analysis of *will* as a modal.

2 Futurity

The first issue to be addressed is why *will* in some cases seems to obviously refer to a future situation, as in (10). The analysis by Yavaş mentioned above accounts for this fact by stipulating that the relevant modality is prediction, and prediction inherently involves futurity. But prediction is not the only modality that involves the future. For example, deontic modals quantify over possible worlds consistent with what is demanded or required. Pragmatics dictates that what is demanded is that some situation hold in the future. We see this effect in imperatives.

(13) Do fifty push-ups.

(13) demands of the hearer that she do fifty push-ups after the demand. This inherent future with demands also shows up in deontic modals.

(14) You must do fifty push-ups.
(15) Sally may go to the party if she finishes her work.

The time of doing push-ups in (14) and the time of going to the party in (15) are required to be after the utterance time.

Similarly, verbs which express desires or demands require their complements to be evaluated in the future.

(16) I expect to win the race.
(17) John requires us to attend the meeting.

The time of winning in (16) and the time of attending the meeting in (17) must be in the future. Once again, this is not surprising given the lexical meanings of the matrix verbs.

We see in these examples that shifting to the future is a property common to a number of intensional expressions, derived from the lexical meaning of those expressions. Therefore, the fact that *will* shifts to the future does not force us to conclude that it is a future tense. This behavior of *will* is consistent with its being a modal; in fact, it is a consequence of its being a modal of prediction.

3   Sequence of Tense

The second property of *will* to be discussed has to do with the so-called Sequence of Tense (henceforth SOT) phenomenon, and shows that it does not pattern with the past tense. When a stative sentence with past tense is embedded under a sentence with past tense, ambiguity results.

(18)   Mary said that she was tired.

On one reading, (18) is true if at some past time Mary said that she was tired at a prior time, for example if Mary alluded yesterday to her being tired two days before that. In Enç (1987), I have called this reading "the shifted reading", since each past tense shifts one step into the past. On the second reading of (18), the time of being tired is the same as the time of saying, as when Mary says at some past time that she is tired at that time. I have called this reading, where the past tense in the complement does not shift to the past, "the simultaneous reading".[7] This reading is generally taken to be an instance of the sequence of tense phenomenon, where in traditional analyses the past tense in the complement is a morpheme without semantic content, a copy of the higher past tense, and the complement semantically has a present tense (or as in Ogihara (1989), no tense). I am not interested here in how these two readings are obtained.[8] The important point is that these two readings exist.

When we compare *will* to the past tense, we see that we do not get two similar readings.

(19)   Mary will say that she will be tired.

(19) has a shifted reading, and is true if the time of saying is after the speech time, and the time of her being tired is after her time of speaking. Thus both occurrences of *will* shift one step into the future. What is interesting about (19) is that it has only a shifted reading, and that the simultaneous reading is absent. That is to say, (19) cannot mean that Mary will say at a future time that she is tired at the time of her speaking. If *will* is taken to be a tense, we must stipulate that the SOT mechanism that yields the simultaneous readings applies only to the past tense, and not to the future. And since this asymmetry is not derivable, it must be separately stipulated. If, however, we take *will* to be a modal and not a tense, then it is not at all surprising that it does not exhibit SOT effects.

Hornstein (1990) claims that the SOT phenomenon extends to all tenses, including the future.[9] His analysis of SOT, which associates the speech time of the lower sentence with the event time of the higher sentence, derives the simultaneous reading of (18) by assuming that the complement has present tense. As in traditional views, the past tense morpheme is the result of a superficial phenomenon that does not affect interpretation. What I call the shifted reading of sentences like (18) is not discussed by Hornstein, but it can be obtained by applying the SOT rule to the complement when it contains a true past tense. However, Hornstein's analysis predicts a third reading, given that the SOT rule is assumed to be optional. If the SOT rule does not apply and the speech time of the complement with past tense is not associated with the higher event time, this speech time is interpreted as the utterance time by default. As a consequence, both the matrix past tense and the embedded past tense shift into the past of the utterance time independently, and the two situations are not ordered with respect to each other. The sentence is expected to be true on this reading if the time of the saying and the time of being tired are both in the past, regardless of which occurred first. Therefore, this analysis allows the time of being tired to *follow* the time of saying. However, this reading does not exist for (18). One must then further stipulate that an embedded past always signals that the SOT has applied, and the analysis is no longer as general as it is purported to be, even in accounting for the behavior of the past tense.

Hornstein discusses explicitly the sentence in (20) (his (21f) in Chapter 4).

(20) John will think that Mary will be pregnant.

He shows that the reading where each of the *will*'s shifts one step into the future (where Mary's being pregnant is after John's thinking, which is after the time of utterance) can be obtained through the application of his SOT rule. Then the speech time of the lower sentence is associated with the event time of thinking, and since the future requires the event time to follow the speech time, we get the shifted reading. Hornstein claims that this sentence is ambiguous, since the SOT is optional. If the rule does not apply, the speech time of the embedded sentence is left free, and by default is identified as the utterance time. Hornstein seems to think that this yields a correct reading for (20). On this reading, the time of thinking and the time of being pregnant are both claimed to be after the utterance time, but they are not ordered with respect to each other. This reading seems unavailable to native speakers. Furthermore, speakers get no ambiguity for this sentence. (20) has only a shifted reading, like (19). Thus we see that Hornstein's analysis of SOT and his claims that the SOT phenomenon is visible with all tenses including *will* runs into empirical difficulties, and it has not been shown that the behavior of *will* can be collapsed with the behavior of the past tense with respect to SOT.

4 Embedded Present Tense

We now turn to the way *will* and the past tense behave with respect to a present tense embedded under them. Since the particular analysis of the present tense is irrelevant here, I will go along with the accepted view and say that the sentence in (21) has present tense.

(21) Mary is upset.

Present tense does not shift the time of evaluation either to the past or to the future, i.e. it behaves as though it is semantically vacuous. Thus (21) is true if and only if Mary is upset at the original time of evaluation, the time of utterance. Past tense is assumed in most analyses, especially in Priorean analyses (see Prior (1967)), to shift the evaluation time into the past. If this view is correct, then we expect that when a sentence with present tense is embedded under a sentence with past tense, the complement should be interpreted as describing a situation that holds at the past time that the higher tense has shifted to. This prediction is not correct for English.

(22) John said that Mary is upset.
(23) Sarah claimed that she is the best candidate.

(22) does not mean that Mary is upset at the past time of John's speaking. Rather, (22) is interpreted as saying something about Mary's state of mind at the speech time, i.e. at the original evaluation time. Similarly, (23) requires that Sarah be a candidate at the speech time, not just at the past time the claim was made.[10] Partee (1973) argues that the present tense in English has a further property, that it always denotes the utterance time. If we assume this, then the present tenses in (22) and (23) will denote the speech time in spite of the fact that they are embedded under past tense, and we get the desired interpretation.

When we turn to *will*, we see that the present tense embedded under it behaves differently.

(24) John will say that Mary is upset.
(25) Sarah will claim that she is the best candidate.

These sentences allow the complement to be true at the speech time, but they also have a reading where the complement is evaluated only at the future time. In (24), John may be saying something in the future about a state that holds at the time of the saying only. (25) may be true if Sarah makes a claim in the future about her candidacy at that future time. Neither sentence requires the state to hold additionally at the speech time. Thus these sentences seem to be violating the condition that the present tense be linked to the speech time. This is a function of the present tense being embedded under *will*, and therefore *will* clearly behaves differently from the past tense.

We see a similar contrast with present tense in relative clauses.

(26) Mary saw the man who is speaking.
(27) Mary will see the man who is speaking.

In (26), where the matrix clause has past tense, the relative clause is unambiguously interpreted as holding at the speech time. Though Mary saw the man in the past, he must be speaking at the time of utterance. Thus this sentence is not true if Mary sees the man in the past and the man is speaking at the past time of seeing but not at the speech time. (27), on the other hand, has a reading where Mary sees in the future the man who is speaking at the time of seeing, i.e. a reading which does not require the relative clause to be evaluated at the speech time.

One might claim that *will* is a tense, but that some difference between the past tense and the future tense needs to be stipulated. However, further evidence shows that this difference between *will* and the past tense is not random. Consider the following examples with modals in the matrix sentence.

(28) John must claim that he is sick.
(29) Mary may say that she is in charge.
(30) John should talk to whoever is guarding the entrance.

These examples show that both the complement present tense and the relative clause present tense, when embedded under a future-shifting modal, can be anchored to the future time introduced by the modal and need not be anchored to the speech time. That is to say, they behave like *will*. It is not the case that *will* just patterns differently from the past tense. It also patterns exactly like future-shifting modals. Thus when we account for the temporal properties of these modals, we will automatically be accounting for the temporal properties of *will* if we take it to be a modal rather than a tense.

The facts about the embedded present tense can be explained by adopting the usual Priorean view of tenses, not for true tenses, but for modals. Let me assume a referential theory of tenses along the lines of Enç (1986, 1987), with the following properties. Verbs project a temporal argument in the syntax along with their other arguments. A verb like *see*, for instance, takes three arguments, a subject NP, an object NP, and a temporal NP, and describes a situation in which an entity denoted by the subject sees an entity denoted by the object at the time denoted by the temporal argument. A true tense is not a Priorean sentential operator but a referential expression which denotes an interval and binds the temporal argument of the verb. The English past tense, being a true tense, is interpreted according to (31) and denotes a time prior to the evaluation time.

(31) Where w is a possible world and i, i' are intervals, the denotation of PAST at $\langle w,i \rangle$ is an interval i' such that $i' < i$.

The denotation of the tense is determined according to the evaluation time. The evaluation time is also relevant to determining the denotation of other temporal expressions such as *yesterday*, but is otherwise irrelevant to obtaining the denotation of constants like verbs and nouns in the sentence. The tense now binds the temporal argument of the verb and thereby fixes the time at which the situation described by the sentence holds. Crucially, the evaluation time is not shifted by the tense, and remains the same for any embedded sentences, as long as there are no modals in these sentences.

Suppose that modals differ from tenses in this respect. Modals are quantificational; necessity involves universal quantification over possible worlds, and possibility involves existential quantification. Thus it is plausible to treat them as sentential operators. Let us assume further that temporally, they behave like Priorean operators which shift the evaluation time. Some epistemic operators do not replace the evaluation time with a new distinct time, as (32) shows.

(32)   Sally must be in her office now.

These modals are irrelevant to the arguments for *will* and I will ignore them. The discussion below is relevant to modals like the deontic *must* which involve the future. Such modals are interpreted as in (33).

(33)   MODAL[S] is true at $\langle w,i \rangle$ iff in every world w' accessible to w there is an interval i' such that $i < i'$ and S is true at $\langle w',i' \rangle$.

In (33), i is the original time of evaluation, i.e. the utterance time. This time is replaced by a future time and the sentence in the scope of the modal is evaluated with respect to this new time.

How does this affect the temporal argument of the verb in the sentence? Consider (34).

(34)   John must leave.

It is reasonable to assume that there is no tense projected in (34) or that the tense node is empty. Therefore the temporal argument of the verb is not bound. Since the temporal argument is always empty, we can assume that it must somehow be identified.[11] One way of identifying it is through binding by tense. Let us stipulate that when this is impossible, as in (34), there is a default identification mechanism where the denotation of this temporal argument is taken to be the evaluation time.[12] Thus when (34) is interpreted according to (33), the temporal argument of the verb is identified as the future interval i' that the modal shifts to. Thus (34) is true if and only if in every accessible possible world there is a future time and John leaves at that future time.

Compare (34) to (35).

(35)   John will leave.

Now all we have to say is that *will* is one of the modals that is interpreted according to (33), and the correct reading is obtained. With *will*, the worlds are those that are consistent with predictions, and in each of these worlds John is required to leave at a future time.[13]

So far, we have captured the intuition that the futurity in *will* is a consequence of the kind of modal it is, as proposed earlier in the paper. Let us now return to the problems we confronted with the embedded present tense. We will take the present tense to be interpreted according to (36).

(36)   Where w is a possible world and i, i' are intervals, the denotation of PRESENT at $\langle w,i \rangle$ is an interval i' such that $i' = i$.

Like the past tense, the present tense binds the temporal argument of the verb and the correct reading is obtained for matrix present tenses. As for the present tense in complement sentences, recall that in (22) it is linked to the speech time even though it is embedded under a past tense, whereas in (28) it can be linked to a future time.

(22)   John said that Mary is upset.
(28)   John must claim that he is sick.

We noted that we cannot derive the behavior of the present tense in these examples if we adopt the view that it always denotes the speech time in English. However, the analysis outlined above distinguishes tenses from modals by stipulating that only modals shift the time of evaluation. Therefore in sentences like (22), even though the present tense is embedded under a past tense, it denotes the speech time since the original evaluation time (i.e. the speech time) remains unchanged. (28), on the other hand, contains a modal which shifts the evaluation time to the future. Now the evaluation time is no longer the speech time. We obtain the correct reading for (28) because the present tense denotes this new future time of evaluation as required by (33). The difference between (22) and (28) then is due to the fact that tenses and modals affect the evaluation time differently.[14]

Now consider (24).

(24)   John will say that Mary is upset.

If we classify *will* as a modal and not a tense, (24) is interpreted straightforwardly and nothing more needs to be stipulated.[15] The time of evaluation is shifted into the future by *will*, and the complement is evaluated at this new time.

5   The Dual of *Will*

Modals can come in pairs, where they express the same modality but one is a necessity operator quantifying universally, and the other is a possibility operator quantifying existentially. We say then that they are each other's duals.

(37)   You may leave.
(38)   You must leave.

(37) and (38) have readings where *may* and *must* are deontic modals, quantify-ing over possible worlds consistent with obligations and requirements. *May* expresses permission and involves existential quantification, whereas *must* expresses obligation and involves universal quantification. As shown in Kratzer (1981), modals are specified in the lexicon with respect to the kind of possible worlds they can quantify over, or in Kratzer's terms, with respect to the con-versational backgrounds they allow. In addition to deontic modality, both *may* and *must* can express epistemic modality, quantifying over possible worlds consistent with what is known.

(39)   Sarah may be in her office.
(40)   Sarah must be in her office.

According to (39), the set of worlds consistent with what is known contains a world where Sarah is in her office. According to (40), Sarah is in her office in every possible world consistent with what is known. The epistemic *may* then is the dual of the epistemic *must*.

Now consider the pair of sentences in (41) and (42).

(41)   Susan will bring her Finnish friend to the party.
(42)   Susan may bring her Finnish friend to the party.

There seems to be a clear relation between these sentences; they both make predictions about the party. Intuitively, the prediction in (41) is stronger than the prediction in (42). Since *may* is lexically restricted to a possibility operator, we can say that in (42) it quantifies existentially. Thus (42) is true if there is some possible world consistent with current predictions such that Susan brings her friend to the party at a future time in that world.[16] If *will* is treated not as a tense but as a necessity operator quantifying universally over possible worlds consistent with predictions, then this future-shifting *may* is the dual of *will* and the relation between (41) and (42) is captured.

6   Conclusion

I have discussed several semantic phenomena involving the future reading of *will*, and have shown not only that it patterns differently from the past tense, but that it patterns with other future-shifting modals. This is also consistent with its morphological properties, since it is a free morpheme like the modals rather than a suffix like the past tense. If, as is plausible, the present is treated as the absence of past tense (a view that is implemented in different ways in

Ogihara (1989) and Enç (1990)), then the past emerges as the only true tense in English. This is not unusual. Comrie (1985) points out that many languages make only a binary distinction. Some, like English, have a tense that distinguishes the past from the nonpast, and futurity is expressed with a modal or some other form reserved for irrealis. Others, like Hua spoken in New Guinea, have a tense that distinguishes future from nonfuture.[17] Comrie also notes that there are no languages with a tense which distinguishes present and nonpresent. These facts suggest that universally only two tenses are available, the past tense and the future tense. It may also be true that each language is allowed only one tense and other temporal notions are expressed through other syntactic categories.

NOTES

1   The tenses can be further refined in some languages. For example, the African language Haya requires a three-way distinction for the past times 1) earlier on today, 2) yesterday, and 3) earlier than yesterday (Comrie (1985)).

2   If some principle of grammar forced the projection of the tense category for all languages, then we would say that in Chinese there are no lexical items that belong to this category.

3   See Comrie (1985) for examples from a number of languages where the past tense morpheme is used without a past meaning.

4   I do not claim that no language has present tense; the arguments apply only to English. I think that universals about tense are premature at this point.

5   Certainty or probability can be accounted for by ordering the accessible possible worlds. Cf. Kratzer (1981).

6   Note that these truth-conditions still make reference to a future time. We return to this question later.

7   The reader is warned that although Hornstein (1990) claims to adopt this terminology, Hornstein uses the term "shifted reading" for the second reading of this sentence, which I call the "simultaneous reading". He does so because the simultaneous reading is derived in his analysis by the SOT rule which shifts S, the speech time, of the complement to the event time of the higher sentence. What I call the shifted reading is obtained in Hornstein's analysis when the SOT rule does not apply.

8   For the interested reader, recent work on this subject includes Enç (1987), Abusch (1988), Ogihara (1989), and Hornstein (1990).

9   The rule applies vacuously to the present tense.

10   In Enç (1987), I have called the reading of such sentences "the double-access reading", since (22) requires that the state of Mary's being upset extend at least from the past time of saying to the speech time. Similarly in (23), Sarah must be a candidate at the past time when the claim is made and her candidacy must extend to the speech time.

11   It seems natural to view the relation between the tense and the temporal argument as parallel to the relation between the subject and subject agreement.

12 We can implement this in the following way. The empty temporal argument is generated without an index, and must receive an index in order to be interpreted. Binding by the tense morpheme provides an index. When this argument is not bound, it receives an index which denotes the evaluation time.

13 The definition in (33) is a simplification. These modals actually shift into the future twice, as in (i) and (ii).

(i)   If Sally wins the race, Tommy will cry.
(ii) If Eric fails the test, he must drop out of school.

In these sentences, the antecedent of the conditional has to be evaluated at a time after the speech time, and the consequent of the conditional has to be evaluated at a time after that. In (i), for example, the winning of the race is in the future, and Tommy's crying is after the time of winning. Following Kratzer (1981) and Heim (1982), we take the antecedent to be the restrictor of the modal, and the consequent to be the nuclear scope of the modal. We can then redefine the interpretation of the modals in the following way.

(iii) Where S is the antecedent of the conditional and S' is the consequent, MODAL$[S,S']$ is true at $\langle w,i \rangle$ iff in every w' such that w' is accessible to w and there is an interval $i' > i$ such that S is true at $\langle w',i' \rangle$, there is an $i'' > i'$ and S' is true at $\langle w',i'' \rangle$.

Note that once again *will* patterns with the other future-shifting modals.

14 If the view defended in Enç (1990) is correct and there is no present tense in English, then sentences like *John is tired* are tenseless. The temporal argument of the verb once again remains unbound and is identified as the evaluation time by the default identification mechanism outlined above, and the correct interpretation is obtained. Temporal arguments in infinitive clauses are interpreted in the same way.

15 An analysis where *will* shifts the evaluation time but the past tense does not was provided in Dowty (1982b), though there the parallel with modals was not drawn.

16 Toshi Ogihara brought this behavior of *may* to my attention.

17 See the discussion of Hua in Comrie (1985), citing Haiman (1980).

VII Questions

14   The Semantics of Questions

JAMES HIGGINBOTHAM

1   The Problem of Form and Content

The notion of a *question* may be understood in three different, but interrelated ways; a major part of the linguistic problem of the semantics of questions lies in relating these ways to one another.

First of all, questions may be understood as instances of a certain type of linguistic structure; that is, as interrogative forms. In both traditional and contemporary linguistic theory these forms may be *root* forms, constituting interrogative sentences, or *embedded* forms, occurring as complements or subjects, and occupying Θ-positions. Thus (1) is a root interrogative, and the complement in (2) an embedded interrogative:

(1)   Who is Sylvia?
(2)   I want to know [who Sylvia is]

In another common terminology, which we will use here, a root interrogative is a *direct* question, and an embedded interrogative is an *indirect* question.

Second, besides the formal or syntactic conception of a question, there is a semantic conception of a question, as the meaning of an interrogative form. I will uphold here the view that interrogative forms possess meanings peculiar to them, distinct from the meanings of declarative forms.

Third, apart from the purely formal and the purely semantic notions there is yet another conception of questions, as the contents of certain kinds of acts of speech. A person who says (1), for instance, is likely to be expressing a desire to know the identity of Sylvia, and in this sense questioning the hearer. The content of that person's speech act is a question in the third sense of that term.

The ambiguity we have discerned in the notion of a question is matched by that of the notion of a *statement*. We can motivate some of the problems in the linguistic semantics of questions by expounding this ambiguity and the ways in which the different notions of a statement are, on a standard picture, thought to be related. A statement may be a root or embedded declarative form, such as the clause "Sylvia is my friend" in (3) or the complementized clause "that Sylvia is my friend" in (4):

(3)   Sylvia is my friend
(4)   John said [that [Sylvia is my friend]]

Statements are also thought of as the meanings of declarative forms, and as the contents of certain acts of speech, those that consist in stating or asserting something. The relations between these notions are often understood as follows: with a declarative form the semantics of a language associates truth conditions, which constitute the meaning of the form; the speech act of stating has a content that is true if the truth conditions of the form used to express that content are fulfilled, and otherwise false. Thus the form expresses a content, individuated by its truth conditions, and this very content is the object of the speech act. In this way the various notions of a statement are tied together.

A proper theory of statements must also make a distinction between root and embedded statements, of the following kind: a root statement may be used to make an assertion, but an embedded statement preceded by the word "that" or other complementizers merely refers to a content. Thus, to use Wittgenstein's terminology, one can "make a move in the language game" by saying (3), but not by saying (5) (excepting it is understood as an ellipsis, as in "(John said) that Sylvia is my friend"; and in this case what it is elliptical for is itself a root clause).

(5)   (the proposition) [that [Sylvia is my friend]]

We shall suppose that the reason only root clauses can be used to make assertions is that embedded clauses have, whereas root clauses have not, undergone a kind of nominalization, of the sort suggested in Montague and Kalish (1959) (itself having a precedent in Carnap (1947)), as explained below.

If we turn now to questions with this picture in mind, then we should expect a theory of questions to have the following components: (i) a conception of what the interrogative forms are; (ii) a conception of their semantic content, independent of their use; and (iii) a conception of the speech act of questioning that expresses this kind of content. We also anticipate a kind of nominalization in embedded questions, since the distinction between root and embedded constructions holds there as well. Thus one can ask a question by saying (1), but by saying (6) (without ellipsis) one merely refers to a question:

(6)   the question who Sylvia is

In the endeavor to execute a program for questions similar to the familiar program that ties together statements in their syntactic, semantic, and speech act dimensions, there is an immediate difficulty. In the case of statements, it was the truth conditions of a form that served for the content of that form. But interrogative forms do not have truth values, and therefore do not have truth conditions either, or so it would appear. Our problem then is to find a conception of content, different from truth-conditions, that interrogative forms may be said to possess; to show how that content is expressed by such forms; and to show that it is a content suited to the act of questioning. We must also find a way of nominalizing such contents so that the distinction between what one can do with root and embedded questions can be maintained. The analogy between questions and statements breaks down unless such conceptions of content and nominalization can be formulated and defended.

In this article I will examine a way of thinking of the syntax and semantics of questions that sustains the common-sense assumption that interrogative forms do not have truth values, and therefore associates with them a different kind of content from that of declarative forms; and I will argue that the content identified as peculiar to interrogative forms is indeed appropriate for being the content of the speech act of questioning. The path that I will follow differs from that taken in Higginbotham (1993) and (1991) (itself building upon themes expounded in Higginbotham (1978) and Higginbotham and May (1981); the reader is referred especially to Groenendijk and Stokhof (1984) and (1989) for a development in many respects parallel, and to Belnap and Steel (1976) and Belnap (1982) for discussion of controversial issues in the philosophical logic of questions) in that the semantic framework is that of Intensional Logic (IL). I have taken this step partly because of its intrinsic interest, and partly because it facilitates theory comparison appropriate to the context of this handbook.

In the exposition that follows we first consider a certain subset of root questions as syntactic objects. We will isolate a kind of normal syntactic form, congruent with recent developments in syntax, that will then be subjected to semantic analysis. We turn then to the problem of quantifying into questions, and to indirect questions and the matter of nominalization. Finally, we argue in conclusion that the account given satisfies the demands of the program adumbrated above.

2 Syntactic Elements

We assume that the reader is acquainted with the elementary syntax of direct and indirect questions, and here outline the assumptions that will be made in the semantic discussion to follow.

Interrogative forms are taken to constitute a maximal projection CP of the category C = Complementizer, which is marked by some feature, here written as the question mark "?" (the "abstract question morpheme" of early studies in transformational grammar). This feature is taken to be common and peculiar to all interrogative CPs. The complement of C is the *neutral core*, a clausal structure admitting truth conditional analysis. We abbreviate it by the symbol "*S*", as indicating the clausal content without prejudice to its syntactic realization.

A direct "yes-no" question then has the structure in (7):

(7) [$_{CP}$[$_C$?] [$_S$ · · ·]]

where "..." is the neutral core. Like other maximal projections, CP will have a Specifier category Spec(CP). The fuller phrase structure of CP = C″ then follows the familiar pattern of categorial projections under X′ theory, as in (8):

(8) [$_{CP}$Spec [$_C$C S]]

Spec(CP) is the category that is filled by a *Wh*-expression in interrogatives such as "Who left?" in English:

(9) [$_{CP}$[$_{Spec}$Who] [$_C$[$_C$?] [$_S$*t* left]]]

with *t* the trace of *Wh*-movement.

The inversion characteristic of English root forms, as in (10) and (11) has been variously analyzed.

(10) Did John leave?
(11) Who did Mary see?

It appears with all direct questions except those with auxiliaries *have* and *be*, but with no indirect questions. The relevant aspects of structure have been held to involve movement of the inflected (tense) element into C. We will, however, make no semantic distinction (apart from the nominalization of indirect questions to be described) between these examples and the corresponding indirect question forms (12) and (13):

(12) I asked [whether John left]
(13) I wondered [who Mary saw]

which do not show inversion. The word "whether" may be thought of either as the overt counterpart of the feature ?, or as another, special element in Spec(CP).

For languages showing the "Verb-Second" phenomenon, such as German, we follow one standard analysis in assuming that it represents movement of the inflected V into C. Thus the relevant parts of the structure of, e.g. German (14) are taken to be as in (15):

(14) Wem hasst sein Vater?
Who(ACC) hates [his father] (NOM)?
Whom does his father hate?
(15) [$_{CP}$[Wem]$_i$] [[$_C$? + [hasst]$_j$] [sein Vater t_i t_j]]]

We will assume that V-movement, like inversion in English, is semantically empty.[1]

English exhibits *Wh*-movement, which is obligatory in ordinary *Wh*-questions.[2] In some languages the movement of *Wh* is not obligatory, and in others (e.g. Japanese, Chinese) it never occurs at all. Inversely, English *multiple* questions, containing more than one *Wh*-expression, are realized with one and only one of them moving to Spec(CP). In both types of languages, therefore, the question arises how to think of the positions of the *Wh*-expressions in the syntactic forms that are given over to the semantic component of a grammar. In this discussion we will follow the suggestion due to Chomsky (1973) and Huang (1982), and subsequently pursued by many others, that at an appropriately abstract level of syntax, the level LF in the sense of Chomsky (1981) and elsewhere, all *Wh*-expressions are moved to a position outside the neutral core. The exact shape of this movement will be left open, and we can assume without loss of generality that it consists in sequencing the *Wh*-expressions with scope over C' (hence over "?") as well as the core. Thus an English multiple question as in (16) will at LF receive a representation that we can indicate up to the relevant level of detail by (17):

(16)   Who bought what?
(17) $[_{CP}[who_i\,what_j]$ $[?$ $[t_i$ bought $t_j]]]$

English and other languages with overt *Wh*-movement show various patterns with respect to the phenomenon J. R. Ross dubbed *pied piping*, where a maximal projection properly containing the maximal projection dominating the *Wh*-expression undergoes movement. Examples in English include (18) and the like:

(18)   In which box did I put the cigars?

We will assume here that this type of movement is "undone" at LF, so that the syntactic structure delivered up to interpretation is in fact (19):

(19)   [[Which box] [?[did I put the cigars in t]]]

Chomsky (1993) has raised the further question whether it is obligatory to keep anything apart from the *Wh*-expression itself outside the neutral core. Thus one may hypothesize a syntactic structure (20) for (18), either alongside or instead of (19):

(20)   [[Which] [?[did I put the cigars in t box]]]

We will suppose here that this proposal too is semantically neutral.

Summing up, we assume that all human languages present single and multiple *Wh*-questions, both direct and indirect, in the form (21) at LF:

(21) $[_{CP}[Wh_1 \ldots Wh_n)]$ $[?$ $[_S \ldots t_1 \ldots t_n]]]$

where Wh_i is a maximal projection of some category, headed by a single Wh-expression; ? is the feature in C marking questions; (so that if $n = 0$ we have a yes – no question) and S, which may be of any clausal category, is the neutral core. It is with these assumptions that the semantics commences.

3   Semantic Elements

We said above that the neutral core would have a truth conditional semantics. More precisely we take it that with a core S are associated truth conditions along the lines of possible worlds semantics as in (22):

> (22)   S is true in possible world w iff $\phi(w)$

and we assume that native speakers of the language to which S belongs know these conditions. The traces of Wh-expressions, if any, are taken to be free variables. The truth conditions of the neutral core of (16), repeated here, are therefore as in (23):

> (16)   Who bought what?
> (23) $S = [t_i$ bought $t_j]$ is true in w on an assignment f of values to traces iff $f(t_i)$ bought $f(t_j)$ in w

Interpretations of the neutral core along the lines of (23) assign truth conditions directly to syntactic structures. Our exposition here will employ instead a method that is less direct but for our purposes more perspicuous, namely translation of syntactic structures into IL. We will assume that indexed traces are translated as the corresponding variables in IL, and so the translation of the neutral core of (16) will be (24):

> (24)   bought(x_i, x_j)

whose interpretation is straightforward.

   Given that interpretations of the neutral cores are taken over from the usual semantics for declaratives using IL, the content to be assigned to an interrogative form will now depend upon just two factors, namely the action of the mark "?" of the question, and the relation of the fronted Wh-expression to the trace. We concentrate on "?" first.

3.1   Questions as expressed by λ-abstracts: methods of Hamblin and Karttunen

In this subsection we expound and offer some critical remarks on the analyses of questions offered in Hamblin (1973), and in more detail by Karttunen (1977).

By building on this work we set the stage for the view that is supported here. Hamblin (1973), as taken up in Karttunen (1977: 10), suggested that direct yes–no questions, and indirect questions commencing with "whether", had for their semantic value the set of propositions consisting of the proposition expressed by the neutral core, and its negation. A question like (25), then, would be translated as in (26):

(25) Is Sylvia my friend?
(26) $\lambda p[p = {}^\wedge\text{Sylvia is my friend} \vee p = {}^\wedge\neg(\text{Sylvia is my friend})]$

where "Sylvia is my friend" is the translation of the neutral core into the metalanguage. To execute this proposal in respect of the assumed syntactic structure (27) for (26), we use λ-abstraction over possible worlds in the form of intensional abstraction $^\wedge$:

(27) [?[Sylvia is my friend]]

The sign "?" is translated as $\|?\|$, where:

$$\|?\| = \lambda q \ \lambda p[p = q \vee p = \mathbf{N}q]$$

where q and p are propositional variables (of type (s,t)), and $\mathbf{N}q$ is the negation of q, so that for a sentence ϕ of IL we have $\mathbf{N}^\wedge\phi = {}^\wedge\neg\phi$. The rule of combination is (28):

(28) If X is translated as ϕ then $[_C?[_S X]]$ is translated as $\|?\|({}^\wedge\phi)$

which derives the desired result after λ-conversion. Equally, we could treat "?" syncategorematically, and write (29):

(29) If X is translated as ϕ, then $[_C?[_S X]]$ is translated as
      $\lambda p[p = {}^\wedge\phi \vee p = {}^\wedge\neg\phi]$

In an obvious sense, Hamblin's proposal is that yes–no questions express the set of propositions each of which would be an answer to them. Karttunen (1977) modifies Hamblin's original proposal, so that direct questions express, not all their possible answers, but only the true one. We pass over the technicalities of Karttunen (1977: 13–16) here, noting merely that the result corresponding to (29) would be (30):

(30) If X is translated as ϕ, then $[_C?[_S X]]$ is translated as $\lambda p[p = {}^\wedge\phi]$ if ϕ,
      and as $\lambda p[p = {}^\wedge\neg\phi]$ if $\neg\phi$

Karttunen further proposes that in single and multiple *Wh*-questions, what is denoted is the class of true propositions that constitute instances of the neutral core. Thus a question like (16) will be translated as in (31):

(31) $\lambda p(\exists x)(\exists y)[\text{person}(x)\ \&\ \text{thing}(y)\ \&\ p = {}^{\wedge}(x\ \text{bought}\ y)\ \&\ {}^{\vee}p]^{3}$

Apart from the technical details of the derivation of (31), we may call attention to some significant features of Karttunen's proposal.

First of all, *Wh*-expressions are effectively interpreted as existential quantifiers, and in this sense as indefinites, a view that fits well with their syntactic distribution.[4] Second, however, they are treated as unrestricted quantifiers (within the abstract λp). The latter feature appears to create a difficulty for the proposal, in that direct question pairs such as (32) and (33) will be equivalent:

(32)   Which men are bachelors?
(33)   Which bachelors are men?

Intuitively, however, these are different: one answers (32) by enumerating the bachelors amongst the men; but (33) is a silly question, since all bachelors are men.

Karttunen's construction is not easily modified so as to remove the counter-intuitiveness here. We associate (32) with (34), and (33) with (35):

(34) $\lambda p[(\exists x)\ (\text{man}(x)\ \&\ p = {}^{\wedge}\text{bachelor}(x)\ \&\ {}^{\vee}p]$
(35) $\lambda p[(\exists x)\ (\text{bachelor}(x)\ \&\ p = {}^{\wedge}\text{man}(x)\ \&\ {}^{\vee}p]$

These translations have for their values distinct sets of propositions, but do not give rise to distinct true answers.

Consider questions like (36), discussed in Reinhart (1992):

(36)   Which philosophers would you be annoyed if we invited *t*?

Suppose that the interpretation of (36) were the class C of propositions, or true propositions, that are identical, for some value a of x, to

${}^{\wedge}$[if we invited a & a is a philosopher, then you are annoyed]

However the conditional here is understood, C includes propositions for which a is not in fact a philosopher; but these are intuitively irrelevant to the inquiry (36). Again, (36) is conspicuously distinct from (37), but the difference between them would be obliterated:

(37)   [Which invitees]$_i$ are such that you would be annoyed if [they]$_i$ were philosophers?

Now, it is a natural thought that the kind of quasi-quantification illustrated by *Wh*-expressions is restricted after the fashion of more ordinary quantification in natural languages. As applied to (32), for example, the thought is that it restricts the universe to men, and asks which of them are bachelors; as applied to (38) it is that the N appearing with the *Wh* restricts the universe to (a relevant set of) students and asks which of them are in the classroom:

(38) Which students are in the classroom?

Inverting the order, as in (39), gives a non-equivalent question, which restricts the universe to people in the classroom and asks which of them are students:

(39) Which people in the classroom are students?

We shall want a way of distinguishing these questions appropriately.

Thus far we have inquired about the semantics of questions without considering the full explication of the relation of question and answer, which must surely play a significant role in the theory of the content of an interrogative form. The notion of an answer may be understood narrowly, as confined to true answers, or more broadly, as including appropriate answers, whether or not they are true. Since we can recognize an answer as appropriate even when it is not true (as when we say that someone gave "the wrong answer," meaning that the response, although appropriate to the occasion, was mistaken), we should recognize the notion of an answer in the broader sense as fundamental. An answer in the narrower sense is then simply an appropriate response that is also true.

Hamblin's account of yes–no questions might be said to assign to them as their denotation the set of propositions each of which is an appropriate answer (namely, the proposition queried, and its negation); Karttunen's account assigns to them just the one proposition that is the true answer. From the point of view of explicating the question-answer relation in the broader sense, therefore, Karttunen's account appears less than satisfactory, since it does not appear to distinguish wrong answers from irrelevant remarks. (We will consider below some of Karttunen's considerations in favor of the theory he advances.)

Consider now *Wh*-questions ranging over individuals. On either Hamblin's account or Karttunen's, these are sets of propositions in one-to-one correspondence with sets of objects (or n-tuples of objects, in the case of multiple questions). On Karttunen's theory, the interpretation of a concrete example such as (40) is (in one-to-one correspondence with) the class of persons x such that, in fact, x was invited to the party:

(40) Which people were invited to the party?

What are the appropriate answers to (40)? Suppose for simplicity that each person has a unique name, and that each name in the context refers to a unique person: let the names be a_i, $1 \leq i \leq 2n$. Then the true answer to (40), where, let us say, a_i was invited for odd i and not invited for even i, would be as in (41):

(41) a_1 was invited to the party;

a_3 was invited to the party;

. . .

a_{2k+1} was invited to the party;

. . .

a_{2n-1} was invited to the party.

Our question will now be whether this conception allows us to reconstruct the notion of an appropriate answer. There are two major difficulties here.

The first difficulty is that (41) is not, as it stands, a *complete* answer to (40), in the sense that, having enumerated the true instances, it still fails to say that they are *all* the true instances of "*x* was invited to the party". Suppose that Mary asks (40), and John responds with (41). Then Mary will still fail to know on that basis alone whether, say, a_2 was invited to the party. This difficulty shows up in giving the truth conditions of a sentence such as (42) (from Karttunen (1977)), which contains an indirect question:

(42)   John told Mary who passed the test

Karttunen writes (1977: 11) that "[(42)] is true just in case John told Mary every proposition in the set denoted by the indirect question." But it seems that John may tell Mary every such proposition without Mary's coming to know whether a proposition that he did not tell her was true, and so without knowing whether someone whom John did not mention passed the test.

The second difficulty is that the denotation that Karttunen assigns to *Wh*-questions does not make room for answers that give some information but are short of being exhaustive. Thus in response to (40) John's best information may be (43):

(43)   At least six people were invited to the party

(43) is compatible with various possibilities, but not with all. In this sense it gives information, although the information is less than complete.

Let us call responses like (43) *partial answers* to questions like (40). Then our problem is to distinguish partial answers from misplaced or irrelevant remarks. As with the first difficulty, this problem shows up in connection with indirect questions, as in (44):

(44)   John knows something about who was invited to the party

If John's best information is (43), (44) is true; similarly if his best information is, say, (45):

(45) a_1 was invited if and only if a_2 was not

The difficulties just enumerated may lead us to constructions that, taking Karttunen's theory as basic, supplement it with other devices to reconstruct the notions of completeness and partiality of answers. Here, however, we follow a different course, assigning to interrogative forms denotations for which these notions receive a direct interpretation.

3.2   Partitions

Suppose that with an interrogative we associate, not a single set of propositions, but rather a *space of possibilities*, having the property that its elements are mutually exclusive (so that no two elements of the space can both be true), and (in the normal case) jointly exhaustive (so that one element must be true). A person who asks a question wanting to know an answer to it wishes relief from ignorance as to which element of the space of possibilities set up by the question actually obtains. Such a person cannot but be satisfied if a response is forthcoming that narrows the space down to a single element; but the degree of information obtained may vary all the way from complete satisfaction through partial relief from ignorance (when the space is not reduced to a single element but as a result of the response anyway diminished) down to no information at all, as when the response does not eliminate even a single possibility. From this point of view, the complete answers to questions will be responses that (whether true or false) limit the space of possibilities most severely; but there is room for partial answers as well, namely responses that eliminate, by being incompatible with, some of the possibilities that were left open in the question.

Working as we are here within IL, a possibility is simply a set of propositions (that is, a set of sets of possible worlds), and a space of possibilities is therefore a set of sets of propositions. Such a set π is a *partition* if

(46) $\pi(A)$ & $\pi(B)$ & $A \neq B \rightarrow \sim\Diamond(\forall p)[A(p) \vee B(p) \rightarrow {}^{\vee}p]$

The sets of propositions in a partition are mutually exclusive, in the sense that there is no possible world in which all the propositions in two different sets are true. A partition π is *proper* if it satisfies (47):

(47) $(\exists A)[\pi(A)$ & $(\exists q)\,\forall(q)$ & $\Diamond\,(\forall(p)(A(p) \rightarrow {}^{\vee}p)]$

A proper partition, then, is a nonempty set of propositions, one member of which is also nonempty and contains propositions such that it is possible that all of them are true.

The partition or space of possibilities that corresponds to a yes–no question should evidently be the pair represented by the proposition that is the neutral core, and its negation. In place of Hamblin's or Karttunen's conception of the semantics of sentences ?-S, then, we will retain the rule (28), but have (48) instead of (29) or (30):

(48)   If X is translated as ϕ, then $[_{C'}?[_{S}X]]$ is translated as:
$$\lambda A(\forall p)(A(p) \leftrightarrow p = {}^{\wedge}\phi) \vee (\forall p)(A(p) \leftrightarrow p = {}^{\wedge}\neg\phi)]$$

In terms of the type theory, then, partitions are of type $(((s,t),t),t)$ of sets of sets of propositions, and the interpretation $\|?\|$ of the abstract question morpheme "?" is of the type $((s,t),(((s,t),t),t))$, mapping propositions into partitions.

It is convenient to depict the partition given in (48) in the informal notation (49):

(49) $\{\{^{\wedge}\phi\},\{^{\wedge}\neg\phi\}\}$

The operation $\|?\|$ is well defined independently of whether ϕ is a closed sentence, so that (48) extends to the case where the intension of ϕ depends upon an assignment f of values to variables. Consider then how to extend the notion to ordinary *Wh*-questions, such as (40), repeated here:

(40)   Which people were invited to the party?

The representation is as in (50):

(50) $[_{CP}[\text{Which people}]_i \ [_{C'}? \ [t_i \text{ were invited to the party}]]]$

and so the interpretation of C' is (51):

(51) $(\lambda A)[\forall p)(A(p) \leftrightarrow p = {}^{\wedge}(x_i \text{ was invited to the party})) \vee (\forall p)(A(p) \leftrightarrow p = {}^{\wedge}(\neg x_i \text{ was invited to the party}))]$

Suppose that there were, say, 20 potential invitees to the party, and the question (40) as asked in its context was about these people, and no others. The space of possibilities is then generated by taking the possible guest lists in turn, all the way from the one where no one at all was invited to the one where all 20 were invited. For each person a in the context set we have the partition π_a consisting of the singleton set of propositions whose sole member is $^{\wedge}(a$ was invited), and the singleton set whose sole member is $^{\wedge}\neg(a$ was invited). The space may therefore be obtained by taking what we will call the *direct product* of all these partitions, the new partition being obtained by taking all possible ways of combining the partitions in G. More formally, if c is a choice function on G, selecting for each π in G an element $c(\pi)$ of π, then

$$\lambda p(E\pi)((c(\pi))(p) \ \& \ G(\pi))$$

is one such set of propositions, and so we may define the direct product $\mathbf{X}G$ of the elements of G by

$$\mathbf{X}G \ = \ \lambda A\{(\exists c)[(\forall p)[(A(p) \leftrightarrow (E\pi)((c(\pi))(p) \ \& \ G(\pi))]\}$$

To complete the picture for (40) and the like, we want the family G to consist of the set of partitions obtained by assigning as the value of x_i those individuals satisfying the restrictive clause, in this case that x_i is a person (in the context). The translation may be summed up as in (52):

(52) If X is translated as τ, and Y is translated as δ then
$$[_{CP}[Wh\ [_{N'}Y]]_i\ [_{C'}X]]$$

is translated as

$$X\{\lambda\pi[(Ex_i)(\delta\ \&\ \pi=\tau)]\}$$

Note in particular that the variable x_i, free in τ, is bound in the translation by the existential quantifier.[5]

Consider a very simple case, where the context contains only two students, a and b, and the question (53) in this context:

(53) [Which students]$_i$ did you see t_i?

Here we have:

$C' = X$ is translated as in (51), with "you saw x_i" in place of "x_i was invited to the party";
$N' = Y$ is translated as "student(x_i)";

and, abbreviating "$^\wedge$you saw α" by "$^\wedge\phi(\alpha)$", the resulting partition may be depicted as in (54):

(54) $\{\{^\wedge\phi(a),^\wedge\phi(b)\},\{^\wedge\neg\phi(a),^\wedge\phi(b)\},\{^\wedge\phi(a),^\wedge\neg\phi(b)\},\{^\wedge\neg\phi(a),^\wedge\neg\phi(b)\}\}$

We would like to suggest that any of the sentences below would constitute complete answers to (53):

(55) I saw a, but not b
(56) I saw only b
(57) I saw no students

and that the following would constitute partial answers:

(58) I saw a
(59) I saw a or b, but I don't remember which
(60) If I saw a, then I saw b too

The sense in which any one of (55)–(57) is a complete answer is that the truth of these sentences is compatible with one possibility in the space, and incompatible with the others. The sense in which any one of (58)–(60) is a partial answer that is less than complete is that its truth is incompatible with some of the possibilities in the space, but compatible with more than one (for example, the truth of (60) is compatible with every possibility except the one where the speaker saw *a*, but did not see *b*). Obviously, all of (55)–(60) are remarks relevant to the question (53). In fact, we will suggest that what it is for a sentence to be a relevant answer is just for it to be incompatible with some (but not all) possibilities. In the next subsection we develop these ideas more explicitly.

3.3   *Answers and presuppositions*

We turn now to the explication of the notion of an answer to a question (an interrogative form), and to the notion of the *presuppositions* of a question on the view thus far developed. We have said that a question poses a space of possibilities, and that a relevant answer to a question cuts down the space, by being incompatible with certain possibilities within it. Suppose that π is a partition, and that it is proper, in the sense defined above. If p is a proposition, let the *conditionalization* π/p of π by p be the result of (a) adding p to every A such that $\pi(A)$, and (b) deleting from the result any set whose logical product (the intension of the finite or infinite conjunction of the extensions of all its members) is the empty proposition, true in no worlds. Formally:

$$\pi/p = \lambda A\{[\forall q][A(q) \leftrightarrow [q = p \vee (\exists B)(\pi(B) \& B(q))]] \& \Diamond (\forall q)(A(q) \to {}^{\vee}q)\}$$

Then p is *relevant* to π if the elements of π/p are fewer than those of π, otherwise *irrelevant*. Consider then the conditionalization of the question expressed by "Did John leave?" as it would be depicted in (49), by the answer, "John left." At the stage (a) we get

(61)   {{^John left},{^John left,^¬(John left)}}

where the logical product of the second element is the empty proposition ^(John left & ¬(John left)). At stage (b) therefore we get the partition (62)

(62)   {{^John left}}

Supposing the answer was a true one, the questioner will have obtained information from it. But even if it is not true, the answer is (maximally) relevant, since it diminishes the space of possibilities posed by the question to a single one.

The illustration just given for the case of a simple yes-no question extends to *Wh*-questions straightforwardly, and indeed fulfills the desideratum that we should be able to distinguish relevant partial answers, even those that give only very incomplete information, from responses that are not answers at all.

Acts of asking questions carry presuppositions, sometimes present in the situation of utterance without being linguistically triggered, and sometimes present in the form of the utterance itself. Intuitively, a question like (63) presupposes that there was a man in a red hat to be seen:

(63)   Did you see the man in the red hat?

Suppose you ask me (63), and suppose that I am firmly convinced that there are no men with red hats about. I take it, however, that you believe that there are some, indeed a unique salient one that you can indicate to me by using the phrase in your question. Then you make a presupposition in your question, one which I reject, and I do not answer your question with, "No." How can we understand this phenomenon within the theory given here?

First of all, your presupposition that there is a unique man in a red hat can be encoded into the question you express by putting the proposition expressing it into every possibility in the space that you present; that is, by conditionalizing on that presupposition. Where μ is the proposition that there is a unique man in a red hat, and $^\wedge\phi$ is $^\wedge$(you saw the man in the red hat), the partition you express is (64):

(64) $\{\{^\wedge\phi,\mu\},\{^\wedge\neg\phi,\mu\}\}$

This partition is not exhaustive; in fact neither of its members will consist only of true propositions in worlds in which μ is not true. Convinced as I am that there is no man in a red hat, I believe that no element in your space of possibilities answers to reality, and I may repudiate your presupposition by saying (65):

(65)   There is no man in a red hat

If we now conditionalize your partition by the proposition p that I express, the result is the empty partition $\{\phi\}$; and so in particular we violate the condition on π/p that it contain some element that is possibly true. These reflections suggest the following explications:

(66)   A *presupposition* of a partition is any proposition implied by each of its members; to *reject* a presupposition of π is to assert a proposition p such that π/p is undefined.[6]

The constructions and definitions given here comprise a semantics for almost all interrogative forms, direct and indirect, of the kind sketched in section 1; that is, of the kind (21), repeated here:

(21) $[_{CP}[Wh_1 \ldots Wh_n)] \; [? \; [_S \ldots t_1 \ldots t_n]]]$

Our examples have all been questions about ordinary individuals. But *Wh*-questions can be formed from nearly every syntactic category in English, and in principle from any semantic category. Thus we have questions like those in (67):

(67)   How often [does the dog go outside *t*]?
       Why [is grass green *t*]?
       How [did you fix the car *t*]?

The construction given above applies to all these cases, where the normal form at LF has the structure

$$[_{CP}[_{XP}Wh\text{-}R]_i \; [_{C'}? \; [_S \ldots t_i \ldots]]]$$

XP is some category, *R* is the restriction on *Wh*, and $C' = ?[\ldots t_i \ldots]$ is the nuclear scope of XP. In the next section we turn to more complex types.

4   Quantifying Into Questions

Consider how quantifiers might be combined with questions. Interrogative forms such as (68) are known to be ambiguous:

(68)   What did everybody say?

Intuitively, the question might be asking for particular things such that everybody said those things. But there is another (and perhaps more natural) interpretation according to which the question wants to know, for each person, what that person said. Here we shall suppose (with Karttunen) that these questions may arise by exporting the quantifier past the *Wh*-expression, so that we shall have an LF-representation as in (69):

(69)   [[everybody]_i [[what]_j [? t_i said t_j]]][7]

On reflection, it is possible to export not just the universal quantifier, represented in (69) by "everybody", but other quantifiers as well. Nuel Belnap once gave the example (70):

(70)   Where can I find two screwdrivers?

A person who asks (70) may mean to inquire what place is an *x* such that there are two screwdrivers at *x*. But s/he may also mean just to get hold of information that will enable him/her to locate two screwdrivers, and in this sense of the question it arises from the interrogative form (71):

(71)   [[two screwdrivers]$_i$ [[where]$_j$ [? I can find t_i at t_j]]]

The translation of the nuclear scope of the quantifier "two screwdrivers" is unproblematic. It is "$\mathbf{X}G$", where G applies to the partitions given by C', binding the variable "x_i"; "x_j" will appear as a free variable. Our problem is to quantify over this position, in a way dictated by the interpretation of the restricted quantifier "two screwdrivers".

It might be argued that universal quantification into questions is dispensable in principle, in favor of multiple interrogation. However, there is a subtle difference between questions into which there has been universal quantification and multiple *Wh*-questions; that is, between (68) and the closely related (72):

(72)   Who said what?

The difference may be put by saying that (68) and (72) share the same *complete* answers, but have different *partial* answers. A complete answer to either question will, for each person in the relevant context, say what that person said. But suppose that there are three relevant people, and suppose that you know exactly what two of them said, but have no information about the third. Then you may truthfully assert (73):

(73)   I have some information about who said what

but you cannot truthfully assert (74):

(74)   I have some information about what everybody said

The reason is that, to have some information as in (74) you must have *some* information about *each* person, and such information is by hypothesis lacking.

Even if, contrary to the judgement expressed above, the questions (68) and (72) are not distinguished, we must still consider Belnap's case, which is not equivalent to any multiple question. Therefore, we shall have to allow for genuine quantification into questions, in principle by any available quantifier. How is this to be done? The procedure adopted here calls for raising the type of questions with quantification above that of partitions, to sets of sets of them. A set of partitions will be called a *bloc of order 0*, and sets of blocs of order 0 *questions of order 1*. We will suppose that to answer a question of order 1 is to answer every question in one of its blocs. The formal construction proceeds as follows.

In the following definition, we avail ourselves of a (defined) restricted quantifier notation

$[Q^*v{:}\delta]\ \beta$

where δ and β are formulas, v is a variable, and Q^* a quantifier.

(75)   If X is translated as α, Q as Q^*, and Y as δ, then

$$[[Q\ [_{N'}Y]]_i\ [_{CP}X]]$$

is translated as

$$(\lambda V)\{(A\pi)(V(\pi) \rightarrow (Ex_i)\pi = \alpha)\ \&\ [Q^*x_i{:}\delta](E\pi)(V(\pi)\ \&\ \pi = \alpha)\}$$

The first conjunct in the interior of the above formula restricts the partitions in the bloc V to those that are derived from α (within which the variable "x_i" will be bound). The second conjunct restricts blocs V to those that contain a quantity of partitions, in one-to-one correspondence with values of that variable, that make the quantified statement true. Because of the one-to-one correspondence, these will be precisely the extensions which, when assigned to a predicate variable F, would make

$$[Q^*x_i{:}\delta]\ F(x)_i$$

true. The method therefore applies to any quantifier, as determined by its ordinary meaning.

By way of fixing ideas, let us consider (71), repeated here, as a typical example:

(71)   [[two screwdrivers]$_i$ [[where]$_j$ [? [I can find t_i at t_j]]]]

Its (rather formidable) translation has for its interpretation a set Ω of blocs V, each of which is a set of partitions for the question expressed by

Where can I find x_i?

for only screwdrivers as values of x_i, and for at least two such. There being many more than two screwdrivers, Ω will have many blocs. By contrast, the universal question (68) will have only one bloc, namely the one that contains all and only the partitions expressed by

What did x_i say?

for the persons in the context as values of x_i.

We may now put our suggestion above about the answers to questions that exhibit quantification outside the scope of "?" in the form of a definition:

(76)   A *relevant answer* to a question Ω of order 1 is a proposition that, for some bloc V such that $\Omega(V)$, is a relevant answer to every partition in V.

Thus to answer a universal question one must answer its (sole) bloc; but to answer Belnap's question (70) it is sufficient, for any two screwdrivers a and *b*, to answer the question where *a* may be found, and the question where *b* may be found.

It is possible to have iterated quantification into questions, as in one interpretation of (77):

(77) What did everybody say about everybody?

(Imagine this as a request for all the latest gossip.) Our construction, applied to such cases, would yield blocs of order 1, namely sets of questions of order 1, and then questions of order 2, namely sets of blocs of order 1; and so on up, as more quantifiers appear. We may also, more simply, quantify into yes–no questions, as in (78):

(78) For each and every book, is it worth reading?

A relevant answer to this question will answer, for each book, the question whether it is worth reading.[8]

5 Indirect Questions

Recall that an indirect or embedded question is an interrogative form occupying a Θ-position, thus an argument of a head. In standard English, indirect yes – no questions are identified as being marked with "if" or "whether", and although these expressions may differ somewhat in meaning, we shall assume for simplicity that they may be taken as the spellout or reflex of the "?" in C (modulo the question of nominalization, to which we return). Spec(CP) will then be semantically inert even if non-empty, and we begin therefore with the assumption that examples like (79) embed the interrogative form (80):

(79) Mary knows/wonders/told John [whether/if it was raining]
(80) [$_C$? [$_S$it was raining]]

The type of a V with respect to the argument position that is occupied by an indirect question is for the case of "know", "raised" from propositions to a higher type. This V may take for its complement ordinary nominals referring to propositions, and finite clauses, which do the same; and it is natural to suppose that its use as in (79) is derivative from this. Similarly for the sentential complement of "tell", which may be declarative. Not so with the V "wonder", whose complement is necessarily an interrogative form.[9] We are thus led to suppose that the interpretation of the indirect questions is the same as that of the corresponding direct questions, except for the nominalization that makes indirect questions unsuitable as vehicles for asking a question.[10]

Nominalization of a root sentence is expressed in IL by the sign "^" for

λ-abstraction over possible worlds. Complement clauses require nominalization, and it is possible to interpret the ordinary declarative complementizer "that" as expressing it. Root clauses, of type t, have truth values for their extensions; but complementized clauses have propositions for their extensions, and therefore simply refer. For this reason, one makes an assertion by uttering a root clause, but not by uttering a complementized clause. We assume this type of nominalization applies to the contents of questions as well, when they are embedded. If the translation of a root interrogative C' is Σ, then that of the corresponding embedded interrogative is $^\wedge\Sigma$. Note particularly that it may be that $\Sigma = \Gamma$, although $^\wedge\Sigma \neq {}^\wedge\Gamma$; such will be the case for any two *Wh*-questions with the same nuclear scope and having restrictions that, while coextensive in the actual world, diverge elsewhere.

Suppose then that the interpretation of the complement in (79) is the nominalization of the interpretation of the direct question, "Is it raining?" We then take V like "know" and "wonder" as expressing relations between persons (or other agents) and intensions $^\wedge\pi$, where π is a partition. We can now use the theory of conditionalization of partitions together with assumptions about rationality, to explain why, for example, (81) is a natural scenario:

> (81)   Mary wondered whether it was raining; looking outside the window she saw that it was; so (of course) she didn't wonder about that any longer.

Mary is initially in the state

$$\text{Wonder(Mary,}^\wedge\pi,T)$$

for some time T, where π is the partition that interprets the indirect question. Shortly after, say at time T', she comes to be in the state

$$\text{Know(Mary,}^\wedge\text{it is raining,}T')$$

Since Mary is rational, she wonders about an intension $^\wedge\pi$ only if she does not know the complete answer; i.e. only if π has more than one member. So if upon learning that it is raining she conditionalizes upon π by this new information, deriving $\pi' = \pi/^\wedge(\text{it is raining})$, she will not of course wonder about $^\wedge\pi'$, what is left of $^\wedge\pi$ after conditionalization.

The transitions among Mary's mental states, as described in (81) and rationalized by the account given, are like those of a person who asks, desiring relief from ignorance, whether it is raining, and believes the respondent who tells her that it is. In (81), we have Mary looking outside the window, thus putting herself in a position to "answer her own question." But relief from ignorance can occur in the absence of investigation, simply by the coming of new information to the agent. For this reason, the applications of the theory of questions to the theory of rationality are more fundamental than applications to discourse. The latter applications actually derive from the former.

For another example in support of this point, consider the notion of a *test question*, such as might be asked by an examiner of an examinee. In the test setting, the examiner already knows the answer to the question asked, or at least knows how to determine whether the examinee's answer is correct. What the examiner wonders is whether the examinee knows the right answer, for which the examinee's behavior is expected to provide evidence. Given the evidence, what the examiner conditionalizes upon is not the question asked, but the question whether the examinee knows the answer to it, a question that was not asked.

Whereas a V like "wonder" seems to express a relation between agents and the meanings of interrogative forms, a V like "know" may be mediated, in its use with indirect questions, by the ordinary knowledge relation between agents and propositions. One way of interpreting this mediation is as in (82):

(82) $\text{know}(x, {}^\wedge\pi) \leftrightarrow (\exists p)(\text{know}(x,p) \ \& \ p \text{ answers } \pi)$

where (82) is to hold necessarily, for all x, p, and π.

Karttunen (1977) notes that even non-factive V relating agents to propositions generally show a kind of factivity when they are construed with indirect questions. Thus "tell" is certainly not factive, but in either (79) above, or Karttunen's example (42), repeated here, we have the intuition that whatever the agent said was in fact true:

(42) John told Mary who passed the test

It is partly on the basis of this fact that Karttunen proposes that indirect questions denote only true complete answers, rather than all possible complete answers. In the system developed here, where the partition answering to an indirect question is indifferent to which element of it happens to be true, we must account for the factivity in question in a different way. A simple possibility is to modify postulates of the form of (82), so that, for an expression R of the appropriate kind, they incorporate the truth of answers, as in (83):

(83) $R(x, {}^\wedge\pi) \leftrightarrow (\exists p)(R(x,p) \ \& \ p \text{ answers } \pi \ \& \ {}^\vee p)$[11]

6 Conclusion

In the wake of the technical discussion above I return now to the problem with which we began, of how to relate the syntactic and semantic conception of questions to each other, and how to relate them both to the content of acts of speech.

We have the intuition that questions do not have truth values. This intuition is sustained on the present account, because although the elements A of partitions may be said to have truth values, true if all the propositions in A are true, and otherwise false, sets of such elements cannot. The content expressed by a question, the intension of a partition, is in each possible world a logical space, or a space of possibilities. Just as a declarative form has a truth value, and expresses an intension whose value in each possible world is a truth value, so an interrogative form has a value in the realm of partitions, and expresses an intension whose value in each possible world is a partition. An interrogative form is suited to asking a question, because it presents a space of possibilities; and its nominalization is suited to being a complement to states such as wondering because the content of that nominalization in any world is such a space. Finally, indirect questions, the nominalizations of questions, are admitted as the objects of states such as knowing, or activities such as telling, because their relation to intensions $^\wedge\pi$ of partitions π is mediated by the concept of being in the state of knowing, or engaging in the activity of telling, propositions that are true answers to π. Such is the conceptual solution to the problem of the form and content of questions, putting them in proper analogy with statements.

In this article I have concentrated on only some of the most basic formal aspects of the semantics of questions, and have left many complex issues aside. If the reader has seen from this brief outline how much logical structure can be found in problems, simply put, about the syntax and semantics of some of our most ordinary speech, it will have served its purpose.

NOTES

1   Technically, we take movement into C to have the semantics of the type of raising that does not change meaning. Thus the translation into IL of the embedded S in (14) will be

   $F_j(\text{sein Vater}, x_i)$

   with "F_j" a two-place predicate variable. (Strictly speaking, two-place predicates represent an extension of the primitive vocabulary of IL; we use them as making for easier readability.) When the antecedent "hasst$_j$" is encountered in C, the semantic effect is merely to replace (prior to the operation described below triggered by "?") that variable with its antecedent.
2   Besides these, there is a special class of questions marked in English by special (high-pitch) intonation, the so-called *echo* questions, not considered here.
3   Recall that $^\vee p$ is the extension (truth value) of p. I simplify here, in that individual variables are taken as ranging over objects (things of type e) rather than individual concepts, as in Karttunen's original exposition; and I use English words as their own translations into the metalanguage whenever possible.

4   For instance, contexts such as *there*-insertion, which are restricted to indefinites, accept *Wh*-expressions, as in (i):

      (i)   Who said [there was who in the garden]?

5   I omit here the explicit mechanism, required for ordinary quantification as well as for questions, that secures the fact that the variable appearing in the translation of Y is the variable x_i.

6   Naturally, this definition has within IL the consequence that each partition presupposes every necessary truth, and inversely that the assertion of any necessary falsehood constitutes a rejection of the presuppositions of any partition. The essentials of the above account may be retained, however, even under more refined conceptions of propositions and partitions.

7   A number of syntactic questions arise here, for instance whether we should regard this representation as resulting from adjunction to CP, or perhaps as movement into Spec. We shall for the sake of discussion assume the former.

8   There is a further extension to truth functional combinations of questions, omitted here; but see Higginbotham (1993) or (1991), or Groenendijk and Stokhof (1989).

9   There is a somewhat archaic form, exemplified in "I wonder that he went to San Francisco", where "wonder" means *marvel at*. Although this form may have had a historical influence, it seems clearly semantically different, and anyway many English speakers who have the word "wonder" know nothing of this other use.

10   An alternative view, developed especially in Hintikka (1976) and others of his works, would attempt to reduce direct questions to sentences with indirect questions, and these in turn to sentences that embed only declaratives. The existence of V like "wonder", as well as other contexts pointed out in Karttunen (1977), appears to set limits on any such reduction. Among the merits of Hintikka's proposal, however, is that it correlates the utterance of interrogatives with the contents of at least some speech acts, one of the points that we wish to explain. We do not consider this development here, but refer the reader to the work cited.

11   See further Higginbotham (1991), and for a detailed analysis Lahiri (1992).

15 Interrogatives: Questions, Facts and Dialogue

JONATHAN GINZBURG

1 Introduction

This paper focuses on the semantics of interrogative sentences and has three main parts.[1] The first critically reviews some basic issues drawing on the recent literature. In the second, I present and motivate the outlines of a theory of questions and a semantics for interrogatives. Both sections are based on work presented in much fuller detail in Ginzburg (1994a). The third section offers a dialogue setting for the theory developed in the second part.

2 Basic Issues in the Semantics of Interrogatives

2.1 Questions and interrogatives

There is a clear connection between the semantics of interrogatives and the notion of a question. A number of common-noun phrases denote entities of which one can predicate (un)resolvedness, openness and so forth:

(1) a. The question/issue remains unresolved.
     b. The question/issue is still an open one.

Interrogative but not declarative sentences can be used to designate such entities:

(2) a. The question/issue is who left/whether Bill is happy.
     b. # The question/issue is that Bill is happy.

When we try to explain what underlies inference patterns such as the ones in (3a) and in (3b), we see perhaps more strongly the co-dependence of the two issues – what denotation[2] to assign to interrogatives and what (semantic) object a question is.

(3) a. The question is who should be selected for the job. Jill has been investigating this question. Hence, Jill has been investigating who should be selected for the job.

b. The question was who should be selected for the job. However, since we now know that . . . and that . . . , it is clear that this question is now resolved.

The clichéed statement that *how such issues are to be resolved is determined, to a large extent, by the range of phenomena one's theory is intended to cover* applies here with special force, since intuitions on what an interrogative should denote are hard to come by. In light of this, a common approach within the work on interrogatives has been to focus on a particular set of phenomena, find a semantic invariant defined by an interrogative use for that set of phenomena, and then identify the interrogative denotation with that invariant. Distinct phenomena have spawned distinct approaches and conflicting opinions on which is *the invariant* that most adequately serves as the denotation. Focus on how elliptical responses get interpreted shows the importance of associating an n-ary relation with an interrogative use, whereas focus on the use of interrogatives in attitude reports inclines one to the importance of associating a particular proposition, the exhaustive answer, with an interrogative use. It is researchers who noted the use of interrogatives to denote apparently *non*-propositional attitudes from whom proposals have originated that the existing ontology needs to be expanded to include a new class of object, a question, call it. The most influential proposals to this effect have, in fact, proposed a very specific characterization of what a question is: namely, that a question is a property of propositions, that property which specifies what it is to be an *exhaustive answer*.

An important point that will emerge in this first section is that all the invariants noted above, as well as a number of ones hitherto unmentioned, are in one way or another, with certain important modifications, necessary for semantic analysis. Hence, in order to get a viable analysis, the denotation(s) one posits need to be ones from which, in conjunction with the semantic structure provided by other available semantic objects, it is possible to "read off" the requisite invariants.

2.2   *Questions and N-ary relations*

One of the most obvious ways in which a query use of an interrogative i_0 changes the context is to enable elliptical followups that agree with the interrogative phrase(s) of i_0:[3]

(4) a. Who likes Millie? Jill/A friend of Jill's.
   b. Why does Jill like Millie? Because they're cousins.
   c. Are you happy? Yes/Maybe.

A plausible conclusion to draw from this is that each *question* q_0 expressed by an interrogative use is associated with an n-ary relation, say $rel(q_0)$, which is made salient whenever q_0 is. This is what allows a response to a query to be elliptical – the full content of the response is then computed by predicating the elliptical response of $rel(q_0)$:

(5) a. The question expressed by a use of: "Who likes Millie" is associated with $\lambda x LIKES(x,m)$.
   Content of response "Jill": $\lambda P P(j)$.
   Content of response "A friend of Jill's": $\lambda P \exists y$ (*friend* – *of*$(j,y) \wedge P(j)$).
   Full content: $\lambda P P(j)[\lambda x LIKES(x,m)]$.
   Full content: $\lambda P \exists y$ (*friend* – *of* $(j,y) \wedge P(j))[\lambda x LIKES(x,m)]$
   b. The question expressed by a use of: "Does Bill like Mary" is associated with $LIKES(b,m)$.
   Content of response "Yes": $\lambda p TRUE(p)$.
   Content of response "Maybe": $\lambda p MAYBE(p)$.
   Full content: $\lambda p TRUE(p)[LIKES(b,m)]$.

In fact, stronger conclusions from data such as (4) have been drawn: for instance, one can *identify* q_0 with $rel(q_0)$ (see e.g. Keenan and Hull (1973), Hull (1975), Hausser (1983), Hausser and Zaefferer (1979)). In (5), I have strayed from a number of works in this tradition in viewing the *responsive* phrase as the operator, rather than the interrogative:[4] it suggests that the expected semantic category of the responsives is $\langle rel(q_0),t \rangle$, (i.e. a function that takes elements of type $rel(q)$ to propositions). This has two positive consequences: first and more importantly, quantified answers, as in (4a), are directly accommodated and expected. Second, $rel(q)$ for a y/n interrogative "whether p" is p. This is intuitively appealing since a declarative "p" can be used to make a similar query.

There is an important insight emphasized by this approach, namely that a question and answer pair form a dialogue unit. As we shall see when we come to consider naturally occurring dialogue in Section 4, what is required is a more general notion that relates a question to a multiplicity of contributions that pertain to it. In other words, since the discussion of a single question can last over several turns, and elliptical contributions are possible, in principle, arbitrarily far away from the turn in which the question was posed, what will be needed is a notion of context which can express the fact that a particular question is (still) under discussion, and hence its associated relation is (still) salient.

A common argument against identifying questions with n-ary relations dating back to the classical Montagovian era concerns the multiplicity of semantic types that emerge; that is, within a type theory such as that provided by Montague's *IL*, any two interrogatives differing in r-ity (e.g. unary/binary/ternary *wh*-interrogative-sentences) or in the type of argument (e.g. where constituent interrogative is adverbial vs. where constituent interrogative is an argument of a verb) are distinguished. This contradicts a possible methodological constraint that a given syntactic category should map onto a single semantic type. An empirical problem deriving from this concerns coordination: how to interpret a coordinate structure consisting of conjuncts of distinct semantic type? In light of the subsequent relaxation of type discipline, both problems currently seem less acute. In particular, in a setting where λ-abstracts form a single semantic type, one can offer definitions such as the following for coordination:[5]

(6) $\lambda X_1, \ldots, X_n \sigma(X_1, \ldots, X_n) \vee / \wedge \lambda Y_1, \ldots, Y_m \tau(Y_1, \ldots, Y_m)$
   $=_{def} \lambda X_1, \ldots, X_n, Y_1, \ldots Y_m \sigma(X_1, \ldots X_n) \vee / \wedge \tau(Y_1, \ldots, Y_m)$

Below, I shall propose that $rel(q_0)$ is one of two invariants that serve to individuate a question. In addition to its importance in characterizing the context change associated with questions, it turns out that a number of fundamental notions of answerhood are definable on the basis of $rel(q_0)$.

Nonetheless, I do not believe that it is theoretically desirable to *identify* questions with n-ary relations. What is missing is a connection to the world. Let us see why.

2.3   *Questions and propositions*

2.3.1   *Introduction*

There is a well known schema that relates the proposition expressed by a (use of a) declarative sentence *d* to the possibility of embedding *d* as the complement of a predicate drawn from the class of so called *factive* predicates:

(7)   The claim is that *p*.
   Bill V's/has V'ed (knows/discovered) that *p*.
   So, the claim is true.

There is a converse schema that provides a sufficient condition for (the content of) a declarative to be in the positive extension of a factive (and, it is also satisfied by a class of non-factives). The schema relates V'ing of fact nominals to V'ing of 'that' clauses:

(8)   A certain fact is/has been V'ed (known/discovered).
   Which fact? One that proves the claim that *p*.
   So, it is/has been V'ed that *p*.

In Ginzburg (1994a), analogous schemas are pointed out relating questions expressed by interrogative sentences and a class of predicates that includes the factives but also predicates such as "tell", "guess", and "predict". I dub such predicates *resolutive* predicates: whereas we can talk about the *truth* of a proposition, this is not possible with a question. What one can talk about is whether the question is *resolved*:

(9) a. The question is: who left.
       Bill V's/has V'ed (knows/discovered/told me/reported/man-
         aged to guess) who left.
       So, the question is resolved/the question is no longer open.
     b. A certain fact is/has been V'ed (known/discovered/told to me/
         reported/guessed).
       Which fact? A fact that resolves the question of who left.
       So, it is/has been V'ed (known/discovered/told to me/reported/
         guessed) who left.

This analogy makes clear the strong connection between facts, questions and propositions: just as truth is a fundamental property of propositions relating them to the facts and the way the *world* actually is, so *resolvedness* is an analogous property of questions.[6]

However, *identifying* a question q_0 with its $rel(q_0)$ does not offer any obvious account of such a connection to the world.

There have been various accounts of questions that have tied them quite closely to propositions. The issue is: how tight is this connection? One approach initially proposed by Åqvist and Hintikka (e.g. Åqvist 1965, Hintikka 1976, 1978) seeks to reduce interrogative meaning to declarative meaning by means of paraphrases of the following type:[7]

(10) a. John V's who came ↔ Any person is such that if he came, then
         John V's that he came.
      b. John V's whether it is raining ↔ If it is raining, then John V's
         that it is raining, and if it is not raining, then John V's that it is
         not raining. (Hintikka (1976))

An alternative approach, due originally to Hamblin (1973) and to Karttunen (1977), while sharing much of the intuition that inspires (10), seeks to establish the connection at a semantic level, thus recognizing an ontological distinctness between questions and propositions.[8]

One of the main reasons that lead to the prominence of the alternative approach, particularly influential within Montague Grammar, is this: Karttunen points out the existence of a class of predicates which embed interrogative but not declarative complements:

(11) a. Jill asked/wondered/investigated who left.
      b. Jill asked/wondered/investigated # that Bill left.

Moreover, even if one attempts to provide a semantics for some such predicates by means of lexical decomposition, Karttunen's claim is that there is no obvious way to lexically decompose predicates such as those in (12) in a similar way:[9]

(12) a. Who wins the race depends upon who enters it.
      b. When Mary will arrive will be influenced by who drives the bus.

This argument had a compelling force during the early days of Montague Grammar where adherence to surface compositionality was stressed. For those to whom the argument might appear somewhat esoteric ("how often does 'depend on' appear in a corpus?"), there is an interesting correlate to Karttunen's argument within dialogue which is worth pointing out: a sufficient condition for a query use of a question q_1 to be felicitously responded to with a question q_2 is that q_1 *depend on* q_2 (cf. Carlson (1983)):

(13) a. A: Who murdered John?
         B: Who was in town yesterday?
      b. Who murdered John depends on who was in town yesterday.

Predicates such as "depend", then, play an important role in structuring dialogue. For more discussion and a generalization of this see section 4.

2.3.2 Hamblin semantics

Hamblin's view is, apparently, inspired by his earlier work on modelling dialogue (Hamblin (1970)): "Pragmatically speaking a question sets up a choice situation between a set of propositions, namely those propositions that count as answers to it." (Hamblin (1973), p.254) On this view, each question defines a set of alternative propositions, call it *Answer-Set(q)*, each element of which constitutes a valid option for a response. Hamblin chooses to identify a question with its Answer-Set (this is not his terminology.). Hamblin posits the following:

(14) a. Answer-Set("Who likes Bill") $= \lambda p[\exists y(p = LIKES(y, bill))] =$ {LIKES(j,b), LIKES(m,b), LIKES(c,b), ...}
      b. Answer-Set("Who likes whom") $= \lambda p[\exists y \exists x(p = LIKES(x, y))] =$ {LIKES(j,b), LIKES(m,b), LIKES(c,b), ...}
      c. Answer-Set("Does Bill like Mary") $= \lambda p[(p = LIKES(b,m)) \vee (p = \neg LIKES(b,m))] = $ {LIKES(b,m), $\neg$ LIKES(b,m)}

Actually, Hamblin proposes to "type raise" declarative denotations to (singleton) sets of propositions. One can then offer the following algebraical perspective within a lattice of propositional elements: questions are the "non-singular" entities, the "plural propositions". Such a view has been developed further in Belnap (1982) and especially in Lahiri (1991):

(15) $Q' =_{def} \{p : \exists p' | p' \in Power - set(Answer - Set(q)) \setminus \emptyset \wedge p = \wedge p'\}$ (Lahiri p.159)

Therefore, the individual members of the Answer-Set(q) can be construed as the potential partial answers. More on this aspect of Hamblin's theory in Section 3.4.2.

Hamblin's approach is particularly important, historically, in recognizing the need for an independent ontological notion of question. Moreover, construing questions as entities that, in some sense, determine answerhood options is an important, if not unproblematic insight.

On the critical side of things, it is worth noting that the particular composition Hamblin chooses for his Answer-Sets is open to question. It arises by stipulation rather than via a uniform mapping that covers the *wh*-questions and the *y/n*'s questions. Indeed, if one is to construe Answer-Set(q) as characterizing the responsehood options associated with a query involving q, it is clearly inadequate.

For instance, there is a class of propositions that a competent speaker of English recognizes as "intimately related" to a particular question, call it q_0, quite independently of their truth or specificity relative to current purposes. This class consists of those propositions characterizable as providing information *about* q_0.[10]

Ranges of aboutness for questions arising out of yes/no-interrogative uses and simple[11] uses of unary *wh*-interrogatives are exemplified in (16), (17).[12]

(16) a. Jill: Is Millie leaving tomorrow?
        Bill: Possibly/It's unlikely/Yes/No.
      b. Bill provided information about whether Millie is leaving tomorrow. (We have no indication whether this information is reliable.)

(17) a. Jill: Who is coming tonight?
        Bill: Millie and Chuck/Several friends of mine./Few people I've heard of.
      b. Bill provided information about who was coming that night. (We have no indication whether this information is reliable.)

For convenience, let us notate the class of propositions that are *about* q_0 as Aboutness-Set (q_0). Comparison with the answerhood options offered by Hamblin suggests that, in this respect, Hamblin's view of questions is not adequate empirically.

2.3.3   *Karttunen*

To see how the Hamblin view relates to Karttunen's account, it is useful to fix the epistemic setting, since it is within such a setting that the analysis is more persuasive. We have as given a set of entities with which we are familiar to a large extent. In other words, the "essential" properties of these entities are known to us, and with each entity we have, say, associated a name that rigidly designates it. At some point *t*, we get interested in the makeup of a particular property *P*. It is quite natural in such a setting to view our wonderment about the question *who P's* in, as I shall dub it, *alternativist* terms: is it a_1 who *P's*, is it a_1 and a_2 who *P*, etc. More concretely, the desired *end* result of an inquiry or conversation on the topic of who *P's* will frequently be a proposition dubbed the exhaustive answer:

> (18)   a.   Exh-Answer(*q*) = $\wedge$ {*p*| True(*p*) $\wedge$ *p* $\in$ Answer-Set(*q*)}
> b.   Exh-Ans("Who likes Bill") = conjunction of all true instantiations of Likes(*x,b*).
> c.   Exh-Ans("Whether Mary likes Bill") = Likes(*m,b*) if true, otherwise ¬Likes(*m,b*).

That is, we will be happy to assent to the inference that if we know or have been told who *P's*, and a_1 *P's*, then we know that a_1 *P's*.

Karttunen chooses the exhaustive answer as the invariant with respect to which questions are to be identified. More specifically, Karttunen identifies a question with a property of propositions, the property of being the exhaustive answer.

> (19)   a.   *I* = "who walks"
> b.   Karttunen denotation of *I* at $\langle w \rangle$: $\lambda p[TRUE(p) \wedge \exists y(p = WALKS \langle w \rangle (y))]$

Thus, whereas Hamblin sees a question as indicating to us what the options for responding are, what Karttunen is offering is, in terms of the schemas in (9a,9b), a very specific analysis of a question's resolvedness conditions.

Given this, one natural question to ask about Karttunen's approach is whether in an epistemic setting different from the one sketched above, this analysis of the resolvedness conditions holds up. Belnap (1982) is dubious about the analysis on the grounds that a question might have more than one resolving answer, for instance:

> (20)   What is an example of a prime number?

In Section 3.4 I take up this issue in some detail, concluding ultimately that resolvedness conditions are best characterized in agent–relative rather than semantic terms.

Table 15.1 Resolutive and Question predicates

Resolutives		QI
discover	report	ask
find out	tell	wonder
forget	announce	weigh-in-one's-mind
guess	state	investigate
predict	reveal	discuss,
know	remember	talk-about
determine	show	

An additional issue is this: Karttunen provides an argument for assuming that our ontology needs to contain *questions* as the content of *some* interrogative uses. However, for methodological reasons (type hygiene), he actually assumes that *all* interrogative uses denote questions. Thus, in order to relate the interrogative and declarative complements of resolutive predicates Karttunen proposes, for instance, the following meaning postulate for "know":

(21) know(x,Q) ↔ $\forall p$(if $Q(p)$, then know(x,p)) and if ¬$\exists p Q(q)$, then know$(x, ^\wedge¬\exists\ q Q(q))$ (Karttunen (1977, footnote 11, page 18))

We can convert our intuition that not all interrogative complements denote questions into data: Resolutive and factive predicates do not embed question-denoting nominals in a purely referential way, though question predicates do.[13]

This is an intrinsic problem for a Karttunenean strategy for interrogative semantics whereby all interrogative embedding predicates are treated uniformly as having *questions* in their extension.

Substitutivity:
(22) a. Jill asked/investigated an interesting question. The question was who left yesterday. Hence: Jill asked/investigated who left yesterday.
  b. Jill discovered/revealed an interesting question. The question was who left yesterday. It does *not follow* that: Jill discovered/revealed who left yesterday.

Existential generalization:
(23) a. Jill asked/investigated who left yesterday. Hence, there is a question/issue that Jill asked/investigated yesterday. Which question? The question was who left yesterday.
  b. Jill discovered/knows who left yesterday. It does not follow that: there is a question/issue that Jill discovered/knows.

2.3.4   Groenendijk and Stokhof

Groenendijk and Stokhof's approach is one which recognizes the existence of (at least) two kinds of interrogative complements and the need to offer a systematic connection between the two. Groenendijk and Stokhof follow Karttunen in providing questions as semantic entities distinct from propositions. Indeed in explicating what a question is, their approach is close in spirit although quite distinct in execution. In order to gain a systematic correspondence between questions and propositions Groenendijk and Stokhof appeal to the Montague Grammar (MG) distinction between the *intension* and the *extension* of an expression.

The extension of an interrogative is identified with the exhaustive answer. Hence, the intension is that function that maps a world to the proposition that constitutes the exhaustive answer in that world. Within a possible worlds semantics the picture that emerges is this: the extension at w is a set of worlds, those worlds that determine the extension of the queried property equivalently. The intension of the interrogative is the partition of the set of possible worlds induced by this equivalence relation:

> (24)   a.   whether Millie likes Bill.
>   Extension at i: $\lambda j(like(m,b)(j) = like(m,b)(i))$ (All worlds j that agree with respect to the truth value of "$like(m,b)$" at i.)
>   Intension: $\lambda i \lambda j(like(m,b)(j) = like(m,b)(i))$
>
> b.   who likes Bill. Assumed paraphrasable as: "for all x whether x likes b".
>   Extension at i: $\lambda j(\lambda x like(x,b)(j) = \lambda x like(x,b)(i))$ (All worlds j that agree with respect to the extension of "x likes b" at i.)
>   Intension: $\lambda i \lambda j(\lambda x like(x,b)(j) = \lambda x like(x,b)(i))$

Two comments on these definitions. First, Groenendijk and Stokhof offer a single schema covering y/n and *wh*-interrogatives, a constituent of which is indeed $rel(q_0)$. Second, the notion of exhaustiveness that Groenendijk and Stokhof assume is *stronger* than that implemented by Karttunen. Whereas Karttunen sees the end result of an inquiry into a question *who P's* as the acquisition of knowledge of the *positive* extension of P, Groenendijk and Stokhof build in the assumption that it involves knowledge of the negative extension as well. In other words, that "Jill knows who left" is assumed to entail that "Jill knows *whether* a_1 left", for all a_1.

Groenendijk and Stokhof then distinguish between two types of interrogative embedding relations. On the one hand, there are relations that take questions as their arguments. Technically, these relations will take the intension of an interrogative as their argument. Relations of this kind include "wonder" and "ask". However, relations such as those denoted by interrogative complement embedding "*know*", "*tell*" *etc.* are not treated as relations that take questions. Rather, the argument in this case is the extension of an interrogative which, like the *intension* of a declarative, is taken to be a proposition. I will argue in Section 3.2 that the ontological distinction between resolutive / factive predicates and question predicates is of a different nature.

2.4   Recap: what is a question?

I have surveyed a number of different approaches to the semantics of interrogatives and to the related issue of what is a question. As I mentioned in the introduction, a general approach has been to find a semantic invariant needed to analyze an interrogative use for a particular class of phenomena and then identify the interrogative denotation with that invariant. I have mentioned the following as fundamental invariants associated with a question q_0:

- Rel(q_0): each question is associated with an n-ary relation. This is needed for the semantics of elliptical responses.

- Aboutness-Set(q_0): each question is associated with a class of propositions, those characterizable as providing information *About*(q_0) – those a competent speaker of English recognizes as "intimately related" to any given question, call it q_0, quite independently of their truth or specificity relative to current purposes. The accounts discussed above do not offer a fully adequate account of this invariant.

- Exh-answer (q_0): each question is associated with the proposition which, for a particular epistemic setting described above, provides an account of when the question is resolved. Resolvedness conditions are required for the semantics of resolutive predicates.

The issue to consider is, then, does one or another of these invariants deserve priority as defining *the essence* of what a question is for semantic purposes? I have already suggested that identifying q_0 with Rel(q_0) is undesirable, primarily because it does not offer any obvious account of how questions are related to facts and the way the *world* actually is, as manifested by a relation of resolvedness.

What about identifying q_0 with Exh-answer (q_0), or rather, with an intensional construct that determines Exh-answer (q_0)? In Section 3.4, I will suggest that this turns out to be undesirable once one takes a wider perspective, both in terms of the different circumstances in which questions are used and by considering questions other than "who-questions". Strengthening Belnap's complaints about the *non-uniqueness* of resolving information, I will demonstrate that whether a particular item of information *resolves* a given question is in part determined by agent-relative rather than by semantic factors. Hence, it is undesirable to reduce the *semantic* identity criteria of a question to its resolvedness conditions.

In the absence of an essential property that *defines* questionhood, the approach I shall ultimately propose will be one that remains agnostic as to what a question is, while at the same time explaining how to characterize its basic properties. In such an approach a question, just like other attitudinal entities, will be treated on a par with other individuals.

3   Towards a Theory of Questions

3.1   *Introduction*

This section is structured as follows: first I motivate the adoption of a somewhat different ontological setting for interrogative and declarative semantics. I then consider the issue of whether a question should be reductively characterized in terms of its "resolvedness conditions" and reach a negative conclusion. I then show how questions and propositions emerge as "derived elements" from a basic situation theoretic ontology consisting of situations, facts, and n-ary lambda abstracts. Finally, this ontology is used to provide a semantics for interrogatives.

3.2   *Ontological considerations*

The initial issue I will pursue is an ontological one. I will suggest that a bifurcation of the kind identified by Groennendijk and Stokhof for interrogatives also arises with declaratives. This evidence points to the need for a modification of some basic ontological assumptions about propositional attitude predicates, along lines originally proposed by Vendler (1972).[14] The overall diagnosis will be the existence of (at the very least) a 3-way split among interrogative and declarative embedding predicates. Certain predicates (*ask, wonder*) take questions as their arguments, certain predicates (*believe, claim*) take propositions as their arguments, whereas resolutive/factive predicates (*know, discover*) take neither questions nor propositions as their arguments, but rather a family of entities which include the class of facts. In particular, the evidence suggests that precisely those declarative embedding predicates whose arguments are required to be propositions on just about anyone's criteria for what constitutes a proposition, namely being a truth or falsity bearer, are inapplicable to interrogative content. This is a fact that goes unexplained on any approach, such as Groenendijk and Stokhof's, in which interrogatives possess a propositional denotation.

The data we saw in (22,23), which shows that questions are not genuine arguments of resolutives/factives, is perhaps not particularly surprising for any semantic approach, such as Hintikka's or Groenendijk and Stokhof's, which analyze interrogatives embedded by resolutives/factives as denoting propositions.

Table 15.2 Resolutive, Factive, Question, TF predicates

Resolutives	Factives	QI	TF
report	reveal	ask	claim
tell	know	wonder	believe
announce	forget	investigate	assume
guess	determine	discuss	assert
predict	discover	ponder	allege
state	remember	about	deny
	show		prove

However, unexpected for the latter type of approach is that a set of data analogous to the one above can be produced with respect to proposition-denoting nominals, ones that denote entities of which one can predicate truth or falsity. In this case, factive predicates do not embed proposition-denoting nominals purely referentially, though TF predicates do.

Substitutivity:
(25) a. The Fed's forecast was that gold reserves will be depleted by the year 2000.
      b. Bill believes/accepts the Fed's forecast. Hence, Bill believes/accepts that gold reserves will be depleted by the year 2000.
      c. Bill discovered/was aware of the Fed's forecast. It does *not follow* that: Bill discovered/was aware that gold reserves will be depleted by the year 2000.

Existential generalization:
(26) a. Bill believes that gold reserves will be depleted by the year 2000. Hence, there is a claim/hypothesis/prediction that Bill believes.
      b. Bill discovered/knows that gold reserves will be depleted by the year 2000. *It does not follow* that there is a claim/hypothesis that Bill discovered/knows.

The main contrast revealed here is highlighted in (27):

(27) a. Jill believed a certain hypothesis. Hence, Jill believed that that hypothesis is true.
      b. Jill discovered a certain hypothesis. It does not follow that Jill discovered that that hypothesis is true.

In fact, this data constitutes the tip of an empirical iceberg that motivates us to discard the label *propositional attitudes* as a catch-all term for the "that-clause" embedders, given the presupposition the label carries that *all* such predicates take propositions as their arguments. There are many explanatory benefits for reserving this term and the presupposition it embodies for TF preds and, moreover, for assuming both that:

> **Non-prop-int**: interrogatives *do not* have a denotation that is propositional.
> and, that
> **Non-prop-decl**: declaratives *do* have a denotation that is non-propositional.

The contrast exemplified above in (25–27) can be formulated more generally in terms of the following inference schema:[15]

(28) $\lceil$ V the N' $\rceil$

   ——————————————

   $\lceil$ V that the N' is true $\rceil$
   T-Pred

T-pred characterizes TF predicates as imposing an appropriateness condition on their arguments, namely that they be truth/falsity predicable. **T-pred** coupled with *Non-prop-int* allows for an ontology in which the following fact about TF predicates can be captured. TF predicates are inapplicable to interrogative content:[16]

(29)   a. # Basil supposes/assumes which pitcher will do what tomorrow.
   b. # Bill claimed/argued who came yesterday.

Notice that these facts remain unchanged if one adds as an assumption that the requisite belief, claim etc. is true.

(30)   Bill knows who left: Jerry, Mike and Marabella. So, # he believes/assumes who left.

This is one indication that a pragmatic explanation of such facts,[17] for instance based on a principle such as *do not fill the cognitive argument of a TF predicate with material already present in the common ground, cannot* be made to work.

Although the data considered so far might suggest that factives affect their NP arguments in some mysterious way, data such as the following indicates that when the common-noun phrase denotes entities which refer to or describe facts, events or other states of affairs that obtain, pure referentiality is evinced:

Substitutivity:
(31)   a. Jill is aware of/reported/revealed that fact. That fact is that Bill has been working hard to destroy the company. Hence, Jill is

aware/reported/revealed that Bill has been working hard to destroy the company.

b. Jill guessed/could have predicted/discovered these basic truths about Bill. One of these is that Bill never finishes writing up. Hence, Jill guessed/could have predicted/discovered that Bill never finishes writing up.

c. Jill regrets/remembers well a particularly gruesome outcome of Bill's pronouncement. That particularly gruesome outcome of Bill's pronouncement was that everyone was required to sign the pledge. Hence, Jill regrets/remembers well that everyone was required to sign the pledge.

Existential generalization: (for declaratives: valid only for factives)

(32) a. Jill discovered/revealed that Bill has been working hard to destroy the company. Hence, there is some fact that Jill discovered/revealed.

b. Jill discovered/told us who Bill has chosen for the job. Hence, there is some fact that Jill discovered/told us.

3.3 Interim conclusion

The data presented in the previous section leads us in the following ontological direction: we need an ontology in which questions, propositions, and facts are distinguished in order to capture the difference between the entities distinct classes of predicates embed *purely referentially* and those to which they are *inapplicable*. Clearly, it will not be satisfactory to posit such an ontology in a wholesale, unstructured fashion. Rather what we desire is to establish how these distinct entities relate to each other and to provide (some of) the basic structure for a semantic universe. One strategy for constructing such a universe will be provided in Section 3.5, after I discuss the issue of questions and resolvedness conditions.

Given such an ontology, we will be able to move more directly to the semantic front. What we have seen is that interrogatives are required to denote both questions and facts, and equally that declaratives are required to denote both propositions and facts. The explanation common to both cases which I will adopt, is that such expressions can be *coerced* to denote facts.

3.4 Questions and resolvedness conditions

Recall that in Section 2.3 I described an epistemic setting which is particularly well suited for the view of questions developed by Karttunen, and Groenendijk and Stokhof. This is a setting where the entities are ones with which we are to a large extent familiar. In such a case it is at least plausible to model our wonderment about a question *who P's*, for some locally salient property *P*, in alternativist lines: is it a_1 who P's, is it a_1 and a_2 who P, etc. Equally, that question's resolvedness conditions are captured fairly well by the exhaustive answer.

However, the epistemic setting described above is far from prototypical. A somewhat extreme case is when the domain of interest is completely unfamiliar. Consider, for example, the following sentence

(33)   What is the word for "relaxation" in Chukotian?

uttered by someone who doesn't know what language family Chukotian belongs to, let alone possible word forms in the language. Clearly, I can ask or understand this question with little or no reference to or acquaintance with *any* singular proposition which instantiates an answer. For such a context, our wonderment about that question does not seem to be plausibly modelled in alternativist terms. In other words, any even *prima facie* psychologically conceivable notion of the update of an epistemic state will not involve the constituents of the Answer-Set.[18]

To see how a change in epistemic setting can actually affect truth conditions, consider the following case: a scientist and an EC politician visit an institute located in a country on the far periphery of observable academic activity. Both people are taken to visit a local research institute where the scientist gives a number of lectures. After the last lecture, each asks (34a). It is clear that neither of them will be satisfied with (34b), to which they would be entitled to react with (34c):

(34)   a.   Q: Who has been attending these talks?
       b.   The director: (Provides list of names)
       c.   I asked the director who had been attending the talks. She didn't really tell me. All she did was recite a list of names, none of which meant much to me.
       d.   The director was asked who had been attending the talks and she told us.

Note that in this case (34b) is, on anyone's account, an *exhaustive* answer since, if true, it fixes the extension of the predicate "has been attending these talks".[19] Nonetheless, neither queriers' wonderment about the question is at all satisfied by the exhaustive answer. But notice that the epistemic setting here is a crucial parameter. If a local researcher, familiar with the lecture attendees, but who had not herself attended the lectures, happened to hear the dialogue in (34), she would, typically, react by saying (34d).

What the visitors would really have welcomed would be responses of the type provided in (35a,b), which could then be reported as (35c):

(35)   a.   [Querier is the high ranking EC politician.] The director: A number of linguists and psychologists.

b. [Querier is the researcher in the field covered by the institute.] The director: A number of cognitive phoneticians and Willshaw-net experts.

c. I asked the director who had been attending the talks and she told me.

Is the contrasting behavior between the two foreigners and the local observer one that can be addressed, say, by positing a kind/individual ambiguity associated with "who"? Apparently not, as a careful examination of (35) shows. Notice that permuting the responses results in inappropriateness. Supplied with the information in (35b), the EC politician would react in terms similar to (34c). Equally, supplying the scientist with the information in (35a) would in all likelihood not satisfy him enough to assert (35c). (For that matter, neither responses would, in all likelihood, be satisfactory for the local observer.)

These examples emphasize that a number of agent-relative factors come in to play in the *truth conditions* of interrogatives embedded by resolutive predicates such as "tell", "know", or "discover", in other words in fixing what information counts as information that resolves a given question. Rather than one, exhaustive answer, there exist a multiplicity of non-mutually entailing items of information that *potentially* resolve a given question. It is only within a particular kind of context that extension-fixing exhaustive answers are particularly favored.

3.4.1 Resolving when and where

In the previous section I argued that the simple picture of what a question is provided by alternativist views of questions is hard to maintain for who-questions. Here, rather briefly, I would like to indicate that when we extend our attention to other types of question, the situation is, if anything, worse for the alternativist.

The examples in (36) illustrate how information ranging from relatively coarse quantificational statements (36b,c) to the ultra-precise (36d,e) can constitute resolving information disquotable as (36f):

(36) a. A: When is the train leaving.
b. [B is a guard at the station.] B: Very soon. Run before you miss it.
c. B: Within the next hour: you better stay in the station.
d. B: At 13:10.
e. [A is about to measure the speed of light:] B: according to our caesium clock at 13:10.88254.
f. B indicated to A when the train is leaving.

Examples (37) and (38) illustrate, respectively, how a particular proposition serves as resolving information in the one context, but no longer does so in another context:

(37) a. [Context: Jill about to step off plane in Helsinki.]
Flight attendant: Do you know where you are?
Jill: Helsinki.
b. Flight attendant: Ah ok. Jill knows where she is.

(38) a. [Context: (Based on a scene from Jim Jarmusch's "Night on Earth") Jill about to step out of taxi in Helsinki.]
Driver: Do you know where you are?
Jill: Helsinki.
b. Driver: Oh dear. Jill doesn't (really) know where she is.

What is the difference between the two contexts? The difference seems to lie in the different causal roles associated with the information Jill possesses. In the former case the information has no role beyond confirming for Jill that she has arrived at the right destination; in the latter case the information cannot be used by Jill to locate the destination she needs. Concretely, assuming Jill's inferential capabilities remain constant across the two contexts, the difference lies in the lower bound, henceforth the *goal*, which the potentially resolving information must be able to entail.

3.4.2   *Partial resolutives*

The overly restricted view of resolvedness I am considering also manifests itself in connection with the issue of what constitutes partial resolvedness. Within an alternativist epistemic setting, it is natural to view partial resolvedness concerning *who P's* as consisting of information about one or more individuals $a_1, \ldots, a_n$ that indicates that they P. However, I suggest such a notion is *not* an adequate, weaker substitute with which to explicate questions.

Berman (1990, 1991) suggests that such partial exhaustive readings arise systematically in interrogatives embedded by resolutives modified by adverbs of quantification. Berman claims that in addition to a reading in which the adverb can be interpreted as quantifying over cases/events/situations, (39a) displays an additional reading, (the *quantificational variability (qv)* reading), paraphrasable as (39b):[20]

(39) a. Jill to some extent/mostly/usually knows which students cheat on the exam.
b. For some/most students x that cheat on the exam, Jill knows that x cheat on the exam.

Berman offers an account for such readings by combining a Hintikka–based approach to interrogatives with a DRT approach to adverbs.

Lahiri (1991) argues that qv readings arise only with adverbs of extent and proposes an account of such readings as involving quantification over the *atomic* elements of a Hamblin semantics Answer-Set:

(40) a. John mostly/partly knows who did well on yesterdays's exam.
      b. Most/Some atomic factual answers to "who did well on the exam" are atomic factual answers such that John knows them.

Let us once more change the epistemic setting to one that includes unfamiliar individuals. The inference from (41a) to (41b) is licensed even on *de dicto* readings of (41a), in which case the inference to (41c) is unjustified:

(41) a. Celia knows that some rather unruly linguists showed up (though she doesn't know who).
      b. Celia knows to some extent who showed up last night.
      c. For some person x that showed up last night, Celia knows that x showed up last night.

Similarly, unexpected on the Hamblin view where no partial information about y/n interrogatives is accommodated, is (42a) licensing a qv reading as in (42b) or (42c):

(42) a. Jill: Is Millie coming tomorrow? Bill: It's possible, (given that she's booked her flight.)
      b. This information indicates to some extent whether Millie will be coming tomorrow.
      c. Bill gave Jill some idea of whether Millie would be coming tomorrow.

In fact, given the strong connection suggested in the schemas in (7), (8) 2.3 between resolutive interrogatives and factive declaratives, we are not surprised to find that similar readings arise with declaratives:

(43) a. The scientist has to some extent established which person committed the crime. (The scientist has established a fact that goes some way towards resolving the question of which person committed the crime.)

      b. The scientist has to some extent established that unpasteurized milk causes botulism in rats. (The scientist has discovered a fact that goes some way towards proving the claim that unpasteurized milk causes botulism in rats.)

3.4.3 Resolvedness: interim conclusions

The data we have seen in the previous three subsections can be summarized as follows: the notion of *resolvedness* is agent-relative.[21,22] A given question defines a class of informational items which can each *potentially* be resolving. Whether a given member of this class, p, is actually resolving *for a given agent* depends on two additional factors: a goal g_0, which determines what p needs to entail, and a knowledge state, ms_0, which determines the resources relative to which p has g_0 as a consequence.

An empirical characterization of the class of potentially resolving information is not entirely straightforward because of the de-contextualization involved. I assume the following:[23]

> (44) a. An informational item τ *potentially resolves* q if either:
> b. τ POSITIVELY-RESOLVES q (for "whether p": any information that entails p; for a *wh*-question: any information that entails that the extension of the queried predicate is non-empty.)
> c. τ NEGATIVELY-RESOLVES q (for "whether p": any information that entails ¬p; for a *wh*-question: any information that entails that the extension of the queried predicate is empty ("who came? No one came".))

Why resolvedness has the parameters that it does becomes more obvious when considered in terms of dialogue. The explication it will receive in Section 4 is as an agent-relative view of when the question has been discussed enough for current purposes to be considered "closed".

3.5 *Characterizing questions and propositions*

3.5.1 *Basic strategy*

How to characterize questions then? The strategy I adopt here in common with past work in situation theory (e.g. Barwise(1989), Barwise and Cooper (1991), Barwise and Etchemendy (1990), Westerståhl (1990), Fernando (1991), Aczel and Lunnon (1991) and in property theory (e.g. Bealer (1982, 1989), Chierchia and Turner (1988), Chierchia (1994), is to characterize semantic objects such as properties, propositions, and in this case questions, in a way that treats their identity conditions very much on a par with "ordinary" individuals. Such entities are taken as basic but arrive on the scene with certain structural constraints that relate them to the other entities.[24]

On this strategy, then, we will find certain parameters with which to individuate questions from each other which can be used in conjunction with the semantic structure provided by other available semantic objects to define a number of the invariants discussed above as requisite invariants, some of which will be parametrized by agent specific parameters. This is quite analogous to associating certain individuating parameters with a human entity, say, her finger-prints, height, weight, profession and date of birth, and using these in conjunction with certain structural social facts to characterize her current properties. There is no temptation to identify the human with her ⟨finger-prints, height, weight, profession, date of birth⟩, though the State occasionally chooses to do so.

3.5.2 Basic ontology

The basic ontology we start out with consists of a non-empty collection of: objects Sit_0 called situations, objects SOA_0 called SOA's,[25] and a set of n-ary SOA-abstracts.[26]

Here situations are partial, actual entities, with uses that include: explicating such objects as states or events, denotations of naked infinitive clauses (see e.g. Barwise and Perry (1983)), and explicating domain restriction in quantification (Gawron and Peters (1990), Ginzburg (1992), Cooper (1993b)).

SOA's here perform a function of describing possible ways the actual situations might be; hence play a similar role to possible worlds in possible worlds semantics, with two obvious differences. SOA's are structured and they are either "atomic" (the *basic* ones), or built up from the basic ones by algebraic operations.

A *basic* SOA is an "atomic possibility" denoted $\langle R,f;i \rangle$, where R is a relation, f is a mapping assigning entities to the argument roles of the R, and i is a *polarity*, i.e. $i \in \{+,-\}$. Basic SOA's come in pairs corresponding to whether the objects assigned to the argument roles stand in the relation R or do not. These are denoted, respectively, as follows:

(45)   a. $\sigma = \langle R,r_1\colon a_1, r_2\colon a_2, \ldots, r_n\colon a_n; + \rangle$
       b. $\overline{\sigma} = \langle R,r_1\colon a_1, r_2\colon a_2, \ldots, r_n\colon a_n; - \rangle$

In the case that a *possibility* represented by some SOA σ is realized, the assumption is that there must be some situation s_0 in the world that *supports the factuality of* σ. This is denoted.

(46) $s_0 \models \sigma_0$

The structure that has typically been proposed for this ontology includes at least the following:

- The SOA's form a Heyting algebra under a partial order "$\rightarrow$" ("informational subsumption"). This means that we get a structure that is closed under arbitrary meets ($\wedge$) and joins ($\vee$).

- The situations and SOA's together form a SOA-algebra:
  1. If $s \models \sigma$ and $\sigma \rightarrow \tau$, then $s \models \tau$.
  2. $s \not\models 0$, $s \models 1$.
  3. If Σ is any finite set of SOA's, then $s \models \wedge \Sigma$ iff $s \models \sigma$ for each $\sigma \in \Sigma$.
  4. If Σ is any finite set of SOA's, then $s \models \vee \Sigma$ iff $s \models \sigma$ for some $\sigma \in \Sigma$.

- An operation of application is defined which satisfies an analogue of β-reduction:

(47)   a. λx $\langle$**LIKE,liker:jill,likee:x;+**$\rangle$ $[x \rightarrow$ **mike**$]$ =
$\langle$**LIKE,liker:jill,likee:mike;+**$\rangle$
b. $\lambda x,y\langle$**HOT,location:x,time:y;+**$\rangle[x \rightarrow$ **HCRC**, $y \rightarrow$ **3am**$]$ =
$\langle$**HOT,location:HCRC,**time:3am;+$\rangle$

3.5.3   *Propositions*

Given these "basic" entities of the ontology, we can now introduce propositions and questions. In situation theory, a *proposition* is constructed as a relational entity $p = (s!\tau)$ in terms of a situation s and a SOA τ. In other words, we
assume as a basic identity criterion that in order for two propositions p_1, p_2 to
be identical, their "defining components" have to be identical: $p_1 = {}_{def}(s_1!\tau_1) =$
$p_2 = {}_{def}(s_2!\tau_2)$ iff $s_1 = s_2$ and $\tau_1 = \tau_2$.

The sense in which a proposition is constructed from a situation and a SOA
is that the basic properties of the proposition are fixed by the situation/SOA
pair that individuate it.

(48) $p = (s!\tau)$ is TRUE iff τ is a *fact* of s: denoted as: $s \models \tau$

Thus, the proposition $(s!\langle WALK,j;+\rangle)$ is TRUE iff $s \models \langle WALK,j;+\rangle$. That is,
intuitively, if j's walking is a fact of s.

For many semantic applications, what is needed is a more relativized notion. Factivity, for instance, concerns itself not with absolute truth, but with
information that has already been established for an agent or set of agents.
Hence, we have the following notion of *provability* relativized to an agent's
mental situation ms. This holds between a SOA σ and a proposition $p = (s!\tau)$
("σ proves p") iff σ is a fact from which the truth of p (or equivalently: the
facticity of τ) can be deduced relative to the *notion of consequence* provided by
ms.

(49)   PROVE($\tau,(s!\sigma),ms$) iff
a. $\tau \Rightarrow_{ms} \sigma$
b. $s \models \tau$

Here $\Rightarrow_{ms}$ is taken to be a sound notion of consequence available to the
mental state ms of an agent a.[27]

3.5.4   *Questions*

A question will be an entity $(s?\mu)$, constructed from a situation s and an n-ary
abstract $\mu = \lambda X_1, \ldots, X_n \sigma (X_1, \ldots, X_n)$ $(n \geq 0)$. This latter is, of course, Rel(q_0)
discussed previously in Section 2.2, whereas s is the parameter that provides
the connection to the world. For instance, the rules I will posit in Section 3.6
will associate:

(50) a. a use of "Did Bill leave" with the question $(s?\langle LEFT,b;+\rangle)$,
      b. a use of "who left" with the question $(s?\lambda x \langle LEFT,x\rangle)$

I have noted before that relations definable *semantically* by a question should include the notions of *aboutness*, the exhaustive answer, and the facts that *potentially* resolve the question. Indeed, I say that $q = (s?\mu)$ is constructed from s and μ because:

1. μ constitutes an "underspecified" informational item from which the class of informational items, SOA's, that are *about* q can be characterized (recall that intuitions concerning *aboutness* are independent of truth or specificity; they pertain solely to "subject matter")
2. Those SOA's which are facts of s and informationally subsume a level determined by μ constitute the class of SOA's that *potentially* resolve q.

(For formal definitions for aboutness, potential-resolvedness and an analogue of the exhaustive answer see Ginzburg (1994a).)

I have emphasized above that the notion of *resolvedness* relevant for natural language semantics is in part agent-relative. Where the agent-relativity comes in is in determining the degree of the specificity of the information ("the goal") and the informational means relative to which this specificity must be attained. Hence, we have the following definition which is stated relative to an agent's mental situation that supplies a *goal g* and a *notion of consequence*:

(51) A fact τ RESOLVES $(s?\mu)$ relative to a mental situation *ms* iff
      1. Semantic condition: τ is a fact of s that potentially resolves μ
      2. Agent relativization: $\tau \Rightarrow_{ms}$ Goal-content(ms) (Intuitively: τ entails the goal represented in the mental situation *ms* relative to the inferential capabilities encoded in *ms*.)

3.6 *Meanings for interrogatives*

Given the emphases of this current paper, I will provide a minimal discussion of *wh*-phrase meaning, limiting myself to a sketch of how meanings for a number of rather simple interrogative sentences can be compositionally constructed. More specifically, I limit myself here to a discussion of individual uses of *wh*-phrases, though some discussion of echo uses will be provided in Section 4.4.

3.6.1 *Meaning in situation semantics*

In situation semantics an *utterance* is reified as a situation, one that supports the various contextual facts needed to obtain a content from a meaning. A meaning for an expression will be an n-ary abstract in which the contextual parameters are abstracted away subject to certain *restrictions*, facts that must hold in any utterance (situation) of that expression.[28] For example: a simplified, tenseless meaning for an assertoric use of (52a) is given in (52b):

(52)   a. Bill likes me
       b. $\lambda ub,\ a,\ s\ \langle ASSERT,a,(s!\langle LIKE,b,a;+\rangle)\rangle$
          RESTRICTIONS: $u \models \langle NAMED,"Bill",b;+\rangle$.
          $u \models \langle SPEAKER,a;+\rangle\ u \models \langle DESCRIBING,a,s;+\rangle$

For its full effect to go through, the utterance situation needs to provide values for a speaker a, the situation described s, and a referent b for the NP "Bill". We shall see in Section 4.4 how, given this view of meanings and utterances, we can attempt to characterize what possible clarification-questions an utterance of this sentence can give rise to.

As a notational convention, I will generally write meaning descriptions as follows:

(53)   a. ["a"] $(x_1, \ldots ,x_n)$ = B.
          RESTRICTIONS: $C(x_1, \ldots ,x_n, \ldots ,y_1 \ldots ,y_m,B)$.

Here $x_1, \ldots ,\ x_n$ are contextual parameters introduced by this grammar rule, usually including the utterance notated as *utt – sit*. $y_1, \ldots ,\ y_m$ are contextual parameters (possibly) introduced by the constituents.

Compositionality is assumed to hold of meanings. For instance, a tense-less meaning description of a (simple, quantifier-less, declarative) sentence is the following:

(54)   a. $S \rightarrow$ NP, VP
       b. [S] $(utt - sit)$ = $\langle$Cont(VP),Cont(NP)$\rangle$;
          RESTRICTIONS: combine the RESTRICTIONS(NP) with the RESTRICTIONS(VP).

with the following simplified example of a derivation:

(55)   a. ["You walk"] $(utt - sit)$ = $\langle WALK,s\rangle$.
          RESTRICTIONS: $utt - sit \models \langle ADDRESSED\text{-}WITH\ "You",s\rangle$.
       b. ["walk"] $(utt - sit)$ = WALK.
          RESTRICTIONS: (none).
          ["You"] $(utt - sit)$ = s.
          RESTRICTIONS: $utt - sit \models \langle ADDRESSED\text{-}WITH,"You",s\rangle$.

Following up on this, we can provide rules for that/whether clauses using HPSG-like syntax. The content of a "that clause" is a proposition, one whose constituents are the SOA provided by the unmarked clause and a contextually provided situation:

(56) a. S[fin,+DECL,+marked] $\rightarrow$ Marker: that, H: S[fin,+DECL, -marked]

  b. S[fin,that]] $(utt - sit, descr - sit_0) = $ (descr-sit_0 ! Cont(H))
     RESTRICTIONS: Identical with RESTRICTIONS(H)

I analyze "whether-clauses" analogously: hence, in line with the above discussion, the content of a "whether-clause" is a question, one whose constituents are the SOA provided by the unmarked clause and a contextually provided situation:

(57) a. S[fin,+INT,+marked] $\rightarrow$ marker: whether, H: S[fin,+DECL, -marked]

  b. [S[fin,+INT,+marked]] $(utt - sit, descr - sit_0) = $ (descr-sit_0 ? Cont(H))
     RESTRICTIONS: Identical with RESTRICTIONS(H)

3.6.2 Constructing question meanings

Let us now bring *wh*-phrases into the picture. The simplified account provided here is based on that of Ginzburg (1992), where an account of *wh*-phrase meaning is developed in which these denote restriction carrying variables that get *closured* in with wider scope than nominal quantifiers.[29] This is described by the following modification to (54):

(58) a. S[fin,+INT,-INV][1] $\rightarrow$ H: V[fin], C: NP[nom]

  b. [S] $(utt - sit, descr - sit_0) = $ (descr $- sit_0$? Λ-CLOSURE($\langle$Cont(H), Cont(C)$\rangle$))
     RESTRICTIONS: combine the RESTRICTIONS(C) with the RESTRICTIONS(H)

Here the question-situation is provided by context. Λ-CLOSURE is an operator that abstracts over the variables introduced by each *wh*-phrase that gets closured at that sentential level to form an abstract. We appeal here to the existence of a notion of simultaneous abstraction (as in e.g. Aczel and Lunnon 1991):

(59) Λ-CLOSURE($\langle Q, \ldots r_1 : x_1, \ldots, r_n : x_n \rangle$) $=_{def}$
     $\lambda x_1 \ldots, x_n \langle Q, \ldots r_1 : x_1, \ldots, r_n : x_n \rangle$

Given the lexical entries for "who" and "what" in (60a,b) and the rule in (58), this will yield the following derivation for "who likes what":

(60) a. ["who"]$(utt - sit_0) = t$;
     RESTRICTIONS: $dis - sit_0 \models \langle$PERSON,$t\rangle$

  b. ["what"]$(utt - sit_0) = v$;
     RESTRICTIONS: $dis - sit_0 \models \langle$INANIMATE,$v\rangle$

c. ["likes what"] $(utt - sit_0) = \lambda x \langle$LIKE, liker:$x$, likee:$v\rangle$
RESTRICTIONS: $dis - sit_0 \models \langle$INANIMATE,$v\rangle$

d. ["who likes what"] $(utt - sit_0, s) = (s\ \lambda t,\ v\langle$LIKE, liker:$t$, likee:$v\rangle)$
RESTRICTIONS: $dis - sit_0 \models \langle$INANIMATE,$v\rangle \wedge \langle$PERSON,$t\rangle$

I treat "when", "where", and "why" as sentential modifiers, whose argument is a SOA, restricted to be factual. Given the rule in (61a–c), we get the derivation for "why does Bill like Mary" in (61d,e):

(61) a. S[+fin,–marker] $\rightarrow$ ADJ: ADVP, H: S[+fin,-marker]

b. $[S](utt - sit_0) = \Lambda$-CLOSURE($\langle$Cont(ADJ),Cont(H)$\rangle$)
RESTRICTIONS: combine the RESTR(ADJ) and RESTR(H).

c. Cont("why") $= \lambda P\langle$BECAUSE,cause:c,effect: $P\rangle$
RESTRICTIONS: $utt - sit_0 \models P$

d. ["does Bill like Mary"] $(utt - sit_0) = \langle$LIKE, liker:b, likee:$m\rangle$
RESTRICTIONS: $utt - sit_0 \models \langle$NAMED,"Bill",$b\rangle \wedge$ $\langle$NAMED,"Mary" $m\rangle$

e. ["why does Bill like Mary"]$(utt - sit_0,s) = (s?\lambda c\langle$BECAUSE, cause: c, effect: $\langle$LIKE, liker:b, likee:$m\rangle\rangle)$
RESTRICTIONS: $utt - sit_0 \models \langle$LIKE, liker:$b$, likee:$m\rangle \wedge \langle$NAMED, "Bill",$b\rangle \wedge \langle$NAMED,"Mary" $m\rangle$

"when" and "where" are identical save that instead of an operator "BECAUSE"; "when" will have an operator "DURING" with argument roles **time** and **event**, whereas "where" will have an operator "IN" with argument roles **location** and **event**.

3.7 *Factives and resolutives*

The need for a coercive analysis of declaratives and interrogatives embedded by factives and resolutives respectively was motivated in Section 3.2.

The coercion process we require is intended to achieve two effects. On the one hand, it is supposed to enable both an interrogative I and a declarative D to describe facts.[30] On the other hand, the two coercions are required to provide facts with slightly different pedigrees. The interrogative coercion needs to yield (a description for) a fact that in that context resolves the question denoted by I, whereas the declarative coercion should yield (a description for) a fact that proves the truth of the proposition denoted by D. In this way, we achieve both the right content-type for resolutives and factives and ensure that the requisite inference patterns are satisfied.

In light of this we define the following sets of facts:

(62) a. $f \in$ RESOLVING-FACTS[q,ms] iff RESOLVES(f,q,ms)

b. $f \in$ PROVE-FACTS[q,ms] iff PROVES(f,q,ms)

We need to achieve the effect of:

(63) $\ulcorner V\ S[+\text{Int}]\urcorner$ denotes $\lambda x \exists f\langle \text{CONT}(V),x,f,ms\rangle$ where
$f \in$ RESOLVING-FACTS$[\text{CONT}(S{:}[+\text{Int}]),ms]$

This can be achieved along lines made familiar in PTQ (Montague 1970): the interrogative is coerced to denote an existential quantifier over facts f, restricted so that f resolves the question denoted by the embedded complement relative to ms; the embedding predicate is postulated to satisfy a constraint similar to PTQ's MP1 for extensional verbs. How do we know the set RESOLVING-FACTS$[\text{CONT}(S[+\text{Int}]),ms]$ is non-empty? The coercion process will be well-defined if and only if the question is resolved. In other words, it is a presupposition of the coercion that the question is resolved. Thus, going along the coercion route, allows for the resolvedness presupposition to emerge without further stipulation.

Similar reasoning can be applied to the declarative case with factives. Given this, we postulate the following rules:

(64) a. An interrogative I can be coerced to denote $\lambda \mathcal{P} \exists f[\mathcal{P}(f)]$
RESTRICTIONS: $utt - sit_0 \models f \in$ RESOLVING-FACTS$[\text{CONT}(I),ms]$
b. A declarative D can be coerced to denote $\lambda \mathcal{P} \exists f[\mathcal{P}(f)]$
RESTRICTIONS: $utt - sit_0 \models f \in$ PROVE-FACTS$[\text{CONT}(D),ms]$
c. If V is a resolutive/factive predicate and $\mathcal{P}$ a quantifier, then
$\langle V, V'\text{er}{:}x, \text{content-role: } \mathcal{P}, \text{cog-role:}ms\rangle \leftrightarrow$
$\mathcal{P}(\lambda f\langle V, V'\text{er}{:}x, \text{content-role:}f, \text{cog-role:}ms\rangle)$

These rules are not overly complicated. What might be less obvious is *why* such an ontology arises. Let us then change perspective and adopt the perspective of dialogue to see how *inter alia* resolvedness emerges as a dynamic "control principle" that relates questions and facts.

4 Dialogue Dynamics

4.1 Introduction

Various phenomena relating to questions warrant adopting a dynamic perspective, where by *dynamic* I mean an approach wherein the meaning of a linguistic form is explicated in terms of the effect its use has on existing commonly shared "resources". Posing a question changes a context in such a way as to (a) significantly restrict the space of felicitous follow-up assertions or queries, (b) to license an elliptical form which (overtly) conveys only the *focus* component of the response. Nonetheless, whereas the setting for most dynamic theories of meaning has, since Stalnaker's (1978) pioneering paper on assertion and presupposition, been monologual *discourse*, it is clear that the natural setting for question use is a conversational setting consisting of at least two speakers, i.e. *dialogue*.

In fact, since dialogue is the basic form of conversational interaction, a strong case can be made that this should be the appropriate setting for semantic theory in general, requiring both a more *individualistic* and a more *structured* view of context. At a given point, *distinct* individuals can have *distinct* semantic options; context has *components* only some of which a given conversational contribution need interact with. (See Ginzburg (1994b,c) for detailed argumentation to this effect.)

Here my aims will be relatively restricted. The first aim is to sketch a framework, one which conservatively extends the Stalnakerian view, in which it is seen how the semantic entities motivated in the previous section, questions, propositions, and facts, both are manipulated in and structure language use. In particular, I am concerned to explain how such "pragmatically conditioned" presuppositions as *resolvedness* emerge, but also how the fact that a particular question is *under discussion* influences topic choice and licenses ellipsis. Second, I will offer notions of querying and assertion that capture the interactive nature of these acts in dialogue. For instance, B1–B3 are all felicitous followup moves by B either to the query in (65a) or the assertion in (65b):

(65)   a. A: Does Bill know Mary?
      b. A: Bill knows Mary.
      c. B1: yeah.
      d. B2: I don't think so.
      e. B3: Mary?

Thus, within a dialogue perspective, it is not only queries that elicit responses; rather any move after which the turn is surrendered to another participant will require us to offer a characterization of the available follow-up moves. My third aim derives from the existence of one class of such followups common to all utterances, namely those whose primary function is to indicate comprehension or the need for clarification. Most formal semantic models have hitherto abstracted away from issues pertaining to communication, such as the fact that one participant's utterances are not automatically and identically comprehended by the other participants. The consequence of this has been that many actually occurring dialogue contributions cannot be analyzed. I will show how the conception of question developed here allows us to offer an analysis of such utterances and take an initial step towards integrating semantics and communication. More generally, the aim is to show that, given the notion of question we have available to us and given the notion of context we develop, many responses whose post-query felicitousness has previously been relegated to "pragmatics" can now be provided with a more principled semantic account.

4.2 Structuring the common ground

How to talk about a dialogue participant (DP)? I propose the following schematic partition. On the one hand, we need a way of talking about some *quasi-shared* object, each DP's version of the common ground, relative to which conventionalized interaction will be assumed to take place. This is because I adopt the assumption, built into the notion of a *dialogue game*, (e.g. Hamblin (1970), Carlson (1983), Houghton and Isard (1986)), that interaction in conversation can be characterized in terms of a limited number of primitive move types which set up a restricted set of options or, perhaps obligations (Traum and Allen (1994)). I will call this component the *DP's gameboard* (cf. Hamblin's (1970) notion of "individual commitment slate").

Separate from this will be the *non-publicized* aspects of each participant's individual mental state. I will call this the DP's *unpublicized mental situation* (UNPUB-MS(DP)). Typically, such things as goals and general inferential capabilities will be represented here. We saw in Section 3.4 that the notion of *resolvedness* is agent-relative, and hence within the current terms we would say it is relative to the UNPUB-MS(DP).

Thus, a participant in a dialogue is modelled as a set of triples, each triple of the form $\langle GB, ms, t \rangle$ ("a gameboard configuration GB, with a mental situation ms at time t"). A gameboard is a situation which represents a DP's view of certain attributes of the dialogue situation. Which attributes?

Stalnaker limited himself to the contextual change brought about by assertion, and hence the sole contextual resource that he was concerned with was the set of assumptions the conversational participants hold commonly at t. For reasons already discussed in Section 3.2, rather than identify this as a set of true propositions, I will propose this resource should be the set of commonly accepted FACTS. Once we bring querying into the picture, what other attributes should the gameboard be specified for?

Our starting point is the observation that conversation is structured: at any given point, what speakers can talk about and how is constrained by the history of the conversation. More particularly, and with certain caveats to be discussed below, more recent moves have more influence on what can be said and how than moves that occurred further back in the past.

How does structure emerge? I recognize here two basic sources, both of which have figured in the conversation analysis tradition. The first is *the latest-move* made. I will assume, then, that as soon as illocutionary information is *accepted*, it serves as the value of a contextual attribute which I dub *LATEST-MOVE*. Once we allow this context attribute, we can offer an initial repertory of *reactions* to queries and assertions, a task I shall come to shortly.

The second source of structure derives, not surprisingly, from questions: both the formal semantic (see above) and the Conversation Analysis literature (Sacks and Schegloff (1973), Levinson (1983)) have long emphasized that a question and answer pair form a single discourse unit.

What we can see clearly from the examination of actual dialogue, for instance the one in figure 15.1 taken from the London-Lund corpus, is that the discussion of a single question can last over many conversational turns and be separated by other questions that have been introduced in the meantime. In particular, "answer ellipses" can occur arbitrarily far away from the questions they relate to. Thus, the discussion of the question raised in (1) by B in dialogue 1 is finally concluded 14 turns later in (15) by the ellipse "a half generation then", taken to mean "father of *a* is a half generation younger than the father of *B*":

Figure 15.1   Dialogue 1: Extract from (London Lund, S.1.13, p.333)

B(1): after all your father's a generation younger than my father isn't he, basically
a(2): well I should think so
B(3): cos your father's now SEVENTY is he
a(4): seventy two or (simultaneous with next turn:) seventy three B(5): SEVENTY TWO. yes. well father would have been seventy eight I suppose. if he had been alive still
C(6): good lord
a(7): that all
?(8): goodness
C(9): my father would have been a hundred and twenty seven
B(10): no, not seventy eight, eighty eight
a(11): (coughs)
B(12): yes. (simultaneous with next turn:) no. yes
a(13): as bad as Charlotte's
B(14): no, not seventy eight. yes, eighty eight. no, I'm sorry, sixteen years, yes eighty eight, that sort of thing
C(15): a half generation then

In order to keep track of the class of questions that are (potentially) under discussion at a given point, I assume that the gameboard, in addition to FACTS and LATEST-MOVE, must also provide as value for an attribute QUD (Question Under Discussion), a partially ordered set of questions. The maximal element of QUD corresponds to the current topic of discussion.[31]

Summarizing for the moment: we have the following view of a participant in a dialogue:

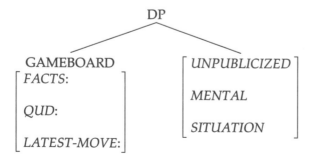

The gameboard representing each DP's version of the common ground is structured as follows:

FACTS: set of commonly agreed upon facts;

QUD ("questions under discussion"): partially ordered set that specifies the currently discussable questions. If q is topmost in QUD, it is permissible to provide any information specific to q.

LATEST-MOVE: content of latest move made: it is permissible to make whatever moves are available as reactions to the latest move.

4.3 Querying and assertion

Let us now move to consider how querying and assertion are viewed within this perspective. What principles govern the manipulation of questions and propositions until they finally lead to an incrementation in the set of commonly accepted facts? I make two simplifying assumptions, the first of which will be dropped in Section 4.4: first, perfect communication obtains between the participants, and second, each participant performs at most one move per turn (a query or an assertion). That is, a turn containing two separate queries or a query followed by an assertion is not accommodated. Such possibilities are the rule rather than the exception in actual dialogue. They do, I believe, strengthen the need for certain aspects of the setup described here, namely the ordering in QUD and the potential for mismatch among the participants.

For querying we identify the following three as definitive issues:
1. How does a particular question get adopted as *the question to be discussed*?
2. What class of utterances is available as replies specific to a question q?
3. Until when does a question's discussion continue?

The importance of the first issue becomes clear as soon as one reflects on the fact that the development of a dialogue depends on both participants. That is, one needs to make allowances for the fact that the person who responds to the query might not wish to adopt the question posed by the querier, although an initial rejection of discussion does not mean that the original question gets erased from the context. This is illustrated in the (constructed) dialogue in (66), where on her final turn the responder exploits the presence of the original question in her context in providing an elliptical answer specific to that question:

(66) (14a) A: Hey, guess who showed up to lunch.
     (14b) B: I don't want to.
     (14c) A: Why not?
     (14d) B: Don't want to.

(14e) A: Please.
(14f) B: Oh ok. Millie.

This motivates the following basic protocol for querying: if DP_1 poses the question q he adds q as topmost element in (his own) QUD. Assume all has gone well on the communication side of things, as we shall for the moment. Then, DP_2 will register in her LATEST-MOVE that:

(67)   LATEST-MOVE: DP_1 QUERY q

Now DP_2 has two options: she can either

Accept q for discussion: update QUD so that q becomes topmost and provide a q-specific utterance.

Reject q for discussion: in this case DP_2 also adds q to her QUD, but rather than make q *the* question to be discussed, she asserts her unwillingness to discuss q. This involves making the question pertaining to this, viz. "whether DP_2 will discuss q" as topmost in her QUD. DP_2 can now utter a rejection phrase ("I don't want to talk about that", "Never mind q" etc.)

Given a question $q = (s?\mu)$, a q-specific utterance will be one that either:
1. Conveys information ABOUT q.
2. Conveys a question q_1 on which q depends.[32]

Here, then, the notion of *q-specific utterance* allows in either (potential) partially resolving answers or questions the resolution of which is a necessary condition for the resolution of q. In the latter case, the question offered as a reply will typically become the question under discussion:

(68)   a. A: Who killed Bill?
           B: Who was in town at the time?
           A: Do you think that Mary was?
           B: Probably.
           A: And Jill?
           B: Yes. Which one of them had a motive?

Now regardless of which option DP_2 adopted, we face the third definitive issue: how long does a question remain under discussion? The basic principle that seems to be at work here is the following:

(69)   **QUD DOWNDATING**: Assume q is currently maximal in QUD, and that ψ is a fact that either

(a) *resolves q relative to UNPUB-MS(DP)* Or,

(b) indicates that *no information about q* can be provided.

Then, adding ψ to FACTS licenses

(1) removing q from QUD, and

(2) if (a) applies, adding the fact ϕ to FACTS, where ϕ is **the fact that ψ RESOLVES** q *relative to UNPUB-MS(DP)*

The QUD downdate principle suggests a construal of the notion of *resolvedness* that I have been hinting at above, namely that it is an agent-relative view of when the question has been discussed sufficiently for current purposes to be considered "closed". Equally, (69) provides a source for the emergence of resolvedness presuppositions to which we appealed in our coercive analysis of interrogative complements embedded by resolutive predicates. We can summarize the emergence of these presuppositions as in (70):

(70) I wondered about q, so I asked q. She told me that . . . and that . . . etc. This was true. The question q is now resolved, so now I know q.

Let us return to explicating a query sequence. If DP_2 accepts q for discussion, then as stated above, discussion of q will proceed in accordance with the QUD downdate principle above. Otherwise, DP_1 has the option of accepting DP_2's rejection, in which case q will be removed from QUD in accordance with the downdate principle, or DP_1 can discuss DP_2's rejection and try to convince her that q should be discussed and so on. If he succeeds, then "whether DP_2 will discuss q" gets eliminated from both DP's QUD's, q is now topmost and will be discussed afterall.

Let us now turn our attention to assertion. Here two issues arise:

1. How to provide an account of an assertion sequence that allows, in addition to acceptance and rejection, also the option of *discussion*?
2. When and how can an asserter assume his assertion is *part of the common ground*?

Consider a sequence in which DP_1 makes an assertion *that p*. If FACTS is to serve as some sort of common ground repository, DP_1 cannot, with an important caveat to which I shall come later, update FACTS *before* receiving acceptance from DP_2. What does he do in the meantime? I suggest that what he does is update his QUD with the question *whether p* as its topmost element.

What options does DP_2 have now? Her LATEST-MOVE now contains the information:

(71) LATEST-MOVE: DP_1 asserts that p.

DP_2 now has two possible classes of reactions:

Accept p: in this case, DP$_2$ *adds* to her FACTS attribute *the fact that p*. At this point, she can either explicitly utter an acceptance phrase ("I see", "uh huh", head nod); Or move on: DP$_2$'s QUD at this point is a (not necessarily proper) subset of what it was before DP$_1$'s assertion. So DP$_2$ can introduce a new question for discussion, either by assertion or by querying.

Discuss whether p: in this case DP$_2$ adds as the topmost element in *her* QUD the question *whether p* and produces an utterance specific to the question.

This perspective on assertion leads to the expectation of three possible routes for the conversation: If DP$_2$ explicitly chooses *not* to accept the assertion that *p*, a discussion of *whether p* will ensue which, by the QUD downdate principle, should continue until either the question is resolved or one DP indicates she can/will not provide more information concerning that question.

Alternatively, if DP$_2$ *explicitly* accepts DP$_1$'s assertion, then since the acceptance constitutes information that resolves the question *whether p*, currently topmost in his QUD, then DP$_1$ can utilize the QUD *downdating* principle: *whether p* gets removed from QUD and the resolving information, in this case *the fact that p* gets added to FACTS. So, at this point *the fact that p* is in FACTS on both gameboards.

Quite frequently, nonetheless, an assertoric move is unlikely to provoke controversy or response from other DP's, whether someone is giving a lecture, engaged in instruction, or, there is a certain "meta-linguistic" interaction that I shall come to shortly. We therefore need to allow an option which introduces a potential for mismatch among the participants, for a DP to accommodate into FACTS the fact that the topmost question in QUD is *positively resolved* even if DP$_2$ has not accepted this move.[33]

(72) **ACCOMMODATE QUESTION:**
      if *q* is topmost in QUD, it is permissible to add the fact *that there exists a fact* **positively resolving** *q* to FACTS. Optionally, remove *q* from QUD.

The relation POSITIVELY-RESOLVES was defined in (44). Since it is the case that for a question of the form *whether p*, all and only facts proving *that p* stand in this relation to the question, it follows that if DP$_1$ receives neither explicit acceptance nor discussion, he is entitled to update FACTS with *the fact that p*, the point of his original assertion.

4.4 *Questions and meta-linguistic interaction*

Finally, I want to show how within the framework described above the potential for moves indicating successful comprehension or the need for clarification can be explained as a consequence of the fact that an utterance of a particular linguistic form with a particular meaning has occurred.

(73) a. A: Bill left last night.
      b. B: Bill, mmh.
      c. B: Bill?
      d. B: He left when?

Recall that within the situation semantics described above a meaning is an n-ary abstract where the variables abstracted over correspond to the contextual parameters. An utterance is reified as a situation, one that supports the various contextual facts needed to obtain a content from a meaning.

Given this and the notion of question described in the previous section, it follows that an utterance u and a meaning μ of a sentence S, serve to define a question $q(u,S) = (u?\mu)$. This question can be paraphrased approximately as: *what values are assigned to the contextual parameters of μ.*

The analogy to the view of assertion presented above is strikingly clear. Rather than assume that information about the *content* of the utterance that requires fixing by the context is necessarily available to the addressee (in other words can be automatically added in as part of the gameboard), we allow for the option of discussing any of these contextual parameters.

How do we revise our original dialogue move rules to take these issues into consideration? The moves previously described will now be altered by composing any move that involves producing an utterance u of sentence S with a potential discussion sequence of $q(u,S)$.

The basic idea is this: once an utterance has been posed, if the stimulus of an utterance u of a sentence S is good enough for the addressee to recognize what sentence has been uttered, she is expected to act as follows:

(74) If DP_2 believes that S was uttered, she updates QUD with $q(u,S)$

u will be *grounded* if and only if there is a fact that the addressee knows and which resolves the question $q(u,S)$ relative to her UNPUB-MS.[34] In this perspective, grounding involves the utterer and addressee coming to be satisfied that the addressee knows an answer to the meaning question, specific enough for current purposes. In such a case, just as with an assertion, the addressee has the option of explicitly accepting the utterance, as in (73b).

Otherwise, DP_2 has the option of following up DP_1's utterance of S with any clarification question on which $q(u,S)$ *depends*.

Let us consider an example: why does (75a) license (75b) as a clarification?

(75) a. Bill left.
      b. WHO?

On an analysis of the content of echo queries as in Ginzburg (1992, 1994b), (75b) gets a reading with content (76b):

(76) a. $(u?\lambda ub,a,s\langle ASSERT,a,(s!\langle LEAVE,b\rangle)\rangle)$
      b. $(u?\lambda x\langle ASSERT,a,(s!\langle LEAVE,x\rangle)\rangle)$ ("who does A assert that left")

Given that the meaning question defined by (75a) is (76a) (ignoring the associated restrictions here for simplicity), (76b) is a $q(u,$ "Bill left")-specific utterance. (76a) is a question that depends on (76b), and (76b) hence is licensed.

NOTES

1   Extensive discussion of the semantics of *wh*-phrases can be found in Groenendijk and Stokhof (1984), May (1985), Engdahl (1986), Berman (1991), Ginzburg (1992), Chierchia (1993).
2   Here and elsewhere I use "denote" as shorthand for "its content on a particular use is". In particular, no associations whatever should be made between this usage and ones that pertain to the Fregean distinction between sense and denotation.
3   I restrict myself here to English. In languages with overt case-marking, the elliptical phrase has to concord in case with the relevant interrogative phrase.
4   Such a strategy, with certain modifications, is adopted in Groenendijk and Stokhof (1984).
5   This particular definition is taken from Cooper (1993) who proposes that DRS's in the sense of Kamp (1981) comprise a semantic type consisting of n-ary abstracts.
6   Lappin (1982) identifies the meaning of a query use of an interrogative with the conditions under which it is answered where the fulfillment (answering) conditions of the query are the interrogative counterpart of the truth conditions of an assertive use of a declarative.
7   Stenius (1967) proposes an alternative reductionist account in which questions are analyzed into an interrogative operator and a truth-conditional "sentence radical" to which the operator applies.
8   For additional discussion of Hamblin (1973) and Kartunnen (1977), and for an alternative approach to the semantics of interrogatives see Higginbotham (this volume).
9   However, see Boër (1978) and Hand (1988) for a semantics for "depend wh" which share important assumptions with Hintikka interrogative semantics.
10 "concerning", "on", "as–to", and "regarding" are close synonyms of this sense of "about".
11 "simple" in the sense that functional/pair-list/echo uses are ignored.
12 The ranges described here should probably be viewed as base cases, since, for instance, if p constitutes information about q_0, it would appear that $(p,$ if $r)$ does too:

    (i)   A: Will Mary come? B: She probably will, if it isn't raining.

    I owe this point to David Milward.
13 The term "pure referentiality" and tests associated with it are taken from Quine (1953a), especially $p.139$–145. See Ginzburg (1994a), Section 7.2 for assumptions on how such tests are to be construed in attempts at establishing the ontological correctness of a denotation type.

14 Philosophical motivation for distinguishing facts and true propositions is offered by Austin (1950, 1954).
15 This schema is inspired by observations of Vendler (1972), chapter 5.
16 These facts are apparently stable across a wide range of languages, including English, Hebrew, Japanese, Greek, and Turkish.
17 Boër (1978) seems to advocate such a solution: "it is the inherent factivity of 'who' clauses which makes them bad company for most non-factive verbs of propositional attitude. Usually, the pragmatic point of using a non-factive verb of propositional attitude is to leave open the question of truth value of the proposition which is the object of that attitude, and this point is frustrated by the semantics of 'who' clauses . . ." (Boër 1978, p.333).
18 Note that these considerations apply equally to Hamblin's approach.
19 Indeed, to remove a possible objection about the role of proper names in this example, one could change the example to one where the director responds deictically by pointing at the crowd: "this person and that person and that one and that one . . .".
20 For discussion of this and other aspects of the quantificational variability effect (QVE), see Berman (1990, 1991, 1994), Lahiri (1991), Groenendijk and Stokhof (1993), and Ginzburg (1994a, 1995).
21 Hintikka (1976, 1983a), Boër (1978) and Boër and Lycan (1985) represent approaches, which although they do not countenance an independent notion of question, can be construed as providing notions of resolvedness which are parametrized. Boër and Lycan's (1985) work on the semantics of "knowing who", in particular, develops an account where these parameters can be identified with the reported agent's purpose and mental capacities.
22 Groenendijk and Stokhof do show how to relativize their notion of answerhood to individual epistemic states. What this allows is for a refinement of the partition of the set of possible worlds defined by an interrogative intension.
    (i) Assume I/Q is a partition of the set of possible worlds I determined by the question Q. An information set J is a non-empty subset of I. Then, the set of answers compatible with J is: $\{X \in Q \mid X \cap J \neq \emptyset\}$ (See Groenendijk and Stokhof (1984), p.222.)
    Nonetheless, Groenendijk and Stokhof view such a relativization as an explanatory tool for the pragmatics of query/response interaction and do not try to build it into the semantics of embedded interrogatives. Moreover, such a relativization does not deal with fluctuations of *the goal* associated with an (embedded) question.
23 Based on data in Ginzburg (1994a). See also Belnap (1982) p.196 for apparently similar intuitions.
24 As per Chierchia (1994): "it doesn't matter what propositions are to the extent that they have enough logical structure to support a comprehensive semantic program and plausible view of mental attitudes." (Chierchia (1994), p.147.)
25 Also referred to as *infons* in the literature.
26 I will proceed informally here. For a careful development of such a universe *sans* questions see Barwise and Etchemendy (1990), Barwise and Cooper (1991), Cooper and Poesio (1994b).
27 See e.g. Barwise (1986) for one such situation theoretic notion of $\Rightarrow$. For more recent developments see Barwise (1993). Of course, in the current paper nothing hinges on the particular notion of $\Rightarrow$ chosen.
28 For an introduction to a current version of situation semantics see Gawron and Peters (1990), Cooper and Poesio (1994b).

29   Motivation for this view of scopal interaction includes evidence, based on data from Berman (1990), that whereas indefinite descriptions interact scopally with adverbs of quantification, *wh*-phrases do not. Similarly whereas it is possible to get crossing co-reference readings in multiple-*wh* versions of Bach Peters sentences, this does not seem possible in such sentences containing a *wh*-phrase and a quantifier. A non-quantificational view of *wh*-phrase meaning is, in addition, particularly well suited to deal with echo uses of *wh*-phrases, where the echo-*wh*-phrase(s) scope over all other constituents, including a contextually supplied illocutionary matrix representing the force of the previous speech act. See Ginzburg (1992) for further details and a fragment that includes functional and echo uses. A restricted and somewhat modified version which also includes a semantics for attitude reports is presented in Ginzburg (1994a).

30   The need to quantify over rather than directly denote facts is discussed in Ginzburg 1994a. The intuition for resolutive complements should be clear: resolutive complements provide us with the ability to make statements about the at times arbitrary/non-familiar facts that resolve a given question.

31   As will become clear below, the partial ordering is to an important extent semantically driven; when semantics does not determine which question has precedence, however, the DP's will need to negotiate the ordering amongst each other.

32   Here, inspired by Karttunen (1977), I define the relation of dependence between two questions as follows: q_1 DEPENDS-ON q_2 iff q_1 is *resolved* by a fact τ only if q_2 is also resolved by τ. The insight behind this option is drawn from Carlson (1983), p.101.

33   Ginzburg (1994c) offers independent motivation for this rule from considerations pertaining to sluicing.

34   The term "grounded" is from Clark and Schaefer 1989.

VIII Plurals

16 Plurality

FRED LANDMAN

1 Cumulative Readings

In his seminal paper, (Scha (1981)), Remko Scha discusses what he calls the **cumulative reading** of sentences like (1):

(1)   Three boys invited four girls.

On this reading, what the sentence expresses is the following: the total number of boys that invited a girl is three and the total number of girls that were invited by a boy is four. (Such and similar readings have also been discussed by others, e.g. Langendoen (1978), Carlson (1980), Higginbotham and May (1981) and Gil (1982).) Scha distinguishes cumulative readings from **collective** and **distributive** readings, and he introduces a mechanism of **binary quantification** to deal with cumulative readings. In Scha's analysis, sentence (1) involves a binary determiner [three-four]$_{DET}$ which combines with a binary noun [boys–girls]$_N$ to form a binary noun phrase. Thus, at the semantically relevant level of representation (1), has the structure (1a):

(1)   a.   [[[three–four]$_{DET}$ [boys–girls]$_N$]]$_{NP}$ [invite]$_{VP}$]

The rationale for this analysis is that on the cumulative reading the interpretation of each noun phrase seems to require information expressed by the other noun phrase: the sentence does not talk about three boys and four girls, but about boys that invited a girl and girls that were invited by a boy. We seem to need to access the information expressed by the noun phrases simultaneously, and we can do that by encoding this in the meaning of the binary determiner:

> [three–four]$_{DET}$ denotes the relation that holds between a binary noun *boys–girls* and a transitive verb *invite* iff the number of boys that invite a girl is three and the number of girls invited by a boy is four.

The analysis of cumulative readings in terms of binary quantification is rather complicated and introduces categories into the grammar (like binary determiners) that one would want to have independent justification for. Since Scha's paper, several people have argued that we do not need to add a mechanism of binary quantification to the grammar to deal with cumulative readings, because we do not need to recognize cumulative readings as an independent category that the grammar needs to account for. This is most explicitly argued by Craige Roberts (1987). She argues that we do not need to generate cumulative readings, because we can reduce them to collective readings. The grammar will generate a reading where both *three boys* and *four girls* get a collective reading, as in (1b):

>   (1)   b.   A group of three boys invited a group of four girls.

Following Dowty (1986), we can assume that such a collective reading of (1) may in context have implicatures concerning whether, and if so how, the inviting is distributed over the members of these two groups. This means that the reading that the grammar generates for (1) is underspecified as to how the inviting is actually done. The cumulative reading is not a separate reading, but one instance of a situation in which the double collective reading is true. Hence, Roberts argues, the grammar does not have to deal with cumulative readings.

This approach is tempting, but it requires in turn a re-evaluation of what is to count as a collective or a distributive reading. In the first part of this paper, I will discuss the notions of distributivity and collectivity and propose a criterion for telling whether or not we are dealing with a collective reading or not. I will argue that on this criterion, both distributivity and cumulativity are to be distinguished from collectivity. Moreover, I will argue that distributivity and cumulativity are in essence the same semantic phenomenon: semantic plurality. In the second part of this paper, I will develop (the beginnings of) an event-based theory of plurality, and use this as a framework for comparing different proposals concerning distributive, collective, cumulative (and other) readings of sentences like (1).

2   Distributivity and Collectivity in Landman (1989a)

Godehard Link (1983) introduced an operation of semantic pluralization *. Link assumes that the domain of individuals consists of singular, or atomic, individuals, plus plural individuals, where plural individuals are regarded as sums of singular individuals under an operation of sum-formation $\sqcup$; equivalently, the domain is ordered by a part-of relation $\sqsubseteq$, and singular individuals are those individuals that have only themselves as parts. In Link's semantics, a singular predicate like BOY denotes a set of singular individuals only, a set of atoms. Pluralization is closure under sum: *BOY adds to the extension of BOY all the plural sums that can be formed from elements of BOY:

$$*BOY = \{d \in D: \text{for some non-empty } X \subseteq BOY: d = \sqcup X\}$$

It can be shown that when we restrict the domains of interpretation properly (essentially to structures isomorphic to Boolean algebras with the bottom element removed, structures which I will call atomic part-of structures), Link's operation of pluralization predicts some very general properties of plural nouns. In particular, the pattern in (2) becomes valid:

(2)　　John is a boy and Bill is a boy iff John and Bill are boys.
(2)　a.　$BOY(j) \wedge BOY(b) \leftrightarrow *BOY(j \sqcup b)$

The inference pattern that we find for plural nouns in (2) is exactly the same as what we find for verbs, when they are interpreted distributively, as in (3):

(3)　John carried the piano upstairs and Bill carried the piano upstairs iff John and Bill carried the piano upstairs (on the distributive interpretation of *carry the piano upstairs*).

In view of this, I argued in Landman (1989a) for reducing distributivity to semantic plurality. I assumed that the grammar contains a single operation that forms semantically plural predicates out of semantically singular predicates. In the nominal domain, the operation of pluralization leads to plural nouns. In the verbal domain, pluralization creates distributive interpretations. The aim of this proposal was to give a unified account to examples like (2) and (3). A special problem is raised by cases of distribution to collections like (4):

(4)　The boys meet and the girls meet iff the boys and the girls meet (on the distributive interpretation of *meet*. This interpretation is triggered for instance when we add *but not in the same room*).

We would like to give a unified explanation for the patterns in (2), (3) and (4), but this leads, in the case of (4) to a problem or grid: if *the boys and the girls* in (4) denotes the sum of the boys and the girls, then pluralization will distribute the predicate MEET to the individual boys and girls. The problem is that on the relevant interpretation, we *do* want the predicate to distribute, but only to the sum of the boys and to the sum of the girls, and not all the way down to the individuals. The solution that I proposed (in part following Link (1984)) was to assume that the noun phrase *the boys* can shift its interpretation from a plural interpretation, $\sigma(*BOY)$, the sum of the individual boys, to a group interpretation, $\uparrow(\sigma(*BOY))$, **the boys as a group**. Here the group-forming operation $\uparrow$ is an operation that maps a sum onto an atomic (group) individual in its own right.

I assumed then that collective interpretations are group interpretations. In essence, what I assumed was that the collective reading of sentence (5) comes about through an implicit group-operator, an operator which is explicit in (6):

(5)   the boys carried the piano upstairs.
(6)   the boys, as a group, carried the piano upstairs.

In this view, collective predication is singular predication: a semantically singular predicate is predicated of an atomic individual, a group: $P(\uparrow(\sigma(*BOY)))$. On the other hand, distributive predication is plural predication: a semantically plural predicate is predicated of a plural individual: $*P(\sigma(*BOY))$. Furthermore, the capacity to shift from sum interpretations to group interpretations introduces the required grid to give a unified account of pluralization that applies to (4) as well. If we assume that *the boys and the girls* can denote the sum of the boys as a group and the girls as a group, we get exactly the pattern of distribution to collections:

(4)   a. $\text{MEET } (\uparrow(\sigma(*BOY))) \wedge \text{MEET } (\uparrow(\sigma(*GIRL))) \leftrightarrow$
$*\text{MEET } (\uparrow(\sigma(*BOY)) \sqcup \uparrow(\sigma(*GIRL)))$

In sum, then, in Landman (1989) I assumed the following:

- all basic predicates, nominal or verbal, are semantically interpreted as sets of atoms;
- there are (at least) two modes of predication:

    1. **singular predication** applies a basic predicate to an atomic (singular or group) individual;
    2. **plural predication** applies a plural predicate distributively to a plural sum of such atomic individuals.

- noun phrases like *John and Bill* and *the boys* can shift their interpretation from sums to groups (the boys as a group).

3   Thematic and Non-thematic Roles

Above I have made the distinction between basic, singular predicates and plural predicates that are pluralizations of basic predicates. These are not the only kinds of predicates that need to be distinguished. The grammar will contain, besides pluralization, operations that turn plural predicates into complex plural predicates, and the latter need not be pluralizations of basic, singular, predicates. However, all this stays rather abstract theorizing, as long as we do not determine what counts as a basic predicate.

I think of basic predicates as by and large corresponding to those lexical items that assign thematic roles (though not all of them, some lexical items like for instance *look alike* – if that is a lexical item – I would assign internal logical structure, making it in effect a plural predicate). Basic predicates are predicates that have **thematic** commitment. If a basic, singular predicate applies to a certain argument, that argument fills a thematic role of that singular predicate. This means that whatever semantic properties are associated with that thematic role, the object that fills that role in that predication has those properties. Thus, for example, I assume that *sing* is a basic predicate assigning the agent role to its subject. By that, I assume that whatever semantic inferences and implicatures follow from filling the agent role of *sing*, if *John sings* is true then those inferences and implicatures hold with respect to John. This is rather straightforward. But it has an interesting consequence. I have assumed in the previous section that collective predication is an instance of singular predication. If singular predication is thematic predication, it follows that collective predication is thematic predication. Moreover, if collective predication is nothing but singular, thematic predication, it follows that there is no place in the grammar for a separate theory of collective predication, i.e. there is no separate theory of collective inferences. This means that all inferences and implicatures associated with collective readings have to be derived from two sources: the general theory of thematic roles and inferences associated with those, and the nature of the argument filling the role, i.e. the fact that a group, rather than an individual fills a role. (This idea is, I think, in the spirit of some of the discussion of Scha (1981). The alternative, i.e. trying to delineate a theory of collective inferences, finds, I think, its origin in Dowty (1986), and is most worked out in Lasersohn (1988).)

Let me give some examples.

Example 1. **Collective body formation**:

> (7)   a. The boys touch the ceiling.

This example is a variant of an example discussed in Scha 1981. For (7a) to be true on a collective reading, there is no need for more than one boy to do the actual touching: (7a) is true if the boys form a pyramid and the topboy touches the ceiling. A theory of collective inferences would explain this by assuming that the predicate *touch* as applied to a collection distributes semantically to at least one of the members of the collection, while the involvement of the others is a matter of cancelable implicatures. The alternative explanation that I would propose (following basically Scha 1981) is the following: Compare (7a) with (7b):

> (7)   b. I touch the ceiling.

What does it mean for me to touch the ceiling? It means that part of my body is in surface contact with part of the ceiling. This follows from the meaning of *touch*: part of the agent is in surface contact with part of the theme. Exactly the same meaning is involved in (7a). The only difference between (7a) and (7b) is that in (7a) it is a collection that fills the agent role and a collection has different parts than an individual does. In particular it can be individuals that are part of collections (in a sense of part-of which is analogous to the relation between me and my body parts). Thus, we do not need to assume anything special about collective predication to explain this case.

Example 2: **Collective action**:

    (8)   a. The boys carried the piano upstairs.

In a collective action, the predicate does not necessarily distribute to each of the boys (the actual predicate needn't distribute at all), nor does it have to be the case that all the boys in (8a) have to be directly involved in the action, i.e. not all boys have to do actual carrying (like the one who is walking in front with a flag). In a normal context, (8a) will implicate some other things about the boys, like that some of them are (at least partly) under the piano some of the time, and that some of them move up the stairs. However, let us again compare this with the singular case (8b):

    (8)   b. I carried the piano upstairs.

Also in (8b), not all my parts do the carrying (my big toe doesn't). While it tends to be the case that when I carry the piano upstairs all my parts move up the stairs, such differences can easily be attributed again to the differences in the relation between me and my parts and collections and their parts: collections can be spatially discontinuous.

Example 3: **Collective responsibility**:
Lasersohn (1988) argues that often in collective readings, we do not require that the individuals are directly involved in the action, but that they do share in the responsibility: we ascribe collective responsibility to the agent in a collective predication. Cf. (9a):

    (9)   a. The gangsters killed their rivals.

While not every gangster may have performed any actual killing, that will not help them in court: the individual gangsters are co-responsible for the killings. Again this is not different from the singular case, cf. (9b):

    (9)   b. Al Capone killed his rivals.

It is a general property of agents (of verbs like *kill*) that we can assent to the truth of the sentence, even though the agent does not literally perform the action: (9b) is true even if Capone didn't pull the trigger himself, because he bears the responsibility for the action (the difference being that responsibility tends not to carry over to non-sentient parts of an agent, though Capone's bad liver may have had something to do with it).

The conclusion is: all these cases involve thematic predication where a collection fills a thematic role. Differences with singular predicates are reduced to the differences between individuals and collections.

It now becomes interesting to compare these cases with what I have called **plural predication**. Look at (10) on the distributive reading:

(10) The boys sing.

The crucial difference with the previous cases is that on the distributive interpretation of (10), it is not the entity that is the subject in the predication, the denotation of *the boys*, that is claimed to have the semantic properties that agents have, but the individual boys. On this reading, no thematic implication concerning the sum of the boys follows. This means that the distributive predication is not an instance of thematic predication of the predicate *sing* to its subject.

This has an important theoretical consequence about the way we set up the grammar. Some analyses of plurality assume that also in a distributive predication in (10), *the boys* fills the agent role of a basic predicate *sing*. This is, for instance, what Scha (1981) does for examples like (10). Scha, and others following him, would derive the distributive reading through an optional meaning postulate on *sing* (on one of its meanings X *sings* is equivalent to *every part of* X *sings*). However, since there are no thematic inferences concerning what fills the agent role in the distributive reading, on such a theory, it follows that **there cannot be any semantic content to the notion of agent at all**. That is, this approach is incompatible with any theory that assigns any semantic, thematic property to a thematic role, because in the distributive cases the entity that fills the role doesn't have the relevant property. (Note that I have formulated the problem in terms of thematic roles, but the problem is just the same in an ordered argument theory: we would want the lexical predicate to constrain its arguments in certain ways, but in the distributive case, those arguments aren't constrained in those ways.) This would mean that thematic roles cannot have any content. Not even a weak theory of thematic roles, like the one in Dowty 1989 would be possible: thematic roles become meaningless labels. Now, some might be willing to accept the impossibility of a theory of thematic roles without batting an eyelid. My feeling is that whatever the possibility of a contentful theory of thematic roles, it is not the business of the theory of plurality to make it impossible.

This means, then, that in plural, distributive, predication in (10), the subject *the boys* does not fill a **thematic** role R of the predicate *sing*. I will assume that it does fill a role, and that the role that it fills is a **non-thematic**, plural role defined on R.

I define thematic predication as predication of a thematic basic predicate to an argument, predication where the argument fills a thematic role of a basic predicate. (A remark: I am not assuming that basic predicates have to assign thematic roles to all their arguments, I don't want to commit myself here, for instance, to a particular view on raising predicates. Furthermore, I don't assume that basic predicates cannot have internal lexical structure, like aspectual structure in say Dowty's (1979) theory, and other theories following that. Basic here means basic as far as plurality and scope phenomena are concerned.)

In theories of plurality, including my own, a lot of unclarity exists about what counts as a collective reading and how to distinguish collective readings from non-collective readings. The framework that I am developing here suggests a criterion for determining when we are dealing with a collective reading:

> **The collectivity criterion**:
>
> The predication of a predicate to a plural argument is **collective** iff the predication is predication of a **thematic** basic predicate to that plural argument, i.e. is a predication where that plural argument fills a **thematic** role of the predicate.

One side of this criterion is the proposal that I made before: there is not a special theory of collectivity implications. Collectivity implications are instances of thematic implications:

> **The presence of collectivity implications indicates that the predication is thematic predication**.

I think that, though not much discussed explicitly in this form, this part of the collectivity criterion is widely accepted in the literature on plurality. What turns it into a criterion is the other direction:

> **Lack of collectivity implications indicates non-thematic predication**.

This part tells us that we cannot use the notion of collectivity as a plural waste-paper basket. It tells us that if a certain predication arguably lacks collectivity implications, we cannot subsume it under collective predication, and this means that we cannot leave it unanalyzed: we have to assume that it is a complex plural predicate, derived from other predicates through the plurality operations that are available in the grammar (of which simple pluralization of a basic predicate is an instance). The interesting thing is that when one reads the literature (for instance the literature arguing in favor of a distributive operation, e.g. Link (1991), Roberts (1987), Hoeksema (1988), Landman (1989a), and many others), one gets the impression that also this part is widely accepted (though implicitly) in the literature. If so, then it is more accepted as a virtuous ideal than as a matter of praxis, because I don't know a single theory that actually manages to live up to this part. And the reason is that, while it has the great advantage of clarifying the notion of collectivity, it makes life difficult. For instance, many cases that I regarded in Landman (1989a) as instances of collective predication that maybe the lexicon, but not the grammar needs to analyze further, can no longer be regarded as such. Applying the collectivity criterion to predicates like *look alike, separate* or *sleep in different dorms* tells us that these predicates cannot be regarded as collective predicates, and shows (in line with Roberts (1991), Schwartzschild (1991, 1992), Carlson (1987), Moltmann (1992)) that we need to regard these as complex plural predicates. I do not have space in this paper to discuss these cases more. While I am aware that the application of the collectivity criterion is difficult in various subtle cases, and while I am not sure that in a final account (if there is such a thing) the criterion can hold unmodified, I think (and hope to show) that the criterion has very interesting empirical and theoretical consequences, and provides a healthy methodology in determining what should be part of the grammatical theory of plurality and what can be left to the lexicon.

4 Application 1: Partial Distributivity and Distributivity

As an application of the collectivity criterion, let us look at the following examples from the literature:

(11) The marines invaded Grenada.   (Carlson (1977b))
(12) The leaves of tree A touch the leaves of tree B.   (Scha (1981))
(13) The journalists asked the president five questions. (Dowty (1986))

These are all cases where for the sentence to be true, it is not necessary that **all** individual parts of the plural entities involved have the relevant property, **invading, touching, asking**. But it does seem to be necessary that **some** individual parts have the relevant property. One could call this phenomenon **partial distributivity**: the relevant property distributes to some, but not necessarily all parts of a plural argument. Since total distributivity is the borderline case of partial distributivity, one could use this as an argument to eliminate distributivity from the grammar. The argument would go as follows: the lexical meaning of the predicates in (11)–(13) tells us that some parts have the relevant property. Total distributivity is compatible with that. The so-called distributive reading is not a separate reading, but an instance of the basic reading, i.e. it represents one type of situation in which the basic reading of (11)–(13) is true. Given this, we would not need a separate distributive operator or a pluralization operator.

The problem with this proposal is that in all cases (11)–(13) there are collective, thematic implications. Another way to say this is that all these cases are **non-inductive**.

Take (11): Suppose that two members of the Marine Corps in a totally un-authorized action land on Grenada. Would we say that this is **sufficient** to make (11) true? I don't think so. Now, maybe if we increase the number of Marines landing we reach at a certain moment a point where we're inclined to count (11) as true. But crucially, this is not because of the numbers, but because at a certain moment, this becomes an action that reflects on the whole Marine Corps, a collective responsibility. And it is this collective responsibility, rather than the number of individual Marines involved, that makes (11) true.

Similarly, in (12), it is because we easily conceive of the leaves on a tree as a coherent body (the foliage) (and there is surface contact) that we regard (12) as true. (14) is a funny sentence:

(14)   The green leaves in Holland touch the yellow leaves in Holland.

If (12) were inductive, then the touching of two individual leaves would be sufficient to make (12) true. But then there is no reason why (14) shouldn't be a perfectly fine and true sentence. But (14), out of the blue, is weird, and the reason is collectivity: out of the blue it is difficult to turn the green and the yellow leaves in Holland into coherent bodies (coherent enough to make "touching" a sensible relation between them). (13) may seem more inductive: if five individual journalists happen to ask a question, isn't that sufficient to call (13) true? While it is harder to detect, I think that also (13) is in fact not inductive and involves collective responsibility. A press-conference is a kind of allegorical play with fixed roles filled by certain individuals or groups (The President, The Press); it is the business of journalists at a press-conference to ask questions and it is part of the play that this is done in a certain way (distributing question asking over journalists). Yet, (13) makes an evaluative statement about the functioning of the whole Press-corps: they got in five questions, which means, depending on the press-conference, that THEY (the press) did or didn't do their job well. Another reason to assume that (13) involves a collective reading is the following. Look at (15):

(15)   The press asked the president five questions.

(15), I think, does not differ at all from (13) in how inductive or non-inductive it is. But (15) involves a singular collective expression. While Schwarzschild (1991) argues convincingly (against Landman (1989)) in favor of distinguishing such singular collective expressions from plurals in collective readings, there doesn't seem to be a difference here, and since also for Schwarzschild, singular collective expressions are as prototypically collective as you get, this provides another reason to assume that partial distributivity is a collectivity effect.

In all these cases, then, there are collectivity implications. By applying the collectivity criterion, this means that in all the cases (11)–(13) we are in fact dealing with collective readings. Now compare the previous cases with the distributive interpretation of (16):

(16)   The boys carried the piano upstairs.

Think of the following context: in a game show the girls each have to swim fifteen meters, while each of the boys carries a toy-piano upstairs (which then, each time, is brought down again for the next boy. To make it difficult, we assume that the stairs are greased). In that context, the distributive interpretation of (16) is fine after the following question: What were the boys doing while the girls were swimming?

The important thing here is that, on this interpretation, (16) is **purely inductive**: if boy 1 carried the piano upstairs, ... , boy n carried the piano upstairs, then we can truthfully say (16) on the distributive interpretation. This means that (16) does not involve any thematic implications concerning the plural argument of the predication, the boys, itself. Applying the collectivity criterion, it follows that (16) is not a collective reading, and does not involve a basic, thematic predicate. It follows then from the collectivity criterion, that the attempt to eliminate distributivity from the grammar by trying to reduce it to lexical partial distributivity fails: partial distributivity is collectivity, and hence thematic predication, while true distributivity is non-thematic predication.

5   Application 2: Partial Cumulativity and Cumulativity

Now let us look at (17):

(17)   Forty journalists asked the president only seven questions.

(17) looks like a cumulative reading, except that, because of the distribution of the numbers (assuming that questions don't get asked more than once), if it is a cumulative reading, it can only be a partial cumulative reading. But (17) isn't different from (13), so by the same argument as before, we should conclude that (17) is a collective reading, and that the partial cumulativity effect is really a thematic, collectivity implication. More evidence for this is example (18):

(18)   Fifteen women gave birth to only seven children.

Out of the blue, (18) is weird. The natural reaction to (18), out of the blue, is something like: how did they manage to do that? There is a natural explanation for this: *give birth to*, as a relation between women and children, is a relation that strongly resists its first argument being interpreted collectively:

give birth to is a hyper-individual relation between a woman and a child: we do not think of women as giving birth to children in groups. Thus, (18) does not, out of the blue, have a collective reading, and that's why it is weird. Compare (18) with (19):

(19)   Seven hundred chickens laid fifty eggs.

Unlike (18), (19) is not weird out of the blue. In the context of what is called in Dutch the Bio Industry, (19) can easily be interpreted as a comment on the malfunctioning of a particular chicken battery. The reason is that the role of chickens in a battery is similar to that of journalists at a press conference: who cares that a chicken also has a hyper-individual relation to her egg: for us, chickens are means of producing eggs: it is the business of chickens in a battery to produce a certain quota of eggs. For that matter, it is easy for us to ascribe collective responsibility to the chickens in a certain battery for the malfunctioning of the battery. For this reason, a collective reading of (19) is easily available. This is much more difficult in (18). I'm not claiming that (18) doesn't have a collective reading. For instance in the not so natural context of hospital statistics, (18) can get a collective reading as well, and it can be seen as a comment on the malfunctioning of the maternity ward. Nevertheless, out of the blue, this reading is not available for (18). Now look at (20):

(20)   Seven women gave birth to fifteen children.

There is a sharp difference, out of the blue, between (18) and (20). Unlike (18), (20) is fine and the reading that is in fact most prominent is the **cumulative reading**: seven women gave birth to children and fifteen children were born to them.

These facts form a serious problem for Roberts' (1987) proposal to reduce cumulative readings to collective readings. If cumulative readings are collective readings, then the cumulative reading of (20) should be a collective reading, like (18). But we have seen that (18) doesn't have a collective reading. (18) is weird out of the blue. But if (18) doesn't have a collective reading out of the blue, neither should (20): i.e. (20) should be just as weird as (18). But (20) isn't weird out of the blue. It is fine. Hence we have a strong argument here that cumulative readings are in fact not collective readings.

In sum: (18) is weird because it does not naturally have a collective reading and it cannot have a cumulative reading (because of the numbers). (20) is weird on a collective reading, just like (18), but it is fine on a cumulative reading.

A second argument that cumulative readings should not be reduced to collective readings involves the collectivity criterion directly. Cumulative readings are as inductive as distributive readings (as argued in Krifka (1989, 1990a), and in other work by him). If Sarah gave birth to Chaim and to Rakefet, and Hanah gave birth to Avital, we can truthfully say (21) on a cumulative reading:

(21) Sarah and Hanah gave birth to Chaim, Rakefet and Avital.

The collectivity criterion then tells us that cumulative readings are non-thematic, and hence non-collective. This means that Roberts' attempt to eliminate cumulativity from the grammar by reducing it to collectivity fails, and we have strong arguments that the grammar needs to deal with cumulative readings after all. In fact, cumulative readings are not like collective readings at all, rather they are very closely related to distributive readings. Hence, if we want to reduce cumulative readings to something else, it shouldn't be collectivity, but plurality. In the remainder of this paper, I will develop the beginnings of a theory of plurality and scope, which will present a unified analysis of distributive and cumulative readings: both are reduced to plurality. Cumulative readings are plural readings, like distributive readings, but unlike distributive readings, they are scopeless. What we need then is a theory of plurality, scope and scopelessness. To this I now turn.

6 A Neo-Davidsonian Theory of Events and Plurality

I will now sketch the (bare) outlines of the language of events and plurality that I will assume. The language has lambda-abstraction and set-abstraction (following Scha (1981)), includes a neo-davidsonian theory of events (following Parsons (1990)), and a theory of plurality. In particular with respect to the analysis of cumulativity, the theory is very close to Schein (1993) and Krifka (1989). It differs from both by strictly adhering to the collectivity criterion.

The language is based on the following types:

– the type of events *e*.

e is interpreted as a structure ⟨E,⊔,ATOM⟩, an atomic part-of structure: this is a structure of atomic (singular) events and their (plural) sums. (These structures are in essence atomic boolean algebras with their bottom element removed. For discussion of these structures, see Landman (1989a), Landman (1991), Lønning (1989), Krifka (1990a).) An example:

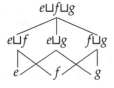

plural events

ATOMS: singular events

– the type of individuals *d*

d is interpreted as a structure $\langle D,\sqcup,\text{IND},\text{GROUP},\uparrow,\downarrow\rangle$, an atomic part-of structure of singular individual and group atoms (IND and GROUP) and their plural sums, with an operation of group formation $\uparrow$. SUM is the set of sums of individuals. $\uparrow$ turns a sum of individuals (a$\sqcup$b) into a group atom $\uparrow$(a$\sqcup$b): a $\sqcup$ b as an entity in its own right, a group, more than the sum of its parts. The definition of $\uparrow$ and $\downarrow$ follows Landman (1989a), but includes some improvements from Schwarzschild (1991):

> $\uparrow$ is a **one-one** function from SUM into ATOM such that:
> 1. $\forall d \in$ SUM-IND; $\uparrow(d) \in$ GROUP
> 2. $\forall d \in$ IND: $\uparrow(d) = d$
>
> $\downarrow$ is a function from ATOM onto SUM such that:
> 1. $\forall d \in$ SUM: $\downarrow(\uparrow(d)) = d$
> 2. $\forall d \in$ IND: $\downarrow(d) = d$

Example (partial):

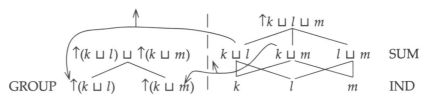

- the type of sets of individuals, pow(d)
- the type of sets of events, pow(e)

Nominal predicate constants like BOY, GIRL are of type pow(d) and denote sets of **atomic** individuals.

Verbal predicate constants like SING, KISS are of type pow(e) and denote sets of **atomic** events.

Pluralization is a predicate operation and is defined on pow(d) and on pow(e): *P is the closure of P under sum. Hence,

> *BOY is the set of individual boys and their plural sums.
> *SING is the set of atomic singing events and their plural sums.

– further we have the usual function types: $\langle a,b \rangle$ is the type of functions from type a into type b. Of special importance is the type $\langle e,d \rangle$: $\langle e,d \rangle$ is the type of thematic and non-thematic roles. I assume that the theory incorporates an undefined object and a theory of partiality: these roles are partial functions from events into individuals. This incorporates the Unique Role Requirement (cf. Carlson 1984, Parsons 1990): no event has more than one agent, theme, etc.

The language contains Role constants: Ag, Th, . . . , which denote **thematic roles**. I assume that the domain corresponding to $\langle e,d \rangle$ contains a subset TR, the set of **thematic** roles. Thematic constraints are constraints on the members of TR. In line with the collectivity criterion, thematic roles will indicate thematic, singular or collective, predication. This is captured as a singularity constraint:

Singularity constraint on thematic roles:
1. thematic roles are only defined for atomic events.
2. thematic roles only take atomic individuals (singular individuals or groups) as value.

We define: $AT(x) = \{a \in AT: a \sqsubseteq x\}$

$AT(x)$ is the set of atomic parts of x.

We have in the theory up to now singular events and singular individuals (and groups), which are linked by singular thematic roles. Pluralization of event predicates adds sum events, pluralization of nominal predicates adds sum individuals. We now add pluralization on roles, which creates **plural roles**:

Plural roles:
Let R be a role.
$*R$, the plural role based on R is defined by:
$*R(e) = \sqcup(\{R(e'): e' \in AT(e)\})$
if for every $e' \in AT(e)$: $R(e')$ is defined; otherwise undefined.

This tells us that the plural agent, theme, . . . of a sum of events is the sum of the agents, themes, . . . of the atomic parts of that events. (This is very similar to Krifka's (1989) cumulativity requirement.) If e is an event of John singing and f is an event of Mary singing, then the **thematic** role Ag is defined for e ($Ag(e) = j$) and for f ($Ag(f) = m$), but not for the sum event $e \sqcup f$, because thematic roles are only defined for singular events. However, the plural role $*Ag$ is defined for $e \sqcup f$: the agents of the atomic parts of $e \sqcup f$ are j and m, hence the plural agent of $e \sqcup f$ is $j \sqcup m$: $*Ag(e \sqcup f) = j \sqcup m$.

The ideas about thematic and non-thematic predication are captured in this theory as follows:

- singular verbal constants are sets of atomic events.
- plural verbal constants are sets of plural events.
- Singular predication is predication where an atomic individual (individual or group) fills a thematic role (in TR) of an atomic event. Since lexical constraints are constraints on thematic roles in TR, such predication is indeed thematic.
- Plural predication is predication where a plural individual fills a plural role of a plural event. This predication is non-thematic, the plural object that fills the plural role is not itself required to satisfy the thematic constraints imposed in thematic roles.

7   The Grammar

7.1   Verbs

In a classical Montague style analysis (with type shifting), verbs are interpreted as **n-place properties** of type $\langle d, \ldots, \langle d,t \rangle \rangle$ (*n*-times *d*): functions that taken-arguments into a truth value. In the present theory (in essence following Parsons (1990)), verbs are interpreted as **n-place scope domains** of type $\langle d, \ldots, \langle d, \mathrm{pow}(e) \rangle \rangle$ (*n*-times *d*): functions that take n-arguments into a set of events. A (0-place) scope domain is a set of events tied together by roles.

We associate with each verb a verbal predicate constant of type $\mathrm{pow}(e)$. The basic interpretation of the verb is unmarked for semantic plurality. However, since for any predicate P the singular form P is a subset of the plural form $^*P$, this means that the plural form is the unmarked form. We have the following interpretations:

> $walk \rightarrow \lambda x.\{e \in {}^*\mathrm{WALK}: {}^*\mathrm{Ag}(e) = x\}$
> $kiss \rightarrow \lambda y \lambda x.\{e \in {}^*\mathrm{KISS}: {}^*\mathrm{Ag}(e) = x \wedge {}^*\mathrm{Th}(e) = y\}$

i.e. *kiss* is a function (of type $\langle d, \langle d, \mathrm{pow}(e) \rangle \rangle$) that maps an object and a subject onto the set of (sums of) kissing events with that subject as plural agent and that object as plural theme.

We can now illustrate the predictions of the theory concerning thematic and non-thematic predication. Look at examples (22) and (23):

> (22)   John sings.
> (23)   John and Mary sing.

As will become clear presently, the grammar derives the following interpretation for (22):

> (22)   a. $\exists e \in {}^*\mathrm{SING}: {}^*\mathrm{Ag}(e) = j$
> There is a sum of singing events with plural agent John.

For (23), two interpretations will be derived:

> (23)   a. $\exists e \in {}^*\mathrm{SING}: {}^*\mathrm{Ag}(e) = {\uparrow}(j \sqcup m)$
> There is a sum of singing events with the group of John and Mary as plural agent.

> (23)   b. $\exists e \in {}^*\mathrm{SING}: {}^*\mathrm{Ag}(e) = j \sqcup m$
> There is a sum of singing events with the sum of John and Mary as plural agent.

Let's concentrate first on (22a) and (23a). Clearly, these interpretations sound much too plural. However, since j and $\uparrow(j \sqcup m)$ are atoms, they have only themselves as parts. Hence, an atom is the plural agent of a sum of singing events iff it is the agent of all the atomic part events. This means that (22a) and (23a) are equivalent to (22b) and (23c) respectively:

(22)   b. $\exists e \in$ SING: Ag(e) = j
(23)   c. $\exists e \in$ SING: Ag(e) = $\uparrow(j \sqcup m)$

In (22b) and (23c) the predication is thematic: hence (23a) and (23c) are the collective interpretation of (23).

Now look at (23b). The atomic parts of the sum $j \sqcup m$ are j and m. *Ag(e) = $\sqcup$ {Ag(e'): $e' \in$ AT(e)}. This means that some of the atomic parts of e will have to have j as agent, and the rest m. This means that (23b) is equivalent to (23d):

(23d) $\exists e \in$ SING: Ag(e) = $j \wedge \exists e \in$ SING: Ag(e) = m

This means that (23b) indeed is the distributive interpretation of (23), and, as can be seen from the equivalence with (23d), the predication in (23b) is non-thematic.

7.2   Noun Phrases

The theory will treat non-quantificational noun phrases differently from quantificational noun phrases. Non-quantificational NPs are proper names, definites and indefinites. For these, I will assume, following Landman (1989a), that they can shift their interpretation from plural to group interpretations. This gives two interpretations for *John and Mary* and *three boys*:

John and Mary $\rightarrow j \sqcup m,\ \uparrow(j \sqcup m)$
three boys $\rightarrow \lambda P.\exists x \in$ *BOY: $|x| = 3 \wedge P(x)$ (sum)
The set of properties that a sum of three boys has.
           $\rightarrow \lambda P.\exists x \in$ *BOY: $|x| = 3 \wedge P(\uparrow(x))$ (group)
The set of properties that a group of three boys has.

(Note that for most purposes in this paper – with the exception of problems of grid – I could have taken an alternative road, and worked the shift between plural and collective predication into the predicates, i.e. choose, say, only the sum interpretation for the NPs, and let a shift operation on the verbs option- ally introduce the $\uparrow$ operation, or the other way round. I think that in a full- fledged theory we need both options; just as I think that for examples like *The boys, as a group, left*, the grammar will need to deal both with collective NPs like *the boys, as a group* and collective predicates *left, as a group*. I do not have space here to pursue this further.) Since I do not have space to go into the subtleties of quantificational NPs, I will just assume that they get their standard interpretation:

> *every girl* → $\lambda P.\forall x \in$ GIRL: $P(x)$
> *no girl*   → $\lambda P.\neg\exists x \in$ GIRL: $P(x)$

7.3   *In-situ Application*

In-situ application is the mechanism with which arguments are associated with verbs. This is constrained by the following **scope domain principle**:

> **Scope domain principle**:
> Non-quantificational NPs can be entered into scope domains. Quantificational NPs cannot be entered into scope domains.

The second part is a standard assumption in neo-Davidsonian theories. It has the consequence that quantificational NPs take scope over the event argument. The first part is particular to the present theory: the possibility of entering non-quantificational NPs into the scope domain will create **scopeless** readings.

I assume that verbs are functions on all their arguments. In-situ application is in essence functional application, except that I assume a type shifting theory (e.g. Partee and Rooth (1983)). Functional application gets generalized to an operation APPLY which does the following: APPLY does functional application if the types fit; if they don't fit, it lifts the function or the argument to make them fit and then does functional application.

More precisely:

> The type shifting operation LIFT has three instances:
>   NPs: LIFT$[\alpha] = \lambda P.P(\alpha)$ (α of type d)
>   VPs: LIFT$[\beta] = \lambda T.\{e \in$ E: $T(\lambda x.e \in \beta(x))\}$
>   (T of type $\langle\langle d,t\rangle,t\rangle$, x of type d, β of type $\langle d,\text{pow}(e)\rangle$)
>   TVs: LIFT$[\beta] = \lambda T\lambda x.\{e \in$ E: $T(\lambda y.e \in [\beta(y)](x))\}$
>   (T of type $\langle\langle d,t\rangle,t\rangle$, x, y of type d, β of type $\langle d,\langle d,\text{pow}(e)\rangle\rangle$)

APPLY is defined as:
APPLY: 1. If α is of type $\langle a,b\rangle$ and β of type a then:
            APPLY $[\alpha,\beta] = \alpha(\beta)$
       2. If LIFT$[\alpha]$ is of type $\langle a,b\rangle$ and β of type a then:
            APPLY $[\alpha,\beta] = \text{LIFT}[\alpha](\beta)$
       3. If α is of type $\langle a,b\rangle$ and LIFT $[\beta]$ of type a then:
            APPLY $[\alpha,\beta] = \alpha(\text{LIFT}[\beta])$

Given this, in-situ application is defined as follows:
IN-SITU APPLICATION:

$$\text{TV} + \text{NP} \Rightarrow \text{VP}; \quad \text{VP}' = \text{APPLY}[\text{TV}',\text{NP}']$$
$$\text{NP} + \text{VP} \Rightarrow S; \quad S' = \text{APPLY}[\text{VP}',\text{NP}']$$

The effect of in-situ application is that the noun phrase meaning is fed into the scope domain. We will see this shortly, when I discuss the predictions of the theory.

7.4 Existential closure

After in-situ application, but before quantifying in, existential closure takes place. This again follows Parsons' neo-Davidsonian theory:

EXISTENTIAL CLOSURE: Let α be a scope domain (type pow(e)):
$$\text{EC}(\alpha) = \exists e \in \alpha$$

7.5 Scope and quantifying in

The theory has a scope mechanism. Any of the well-known scope mechanisms can be used here. I will choose storage (Cooper (1983)).

7.5.1 Storage

In a storage theory, the scope domain principle gets the following form: quantificational NPs are obligatorily stored, non-quantificational NPs can be stored with the following rule of

STORE$_n$:
Let α be an NP meaning and S the quantifier store:
$$\text{STORE}_n (\langle \alpha, S \rangle) = \langle X_n, S \cup \{\langle n, \alpha \rangle\}\rangle$$

The meaning of α is stored, and in-situ application will use a variable instead. As usual, stores are inherited in building up meanings.

7.5.2 Quantifying in

In the next section I will compare different theories of plurality and scope that can be found in the literature. For reasons of comparison, I will present here three possible rules of quantifying in:

Non-scopal quantifying in:
$$\text{NQI}_n(\langle \varphi, S \rangle) = \langle \text{APPLY} [\alpha, \lambda x_n \varphi], S - \{\langle n, \alpha \rangle\}\rangle$$

This is just Montague's rule. It forms the property $\lambda x_n \varphi$ which (as we will see) is a non-scopal property: "the property that you have if you have φ".

Scopal quantifying in:

$SQI_n(\langle\langle\varphi,S\rangle\rangle) = \langle APPLY[\alpha,\lambda x.\forall\ x_n \in AT(x)\varphi], S - \{\langle n,\alpha\rangle\}\rangle$

This is the rule that I will assume myself. It forms the property $\lambda x.\ \forall x_n \in AT\ (x): \varphi$, which is a scopal property: "the property that you have if all your atomic parts have φ".

Distributive quantifying in:

$DQI_n(\langle\langle\varphi,S\rangle\rangle) = \langle APPLY[\alpha,\lambda x.\forall x_n \in AT(\downarrow(x))\varphi], S - \{\langle n,\alpha\rangle\}\rangle$

This rule is almost the same as SQI except that it works on groups rather than sums. It forms the property $\lambda x.\ \forall x_n \in AT(\downarrow(x)) : \varphi :$ "the property that you have if all the atomic parts of the sum corresponding to the group have φ".

8   Three Theories of Scope and Plurality

We will now be concerned with examples like (24)

(24)   Three boys invited four girls.
(25)   Exactly three boys invited exactly three girls.

The question is: how many readings should the grammar generate for sentences like (24), and what should they be? The abundant literature on sentences like (24) is far from unanimous on this. In fact, proposals range between one reading and infinitely many readings, and basically everything in between.

The difficult question, which seems to be underdetermined by native (and non-native) speakers' judgements is how to distinguish between a reading of (24) and a situation in which (24) is true. Given the problems with intuitions, the empirical basis for any grammar proposal for (24) is somewhat shaky. Nevertheless, I do think that there are empirical and theoretical considerations that allow us to compare and evaluate different proposals. In this section I will compare three such proposals.

Even with the data as muddled as they are, there is one piece of data that does constrain possible grammars for examples like (24). The constraint is in fact clearer in (25), which avoids the problems of at least/exactly readings. The constraint is the following:

> **Distributive scope generalization**:
> When we look at all situations where (25) is true, the number of girls invited can vary between 4 and 12: (25) is not true if less than four girls are invited, and (25) is not true if more than 12 girls are invited.

This seems to be a solid fact, and it provides an argument that the grammar has to generate at least two readings. One could be the double collective reading (which says that a group of three boys invites a group of four girls). But this reading will not cover situations where all in all twelve girls get invited. The standard explanation, which is very sensible, is that the other reading is derived through a scope mechanism in the grammar. A scope mechanism can interpret the NP *four girls* in the scope of *three boys* and derive an interpretation where it is four girls per boy (giving maximally twelve girls).

Thus a scope mechanism will add at least one more reading for examples like (24) and (25), a scoped reading.

In its most general form, a scope mechanism has the following four properties: it is optional (in particular, non-quantificational NPs are not obligatorily scoped out); it is iterable (the mechanism can apply to a structure to which it has already applied before); it defines and uses a (transitive) notion of scope, and scope sets up a relation between a scopal element (say an NP) and its scope (this means that scope is only indirectly a relation between NPs, and hence that the mechanism applies to cases that involve only one NP); finally, the mechanism creates a scope dependency, a situation where an expression is interpreted as dependent on a (quantificational) operator.

For quantificational NPs, Montague's quantifying-in rule NQI is a scope mechanism in the above sense. For non-quantificational NPs (in particular plural NPs), Montague's NQI is not a scope mechanism, because it is in fact not capable of creating a scope dependency. The other two quantifying-in rules, SQI and DQI, are scope mechanisms.

Now, the situation is that – while we have empirical evidence from the distributive scope generalization that we need a scope mechanism to create a scoped reading – because of the properties listed above, a general scope mechanism (without separate restrictions) will in fact add not just one reading, but four. This can be seen by discussing the first theory.

THEORY I: Lakoff 1970

On this theory, collective readings are in-situ readings. Distributivity is not reduced to plurality, but to scope: distributivity is created by the scope mechanism. In Lakoff's theory, the scope mechanism is quantifier lowering. Equivalently, this theory assumes that quantifier raising, QR, creates scope dependencies. This theory can be modeled in the framework given before as follows. We assume that NPs have only collective interpretations (i.e. we allow no shifting to sum interpretations). Furthermore, we take as our quantifying-in rule the rule DQI. This theory produces five readings.

1. Cs–Co: leave subject and object in situ.
This is the double collective reading.

Derivation:
$Invite \rightarrow \lambda y \lambda x. \{e \in {}^*\text{INVITE}: {}^*Ag(e) = x \wedge {}^*Th(e) = y\}$
$Three\ boys \rightarrow \lambda P. \exists x \in {}^*\text{BOY}: |x| = 3 \wedge P(\uparrow(x))$
$Four\ girls \rightarrow \lambda P. \exists y \in {}^*\text{GIRL}: |y| = 4 \wedge P(\uparrow(y))$

Enter *four girls* into the scope domain with in-situ application; enter *three boys* into the result with in-situ application; apply existential closure. The result (after reduction) is:

$\exists e \in {}^*\text{INVITE}$: $\exists x \in {}^*\text{BOY}$: $|x| = 3 \wedge {}^*\text{Ag}(e) = \uparrow(x) \wedge$
  $\exists y \in {}^*\text{GIRL}$: $|y| = 4 \wedge {}^*\text{Th}(e) = \uparrow(y)$

Both plural agent and plural theme are atoms, so we derive the thematic statement:

$\exists e \in \text{INVITE}$: $\exists x \in {}^*\text{BOY}$: $|x| = 3 \wedge \text{Ag}(e) = \uparrow(x) \wedge$
  $\exists y \in {}^*\text{GIRL}$: $|y| = 4 \wedge \text{Th}(e) = \uparrow(y)$

There is an event of a group of three boys inviting a group of four girls.

A model where this reading is true is:

$$\uparrow(a \sqcup b \sqcup c) \rightarrow \uparrow(1 \sqcup 2 \sqcup 3 \sqcup 4)$$

The operation of QR, interpreted as DQI, creates a distributive dependency: the scope of the QR-ed NP is interpreted relative to the atomic parts of the QR-ed NP. We can apply QR in four ways: we can either QR the subject, or QR the object, or QR both in two orders. This gives four scoped readings:

2. *Ds(Co)*. QR the subject: A GROUP OF FOUR GIRLS PER BOY

$\exists x \in {}^*\text{BOY}$: $|x| = 3 \wedge \forall a \in \text{AT}(x)$:

  $\exists e \in \text{INVITE}$: $\text{Ag}(e) = a \wedge \exists y \in {}^*\text{GIRL}$: $|y| = 4 \wedge \text{Th}(e) = \uparrow(y)$

There are three boys such that each boy invites a group of four girls.

  $a \rightarrow \uparrow(1 \sqcup 2 \sqcup 3 \sqcup 4)$
  $b \rightarrow \uparrow(5 \sqcup 6 \sqcup 7 \sqcup 8)$
  $c \rightarrow \uparrow(9 \sqcup 10 \sqcup 11 \sqcup 12)$

3. *Do(Cs)*: QR the object: A GROUP OF THREE BOYS PER GIRL

$\exists y \in {}^*\text{GIRL}$: $|y| = 4 \wedge \forall b \in \text{AT}(y)$:

  $\exists e \in \text{INVITE}$: $\exists x \in {}^*\text{BOY}$: $|x| = 3 \wedge \text{Ag}(e) = \uparrow(x) \wedge \text{Th}(e) = b$

There are four girls such that each girl is invited by a group of three boys.

  $\uparrow(a \sqcup b \sqcup c) \rightarrow 1$
  $\uparrow(d \sqcup e \sqcup f) \rightarrow 2$
  $\uparrow(g \sqcup h \sqcup i) \rightarrow 3$
  $\uparrow(j \sqcup k \sqcup l) \rightarrow 4$

4. $Ds(Co\ ())$: QR the object, then the subject: FOUR GIRLS PER BOY

$\exists x \in {}^*BOY: |x| = 3 \wedge \forall a \in AT(x): \exists y \in {}^*GIRL: |y| = 4 \wedge \forall b \in AT(y):$
  $\exists e \in INVITE: Ag(e) = a \wedge Th(e) = b$

There are three boys such that for each boy there are four girls such that that boy invites each of those four girls.

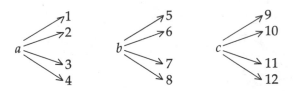

5. $Do(Ds\ (\ ))$ QR the subject, then the object: THREE BOYS PER GIRL

$\exists y \in {}^*GIRL: |y| = 4 \wedge \forall b \in AT(y): \exists x \in {}^*BOY: |x| = 3 \wedge \forall a \in AT(x):$

  $\exists e \in INVITE: Ag(e) = a \wedge Th(e) = b$

There are four girls such that for each of those girls there are three boys such that each of those boys invites that girl.

Note: 3. and 5. are inverse scope readings. They are usually exceedingly difficult to get (some, like Scha (1981), set up the scope mechanism in such a way that these readings are not produced by the basic scope mechanism, but only as part of an optional principle).

Now, we can argue the reasonableness of these results as follows: The collectivity criterion requires us to distinguish between readings 2. and 4. (where the object is collective and distributive, respectively). The distributive scope generalization distinguishes reading 1. from both 2. and 4. The opinion of the theory on inverse readings 3. and 5. is less compelling. These readings are produced by the general scope mechanism and are not independently motivated. If wanted, a separate condition forbidding inverse scope could get rid of these. On the other hand, in some cases inverse scope seems to be less of a problem. For that reason, one could let the grammar generate them and try to give an independent reason why these readings are usually so difficult to obtain.

Thus Lakoff's theory produces five readings, three of which are well motivated independently, and it seems that this is the minimum number of readings that any grammar will have to generate (again, except for the problem of inverse readings).

Roberts (1987) discusses various problems with Lakoff's theory, arguing that the theory undergenerates. I will here discuss yet another problem showing the same. Look at the situations 6. and 7., where as before letters indicate boys, numbers girls, and the arrows inviting.

6. $a \longrightarrow$
   $b \Longrightarrow \uparrow(1 \sqcup 2 \sqcup 3 \sqcup 4)$
   $c \longrightarrow$

7.
   $\uparrow(a \sqcup b \sqcup c) \xrightleftharpoons{\quad} \begin{array}{l} 1 \\ 2 \\ 3 \\ 4 \end{array}$

When we evaluate sentence (24) in either of these situations, we observe that these are situations where it is very easy to agree that (24) is true. The readings corresponding to these situations are the following:

6. *Ds–Co*:

$\exists x \in {}^*\text{BOY}: |x| = 3 \wedge \exists y \in {}^*\text{GIRL}: |\,y| = 4 \wedge \forall a \in \text{AT}(x):$

$\exists e \in \text{INVITE}: \text{Ag}(e) = a \wedge \text{Th}(e) = \uparrow(y)$

There are three boys and there is a group of four girls such that each of those boys invites that group of girls.

7. *Cs–Do*

$\exists x \in {}^*\text{BOY}: |x| = 3 \wedge \exists y \in {}^*\text{GIRL}: |y| = 4 \wedge \forall b \in \text{AT}(y):$

$\exists e \in \text{INVITE}: \text{Ag}(e) = \uparrow(x) \wedge \text{Th}(e) = b$

There is a group of three boys and there are four girls such that that group of boys invites each of those girls.

Lakoff's theory does not generate these readings.

There is a ready response to this. One could argue the following: reading 6. is the borderline case of reading 2. and reading 7. is the borderline case of reading 3. Thus, reading 2. is in fact true in situation 6., and reading 3. is true in situation 7. Thus Lakoff's theory does generate two readings of sentence (24) that are true in situations 6. and 7. Hence, we could say: even better that the theory doesn't generate readings 6 and 7, it doesn't have to generate these.

There is a serious problem with this argument. As we have seen, reading 3. is an inverse reading, and very difficult to get. If our judgement that sentence (24) is true in situation 7. involves interpreting (24) on reading 3., we predict that it should be at least as difficult to judge (24) to be true in situation 7., as it is in situation 3. But this is not the case. It is very easy to judge (24) to be true in situation 7., hence the truth of (24) in situation 7. cannot be reduced to reading 3. In fact, it can't be reduced to any of the other readings either. This means that we need a mechanism producing reading 7. Now, since reading 2. is not an inverse reading, we don't have a similar argument for reading 6. However, typically a general mechanism that will produce reading 7. will produce reading 6 as well. This means then, that we have evidence for seven readings, two more than Lakoff's theory gives.

THEORY II: Roberts 1987

Such a theory is provided by Roberts' 1987 theory of scopal and non-scopal derived predicates. I do not have space to present the details of Roberts' theory, but in terms of QR, the theory can be reconstructed as follows:

Let us assume that we have two flavors of QR: QR_1 moves and creates a scopal dependency, while QR_2 moves or does not create a scopal dependency. In the present framework, this comes down to the following extension of Lakoff's theory: As before, we assume that we have only collective NPs. The two flavors of QR correspond to two quantifying-in rules: as before we have distributive quantifying-in DQI, but we add to the theory also non-scopal quantifying-in NQI. Thus, both these rules are available. This gives us indeed seven readings. Lakoff's five readings, plus readings 6. and 7.:

6. *Ds–Co*: quantify in the subject with DQI, after that quantify in the object with NQI
7. *Cs–Do*: quantify in the object with DQI, after that quantify in the subject with NQI

In this way, we solve the problem with situation 7.: Roberts' theory generates reading 7., hence the truth of (24) in situation 7. no longer relies on inverse reading 3. There is still a problem: readings 6. and 7., as I argued, are very easy to get. Yet in a sense, they have a more complicated derivation than the other readings. Moreover, in this theory now reading 6. becomes an inverse scope reading. But clearly it is much easier to judge (24) to be true in situation 6., than it is to judge the other inverse scope readings to be true in their characterizing situations. While not as serious a problem (for one thing, 6. is the borderline of 2.), there seems to be something unsatisfactory about the situation.

THEORY III: my proposal

Let us now see what the grammar that I have set up in this paper predicts. On my theory, non-quantificational NPs can shift their interpretation between collective and plural interpretations. The scope mechanism (and the only scope mechanism) is SQI.

This theory produces eight readings:

The scope mechanism SQI brings in four scoped readings. These are exactly the four scoped readings from Lakoff's theory (which shouldn't come as a surprise, since SQI is in essence the same rule as DQI). However, the simplest derivations are simpler than in Lakoff's theory, because in each case we only need to invoke the scope mechanism once:

2. *Ds(Co)*: group object in-situ, quantify-in sum subject
3. *Do(Cs)*: group subject in-situ, quantify-in sum object
4. *Ds(Do)*: sum object in-situ, quantify-in sum-subject
5. *Do(Ds)*: sum subject in-situ, quantify-in sum-object

Besides these readings, the theory produces four **scopeless** readings, readings that do not invoke the scope mechanism at all, but only use in-situ application:

1. *Cs–Co*: group subject and group object in-situ
7. *Cs–Do*: group subject and sum subject in-situ
6. *Ds–Co*: sum subject and group object in-situ
8. *Ds–Do*: sum subject and sum object in-situ

For example, for reading 7. we enter first the sum interpretation of *four girls* and then the group interpretation of *three boys* into the scope domain. We get:

$$\exists e \in {}^{*}\text{INVITE}: \exists x \in {}^{*}\text{BOY}: |x| = 3 \wedge {}^{*}\text{Ag}(e) = \uparrow(x) \wedge$$
$$\exists y \in {}^{*}\text{GIRL}: |y| = 4 \wedge {}^{*}\text{Th}(e) = y$$

There is a sum of inviting events with a group of three boys as plural agent and a sum of four girls as plural theme.

This group of three boys will be the agent of each atomic sub-event, while the four girls are distributed as themes over the atomic sub-events. Hence this means:

There is a group of three boys and there are four girls such that for each of those girls there is an event of that group inviting that girl.

This is equivalent to reading 7.

The interesting case is, of course, the one reading that is not produced by Roberts' theory, reading 8.:

8. *Ds–Do*: scopeless plural reading:

$$\exists e \in {}^{*}\text{INVITE}: \exists x \in {}^{*}\text{BOY}: |x| = 3 \wedge {}^{*}\text{Ag}(e) = x \wedge$$
$$\exists y \in {}^{*}\text{GIRL}: |y| = 4 \wedge {}^{*}\text{Th}(e) = y$$

There is a sum of inviting events that has a sum of three boys as plural agent and a sum of three girls as plural theme.

This tells us that every atomic part of *e* has one of these boys as agent and every atomic part of *e* has one of these girls as theme. In other words, every one of these boys invites one (or more) of these girls and every one of these girls is invited by one (or more) of these boys.

This is the cumulative reading (apart from the exactly part, which Scha (1981) builds into the meaning of the cumulative reading, but which is arguably a matter of conversational implicatures, e.g. Horn (1972), Kadmon (1987)).

A situation in which 8 is true:

In this theory, then, in the case of one-place predicates, distributive readings fall out of the theory as plural readings. In the case of two-place predicates, plural readings come in two varieties: scoped plural readings, which are also distributive readings, and scopeless plural readings, which are cumulative readings.

We can list the following advantages of this theory over the other theories discussed:

In the first place, the two natural readings 6. and 7. do not rely on inverse scope. The fact that they are easy to get, can be explained by the fact that they do not involve the scope mechanism as all: 6. and 7. are scopeless readings.

Second, cumulative readings fall out of the theory, and they fall out of the theory without invoking the complicated mechanism of binary quantification.

Third, cumulative readings are independent from collective readings. They are not reduced to collective readings. Hence the theory obeys the collectivity criterion.

Fourth, cumulative readings are, like distributive readings, non-thematic. Both are reduced to plurality.

Obviously, this is not a full theory, but only the beginning of a theory. For one thing, I am not dealing in the present paper with the urgent problem of how to extend the present theory to cumulative readings of other NPs, like downward entailing NPs, as in (26):

(26)   At most three boys invited at most four girls.

I discuss this and many other aspects of the present framework elsewhere (Landman (1994)).

9   Cover Readings

There is one more type of reading of sentences like (24) that I have not yet discussed. These are what Scha (1981) calls second collective readings, and which have since become known as cover readings or partitive readings. Look at (27):

(27)   Four hundred fire fighters put out twenty fires.

The reading that we are interested in is the reading where the sentence expresses that some **groups** of fire fighters put out fires, these groups altogether consist of four hundred fire fighters and altogether twenty fires were put out by these groups. Theories of cover readings are developed, among others, in Scha (1981), Verkuyl and van der Does (1991), Gillon (1987), van der Does (1992), and Schwarzschild (1991). Scha (1981) (and after him Verkuyl and van der Does (1991)) assumes an interpretation for the NP *four hundred fire fighters* which breaks up a group of four hundred fire fighters into subgroups covering that group. This approach is untenable, because it conflicts with the distributive scope generalization. If the cover is part of the noun phrase interpretation, the scope mechanism will predict that when the cover NP is scoped, the rest of the sentence will take scope dependent on not the individual fire fighters but on these subgroups (i.e. the reading will be *twenty fires per group of fire fighters*). Since there can be far more than four hundred subgroups involved, we predict that the sentence can be true in situations involving far more than 400×20 fires, contradicting the distributive scope generalization.

The relevant observation concerning cover interpretations is that they are closely related to cumulative readings: like cumulative readings, they are **plural**, non-thematic readings, and like cumulative readings they are scopeless. This means that the cover effect should not be regarded as contributed by the noun phrase interpretations, but rather, like cumulative readings, by the verb or the predication.

I will extend the theory with **cover roles**. For simplicity, I will restrict the models to models where $\text{ATOMd} = \text{ran}(\uparrow)$. In such models cover roles can be truly roles (otherwise we have to define cover relations). Cover roles will be non-thematic roles, defined in terms of plural roles. They will be partial functions from sum events into atoms.

Let R be a thematic role.
   ^cR, the **cover role based on** R, is the partial function from De into Dd defined by:
   $^cR(e) = a$ iff $a \in \text{ATOM} \wedge \sqcup(\{\downarrow(d) \in \text{SUM}: d \in \text{AT}(*R(e))\}) = \downarrow(a)$
      undefined otherwise.

To show how this works, suppose the following:

$Ag(e) = \uparrow(j \sqcup b)$
$Ag(f) = \uparrow(j \sqcup m)$
$Ag(g) = \uparrow(b \sqcup m)$
then: $*Ag(e \sqcup f \sqcup g) = \uparrow(j \sqcup b) \sqcup \uparrow(j \sqcup m) \sqcup \uparrow(b \sqcup m)$

$\{\downarrow(d): d \in AT\ (*Ag(e \sqcup f \sqcup g))\} = \{j \sqcup b, j \sqcup m, b \sqcup m\}$.
Hence: $\sqcup\ (\{\downarrow(d): d \in AT(*Ag\ (e \sqcup f \sqcup g))\}) = \sqcup\ (\{j \sqcup b, j \sqcup m, b \sqcup m\})$
$= j \sqcup b \sqcup m = \downarrow(\uparrow\ (j \sqcup b \sqcup m))$.
Hence $^cAg\ (e \sqcup f \sqcup g) = \uparrow(j \sqcup b \sqcup m)$

Let us define a **subgroup** of a group α as a group β such that $\downarrow(\beta) \sqsubseteq \downarrow(\alpha)$. Let us define: set X of subgroups of group α covers α iff $\sqcup\ \{\downarrow(x): x \in X\} = \downarrow(\alpha)$. Given this terminology, a group α is the cover agent of sum-event e if the plural agent of e is a sum of subgroups of α that together cover α.

In the grammar, we now assume a type shifting principle for verbs, which says that verbs can switch from n-place scope domains with a plural role $*R$ to n-place scope domains with a cover role ^cR:

$$\lambda x_n \ldots x \ldots x_1.\{e \in *V: \ldots *R(e) = x \ldots\} \Rightarrow$$
$$\lambda x_n \ldots x \ldots x_1.\{e \in *V: \ldots ^cR(e) = x \ldots\}$$

Let us look once more at (24):

(24)   Three boys invited four girls.

If we start with the following scope domain:

$$\lambda y \lambda x.\{e \in *INVITE: ^cAg(e) = x \wedge ^cTh(e) = y\}$$

and enter the group object and group subject into the scope domain, we get the following interpretation:

Ps-Po:
$$\exists e \in *INVITE: \exists x \in *BOY: |x| = 3 \wedge ^cAg(e) = \uparrow(x) \wedge$$
$$\exists y \in *GIRL: |y| = 4 \wedge ^cTh(e) = \uparrow(y)$$

Working this out, we get:

$$\exists e \in *INVITE: \exists x \in *BOY: |x| = 3 \wedge \sqcup\ (\{\downarrow(d): d \in AT\ (*Ag(e))\}) = x \wedge$$
$$\exists y \in *GIRL: |y| = 4 \wedge \sqcup\ (\{\downarrow(d): d \in AT\ (*Th(e))\}) = y$$

There is a sum of inviting events, a sum of three boys and a sum of four girls and the plural agent of the sum of inviting events is a sum of groups covering that sum of boys, and the plural theme of the sum of inviting events is a sum of groups covering that sum of girls.

In other words: there is a sum of inviting events with as plural agent a sum of groups of boys (making up three boys in total) and as plural theme a sum of groups of girls (making up four girls in total).

We see that cover readings are really analyzed in terms of distribution to subgroups. A situation where this reading is true is:

$$\uparrow(a \sqcup b) \rightarrow \uparrow(1 \sqcup 2)$$
$$\uparrow(a \sqcup c) \rightarrow \uparrow(3 \sqcup 4)$$

Adding the possibility to shift to cover readings adds five more readings to the theory: basically, for every reading where one of the NPs has a group interpretation, a reading is added where that NP has a cover interpretation.

Following Schwarzschild (1991), we assume that if $a \in$ IND: $a = \uparrow(a)$. This means that individuals are their own subgroups. It follows from this that if $*R(e) = x$, where $x \in$ SUM, then also $^cR(e) = \uparrow(x)$: if, say, the plural agent of e is a sum of individuals x, then those individuals are subgroups that cover $\uparrow(x)$. Similarly, if $*R(e) = \uparrow(x)$, then also $^cR(e) = \uparrow(x)$: in this case $\uparrow(x)$ is covered by $\{\uparrow(x)\}$. This means that all the four scopeless readings we had before, plus the new ones that are added, are in fact, all borderline cases of the double cover reading. This suggests an alternative to the theory that I am proposing, which actually reduces the number of readings:

THEORY IV: Schwarzschild 1991

This theory makes the following assumptions:
1. NPs have only group interpretations; 2. Verbs have only an interpretation as scope domains where all roles are cover roles; 3. The scope mechanism is DQI.

This theory reduces distributivity to scope and cumulativity to cover effects. The theory generates five readings for sentence (24): One scopeless reading: *Ps–Po* and four scoped readings: *Ds(Po); Do(Ps); Ds(Do()); Do(Ds())*.

The theory does not generate the other scopeless readings, i.e. it doesn't generate directly collective or cumulative readings. But, in the light of the above, it doesn't have to, because those are all special cases of the one scopeless reading it does generate, the double cover reading. Apart from some differences that are irrelevant in the present context, this theory represents the position of Schwarzschild (1991) quite closely, and probably also that of Gillon (1987).

Note that the arguments that I brought up against the theories I and II do not carry over to theory IV. The readings *Ds–Co* and *Cs–Do* are not generated by the scope mechanism, neither do they have to be regarded as borderline cases of readings that are generated through inverse scope. They are borderline cases of the most basic scopeless reading: *Ps–Po*.

If it is the number of readings that we're most interested in, then it is quite clear that theory IV is the most attractive of the theories I have discussed here: It generates only five readings, four of which we get just because we have a scope mechanism; it doesn't overgenerate like Scha's theory and all readings discussed in this paper are special cases of readings generated by theory IV.

In fact, I do not have strong arguments against theory IV, I think it is a very strong alternative to theory III. I will end this section with some discussion.

Theory III is based on the distinction between two basic kinds of predication: thematic predication and plural predication. The assumption that there are collective readings corresponds to the assumption that verbs can directly express thematic predication to plural arguments. The assumption that there are plural readings (distributive/cumulative) corresponds to the assumption that semantic pluralization is freely available in the verbal domain. Theory IV argues correctly that the effect of cover readings, or partitivity, as defined here, is a generalization of both, and hence can replace them in the grammar. This is technically correct, but has consequences for the overall architecture of the theory that I find dubious. Rather than making partitivity the center of the theory of plurality, I suggest that we regard it as a special interpretation strategy of verbs, made available by the connections between different semantic domains.

The main problem with theory IV is that the process of generalization, and the weakening of the readings cannot stop here. Look at (28):

(28)   Three boys ate fifteen breads.

The cover interpretation for (28) tells us that there is a cover of these three boys and a cover of these fifteen breads, and each block of boys eats some block of breads, while each block of breads gets eaten by some block of boys. But as is well-known, this is not the only interpretation possible. ^cR is a **plural partition** of the verbal arguments into subgroups, but (28) also allows a **mass partition** of those arguments that allows a mass interpretation (in (28) the theme) into sub-mass parcels. On that interpretation we associate groups of boys with entities that are not groups of breads.

Given the way we have defined ^cR, we can express such mass-partition in a completely analogous way to plural partition. We assume that we have a mass domain MASS, which is a part-of structure, and we assume that just as ↑ and ↓ associate the domain SUMd with the domain ATOMd, there are two similar operations p (package) and g (grind) between MASS and ATOMd (for details, see Landman (1991)). Given this we can define a mass-cover role as:

Let R be a thematic role.
^mR, the **mass-cover role based on** R, is the partial function from De into Dd defined by:
$^mR(e) = a$ iff $a \in$ ATOMd $\land \sqcup (\{g(d): d \in \text{AT}(^*R(e))\}) = g(a)$
undefined otherwise

Assuming that, for roles that in a predication can have a mass-interpretation, we can shift from a plural role to a mass-cover role, we get (28a) as an interpretation for (28):

(28)   a. $\exists e \in {}^*\text{EAT}: \exists x \in {}^*\text{BOY}: |x| = 3 \wedge \sqcup (\{\downarrow(d): d \in \text{AT}({}^*\text{Ag}(e)\}) = x \wedge$
$\exists y \in \text{BREAD}: |y| = 15 \wedge \sqcup (\{g(d): d \in \text{AT}({}^*\text{Th}(e)\}) = g(\uparrow(y))$

Note that, unlike in the plural case, a mass partition of an atom does not necessarily reduce to thematic predication to that atom: The plural partition of (29) reduces to (29a); the mass partition is (29b):

(29)   A boy ate a bread.
(29)   a. $\exists e \in \text{EAT}: \exists a \in \text{BOY}: \exists b \in \text{BREAD}: \text{Ag}(e) = a \wedge \text{Th}(e) = b$
(29)   b. $\exists e \in {}^*\text{EAT}: \exists a \in \text{BOY}: {}^*\text{Ag}(e) = a \wedge$
$\exists b \in \text{BREAD}: \sqcup (\{g(d): d \in \text{AT}({}^*\text{Th}(e)\}) = g(b)$

(29b) says: there is a sum of events of eating chunks of bread by some boy, all together making up a bread. We can think of (29b) as representing a subtle shift of meaning of *eat*, focusing on the actual process of eating.

Now, it seems that the logic of the argument in favor of theory IV – the reduction of readings and the notion of partitivity as the basis of the theory of plurality – leads to the conclusion that, given the obvious similarities between these two forms of partitivity, the theory cannot stop at plural partitivity, but has to define a notion of cover role that generalizes over these two. This means that the basic representation of sentences will become once more weaker. And it is not clear that the process will stop here. Other semantically relevant part-of relations have been proposed as related to the domain of individuals (like the domain of stages of individuals, see Carlson (1977b), Hinrichs (1985), Krifka (1990a), Moore (1993)), and there is no reason to expect that we cannot partition individuals along those other part-of dimensions as well. For each of these cases the basic representation of the verbs would have to be weakened. My feeling is that this makes the basic representations exceedingly weak, in my view too weak.

Theory III fits in the following more general semantic picture. I assume that we have basic domains of atoms: individuals and events. The theory of plurality associates with these domains of atoms part-of structures of sums. Just as the domains of plurality (sums) are associated with the basic domains of atomic entities (individuals and events), so are other semantic domains that form part-of structures associated with these atomic domains: the mass domain (Link (1983), Landman (1991)), aspectual domains like the domain of processes and their stages (Bach (1986), Landman (1992)), the domain of states and their parts, presumably domains of stages of individuals (or eventual individuals, see Moore (1993)), and probably others. I assume that these partially ordered domains are connected to the domain of atoms through shifting operators. The most important of these is **promotion**: partially ordered entities can be promoted to individuals (atoms): all partially ordered entities can be shifted to entities that are no longer fully determined by the relations to their parts, and in this way be treated as individuals in their own right. This brings them into the domain of atoms, and there they form input to the theory of plurality. For entities in the plural domain (sums), this is what group formation does. I argue in Landman (1991) for packaging as an operator shifting mass-entities into count atoms. Moore (1993) argues for a similar shift from stages to individual atoms. I would argue that quantified states (as in *I was in Amsterdam three times last year*) involve a similar shift. On this perspective, it is natural to see partitivity as a shift operation as well: an operation breaking up atoms, shifting an atom to a sum of constituting atoms, where constitution is defined in a related partially ordered domain. I regard partitivity shifts as shifts of meaning of the verbs. The shift from a plural role of the verb to a cover relation can be seen as a shift in perspective of the verb: from the perspective of predication to entities just as entities, to a perspective of predication to entities as made up from parts of a particular kind. For some part-of relations such a shift can be readily available (like from groups to sums of subgroups), for others, this may be much more restricted. The theory of collectivity, plurality and scope I have developed in this paper assigns to a sentence like (24) four scopeless readings and four scoped readings, all of which are plausible. These readings I regard as the primary readings. Other readings, like partitive readings, can be derived in context through optional shifting of the meaning of the verb.

ACKNOWLEDGEMENTS

Most of the research for this paper was done while I was a Lady Davis Fellow in the English Department at the Hebrew University of Jerusalem in 1992 and I gratefully acknowledge the financial support of the Lady Davis Fellowship Fund. The material in this paper was presented in lectures at the Hebrew University in 1992, in lectures at Cornell University in 1993, in colloquiums at Cornell University and at the CUNY Graduate Center, and at the conference Events and Grammar held at Bar-Ilan University in November 1993. I thank the audiences of all these events for their stimulating discussion and comments.

IX Computational Semantics

17 Computational Semantics – Linguistics and Processing

JOHN NERBONNE

1 Introduction

Computational linguistics assumes from linguistics a characterization of grammar – the relation between meaning and form – in order to focus on processing, e.g. the algorithms needed to compute meaning given form (parsing), etc. Computationalists naturally construe grammar as a set of constraints on the meaning-form relation, which suggests constraint-resolution as a processing strategy. This paper illustrates the constraint-based view of semantics and semantic processing and attempts to draw implications for semantic theory. This introductory section explains background assumptions, particularly about the division of labor between linguistics and computational linguistics and also about constraint-based linguistic theory. Section 2 illustrates how constraint-based theory reconstrues the syntax-semantics interface, and Section 3 illustrates how constraint resolution provides a welcome freedom for processing. Section 4 offers some modest conclusions about this work.

The present paper is NOT an attempt to provide a picture of the state of the art in computational semantics, which includes some sensible attention to Artificial Intelligence, and also to the needs of attempting to deal with applications. The papers in Rosner and Johnson (1992) provide a good overview of trends in the fields (see also the review in Nerbonne 1994) while Nerbonne et al. (1993) sketches one approach to trying to accommodate applications even while making use of work in theoretical semantics. The present paper focuses on topics which lie closer to the core of interest in theoretical semantics – the syntax-semantics interface and the processing of semantic information.

1.1 What is computational semantics?

There is a natural division of THEORETICAL labor between the disciplines of linguistics and computational linguistics, namely that linguistics is responsible for the description of language and computational linguistics for the algorithms and architectures needed to compute with these. On this view the theoretical fields are related by their common focus on language, and moreover, computational linguistics is dependent on linguistics for the characterization of the relations it computes. Kaplan (1987) articulates this view further, and it is popular among computationalists.

Each of the fields has its more empirical and more theoretical aspects – the distinction at hand is orthogonal. Linguistics has its descriptive and theoretical perspectives, and so does computational linguistics. Computationalists DESCRIBE concrete algorithms and architectures (and report on their relative successes), but they also analyze these theoretically – in terms of their decidability, time/space complexity, the data structures they require, and, in the case of parallel algorithms, the communication protocols needed.

The division of theoretical labor suggested here is sometimes obscured by the many other purposes which computers serve in linguistic research, e.g. as vehicles for projects in applied linguistics (natural language interfaces, information retrieval, computer-assisted language learning, etc.); as visualization tools; as laboratories for linguistic experiments; as channels to immense data reserves in the form of corpora; as repositories for data organization, storage, and retrieval; etc. But clearly the use of computers cuts across the usual divisions of theory/application, theory/experiment and theory/data.

1.2   Feature-based theories

The extensive use of features and various concepts of feature matching gave rise in the eighties to "feature-based grammars" and eventually "feature logics" (Bresnan 1982, Gazdar et al. 1985, Carpenter 1992). Although these were initially developed by linguists, mathematical work on feature-based formalisms was also taken up by computational linguistics. The present paper is too limited in scope to provide an introduction to all this work; Shieber (1986) is the fundamental introduction and may be studied accompanied by PATR-II (Shieber et al. 1983), an implementation of the basic mechanisms. The uses we make of the work should be clear from the informal illustrations. The main aspects of feature grammars we wish to exploit here is their ability to encode PARTIAL INFORMATION, including information specified variably. We turn to this below after providing some illustration of the use of feature description languages in semantics.

1.3   A simple illustration

There are several alternative means of specifying the constraints associated with a grammar (cf. Bresnan (1982), Gazdar et al. (1985), Carpenter (1992)). The simplest formalism, PATR-II (Shieber 1986), sees linguistic objects as trees with feature-value decorations. We might have used this simplest theory to emphasize that no parochial assumptions bear on the points below, but for the sake of conciseness, we use an attribute-value representation. The relation to PATR-II is illustrated in a first version of a grammar, to which we now turn.

The fundamental idea is simply to use feature structures to represent semantics. If one wishes to compute the semantics of a sentence such as *Sam runs*, one first defines a primitive grammar which admits this. In PATR-II this can take the following form:

```
; ; Lexicon (cont.)
; ; = = = = =
```

Word Sam: ⟨cat⟩ = NP   Word runs: ⟨cat⟩ = VP
         ⟨agr⟩ = sg   ⟨agr⟩ = sg
         ⟨sem⟩ = m.   ⟨sem pred⟩ = run
                                      ⟨sem arg⟩ = ⟨subj sem⟩.

```
; ; Grammar Rule
; ; = = = = = = = = =
```

Rule {Sentence}

S → NP VP   ⟨NP agr⟩ = ⟨VP agr⟩
            ⟨sem⟩ = ⟨VP sem⟩
            ⟨NP sem⟩ = ⟨VP subj sem⟩.

The context-free notation in this example grammar can be read in the usual way, while the equations constrain properties of the grammatical objects. For example, the first equation associated with *Sam* specifies that its category is NP, while the first equation associated with the rule specifies that the agreement of NP and VP must coincide. Note that equations specifying syntactic as opposed to semantic properties have no special status. Accordingly, various strategies about the optimal order in which to process constraints are possible.

The feature SEMANTICS (sem) is included in this example in order to show how the mechanism can be used to encode semantics. The semantics feature is lexically provided for in the case of *Sam* and *runs*, and is specified for the example sentence on their basis. As primitive as this example is, it illustrates two techniques crucial to using features-based systems to specify semantics: first, specifications may be complex, as the lexical semantics for *runs* (involving ⟨**sem pred**⟩ and ⟨**sem arg**⟩) illustrates. Second, variables may be employed especially to specify the semantics of complex expressions. Thus the semantics of sentences is specified via a variable (required to be equal to the VP semantics). Figure 17.1 illustrates this employing a more popular representation.

Syntax/Semantics interfaces using feature-based formalisms may be found in Shieber (1986), Pollard and Sag (1987), Fenstad et al. (1987), and Moore (1989). The motivation for these early attempts was certainly the success feature-based descriptions enjoyed in syntax. Treating semantics in the same way meant that syntactic and semantic processing (and indeed all other feature-

Figure 17.1 A sketch of the semantic derivation of *Sam runs*, **run′**(*s*) as this would proceed using unification. Unification applies to syntactic and semantic representations alike, eliminating the need to compute these in distinct processes, and unification is employed to bind variables to argument positions, eliminating the need for (a great deal of) β-reduction as used in schemes derived from Montague and the lambda calculus. The reader may verify that the matrices of feature-value specifications are equivalent to those in the PATR-II grammar in the text, but the representation of shared structure via the boxed numbers allows grammars to be more concise.

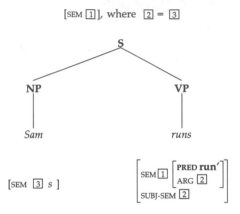

based processing) can be as tightly coupled as one wishes – indeed, there needn't be any fundamental distinction between them at all. In feature-based formalisms, the structure shared among syntactic and semantic values constitutes the syntax/semantics interface.

Our earlier papers have explored several advantages of the constraint-based view of the syntax/semantics relation over standard views, including (i) the opportunity to incorporate nonsyntactic constraints on semantics, such as those arising from phonology or context (Nerbonne 1992a); (ii) the opportunity to formulate principles which generalize over syntax and semantics, such as those found in HEAD-DRIVEN PHRASE STRUCTURE GRAMMAR (Pollard and Sag (1987), Nerbonne (1992a)). Halvorsen (1988), Nerbonne (1992a) elaborate on the virtue of understanding feature-based semantics as specifying constraints on logical forms, not model structures. The virtues of viewing semantic processing as manipulation of logical form descriptions includes not only a characterization of semantic ambiguity, which in turn provides a framework in which to describe disambiguation, but also the opportunity to underspecify meanings in a way difficult to reconcile with other views. The latter point is illustrated with an application to the notorious scope ambiguity problem.

1.4   *The constraint-based view*

Montague's famous characterization of the relation between syntax and semantics as a homomorphism naturally gives way here to a CONSTRAINT-BASED view. The constraint-based view was originally motivated by the close harmony it provides with syntax, which is universally processed in a constraint-based fashion. Employing the same processing discipline in syntax and semantics allows that their processing (and indeed other processing) can be as tightly coupled as one wishes – indeed, there needn't be any fundamental distinction between them at all.

In this paper we shall focus on two consequences of the constraint-based view – one linguistic, one computational. Given our own interests it will not be surprising that the lion's share of attention is paid to the computational point. We discuss a linguistic consequence of the constraint-based view in order to give some of the flavor of the linguist-computationalist dialectic.

Given a constraint-based view, it is natural to formulate hypotheses about syntax/semantics interfaces as manipulations of *constraints* rather than as functions on the *semantic objects* directly. This leads immediately to a relaxing of the compositionality requirement, i.e. the requirement that the meanings of phrases be the values of functions defined on the constituents' meanings. We illustrate this linguistic point briefly with an eye toward illuminating the computational perspective on linguistic theory.

The computational point is addressed at more length. In order to view semantics as a homomorphic mapping from syntax, Montague needed an artificially "disambiguated syntax" – the only plausible candidate to serve as the basis for a *function* from syntax to semantics: $f: DS \mapsto S$. DS, the level of disambiguated syntax, was normally seen as a minor technical inconvenience in the Montague framework. After all, one may always eliminate the apparent unnaturalness by viewing the "real relation" as the image of the disambiguated mapping under a suitable notion of syntactic equivalence (perhaps string identity). $R: sR\sigma \leftrightarrow \exists s'$ **disambig** $(s', s) \wedge f(s') = \sigma$. It has always been clear that syntax/semantics constraints may not uniquely determine a semantics. Instead, the constraints UNDERSPECIFY the semantics (in general). We interpret this technically in the following way: the syntax/semantics interface is a relation between syntactic structures (decorated trees) and formulas in a meaning representation language. The relation is underspecified if a single syntactic structure is interpreted as two or more formulas (which are moreover not merely alphabetic variants). Of course the formulas may normally have a good deal in common. We then ignore the function f above and attempt to specify R directly.

This wider view of the syntax/semantics interface has a liberating effect: it becomes quite natural to exploit the set of constraints associated with any stretch of syntactic material – even if that material does not form a constituent. We shall exploit this property in order to illustrate how constraint-based semantics allows a particularly simple approach to the problem of computing semantics incrementally. In this case the partial constraints may combine to restrict syntactic processing hypotheses significantly. The advantage that our approach has over others here lies in the fewer assumptions we make about syntactic structure.

There is finally a deeper perspective on our eschewing compositionality. Our motivation for exploring constraint-based formulations of grammar is the freedom this allows in processing. Concretely, this means that we wish to experiment with the order in which information is combined, which translates mathematically into the requirement that we base our semantic specifications on information-combining operations which are COMMUTATIVE – which composition most clearly is not: $f \circ g \neq g \circ f$. This also explains the preference for UNIFICATION as an information-combining operation in constraint-based theories, but, in fact, it is only one of several choices.

2   Noncompositional Constraints

In this section we illustrate the linguistic benefits of focusing on constraints. Into the primitive grammar above we successively introduce lexical ambiguity, phrasal ambiguity, and noncompositional constraints on interpretation.

The constraint-based view has a RELATIONAL take on ambiguity that is fundamentally different from that of the homomorphic view. Consider further the example in Figure 17.1 by way of illustration. The verb *runs* is, like most natural language words, highly ambiguous. It can mean 'to go quickly by foot' *She's running in the Marathon*, but also 'to function' *The printer's not running*, 'to flow' *Your mascara is running*, 'to flee' *At the first sign of danger, they ran*, etc. (any large dictionary will list several more). Now, if we require a homomorphic relation between syntax and semantics, then we must define a mapping with this range. Since the mapping must be functional, we can only do this by assuming the ambiguity in the syntax, and then carrying it forward into the semantics. The constraint-based view suggests postulating a nonfunctional relation between syntax and semantics. There is then a single syntactic item corresponding to *run*, which is constrained to mean one of the things in its dictionary entry. This may be accomplished by changing the specification for *runs*'s semantics (we continue here and throughout with the notation of Figure 17.1):

$$\begin{bmatrix} \text{HEAD|CAT} & \text{VP} \\ \text{SEM|PRED} & \{\textbf{go-fast', function',flow', flee',} \dots \} \end{bmatrix}$$

This is a disjunctive specification with the content: the semantic predicate is exactly one of the values **go-fast',** . . . .[1] It is quite simple, but it already breaks the compositional mold: a single syntactic entity is mapped to several semantic entities. Of course, it is a simple matter to "carry" the ambiguity back into the syntax, and so preserve compositionality, but there is no need to.[2] In fact on reflection it seems strained to postulate various lexical items for *run* – all sharing the same syntactic and morphological properties. The approach taken here can postulate a single lexical item with a variety of semantics interpretations.[3]

Before continuing to remark on issues of "compositionality", we need to clarify the sense in which we use this term. In linguistic semantics the term has normally been taken to require that the meaning of a phrase be the value of a function defined on the meanings of its subconstituents. Taken this way, compositionality is a hypothesis about the semantics of natural language – i.e. the hypothesis that the correct semantics for a natural language is such that, for any construction (grammar) rule, there is a function which takes the meanings of its constituents as arguments, and yields the meaning of the composed phrase as value. Now, Zadrozny (1994) has shown that, if any semantic mapping exists, then it has a compositional reformulation, which shows the hypothesis to be unfalsifiable. Zadrozny adds that the functions in question are not guaranteed to be computable or even finitely specifiable, and that there may well be nonvacuous hypotheses about compositionality if limited to particular classes of functions, but this is not our concern here. The compositionality hypothesis has such widespread acceptance that in fact grammatical descriptions and description schemes normally simply assume it – and implicitly or explicitly require it. Our point is just that stepping back from this common assumption allows one to assume a different perspective on some problems of grammatical description and processing.

A relational treatment of lexical ambiguity is a harmless deviation from compositionality introduced here for the sake of suggesting that the semantic community has come to assume compositionality rather too automatically. A more interesting variation occurs when we begin treating semantics by manipulating constraints rather than writing functions. In compositional treatments the function yielding the semantics of a mother node views the semantics of daughter constituents as black boxes – as units whose internal make-up is ultimately irrelevant. We automatically shed such blinkers when we manipulate constraints.

Consider the case of prepositional phrases used on the one hand as free adjuncts and on the other as optionally subcategorized arguments. These are quite common, as a few examples easily suggest:

(1)   a. The mill ran on Wednesday
      a'. The mill ran on methane
      b. Sam waited on Wednesday/Mary
      c. Sam waited for hours/Mary
      d. Sam decided on Wednesday (ambig., cf. on Mary)
      e. Sam decided about Wednesday/Mary
      f. Sam voted for Mary (ambig.)
      g. Sam invested in May/Texaco
      h. Sam went on about Christmas (ambig.)

Clearly some strings (e.g. (1d)) are ambiguous. In the adjunct reading, Wednesday was the time Sam's decision was made; in the argument reading it was (part of) the decision itself (in this case the sentence might be taken to mean that Sam decided on Wednesday as the day for a meeting, for example, but the decision might have been made on another day). The analytic question is not vexing: the ambiguity correlates with the argument/adjunct distinction.

But now consider just the prepositional phrase *on Wednesday* in isolation: what meaning should it be assigned in a compositional treatment? In case it appears as a temporal adjunct, it expresses a relation between an event and a time, but in case it's a subcategorized-for argument (as it might also be interpreted in (1d)), it seems merely to denote the day Wednesday. Thus the meaning of the PP phrase seems to depend, not just on the meanings of its parts, but rather on its syntactic context – the fact that it occurs in construction with a particular verb. The difference in the two kinds of PPs is particularly striking in some cases, e.g. (1c), where the subcategorized phrase is interpreted merely as standing in a particular relation to the rest of the arguments, while the adjunct is interpreted as scoping over the relation denoted by the verb (this is a standard analysis for duratives – cf. e.g. Dowty 1979).

In the adjunct (frame adverbial) reading, the preposition makes an independent contribution to semantics, at the very least distinct from other adpositions which can head free adjuncts such as *with, on, in spite of, notwithstanding* etc., or the other temporal or locative prepositions such as *before* or *after*. In the argument (co-specifying) case the preposition is simply required, so that no independent contribution to semantics is discernible (which is not to deny that the choice of preposition is "partially motivated", i.e. semantically rather better suited to function here than most alternatives). I believe that semanticists are agreed that very different treatments of these phrases are required. Although both types of phrase are optional, the adjuncts may occur multiply in a single clause, which requires recursive structure in representation. (Benefactives are admittedly strained if iterated, so perhaps they ought to be classed with optional arguments.) Arguments, on the other hand, occur once or not at all. It is most straightforward to simply reserve a position for them in a relation.[4]

Just as in the case of lexical ambiguity, one can avoid noncompositional treatments in this phrasal case by postulating ambiguity – beginning with the preposition *on*, which can be translated as expressing a relation in the adjunct case, and as vacuous (an identity function) in the argument case. The ambiguity percolates naturally to the PP. Technically, there is nothing amiss with such a treatment, but it seems counterintuitive – in particular, in locating the ambiguity in the preposition, rather than the combination of verb plus prepositional phrase.

We now sketch an alternative; continuing to focus discussion on (1d), because its representation is logically simple. For the sake of concreteness, let's suggest representations: the meaning of the optional argument as part of the relation denoted by *decide*: **decide-on**$'(e,s,w)$ holds iff e is an event of Sam deciding in Wednesday's favor. We'll then represent the temporal adjunct *on Wednesday* as a relation between the event denoted by the verb and Wednesday: $\sqsubseteq_t(e,w)$, i.e. a relation which holds just in case the event is temporally contained within Wednesday. More generally, any theme argument may be specified to stand in the containment relation with respect to the object of the preposition *on*, but we focus on the example (1d).

This is the puzzle for compositional treatments: how can the semantics of the PP construction be a function yielding m (from **on'** and m) (*Sam decided on Mary*), but **on'**(e,w) (from **on'** and w) (*Sam decided on Wednesday*)? One might hypothesize a type sensitivity (distinguishing the PERSON m from the TIME w), but the ambiguous examples (e.g. (1d,f,h)) indicate that this does not generalize – more is at stake than polymorphic functions. We seem ultimately forced to postulate ambiguity in the semantics of *on* (and the phrases headed by it), which seems counterintuitive.

Proceeding from a constraint-based perspective, we have a slightly different response available – *viz.* that there is a single set of constraints which entail that the semantics of the PP is *always* **on'**$(e,$**NP'**$)$, but that the constraints specifying the semantics of the VP sometimes use this entirely, and sometimes use only the semantics of the NP object – a clearly noncompositional step (see Davis (1995) for a more compositional suggestion in a constraint-based vein). Below, we extend the grammar presented in Section 1.

Before presenting the extended grammar, it is worth noting two things about this sort of effort. First, by virtue of its being concrete (and implemented), the example grammar is specific about some irrelevant points. This can be distracting, but it has the advantage of being more reliable and perhaps more easily understandable (for being concrete). Second, the example is formulated in an "HPSG" style (à la Pollard and Sag 1987, Pollard and Sag 1994), but this is strictly inessential to the points being made. The same demonstration could be given in LFG, Word Grammar, Definite Clause Grammar, or a logical formulation of GB or minimalism (e.g., that of Stabler 1992). HPSG is used here because I use it elsewhere, and its attribute-value "boxes" may be easier to read.

We first need to encode the new lexical items. In a larger fragment, most of the specifications included here would be "inherited" from more abstract word class specifications (see Flickinger and Nerbonne (1992) for an extended presentation).

$$
on \quad
\begin{bmatrix}
\text{HEAD|CAT } p \\
\text{SUBCAT } \left\langle \begin{bmatrix} \text{HEAD|CAT } np \\ \text{SEM } \boxed{2} \end{bmatrix} \right\rangle \\
\text{SEM } \begin{bmatrix} \text{PRED } \sqsubseteq_t \\ \text{THEME } \boxed{1} \\ \text{GOAL } \boxed{2} \end{bmatrix}
\end{bmatrix}
$$

$$
decided \quad
\begin{bmatrix}
\text{HEAD|CAT } v \\
\text{SUBCAT } \left\langle \begin{bmatrix} \text{HEAD|CAT } \textit{PP-on} \\ \text{SEM } [\text{GOAL } \boxed{2} \ ] \end{bmatrix} \right\rangle \\
\text{SUBJ|SEM } \boxed{1} \\
\text{SEM } \begin{bmatrix} \text{PRED } \textbf{decide-on'} \\ \text{EVENT } \boxed{3} \\ \text{SOURCE } \boxed{1} \\ \text{THEME } \boxed{2} \end{bmatrix}
\end{bmatrix}
$$

Like all our specifications, these are partial. (We shall have occasion to flesh out the prepositional specifications directly.) In comparison with the earlier example, we have first complicated the verb semantics by adding the event argument (to allow a simple treatment of the time adverbial). Second, we make use of a SUBCATEGORIZATION feature to specify the complements which these words select. Its value is enclosed in angle brackets because it is a list (of potentially several items). The specification of the prepositional phrase selected by *decide* is further enclosed by parentheses to indicate that it is optional, as is standard. Finally, we assume that *Mary* is entered in the lexicon as *Sam* is.

A sketch of a (partial) analysis tree is provided in Figure 17.2. What is noncompositional here is the specification of the THEME semantics of *decide* as covarying NOT with the semantics of the selected complement, but rather with the semantics of its complement's complement. This is a natural non-compositional specification in the formalism here. The (single) rule licensing the different head-complement combinations in the two interior nodes has not been provided, but it is just the head-complement schema of HPSG (Pollard and Sag 1994, p.38), which is subject to the subcategorization principle (*ibid.*, p.34), requiring that specifications imposed by the head must unify with those on complement daughters. The example likewise assumes (uncontroversially) that semantic specifications follow head lines (in head-complement structures).

In order to contrast the adjunct reading to this we need to sketch a treatment of adjuncts. We assume, fairly standardly, that adjuncts select the heads they combine with, rather than *vice versa*, and we encode selection in the feature MOD.

Like subcategorization information, this will unify with the information associated with structures admitted by the rule. The earlier lexical entry for the preposition *on* suppressed this information, which we therefore now supplement:

$$
on \quad \begin{bmatrix} \text{HEAD} \begin{bmatrix} \text{CAT } p \\ \text{MOD} \left[\text{SEM } \boxed{4} \; [\text{EVENT } \boxed{1} \;] \right] \end{bmatrix} \\ \text{SUBCAT} \left\langle \begin{bmatrix} \text{HEAD|CAT } np \\ \text{SEM } \boxed{2} \end{bmatrix} \right\rangle \\ \text{SUBJ|SEM } \boxed{1} \\ \text{SEM} \begin{bmatrix} \text{PRED } \sqsubseteq_t \\ \text{THEME } \boxed{1} \\ \text{GOAL } \boxed{2} \end{bmatrix} \end{bmatrix}
$$

Note that the argument position bound to the variable '$\boxed{1}$' is now further specified as the EVENT (time) of the object modified. This will eventually account for the semantic effect of the frame adverbial – that of restricting the time at which the event is said to take place.

Figure 17.2 A sketch of the semantics of the VP *decide on Mary*, as it is derived from noncompositional specifications. The semantics of the verb *decide* is specified to bind its theme role to the semantics of the object (goal) of the preposition – without intermediate reference to the semantics of the prepositional phrase it stands in construction with.

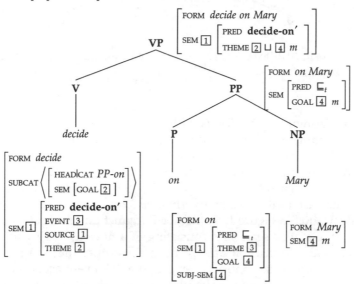

The received view of the semantic contribution of adjuncts is that they fall into two classes – one class, typified by conditional clauses, serves as an OPERATOR scoping over the head it is in construction with, and a second class, typified by locative and most temporal adverbials, serves as a RESTRICTOR of some argument position within the head. Kasper (1994) provides an elegant means of reducing the second class to the first, so that the apparent grammatical distinction may be reduced to a purely lexical one. Kasper's specifications are too sophisticated to be introduced and explained here in full (but see note). We shall assume the effect of his specifications: the semantics of a head-adjunct construction with a restrictor adjunct will be assumed from the head, and the adjunct semantics will serve to restrict some argument with the head semantics.[5] In order to implement Kasper's ideas on restrictive adjunction, we require a minor complication of the grammar: the feature SEMANTICS (abbreviated 'SEM' above), which has heretofore specified the semantic translations of words and phrases, will now be divided into NUCLEUS (abbr. NUCL), the core around which the full-fledged semantics is built, and RESTRICTIONS (abbr. RSTR), which describe constraints the arguments in the nucleus are subject to. The few examples treated thus far may all be construed as manipulating only the nucleus part of the semantics.

The specifications foresee the following schema for this restricting class of adjuncts:

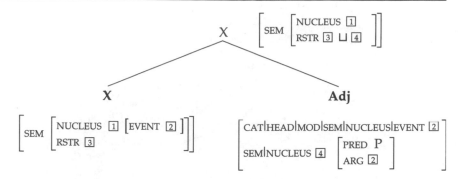

The schema distinguishes a nucleus within the semantics from a set of restrictions on its arguments. Within a head-adjunct phrase (involving the class of adjuncts under discussion), the head determines the semantic nucleus of the phrase and contributes whatever restrictions it has accumulated, while the adjunct adds its own restriction. Figure 17.3 illustrates how this scheme is applied to the case of the frame adverbial *on Wednesday*.

In the illustration in Figure 17.3, the head-adjunct phrase *decided on Wednesday* would have a head semantics consisting of a nucleus specifying an event of deciding, and a restriction arising from tense that the event be past. It would have an adjunct semantics specifying that the event occur on (a contextually determined) Wednesday. The phrasal semantics has the same nucleus as the head and contains all the daughters' restrictions.

The purpose of this section has been the illustration of the advantage of the added freedom which constraint-based semantics allows as compared to strictly compositional treatments of syntax-semantics interaction. For further applications of constraint-based semantics, the reader is referred to the references in this section, but also to Dalrymple et al. (1991), which contains an interesting treatment of ellipsis which makes essential use of constraint-based description.

3   "Noncompositional" Processing

In this section we interpret "selectional restrictions" semantically, exploiting the fact that they can be used to reduce the number of parses available.[6] Once one takes this step, it is natural to try to take advantage of such information early in processing – maximizing the efficiency benefits, and plausibly modeling human language users more faithfully in this respect as well. Taken to its extreme, this means that semantic processing must allow information flow along noncompositional lines. This does NOT reject the grammatical thesis that syntax-semantics dependence is ultimately compositional, only that processing is organized along the same lines.

COMPOSITIONALITY concerns the relation between syntax and semantics – i.e.

Figure 17.3 A sketch of the semantics of the VP *decide on Wednesday*, as it is derived from (incidentally) compositional specifications. The semantics of the verb *decide* includes a set of restrictions to which the adjunct semantics is added.

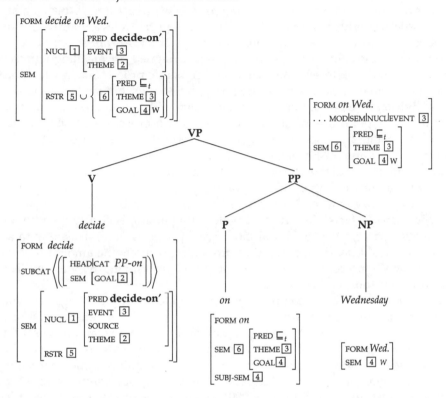

(static) linguistic structure, not processing. Nonetheless, the compositional view often extends to a natural and popular procedural interpretation, that of bottom-up processing. This is a natural interpretation because compositional semantics specifies the semantics of phrases via functions on the semantics of their daughters. It is natural to evaluate arguments before attempting to apply functions to them (although partial and so-called "lazy" evaluation schemes certainly exist) (see, e.g. Kahn (1987)). We will use the term BOTTOM-UP EVALUATION for semantic processing which proceeds bottom-up in the analysis tree, evaluating arguments and then functions applied to them along the lines suggested by compositional grammatical theory. We will therefore try to reserve the term COMPOSITIONAL for theses about grammatical structure (or the formulation of hypotheses about this) – the title of the present section notwithstanding. But the general subject will be processing, so if a bit of metonymy creeps into the discussion, it should not be overly distracting. To forestall misunderstanding, let us reiterate immediately our position that processing considerations may not be conflated with linguistic ones. The fact that purely bottom-up processing is less than optimal is completely consistent with there being a compositional syntax-semantics interface.

For the purposes of the present section, we may view semantic interpretation as a form of PARSING, i.e. computing the (set of) structure(s) which a grammar associates with a string. In syntactic parsing the relevant structures are syntax trees, while in semantic processing the structures are semantic representations – normally, expressions in a logic designed for meaning representation. It is possible to separate syntax and semantic processing, in which case one views semantic processing as inputting, not strings, but syntactic analyses. This division of labor is normal, practical, and – depending on assumptions about the temporal organization of the putative processes – possibly tenable from computational and psychological viewpoints as well. This section will not simply assume this, however. The ideas advanced here are independent of whether there are distinct processes for syntax and semantics.

Bottom-up processing is only one of many possibilities, not distinctly superior either by virtue of its technical properties or by its fidelity to the psycholinguistic facts.[7] In fact, pure bottom-up parsing is clearly poor both in efficiency and as a psychological model (see previous note). It is easy to see why this should be, since bottom-up processing restricts the amount of information which is accessible when forming and prioritizing hypotheses. Top-down information can be useful.

INCREMENTAL PROCESSING computes analyses while inputting strings one word at a time, in the order in which they're heard or read (the left-right order in text). It enjoys wide acceptance in psycholinguistic research, and it is useful in many applications, since it exploits information as quickly as it is available. The intuitive notion of "incremental processing" requires some sharpening: after all, almost all parsing algorithms – including bottom-up ones – read input from left to right. Schabes (1990) suggests that procedures be regarded as incremental when they obey the VALID PREFIX PROPERTY:

> If the input tokens $a_1 \ldots a_k$ have been read then it is guaranteed that there is a string of tokens $b_1 \ldots b_m$ (b_i may not be part of the input) such that the string $a_1 \ldots a_k b_1 \ldots b_m$ is a valid string of the language. (Schabes 1990, p.54)

That is, an incremental procedure must reject a string as soon as there is no valid continuation. This seems like a good definition; in particular, purely bottom-up and purely top-down parsing algorithms certainly do not count as incremental according to this definition, which is just as it should be.

We turn now to an illustration of how the computation of partial constraints on semantics can be useful in incremental evaluation. This should also further serve to clarify the distinction between incremental and nonincremental processing. For this purpose, we provide a brief feature-based treatment of selectional restrictions (see Nerbonne 1992b for further detail).

The word *chair* is ambiguous, possibly referring to a piece of furniture but also to the head of an organization, as in *the chair of the committee*. In a sentence such as *The chair decided on Mary*, we spontaneously understand only the reading of *chair* as human – or, at least as a mental agent.[8] It is trivial to write feature specifications which enforce the requirement that subjects of *decide* be things capable of mental agency. We simply introduce a feature, e.g. M-AGT and then require that subjects of *decide* be compatible with this feature:

$$\begin{bmatrix} \text{FORM } decide \\ \text{SEM}|\text{NUCL} \begin{bmatrix} \text{PRED } \textbf{decide-on}' \\ \text{SOURCE}|\text{M-AGT } + \end{bmatrix} \end{bmatrix}$$

Similarly, we shall wish to differentiate the readings of *chair* using this same feature:

$$\begin{bmatrix} \text{FORM } chair \\ \text{SEM}|\text{NUCL} \left\{ \begin{bmatrix} \text{PRED } \textbf{furn-for-sitting}' \\ \text{THEME}|\text{M-AGT } - \end{bmatrix}, \begin{bmatrix} \text{PRED } \textbf{org-head}' \\ \text{THEME}|\text{M-AGT } + \end{bmatrix} \right\} \end{bmatrix}$$

(We again employ set braces to denote a disjunction of potential readings, as in the first example in Section 2 above.) The SOURCE role of *decide* is thus incompatible with the THEME role of *chair* in the furniture reading – the two values do not unify and therefore cannot be identified. This is sufficient to guarantee that any attempt to use *chair* as the subject of *decide* will force the reading in which the chair is a potential mental agent. The other reading is simply unavailable given these specifications (see previous note for discussion).[9]

We are deliberately vague about the details of the grammatical specifications that necessitate the identification of the subject's features and those of the verb's subject specification, since these vary rather a lot depending on one's grammatical assumptions. For the sake of concreteness, we sketch how the identification would be effected in HPSG (Pollard and Sag 1994). In HPSG the subcategorization principle would ensure that the **VP** would assume the undischarged (subject) valence requirements of its lexical head **V**, and a grammatical rule (Schema 1) would allow the sentential node only where the **NP** could be identified with the **VP**'s subject specifications. The relation between the **NP** and its head **N** is analyzed variously, and surely not many researchers would simply identify the semantic specifications of the two (preferring perhaps to view the semantics of the **N** as a predicate, and that of the **NP** as a generalized quantifier). But that is not essential, only that the sortal information associated with the noun somehow continue on to the **NP**, and that this be required to unify with the verb's subject specifications. In the examples below we assume that such a requirement is enforced without providing the specifications on rules, etc., which would effect it.

The purpose of developing this (perhaps overly brief) treatment of selectional restrictions is to provide an example to illustrate the consequences of some

Figure 17.4 In (pure) bottom-up processing, no parent node is processed until all of its daughters are. The coindexing noted as ' 1 ' is compatible only with the second, lower construal of the word *chair*. In bottom-up processing the alternative, incompatible reading cannot be noted (and rejected) until the sentence level (given standard assumptions about constituent structure). The traversal indicated above by the numerical node annotations is the optimally incremental bottom-up traversal of the example sentence *The chair decided on Mary*. Since it is effectively the sentence node at which subject-verb agreement is enforced, including agreement of semantic selectional restrictions, there is no way to reject the senseless reading until the entire sentence is processed. Given the strong preference for right-branching structures in grammar, purely bottom-up processing can have no account of incremental understanding.

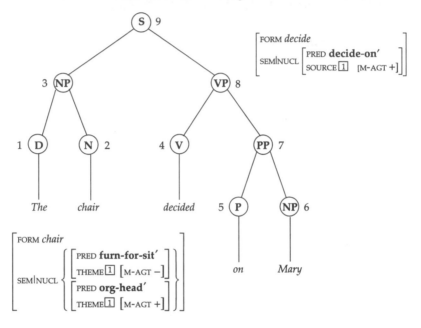

assumptions about semantic processing. The incompatibility of the furniture reading of *chair* with the mental agency required of subjects of *decide* must be enforced in any correct processing scheme – but in incremental schemes, it must be enforced at the point at which the word *decide* is encountered.

Figure 17.4 illustrates why purely bottom-up processing cannot be incremental (at least for standard grammars).

Since the meaning of a phrase depends on its daughters' meanings (compositionality), there cannot be a (final) computation of phrasal meaning before all the daughters' meanings have been processed. One could imagine an argument for bottom-up evaluation proceeding from linguistic compositionality in this way. But several escape routes open before this conclusion is reached. The two most prominent ones are (i) currying and (ii) using partial specifications. If one curries an *n*-place function, one expresses it as a one-place function whose values are (*n*-1)-place functions. Thus, even if the value of the function cannot be determined in general, there will be circumstances in which the

Figure 17.5 The flexible categorial grammar solution to incremental, bottom-up processing. Since no parent node is processed until all of its daughters are, the scheme indicated by the numerical traversal annotations is bottom-up. Since the grammar is left-associative, the processing can also be incremental. This solution is formally sound, but its linguistic assumptions are heterodox. It is safe to say that *no* evidence exists for most of the novel constituents posited on the left-associative view. If, on the other hand, the view is tenable, it indicates that constituent structure – the primary explanatory device in syntax – is relatively insignificant.

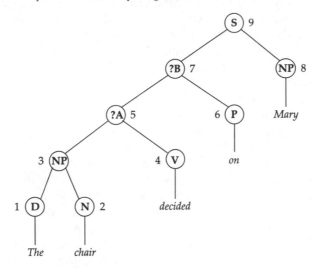

curried function can usefully be applied. In this paper we shall focus on the other possibility however, that of using the partial specifications which are the trademark of feature-based theories. Thus, even though we cannot derive a complete semantics for a sentence before processing the entire VP, we shall be able to derive some properties of the sentential semantics early. In particular, we will be able to exclude some hypotheses about subject meanings based only on the verb – without waiting for the VP meaning to be computed. (We could in a parallel way illustrate how some hypotheses about verb meaning may be excluded on the basis of subject meaning, but this would add little.) Thus the programmatic point of this section is that computation with partial descriptions of semantics – as is common in feature-based theories – provides a basis for explaining the possibility of incremental understanding.

Steedman (1987a and elsewhere) and Haddock (1988) have championed an approach to incremental interpretation which allows processing to be both incremental AND bottom-up. This approach has come to be known as FLEXIBLE CATEGORIAL GRAMMAR, (hence: flexible CG) and an illustration of its application to our example may be found in Figure 17.5.[10] The key to Steedman's solution lies in the wholesale abandonment of standard assumptions about constituent structure (see example), which Steedman takes to be rigorously left-branching in order to reconcile bottom-up and incremental processing. Since the syntax is completely left-branching, EVERY initial segment is a constituent. In fact, as

Steedman (1987a) argues, under the "strong competence hypothesis" of Kaplan and Bresnan (1982) – the assumption of parallelism between linguistic structure and processing – the left-branching structure would appear to be necessary.

The flexible CG analyses have attracted attention because of their application to difficult problems of the grammatical analysis of coordination, including gapping and right-node raising (Steedman 1990). Here they have had some success, especially compared to other frameworks. But several aspects of the overall position remain unconvincing. First, the "flexibility" promised by the approach cuts both ways – even if it seems appealing to posit alternative constituent structures for coordination (which motivated a great deal of the work in question), it seems difficult to accept the wholesale ambiguity in constituent structure which is the consequence of the flexibility. It is trivial to find sentences in which some initial segments would constitute ridiculous constituents (the node marked "?B" in Figure 17.5 is only suggestive – much less plausible examples are readily constructed). The postulation of such constituents is incompatible with most syntactic theory, which relies crucially on constituent structure to account for a great deal of syntax – e.g. word order, long-distance dependence, island constraints, restrictions on anaphoric relations ("binding theory"). For most syntacticians, constituent structure is the primary explanatory mechanism, so many syntactic explanations are lost if constituency is simply left-associative. Second, even within CG, the use of calculi flexible to this degree is controversial: Houtman (1994, pp.74–90) devotes most of a chapter to "Arguments against Flexibility" (focusing his attack, however, not on the combinatory grammars which Steedman advocates, but rather on Lambek-style CG). It is controversial not only because it fails to account for the coordination phenomena as generally as it was originally claimed to (Houtman 1994), but also because it leads to a counterintuitive collapse of categories in the analysis of adjuncts ("Dekker's paradox", discussed by Houtman, pp.85–89). Third, and perhaps less directly applicable to the point at hand, the flexibility in this approach is now overused. Joshi (1990) notes that "flexibility" is variously deployed, not only to enable incremental, bottom-up processing, but also to allow constituent structure to match intonational grouping, and to allow constituent structure to match coordination. These three requirements are certainly not simultaneously satisfiable. (This point is less directly applicable because it would be conceivable to focus only on the left-associative treatments, ignoring other applications of flexibility. But this would rob flexible CG of its most impressive success, in the analysis of coordination.)

Shieber and Johnson (1993) contains a rather different view of the work on incremental understanding in flexible CG, objecting that its conclusions follow only under the implicit assumption of synchronous computation of semantics. They claim that incremental interpretation follows not from grammatical structure (the flexible CG position), nor even from the control structure of particular algorithms (the position to be illustrated below), but rather from the asynchronous nature of understanding. While we find this alternative interesting psychologically, we take it that an algorithmic solution remains of interest, at least technically. We turn to this now.

It seems best not to explain incremental understanding on the basis of grammatical structure, but rather to ask how might incremental understanding be possible if grammatical structure is roughly as we know it (in fact, mostly right-branching). Given our construal of understanding as parallel to parsing, we have a rich choice of incremental processing algorithms. To illustrate how the constraint-based view of semantics processing enables incremental semantic evaluation, we need only choose one. A popular choice for incremental parsing is (predictive) LEFT-CORNER (hence: LC) parsing. It is popular because it makes use of both bottom-up (lexical) and also top-down (grammatical) information.

An LC parser may be viewed as a process which constantly attempts to extend the analysis of an initial segment ("left corner") of a string.[11] The LC parser begins with the assumption that the empty string has an analysis as the initial segment of **S** (the category to be found), and then reads words. After reading each word, it fills in as much of the analysis as is necessary to verify that there is a way of filling in the analysis tree from **S** to the segment, i.e. that the initial segment is possible in the language. The algorithm is easiest to understand as a mutual recursion between the following pair of routines:

```
proc parse (α:nonterminal-category);
    begin
            read next word W;
            CAT ← CAT(W);
            if CAT = α
                then SUCCESS
                else if ◊-lc(CAT,α)
                        then expand-lc(CAT,α)
                        else FAIL
                    endif
            endif
    end parse
proc expand-lc(CAT,goal)
    begin
            for-each rule β → CAT γ
                if ◊-lc(CAT,goal)
                    then parse(γ);
                        if end-of-input
                            then SUCCESS
                            else expand-lc(β,goal)
                        endif
                endif
            end-for-each
    end expand-lc
```

We omit the definition of the relation '◇-lc', which holds between a top category and a bottom category intuitively just in case there is path from the top to the bottom along the leftmost categories in (the right-hand) sides of grammar rules. Thus, in a grammar with **S → NP VP.**, **NP → Det N**, the relation would hold of the pair (**S,Det**), and trivially of the pairs (**S,NP**) and (**NP,Det**).

To appreciate the workings of the LC parser, let's fill out the grammar just mentioned by adding the usual **VP → V NP** rule, and the lexical items *the* (**Det**), *saw* (**V**), and *child* and *toy* (**N**). Then Table 17.1 traces the execution of the LC parser on this grammar on the input string *The child saw the toy*. We seek an **S**, and therefore invoke parse (**S**). The table below provides a trace of the execution:

Table 17.1

		parse			*expand-1c*		
step	*reader*	*α*	*word*	*CAT*	*CAT*	*goal*	*rule*
1	↑ *The child saw the toy*	**S**	*The*	**Det**			
2	*The* ↑ *child saw the toy*				**Det**	**S**	**NP → Det N**
3	*The* ↑ *child saw the toy*	**N**	*child*	**N**			
4	*The child* ↑ *saw the toy*				**NP**	**S**	**S → NP VP**
5	*The child* ↑ *saw the toy*	**VP**	*saw*	**V**			
6	*The child saw* ↑ *the toy*				**V**	**VP**	**VP → V NP**
7	*The child saw* ↑ *the toy*	**NP**	*the*	**Det**			
8	*The child saw the* ↑ *toy*				**Det**	**NP**	**NP → Det N**
9	*The child saw the* ↑ *toy*	**N**	*toy*	**N**			

The table fills in cells only where the procedure is active. Thus, at Step 1, values are supplied for the local variables in the parse routine, but not in the routine expand-lc, which has not been called. At Step 2, expand-lc is executing so its variables are filled in, and parse's variables are omitted.

The table provides snapshots of the execution of the routines. As **parse** is first called (with argument **S**), nothing has been read. We picture the sentence being processed as having a pointer indicating how much has been read. So initially, the pointer is before the first word:

> ↑ *The child saw the toy*

This is reflected in the table. Since parse reads the first word, the pointer is advanced before the following word is read. For this reason, the reader in the second row of the table shows the pointer after the first word. And in general, whenever parse executes, there is an advance of the pointer.

Once the word has been read (*The*), and its category determined (**Det**), parse notes that there is no match between the category determined and the goal α (bound to **S**). Therefore, expand-left-corner is called (line 2 of the table), with parameters CAT and goal bound to **Det** and **S**. expand-lc hypothesizes about rules with LC **Det** (CAT), and we show the result of hypothesizing with the rule **NP** → **Det N**. Since **Det** is a possible left-corner of **S**, parse is recursively called (line 3), now with the goal parameter bound to **N**. In this case, the category matches, and control is passed back to expand-lc, which calls itself, this time with arguments **NP** and **S**. Given this much explanation, the rest of the trace should be fairly straightforward to follow. The rule column of the expand-lc part of the table is interesting because it is there one can see how the structure for the initial segment is being built up as the parse progresses.

This procedure is indeed incremental in the relevant sense – if there is no possible continuation of an initial segment, processing will fail immediately, without continuing. This can be verified by attempting to execute the procedures on such input, for example, the string *The child saw* . . . This would proceed exactly as the execution in the table, but would fail at step 3 – on determining that **Det** is not a possible left corner of **N**.[12]

Figure 17.6 shows an application of a left-corner traversal to the sentence used as an example of the utility of incremental processing. To make the illustration water-tight, the LC routines above should be modified to process not only the category information on nodes, but also the feature decorations associated with them. It is essential that these too be checked as the parse progresses. If this is done, then the value of the subject's feature [SEM|NUCL|THEME|M-AGT ±] will be constrained to be identical to the verb's subject specification, which in turn will be lexically constrained to be + in the case of *decide*, just as in Figure 17.4. This filters out the furniture sense of *chair* from further consideration.

As long as the feature specifications associated with the rules are being checked as the rules are, then the objectionable analysis must be detected at the time the verb is read (more exactly, once its feature specifications are processed).

4 Conclusion

While linguistics characterizes grammar – the relation between meaning and form – computational linguistics focuses on processing, e.g. the algorithms and data structures needed to compute meaning given form (parsing), or form given meaning (generation), etc. Of course work in one field may have ramifications in the other.

Given this division of labor, it is natural to view grammar as a set of constraints on the meaning–form relation, whose computation is to be considered independently. The present paper focuses on consequences of this view for the

Figure 17.6 In left-corner processing, a parse is sought by continually seeking to extend the analysis of an initial segment of the string to be parsed (prefix). This leads to a complex traversal, allowing information to flow both bottom-up and top-down (see text for details). The processing is incremental in Schabes's sense, since impossible prefixes must be recognized as such. The traversal indicated below by the numerical node annotations is the record of the first visits to the node by the parsing traversal. Since subject properties are available for computation when the verb is visited, subject-verb agreement can be enforced at the earliest possible moment, including agreement of semantic selectional restrictions. Thus senseless readings may be rejected even before the entire sentence is processed. Given the strong preference for right-branching structures in grammar, (somewhat) elaborate processing models seem necessary.

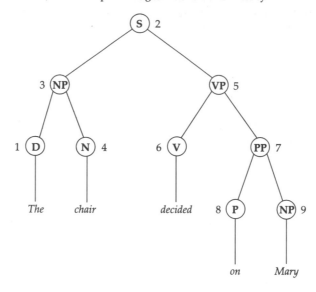

syntax–semantics interface and the processing of semantic information. The interface topic is, properly speaking, linguistic, and was developed to illustrate the dialectic between grammar and processing which computational linguistics encourages. The processing topic is computational, and the present contribution advocates an approach which minimizes linguistic assumptions. In particular, it is argued that we need not assume that grammar is left-associative in order to account for incremental understanding. This can arise using standard processing techniques, as long as semantic processing consists of collecting and resolving constraints on semantic representation.

NOTES

* I had hoped to coauthor this with Per-Kristian Halvorsen of Xerox PARC, but we both became too busy for effective collaboration. He certainly influenced my ideas on these matters, as did the audience at the 1990 Annual Meeting of the Associa-

tion for Computational Linguistics, where he and I presented related material as a tutorial. Thanks too to Ron Klopstra, who implemented a parser illustrating the ideas in Section 3, as part of his 1993 Groningen Master's Thesis.

1   In fact, this involves a mild (and well-studied) extension of the PATR-II formalism to allow disjunction. Kasper and Rounds (1986), Carpenter (1992) have details.

2   More interesting (but also more difficult to illustrate briefly) are attempts to provide constraint-based theories of nonlexical ambiguity. Nerbonne (1993) provides the foundation for a constraint-based treatment of quantifier scope ambiguity, but it would take us too far afield to present it here.

3   Of course, this is not the same as a single disjunctive semantics, either. See Nerbonne (1992a) for discussion.

4   Of course this means that provision must be made for the case where arguments are missing. In fact there is a variety of interpretation, depending on the verb, but including at least the narrow scope existential (*He sang* iff *He sang something*), contextually definite (*He noticed* iff *He noticed what is contextually definite*), and reflexive (*wash*). We shall simply use the appropriate meaning for the case at hand, the narrow scope existential (*decide*).

5   Kasper's treatment is particularly attractive in that it requires no idiosyncratic assumptions about syntactic structure; in particular, it is compatible with there being multiple adjuncts within a single (nonrecursive) VP node. The following contains (a simplification of) the relevant specifications (from Kasper (1994), p.63, which contains full explanation and justification):

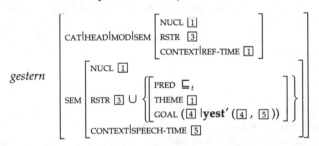

The features SEM|NUCL "semantic nucleus" and HEAD|MOD|SEM|NUCL are coindexed to require that the semantics of the adjunct (which is to be passed on as the semantics of the adjunct-head phrase) be taken from the head it modifies. The effect is that the semantics of head-adjunct constructions involving this class of adverbials is determined by the head. The contribution of the adjunct itself is to contribute to the set of restrictions associated with this semantics. This may be found in SEM|RSTR, in the right side of the set-union operator, where it is specified that the time "[1]" (reference time of the head semantics) fall within the day before speech time. This sort of specification is itself a further example of the sort of noncompositionality possible in this approach.

6   This has been common practice in computational linguistics at least since Wilks (1975). But see Gale et al. (1992) for arguments that some such selection is not semantic.

7   It would far exceed the bounds of this contribution to attempt to review the range of possibilities or issues in parsing. Some recent surveys are useful. Sikkel (1993) reviews the formal properties of a very wide range of parsing algorithms, Bouma and van Noord (1993) reviews the practical performance of a range of algorithms,

controlling for grammar type, and Mitchell (1994) reviews the psycholinguistics of human parsing.

8   We ignore here and henceforth the status of the problematic "reading" in which a decision is attributed to a piece of furniture. Nothing crucial seems to hinge on it. There is a tricky issue associated with the exact representation of the deviant "reading", however. Suppose it is a genuine reading, and therefore something which should be accounted for linguistically. Then it would seem wrong to provide a *linguistic* account of its ill-formedness, as we are about to do. We do not simply embrace this conclusion, because it seems equally plausible that what happens here is that the "normal" linguistic construal of furniture as non-agentive is put aside. A deeper reason for not caring whether this attribution is, strictly speaking, linguistic, is that we shall want to represent *all* the information needed to support linguistic processing, and if this leads us into borderline areas, so be it.

9   The treatment suggested above may be extended to be compatible with the existence of a complex hierarchy of sorts of the kind found in knowledge-representation systems. Some further details may be found in Nerbonne (1992b), but we shall omit them here.

10   See Jacobson (this volume) for more on semantics and categorial grammar. See Stabler (1991) for a similar critique of Steedman's position, i.e., that Steedman's argument fails to consider that one might compute semantics for syntactically incomplete constituents. Stabler also indicates how semantic evaluation might be coupled to the assigning of semantic representation in his proposal. Stabler's work is couched in a tree-like representation of logical form which he shows can be construed as left-branching. The present work differs, however, in using examples which hinge not on logical form, but selection restrictions, and in making no assumption about logical form (except that it can be described in a language of constraints).

11   Pereira and Shieber (1987, pp.178–82) describes a nonpredictive LC parser. Cf. note 6 for general literature on parsing. The parser and grammar (slightly modified for presentation) described in this section were implemented by Ronald Klopstra in his Groningen Master's Thesis (Klopstra 1993).

12   The careful reader will note that this will end one execution path, using the hypothesis that the initial *The* is licensed by the **NP** → **Det N**, and that in principle all the rules may be tried. But of course none of the other rules have **Det** as a leftmost category on the righthand side. So this does indeed end the parse (in failure).

X Lexical Semantics

18 Lexical Semantics and Syntactic Structure

BETH LEVIN and MALKA RAPPAPORT HOVAV

The past ten years have been marked by a resurgence of interest in lexical semantics, which has resulted in part from the assumption common to many current syntactic theories that various aspects of the syntax of a sentence are determined by the meaning of the predicator[1] in that sentence (for discussion see Wasow 1985). The most striking illustration of the role of meaning in the determination of syntax comes from the existence of regularities in the syntactic expression of the arguments of predicators, which we call, following Carter (1988), "linking regularities." These regularities are usually formulated in terms of "linking rules," which associate arguments bearing certain semantic roles with certain syntactic expressions. For example, in English, arguments bearing the agent semantic role are most commonly expressed as the syntactic subject of the sentence. Thus to the extent that the semantic role of an argument is determined by the meaning of the predicator selecting it, the meaning of predicators is a determining factor in the syntax of a sentence. Not only do linking regularities govern the expression of arguments within a given language, but there are impressive similarities in the linking regularities found across languages (Fillmore 1968; Carter 1976, 1988; among others). For example, the generalization concerning the expression of arguments bearing the agent semantic role extends beyond English to the majority of the world's languages.

The existence of linking regularities has long been recognized. One of their earliest instantiations is found in the work of the Sanskrit grammarian Panini, while the more recent "subjectivalization" and "objectivalization" rules of Fillmore (1968), stated in terms of deep case relations, can be seen as the inspirations for current formulations of such rules. Although it is widely acknowledged that linking regularities exist, the development of a full theory of the mapping between lexical semantics and syntax requires that certain unresolved issues be addressed.

The first question concerns the extent to which the syntactic expression of arguments is predictable. Chomsky (1986b), following Stowell (1981) and

Pesetsky (1982), has suggested that subcategorization frames, the part of the lexical entry of a word which encodes the syntactic environment it can be found in, can be dispensed with completely, with the information they encode being derivable from rules which determine the syntactic realization of the semantic arguments of the word. This approach takes the syntactic expression of arguments to be fully predictable. Others, including Jackendoff (1990), Rosen (1984), and Rothstein (1992), are more skeptical about whether this is possible. It is clear that there are certain idiosyncrasies in the syntactic expression of arguments, as when a verb governs a particular morphological case or preposition. The question is whether this type of idiosyncracy is all that is unpredictable about a word.

The assumption which has guided our own work in this area and which serves as the starting point for the case study presented in this paper is that the mapping between the lexical semantic representation of a predicator and the syntactic expression of its arguments is fully predictable. Testing the limits of this hypothesis has proven to be a particularly fruitful way of deepening our understanding of the lexical semantics-syntax interface; in contrast, research which emphasizes the unpredictable aspects of the mapping from lexical semantics to syntax is unlikely to make such a contribution. We hope to demonstrate this through the case study presented in this paper.

The second open question concerns the nature of the lexical semantic representation. The linking rules are formulated in terms of elements of this representation; therefore, a theory of linking clearly has to make use of a fully articulated theory of lexical semantic representation. To date there is little consensus regarding the nature of the lexical semantic representation. One point we will make in this paper is that such a theory can be developed only once the syntactically relevant components of meaning are isolated. Using the wrong aspects of verb meaning as a basis for the lexical semantic representation may preclude the successful formulation of linking rules. The earliest theories of lexical semantic representation, such as Fillmore's (1968) Case Grammar or Gruber's (1965) thematic relations, were what Levin (1995) calls "role-centered;" that is, representations were formulated in terms of the names of the semantic relations that arguments bear to their predicators such as agent, patient, theme, and goal. More recent approaches, such as those taken by Jackendoff (1983, 1990), Carter (1976, 1988) and Pinker (1989), have been "predicate-centered," taking the form of predicate decompositions. Such representations focus on those aspects of the meaning of a predicator which are relevant to the syntax. It appears that the syntactically relevant components of meaning can be better expressed in predicate-centered approaches to lexical semantic representation (Jackendoff 1983, 1990; B. Levin & Rappaport 1988; Pinker 1989).

Recently attention has been focused on what Talmy (1985) has called the lexicalization patterns of a language and their relevance to linking. The term "lexicalization patterns" refers to generalizations concerning the types of meaning that can be associated with the verbs of a language, whether morphologically simple or complex. Often verbs have several meanings which share a common core but which differ with respect to the other meaning components they include. It is important to study the patterns of lexicalization in a language since the elements of meaning lexicalized along with the common core may influence the linking of a verb's arguments.

The third question concerns cross-linguistic variation in the mapping between lexical semantics and syntax. Once again, it is clear that a certain degree of variation exists between languages, and future research will have to determine the extent of variation, as well as its sources. With respect to the sources of variation, we venture as a hypothesis that much of the observed variation can be attributed to differences in lexicalization patterns, rather than to the set of meaning components which are relevant to linking or to the linking rules themselves. For example, words which seem to be translation equivalents in two languages may nevertheless differ in the syntactic expression of their arguments due to the fact that the elements of meaning lexicalized along with the core meaning differ in the two languages. Variation may also arise from the way in which languages calculate how the pertinent components of meaning contribute to the expression of arguments. Languages may not give the same weight to each component, with the result that a particular argument may not receive the same expression in different languages.

One of the striking properties of the organization of the lexicon is the existence of semantically coherent classes of verbs. Many aspects of a verb's behavior, including the syntactic expression of its arguments, appear to be determined by membership in these classes, which often receive quite a fine-grained semantic characterization (Levin 1993; Pinker 1989). Since there are many facets to a verb's meaning, it is not always *a priori* clear what aspects of meaning are relevant to the determination of its class membership, that is, what the syntactically relevant semantic components are. A point we hope to underscore in this paper is that detailed studies of the syntactic behavior of the members of these semantically-defined verb classes can help to isolate those aspects of meaning and to answer the three questions posed above concerning the nature of the lexical semantics-syntax mapping. For example, if it appears that there are two classes of verbs in some language whose members share the same semantic characterization but differ in the syntactic expression of their arguments, this could either show that a certain degree of idiosyncracy is allowed in that language, or it could indicate that there is an aspect of meaning which distinguishes between the two classes and which is in fact relevant to the linking rules.[2]

In this paper, we present a case study in lexical semantic analysis of two such semantic classes of verbs: verbs of sound and verbs of manner of motion. We will see that the behavior of these verbs can be understood only once the syntactically relevant aspects of meaning are isolated and the lexicalization patterns available to a language are understood. We consider the behavior of these verbs in the context of a much-studied hypothesis about the mapping between lexical semantics and syntax known as the Unaccusative Hypothesis (Perlmutter 1978; Pullum 1988; Burzio 1986).

1   A Brief Introduction to the Unaccusative Hypothesis

The relationship between lexical semantics and syntax has received substantial attention over the last fifteen years in the context of the Unaccusative Hypothesis (UH), introduced by Perlmutter (1978). This hypothesis proposes that intransitive verbs fall into two sub-classes, the unaccusative and unergative classes, whose members are associated with distinct syntactic configurations. The central idea is that the subject of an unaccusative verb is a derived subject, being a direct object at some underlying level of syntactic representation, while the subject of an unergative verb is a subject at all levels of syntactic representation. This idea is implemented differently in different syntactic frameworks. In the Government-Binding framework (Chomsky 1981), for example, unaccusative verbs have a d-structure object but no subject, while unergative verbs have a d-structure subject but no object, as schematized below.

(1)   a.   Unaccusative Verb: __ [$_{VP}$ V NP]
      b.   Unergative Verb: NP [$_{VP}$ V]

In English, due to independent principles of grammar, the single argument of an unaccusative verb surfaces as a subject, giving the impression of a single homogeneous class of intransitive verbs (Burzio 1986).

It is important to note that the UH in its original formulation attributes different syntactic properties to the two classes of intransitive verbs. The strongest support for the UH has come from differences in the syntactic behavior of the two classes of intransitive verbs which are said to be explained by appeal to the distinct syntactic configurations that the UH associates with each class. But although the two classes of verbs receive a syntactic characterization, there are important semantic generalizations regarding class membership. Moreover, cross-linguistically there are impressive similarities in class membership. Noting the existence of such semantic correlates in his original paper on unaccusativity, Perlmutter hypothesized that the class membership of intransitive verbs is fully predictable semantically. Due to this conjunction of semantic and syntactic properties, unaccusativity provides fertile ground for the exploration of the relationship between lexical semantics and syntax in general and for the isolation of the syntactically relevant components of meaning in particular. The literature on the semantic underpinnings of unaccusativity has cited various semantic determinants of verb classification. Although the identification of the correlates is the topic of active research, commonly cited correlates include telicity, stativity, and agentivity (Dowty 1991; L. Levin 1986; Van Valin 1990; Zaenen 1993; among others).

The approach to unaccusativity just outlined has not gone unchallenged (Dowty 1991; Van Valin 1990; Zaenen 1993). In this paper we address the challenges posed by phenomena which suggest that the class membership of verbs is not fully predictable semantically. We do this through an examination of what we refer to as "variable behavior" verbs: verbs which sometimes display unaccusative behavior and sometimes display unergative behavior. The existence of such verbs seems at odds with the hypothesis that class membership is predictable semantically, since if a verb's meaning determines its classification, its classification should be determined once and for all. It turns out, however, that these verbs seem problematic only because their correct semantic classification is not immediately clear. Once the syntactically relevant components of meaning are isolated and the linking rules which make reference to these components are formulated, the solution to the quandary posed by these variable behavior verbs becomes apparent. A close look at such verbs reveals that they are always associated with more than one meaning. Furthermore, when such a verb displays unaccusative behavior it is associated with a meaning which is independently correlated with membership in the unaccusative class, and when it displays unergative behavior it is associated with a meaning which is independently correlated with membership in the unergative class. Variable behavior verbs are useful as a probe into the syntactically relevant meaning components since contrasting the meaning of a verb when it behaves as an unaccusative verb with the meaning of the same verb when it behaves as an unergative verb will help to isolate precisely those aspects of meaning which play a part in the syntactic classification of verbs.

2   Verbs of Sound: an Introduction

In the remainder of this paper we present a case study involving verbs of sound, a set of verbs whose variable behavior has not to our knowledge been noted in the literature on unaccusativity.[3] Verbs of sound in English form a large class – one of the largest classes listed in B. Levin (1993) – whose members describe the emission or production of a sound.[4] Verbs of sound are differentiated from each other by the physical properties of the sound that they lexicalize and by its manner of production. Representative verbs are listed in (2) and typical uses from the BCET corpus (Sinclair 1987), cited in Atkins and B. Levin (1991), are given in (3).

(2)   beep, buzz, creak, gurgle, jingle, ring, roar, rumble, screech, thud, tick, whistle, . . .
(3)   a. cars honked and hummed in the road
      b. I hissed and snarled and ground my teeth at them.
      c. the line of wart-hogs moved snuffling and grunting across the trail

Verbs of sound are intransitive verbs, taking the emitter argument as subject. Although these verbs do not permit abstract nouns as their subjects (**Peacetime* *cooed*, **Industriousness buzzed*), these verbs nevertheless take a range of subjects: animate (human or not) and inanimate concrete nouns. Due to the nature of the associated sounds, individual verbs differ in the range of subjects available to them. What is distinctive about the verbs of sound is that many are either necessarily nonagentive (e.g. *creak, whir*) or nonagentive at least for some choices of emitter argument (e.g. *groan, whistle*).

Since verbs of sound are intransitive, the question arises as to their classification with respect to the UH. Although Perlmutter (1978) included verbs of sound that take inanimate arguments among the unaccusative verbs, their classification is not immediately apparent. On the basis of two commonly cited semantic determinants of unaccusativity, telicity and agentivity, they do not fall clearly into either the unaccusative or the unergative class. As atelic verbs they might seem to belong to the unergative class, but as verbs that are nonagentive when they take inanimate arguments they might seem to belong to the unaccusative class. This fact in itself makes the study of verbs of sound important, since their behavior will help shed light on the way various aspects of meaning are implicated in the classification of verbs. In Section 6 we discuss how the behavior of verbs of sound helps clarify the nature of linking rules.

A study of the syntactic behavior of these verbs points to an unergative classification for the simple sense discussed so far. We briefly review some evidence in favor of this suggestion; for further discussion see B. Levin & Rappaport Hovav (1995). First, in some languages unaccusative and unergative verbs select different auxiliaries in certain tenses, with selection of the counterpart of the English auxiliary *be* being taken as evidence for unaccusative status (Burzio 1986; Hoekstra 1984; L. Levin 1986; Rosen 1981, 1984; among others). Italian is such a language, and in Italian verbs of sound do not select the unaccusative auxiliary *essere* "be", but rather select the auxiliary *avere* "have" associated with unergative verbs. (See B. Levin & Rappaport Hovav (1995) for discussion of comparable facts from other languages).

(4)   ha cigolato "creaked", ha stormito "rustled" (Rosen 1984, (77))

Further evidence that these verbs are unergative comes from their case-assigning properties. As discussed by Burzio (1986), unaccusative verbs cannot assign accusative case and, therefore, cannot be found with direct objects – even nonsubcategorized objects – since there is no case available for such an object. In contrast, unergative verbs can assign accusative case, but since they do not select an internal argument, they can only assign this case to a nonsubcategorized object. Verbs of sound are found with a range of objects, as the following examples show.[5]

(5)   a. ... the bell above her head had jangled its first summons ...
         (L. Talbot, *The gentlewomen*, Macmillan, London, 1952, p.7)
      b. The grandfather clock ... ticked its majestic tread through the
         Hall of Silence ... (A. W. Upfield, *Bony and the Kelly Gang*, Collier,
         New York, 1988, p.48)

  c. The very word was like a bell that tolled me back to childhood
   summers . . . ("Hers; Child's play, women's sway," *The New York
   Times*, July 17, 1988, Article 248)

One of the constructions with nonsubcategorized objects is the *"X's way"* construction discussed by Goldberg (1995), Jackendoff (1990), Marantz (1992), and
Salkoff (1988). In this construction, exemplified in (6), an unergative verb is
followed by an object consisting of a noun phrase headed by the noun *way*
with a possessive modifier whose form is determined by the subject of the
verb. This object is used to predicate an XP describing a result state or location
of the subject.

 (6) The candidate off in the provinces, plotting and planning and dream-
   ing his way to the nomination . . . (R. Toner, "While others shrank
   from race, Clinton clung to dream of presidency," *The New York
   Times*, July 12, 1992, p.14)

Marantz argues that the verb in this construction is necessarily unergative,
allowing this construction to be used to diagnose a verb's classification. This
construction is found with verbs of sound both with inanimate subjects, as in
(7), and animate subjects, as in (8), supporting the classification of these verbs
as unergatives.

 (7) a. Then he watched as it gurgled its way into a whiskey tumbler.
    (M. Grimes, *The Five Bells and Bladestone*, Little, Brown and Com-
    pany, Boston, 1987, p.200)
   b. . . . as the huge vehicle groaned and belched its way up the stony
    slope as steep as a house roof. (A.W. Upfield, *Sinister stones*, 1954;
    Collier reprint, New York, 1986, p.26)

 (8) a. . . . showing Marlon Brando mumbling his way through "The
    Godfather". (AP90 35497690)
   b. A singer warbled her way through "Georgia On My Mind". (AP90
    24608885)

3 The Variable Behavior of Verbs of Sound

In this section we demonstrate how verbs of sound show variable behavior
and propose an explanation for their variable behavior. We illustrate this point
through the behavior of this class of verbs in the resultative construction, a
widely cited unaccusative diagnostic (Simpson 1983; Hoekstra 1988; B. Levin
& Rappaport Hovav 1995). This construction takes distinct forms with unaccusative and unergative verbs, allowing a verb's classification to be discerned from the form of the construction that it is found in. The hallmark of

the resultative construction is the resultative phrase: an XP which denotes the state achieved by the referent of the NP it is predicated of as a result of the action denoted by the verb in the construction. This construction is illustrated in (9) with a transitive verb. Note that the resultative phrase *clean* is predicated of the object, *the floors*.

(9)   They scrubbed the floors clean.

As the examples in (10) and (11) show, there are two patterns of resultative constructions found with intransitive verbs.

(10)   The bottle broke open. (cf. She broke the bottle open.)
(11)   a. . . . the other officers laugh themselves helpless. (P. Lively, *Moon tiger*, Grove, New York, 1988, p.112)
           (cf. *The officers laughed helpless.)
        b. You may sleep it [= the unborn baby — MRH & BL] quiet again . . . (E. Bagnold, "The squire," in *The girl's journey*, Doubleday, Garden City, NY, 1954, p.285)

In one pattern, which is attested only with unaccusative verbs, the resultative XP is predicated of the surface subject of the verb and there is no object, as in (10). In the second pattern, illustrated by (11), the resultative XP is predicated of the object; this pattern is found with unergative verbs (it is also the pattern found with transitive verbs; see (9)). Thus when an intransitive verb is found in the resultative construction its status as unaccusative or unergative can be directly determined.[6]

Verbs of sound are found in the resultative patterns associated with both unergative and unaccusative verbs, as shown in (12) and (13), respectively.

(12)   a. We searched the woods and cliffs, yelled ourselves hoarse and imagined you drowned . . . (M. Wesley, *A sensible life*, Viking, New York, 1990, p.327)
        b. Well, the conclusion was that my mistress grumbled herself calm. (E. Brontë, *Wuthering Heights*, 1847; Penguin edition, London, 1965, p.78)

(13)   a. . . . the curtains creak open and radiant evening light streams into the cluttered room. (S. Cheever, *Elizabeth Cole*, Farrar, Straus & Giroux, New York, 1989, p.70)
        b. The lid of the boiler clunked shut. (P. Lively, *The road to Lichfield*, Grove Weidenfeld, New York, 1991, p.52)

Given our initial classification of verbs of sound as unergative, the appearance of these verbs in the unaccusative resultative pattern demands an explanation. However, the variable behavior is problematic only to the extent that the verbs manifest a single meaning in both constructions. We will show that verbs of sound have two different but related meanings, each correlated with a different classification. When such a verb is found in the unaccusative resultative pattern it has a meaning correlated with the unaccusative classification; when it is found in the unergative pattern it has a meaning correlated with the unergative classification.

More specifically, verbs of sound in English have the option of becoming verbs of directed motion. When a verb of sound shows the directed motion meaning, it requires a directional phrase as a complement, be it a directional PP or, as we discuss below, some other XP with a directional interpretation such as the result locations and positions of the unaccusative resultative construction. Examples of the directed motion sense of verbs of sound with a directional PP are given in (14).

> (14) a. . . . the elevator wheezed upward. (M. Muller, *There's nothing to be afraid of*, St. Martin's, New York, 1985, p.3)
> b. . . . a flatbed truck . . . rumbled through the gate. (M. Muller, *There's nothing to be afraid of*, St. Martin's, New York, 1985, p.39)
> c. The kettle clashed across the metal grid. (S. Miller, *Family pictures*, Harper & Row, New York, 1990, p.34)

In the directed motion sense, the verbs describe the motion of an entity where the motion is characterized by the concomitant emission of the sound whose nature is lexicalized in the verb. Sentence (14a), for example, can be paraphrased as "The elevator moved upward while wheezing."

When verbs of sound become verbs of directed motion, they take on syntactic properties manifested by verbs which are inherently classified as verbs of directed motion. Such verbs specify an inherent deixis of motion (e.g. *arrive*, *come*, *go*) or an inherent direction (e.g. *descend*, *rise*). They differ from the other major class of verbs of motion – the verbs of manner of motion (e.g. *run*, *swim*, *amble*) – in being unspecified for the manner of motion: someone can arrive by walking or running or jogging. Verbs of directed motion are independently known to be unaccusative (Hoekstra 1984; B. Levin & Rappaport Hovav 1992; L. Levin 1986; Rosen 1984; Van Valin 1990). The most frequently cited evidence for their status is their ability to take the unaccusative auxiliary *essere* "be" in Italian, as well as their behavior with respect to *ne*-cliticization; both these properties have been associated with the unaccusative syntactic configuration (Belletti and Rizzi 1981; Burzio 1986; Perlmutter 1989; Rosen 1981).[7]

> (15) Ne sono arrivati molti.
> "Many of them arrived."

If verbs of directed motion are unaccusative, and verbs of sound have the option of becoming verbs of directed motion, then they would be expected to show unaccusative behavior only on their directed motion sense.

Evidence that this is indeed the case comes from an examination of the resultative XPs in (12) and (13). Although most phrases that have come under the label "resultative phrase" semantically describe result states, the phrases found in the problematic unaccusative resultative constructions are better characterized as result positions. For example, although the XP *shut* usually describes a state, in *The door banged shut*, the XP *shut* describes not a state, but rather a position associated with the state of being shut. Another type of resultative phrase found when these verbs are in the unaccusative resultative pattern takes the form of an intransitive preposition that denotes a location such as *apart* and *away*, as in *The gates slowly creaked apart*. The basic claim is that the result position and location phrases reflect the meaning shift that the verb has undergone to become a directed motion verb.[8]

Further support for our analysis comes from the fact that resultative phrases that unambiguously denote result states are excluded from the unaccusative pattern and are found with the unergative (and transitive) pattern with verbs of sound. If such resultative phrases are inserted into the unaccusative pattern, the outcome is unacceptable, as shown in (16), though they may be found in the unergative pattern, as shown in (17).

(16) a. *The skylight thudded to pieces.
      b. *The curtains creaked thin.
      c. *The phone rang to death.

(17) a. ... you can't just let the thing ring itself to death, can you? ("OBSERVER; Trace that call no more!," *The New York Times*, March 8, 1989, Article 55)
      b. He had set an alarm, which rang at five thirty the following morning, shrilling them both awake. (R. Pilcher, *Voices in summer*, St. Martin's, 1984, p.116)

The problem cannot be attributed to a general incompatibility between result state phrases and the unaccusative resultative pattern, since, as the examples below show, unaccusative verbs can be found in resultative constructions with result state phrases.

(18) a. The bag of flour broke open.
      b. The lake froze solid.
      c. The cookies burnt to a crisp.

4   Further Confirmation for the Semantic Class Shift

As noted in Section 2, many verbs of sound allow animate agentive subjects as well as inanimate nonagentive subjects. Agentive verbs of sound cannot in general become verbs of directed motion, as shown in (19); instead the intended sense must be expressed periphrastically, as in (20).

(19) a. *He yelled/shouted down the street.
          (cf. He yelled/shouted his way down the street.)
      b. *The frogs croaked to the pond.
          (cf. The frogs croaked their way to the pond.)

(20) a. the line of wart-hogs moved snuffling and grunting across the trail (= (3c))
      b. But as he reached for the bird it dodged out of the window and flew away, squawking. (M. Wesley, *A dubious legacy*, Viking, New York, 1992, p.88)

However, occasionally verbs of sound taking animate subjects are found with directional phrases: (21)

(21) a. . . . Sedgwick often clanked into town in sabre and spurs from the cavalry camp. (E. Thane, *Yankee stranger*, People's Book Club, Chicago, 1944, p.133)
      b. She rustled out of the room without waiting for a word from Lind. (M. Ostenso, *Wild geese*, New Canadian Library, Toronto, 1961, p.30)

As discussed in B. Levin (1991) and B. Levin & Rappaport Hovav (1991), in order for a verb of sound to be used as a verb of directed motion the sound must be emitted as a concomitant of the motion. Typically verbs of sound that take an animate argument describe a sound emitted via the vocal tract under the control of an animate entity, particularly for purposes of communication. The sound is not emitted as a consequence of motion; therefore, such verbs do not qualify for a directed motion sense. The verbs of sound taking animate subjects which *can* be used as verbs of directed motion, like *clank* and *rustle* in (21), involve sounds that are never emitted by the vocal tract; furthermore, as pointed out to us by Mary Laughren, these sounds are emitted by articles of clothing and accessories and not directly by the animate entity itself. In the examples in (21) the emitter, though animate, is treated no differently than the inanimate emitters in (14).

Returning to the resultative construction, verbs of sound, as expected, cannot appear in the unaccusative resultative pattern when they denote sounds emitted via the vocal tract, as shown in (22), but are allowed when the sound is emitted as a concomitant of the motion, as shown in (23).

(22) a. *He yelled clear of the falling rocks.
      b. *The frogs croaked apart.
      c. *They shouted free of their captors.

(23) We splashed clear of the oncoming boat.

In contrast, verbs of sound with animate subjects are found freely in the unergative resultative pattern, just as might be expected, with resultative phrases clearly denoting result states, as in (12).

5   The Scope of the Semantic Class Shift

The class shift phenomenon described in the previous section is an instance of a phenomenon that is more widespread in English: verbs from several semantic classes may become verbs of directed motion. Like verbs of sound, verbs of manner of motion (e.g. *run, shuffle,* and *walk*) and verbs of exerting force (e.g. *push* and *pull*) can become verbs of directed motion in the presence of a directional phrase, although they do not in their basic sense describe directed motion.

(24)   a. The children ran into the room.
       b. Sally shuffled over to the counter.

(25)   a. Kim pushed the stroller into the store.
       b. Peter pulled the books out of the package.

Verbs of manner of motion, being intransitive, are of particular interest here. They too are unergative in their basic (i.e. nondirected motion) sense (Hoekstra 1984; B. Levin & Rappaport Hovav 1992; L. Levin 1986; Van Valin 1990; Zaenen 1993; among others), as expected from their agentive nature, but they display unaccusative behavior in their directed motion sense. For example, in some languages with auxiliary selection, the two senses of these verbs select different auxiliaries: the counterpart of *have* for the simple sense and the counterpart of *be* for the directed motion sense, as shown in the Italian and Dutch examples below. As discussed above, selection of the auxiliary *be* is taken as evidence for unaccusative status.

(26)   a. Ugo ha corso meglio ieri.
          "Ugo ran better yesterday." (Rosen 1984, (86a))
       b. Ugo è corso a casa.
          "Ugo ran home." (Rosen 1984, (86b))

(27)   a. Hij heeft/*is gelopen.
          He has/is run. (Zaenen 1993, (22a))
       b. Hij is/?heeft naar huis gelopen.
          He is/has run home. (Zaenen 1993, (22b))

There is further independent evidence for the dual classification of verbs of manner of motion. Like verbs of sound, verbs of manner of motion are found in both the unergative and unaccusative resultative patterns, as illustrated in (28) and (29), respectively.

(28) a. Don't expect to swim yourself sober!
b. He danced his feet sore.

(29) a. She danced/swam/sprinted free of her captors.
b. However, if fire is an immediate danger, you must *jump clear of the vehicle*. (*Illinois rules of the road*, 1989 edition, p.81) [italics in original – BL&MRH]

The presence of verbs of manner of motion in the unaccusative resultative pattern was first noticed in Simpson (1983), who points out that this pattern is found with a restricted group of adjectives which includes *free* and *clear*; it is also found with some intransitive prepositions such as *apart* and *away*.[9]

The data in (28) and (29) receive the same analysis as the comparable data involving verbs of sound: the verbs appear in the unaccusative resultative pattern only on their directed motion sense, as expected from the unaccusative classification of verbs of directed motion. The choice of resultative phrases reflects the different senses of the verbs in the two patterns. The examples in (28) contain result states, while those in (29) contain result positions. Furthermore, the resultative XPs found in the unaccusative and unergative resultative examples are not interchangeable, as shown below. The examples in (30) illustrate the unaccusative pattern with the resultative phrases from the "unergative" examples in (28); those in (31) illustrate the unergative pattern with the resultative phrases from the "unaccusative" examples in (29).

(30) a. *She danced/swam/sprinted sober.
b. *The jogger ran sore.

(31) a. *You must jump yourself clear of the vehicle.
b. *They swam themselves free of their captors.

Thus verbs of sound and verbs of manner of motion show parallel variable behavior in the resultative construction since they both allow directed motion senses.

The behavior of verbs of sound and verbs of manner of motion with respect to the causative alternation further supports our contention that they have two meanings, each associated with a different syntactic classification. Members of both classes may be found in the causative alternation in English (*Kelly broke the glass/The glass broke*) – a context said to be restricted to unaccusative verbs (B. Levin & Rappaport Hovav 1995; Burzio 1986; Rosen 1981; among others).[10] The parallel between the two classes of verbs involves the circumstances under which they are found in the causative alternation; members of both classes require the presence of an overt or implicit directional phrase in their causative use.[11]

(32) a. . . . several strong Teamsters . . . shuffled Kit out of the room . . .
            (L. Matera, *A radical departure*, 1988; Ballantine, New York, 1991,
            p.79)
      b. ". . . I promised Ms. Cain I would ride her around the ranch . . .
            (N. Pickard, *Bum steer*, Pocket Books, New York, 1990, p.92)

(33) a. *Several strong Teamsters shuffled Kit.
      b. *I promised Ms. Cain I would ride her.

(34) a. Slowly, they rumbled the Big Wheel across the sidewalk . . .
            (R. Robinson, *Summer light*, Viking, New York, 1988, p.28)
      b. The driver roared/screeched the car down the driveway.

(35) a. *They rumbled the Big Wheel.
      b. *The driver roared/screeched the car.

In B. Levin & Rappaport Hovav (1995) we propose an account of the causative alternation that sheds light on this requirement. An unergative verb is prevented from having a causative use for syntactic reasons: its single argument fills the position needed for the "causer" argument which would be introduced by such a use. However, as we have argued, verbs of sound and verbs of manner of motion receive an unaccusative classification in their directed motion sense. Given this classification, their single argument is a d-structure object, allowing for the introduction of a "causer" argument. The directional phrase requirement associated with their causative use then follows. Thus the causative alternation provides further support for positing two meanings – and, as a consequence, two syntactic representations – for members of both classes of verbs.

6   Implications for the Theory of Linking

In this section we assess two of the more widely cited semantic correlates of unaccusativity – telicity and agentivity – in the context of our case study. Simplifying somewhat, agentivity has been said to determine unergative classification, while telicity has been said to determine unaccusative classification (Dowty 1991; Tenny 1987; Van Valin 1990; Zaenen 1993). Given these correlations, the question arises as to the classification of verbs which are neither telic nor agentive and verbs which are both telic and agentive since the correlates suggest conflicting classifications for such verbs. An examination of verbs which are neither agentive nor telic will lead us to suggest that the notion of "agent" does not figure directly in the linking rule which maps certain arguments onto d-structure subjects and that another semantic notion figures instead. We will then show how telicity interacts with the concept that replaces agentivity.

In their basic (nondirected motion) sense, verbs of sound with inanimate emitters exemplify verbs which are both atelic and nonagentive. Since these verbs behave as unergative verbs, it might seem that only telicity – and not agentivity – is relevant to their classification, with telic verbs being unaccusative and atelic verbs being unergative. However, in B. Levin & Rappaport Hovav (1995) we show that there are atelic unaccusative verbs (verbs such as *rock* and *roll* which participate in the causative alternation) suggesting that the absence of telicity does not necessarily determine an unergative classification.

What then could be responsible for inanimate emitters being expressed as d-structure subjects, so that verbs of sound would be classified as unergative? We suggest that verbs, including intransitive verbs, should be subdivided into those which denote internally caused eventualities and those which denote externally caused eventualities.[12] When an intransitive verb denotes an internally caused eventuality, some property of the entity denoted by the argument of the verb is responsible for the eventuality; we call this argument the "causer" argument. We propose that there is a linking rule – call it the Causer Linking Rule – associating causers with the d-structure subject position.

An agent is one type of causer argument since the agent argument of a verb is almost by definition responsible for the eventuality denoted by that verb. But the notion of causer is not equivalent to that of agent; it is meant to subsume notions which are not traditionally seen as causes. In particular, this notion is intended to encompass the emitter argument of verbs of sound (and other verbs of emission), since it is some property of the emitter, or perhaps the emitter itself, which is responsible for the emission of the sound denoted by the verb. It is also intended to subsume the single argument of verbs like *blush* and *shudder*, which, although not an agent, is still the source of the eventualities denoted by these verbs.

The notion of causer should also not be identified with any argument position of the putative primitive predicate CAUSE, often postulated and used in decompositional representations of verb meaning (e.g. Carter 1988; Dowty 1979; Jackendoff 1983, 1990; among others). In such decompositions, CAUSE is a dyadic predicate which takes a causer or causing event argument and a second argument which is necessarily an event, specifically the event that is caused. However, a causer on our definition may be the argument of an intransitive verb, and the verb may even be stative (e.g. the verb of smell emission *stink*).[13] We suggest, then, that the behavior of verbs of sound supports the replacement of agentivity with the notion of causer as a determinant of which intransitive verbs are unergative.

We turn next to externally caused eventualities. These eventualities typically involve two subevents: the causing event, which includes the causer as an argument, and the caused event (Dowty 1979; Parsons 1990; among others). The Causer Linking Rule is applicable, then, to transitive verbs as well as to intransitive verbs; it is responsible, for example, for associating the causer of transitive verbs such as *break* – be it an agent, an instrument, or a natural force – with the d-structure subject position. We propose that the same analysis also applies to the intransitive forms of verbs like *break*. These intransitive verbs describe externally caused eventualities; they arise from a process which allows their causer argument not to be expressed syntactically. Therefore, although the intransitive form of a verb like *break* has only one argument, this argument, as the noncauser argument of an externally caused eventuality, will not be a d-structure subject since the Causer Linking Rule does not apply to it. This treatment is consistent with the classification of such intransitive verbs as unaccusative. The linking rule which we introduce in B. Levin & Rappaport Hovav (1995) to associate this argument with the d-structure object position is not tailored only to these particular intransitive verbs. Thus we can identify unergative verbs with internally caused intransitive verbs, and unaccusative verbs with the intransitive variant of externally caused verbs.[14]

As verbs which are both telic and internally caused, agentive verbs of manner of motion in the directed motion sense allow the interaction of internal causation and telicity to be investigated. Telic verbs typically have an argument associated with some property which determines the temporal progress of the eventuality they denote (Dowty 1991; Tenny 1987, 1994; among others). Simplifying somewhat, it is this argument which denotes the entity which undergoes the change specified by the verb. For example, with a telic verb like *harden*, the hardness of the entity denoted by the direct object is the property in terms of which the change specified by the verb is measured and which determines when the change is complete. With verbs of directed motion, the argument undergoing the motion has a property, its location, which determines when the event is complete. We call such an argument the theme argument. This argument is typically associated with the d-structure object position by what we call the Theme Linking Rule.[15] When an agentive verb of manner of motion is used in the directed motion sense, it has an argument which qualifies both as causer and as theme. The fact that such verbs are unaccusative shows that the Theme Linking Rule takes precedence over the Causer Linking Rule in the calculation of the syntactic expression of an argument.

Bringing these results together, we have shown that a telic single argument verb is unaccusative independent of whether it denotes an internally or an externally caused eventuality, but that the classification of an atelic single argument verb depends on the classification of the verb in terms of the nature of the eventuality it denotes. More importantly, we have shown how a detailed study of the syntactic behavior of verbs belonging to particular semantic classes can play an important part in the formulation of the linking rules which are ultimately responsible for the classification of verbs.

7   The Source of the Multiple Meanings

We have explained the variable behavior of verbs of sound and verbs of manner of motion by positing a process of meaning shift, which allows verbs in certain semantic classes to regularly manifest several meanings. We can think of these class shifts as instances of the phenomenon of "regular polysemy" which has been extensively documented by Apresjan (1973, 1992) in the noun as well as the verb lexicon. Once these meaning shifts are recognized, it becomes clear that the syntactic expression of arguments of variable behavior verbs is consistent with the linking rules of a language. Rather than undermining the thesis that the syntactic behavior of verbs is determined by their meaning, it actually supports it. In this section we further explore some of the central properties of such processes of meaning shift.

Meaning shifts are productive across semantically coherent classes of verbs. That is, members of specific semantic classes of verbs regularly map onto other semantic classes of verbs. For example, although we have seen that both verbs of manner of motion and verbs of sound map onto the class of directed motion verbs, this process is not completely general. Even among the set of verbs which are atelic – the most evident property that verbs of manner of motion and verbs of sound share – not all intransitive activity verbs can become verbs of directed motion in English; as expected, only those which can show this shift are found in the unaccusative resultative pattern.

(36) a. *Kelly laughed/sang/swore/cried out of the room.
(on the interpretation: Kelly went out of the room laughing/singing/swearing/crying.)
b. *The boys laughed/sang/swore/cried clear of oncoming traffic.
(on the interpretation: The boys moved clear of oncoming traffic, laughing/singing/swearing/crying.)

These data, and data from other meaning shifts, suggest that meaning shifts are rule-governed processes: they are both regular and productive, although their existence and scope need to be stipulated in the lexicon of a language.

Further evidence for this comes from the fact that the availability of meaning shifts varies from language to language as shown by studies of lexicalization patterns such as those presented in Talmy (1975, 1985b, 1991). As Talmy shows, verbs of manner of motion can regularly become verbs of directed motion in English and some other languages. Examples of such shifts from German and Hebrew are given below, in (37) and (38), respectively.

(37) a. Die Kinder liefen in das Zimmer (hinein).
the children ran into the-ACC room (into)
"The children ran into the room."
b. Die Kinder sind an das andere Flußufer geschwommen.
the children are to the-ACC other riverbank swum
"The children swam to the other side of the river."

(38) a. Hu rakad el mixuts laxeder.
"He danced out of the room."

b. Habakbuk tsaf lagada haSniya Sel hanahar.
"The bottle floated to the other side of the river."

However, not all languages allow verbs of manner of motion to show this type of regular polysemy (Carter 1988; B. Levin and Rapoport 1988; B. Levin & Rappaport Hovav 1992; Talmy 1975, 1985). French is such a language. Although the English sentence (39a), the word-for-word translation of the French example in (39b), is ambiguous between a reading in which the boat is floating at a location under the bridge (simple manner of motion reading) and a reading in which the boat floats to a point under or even on the other side of the bridge (the directed motion reading), the French sentence can only mean that the boat is floating at a location under the bridge, demonstrating the unavailability of the directed motion sense in French.

(39) a. The boat floated under the bridge.
      b. Le bateau a flotté sous le pont. (B. Levin & Rapoport 1988, (17))

Languages in which verbs of manner of motion cannot be used as verbs of directed motion differ in the strategies they make available for expressing the meaning conveyed by the English directed motion sense of verbs of manner of motion. For example, studies in comparative stylistics such as Vinay & Darbelnet (1958) point out that the directed motion sense of English verbs of manner of motion is expressed periphrastically in French.

(40) a. Blériot flew across the Channel.
      b. Blériot traversa la Manche en avion.
         Blériot crossed the Channel by plane
         (Vinay & Darbelnet 1958, p.105)

Just as the shift from verb of manner of motion to verb of directed motion is not manifested in all languages, neither is the shift from verb of sound to verb of directed motion. Our initial investigations suggest that the set of languages in which verbs of sound show this shift is the same set of languages in which verbs of manner of motion show this shift. Thus German and Hebrew, like English, allow both verbs of manner of motion and verbs of sound to become verbs of directed motion, as shown in (41) and (42), respectively.

(41) a. Die Kugel pfiff durch die Luft.
         "The bullet (lit. sphere) whistled through the air."
      b. Der Lastwagen rasselte den Berg hinunter.
         "The truck rattled down the hill."

(42) a. Hakadur Sarak le'evra.
         "The bullet whistled towards her."
      b. Hatankim ra'amu el me-ever lagvul.
         "The tanks roared across the border."

In contrast, in French, which does not allow verbs of manner of motion to be used as verbs of directed motion, verbs of sound also cannot be used as verbs of directed motion. In general, it is unnatural in French to attempt to mention a sound when the motion of an entity is being described. Meanings comparable to the English (a) sentences of (43) and (44) might be expressed periphrastically in French as in the (b) sentences, but even such translations would be considered poor and unnatural versions of the English sentences.[16]

(43) a. The car roared down the street.
      b. La voiture descendit la rue en vrombissant.
         the car went down the street in roaring

(44) a. The truck rumbled into the yard.
      b. Le camion entra dans la cour dans un grand fracas.
         the truck entered in the yard in a big din

These data suggest that if a language allows one class of verbs to shift, it will allow the other class to shift as well. However, much more cross-linguistic research needs to be carried out in order to determine the precise restrictions on meaning shifts.

8 Conclusion

The case study presented here was chosen to demonstrate that many facets of the syntax of a sentence are determined by the meaning of its predicator. This point was illustrated in the context of the semantic underpinnings of the Unaccusative Hypothesis and, specifically, by examining variable behavior verbs – verbs whose behavior appears initially inconsistent with a regular mapping from lexical semantics to syntax. Not only have we shown that the variable behavior of verbs of sound and verbs of manner of motion does not pose a problem for the hypothesis that unaccusativity is semantically determined, but we have provided new insights into lexical organization by uncovering relationships between several verb classes. Specifically, verbs of manner of motion behave more like verbs of sound than like verbs of inherently directed motion, a class that *a priori* might have been expected to be more syntactically similar to verbs of manner of motion since both classes can be characterized as verbs of motion. This parallel illustrates that the components of meaning relevant to the syntax may not always be the obvious ones. It is such unexpected, though on reflection perhaps not altogether surprising, parallels that bring out the value of seriously pursuing the hypothesis that the meaning of a verb determines its syntactic expression.

NOTES

Acknowledgments   This work was presented at the Research Institute for Language and Speech, University of Utrecht, November 1992; the Workshop on Thematic Roles in Linguistic Theory and Language Acquisition, University of Kansas, January 1993; and the Dagstuhl Seminar on Universals in the Lexicon, March 1993. We thank the participants for their comments. We would also like to thank Grace Song for her comments on a draft of this paper and John Wickberg and David Yarowsky for helping us find relevant examples in on-line texts. This research was supported in part by NSF Grants BNS-8919884 and DBS-9221993.

1   By "predicators" we mean verbs and other argument-taking lexical items.
2   The class of psychological predicates illustrates this point. As is well-known, these verbs fall into two subclasses in terms of argument expression, and researchers have been divided as to whether this subclassification is attributable to differences in meaning (see, for example, Pesetsky 1987, 1995) or to variability in the expression of certain arguments (see, for example, Belletti and Rizzi 1988).
3   The material in this case study is drawn from the more extensive discussion of verbs of sound in B. Levin & Rappaport Hovav (1995).
4   These verbs belong to the larger class of verbs of emission, which includes verbs that describe the emission of a stimulus (light, sound, smell) or a substance. All verbs of emission share certain properties, such as participation in the intransitive form of the locative alternation. Verbs of sound show a wider range of senses than verbs in the other subclasses because they can be used as verbs of communication. See B. Levin (1991, 1993) for more discussion.
5   In some of the examples, the object might be characterized as the emitted sound; in such instances it is not clear that the object is nonsubcategorized. What is relevant here is that these verbs, like other unergative verbs, are able to assign case.
6   A diagnostic is convincing only to the extent that the differential behavior of the verbs can be explained by appeal to the different syntactic representations of the verbs. See B. Levin & Rappaport Hovav (1995) and Hoekstra (1992) for two possible explanations of the different behavior of unaccusative and unergative verbs in the resultative construction. These studies explain why a resultative phrase can only be predicated of a d-structure object, thus explaining why only unaccusative verbs have resultative phrases predicated of a surface subject.
7   See B. Levin & Rappaport Hovav (1992, 1995) for further discussion.
8   We deliberately use the term "position" rather than location since the result phrases in (13) need not involve an actual displacement. A change of position might be viewed as a change of location with no necessary displacement.
9   The adjective-headed result phrases which can be predicated of animates are typically *free* and *clear*, while those predicated of inanimates are typically *open, closed,* and *shut*. This difference in distribution reflects whether or not the adjective can be predicated of animates.
10 Although we argue that only unaccusative verbs participate in this alternation, it is not the case that all unaccusative verbs do. See B. Levin & Rappaport Hovav (1995) and Pinker (1989).
11 It is clear from the full context that in (32b) the riders are on separate horses; that is, the example does not have the accompaniment interpretation found in

sentences such as *Tina walked her dog*, which might be argued to instantiate a phenomenon distinct from the one being discussed here.

As we discuss in B. Levin & Rappaport Hovav (1995), due to the manipulability of some entities which emit a sound, causative uses of some verbs of sound are found without directional phrases, as in *Tracy jingled the coins*; comparable uses are not found with agentive verbs of manner of motion, as these necessarily take agentive subjects. When manipulability is not at issue, the directional phrase requirement comes to the fore for verbs of sound as well. See B. Levin & Rappaport Hovav (1995) for more discussion.

12 This analysis owes much to the insightful discussion of intransitive verbs in Smith (1970).

13 This approach is consistent with Wilkins and Van Valin's (1993) suggestion that the notion "agent" should not be considered primitive and cannot be defined as the argument filling a particular position in a decompositional representation of verb meaning (as in, for example, Jackendoff 1972, 1983, 1987b).

14 This statement is somewhat of a simplification; see B. Levin & Rappaport Hovav (1995). First, there may be a class of internally caused unaccusative verbs: internally caused verbs of change of state such as *bloom* and *blossom*. Second, there is evidence for a class of unaccusative verbs, the verbs of existence and appearance, that cannot be associated with the intransitive variant of externally caused verbs.

15 See Dowty (1991), B. Levin & Rappaport Hovav (1995) and Tenny (1987) for fuller and more explicit formulations of the Theme Linking Rule.

16 We thank Sue Atkins and Henri Béjoint for the examples in (43) and (44) and for discussion of this point. Some notes about the French examples. In (43b) the French verb *vrombir* is a very literary word, unlike the English verb *roar*. In (44b) the noun *fracas*, like the English noun *din*, can be used for a range of loud noises and thus does not capture any of the properties that make the sound associated with the verb *rumble* different from those associated with other verbs describing loud sounds.

XI Semantics and Related Domains

19 Semantics and Logic

GILA Y. SHER

Tarski's seminal work on truth and logical consequence is, perhaps, the single most important contribution to modern semantics. The recursive definition of truth in terms of satisfaction and the inductive, step-by-step definition of the logical syntax on which it is based, the notion of semantic model, the definitions of logical truth and logical consequence, are at the core of contemporary semantic theories.[1] Model-theoretic semantics (abstract logic), possible-world semantics, theories of meaning such as Davidson's and others', Montague semantics and even logical form (LF), a branch of generative syntax, all incorporate Tarskian principles.[2] Tarski's theory, however, is a logical semantics, resting, as it does, on an essential division of terms into logical and extralogical. In the mid-fifties a generalization of logical terms led to a substantial expansion of Tarskian semantics with important advances in logic and, more recently, in linguistics. Philosophically, the new generalization has raised, as well as provided tools for answering, important questions about logical semantics and its relation to linguistic semantics. In this paper I will discuss Tarskian semantics and the generalizations that followed in an attempt to answer some of the ensuing philosophical questions.

1 Tarskian Semantics Before 1957

In "The concept of truth in formalized languages" (1933) Tarski observed that the task of defining truth for a language with infinitely many sentences is complicated. We cannot refer to infinitely many sentences directly in a finite discourse, hence an indirect method is called for. The recursive method naturally suggested itself. The recursive method allows one to define predicates in a finite manner provided the domain of objects over which they range is itself finitely definable in a certain specified sense. In particular, if we construct the domain of objects inductively – i.e. generate it from a directly specified "base" (a non-empty set of objects) by means of a finite number of operations – if, furthermore, the domain is freely generated by this construction (i.e., an object cannot be constructed in more than one way), and if, finally, we limit our-selves to predicates whose satisfaction is a matter of the inductive structure of the objects involved, then we can define the extension of these predicates over the given domain recursively. Given a set S with a base B and, say, two freely generating operators, f^1 and g^2, the recursive definition of a predicate $\mathcal{P}$ (i) specifies for each atomic element whether it satisfies $\mathcal{P}$, (ii) provides a recur-sive rule for each generative operator: a rule that shows whether $f(a)$ satisfies $\mathcal{P}$ based on whether a satisfies $\mathcal{P}$, and a rule that shows whether $g(a,b)$ satisfies $\mathcal{P}$ based on whether a, b satisfy $\mathcal{P}$.[3] In Tarskian semantics the domain of objects is a set of formulas, and complex formulas are generated from simpler ones by means of certain logical operators. Another logical term (identity) participates in the construction of atomic formulas, although atomic formulas do not, in general, require logical terms. The definition of truth (in terms of satisfaction) specifies how the truth (satisfaction) of a complex formula is determined by the truth (satisfaction) of its constituent subformulas and the logical operators involved. The basic, non-recursive clause includes a specific rule for atomic formulas containing a logical term (identity) as a constituent, and a general rule for all other atomic formulas. Briefly, the definitions of the syntax and the semantics go as follows (I restrict myself here to 1st-order languages with no functional constants):

1.1 Syntax

Let L be a 1st-order language. We distinguish L by its non-logical constants: individuals, $c_1, \ldots, c_j$, and k_i-place predicates, $\mathcal{P}^{k_1}_1, \ldots, \mathcal{P}^{k_m}_m$, where j, $m \geq 0$ and $k > 0$. (The variables, logical symbols and punctuation marks (brackets) are the familiar ones, and they are common to all 1st-order languages.)

1.1.1 Inductive definition of well-formed formula (wff) of L

Base:

- If $\mathcal{P}^n$ is a non-logical predicate constant and $t_1, \ldots, t_n$ are individual terms (individual constants or variables), then $\ulcorner \mathcal{P}t_1, \ldots, t_n \urcorner$ is a wff.
- If t_1, t_2 are individual terms, then $\ulcorner t_1 = t_2 \urcorner$ is a wff.

Inductive clauses:

- If Φ is a wff, then $\ulcorner {\sim} \Phi \urcorner$ is a wff.
- If Φ, Ψ are wffs, then $\ulcorner \Phi \vee \Psi \urcorner$ is a wff.
- If Φ is a wff and x is an individual variable, then $\ulcorner \forall x \Phi \urcorner$ and $\ulcorner \exists x \Phi \urcorner$ are wffs.
- Only expressions obtained by one of the base or inductive clauses above are wffs.

1.2 Semantics for L

1.2.1 Recursive definition of satisfaction for L (a modern version):

Let A be the universe of discourse (a non-empty set of individuals) and d a denotation function which assigns to each individual constant c of L a member of A and to each non-logical n-place predicate constant $\mathcal{P}^n$ of L a subset of A^n (an n-place relation on A or a subset of A when $n = 1$). Let G be the collection of all functions from the set of variables of L into A. For each $g \in G$ let $\bar{g}$ be its extension to all the individual terms t of L: $\bar{g}(t) = g(t)$ if t is a variable, $\bar{g}(t) = d(t)$ if t is a constant. Then, relative to A and d, satisfaction of a wff Φ by a $g \in G$ – or, as I will present it here, the *truth value of Φ under g, $v(\Phi[g])$,* (where $v(\Phi[g]) \in \{T,F\}$) – is defined recursively as follows:

Base:

- $v(\ulcorner \mathcal{P}t_1, \ldots, t_n \urcorner[g]) = T$ iff (if and only if) $\langle \bar{g}(t_1), \ldots, \bar{g}(t_n) \rangle \in d(\mathcal{P})$.
- $v(\ulcorner t_1 = t_2 \urcorner[g]) = T$ iff $\bar{g}(t_1)$ **is the same as** $\bar{g}(t_2)$.

Recursive clauses:

- $v(\ulcorner \sim\!\Phi \urcorner[g]) = T$ iff **not** $v(\Phi[g]) = T$.
- $v(\ulcorner \Phi \lor \Psi \urcorner[g]) = T$ iff $v(\Phi[g]) = T$ **or** $v(\Psi[g]) = T$.
- $v(\ulcorner \forall x\Phi \urcorner / \ulcorner \exists x\Phi \urcorner[g]) = T$ iff for **every** / **some** individual a in A, $v(\Phi[g(a/x)]) = T$, where $g(a/x)$ assigns a to x and otherwise is the same as g.

1.2.2 Definition of truth:

A sentence (closed wff) σ is <u>true</u> (relative to A,d) iff its truth value under every (or some) $g \in G$ (it comes to the same thing) is T.

In order to define the notions of <u>logical truth</u> and <u>logical consequence</u>, Tarskian semantics introduces an apparatus of models. Given a 1st-order language L (as above), a *model* $\mathfrak{A}$ for L is a pair $\langle A,d \rangle$ where A is any universe (non-empty set of objects) and d a denotation function defined relative to A as above. The definitions of truth and satisfaction in a model are also the same as above, only now A is the universe of the given model and d its denotation function.

1.2.3 Definitions of logical truth and consequence:

- A sentence σ of L is a *logical consequence* of a set Γ of sentences of L iff there is no model $\mathfrak{A}$ for L in which all the sentences of Γ are true and σ is false.
- A sentence σ of L is *logically true* iff it is a logical consequence of any set of sentences of L (equivalently: iff it is true in every model $\mathfrak{A}$ for L.)

2   Unanswered Questions

Tarski's work in semantics led to a torrent of philosophical writings, but several important questions concerning the nature of logical semantics and semantics in general were rarely raised. In particular, the role, scope and nature of logical terms in Tarskian semantics as well as the relation between logical and non-logical semantics were never adequately clarified.

(A) The role of logical terms in Tarskian semantics is critical. The construction of the syntax as well as the definition of truth via satisfaction are based on fixed functions that correspond to particular constants – identity, truth-functional connectives, the existential and/or universal quantifiers. It is usually taken for granted that these constants are logical – that, furthermore, these are all the logical constants there are. With the exception of Tarski, the early logicians, and many of their successors, were content with this state of affairs. No one proposed a direct justification for his choice of quantifiers, though some produced indirect justifications. Thus, Frege and Russell believed that all of mathematics is reducible to logic with the "standard" logical terms, and Quine (perhaps the most influential of the later philosophers of logic) believed the "remarkable concurrence" of the semantic and proof-theoretic definitions of logical truth and consequence in "standard" 1st-order logic – completeness – justified drawing the boundary in the standard way. But the questions naturally arise whether mathematics cannot be reduced to logic with other logical terms, and whether no other (interesting) logical systems are complete. (Indeed, we now know that some interesting non-standard systems are.[4]) Frege referred to the standard quantifiers as expressions of generality, and in many textbooks logic is characterized as "general" and "topic neutral" and logical truths as "necessary." But in the absence of adequate criteria for generality, topic neutrality and necessity, why should we think that "not," "or," "is," "all" and their derivatives are the only carriers of general, topic neutral, necessary truths? Moreover, why should we think that the attributes of generality, topic neutrality and necessity uniquely identify logical truth at all (rather than a more inclusive – or a narrower – category of truths)?

Already in 1936 Tarski realized the issue of logical terms is crucial for logical semantics:

> Underlying our whole construction [of the semantic definition of logical consequence] is the division of all terms of the language discussed into logical and extra-logical. This division is certainly not quite arbitrary. If, for example, we were to include among the extra-logical signs the implication sign, or the universal quantifier, then our definition of the concept of consequence would lead to results which obviously contradict ordinary usage. On the other hand, no objective grounds are known to me which permit us to draw a sharp boundary between the two groups of terms. It seems to me possible to include among logical

terms some which are usually regarded by logicians as extra-logical without running into consequences which stand in sharp contrast to ordinary usage. In the extreme case we could regard all terms of the language as logical. (Tarski 1936a: 418–9)

The extreme case Tarski referred to is one in which the boundary between logical and material consequences largely disappears. Such materially valid arguments as "Bush lost the 1992 US presidential elections; therefore, Clinton is the US president in 1994" come out logically valid. To avoid this result, a reasoned distinction between logical and extra-logical terms has to be established. Clearly, the task of establishing such a distinction is of utmost importance for logic. For many years, however, philosophers of logic took the standard division of terms into logical and extra-logical as given. This was not so much a matter of choice, but a matter of not knowing how to go about establishing a reasoned distinction.

(B) The Tarskian definition of truth in the form given above (or in any of the common forms) is inherently uninformative: Essentially, what this definition says is that $\ulcorner \Phi$ or $\Psi \urcorner$ is true iff Φ is true or Ψ is true, $\ulcorner$Some x is $\Phi x \urcorner$ is true iff some individual in the universe satisfies $\ulcorner \Phi x \urcorner$, and so on. If "or" in $\ulcorner \Phi$ or $\Psi \urcorner$ or "some" in $\ulcorner$Some x is $\Phi x \urcorner$ is unclear, ambiguous, or imprecise, the above definition of truth does not assist us in clarifying, disambiguating, or rendering it precise. For the connectives, however, we do have an informative definition available, tied up with a precise criterion of logicality. In the early days of modern logic the distinctive feature of logical connectives was determined to be truth-functionality, and, based on this feature, logical connectives were identified with certain mathematical functions, namely Boolean truth functions (functions from sequences of truth values to truth values): Negation was identified with the 1-place function $f_\sim$, where $f_\sim(T) = F$ and $f_\sim(F) = T$, disjunction was identified with the 2-place function, f_v, where $f_v(T,T) = f_v(T,F) = f_v(F,T) = T$ and $f_v(F,F) = F$, etc. The semantic identification of logical connectives with Boolean functions led to the following criterion for logical connectives:

> (LC)   A term C is a logical connective iff there is a natural number n and a Boolean function $f_c:\{T,F\}^n \rightarrow \{T,F\}$ such that for any n-tuple of well-formed sentences $\sigma_1, \ldots, \sigma_n, \ulcorner C(\sigma_1, \ldots, \sigma_n) \urcorner$ is a well-formed sentence and its truth value is determined by $f_c[v(\sigma_1), \ldots, v(\sigma_n)]$, where for $1 \leq i \leq n$, $v(\sigma_i)$ is the truth value of σ_i.

This criterion gives a precise and informative answer to the questions: "What is a logical connective?", "What are all the logical connectives?". It decides the adequacy of a given selection of logical connectives ($\sim$ and V constitute a "complete" selection but & and V do not: we can define all truth-functional connectives in terms of $\sim$ and V, but not in terms of & and V). And it enables us to give a more informative account of the truth conditions of sentential compounds:

- $v(\ulcorner {\sim}\varPhi\urcorner [g]) = T$ iff $f_{\sim}(v(\varPhi[g])) = T$,
- $v(\ulcorner \varPhi V \varPsi\urcorner [g]) = T$ iff $f_v(v(\varPhi[g]),v(\varPsi[g])) = T$.

Whereas in the earlier version the definiens simply simulated the definiendum, here the definiens includes a precise and informative rendition of the latter. (Thus, if the colloquial "or" is ambiguous between the exclusive and inclusive reading, the Boolean function associated with "or" resolves the ambiguity.)

Unlike the logical connectives, the logical predicates and quantifiers are usually defined by enumeration and the meta-theoretical account does little more than translate them into colloquial language. It is true that their frequent use in mathematics has made these terms precise, but no systematic identification of the logical predicates and quantifiers with mathematical functions based on a general criterion of logicality is given.

(C) Tarski's recursive definition of truth is limited to sentences generated by means of *logical* operators. In this definition each logical term receives special treatment, but all non-logical terms of a given grammatical category are treated "en masse." The question naturally arises whether Tarskian semantics is inherently logical. Clearly, in logic, we are interested in studying the contribution of logical structure to the truth value of sentences, but logical structure is not the only factor in the truth or falsity of sentences. To what extent is Tarski's method limited to logical semantics? Should we think of natural language semantics as a straightforward extension of Tarski's theory?

These questions, thus, are awaiting an answer: (A) Is there a philosophical basis for the distinction between logical and non-logical terms? (B) Can we develop a precise mathematical criterion for logical constants and, based on it, an informative definition of truth? (C) What is the relation between logical and general semantics? Before 1957 it was hard to answer the first two questions since no systematic study of logical terms (other than connectives) existed. But the generalization of the standard quantifiers by Mostowski (1957) changed this situation: it created a framework within which to develop, compare and investigate alternative answers to questions about logical terms.

3   Mostowski's Generalization of the Logical Quantifiers and Further Developments

In his 1957 paper, "On a generalization of quantifiers," Mostowski proposed a semantic criterion for logical quantifiers leading to a new notion of logical term, considerably broader than the standard one. Before I describe Mostowski's criterion I would like to introduce a syntactic–semantic classification of primitive terms that is independent of their logical status. Relative to this classification we will be able to view Mostowski's generalization as a first step in answering the question: "What terms of what categories are logical, and why?"

Adopting a Fregean conception of quantifiers as properties (relations) of properties (relations) of individuals, I will present a syntactic classification of terms into *orders* and *types* based on semantic considerations. The order of a term depends on whether its extension or denotation (in what may be called its "intended model") is an individual, a set or n-tuple of individuals, a set of sets of individuals, etc. (I assume the notion of an empty set of individuals is distinguished from that of an empty relation of individuals, an empty set of sets of individuals, etc.) I am leaving functional terms and sentential connectives out, the former for the sake of simplicity, the latter because the problem of providing a precise criterion of logicality for the connectives has its own, independent, solution. (See above)

Order:

- A primitive individual term (a term denoting an individual), t. *order* 0.
- A primitive n-place predicative term (a term whose extension is a set or relation), P (where $n > 0$): *order* $m + 1$, where m is the order of the highest argument of P.

On this classification, a 1st-order system consists of primitive terms (or schematic representations of primitive terms) of orders 0, 1 and 2, where all variables are of order 0 and all primitive terms of order 2 are logical. I.e. a 1st-order system is a system whose non-logical constants and variables are of order ≤ 1. Primitive terms of order 0 are called individual constants, of order 1 – predicates, and of order 2 – quantifiers. Restricting ourselves to constants of orders 0, 1 and 2, we can determine their place in the hierarchy uniquely by means of a simple classification into "types."

Type:

The type of a primitive term provides information about its arguments.

- A primitive individual term, t. *no type* (no arguments).
- A primitive n-place predicative term, P: *type* $\langle t_1, \ldots, t_n \rangle$, where for $1 \leq i \leq n$, t_i = the number of arguments of the i-th argument of P.

Predicates are of type $\langle t_1, \ldots, t_n \rangle$, where for all $1 \leq i \leq n$, $t_i = 0$; quantifiers are of type $\langle t_1, \ldots, t_n \rangle$, where for each $1 \leq i \leq n$, $t_i \geq 0$, and for at least one $1 \leq i \leq n$, $t_i > 0$. Identity is of type $\langle 0,0 \rangle$; the existential and universal quantifiers are of type $\langle 1 \rangle$. Natural language constants are naturally classified as follows: "John" – no type; "is tall" – type $\langle 0 \rangle$; "loves" – type $\langle 0,0 \rangle$. Mathematical constants receive the following classification: "one" – no type; "there is exactly one" – type $\langle 1 \rangle$; "there are finitely many" – type $\langle 1 \rangle$; "most . . . are ---" – type $\langle 1,1 \rangle$; "is a well ordering" – type $\langle 2 \rangle$; the membership predicate of 1st-order set theories (e.g. ZF) – type $\langle 0,0 \rangle$; the 2nd-order membership predicate – type $\langle 0,1 \rangle$, and so on.

Mostowski's generalization can be seen as an answer to the question: "What primitive terms of type $\langle 1 \rangle$ (i.e. quantifiers of type $\langle 1 \rangle$) are logical?" His answer is given by the following semantic criterion:

> (M)   "[Logical] quantifiers should not allow us to distinguish between different elements of [the underlying universe]." (Mostowski 1957: 13)

Two questions naturally arise: (1) What is the precise content of (M)? In particular: What does "not distinguishing between different elements" come to? (2) What is the intuitive justification for viewing logical quantifiers as in (M)? Mostowski did not give an answer to (2), but he did give a precise answer to (1). I will begin with Mostowski's syntactic notion of quantifier.

Syntactically, any predicate of type $\langle 1 \rangle$ can be construed as a 1-place operator binding a formula by means of a variable, i.e. as a quantifier. A quantifier (of type $\langle 1 \rangle$) satisfying (M) is a logical quantifier. To incorporate 1-place quantifiers in a 1st-order syntax we replace the entry for quantification in the standard definition by:

- If Φ is a wff, x is a variable and Q is a logical quantifier, then $\ulcorner Qx\Phi \urcorner$ is a wff.

Disengaging ourselves from the notion of "intended model," we can view quantifiers, semantically, as functions that assign to each universe A an A-quantifier, where an A-quantifier is a set of subsets of A or a function from subsets of A to $\{T,F\}$. Thus, the universal quantifier is a function $Q^\forall$, or shortly, $\forall$, such that for any set of objects, A, $\forall(A) = \forall_A : P(A) \rightarrow \{T,F\}$, where $P(A)$ is the power set (set of all subsets) of A. $\forall_A$ is defined by: given a subset B of A, $\forall_A(B) = T$ iff $B = A$. $\exists_A$ is defined by: $\exists_A(B) = T$ iff $B \neq \phi$. Mostowski interpreted the semantic condition (M) as saying:

> (M*)   An A-quantifier is logical iff it is invariant under permutations of A (or, more precisely, permutations of $P(A)$ induced by permutations of A).

I.e. Q_A is logical iff for any permutation p of A and any subset B of A, $Q_A(B) = Q_A(p'(B))$, where p' is the permutation of $P(A)$ induced by p. (M*) can also be formulated in terms of (weak) automorphisms (isomorphisms of A-structures):

> (M**)   An A-quantifier is logical iff it is invariant under automorphisms of set A-structures.

I.e. Q_A is logical iff given a non-empty set A and B, $B' \subseteq A$: if $\langle A,\langle B \rangle\rangle \cong \langle A,\langle B'\rangle\rangle$ ($\langle A,\langle B\rangle\rangle$ and $\langle A,\langle B'\rangle\rangle$ are isomorphic), then $Q_A(B) = Q_A(B')$. It is easy to see that the standard quantifiers satisfy Mostowski's condition.

Now, as in sentential logic, Mostowski was able to represent the truth (satisfaction) conditions of logical A-quantifiers by correlating them with certain mathematical functions. Given a logical A-quantifier, Mostowski observed that its truth conditions have to do with the *cardinalities* of subsets of A and their complements (in A) and nothing else. Accordingly, $\exists_A$ and $\forall_A$ can be defined in the following way: Given a set $B \subseteq A$, $\exists_A(B) = T$ iff $|B| > 0$, $\forall_A(B) = T$ iff $|A - B| = 0$ ($|\ldots|$ is the cardinality of $\ldots$). We can thus identify $\exists_A$ and $\forall_A$ with *cardinality functions*, $\exists_{|A|}$ and $\forall_{|A|}$, from pairs of cardinals (β,γ) such that $\beta + \gamma = |A|$ to T and F, defined by: $\exists_{|A|}(\beta,\gamma) = T$ iff $\beta > 0$, $\forall_{|A|}(\beta,\gamma) = T$ iff $\gamma = 0$. More generally, any function $q_\alpha : (\beta,\gamma)_\alpha \rightarrow \{T,F\}$, where α is a cardinal number larger than 0 and $(\beta,\gamma)_\alpha$ is the set of all pairs (β,γ) such that $\beta + \gamma = \alpha$, is an α-quantifier. Mostowski proved that there is a 1–1 correlation between logical A-quantifiers, i.e. A-quantifiers satisfying (M*), and α-quantifiers.

How shall we extend (M*) to logical quantifiers of type $\langle 1 \rangle$ in general, i.e. unrestricted to A? Mostowski did not go beyond A-quantifiers, but we can easily extend his criterion based on the following considerations:

(a) It is natural to view a quantifier Q as logical iff for any universe A, Q_A is a logical A-quantifier.

(b) It is natural to require that a logical quantifier Q be correlated with the same α-quantifier in any two universes of the same cardinality.

(a) and (b) lead to the following extension of (M**):

(M***) A quantifier Q (predicate of type $\langle 1 \rangle$) is logical iff it is invariant under isomorphisms of set structures.

I.e. Q is logical iff for every $A \neq \phi$, $A' \neq \phi$, $B \subseteq A$ and $B' \subseteq A'$: if $\langle A,\langle B\rangle\rangle \cong \langle A',\langle B'\rangle\rangle$, then $Q_A(B) = Q_{A'}(B')$. Quantifiers satisfying (M***) are often called "Mostowskian" or "cardinality quantifiers." Among the many quantifiers falling under this category is M, standing for some mathematically precise rendition of "most." If "most" is taken as "more than half," then it is defined by $M_\alpha(\beta,\gamma) = T$ iff $\beta > \gamma$. Other Mostowskian quantifiers are $!\delta$, standing for "exactly δ" and defined by $!\delta_\alpha(\beta,\gamma) = T$ iff $\beta = \delta$; E, standing for "an even number of" and defined by $E_\alpha(\beta,\gamma) = T$ iff β is an even positive integer; $!1/2$, standing for "half" and defined by $!1/2_\alpha(\beta,\gamma) = T$ iff $\beta = \gamma$, and $\mathcal{F}$, standing for "finitely many" and defined by $F_\alpha(\beta,\gamma) = T$ iff $\beta < \aleph_0$. These quantifiers appear in such sentences as "Most things are different from what you think they are," "There are exactly two pennies in my pocket," "There is an even number of letters in the English alphabet," "Half the things are yours," "There are finitely many rows in a truth table," symbolized by $\ulcorner(Mx)\mathcal{D}x\urcorner$, $\ulcorner(!2x)\mathcal{P}x\urcorner$, $\ulcorner(Ex)\mathcal{L}x\urcorner$,

⌜$(!1/2x)\mathcal{Y}x$⌝ and ⌜$(\forall x)[\mathcal{T}x \supset (\text{F}y)\mathcal{R}yx]$⌝, respectively, with the obvious reading of $\mathcal{D}$, $\mathcal{P}$, $\mathcal{L}$, $\mathcal{Y}$, $\mathcal{T}$ and $\mathcal{R}$. We can replace the entry for quantifiers in Tarski's semantic definition of truth under g as follows: Given a universe A of cardinality $\alpha > 0$,

- $v(⌜Qx\Phi⌝[g]) = T$ iff $Q_\alpha(\beta,\gamma) = T$, where $\beta = |\{a \in A: v(\Phi[g(a/x)]) = T\}|$ and $\gamma = |\{a \in A: v(\Phi[g(a/x)]) = F\}|$.

Intuitively, what this definition says is that ⌜$Qx\Phi x$⌝ is true in a model $\mathfrak{A}$ with a universe A of cardinality α iff the number of objects in A satisfying ⌜Φx⌝ and the number of objects in A not satisfying ⌜Φx⌝ is as Q says. Mostowski's generalization was further extended in 1966 by Lindström and Tarski (independently of one another). The extended criterion applies to all terms of orders 0–2, regardless of type. Following common practice, I will name the criterion after Lindström:

(L)   A term is logical iff it is invariant under isomorphic structures,[5]

where a structure is an $n + 1$-tuple, $\langle A, \langle D_1, \ldots, D_n \rangle \rangle$, $A \neq \phi$ and D_i, $1 \leq i \leq n$, is a member of A, a subset of A or a relation of A. The idea is, roughly, that if a term is logical, it does not distinguish between structurally identical arguments. I.e. if $\langle A, \langle D_1, \ldots, D_n \rangle \rangle \cong \langle A', \langle D'_1, \ldots, D'_n \rangle \rangle$, then a logical term assigns the same truth value to $\langle D_1, \ldots, D_n \rangle$ in the universe A as to $\langle D'_1, \ldots, D'_n \rangle$ in the universe A'. Since individual terms have no arguments, they cannot be said to give the same truth value to structurally identical arguments, and we stipulate that they do not satisfy the criterion (L). Among the predicates falling under Lindström's criterion are, in addition to Mostowskian quantifiers, the 1st-order identity relation and the 2nd-order binary predicate "Most" (type $\langle 1,1 \rangle$), appearing in such sentences as "Most students passed the test" and symbolized ⌜$(M^{1-1}x)(Sx,Px)$⌝. Intuitively, ⌜$(M^{1-1}x)(Sx,Px)$⌝ is true iff most of the S's in the universe of discourse are P's, i.e. iff the pair $\langle S,P \rangle$, where S, P are the extensions of ⌜Sx⌝, ⌜Px⌝, respectively, satisfies "Most".[6] "Most" is logical according to (L) since for any universes A and A', and $S,P \subseteq A$, S', $P' \subseteq A'$: if $\langle A, \langle S,P \rangle \rangle \cong \langle A', \langle S',P' \rangle \rangle$, then $\langle S,P \rangle$ satisfies "Most" iff $\langle S',P' \rangle$ satisfies it. Other terms satisfying (L) include the 2nd-order ternary predicate, "More . . . than --- are***" (type $\langle 1,1,1 \rangle$), as in "More girls than boys passed the test," symbolized by ⌜$(M^{1-1-1}x)(Gx,Bx,Px)$,⌝ the 2nd-order membership predicate, where "t is a member of $\mathcal{B}$" is symbolized ⌜$(MEM^{0-1}x)(t,Bx)$⌝, the 2nd-order relational predicate "Well-ordering", where "$\mathcal{R}$ is a well ordering" is symbolized: ⌜$(WO^2xy)\mathcal{R}xy$⌝, etc.

Among the predicates which do not satisfy (L) are all the predicates of type 1 which fail to satisfy (M***), the predicate "is tall", the 1st-order membership predicate, the 2nd-order predicate "is a relation between humans" (type $\langle 2 \rangle$), and many others. Comparing the two membership predicates, $\in^{0-0}$ and $\in^{0-1}$, we see the difference between them intuitively as follows: $\ulcorner t_1 \in {}^{0-0}t_2 \urcorner$ is true in a universe A iff the two individuals assigned to t_1 and t_1 in A, a_1 and a_2, are such that $a_2 = \{a_1, \dots\}$. But as members of A (as individuals) a_1 and a_2 are atomic objects. Therefore, the structures $\langle A, \langle a_1, a_2 \rangle \rangle$ and $\langle A, \langle a_2, a_1 \rangle \rangle$ are isomorphic and no term satisfying (L) distinguishes between them. I.e. for any terms of type $\langle 0, 0 \rangle$, C^{0-0}, satisfying (L): $C_A^{0-0}(a_1, a_2) = T$ iff $C_A^{0-0}(a_2, a_1) = T$. Since $\in^{0-0}$ does distinguish between the structures $\langle A, \langle a_1, a_2 \rangle \rangle$ and $\langle A, \langle a_2, a_1 \rangle \rangle$ (if $a_1 \in_A^{0-0} a_2$ then $a_2 \notin_A^{0-0} a_1$), $\in^{0-0}$ does not satisfy (L). The situation is different with respect to $\in^{0-1}$: $\in_A^{0-1}$ holds between a member and a subset of A, not between two members of A. Therefore, the problem indicated above does not arise: $\langle A, \langle a, B \rangle \rangle$ is never isomorphic to $\langle A, \langle B, a \rangle \rangle$. It is easy to see that $\in^{0-1}$ satisfies (L): Given any non-empty sets A and A', if $\langle A, \langle a, B \rangle \rangle \cong \langle A', \langle a', B' \rangle \rangle$ then $a \in B$ iff $a' \in B'$, i.e. $\in_A^{0-1}(a, B) = T$ iff $\in_{A'}^{0-1}(a', B') = T$.

Lindström's criterion satisfies Mostowski's initial condition, (M): A term invariant under isomorphic structures takes into account only the mathematical structure of its arguments in a given universe. Since individuals are, semantically, atomic elements, they are all structurally identical, and their difference is not detected by any logical (structural) term. Taking Lindström's criterion as my starting point I will now turn to the three questions posed in Section 2. I will begin with the second, meta-logical, question: Is there an informative, constructive definition of logical terms, which exhibits their truth (satisfaction) conditions in accordance with (L) and shows how to build up extensions that satisfy them? In Section 6 I will propose an answer to the question concerning the philosophical foundation of the distinction between logical and non-logical terms, and in Section 7 I will briefly comment on the relation between logical and linguistic semantics.

4   A Constructive Definition of Logical Terms

My answer to the second, meta-logical question is positive. I will present two "constructive" definitions of logical terms: (a) a definition of n-place cardinality quantifiers, based on Lindström (1966), and (b) a definition of logical terms in general, based on Sher (1991).

4.1   A constructive definition of n-place cardinality quantifiers

In his 1966 paper Lindström extended Mostowski's "constructive" definition to *cardinality quantifiers* in general. Lindström proved that if a logical term of type $\langle 1, 1, \dots, 1 \rangle$ satisfies (L), then all it takes into account is the *cardinalities* of 2^n sets in a given universe. More particularly, if a quantifier Q^{1-1} satisfies (L), then the truth of "$Q^{1\text{-}1}$ $\mathcal{B}$'s are C's"[7] is fully determined by the cardinalities of B–C, C–B, $B \cap C$ and A–$(B \cup C)$, where B and C are the extensions of $\mathcal{B}$ and C', respectively, and A is the universe of discourse. (Mathematically, the truth-conditions of $Q^{1\text{-}1}$ are based on the size of the atoms of the Boolean algebra generated by B and C in A.) We can thus identify $Q^{1\text{-}1}$, semantically, with a function, $Q^{1\text{-}1}$, from cardinal numbers α (sizes of universes) to α-quantifiers, $Q_{\alpha}^{1\text{-}1}$, where $Q_{\alpha}^{1\text{-}1}$ is a function from quadruples of cardinals, $(\beta, \gamma, \delta, \zeta)$, whose sum is α into $\{T,F\}$.[8] (If α represents the size of A, then $\beta,\gamma,\delta,\zeta$ represent the cardinalities of B–C, C–B, $B \cap C$ and A–$(B \cup C)$, respectively, where B and C are any subsets of A.) For example, we identify $Most^{1\text{-}1}$ with $M^{1\text{-}1}$, defined by: for any cardinal α, $M_{\alpha}^{1\text{-}1}(\beta,\gamma,\delta,\zeta) = T$ iff $\delta > \beta$. The totality of 4-place cardinality functions as above determines the totality of binary "cardinality" quantifiers, and each cardinality function embeds a set of instructions for constructing an n-tuple of sets that satisfy the corresponding logical term. (To construct a pair of sets such that $\langle B,C \rangle$ satisfying $M^{1\text{-}1}$ in A we partition A to four subsets, A_1, A_2, A_3 and A_4 such $|A_3| > |A_1|$, and we let $B = A_1 \cup A_3$ and $C = A_2 \cup A_3$.)

We incorporate 2-place cardinality quantifiers in a 1st-order Tarskian system by adding a new entry to the syntax and the semantics:

- If Φ, Ψ are wffs, x is a variable and $Q^{1\text{-}1}$ is a 2-place quantifier, then $\ulcorner Q^{1\text{-}1}x(\Phi,\Psi) \urcorner$ is a wff.
- $v(\ulcorner Q^{1\text{-}1}x(\Phi,\Psi) \urcorner[g]) = T$ iff $Q_{\alpha}(\beta,\gamma,\delta,\zeta) = T$, where $\beta = |\{a \in A: v(\Phi[g(a/x)]) = T$ and $v(\Psi[g(a/x)]) = F\}|$, $\gamma = |\{a \in A: v(\Phi[g](a/x)]) = F$ and $v(\Psi[g(a/x)]) = T\}|$, $\delta = |\{a \in A: v(\Phi[g(a/x)]) = v(\Psi[g(a/x)]) = T\}|$, and $\zeta = |\{a \in A: v(\Phi[g(a/x)]) = v(\Psi[g(a/x)]) = F\}|$.

4.2   A constructive definition of logical terms in general

Not all logical terms satisfying (L) are cardinality quantifiers, therefore a general definition of logical terms requires a different method from the one employed above. Presently, I will give an outline of such a general definition. For the purposes of demonstration I will limit myself to terms of types $\langle 0,0 \rangle$, $\langle 1 \rangle$ and $\langle 2 \rangle$. The account will proceed from the bottom up: starting with a universe A, I will describe a method for determining (or constructing) the extensions of all logical terms in A. This method will produce a set-theoretical representation of logical terms in general. I will proceed in four steps.

Step 1. Take any model $\mathfrak{A}$ with a universe A of cardinality α and consider three sets: $S1$ – the set of all pairs of individuals in A ($S1 = A \times A$), $S2$ – the set of all subsets of A ($S2 = P(A)$), and $S3$ – the set of all sets of pairs of individuals in A ($S3 = P(A \times A)$). Subsets of $S1$ constitute extensions of terms of type $\langle 0,0 \rangle$ (e.g. =) in A, subsets of $S2$ constitute extensions of terms of type $\langle 1 \rangle$ (e.g. $\forall$ and $Most^1$) in A, and subsets of $S3$ are extensions of terms of type $\langle 2 \rangle$ (Is–Symmetric[2]) in A. Our first task is to construct the extensions of logical terms of these types in $\mathfrak{A}$.

Step 2. We know that logical terms do not distinguish between objects (pairs of individuals, sets, relations) which are structurally identical. So we can think of logical terms in the following way: if a logical term holds of an object with structure $\mathcal{S}$ in $\mathfrak{A}$, then it holds of all objects with structure $\mathcal{S}$ in $\mathfrak{A}$. Thus, given any subset of $S1$, $S2$ or $S3$, we extend it to an extension of a logical term (of type $\langle 0,0 \rangle$, $\langle 1 \rangle$ or $\langle 2 \rangle$) by closing it under automorphisms. For example, if $A = \{a,b,c,d\}$ and $S \subseteq S2 = \{\{a\},\{b,c\}\}$, then, since $\langle A,\langle\{a\}\rangle\rangle \cong \langle A,\langle\{b\}\rangle\rangle \cong \langle A,\langle\{c\}\rangle\rangle \cong \langle A,\langle\{d\}\rangle\rangle$ and $\langle A,\langle\{b,c\}\rangle\rangle \cong \langle A,\langle\{a,b\}\rangle\rangle \cong \langle A,\langle\{a,c\}\rangle\rangle \cong \langle A,\langle\{a,d\}\rangle\rangle \cong \langle A,\langle\{b,d\}\rangle\rangle \cong \langle A,\langle\{c,d\}\rangle\rangle$, the closure of S, $S*$, is $\{\{a\},\{b\},\{c\},\{d\},\{a,b\},\{a,c\},\{a,d\},\{b,c\},\{b,d\},\{c,d\}\}$. By construction, $S*$ satisfies the invariance condition (L) for A-structures (structures with A as their universe), hence $S*$ is the extension of some logical term over all models with universe A, namely the logical quantifier "either-one-or-two$^1_{A}$," or, shortly "1–2$^1_{A}$," whose syntactic correlate appears in formulas of the form $\ulcorner(1\text{–}2^1x)\Phi x\urcorner$. In this way the closure of each subset of $S1$, $S2$ and $S3$ constitutes the extension of some logical term restricted to A.

Step 3. Logical terms, however, satisfy the invariance condition (L) not only relative to one universe, but also across universes. Therefore, logical terms over $\mathfrak{A}$ should not be constructed from elements of A, but from "neutral" elements, elements that can be used to identify extensions in any universe of cardinality $\alpha = |A|$. One way to satisfy this requirement is to construct logical terms using indices of members of A as our building blocks. We can take α itself, i.e. the set of ordinals smaller than α, as our index set.[9] We start by assigning indices to elements of A by some (any) index function i from A *onto* α. We then replace the extensions of the logical terms over $\mathfrak{A}$ by their indices. Thus, in the example above, we assign to a,b,c,d the indices $0,1,2,3$ and we replace $S*$ by $S^+ = \{\{0\},\{1\},\{2\},\{3\},\{0,1\},\{0,2\},\{0,3\},\{1,2\},\{1,3\},\{2,3\}\}$. The result is an extension of an α-logical-term, in this case, a logical quantifier, 1–2$_\alpha$. We say that a $B \in S2$ satisfies 1–2$_\alpha$ (in $\mathfrak{A}$) iff for some indexing of A by α, the index image of B is in the extension of 1–2$_\alpha$ (i.e. is a member of S^+). In a similar way we construct α-logical-terms of types $\langle 0,0 \rangle$ and $\langle 2 \rangle$.

Step 4. Finally, we "construct" unrestricted logical terms by grouping α-logical-terms together into classes, where each class contains exactly one α-logical-term for each cardinal α. Each class is a logical term (an unrestricted logical term), and the construction of each logical term embeds a structural description of the objects satisfying it in each model. Put otherwise, the representation of each logical term includes "instructions" for constructing its extension in a given model as well as determining, with respect to any given element (in our example, a pair of individuals, a subset of the universe, or a binary relation on the universe) whether it satisfies the given logical term in that model. Technically, I will construe both α-logical-terms and (unrestricted) logical terms as functions. A logical term assigns to each cardinal α an α-logical-term, and an α-logical-term assigns to each element of α of the right type (a pair of ordinals, a set of ordinals, a set of pairs of ordinals, etc.) a truth value, T or F. Thus, if $\alpha = 4$, $1\text{–}2^1_\alpha(\{1\}) = 1\text{–}2^1_\alpha(\{0,3\}) = T$ and $1\text{–}2^1_\alpha(\phi) = 1\text{–}2^1_\alpha(\{0,1,2\}) = F$.[10]

This completes my construction. The construction is, of course, an idealized one, using resources (i.e. proper classes) that go beyond standard set theories. But it gives us a definition analogous to the Boolean definition of the logical connectives: i.e., a definition that embeds rules for determining what satisfies a given logical term. In sentential logic logical terms do not distinguish between sentences with the same truth value, hence sentences are represented by truth values and logical terms are defined as functions on truth values. In (Lindström) 1st-order logic logical terms do not distinguish between objects (denotations and extensions of expressions) with the same mathematical (set theoretical) structure, hence objects are represented by mathematical (set theoretical) structures and logical terms are defined as functions on such structures. The semantic construction of Lindström logical terms is of course more complex than that of the logical terms of sentential logic, but that was to be expected.

To include logical terms of types $\langle 0,0 \rangle$, $\langle 1 \rangle$, and $\langle 2 \rangle$ in a 1st-order Tarskian system, we adjust the syntax and the semantics in the following way:

4.3 Syntax

- If R^{0-0} is a logical term of type $\langle 0,0 \rangle$ and t_1, t_2 individual terms, then $\ulcorner R^{0-0}t_1t_2 \urcorner$ is a wff.
- If Q^1 is a logical term of type $\langle 1 \rangle$, Φ is a wff and x is a variable, then $\ulcorner (Q^1x)\Phi \urcorner$ is a wff.
- If Q^2 is a logical term of type $\langle 2 \rangle$, Φ is a wff and x, y are variables, then $\ulcorner (Q^2xy)\Phi \urcorner$ is a wff.

4.4 Semantics

Relative to a universe A of cardinality α, a denotation function d, an assignment g and an indexing i of A by α,

- $v(\ulcorner R^{0-0}t_1t_2 \urcorner[g]) = T$ iff $R_\alpha^{0-0}(i(\bar{g}(t_1)),i(\bar{g}(t_2))) = T$, where $i(\bar{g}(t_1))$, $i(\bar{g}(t_2))$ are the indices of $\bar{g}(t_1)$, $\langle\bar{g}(t_2)\rangle$, respectively.
  Informally: g satisfies $\ulcorner R^{0-0}t_1t_2 \urcorner$ iff R_α^{0-0} assigns the value T to the pair of indices of the individuals assigned to t_1 and t_2 by g/d.
- $v(\ulcorner (Q^1x)\Phi \urcorner[g]) = T$ iff $Q_\alpha^1(I\{a \in A: v(\Phi[g(a/x)]) = T\}) = T$, where $I\{\dots\}$ is the set of indices of all members of $\{\dots\}$.
  Informally: g satisfies $\ulcorner (Q^1x)\Phi x \urcorner$ iff Q_α^1 assigns the value T to the set of indices of all $a \in A$ such that $g(a/x)$ satisfies $\ulcorner \Phi x \urcorner$.
- $v(\ulcorner (Q^2xy)\Phi \urcorner[g]) = T$ iff $Q_\alpha (I\{\langle a,b \rangle \in A \times A: v(\Phi[g(a/x)(b/y)]) = T\}) = T$.
  Informally: g satisfies $\ulcorner (Q^2xy)\Phi xy \urcorner$ iff Q_α^2 assigns the value T to the set of all pairs of indices of a, $b \in A$, such that $g(a/x)(b/y)$ satisfies $\ulcorner \Phi xy \urcorner$.

While Lindström's criterion does lead to a precise, informative definition of logical terms (and truth), no rationale was offered for his criterion. True, his notion of logical term satisfies Mostowski's requirement that logical terms do not distinguish the identity (individuality) of objects in a given universe, but why should we take Mostowski's requirement as a criterion for *logicality*? A partial justification was given by Tarski who arrived at (essentially) the same criterion as Lindström. Taking his cue from Klein's program for classifying geometric disciplines according to the transformations of space under which their concepts are invariant, Tarski suggested:

> ... suppose we continue the idea, and consider still wider classes of transformations. In the extreme case, we would consider the class of *all* one–one transformations of the space, or universe of discourse, or 'world', onto itself. What will be the science which deals with the notions invariant under this widest class of transformations? Here we will have very few notions, all of a very general character. I suggest that they are the logical notions, that we call a notion 'logical' if it is invariant under all possible one–one transformations of the world onto itself. (Tarski 1986/1966: 149)

By way of justifying his proposal, Tarski said: "[This] suggestion perhaps sounds strange – the only way of seeing whether it is a reasonable suggestion is to discuss some of its consequences, to see what it leads to, what we have to believe in if we agree to use the term 'logical' in this sense." (Tarski 1986/1966: 149–50) And what this criterion commits us to believe in, Tarski went on to say, is that no individual constant expresses a logical notion, that the only binary logical relations of order 1 are the universal relation, the empty relation, identity and diversity; that the only logical notions of order 2, type $\langle t_1 = 1, \ldots t_n = 1 \rangle$ are cardinality notions; that all classical mathematical notions of order >1 are logical notions, etc. The totality of logical notions under this criterion coincides with the totality of terms definable by "purely logical means" in the system of *Principia Mathematica*, hence, Tarski concluded, the criterion stands "in agreement, if not with all prevailing usage of the term 'logical notion', at least with one usage which actually is encountered in practice." (Tarski 1986/1966: 145) Tarski, however, did not tell us why, or even whether, this particular usage should be preferred to others. Why should we not prefer a more restricted usage? a more liberal usage? an altogether different usage?

At least one philosopher, Etchemendy (1990), claims that Tarskian logic does not embed any rational criterion for logical terms, that, in fact, any term whatsoever can serve as a logical term in Tarskian logic. The inevitable consequence is that the very distinction between logical and non-logical truths (consequences) collapses. (Assume "is human" and "is mortal" are included in a Tarskian system as logical terms, based on the following semantic rules:

- $v(\ulcorner \text{Is human } (t)\urcorner[g]) = T$ iff $\bar{g}(t) \in \{a \in A: a \text{ is human}\}$.
- $v(\ulcorner \text{Is mortal } (t)\urcorner[g]) = T$ iff $\bar{g}(t) \in \{a \in A: a \text{ is mortal}\}$.

Then the intuitively logically indeterminate sentence "All humans are mortals" comes out logically true.)

Other questions regarding the distinction between logical and non-logical terms come from *linguistics*, especially the linguistic theory of generalized quantifiers.

5   The Linguistic Theory of Generalized Quantifiers

Linguists have found the logical theory of generalized quantifiers a fertile ground for applications. We can divide the surge of linguistic investigations of generalized quantifiers into two waves.[11] In the first wave linguistic determiners were correlated with 2-place cardinality quantifiers; in the second various linguistic constructions were analyzed as "polyadic" quantifiers. The first wave began with Barwise and Cooper (1981), Higginbotham and May (1981) and Keenan and Stavi (1986/1981). Influenced by Montague's analysis of noun phrases as 2nd-order entities on the one hand and by Mostowski's generalization of the logical quantifiers on the other, Barwise and Cooper suggested that NP's in general are generalized quantifiers. The logician's quantifiers correspond to the linguist's determiners, and the linguist's quantifiers are NP's. A quantified formula is obtained in two steps: First a determiner is attached to an open formula to form a quantifier, then the quantifier is attached to an open formula to form a quantified formula. The combination of "most" (a determiner) and "students" (an open formula, "x is a student") yields a quantifier, "most students," and the combination of "most students" and "passed the test" (an open formula) yields a sentence, "Most students passed the test," symbolized $\ulcorner$Most (students) $\hat{x}$[Passed the test (x)]$\urcorner$. What is, for the logician, a 2-place quantification of the form $\ulcorner Q^{1-1}x(\Phi x, \Psi x)\urcorner$ is, for the linguist, a 1-place quantification of the form $\ulcorner D(\Phi) \hat{x}[\Psi x]\urcorner$. Semantically, determiners are defined as functions from sets to quantifiers (construed as sets of sets). E.g. *Most*({x: x is a student}) = *Most–students* (the set of all sets which include most students as members). Quantifiers are defined as functions from sets to truth values. E.g. *Most–students*({x: x passed the test}) = T/F. (*Most–students*(X) = T iff $X \in$ *Most–students*.) Some determiners are logical, others are non-logical. Determiners expressing the standard logical notions (e.g. "all," "some," "no," "neither," "at least/at most/exactly 2") are logical; determiners expressing other notions (e.g. "most," "many," "few," "a few," "all but John") are non-logical.[12] Quantifiers are, in general, non-logical: "most students," "most teachers," "all children," "all elephants" are distinct non-logical quantifiers. Since NP's in general are quantifiers, proper names are also quantifiers: "Mercury is a planet" has the form $\ulcorner$Mercury $\hat{x}[x$ is a planet]$\urcorner$. This sentence comes out true iff the quantifier "Mercury" (the set of all sets which include Mercury as a member) assigns the value T to the set of all planets. The account also accommodates quantifications with a single open formula. In "Something is blue," for example, "Some" is a determiner, "thing" is an open formula and "Some(thing)" is a quantifier. The sentence is symbolized: $\ulcorner$Some(thing) $\hat{x}[\mathrm{Blue}(x)]\urcorner$.

The only rule that applies to quantifiers (non-logical entities) as "part of the logic," according to Barwise and Cooper, is *conservativity* (or the "living on" condition). We can express this rule in terms of the linguist's quantifiers by: $D(B)[C] = T$ iff $D(B)[B \cap C] = T$, and in terms of the logician's quantifiers by: $Q(B,C) = T$ iff $Q(B,B \cap C) = T$. Informally, conservativity says that the first set (the extension of the left open formula) in a linguistic quantification determines the relevant universe of discourse. "All," "some," "most," are conservative ("Most students passed the test" is equivalent to "Most students are students who passed the test"), while "only" and "There are more . . . than ---" are not conservative ("Only women are allowed in the club" is not equivalent to "Only women are women who are allowed in the club").

Whereas Barwise and Cooper accepted only determiners defined in terms of the standard logical quantifiers as logical, other linguists and logicians (Keenan & Stavi 1986/1981, van Benthem 1983, Westerståhl 1985) took Lindström's criterion as a criterion for logical determiners, viewing invariance under isomorphic structures as expressing the idea that logical terms are topic neutral (van Benthem and Westerståhl). But, according to some of these researchers, various conditions restrict the scope of logical (and non-logical) determiners. Among these are, in addition to *conservativity*, (i) *Continuity* (van Benthem, 1983): a determiner D assigns the value T "continuously," i.e. if $C_1 \subseteq C \subseteq C_2$ and $D(B)[C_1] = D(B)[C_2]$, then $D(B)[C_1] = D(B)[C] = D(B)[C_2]$. This is a particular case of *graduality*: "a determiner should not change its mind too often." (457) (ii) *Constancy* (Westerståhl 1985): if $A \subseteq A'$ and D is a determiner, then D_A and $D_{A'}$ coincide over A. (iii) *Uniformity* (van Benthem, 1983): "the behaviour of D should be regular ("the same") across all universes" (457), where "regular (is the same)" is open to a "hierarchy" of interpretations. None of these requirements is satisfied by all binary Mostowskian quantifiers: "Only" is not conservative, "An even number of" is not continuous, "Half the objects in the universe are both . . . and ---" is not constant, and the quantifier Q defined by: $Q(\alpha) = Most_\alpha$ if α is even and Few_α if α is odd or infinite, is not uniform.

The second wave of linguistic applications of generalized logic centered around polyadic quantifiers, quantifiers binding a formula, or a finite sequence of formulas, by means of two or more variables. (See, among others, Higginbotham & May 1981, Keenan 1987b, May 1989, van Benthem 1989, Sher 1991.) Already in 1981 Higginbotham and May suggested that polyadic quantifiers will help us solve nagging problems of cross reference and "bijective" *wh*-questions. Thus by positing a polyadic, "All–Some" quantifier in two variables, we can explain the anaphoric relations in cross reference (Bach–Peters) sentences like "Every pilot who shot at it hit some Mig that chased him." Polyadic analysis can also explain how questions with multiple singular *wh*-phrases have a bijective interpretation, e.g. how "Which man saw which woman?" allows the bijective answer: "John saw Jane, and Ron saw Nancy."

Other examples of polyadic constructions in natural language are "Different students answered different questions on the exam" (Keenan 1987b), "No one loves no one" (May 1989), "For every drop of rain that falls, a flower grows" (Boolos 1981)[13], etc. Branching quantifiers, or non-linearly ordered quantifier prefixes, can also be regarded as polyadic quantifiers (Van Benthem 1989). Examples of statements analyzed in the literature as branching quantifications are "Some relative of each villager and some relative of each townsman hate each other" (Hintikka 1973b), "Quite a few boys in my class and most girls in your class have all dated each other" (Barwise 1979), "Most of my friends have applied to the same few graduate programs" and "Most of my right hand gloves and most of my left hand gloves match (one to one)" (Sher 1990). What is distinctive of these sentences is the occurrence of two or more Mostowskian quantifiers neither one of which is in the scope of the other.

None of the conditions mentioned above has survived the passage from determiners to polyadic quantifiers: the only constraint on polyadic quantifiers is logicality, construed as invariance. But the nature of invariance ("Invariance under what?") is an open question. Some have interpreted invariance in Lindström's sense (Keenan 1987b, van Benthem 1989), but others have questioned the type of invariance involved. Thus Higginbotham and May (1981) asked whether for binary polyadic quantifiers the condition is invariance under isomorphisms based on permutations of individuals (Lindström), permutations of pairs of individuals, permutations of pairs of individuals with a distinguished first or second element, etc.

Mostowski, Lindström, Tarski, Etchemendy, linguists studying natural language quantifiers, and others (Tharp 1975, Peacocke 1976, Hacking 1979, McCarthy 1981, etc.) have come up with an array of views (and points of view) regarding the existence and content of criteria for logicality. One way to approach the issue is to predicate it on a more fundamental question, for example (Tharp 1975): "What is the task (the point, the intended contribution) of logic?" If we can identify a central task of logic and determine what role logical terms play in carrying out this task, we will be able to view the distinction between logical and non-logical terms as a distinction between terms that can and terms that cannot fill this role, or terms that will and terms that will not contribute to the logical project by "acting" as logical terms. Below, I will present my own solution to the question of logicality based, in part, on Sher 1991. Although my general approach is influenced by Tharp, my analysis and subsequent solution are very different from his.

6   A Philosophical Basis for the Distinction Between Logical and Non-Logical Terms

The primary task of logic is often conceived of as the development of a method for identifying logical consequences, logical truths being a particular case. But given this conception, the question immediately arises: "What kind of consequences are logical?" Many say that logical consequences are due to the structure of sentences, where structure is a function of the specific logical terms present and their arrangement. Thus, Quine (1970: 48) says: "Logical implication [consequence] rests wholly on how the truth functions, quantifiers, and variables stack up. It rests wholly on what we may call, in a word, the logical structure of the . . . sentences [involved]." This characterization, however, gives rise to the question: "Which terms are logical? (What is the *logical* structure of a given sentence?)" So, from the point of view of our present inquiry (into the notion of logical term) this approach is unhelpful. What we need, in order to demarcate the logical terms, is an intuitive characterization of logical consequence that is independent of this demarcation.

A characterization of logical consequence satisfying this requirement was given by Tarski in "On the Concept of Logical Consequence" (1936a). According to Tarski (as I read him), a consequence is logical iff it satisfies two fundamental conditions: (a) *necessity*, and (b) *formality*. In Tarski's words: "Certain considerations of an intuitive nature will form our starting point. Consider any class K of sentences and a sentence X which follows from the sentences of this class. From an intuitive standpoint it *can never happen* that both the class K consists only of true sentences and the sentence X is false. Moreover, . . . we are concerned here with the concept of logical, i.e. *formal*, consequence. . . ." (Tarski, 1936a: 414)[14] In some accounts of logical consequence necessity, but not formality, is mentioned as a primary trait (see Etchemendy, 1991, and references there). But these accounts, Tarski tells us, miss the distinctive feature of *logical*, as opposed to other types of consequence. Logical consequence satisfies a more stringent condition than mere necessity: logical consequence is *formal and necessary* (formally necessary).

Taking Tarski's characterization as my starting point, I would first like to say a few words about formality. It is common to view formality as a syntactic condition: the formality of logical consequence is captured by the various syntactic definitions, while its necessity is captured by the semantic definition. I believe this approach is wrongheaded. The intuitive notion of logical consequence includes the idea that logical consequence is necessary in a special way, namely, in a *formal* way. To capture the intended notion of logical consequence, the semantic account cannot disregard the formal nature of intuitively logical consequences. Two examples of intuitively necessary but non-formal consequences are: (i) "The ball is all blue; therefore, it is not yellow," and (ii) "John is a bachelor; therefore he is unmarried." These inferences clearly rest on non-formal principles – metaphysico-physical principles in the first case and lexical conventions in the second – and this fact can be used to explain why we tend not to view them as strictly logical.

Tarski examined two syntactic definitions of logical consequence and found them lacking: the standard proof theoretical definition, and a substitutional definition. I will begin with the proof theoretical definition. In modern terminology we can formulate this definition as follows: Given a standard 1st-, or higher-order, logic $\mathscr{L}$ with a set of axioms, $\mathscr{A}$, and a set of rules of proof, $\mathscr{R}$: if Γ is a set of sentences of $\mathscr{L}$ and σ is a sentence of $\mathscr{L}$, then σ is a logical consequence of Γ iff there is a (finite) proof of σ from Γ (using the axioms in $\mathscr{A}$ and the rules in $\mathscr{R}$). Now, consider the inference "P(0), P(1), . . . , P(n), . . . ; therefore all natural numbers have the property P," expressed either in 1st- or in higher-order logic. This inference is intuitively formal and necessary, yet it cannot be established by means of the standard proof method. Furthermore, it follows from Gödel's incompleteness theorem that not even by adding (reasonable) rules of proof can we establish all intuitively formal and necessary consequences.

The second syntactic definition of logical consequence is substitutional. This definition says that given a natural (interpreted) language L, σ is a logical consequence of Γ iff there is no uniform substitution for the primitive non-logical constants of L (by grammatically compatible primitive terms of L) under which all the sentences of Γ come out true and σ comes out false. There are (at least) three problems with this definition: the first was pointed out by Tarski (1936a) and the other two are drawn from an analysis of Etchemendy (1990).[15]

(i) The substitutional definition is exceedingly sensitive to the richness of the non-logical lexicon: if L has a limited non-logical vocabulary, then certain consequences which fail the intuitive test pass the substitutional test. For example, let "Tarski," "Gödel," "is a logician" and "is a male" be the only non-logical constants of L. The intuitively incorrect consequence "Tarski is a male; therefore Tarski is a logician" comes out logically valid in L.

(ii) The substitutional method does not have the resources for distinguishing between logical and non-logical terms. Its only resources are grammar, lexicon and the notion of preservation of material truth under substitutions, and these do not suffice to decide the logical status of a given term. The substitutional method, therefore, reduces the distinction between logical and non-logical terms to an arbitrary, or conventional, distinction between "fixed" and "non-fixed" terms, and the notion of logical consequence is relativized to arbitrary divisions of terms into fixed and non-fixed.[16] It can easily be seen that relative to some selections of fixed terms, the "wrong" consequences pass the substitutional test, while relative to others, the "right" consequences fail. Thus, if "Tarski" and "is a logician" are among the fixed terms, "Tarski is a male; therefore Tarski is a logician" passes the substitutional test (and this happens no matter how rich the lexicon of L is). And if "(" and ")" are the only fixed terms, then, assuming the language is modestly rich, "$P\&(Q\&R)$; therefore $(P\&Q)\&R$" fails the substitutional test.

(iii) The substitutional method takes into account only facts about the *actual* world. According to the substitutional definition a sentence is logically true iff all its substitutional variants are true – true simpliciter, i.e. true in the actual world. Thus, from the point of view of the substitutional theory logical truth is *actual* truth preserved under variations in language (non-fixed constants). It follows that if a non-formal, non-necessary truth is insensitive to the non-fixed constants of the language, in particular, if it does not contain non-fixed terms, it is automatically judged to be logically true. This problem arises even on the standard selection of logical terms: "There are at least two objects" is expressible by purely logical vocabulary ($\ulcorner\exists x\exists y(x \neq y)\urcorner$), hence its truth is equated with its logical truth. This sentence is a paradigm of logical indeterminacy, but having no substitutional instances other than itself, it comes out logically true. The same distortion occurs in the case of logical consequence: Assuming the standard selection of logical terms, "There are exactly two objects; therefore X" passes the substitutional test for any sentence X.[17]

Tarski rejected the proof-theoretical and substitutional definitions and decided to use a different method. The "semantic" method, developed in Tarski (1933) naturally suggested itself to him. Below I will present my own version of Tarski's theory. I will show how the considerations motivating this theory provide a philosophical foundation for Lindström's criterion, and how, given this criterion, the theory avoids the limitations and pitfalls of the proof–theoretical and substitutional definitions.

What is a semantic theory? Following Tarski I view semantic theories as theories that deal with concepts relating language to the world (in a broad sense): "We shall understand by semantics the totality of considerations concerning those concepts which, roughly speaking, express certain connexions between the expressions of a language and the objects and states of affairs referred to by these expressions." (Tarski 1936b: 401) There are two types of semantic concepts: those that satisfy this characterization directly and those that satisfy it indirectly. "Reference" and "satisfaction" fall under the first category, "truth" and "logical consequence" under the second. Reference is a relation between a term and an object it refers to, and satisfaction is a relation between a formula and an object (a sequence of objects, a function from the variables of the language to objects in the universe) satisfying it. Truth and logical consequence, however, are linguistic properties (relations): truth is a property of sentences, and logical consequence is a relation between a sentence and a set of sentences. Why do we view them as semantic? One common answer is that truth and logical consequence are semantic because they are definable in terms of semantic relations (reference and satisfaction). I think this answer puts the cart before the horse. Truth is definable in terms of reference and satisfaction because it has to do with objects and their relations to language. Truth holds or does not hold of a given sentence *s* iff the objects referred to in *s* possess the properties (stand in the relations) attributed to them by *s*. More generally, a linguistic property is semantic iff it holds (or fails to hold) of a given linguistic entity ℓ due to certain facts about the objects referred to in ℓ; and similarly for relations. To view logical consequence as a semantic relation is, thus, to view it as a relation between linguistic entities, based on a relation between the objects referred to by these entities. Semantics reduces statements about language to statements about objects. I will not be able to discuss the reduction of "truth" here,[18] but in the case of "logical consequence" semantics reduces "The sentence σ is a logical consequence of the set of sentences Γ'' to something like "The properties attributed to objects by σ stand in the (objectual) relation $\mathcal{R}$ to the properties attributed to objects by Γ." To understand the nature of logical consequence as a semantic relation is thus to understand (i) the nature of reference, and (ii) the nature of the objectual relation $\mathcal{R}$. Leaving reference aside, we can view the intuitive conditions on logical consequence – necessity and formality – as conditions on $\mathcal{R}$. Necessity requires that $\mathcal{R}$ hold *necessarily;* formality – that $\mathcal{R}$ take into account only *formal* features of the objects and properties (relations) involved. What is the objectual relation $\mathcal{R}$?

Consider the intuitively logically valid inference, (1): "Something is white and tasty; therefore, something is tasty." Why is (1) logically valid? Adopting Mostowski's way of viewing quantifiers, we can say that (1) is logically valid because (i) its premise says that the intersection of the sets of white and tasty things is not empty, (ii) its conclusion says that one of the intersected sets, namely the set of tasty things, is not empty, and (iii) *whenever* an intersection of sets is not empty, each of the intersected sets is not empty. Looked at in this way, semantics reduces "σ is a logical consequence of Γ" to "$f(\sigma)\ \mathcal{R}\ f(\Gamma)$," where f extracts the relevant content of σ and Γ (in our example: a set is not empty [$f(\sigma)$], its intersection with another set is not empty [$f(\Gamma)$]), and $\mathcal{R}$ is an objectual expression of generality, roughly "whenever."

In *Tractatus Logico–Philosophicus*, 6.1231–6.1232, Wittgenstein seemingly rejected this way of looking at logical consequence. Speaking in terms of "logical truth" ("logical proposition", in his terminology), Wittgenstein said: "The mark of a logical proposition is *not* general validity. To be general means no more than to be accidentally valid for all things." This observation led Wittgenstein to object to the reduction of logic to generality, and a similar objection was made recently by Etchemendy (1990).[19] But Wittgenstein's problem does not arise on our analysis: logical consequence is not reducible to just any kind of generality, logical consequence is reducible to a special kind of generality, to generality satisfying the intuitive constraints of necessity and formality. Necessity and formality constrain both the function f and the scope of "*whenever*". Formality requires that logical consequence depend only on formal features of the objects involved (non-emptiness of sets and intersections), not their material features (whiteness and tastiness of things), and necessity requires that "whenever" not be restricted to any particular universes, but range over all possible universes. Combining necessity and formality, we can say that logical consequence is reducible to *formal generality*. It is a formally universal fact (a fact that holds in all formally possible structures of objects) that if an intersection of sets is not empty, each of the intersected sets is not empty, and it is due to this formal and necessary fact that (1) is logically, i.e. formally and necessarily, valid.

Tarskian semantics systematizes the reduction of logical truth and logical consequence to formal universality. What is the role of logical terms in this reduction? Consider (1) above. The formal relation underlying (1) is not affected by changes in the extensions of "white" and "tasty," but changes in the extension of "something" and "and" may very well affect it. We can explain the difference between the two pairs of terms by the fact that the formal relationship underlying (1) holds no matter what (formally possible) sets of individuals "white" and "tasty" denote: Given any formally possible universe of individuals and any two sets of individuals in this universe (sets of white and tasty things, sets of black and sour things, etc.), if the intersection of the two sets is non-empty, so is each set non-empty. But the same does not hold for unions: It is formally possible for a union of two sets to be non-empty while one of the sets is empty. Similarly, it is formally possible for an intersection of two sets to be empty without either set being empty. This is the reason the validity of (1) depends on "and" and "something." If we replace the denotation of "and" by the denotation of "or" or the denotation of "something" by the denotation of "nothing," (1) will turn logically invalid. "And" (in $\ulcorner \ldots x \ldots$ and $\_\_\_ x \_\_\_ \urcorner$) denotes an intersection, "something" denotes the property of being non-empty, and the laws governing the intersection and non-emptiness of sets hold in all formally possible structures.

The role of logical terms in Tarskian logic is, thus, to mark formal features and structures of objects, the kind of features and structures responsible for logical consequences. Since logical terms have denotations in all formally possible structures of objects, logical terms are "universal" terms, terms denoting properties applicable to all formally possible objects: humans, dogs, cells, atoms, colors, natural numbers, real numbers, etc. The standard logical terms satisfy this requirement, hence consequences based on these terms are genuinely logical. But the question naturally arises whether all formally necessary consequences are based on the standard logical terms. Consider the inferences (1) "There is exactly one human; therefore, there are finitely many humans," and (2) "There is exactly one human; therefore there are at most ten humans." In standard 1st-order logic (2) is considered logically valid while (1) is logically indeterminate. But is (1) less formally necessary than (2)? Is it intuitively more possible for a singleton set to be infinite than to include ten elements and above?

The task of Tarskian semantics, as I understand it, is to provide a "complete" system for detecting logical, i.e. formal and necessary, consequences. One way of achieving this result is by turning to standard higher-order logic, but another way is to extend standard 1st-order logic by adding new logical terms (e.g. the quantifier "there are finitely many x"). How do we determine the totality of logical terms? To determine the totality of logical terms is to determine the totality of formal (universal) structures of objects. Each formal structure is the extension of some logical term, and each logical term denotes a formal structure. To identify formal structures we will use the best universal theory of formal structure available (a theory applicable to structures of any kind of individuals). Currently ZF (with urelements) or one of its variants appears to be a reasonable choice. Based on this theory we will develop a criterion for formal identity of structures, and based on this criterion we will say that a term is logical iff it does not distinguish between formally identical structures. But this is exactly what Lindström's criterion says, based on the model-theoretic notion of structure. A term is logical iff it is invariant under isomorphic structures. I.e. a term is logical iff it does not distinguish isomorphic extensions of its arguments. Based on this criterion, all cardinality quantifiers are logical, the 2nd-order property of being a symmetric (transitive, reflexive) relation is logical, etc. More generally, any mathematical term definable as a higher-order term is essentially logical. Take, for example, the term "two." As an individual term "two" denotes a particular individual – the number two – hence it fails the logicality test, but as a higher-order term "2" denotes a formal structure – the set of all sets isomorphic to {0,1} – hence is a bona fide logical term. (This comparison explains why individual constants are not included in (L): individual constants denote atomic objects, objects with no structure, formal or non-formal.)

The characterization of logical terms as universal and formal allows us to explain how Tarskian semantics avoids one of the stumbling blocks of substitutional semantics, namely, the relativity of its notion of consequence to arbitrary selections of fixed terms: Lindström's criterion precludes the use of any non-formal or non-universal terms ("Tarski," "is a logician," etc.) as logical (fixed) terms, ruling out inferences obtained by holding such terms fixed. The two remaining problems are circumvented by the introduction of Tarskian models and their specific features. Models, in Tarskian semantics, represent formally possible structures of objects, and the notion of truth in all models (truth in all models of Γ) is not dependent either upon the size of the non-logical vocabulary or upon the size (and other contingent traits) of the actual world: Whether "Tarski" is the only singular term of L or not, "Tarski" is assigned a great many distinct individuals in different models for L, enough to establish a counter-example to "Tarski is X", for any non-logical primitive predicate X. Likewise, truth in a Tarskian model is not truth in the actual world, but truth in a formally possible structure, and the notion of formally possible structure is not constricted by contingent facts (e.g. the cardinality of the actual universe).[20]

7   The Logical Nature of Tarskian Semantics

The third question I raised in this paper was: Is Tarskian semantics specifically designed to accommodate the needs of logic, or can the same apparatus be used to explain other aspects of the relation between language and the world? A complete answer to this question is beyond the scope of the present paper, but I would like to point out two ways in which Tarskian semantics is inherently logical: (a) its choice of "fixed" terms, (b) its method of representing objects and states of affairs. The first point should be obvious by now: Tarskian semantics, even Tarski's general definition of truth (Tarski 1933), is restricted to languages whose "fixed" terms are *logical*, and the recursive definition of truth via satisfaction reflects this fact. This definition employs "fixed" functions which correspond to the logical terms of the language, and these functions take into account only formal features of objects in their domain.

The second point has to do with the way objects and states of affairs are represented in Tarskian semantics, i.e. with its apparatus of models. Briefly, we can present this point as follows: As a logical semantics, Tarskian semantics is interested in features of objects and states of affairs that contribute to logical consequences and only those. That is to say, Tarskian semantics is concerned with (universal) formal features of objects and states of affairs and nothing else. Tarskian models disregard the diversity of objects and the multitude of non-formal properties they possess (non-formal relations in which they stand). All objects, physical and mental, abstract and concrete, microscopic and macroscopic, fictional and real, are represented as members of a set theoretical entity, the "universe" of a model, i.e. a set. All properties of these diverse objects are represented as sets of members of the universe, all relations are represented as sets of n-tuples of members of the universe, etc. Nothing is possibly both dead and alive, but in some Tarskian models things are. Tarskian semantics respects the exclusionary relation between "Exactly two things are X" and "Exactly three things are X" since this relation is formal, but it does not respect the exclusionary relation between "x is dead" and "x is alive" since this relation is not formal. Similarly, Tarskian semantics reduces the multitude of ways in which objects possess properties and stand in relations to a single formal relation, set membership, in spite of the fact that an object possesses, say, a moral property (e.g. being virtuous), or a propositional attitude property (e.g. wishing to be president) in a largely different way from that in which it possesses a physical property (e.g. occupying spatio–temporal region $xyzw$). But Tarskian semantics is not interested in these differences. Set membership is adequate for possession of formal properties, and for the purposes of Tarskian semantics, there is no need for something more elaborate. From the point of view of Tarskian semantics, only the formal skeleton of "object x possesses property P" is relevant.

With this my discussion of semantics and logic has come to an end. I have asked three questions in this paper: (A) Is there a philosophical basis for the distinction between logical and non-logical terms? (B) Can we develop a constructive definition of logical terms based on (A)? (C) To what extent is modern semantics tied up with logic? I proposed an outline of a positive answer to (A) and (B) and some considerations pertaining to (C). Modern semantics sprang out of a distinctly logical conception of semantics. This conception originated in Tarski's theories of truth and logical consequence in the 1930s and has recently been extended following the generalization of logical terms by Mostowski and others. I have shown that the line drawn by Lindström (and the later Tarski) between logical and non-logical terms is philosophically sound, and I have given an outline of a constructive definition of logical terms modeled after the Boolean definition of the logical connectives. As for the many branches and developments in modern semantics, to the extent that these are an outgrowth of Tarskian semantics they are rooted in a *logical* theory of the relation between language and the world. How far semantics can and should go beyond its logical roots is left an open question.

NOTES

1   See Tarski (1933) and (1936a). The inductive definition of syntax is not original with Tarski (note Hilbert and Ackermann 1928), but its central place in semantics is due to Tarski.

2   See, among others, Barwise and Feferman (1985), Hughes and Cresswell (1968), Hintikka (1969), Davidson (1984), Montague (1974), May (1985) and many of the references below.

3   See Enderton (1972), Section 1.2.

4   For an example, see Keisler (1970).

5   Lindström's criterion is slightly different from (*L*): (i) it includes connectives, (ii) it does not apply to all predicates of orders 1–2. More specifically, it does not apply to relations involving individuals (e.g. the relation $\mathcal{R}$ of type $\langle 2,0 \rangle$, where $\langle R, a \rangle \in \mathcal{R}$ iff R is an ordering relation with a smallest element and a is its smallest element.) Tarski's criterion does apply to all predicates, but he uses a slightly different conceptual scheme.

6   Lindström's symbolization is slightly more complicated. He would write "$Qxy(\Phi x, \Psi y)$" where I write "$Qx(\Phi x, \Psi x)$".

7   I use "$Q^{1\text{-}1}$ B's are C's" to represent the general case of a predication of type 1–1 although some predications of this type (e.g. "There are more B's than C's") would be more naturally represented by a different locution.

8   Unlike $Q_\alpha^{1\text{-}1}$, $Q^{1\text{-}1}$ is a "class" function rather than a "set" function, i.e. a *class*, rather than a <u>set</u> of pairs. In what follows I use the term "function" for both. It should be clear from the context whether "set" or "class" is meant.

9   Here I treat cardinals as sets of ordinals, but ordinals have to be treated as atomic elements: {1} and {{0}}, for example, represent different extensions, indeed, extensions of terms of different types.

10   It follows from this step that logical terms may "mean" different things in universes of different cardinalities. Thus, a function, $\exists_F \forall_I$, that assigns to all finite universes A the quantifier $\exists_A$ and to all infinite universes B the quantifier $\forall_B$ is a logical term. This may sound strange at first, but we must remember that even if $C = D$, $\langle A, \langle C \rangle \rangle$ and $\langle B, \langle D \rangle \rangle$ are structurally different, and so various logical quantifiers distinguish between them. In fact, many "natural" quantifiers are sensitive to the size of the underlying universe. Thus "most[1]" assigns the value T to $\{a,b,c,d\}$ in a universe with 6 individuals but not in a universe with 60,000 individuals. Ratio quantifiers can be construed as exploiting the fact that quantifiers may vary according to the size of the given universe: "1/2" is "exactly one" in a universe with two elements, "exactly two" in a universe with four elements, etc. In constructing specific logical apparati various considerations beyond logicality are, of course, taken into account: we may wish to restrict ourselves to "natural" logical terms, logical terms that are useful for a particular purpose, etc. Clearly, many factors combine to determine the logical apparatus of natural language.

11 This division is both analytical and historical, although historically, there are a few exceptions (e.g. Higginbotham and May, 1981).

12 It should be emphasized that I am referring to Barwise and Cooper's claim that these determiners are non-logical in the sense that they do not denote unary quantifiers of first-order logic. Van Benthem (1986) and (1989), Westerståhl (1989), and Keenan (this volume) characterize logical determiners as those which denote functions that are permutation invariant for isomorphic structures on the given universe. On the latter view of logicality, "most", for example, can be taken to denote a logical binary determiner relation. See Lappin (1995b) for a discussion of generalized quantifiers and logicality.

13 Boolos identified statements of this kind as "non-firstorderizable" (relative to the *standard* 1st-order system). For a polyadic analysis of such statements, see Sher (1991: 103).

14 The first underline is mine.

15 See Sher (forthcoming).

16 Compare with Quine's analysis of substitutional quantification. In substitutional quantification, according to Quine, the choice of substitution classes is arbitrary: "substitutional quantification makes good sense, explicable in terms of truth and substitution, no matter what substitution class we take – even that whose sole member is the left-hand parenthesis." (1969: 106)

17 The notion "actual world" is ambiguous, but all we need here is the fact that the concept of truth simpliciter involves a more restricted notion of "world" than the concept of formal and necessary truth.

18 I am currently working on a paper on Tarski's theory of truth. My account is revisionist in the sense that it is concerned with what Tarski's theory actually does, not with what "the historical" Tarski said it does.

19 The connection between Etchemendy and Wittgenstein was pointed by Garcia-Carpintero (1993).

20 My reasons for regarding formal terms as logical are primarily philosophical. The question whether linguistically (empirically), too, formal terms should be regarded as logical requires a separate investigation. May (1991: 353) gives a preliminary positive answer based on the difference between the way a child acquires formal terms and the way s/he acquires non-formal terms. The promising work on natural language polyadic quantifiers (i.e. quantifiers based on (L)) also yields support to the "formal" view of logical terms. The difference between philosophical and linguistic conceptions of logicality is discussed in Lappin (1991).

20 Semantics and Cognition

RAY JACKENDOFF

1 The Basic Stance of I-Semantics

Chomsky (1986b) distinguishes between two ways to treat language as an object of inquiry. The study of "externalized language" or *E-language* treats language as an external artifact used by human beings, and seeks to characterize its properties as part of the external world with which humans interact. By contrast, the study of "internalized language" or *I-language* treats language as a body of knowledge within the minds/brains of speakers, and seeks to characterize its properties within the context of a more general theory of psychology. Since at least the time of *Aspects of the Theory of Syntax* (1965), the goal of generative grammar has explicitly been an account of I-language.

Clearly, an account of how humans actually use language in the external world eventually requires an account of their grasp of the principles of language, i.e. a theory of I-language. Thus a theory of I-language is ultimately necessary, whether or not one desires an account of E-language as well. (Chomsky has in fact argued further that E-language is not a rewarding subject of scientific inquiry at all.)

Semantics, the theory of the relation between language and the world, suffers from the same duality: one can examine it either as an abstract relation external to language users (*E-semantics*) or as a body of knowledge within the brain/mind of the language user (*I-semantics*). Again, an account of how humans use language requires an account of how they *grasp* the relationship between language and the world, so ultimately a theory of I-semantics is desirable.

More specifically, if the theories of syntax and phonology are situated within the stance of I-language, semantic theory may be concerned either with the relation of language users' knowledge of language to the external world (I'll call this "semi-E-semantics"), or with the relation of language users' knowledge of language to their *grasp* or *understanding* of the world. In the latter

Figure 20.1

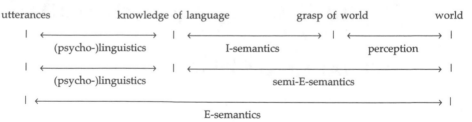

case, a full theory then requires as well an account of the relation between the world and the language user's grasp of it, which falls under the standard topic of "perception and cognition." Figure 20.1 schematizes the relationship of these different approaches.

Most research in semantics either is inexplicit about its stance or else professes E-semantics. However, a growing body of work in several somewhat independent traditions has explicitly adopted the stance of I-semantics, aspiring to study the relation between human language and human concepts, and to use language as a tool for exploring the structure of human cognition. The present chapter discusses the consequences of adopting such a stance and some of the more prominent results and disputes that have emerged.

2   Basic Issues for I-Semantics

Some basic questions for a theory of I-semantics are the following:

(1)   The nature of meaning
    a. What are the terms in which humans grasp the world? That is, what are the formal and substantive properties of human concepts/thoughts/ideas?
    b. How may these properties be formalized so as to develop a fully explicit and predictive theory?

(2)   Correspondence to language
    a. How are the terms in which humans grasp the world related systematically to linguistic expressions?
    b. In what respects, if any, are these terms *not* related systematically to linguistic expressions, being under the influence of nonlinguistic knowledge, context, etc.? Is there a natural division between linguistic and nonlinguistic factors?

(3)   Correspondence to the world
    a. How are the terms in which humans grasp the world related systematically to the world itself through the perceptual systems?

b. In what respects, if any, are these terms *not* related systematically to the physical world? That is, to what extent are human concepts/thoughts/ideas abstract?

These parallel issues familiar from E-semantics. (1) corresponds to the formal problem of creating an intensional language adequate for expressing all the sentences of natural language, such that semantic properties such as sameness and difference of meaning, inference, and presupposition can be computed as formal relations among sentences. (2) corresponds to the problem of mapping syntactic structure into this intensional language. (3) corresponds roughly to the problem of reference (mapping the intensional language onto a model) and the problem of the intentionality of linguistic expressions, though, as will be seen presently, the similarity is only skin-deep.

But in addition, since in I-semantics the formal theories investigated in (1)– (3) are supposed to be instantiated in a human brain, there are fundamental issues that are not shared with E-semantics:

(4) Brain instantiation
   a. How are the systems in (1)–(3) wired in the brain, in terms of both broad localization and local neural connectivity?
   b. To what extent are these systems representative of brain systems as a whole?

(5) Developmental questions
   a. How does a person acquire the terms in which (s)he grasps the world and the systems that relate these terms to linguistic expression and perceptual input?
   b. To what extent is concept acquisition free to adapt to the environment, and to what extent is it guided by genetically determined constraints, at either the individual or species level?

(6) Evolutionary questions
   a. What aspects of the human way of grasping the world can be traced back to nonhuman antecedents, and which represent evolutionary innovations?
   b. To what extent are these innovations representative of evolutionary innovation as a whole?

That is, I-semantics, unlike E-semantics, in principle connects with more general issues of psychology, neuroscience, and biology. Even if such connections are in their infancy, the aspiration to establish them sets boundary conditions on the enterprise that, as will be seen, propel inquiry in directions quite different from traditional semantic theory.

It should also be noticed that the questions in (4)–(6) strongly parallel well-known issues in generative linguistics, because of its focus on I-language. An interesting difference is that evolutionary questions about language tend to be rather obscure, because language *per se* is not attested other than in humans. By contrast, many aspects of the human grasp of the world have obvious animal parallels, so that evolutionary issues can play an interesting role in theory construction.

3 Some References[1]

Some early work on semantics within generative grammar recognized these goals to some degree. Katz and Fodor (1963), Katz (1972), and Weinreich (1966) situate semantic theory in the issue of human competence, but they do not address issues such as (4)–(6). Bierwisch (1967, 1969) is unusual for explicitly linking the search for semantic primitives and semantic universals to perceptual psychology.

In the 1970s a wide range of work developed attempting to link semantics and cognition. Fodor, Bever, and Garrett (1974) and especially Fodor (1975) place traditional philosophical issues about meaning in a psychological framework. Miller and Johnson-Laird (1976) develop a massive account of lexical meaning in a framework that aspires to both computational explicitness and psychological plausibility. Jackendoff (1976, 1978) discusses the relation between grammatical patterns and the cognitive structures they express. Within the AI tradition, Schank's (1973) "conceptual dependencies," Minsky's (1975) "frames," and Schank and Abelson's (1975) "scripts" are all explicitly claimed to be theories of the connection between language and human concepts.

Psychological experiments showing the character of word meanings, calling into question classical theories, were pioneered by Rosch (Rosch 1973, 1975, 1978; Rosch and Mervis 1975; Rosch et al. 1976). Berlin and Kay (1969), Clark and Chase (1972), and Levelt (1984) are other noteworthy pieces of work of this period.

Experimental and theoretical research on semantic development in children also started to develop during this period. Important works include Brown (1973), E. Clark (1973), H. Clark (1973), Bowerman (1974, 1978, 1989), Katz, Baker, and Macnamara (1974), Keil (1979), and, a little later, Macnamara (1982, 1986), Landau and Gleitman (1985), Carey (1985), Pinker (1984, 1989), Keil (1989), Markman (1989), and Bloom (1994).

More recently, two main schools within linguistics can be loosely distinguished whose central tenet is to identify meaning with human concepts. One is *Cognitive Linguistics* or *Cognitive Grammar*, which is (in many cases deliberately) independent of generative grammar. The main figures in this movement are Lakoff (1987, 1990), Lakoff and Johnson (1980), Lakoff and Turner (1989), Langacker (1987, 1991), and Talmy (1978, 1980, 1983, 1985); other important works are Brugman (1981), Fillmore (1982), Fauconnier (1985), Herskovits (1986), Levinson (1992), and Vandeloise (1986). The other school seeks to integrate

I-semantic theory with the syntactic framework of generative grammar. Some major exponents of this approach are Jackendoff (1983, 1987a, 1990, 1992) (who calls the enterprise *Conceptual Semantics*), Bierwisch (1981, 1982), Bierwisch and Lang (1989), Pinker (1989), Nikanne (1990), and Pustejovsky (1991). Zwarts and Verkuyl (1994) recast Jackendoff's approach in model-theoretic terms. Another independent approach is that of Wierzbicka (1980, 1985, 1987, 1988).

The discussion in the rest of this chapter, rather than elaborating the ideas of these trends one by one, concentrates on the issues and results of research in I-semantics as a whole; concurrences and differences among approaches will be mentioned as they arise.

4 The Nature of Truth and Reference in I-Semantics – Preliminaries

In order to treat semantics as an issue about the structure of the human organism, it is necessary to be careful about basic goals of the enterprise. In particular, the traditional preoccupation with explicating the notion of the truth or falsity of a sentence must be re-evaluated. For there is no longer a direct relation between an utterance and the world that renders the utterance true or false; there is instead the sequence of three relations diagrammed in the upper line of Figure 20.1.

As a consequence, a definition of truth for I-semantics parallels the definition of grammaticality for I-linguistics. In I-linguistics, the statement (7a), which appears to be about sentences abstracted away from speakers, is always taken as an abbreviation for statement (7b), which puts grammaticality squarely in the mind of the language user.

(7) a. String S is a grammatical sentence of language L.
    b. A speaker of language L judges string S grammatical (subject to limitations of memory and processing, and under an idealization of uniformity among speakers).

Similarly, the traditional Tarskian definition of truth (8a) must be reinterpreted in I-semantics as an issue of judgment, as in (8b).

(8) a. Sentence S of language L is true iff conditions $C_1, \ldots, C_n$ obtain in the world.
    b. A speaker of language L judges sentence S true iff conditions $C_1, \ldots, C_n$ obtain in his or her construal of the world (subject to limitations of memory and processing, and under an idealization of uniformity among speakers).

That is, truth is no longer regarded as a relation between a sentence and the world, but rather as a relation between a sentence and a speaker's construal of the world. Parallel reinterpretations must be adopted for logical relations such as entailment, presupposition, and so forth.

This reinterpretation places a crucial burden on I-semantic theory. It is no longer possible simply to characterize "the world" logically or set-theoretically, as is frequent in formal semantics. Rather, it is an empirical problem to determine what sorts of entities inhabit the world as humans construe it. These entities may or may not be characterizable in standard logical or set-theoretic terms, and in fact they prove not to be, as will be seen below. Furthermore, truth-conditions must be stated in the vocabulary of human construal of the world.

The claim of this approach is that when people communicate linguistically, they do not communicate about the world plain and simple, but about the world as humanly understood. The entities to which speakers refer are not entities in "the world" plain and simple, but rather entities available in the human construal of the world. These include physical objects and events, illusory objects such as virtual contours, fictional objects such as Santa Claus, social constructs such as marriages and university degrees, mental constructs such as intentions and beliefs, and theoretical constructs such as numbers and logical operators. From the point of view of I-semantics, they all have equally robust status. (This position is worked out in detail by Jackendoff 1983 and Lakoff 1987.)

It is a further empirical question how these different sorts of entities are related to the "real" real world, or alternatively how "meanings in the head" come to be "meaningful." We return to these issues, which are still controversial, at the end of the chapter.

5   Compositionality and Universality of Semantic Vocabulary

Like traditional formal semantics, all approaches to I-semantics are committed to the composition of phrase and sentence meanings from the meanings of constituent lexical items. With the exception of some of the AI-based approaches, all take it for granted that syntactic structure acts as an important guide in the construction of phrase meanings from constituents.

However, nearly all approaches to I-semantics go beyond most work in formal semantics in making a serious commitment to semantic decomposition of lexical items into smaller units.[2] This practice has borne considerable fruit in explaining patterns of inference and patterns of syntactic behavior, some of which will be seen below; this alone is sufficient justification for the undertaking.

But in addition the assumptions of I-semantics lead to foundational questions of lexical decomposition. Parallel to the basic problem in I-linguistics of how a child acquires the grammar of a language, I-semantics faces the question of how a child acquires vocabulary, in particular the meanings of words. Where do the concepts come from that are associated with sounds and syntactic structures?

On the view that the mind can be characterized in terms of formal systems, learning has to be treated as the combining of existing formal units into larger constructs. Moreover, the "existing formal units" must start somewhere: there must be a vocabulary of primitives and principles of combination (i.e. axioms) to get the system off the ground. This system, *by logical necessity*, must be instantiated in the brain innately, since by definition it cannot be learned. (This argument is due to Fodor 1975.)

In fact, *all* theories of learning presuppose some innate basis. It may be something as simple as principles of association, or something as rich as Fodor's (1975) repertoire sufficient to encompass the meanings of all monomorphemic words. The interesting empirical question thus is not whether there is an innate basis behind word meanings, but exactly what this innate basis is. In practice, most approaches to I-semantics assume a fairly rich combinatorial basis for word meanings, with a sizable repertoire of substantive conceptual primitives.

It is sometimes objected (e.g. Partee 1993b) that the innateness of semantic primitives should imply a wider degree of universality in the lexical semantics of languages of the world than actually exists. There are two answers to this objection. The first takes a cue from generative grammar. The innateness of Universal Grammar in phonology and syntax does not imply overwhelming uniformity in these aspects of language: languages can pick and choose among a repertoire of possibilities, some of which are even mutually inconsistent with each other (i.e. accusative vs. ergative case marking). The same could easily be true of semantics: of the concepts made available in the innate basis, languages may choose to grammaticalize or lexicalize different selections, so that different languages may appear semantically incommensurate.

Second, it is not necessarily the case that all (or any) semantic/conceptual primitives are independently expressible *as words*. Just as the smallest isolable speech sounds (phonemes) are composites of distinctive features that cannot appear independently, so it appears to be the case that all word meanings are composite, made up of semantic/conceptual constituents that cannot appear in isolation. That is, word meanings are "molecular" entities in the "chemistry of concepts," while semantic/conceptual primitives are subatomic or even quarklike. This being the case, the ultimate decomposition of a lexical item cannot be expressed in terms of a linguistic paraphrase.

The impossibility of paraphrase definitions is often taken as an argument *against* lexical decomposition (e.g. Fodor, Garrett, Walker, and Parkes 1980), but in fact paraphrase definitions can be expected only if every semantic primitive can itself be expressed by a word, and if every principle of semantic composition can be paralleled by a principle of syntactic composition. Otherwise (as is actually the case), the absence of paraphrase definitions is altogether natural.

How then does one justify a proposed semantic/conceptual primitive? First notice that it cannot be justified in isolation; it makes sense only in the context of the rest of the axiomatic system in which it is situated. In turn, a particular proposal for an axiomatic system is justified not only logically but empirically, in terms of how well it explains the semantic phenomena of language and cognition. Sometimes the issue is raised as how one can ever tell whether a set of proposed primitives is "really" primitive. Suffice it to say that this question seems never to have discouraged physicists, who just take it as a spur to see if deeper decomposition leads to deeper explanation. In practice this is what happens in lexical semantics as well.

6   Relation of Human Concepts to Natural Language Semantics

The last section used the locution "semantic/conceptual" as though the two are one and the same within an I-semantic theory. Most practitioners of I-semantics in fact take for granted the identification of natural language meanings and human concepts, but two alternative positions deserve discussion.

The basic hypothesis in I-semantics is that the syntactic structures of natural language must be related to the concepts they express by a set of rules of translation or correspondence, where "concepts" include all the richness and interconnection of human knowledge (sometimes called "encyclopedic" knowledge and sometimes "pragmatics"). However, the question arises as to whether the relation is direct (Figure 20.2a), or whether there is an independent identifiable level that can be called "semantics proper" intervening between syntax and concepts (Figure 20.2b).

For those advocating a two-stage mapping like Figure 20.2b, the issue is what role the independent level of semantic structure plays. In early work of Katz (1972, for instance), semantic structure is conceived of as a level of representation which captures only semantic relations among sentences such as entailment, synonymy, ambiguity, and anomaly, but which does not represent

Figure 20.2

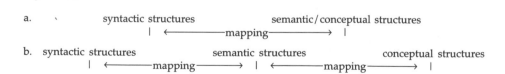

"world knowledge" in general. Such a level of semantics is sometimes assumed by more recent formal semanticists as well. In fact it has proven impossible to separate out purely "semantic" relations from world knowledge and metaphoric construal without massively losing generalizations (Jackendoff 1981, 1983; Lakoff and Johnson 1980; Lakoff 1987), so Katz's conception of semantic structure cannot be maintained.

A second conception of semantic structure has arisen independently in work of, for instance, Pinker (1989) and Bierwisch (1982, 1992), in which it is the level of representation which encodes just those aspects of meaning that make a difference in syntactic structure. For instance, many languages make syntactic distinctions based on number, gender, and animacy, but none make distinctions based on color or the difference between dogs and cats. The idea, then, is that semantic structure encodes number, gender, and animacy but not color or species. Similarly, languages make syntactic distinctions between eventive and stative verbs, but not between verbs of running and verbs of walking; again only the former distinction would appear in semantic structure. Sometimes the implication is that while conceptual structure is universal, semantic structure varies from language to language, depending on what conceptual distinctions are grammaticalized. (See e.g. Talmy 1980, Choi and Bowerman 1991 for discussion of crosslinguistic differences.)

It is possible, however, to reproduce this configuration of facts within a theory structured as in Figure 20.2a, by situating the language-particular aspects of semantics directly in the mapping between syntax and conceptual structure. The idea is that this mapping is only sensitive to a restricted repertoire of conceptual distinctions, so that the rest are necessarily opaque to syntax. The variability among languages in this respect is then attributed to variability in the conceptual factors to which the mapping is sensitive. As a result, no extra level of strictly linguistic semantics is necessary.

Notice how this parallels the behavior of the syntax-phonology interface. There are many phonological distinctions which play no role in syntax; but this does not lead to the postulation of a separate level of representation that contains only the phonological distinctions relevant to syntax. Rather, the idea is that the mapping between phonology and syntax is simply not sensitive to segmental content (say the difference between the phoneme sequences *dog* and *cat*), to number of syllables (*camel* vs. *dromedary*), and so forth. On the other hand, the mapping *is* sensitive to word and phrase boundaries, to affixal structure, and so forth. That is, the mapping between levels of representation is only a partial homology, not a one-to-one correspondence of every element of the structures.

It is unclear which of these views of semantic structure will eventually prevail. The rest of this chapter will assume the latter view without further argument, accepting the identification of semantic representations with (possibly a subset of) human conceptual structures, in accordance with the majority of work in the field.

7   The Noncategorical Nature of Conceptual Categories

The emphasis in I-semantics on lexical meaning has given rise to considerable investigation into the phenomenon of *categorization*: how humans place individuals into categories, and how systems of categories are constructed mentally. As a semantic issue, this problem can be framed in terms of stating the truth-conditions for the sentence *This is an X*, where X is the category in question. By contrast with the main tradition of formal semantics, which adopts rather uncritically the Tarskian criterion of necessary and sufficient truth-conditions, much I-semantic research (in particular Jackendoff 1983 and Lakoff 1987) stresses the insufficiency of Tarskian conditions to characterize the richness of human categories. This section presents examples of some of the problems that have arisen.

7.1   *Categories with graded boundaries*

Consider the category *red*. This cannot be identified with a particular perceived hue, since a broad range of hues are all called *red*. However, as hues shade imperceptibly from red toward orange, there comes a point where observers are no longer clear about their judgments. There may be hesitation and interobserver disagreement. In addition, the judgment of a particular hue may depend on what hues have immediately preceded it in presentation (if presented after focal red, it is judged orange, but if after focal orange, it is judged red). That is, there is a focal range in which judgments are secure and consistent, but this shades into a borderline range in which there is conflict with a neighboring category, and in which judgments become less secure and more context-dependent.

This "fuzziness" in the boundary of a category is not a matter of speakers not "knowing the meaning of *red*"; rather it is inherent in the structure of the concept itself. One can make *red* more "Tarskian" by stipulating rigid boundaries with orange, pink, purple, and brown, but then one is not dealing with the ordinary meaning of the word. Similarly, one can create a new category *red–orange* at the boundary, but then the same sort of fuzziness occurs at the boundary of red and red–orange. (The existence of such phenomena is noted by Putnam 1975; Berlin and Kay 1969 is the classic work on color judgments.)

Similar boundary problems arise with words like *hot* and *tall* that express significant deviation from a norm. What is the lower bound of temperature for, say, *hot soup*, or the lower bound of height for *tall woman*? It is inherent in the structure of these concepts that the boundaries are not classically sharp, in the sense that any particular woman can be definitively said to be either in or out of the set of tall women.

Incidentally, these adjectives also present evidence for the interdependence of linguistic meaning and encyclopedic knowledge in judgments of truth. For, as has often been observed, a *small elephant* is bigger than a *big mouse*: the norm to which the adjective is applied depends on one's knowledge of the standard size of the animals in question. (Bierwisch and Lang 1989 discuss in detail adjectives that relate an instance to a norm.) Similarly (as Talmy 1978 points out), what counts as nearness between stars is metrically quite different from nearness between pieces of furniture; nearness too is defined in terms of the normal distance expected among individuals of the category in question. (See Pustejovsky 1991 for more highly elaborated examples of this sort, having to do with what Millikan 1984 calls the *proper function* of objects; Katz's 1966 treatment of *good* is an early, somewhat clumsily executed example.)

7.2 "Cluster" concepts

The classic example of this phenomenon is Wittgenstein's (1953) analysis of *game*, in which he demonstrates that it is impossible to find a necessary condition that distinguishes games from other activities. He suggests that the word is understood in terms of "family resemblance": there is a cluster of conditions that define games; but no games satisfy all of them, and none of them is shared by all games. That is, none of the conditions is necessary, but various suitable combinations of them are sufficient to permit an individual to be judged a member of the category. Such categories are now called *cluster concepts*.

This analysis is amplified by Rosch (1973, 1975, 1978; Rosch and Mervis 1975), who shows experimentally that categorization judgments may contain a cline of "typicality," ranging from typical exemplars of the category (e.g. a robin is a "typical" bird) to atypical exemplars (e.g. a penguin is an "atypical" bird). Among the various sources for typicality effects,[3] one is a set of conditions that form a cluster concept: examples that satisfy fewer of the conditions are generally regarded as less typical than examples that maximally satisfy the conditions.

The effects of cluster conditions can be observed in concepts involving as few as two conditions. A case first discussed by Fillmore (1982) is the verb *climb*. Consider the following examples:

(9) a. Bill climbed (up) the mountain.
     b. Bill climbed down the mountain.
     c. The snake climbed (up) the tree.
     d. ?*The snake climbed down the tree.

Climbing involves two independent conceptual conditions: (1) an individual is traveling upward, and (2) the individual is moving with characteristic effortful grasping motions (clambering). On the most likely interpretation of (9a), both conditions are met. (9b) violates the first condition, and, since snakes cannot clamber, (9c) violates the second; yet both examples are acceptable instances of climbing. However, if both conditions are violated, as in (9d), the action cannot be characterized as climbing. Thus neither of the two conditions is necessary, but either is sufficient. Moreover, the default interpretation of (9a), in which both conditions are satisfied, is judged more stereotypical climbing; (9b) and (9c) are judged somewhat more marginal but still perfectly legitimate instances.

Parallel analyses have been proposed for the verbs *lie* ("tell a lie") (Coleman and Kay 1981) and *see* (Jackendoff 1983, based in part on Miller and Johnson-Laird 1976). Similar phenomena arise in lexical entries for nouns as well. For instance, a stereotypical *chair* has a stereotypical form and a standard function. Objects that have the proper function but the wrong form – say beanbag chairs – are more marginal instances of the category; and so are objects that have the right form but cannot fulfill the function – say chairs made of newspaper or giant chairs. An object that violates both conditions – say a pile of crumpled newspaper – is by no stretch of the imagination a chair. Lakoff (1987, chapter 4) applies such an analysis to the concept *mother*, which includes the woman who contributes genetic material, the woman who bears the child, and the woman who raises the child. In today's arrangements of adoption and genetic engineering, not all three of these always coincide, and so the term is not always used stereotypically.

Jackendoff (1983) calls a system of conditions of this sort a *preference rule system*; Lakoff (1987) calls it (one aspect of) an *idealized cognitive model*; the *frames* of Minsky (1975) have similar effects. Such concepts, like Tarskian concepts, are combinations of conditions. They differ from Tarskian concepts in that the conditions are combined differently. The combination is not a logical conjunction, since satisfaction of less than the full set of conditions is sufficient to categorize an object. But it is not a logical disjunction either, because a logical disjunction does not make the proper distinction between central and borderline examples. That is, a proper theory of word meanings must be richer than standard logical models. (Default logic comes closer to capturing the effect of such conditions, which function as default values where there is no evidence to the contrary, for instance in (9a).)

Appealing to the psychological goals of I-semantics, such enrichment of the theory proves to be plausible on broader psychological grounds. The manner in which conditions interact in cluster concepts is central in visual perception (Wertheimer 1923, Marr 1982), in phonetic perception (Liberman and Studdert-Kennedy 1977), in musical perception (Lerdahl and Jackendoff 1983), and in Gricean implicature (Bach and Harnish 1979). Moreover, such an interaction is plausibly instantiated in the brain, where the firing of a neuron is normally not a rigid function of other neural firings (like a logical conjunction), but rather a composite of many excitatory and inhibitory synapses of varying strengths. Thus cluster concepts, even though unusual in a logical framework, are quite natural in a psychological framework.

7.3 Image-like components of meaning

Putnam (1975) suggests that for many categories, speakers carry in their heads images of stereotypical instances (though, because he is committed to E-semantics, he does not consider such images part of meanings). Within I-semantics, appeal to image-like representations as part of concepts is widespread, though there are few concrete proposals. Jackendoff (1987a) and Landau and Jackendoff (1993) suggest that entities that are understood spatially (e.g. physical objects and actions) are partially encoded in terms of a *spatial representation* that is an enriched version of Marr's (1982) *3D model structure*. It is widely assumed that other sensory phenomena such as sounds, smells, tastes, and bodily sensations are also encoded partially in modality-specific imagistic terms.

Again, although parsimony might argue against introducing such further kinds of representations into meanings, psychological considerations abundantly support it. Part of the process of identifying a physical object is comparing its appearance to known examples or to a schema that summarizes known examples. Given that the visual system must encode such schemata independently – even in nonlinguistic organisms – there is no reason that the conceptual system should not be able to make use of this information. If it did not, information about appearance would have to be encoded in the conceptual system anyway in order for categorization to take place, resulting in a needless duplication of information.

There is a further reason to accept imagistic encoding as part of word meaning. Many detailed characteristics of shape (as well as sound, smell, taste, and body sensation) do not lend themselves to any sort of algebraic (or propositional) feature decomposition. For instance, the difference between the appearance of a duck and that of a goose can be expressed algebraically only in terms of *ad hoc* features such as [±long neck]. However, such a difference is altogether natural in a system like Marr's 3D model structure, which is adapted to detecting subtle differences of shape and contour.

This is not to say that all categorization can be reduced to imagistic representations. For instance, imagistic representation cannot encode the distinction between types and tokens or the place of ducks in the taxonomy of waterfowl, birds, and animals. Nor can it encode the quantificational aspects of meaning. Rather, it seems appropriate to think of algebraic and imagistic representations as sharing between them the burden of labor of encoding human knowledge of categories – if you will, Putnam's "division of linguistic labor" applied to the modules of the mind.

The linkage thus established between sensory/imagistic encodings and propositional/algebraic encodings also helps explain how it is possible for us to talk about what we see. In order for people to visually identify an entity to which language makes reference, the semantic/conceptual structures derived from language cannot be compared directly against the world. Rather, they must be placed in correspondence with representations arising from the visual modality, so that they may be checked against visual input. This is the *only* plausible causal mechanism by which visual input can have an influence on linguistic expression. Thus an insistence on the psychological principles of I-semantics has important consequences for the theory of reference. We return to this issue in section 10.

8   Spatial Expressions

In contrast with formal semantics, research in I-semantics has consistently been preoccupied with the interpretation of expressions of spatial location and motion. There are a number of natural reasons for this emphasis, all emerging from the fundamental goals of I-semantics. First, the field of spatial location and motion is very rich. Second, because sentences of spatial motion and location are perceptually verifiable (see the previous subsection), judgments of truth, entailment, and ambiguity are quite sharp and highly structured. Third, as will be seen in section 9, many other fields of concepts are structured algebraically along similar lines, so an understanding of spatial expressions potentially yields dividends in understanding language more broadly.

Fourth, again drawing on the biological aspect of semantics, it is to be expected that psychological encoding of spatial location and motion evolved long before language, since all our mammalian antecedents show the capacity to navigate through the world. Fifth, as Piaget (1970) stresses, children show an understanding of spatial concepts in their sensorimotor behavior well before they can speak. In studying spatial concepts, then, one is tapping into a kind of human knowledge that is biologically and developmentally prior to linguistic knowledge, which makes it of exceptional interest. (Many of these reasons are stressed by Miller and Johnson-Laird 1976 as well as later writers.)

There is room here only to touch on one basic phenomenon within this domain: figure-ground organization. However, this phenomenon is central, as it forms the foundation of the theories of Gruber (1965), Talmy (1978, 1983), Langacker (1987), and Jackendoff (1983), and underlies much detailed work on prepositional meanings such as Brugman (1981), Herskovits (1986), Vandeloise (1986), and Landau and Jackendoff (1993).

Consider a simple sentence like *The cat sat on the mat*. The two objects being described, the cat and the mat, are expressed asymmetrically: *the cat* is subject of the sentence, near the top of the syntactic tree, while *the mat* is embedded down inside the prepositional phrase. In principle the spatial relation between the cat and the mat could be encoded conceptually as (10), in which *on* is a two-place relation between the two objects; proposals along these lines are not infrequent.

(10)   sit (the cat) and on (the cat, the mat)

However, the research cited above claims that the meaning of the sentence is asymmetrical in just the way that the syntax is:

1. The mat is conceptualized as a *reference object* or *landmark*.
2. The reference object helps to define a *region* of space. This region of space is expressed by the PP *on the mat*: it is the region in contact with the upper surface of the mat. Different prepositions define different regions based on the same reference object, for instance *under the mat, beyond the mat,* and *off the mat.*
3. The verb uses this region of space to locate a *figural object,* namely the cat. In the present example, the verb *sat* also indicates the posture of the figural object and the past time of the situation in question.

So an informal analysis of *The cat sat on the mat* is something like (11).

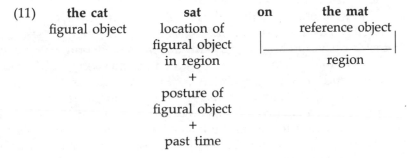

(11)   **the cat**   **sat**   **on**   **the mat**
        figural object   location of   reference object
                              figural object |_____|
                              in region   region
                                  +
                              posture of
                              figural object
                                  +
                              past time

To see the asymmetry more clearly, we may reverse the roles, producing the sentence *The mat lay under the cat.* This sentence sounds distinctly odd, even though the physical situation it depicts is exactly the same; and certainly the grammar is impeccable. In order to see why this should be so, consider a situation in which the roles of the figural and reference objects *can* be satisfactorily exchanged, for instance (12).

(12)   a. The star is inside the circle.
       b. The circle lies around the star.

Even here there is an asymmetry in the concepts expressed by these two sentences, as can be seen by using them as answers to questions. (This argument is due to Gruber 1965.)

(13)   a. Where is the star?   It is inside the circle.
                                   ??The circle lies around it.
       b. Where is the circle?   It lies around the star.
                                   ??The star is inside it.

That is, sentence (12a) is a much better way of saying where the circle is, and sentence (12b) is a much better way of saying where the star is. This difference is explained by the analysis in (11), which says that the reference object (the object of the preposition) is being used to help locate the figural object (the subject of the sentence), not the other way around. In these terms, it is clear why *The mat lay under the cat* sounds odd: it is telling how to find the mat by using the cat as a point of reference; but it is hard to imagine circumstances in which one would want to do this.

For an even more striking case pointed out by Talmy (1983), *next to* appears to be totally symmetrical: if X is next to Y, it stands to reason that Y is next to X. Yet *The bike is next to the house* is fine, but *The house is next to the bike* is distinctly odd. The reason is that relatively large immovable objects are normally used as landmarks for locating small movable objects, but not the other way round. (Notice that if the house in question happens to be a toy "Monopoly" house, so it *is* relatively small and movable, *The house is next to the bike* is much more acceptable.)

The asymmetries in these sentences have nothing to do with the syntax of English, which says only that the subject NP comes first, the object of the preposition follows the preposition, and so forth. And, as (12)–(13) make clear, the asymmetries have nothing to do with the physical world *per se* either. Rather, they have to do with the way the human mind *conceptually organizes* the perceived world: how we use objects to find other objects.

This conceptual organization, and the grammatical organization that goes with it, is replicated in language after language of the world. Thus we have good reason to believe it is part of the innate basis of human concepts.

These examples also show that language expresses the location of objects not in terms of absolute space, but always in terms of figures placed against a background. This background is a region of space whose organization is determined by reference objects (among which may be the speaker and hearer). In terms of a formal logic, this may or may not be a natural way for language to work. But in a psychological context, it is altogether natural, as it accords entirely with the figure-ground organization found in the perceptual systems, and therefore provides a natural mapping to procedures of perceptual verification of the sort discussed in section 7.3.

9   The Same Organization in Abstract Domains of Thought

A second foundational result in I-semantics also originates with Gruber (1965), who showed that many grammatical patterns used to describe physical objects in space also appear in expressions that describe non-spatial domains.

The groups of sentences in (14) through (17) illustrate this result. The first example, (14a), exhibits the figure-ground organization just discussed; the whole set illustrates the larger grammatical and conceptual patterns within which this particular pattern is situated. Notice especially the parallels indicated by the italicized words.

(14) <u>Spatial location and motion</u>
    a. The messenger *is in* Istanbul.   (Location)
    b. The messenger *went from* Paris
       to Istanbul.   (Change of location)
    c. The gang *kept* the messenger
       in Istanbul.   (Caused stasis)

(15) <u>Possession</u>
    a. The money *is* Fred's.   (Possession)
    b. The inheritance finally *went*
       to Fred.   (Change of possession)
    c. Fred *kept* the money.   (Caused stasis)

(16) <u>Ascription of properties</u>
    a. The light *is* red.   (Simple property)
    b. The light *went/changed from*
       green *to* red.   (Change of property)
    c. The cop *kept* the light red.   (Caused stasis)

(17) <u>Scheduling activities</u>
    a. The meeting *is on* Monday.   (Simple schedule)
    b. The meeting was *changed from*
       Tuesday *to* Monday.   (Change of schedule)
    c. The chairman *kept* the meeting
       on Monday.   (Caused stasis)

Each of these groups contains one sentence with the verb *be*, one with *go* or *change*, and one with *keep*. When *be* appears with a preposition (as in (14a) and (17a)), the same preposition can appear with *keep*; if *be* appears without a preposition (as in (15a) and (16a)), so does *keep*. On the other hand, *go* and *change* characteristically appear along with the prepositions *from* and *to*.

There is no reason for these patterns that derives from the physical nature of the situations expressed. Changing possession does not necessarily entail changing location: the sale of a house or stocks does not involve motion at all. An object's color has nothing to do with where it is or who owns it. Setting the appointed time for a meeting or trip bears no apparent relationship at all to the other three.

On a more abstract level, however, the meanings of the four groups of sentences are parallel.

    1. The "be" sentences all describe some state of affairs in which some characteristic is ascribed to the subject of the sentence: location in a

region in (14), belonging to someone in (15), having a property in (16), and having an appointed time in (17).

2. The "go/change" sentences all describe a change involving the subject of the sentence, in which it comes to have the characteristic ascribed by the corresponding "be" sentence. The subject's characteristic at the beginning of the change is described by the phrase following "from," and at the end of the change by the phrase following "to."

3. The "keep" sentences all describe the subject of the sentence causing the object of the sentence to have the characteristic ascribed by the corresponding "be" sentence, and this characteristic persists over a period of time.

In other words, the linguistic parallelism among these sets reveals an underlying conceptual parallelism. Thus it is not accidental that many of the same lexical items recur in (14)–(17).

The idea behind the conceptual parallelism is this: The characteristics that things can be conceived to have fall into broad families or "semantic fields" such as the headings in (14)–(17). Within a field, "be" sentences express simple characteristics such as being in a particular location, belonging to a particular person, being of a particular color, or being scheduled at a particular time. But in addition, the conceptual system contains complex concepts that can be applied to any field, among which are (1) a change from one characteristic to another (the "go/change" sentences) and (2) something making something else have a particular characteristic over a period of time (the "keep" sentences). Because the same abstract system appears in many (and possibly all) semantic fields, it is convenient for the language to use the same words as it switches from one field to another.

In fact, almost any characteristic that varies along a one-dimensional range of values turns out to be expressed in terms of the linear opposites *up* and *down* or *high* and *low*. Numbers (and hence prices, weights, and temperatures) go up and down, military ranks go up and down, pitches on the musical scale go up and down, and so does one's mood. However, as is well known, time concepts are a partial exception to this generalization: in just about every language, they are expressed by terms that also apply to space; but instead of *up* and *down*, they use a front-to-back continuum, for example *before* and *after* in English.

Similar grammatical and lexical patterns appear in language after language. Talmy (1978, 1985a) and Langacker (1987) essentially take them for granted and build theories of conceptual structure around them. Lakoff and Johnson (1980) and Lakoff (1987, 1990) argue that they are part of a vast system of metaphor that is inextricably embedded in the conceptual structure expressed by language. They further argue that the pervasiveness of metaphor makes it impossible to base a semantic theory on a simplistic notion of "literal truth," and impossible to treat metaphor as nontruth-conditional and therefore marginal.

Jackendoff (1983; 1992, chapter 3) and Jackendoff and Aaron (1991), while acknowledging the ubiquity of metaphor, argue for a finer-grained distinction. The traditional notion of metaphor applies to creative, novel expressions, often with a patent semantic clash, used to make speech more colorful. Lakoff et al. extend the term metaphor to *any* extension of terms from one semantic field to another. However, the parallels illustrated in (14)–(17) exhibit no semantic clash, and they are the *only* ways available in English of expressing the concepts in question. Thus they are not metaphorical in the usual sense. Jackendoff argues therefore that the primitives of conceptual structure include a set of precise abstract underlying patterns that can be applied to many different semantic fields such as those in (14)–(17). These patterns are the basic machinery that permits complex thought to be formulated and basic entailments to be derived in any domain. The apparent primacy of the spatial field is then due (1) to its evolutionary primacy and (2) to its strong linkage to perception. (This does not preclude more high-level processes of metaphor as well.)

However this dispute is resolved, all major schools of thought in I-semantics (other than Fodor) agree that the linguistic parallelisms shown in (14)–(17) reflect substantive parallelisms in the concepts these sentences express, and thereby reveal fundamental organization in human conceptual structure.

10 Counterpart of Theory of Reference in I-Semantics

Recall that, in I-semantics, the entities to which language can refer are not entities in "the world" plain and simple, but rather entities in the world *as humans grasp it*. This claim can now be better appreciated in the light of the last three sections. Consider for instance (17b), *The meeting was changed from Tuesday to Monday*. Unlike *The cat sat on the mat*, this sentence points to nothing perceptible. It describes something that takes place only in people's minds, changing their future behavior. In fact, the idea of named time periods like *Monday* is purely a conceptual invention – there is nothing *perceptually* salient about the boundaries of Monday. Yet humans indubitably experience reality as containing Mondays and schedules, and the term *Monday* is taken to refer.

Still more compelling is the case of possession. If something belongs to you, it doesn't belong to me; and our behavior is strongly constrained by this knowledge. Who owns what is an important part of the reality we experience. Yet the predicate of possession has little perceptual basis; it involves strictly conceptual notions such as rights and obligations over potential use of an object.

Returning to categorization, there is nothing *in the world* that demands a sharp boundary between red and orange, and there is nothing *in the world* that sharply distinguishes climbing from other kinds of locomotion. It is the human need to sort the particulars of the world into categories that creates these divisions. In short, many aspects of the concepts expressed by language are purely mental constructs. Nevertheless, they are not fictional or senseless – they are part of the way the world is *for human beings*.

Physical objects and actions tend to have strong perceptual linkages to the "real" world, social constructs less so. However, it is not a matter for semantics *per se* how these perceptual linkages are established; it is part of the theory of perception. What *is* part of semantics is the internal principles of inference among related concepts.

A useful example is the concept of a *strike* in baseball. What makes a particular event count as a strike is its role in a baseball game; a strike is what there are three of when a batter strikes out. The perceptually verifiable conditions are such things as whether the batter swung at a pitched ball and missed, or whether a pitched ball at which the batter did not swing passed through the "strike zone." It is a matter for perceptual theory to determine how the umpire judges where the ball went and what the batter did. The significance of the physical event – whether it takes place as an appropriate subevent of a baseball game, and how it counts in the progress of the game – are all entirely conceptual. Yet the term *strike* can clearly be used referentially. Strikes can be individuated, counted, and quantified; not only that, millions of people care about them.

Such combinations of perceptual and conceptual conditions appear to be pervasive in human concepts (see Carey 1985, Keil 1989 for discussion). In particular, it appears that many theoretical and scientific concepts share the general characteristics of strikes, having an elaborate logico-conceptual organization that is grounded in a scattered array of perceptual observations.

A case sometimes offered against this approach to reference is that of logical and mathematical facts, which, though abstract, are often held to be true independent of human observers. (This is, for example, a major argument of Katz (1981) in his rejection of I-semantics in favor of a Platonistic approach.) Within I-semantics, though, the problem turns inside out: what is it about human beings that (1) permits them to grasp logical and mathematical facts and (2) leads them to believe that these are true independent of human observers? At the moment the jury is out; Macnamara (1986) and Lakoff (1987) have interesting discussions.

There remains an issue that some take to be the pre-eminent issue for any theory of semantics, particularly one that situates meanings in the head. This is the issue of *intentionality*: how a set of formal distinctions internal to the brain can be meaningful, how they can be about "the world." However, in an I-semantic account this issue plays itself out rather differently than usual. I-semantics claims that, although "the world" is experienced as external to the observer, it is full of entities that strictly speaking exist only because of the observer's *construal* of the world – such as the examples just cited. Consequently, the meaningfulness of mental representations are not to be ascribed to any simple relation between symbols in the head and a preexisting, precategorized "real world." Quite different solutions are offered by Fodor (1990), Jackendoff (1987a), and Lakoff (1987), even brief sketches of which would take the present essay too far afield.

However this issue comes to be resolved, it is important to notice that it must be confronted by *any* theory that aspires to account for the human grasp of language. To maintain an E-semantic approach (or a "semi-E-semantic" approach) because it faces no such difficulty simply puts off the issue without solving it.

At the same time, the lack of a firm doctrine on intentionality has not prevented the various schools of I-semantics from producing an array of deep results about the nature of the concepts that language expresses, and the connection of these concepts to human psychology and evolution. It is these results that should command the attention of semanticists in other traditions.

NOTES

1 The list compiled below is by necessity a personal choice. I apologize in advance for any failure on my part to cite work that the reader feels essential.
2 The only major exception is Fodor's (1975) Language of Thought Hypothesis. For reasons too elaborate to go into here, Fodor claims that the meanings of monomorphemic lexical items are undecomposable innate monads. See Jackendoff (1983, Section 7.5; 1992, Section 2.8, chapter 8) for discussion.
3 Typicality judgments occur, for instance, in color concepts, where a focal red is judged more typical than a red tinged with orange. Armstrong, Gleitman, and Gleitman 1983 show that typicality judgments can be obtained even for noncluster concepts; for instance 38 is judged a less typical even number than 4, and a nun is judged a less typical woman than a housewife. Thus typicality in and of itself is only a symptom for a number of underlying phenomena in categorization. But the existence of multiple sources for graded judgments does not undermine the existence of cluster concepts, as Armstrong et al. claim it does. See Jackendoff 1983, chapter 7, note 6 and Lakoff 1987, chapter 9 for discussion.

21 Semantics, Pragmatics, and Natural-Language Interpretation

RUTH M. KEMPSON

Semantics as the study of meaning in natural languages, and pragmatics as the study of how utterances are interpreted, might seem to be one and the same study. Given that the meaning of an expression is the information that that expression conveys, and that interpretation by users of the language is the retrieval of information from expressions, it may be hard to envisage that they could be separable. Nevertheless, semantics and pragmatics constitute two quite discrete programs of research, set within different disciplines. The one is founded in the study of formal systems, the other in cognitive psychology. This chapter argues that developments from both sides of the divide suggest a new view in which the two disciplines can be brought together, a view in which meaning for natural-language systems is defined in terms of the meta-task of building inference-structures. The first move is to establish why semantics and pragmatics are standardly construed as so different (Sections 1–2). Then conflicting semantic and pragmatic claims about natural language content are evaluated (Sections 3–4); and a new proposed proof-theoretic model of utterance interpretation is set out. Finally (Section 5) the consequences of the proof-theoretic mode of analysis are outlined.

1 Formal Semantics: The Starting Point

The starting point for the formal study of semantics of natural languages was the demonstration by Montague (1974) that natural languages can be analysed as formal inference systems in like manner to familiar logical inference systems such as predicate calculus. These logic systems are set up to model truth-preserving relations. Model-theoretic semantics for predicate logic assigns truth-values to well-formed formulae with respect to a model, defines inference in terms of relations between such assigned interpretations, and assigns interpretations to subconstituents of formulae of a type whose outcome will be a truth-value with respect to the model. With otherwise minimal ontological commitments, the system is defined solely in terms of individuals (referred to as having the logical type "**e**" for entity), truth-values (referred to as having the logical type "**t**" for truth-value), and mapping relations from one to the other (functions from **e** to **t**). Such systems have syntactic and semantic characterisations in tandem. The simplest case serves as a pattern. Corresponding to the rule of syntax licensing $F(\alpha)$ as a well-formed formula of predicate calculus is a semantic rule assigning that string $F(\alpha)$ an interpretation with respect to the model M $(= [[F(\alpha)]]^M)$ on the basis of the functional application of the value assigned to the predicate "F" (of logical type $\langle e,t \rangle$) to the value assigned to its argument "α" (of logical type **e**):

> If F is a 1-place predicate, and α an argument, then $F(\alpha)$ is a wff.
> If F is a 1-place predicate, and α an argument, then
> $[[F(\alpha)]]^M = [[F]]^M([[\alpha]])^M$

The overall account is a truth-theoretically interpreted formal system which is rigorously compositional, predicting the meaning of a composite expression solely in terms of some function over the meanings assigned to its parts, those meanings defined relative to a unitary and ontologically parsimonious truth-theoretic concept of semantics (cf. Gamut 1991). The corresponding assertion about natural languages is that a natural language can and should be defined on the same pattern with only minimal extension of the underlying semantic vocabulary (to worlds and times, each world-time pair being a discrete "index of evaluation") to allow, for example, the interpretation of tense as involving truth of an assertion at some given world-time index. The consequence of this commitment is that the relation between string, assigned structure and interpretation must be direct, as in these calculi. There is no place for an intermediate level of representation since if there were, the conception of natural languages as sets of strings over which inference is directly definable would no longer be sustained. In so far as such representations are invoked in talking about meanings, it is assumed that they are for convenience only and are eliminable. Predictably, there is no allusion to psychological properties of reasoning.

2   Pragmatics: The Psychological Perspective

Pragmatics, in contrast, is the study of interpretation from the perspective of psychology, the study of the general cognitive principles involved in the retrieval of information from an uttered sequence of words. Its goal is to explain how from an uttered sequence of words, a hearer can succeed in retrieving some interpretation intended by the speaker, and then from that construal derive yet further information constituting the full import of the utterance. For example, a pragmatic theory is expected to explain how in the conversational sequence

(1) Peter: Is George a good cook?
     Mary: He's a Frenchman.

Peter can succeed in establishing who Mary is referring to in her use of the pronoun *he*, and, further, how he may deduce that George is a good cook (via the retrieval of added information, say that all French people are good cooks). It is widely assumed in cognitive psychology (cf. Fodor 1983) that the cognitive system is a computational device. So the characterisation of how inferences are drawn is presumed to involve sets of representations and relations between them (though cf. Stalnaker 1984, Dennett 1987). In pragmatics too, it is relatively uncontroversial that the recovery of such information involves a psychological process of inference syntactically defined over representations assigned to the string as its interpretation (Cf. Grice 1975, Sperber and Wilson 1986, Atlas 1989). In pragmatic discussions accordingly, the question is not what form the recovered information might take, but how it is recovered (cf. the debate about the status of so-called generalised conversational implicatures; Levinson 1987a, Carston 1988, 1993). The question that is asked is: how does the hearer choose which interpretation to select, given the range of representations she might in principle construct (Grice 1975, Sperber and Wilson 1986)?

The answer to this question is by no means trivial, given the human ability to draw together information from arbitrarily distinct domains (cf. Fodor 1983, who expressed pessimism about the possibility of any theory of central cognitive mechanisms on the grounds of the human ability to make correlations between any arbitrary pair of domains). The first attempt at answering the question of how it is that hearers generally have no difficulty in deciding what interpretation is intended by the speaker was put forward by Grice (1975, 1989a). Grice proposed so-called Maxims of Conversation which constituted principles governing the selection of inferences. These maxims were Maxims of Quality, Quantity, Relevance and Manner, dictating that speakers could be expected to conform to standards of truthfulness, relevance, and saying only as much as is required to achieve the particular inferential effect. Apparent violation of these maxims as in an utterance of *Joan's a vulture* or of *I'm working but I haven't done my teeth today* were said to be the basis whereby extra "conversational implicatures" were derived, thereby explaining how speakers could utter a sentence expressing but a single proposition while nevertheless conveying a whole range of extra effects. The concepts of Relevance, Quantity, etc. were not defined by Grice, but subsequently Sperber and Wilson (1986) argued that relevance could be defined in cognitive terms as achieving an optimal balance between cognitive effort required and richness of inferential effect obtained. They further argued that no maxim was required other than a single invariant Principle of Relevance which guarantees that every utterance conveys a presumption of optimal relevance, all choices of interpretation being made subject to the constraint that the least effort on the part of the hearer to derive an interpretation that the speaker could have intended will be the correct interpretation. The restriction on choice of interpretation is thus not a restriction as to what can count as correlatable domains of interest (Fodor 1983). It is rather a restriction on accessibility of cognitive representations, all interpretations precluded except the candidate representation commensurate with interpretations that the speaker could have intended requiring the smallest search through the cognitive space. The detailed nature of concepts of relevance, etc. remain controversial in pragmatics (Sperber and Wilson 1987a, 1987b, Bach and Harnish 1987, Clark 1987, Gibb 1987, Roberts 1991); but the assumption of a representational base to the explanation is uncontentious.

Of the differences between the semantic and pragmatic approaches, superficially the most prominent is the commitment to formal specification on the one hand contra the extremely informal mode of presentation on the other (cf. Kamp 1979b). More substantial is the difference in mode of explication; the pragmatic assumption being that explanations of utterance interpretation are defined at least in part in terms of the form of the proposition the utterance expresses, the semantic assumption being to the contrary that no explanation of interpretation invokes anything other than a direct mapping from syntactic constructs of the string itself onto model-theoretic objects constituting the interpretation. In the light of these differences, it becomes less surprising that pragmatics and semantics are often assumed to be irreconcilably different enterprises. However, these contrastive forms of characterisation coincide in purporting to provide an explanation of the context-dependence of natural-language interpretation, which is a phenomenon not shared with formal language systems.

3.   The Context-Dependence of Natural-Language Interpretation

The context-dependent nature of natural-language interpretation is the phenomenon that gives the lie to any strict form of the compositionality principle defined for a truth-theoretic account of meaning (cf. Partee 1984). The interpretation of natural-language strings cannot be projected exclusively from the words of the sentence and their mode of combination (as in familiar logic systems), but systematically depends on the environment in which it occurs. Thus a string such as *His mother had died* is subject to different forms of interpretation, depending on whether it is preceded in a single sentence by a quantified expression such as *every boy*, across sentence boundaries preceded by an indefinite NP, or preceded freely in a discourse by a name:

(2)   Every boy was told that his mother had died.
(3)   A student of mine was miserable. His mother had died.
(4)   John was miserable. His mother had died.

The problem is quite general: we cannot even in a simple case such as (4) evaluate the sentence *His mother had died* as true with respect to a model without the referent of the expression having first been established. We know that this phenomenon requires an analysis in terms of some form of underdetermination by the content of the pronoun vis à vis its interpretation, because by strict model-theoretic criteria such a sentence is as many ways ambiguous as the pronoun can be assigned different referents, one and the same sentence being true with respect to some arbitrary model if John's mother had died but false with respect to that same model if Bill's mother was alive (cf. Lewis 1970 and many subsequent references). If we are not to assign this ambiguity to the expression itself, we have to characterise the ambiguity as due to some independently defined concept of "context", characterising the expression in question as projecting some relatively weakly specified input which, when combined with this provided contextual factor, will yield the requisite variety of interpretations.

This phenomenon of context-dependent interpretation is extremely widespread. It affects not only pronouns but also the interpretation of tense, as witness the ambiguity of

(5) John fell. He was pushed.

depending on which event is construed as occurring first. We would not wish here to pinpoint the ambiguity as provided by two discrete forms of past-tense suffix, depending on whether they give rise to the interpretation of propositions in sequence or not. It affects the interpretation of definite NPs. These, like pronouns, are subject to a range of anaphoric effects, as witness

(6) The door was jammed.
(7) I couldn't get out of the car. The door was jammed.
(8) Every car gets the door jammed occasionally.
(9) Every house I put on the market I have checked to make sure that the house is problem-free.

It affects the construal of what set of entities is quantified over (the so called domain selection problem). The following instances of *everyone* are not construed in parallel:

(10) John walked into the room. Everyone stared at him.
(11) John was miserable at the office. Everyone stared at him when he left the meeting.

And so on, through indefinite NPs, demonstrative NPs, VP anaphora, etc.

The question is: how should this phenomenon of context-dependence be explained? There is a range of choices available for each type of case. For any one phenomenon, we have to ask: Should it be explained as a phenomenon of ambiguity, positing different interpretations for the expression itself with no role assigned to the discourse context other than that of disambiguation? Should it be characterised as stemming from an underdetermining input with a process of interpretation reconstructed solely in the semantic algebra? Or should it rather be explained in structural terms as the substitution of one logical expression for another as some representation of content for the string is built up? An analysis failing to grant the pertinence of the general phenomenon of context-dependence to the particular case would put forward the first of these. A semantic explanation suggests the second; a pragmatic explanation the third.

3.1   *The situation-theoretic reconstruction of context*

Out of these, linguists have often chosen the first form of analysis. There are accounts of pronominal anaphora in terms of different types of pronoun (Cooper 1979, Evans 1980, Reinhart 1983a and many syntactic accounts following her, Chierchia 1992, Heim 1990) – indeed few have pressed for a unitary account of anaphora (Kamp 1981 (modulo indexical pronouns), Gawron and Peters 1990, Kempson 1988). There are accounts of indefinite NPs in terms of discrete types of indefinite NP (Fodor and Sag 1982, Kadmon 1990, Chierchia 1992). There are accounts of VP anaphora in terms of different types of content (e.g. Gawron and Peters 1990). There are accounts of different types of ellipsis (Chao 1988, Pesetsky 1982, Lappin, this volume). In each of these, little or no attempt is made to address the problem central to natural language interpretation, that one and the same expression can be used in a multitude of ways with systematic dependence on the context in which it occurs for its particular interpretation. This central point of difference between natural and formal languages is glossed over. The explanations are rather set up as though in the main natural languages pattern like formal languages, with each expression having assigned a fixed interpretation, the problem of context reducing in all such cases to the mere problem of disambiguation.

As the only theories to propose a general solution to the phenomenon of context-dependence,[1] Situation Theory presents the semantic option, Relevance Theory the pragmatic option. Respecting the underdeterminacy of natural-language expressions vis à vis their semantic evaluation, Barwise and Perry (1983) define a semantic framework which allows a range of partial objects (cf. also Devlin 1991); and characterise the interpretation of a sentence as a parametrised object requiring its interpretation to be fixed by anchors to the discourse situation. A sentence such as *She smiled* will be anchored to the speech situation by connections which fix the referent of *she*, the time and location at which the smiling took place. The sentence will thus be predicted to have discrete interpretations depending on the nature of the anchoring, but a single parametrised content:

$$\langle\langle x \; smile, l, t \rangle\rangle$$

with *x*, *l*, *t*, to be fixed subject to constraints that *x* be female, and that *t* be fixed as preceding the time of evaluation. Indeed one of the major contributions of Situation Theory to natural language understanding has been the extended discussion within that framework of the nature of such under-determined contents (Barwise and Perry 1983, Barwise 1988b, Devlin 1991).

Barwise uses this mode of explanation as an attack on representationalist analyses of human inference in general (Barwise 1988b). He argues that the phenomenon of context-dependence immediately demonstrates the falsity of the Fodor view of the cognitive system as a formal (syntactically definable) inference device, on the grounds that a syntactic definition of inference for natural-language strings is not possible. If we grant the Situation Semantics assumption that there is no form of representation associated with a natural language string other than a structural assignment to the words of the string this conclusion certainly follows. One cannot validly infer the truth of (12) from (13) and (14) without fixing the parameters external to the sentence itself which determine that *she* is construed as referring to Sue, *him* as referring to John:

(12) She will follow him.
(13) If John is the leader, Sue will follow him.
(14) John is the leader.

If a natural language is indeed the sole inference system a human being uses, then the human activity of inference requires, as Barwise suggests, a "situated" form of inference, and is not amenable to a purely syntactic definition.

However, rather than take such evidence as denying the Fodor view that the cognitive system is a computational system whose properties can be defined exclusively in terms of the formal properties of the system, one might propose instead that natural languages are not straightforward inference systems of a classical sort, but require a mixed mode of evaluation, their interpretation requiring first the building of some structure corresponding to the truth-theoretic content of the string as so asserted on an occasion of its use prior to the truth-theoretic evaluation of that assigned structure. Interpretation of (12) for example will involve building the structure corresponding to "Sue will follow John", replacing the pronouns with logical constants denoting some particular individuals named *Sue* and *John* respectively. The phenomenon of natural language underdeterminacy and its resolution in specific contexts on this alternative view then becomes the assignment to a string of some structural representation, with structural choices being made as to the form of the intermediate representation, that representation being taken to reflect the content of the proposition the speaker is presumed to have conveyed. Such a move enables us to retain a representationalist view of the mind, while agreeing with Barwise that a formal account of inference defined directly over natural language strings is problematic.

3.2   *A deductive model of utterance processing*

It is this latter view which has been proposed by pragmatists (e.g. Sperber and Wilson 1986). According to Sperber and Wilson's analysis, the task for the hearer is two-fold. In processing an utterance, the hearer has to decode the information intrinsic to the lexical expressions of the sequence. But then the hearer builds a structured object corresponding to the proposition expressed, choosing also a context set of premises with which that proposition can be said to combine to yield the requisite array of indirect effects. This task of building some such requisite representation as the interpretation of a given string can be reconstructed as a sequential reasoning task, taking each word in turn and establishing what the requisite interpretation should be, either by deduction or by abductive choice. It is modelled (Gabbay and Kempson 1992) as a reasoning task over logical type specifications driven by lexical input, with additional choices being made by the hearer in all cases where the input does not fully dictate the selected interpretation. The format adopted is that of a Labelled Deductive System (LDS: cf. Gabbay forthcoming).

In Labelled Deductive Systems, the unit over which inference is defined is a declarative unit, a pair of label-plus-formula, $\alpha{:}A$, to be read as "α labels A". Thus Modus Ponens:

$$\frac{\begin{array}{l} \alpha{:}P \\ \beta{:}P \to Q \end{array}}{\mu(\alpha\beta){:}Q}$$

where μ is some operation on the pair α,β such as functional application. These labels can be used for a variety of purposes: (i) to bring semantic information about the premises used into the proof; (ii) to define extra controls on their combination to allow for a range of related logical systems, (cf. the label-theoretic characterisation of the family of conditional logics, Gabbay and de Queiroz 1992), (iii) to define composite logical systems with the label carrying information about one kind of system, the formula carrying information about another. The first developed example of an LDS framework was the natural deduction system for temporal logic with $t_i{:}P$ to be read as "P is true at time t_i". The rule of Modus Ponens in this system is defined as:

$$\frac{\begin{array}{l} t_i{:}P \\ t_i{:}P \to Q \end{array}}{t_i{:}Q}$$

Such a system uses a predicate logic expressing relations between temporal units as a labelling algebra, and a conditional logic as the logical language, directly bringing relevant aspects of the semantics, here the index of evaluation, into the proof system. The LDS framework provides a general method for combining two sorts of information in a single system, setting out a composite system in which two possibly independent logical languages are defined in tandem, enabling different facets of the particular inference system to be both systematically correlated and yet nevertheless kept distinct. The LDS double articulation of differentiated aspects of interpretation is ideal for modelling natural language interpretation, because we need to model both the properties of the proposition taken to be expressed by the speaker (the ultimate label derived) and the information provided by the words which drive the meta-task for the hearer of identifying what that proposition might be.

In the LDS model adopted in Gabbay and Kempson (1992) LDS_{NL}, the particular form of $\rightarrow$ Elimination, where μ is functional application, and P, Q range over the logical types e, t, $e \rightarrow t$, is:

$$\frac{\begin{array}{l} \alpha{:}P \\ \beta{:}P \rightarrow Q \end{array}}{\beta(\alpha){:}Q}$$

The system assumes isomorphism between the conditional logic and the functional calculus (on this Curry-Howard isomorphism with types as formulae, cf. van Benthem 1986, Gabbay & de Queiroz 1992). It directly translates semantic constructs into labelled formulae in a proof system. Declarative units to which this Modus Ponens rule applies consist of the concept expressed by the word as label to its logical type as formula in a conditional logic. Each successive step of Modus Ponens will then lead to incremental building up of an interpretation through simultaneous steps of functional application on the labels. *John sneezed* provides the simplest pattern. The premises to which Modus Ponens applies are John:e, sneeze:e $\rightarrow$ t, John labelling the type e as its formula, sneeze labelling the type as formula e $\rightarrow$ t; sneeze:e $\rightarrow$ t is the major premise, John:e is the minor premise; and these combine to yield sneeze(John):t, the tense labelling the whole as fixed at a time s_i preceding the time of evaluation, s_{NOW}:

$$s_i{:}\ s_i < s_{NOW},\ \text{sneeze(John):t}$$

The output is a structural representation of some proposition expressed as holding at some particular point in time s_i. This proof-theoretic presentation of the composite process of semantic interpretation displays how the hearer's task of interpreting a sequence of words is simultaneously a goal-directed task of reasoning and nevertheless a structure-building operation of recovering the proposition expressed by the speaker. (Note its faithfulness to the Fodorian stance of defining human reasoning in structural terms – cf. Gabbay & Kempson 1992). The goal imposed on the hearer's reasoning task is the weakly specified one of building a database of premises capable of proving $\alpha{:}t$ as conclusion, α identified not in advance but only by the words as they are taken in sequence (used once and once only).

In reconstructing utterance interpretation as a deduction task, this model is like other parsing-as-deduction models (Pereira 1991, König 1989, Hepple 1990).

In all such systems, some additional specification has to be added to ensure in a string with two NPs, that whatever is the subject combines last in any minimal sequence of steps of $\rightarrow$ Elimination leading to a α:t. In Labelled Deductive Systems restrictions on inference can be defined through the labelling algebra. Following this pattern, the concept of subject can be defined directly through the labelling algebra as the last minor premise in a set of such premises.[2] The Gabbay–Kempson model is however unlike parsing-as-deduction models whose motivation is largely computational (though cf. Pereira and Pollack 1991), in that it purports to provide a general and psychologically motivated model of the interpretation process. To be minimally successful, such a system must include more than just a parsing device. In particular, an essential extension is some reconstruction of the under-determination of truth-theoretic content presented by the natural-language input. This is modelled by the projection of incomplete premises. In the simplest anaphoric case, the expression is taken to project a premise with a place-holding metavariable as label, together with an associated procedure dictating how that metavariable may be instantiated (by an instantiation function Θ). The process of interpreting an utterance of *John saw Mary. She smiled* by a sequence of establishing premises, making on-line choices, and carrying out steps of Modus Ponens, can be set out as:

s_1	GOAL $\vdash \alpha$:t	
step 1	(John, use last)	: **e**
step 2	see	: **e** $\rightarrow$ (**e** $\rightarrow$ **t**)
step 3	$\Theta s_1 = s_i, \; s_i \langle s_{\text{NOW}}$	
step 4	Mary	: **e**
step 5	see(Mary)	: **e** $\rightarrow$ **t**
step 6	see(Mary)(John)	: **t**

s_2	GOAL $\vdash \alpha$:t	
step 7	(**u**, use last, Θ**u** $\notin s_2$, female (**u**)) : **e**	
step 8	Θ**u** = Mary	
step 9	smile	: **e** $\rightarrow$ **t**
step 10	$\Theta s_2 = s_j, \; s_j \langle s_{\text{NOW}}$	
step 11	smile(Mary)	: **t**

Emboldened variable letters are meta-variables, and these require instantiation by the function Θ. The lexical content of pronouns restricts the choice of value instantiating the projected metavariable to range only over labels outside their most immediately containing database. Relevance considerations dictate that this otherwise free choice involves some smallest search through the database to select an appropriate label with which to instantiate the metavariable **u**. Here the choice is stipulated as "Mary" (step 8).[3] Each database bears its own label, fixing its own construal in a flow of time. This is a process driven by the tense specification as input but involving on-line choice (again through the instantiation function Θ – steps 3 and 10) exactly as pronouns.

With this unfolding proof-structure as the basis for ascribing content to natural-language strings, we can now see the difference between a model-theoretic or situation-theoretic perspective on natural-language content and a proof-theoretic perspective. Both situation theory and model theory character-ise meaning solely in terms of what the expression semantically denotes, whether incompletely or fully specified (e.g. through anchoring of the partial semantic object to other semantically defined constructs). The characterisation is solely in terms of input content and output content. There is no record in the resulting evaluation of how such content is built up. Furthermore informa-tion is systematically removed as the semantic compilation builds up. Lexical input may provide indirect functions from individuals onto truth-value as-signments through complex type assignments made to individual lexical items, but the internal structure of the semantic output is invariably minimal (in the model-theoretic concept just a set of possible worlds, in the situation-theoretic concept a relation between utterance-situation and denoted situation). The significance of the proof-theoretic perspective is its commitment to a structural concept of interpretation. For every step of Modus Ponens structure is built up in the labels; and – this being a natural deduction system in which inference is characterised step by step from input to output – all information is retained. It can therefore be used to model all facets of interpretation as a structural process from (i) the input procedures presented by lexical items, through (ii) the under-determinacy of certain kinds of lexical input, and (iii) the resolution of all such inputs by a structural choice made as part of the interpretation process, to (iv) the structural representation which constitutes the final out-come. Despite the representational commitment, this outcome is one for which a classical semantics can be straightforwardly defined, matching the concept of propositional content provided by more orthodox concepts of semantics. The proof-theoretic perspective on content is therefore richer than the simpler truth-theoretic perspective, incorporating the truth-theoretic content as a subpart.

Proof-theoretic and situation-theoretic modelling of natural-language inter-pretation are thus in potential conflict. On the one hand, we have a monolithic situation-theoretic view of content, with context, traditionally represented as a set of external factors which anchor some partially specified semantic object. On the other hand, we have the view that the concept of content attributable to natural language strings is a composite one, comprising a set of procedures for building labelled databases, the ensuing structures having an associated truth-theoretic evaluation of a familiar kind. On this latter view, the concept of context is reconstructed as the set of representations of the logical language (labels and premises) chosen during the proof-construction process as values to assign to meta-language variables provided as input.

3.3   *Discourse representation theory*

Between these model-theoretic and proof-theoretic stances, we have the mixed vocabulary of Discourse Representation Theory (DRT) (Kamp 1981, Kamp and Reyle 1993). In DRT, an intermediate form of representation is posited in the interpretation of a (sequence of) sentence(s) – a partial model structure which is built by formal algorithm from a given syntactic input. One of the roles of this algorithm is to assign values to anaphoric expressions as an integral part of the mapping from syntactic structure onto the Discourse Representation Structure (DRS). A DRS is made up of a set of entities called discourse referents, marked as ".x", ".y" and predicates on those entities ($P(x),Q(y) \ldots$). It is built by a formal algorithm defined as operating on the syntactic structure of some initiating sentence, the building of DRS for each subsequent sentence being relative to the DRS so far constructed. Sequences of DRS's are licensed by this algorithm which dictates possible mappings from some syntactically analysed string onto the DRS; and the result is subject to model-theoretic evaluation. We have as a DRS built from *John saw Mary. She smiled*:

$$
\begin{array}{|ll|}
\hline
x. \quad y. \quad .e_1 \quad .e_{\text{NOW}} \quad z. \quad e_2 & \\[1em]
\text{John}(x) \qquad\qquad\qquad z = y & \\[0.7em]
\text{Mary}(y) \qquad\qquad\qquad \text{smile}(z) & \\[0.7em]
\text{see}(x,y) \qquad\qquad\qquad \text{precede}(e_2, e_{\text{NOW}}) & \\[0.7em]
\text{precede}(e_1, e_{\text{NOW}}) & \\
\hline
\end{array}
$$

These box structures are model-theoretic in conception. A DRS is a partial model, whose evaluation as true is defined as the embeddability of this partial model in some totally defined model. Nevertheless the structural properties of such DR structures may play a critical role in antecedent resolution (subject to configurational restrictions on the place of antecedent and pronominal in the DRS display, cf. Kamp 1981, Kamp and Reyle 1993). A DRS therefore constitutes an intermediate step in the interpretation process, a structural representation whose formal properties are nonetheless determined exclusively by its semantic properties as a partial model.

4   Natural-Language Interpretation as Structure-Building

These sketches, miniature and minimal though they are, display the essence of the different theoretical claims. We are now in a position to ask: What is the nature of natural-language interpretation? Is it strictly semantic, as the tradition of formal semantics and its continuation in situation theory has led us to presume? Is it interpreted by representations which are nevertheless direct representations of model-theoretic constructs, such as DRS's? Or is it proof-theoretic, a truth-theoretic evaluation being only indirectly defined via the proof-theoretic building of some defined meta-structure corresponding to the parsing process? As so far stated, the three analyses might seem compatible with a situation-theoretic account providing a semantic image of the proof-theoretic LDS formalism.[4] But the distinctiveness of the LDS formalism turns on the details of the proof process whereby the interpretation is incrementally built up. So the success of the one explanation over the others will turn on whether properties of the procedure for building the requisite linked labelled databases are essential to the explanation of natural-language interpretation. And it is from the phenomenon of context-dependence that we can glean deciding evidence.

Inevitably, but disappointingly, many of the phenomena in the literature are analysed in a way that avoids the issue. Faced with divergent structural properties of discrete interpretations for a single sentence, an analyst can always invoke ambiguity of the input string, posit the requisite structure at some abstract level of syntactic assignment with a relatively simple correspondence of form and interpretation for the constructed form, and so evade the problem of having to posit a structure-building process of interpretation (at the cost of failing to provide a unified explanation). So with pronominal anaphora, linguists almost universally invoke different kinds of anaphora (in particular bound-variable anaphora vs. referential uses of pronouns, the dispute as to the amount of variation having continued for over a decade (cf. Reinhart 1983a, Cooper 1979, Evans 1980 etc.)). In the area of ellipsis, different kinds are postulated (Chao 1988, Fiengo and May 1993, Lappin 1993a) according as different syntactic restrictions seem to be imposed. Solutions then reflect a stalemate between analyses positing under-determinacy with the structural nature of the interpretation process itself leading to truth-theoretic diversity (Kempson 1988, Gawron and Peters 1990); and others positing a direct semantic characterisation for some separated n-tuples of abstract structure (Reinhart 1983b, Chierchia 1992). However we can get a clear window onto the nature of natural-language interpretation through considering expressions whose interpretation is built up almost exclusively from the interpretation process itself – so-called "bare-argument ellipsis".

4.1   Bare-argument ellipsis and the island constraints

Bare-argument ellipsis is the phenomenon whereby using but a single constituent, a speaker can nevertheless succeed in conveying some full proposition to which the hearer ascribes truth-theoretic content:

> (15)   John insisted Sue visit Mary in hospital. Bill too.

There is a range of choices as to how to build such content, for the fragment in (15) can mean any one of (15a)–(15c):

> (15a)   Bill insisted Sue visit Mary in hospital.
> (15b)   John insisted Bill visit Mary in hospital.
> (15c)   John insisted Sue visit Bill in hospital.

At first sight, these data seem unsurprising enough. By mere observation, these are uncontentious cases of underdetermination of propositional content by the presented lexical content of the fragment itself, suggesting a semantic or pragmatic explanation in terms of some resolution of context-dependence. The process of the reconstruction of interpretation for a fragment involves the construction of a one-place predicate. We can define such a predicate by identifying a function based on some salient property (Dalrymple et al. 1991). Or, equally, we can do so by defining a process of pragmatic interpretation that creates a one-place predicate which can then be reapplied to the newly presented fragment. This latter option is straightforward within the proposed LDS model of utterance interpretation. → Introduction in the Gabbay and Kempson framework takes the form:

$$
\begin{array}{|ll|}
\hline
\text{Assume} & \alpha{:}P \\
 & \quad . \\
 & \quad . \\
 & \beta(\alpha){:}Q \\
\hline
\end{array}
$$

$$\lambda x\ \beta(x){:}P \rightarrow Q$$

→ Introduction is a rule defined to be founded on Modus Ponens. To prove $\gamma{:}P \rightarrow Q$, one opens a new box, constructs an assumption P with label α. And if steps licensed by the logic enable the conclusion Q to be derived using $\alpha{:}P$, then → Introduction licenses a box-exit step giving up the assumption $\alpha{:}P$ and recording in the label that any such assumption is withdrawn, duly building a λ-abstract in the labels as a record of which assumption has been retracted, and from where. This rule of inference thus leads to the creation of a one-place predicate, presented as the premise "$\lambda x.\beta(x):P \rightarrow Q$". Using this rule, ellipsis construal can be modelled as a process of substitution, retraction of one premise and replacement by another:

(15')

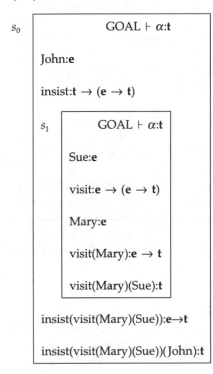

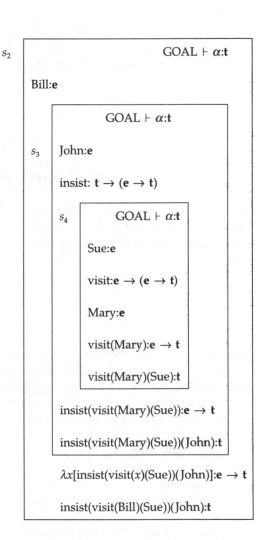

(15') represents the interpretation of the fragment as "John insisted Sue visit Bill in hospital", with Bill:e replacing Mary:e, but choice of either John:e or Sue:e is equally possible. Notice, too, how this reflects the informal pragmatic intuition that the hearer is using the interpretation just built up to reconstruct the fragment (ignoring tense), and does so without invoking any multiplicity of structure in that antecedent clause (contra Pesetsky 1982, Reinhart 1991), thereby preserving the intuition that the phenomenon is one of context-dependence, using information already made available on-line in the discourse.

There is clear initial motivation for such a pragmatic explanation, for the phenomenon displays evidence of restrictions arising from the linear process of interpretation from some immediate discourse context. The phenomenon can occur across speakers:

(16)   John: Mary insists Bill visit Sue in hospital. Angela: Max too.

It requires reconstruction exclusively from its nearest sister:

(17)   We are required to visit Sue in hospital, and John is supposed to be there. Bill too (≠ Bill is required to visit Sue in hospital).

And it is linear left-right, requiring the fragment to follow its host:

(18)   *Bill too, and Mary insists Max visit Sue in hospital.

In particular, the proposed application of a substitution process involving re-use of the most recently constructed database provides the right richness of interpretation possibilities, while preserving the widely observed parallelism between the interpretation of the preceding clausal antecedent and the interpretation of the fragment. An analogous semantic account which reconstructs ellipsis construal as the recovery of some one-place predicate has to trade on some unanalysed concept of discourse salience and semantic parallelism, but appears otherwise equivalent (Dalrymple et al. 1991).

Nonetheless, despite the initial attractiveness of such simple semantic/pragmatic accounts, bare-argument ellipsis is extremely puzzling given standard assumptions. The puzzle is that their reconstruction appears to at least partially parallel standard syntactic restrictions. For example, despite the possibility of reconstructing the fragment to yield interpretations which cross clausal boundaries as in (15), paralleling (19)

(19)   Who does Bill insist that Jo visit *e*?

(21), paralleling the unacceptability of (20), does not allow reconstruction of the fragment across the relative clause boundary as (21′):

(20)   *Which piece has Bill met the student who is playing in *e* at the concert?
(21)   Bill has met the student who is playing in the Bach piece at the concert. But not in the Mozart piano trio.
(21′)   Bill has not met the student who is playing in the Mozart trio at the concert.

Similarly, the fragment in (22) cannot be construed as (22′):

(22) John is going out with a woman who is studying Palestrina. Racine too.

(22′) John is also going out with a woman who is studying Racine.

Of all forms of syntactic restriction, island restrictions have proved amongst the most resistant to pragmatic or semantic explanation despite several attempts (notably Erteschek-Shir and Lappin 1979). By normal methodological assumptions that like phenomena should be assigned an identical form of structure at some level of explanation, such data have been taken to provide strong evidence that the reconstruction of bare argument ellipsis must receive a syntactic solution, with some assigned syntactic configuration providing the basis for predicting that such interpretations are precluded (cf. Neeijt 1979 with the comparable phenomenon of gapping). It has indeed been argued that the reconstruction of fragments is not an ellipsis phenomenon at all (Reinhart, 1991). She argues to the contrary that ellipsis construal involves movement (QR) of the NP in the preceding sentence (movement of *Mary* in the interpretation (15b)), a process which because it involves operator-movement is predicted to display all its properties.[5] Such a syntactic solution invoking application of the process underlying *wh*-gap dependency will predict exact parallelism between the interpretation process and the presented structure of *wh*-initial sentences, but on current assumptions it will preclude even the possibility of a semantic or pragmatic solution, since syntactic principles provide the initial input structure to any process of interpretation. It would therefore mean losing all possibility of explaining the phenomenon in terms of some account of the context-dependent nature of fragment construal, returning to the nonexplanatory stipulation of ambiguity in the intrinsic content of the string as assigned grammar-internally (in this case, ambiguity in the structural analysis of the preceding sentence).

This might seem a clear confrontation between syntacticians and pragmaticists with an easy choice turning on which side has the more successful explanation, but the puzzle runs deeper than that. First there is an added complication which neither form of analysis appears able to address – the parallelism is not more than partial. A *wh*-expression cannot bind a position internal to a clausal subject (the sentential subject restriction), internal to a *wh*-complement headed by e.g. *why* (the *wh*-island restriction), or the subject position of a complement clause marked by *that* (*that*-trace effect):

(23) *Who is that John dotes on *e* obvious?

(24) *What does John wonder why Bill is taking *e*?

(25) *What does John know that *e* is upsetting Bill?

However reconstructions of a bare-argument fragment building interpretations that place the fragment into such a position are fully acceptable:

(26)   That John dotes on Mary is obvious.   Sue too.
                                                                           But not Sue.
(27)   John is wondering why Bill is taking anti-depressants. But not
            diazepam tablets.
(28)   John knows that Sue is upsetting Bill.   Mary too.
                                                                          But not Mary.

(27) for example allows an interpretation of the fragment as "John is not wondering why Bill is taking diazepam tablets". Second, and far more difficult to
square with current assumptions, the data of (21)–(22) are not replicated across
all relative constructions. (29)–(31) seem fully acceptable on an interpretation
which reconstructs across the relative-clause boundary:

(29)   We need a linguist who will work on DRT. Not HPSG.
(30)   I know someone who died of an overdose of cocaine. More surpris-
            ingly, pethadrine too.
(31)   I've read the review that appeared in the Guardian. But not the
            Times.

This array of data is problematic for everyone. It is problematic for syntactic
accounts of ellipsis because of the total lack of explanation of why some
subjacency constraints should be bypassed and others not. The data in (29)–
(31) have to be set aside altogether and a division set up between visible
movement (*wh*-structures), and invisible movement (e.g. for structures for interpretation) to predict the total absence of island effects in (26)–(28) (this is
not unproblematic as quantifier-scope effects are sensitive to these boundaries). The data are also problematic for a purely semantic form of explanation,
since semantic reconstructions of context provide no basis for explaining configurational restrictions. There is no basis for even predicting that an interpretation process such as ellipsis reconstruction would pattern in any way
like *wh*-gap dependency phenomena given the syntactic nature of the latter.
Data such as (29)–(31) have to be taken as definitive, indicating no parallelism
with construal of *wh*-structures, setting aside the data of (21)–(22) as an epi-
phenomenon to be explained some other way (Lappin, this volume). It might
seem that the proof-theoretic mode of interpretation has no greater chance of
success, for the type assignments which drive the combinatorial process merely
reflect the semantic properties of the elements in question. So whatever limits
there are on semantic explanations would surely hold equally of the proof-
theoretic account. However the significance of the proof-theoretic mode of
construal is that it projects structure as it builds interpretation, with the process of interpretation itself defining the structures over which restrictions have
to be satisfied. As we shall see, the dynamics of the logical system itself can
then provide a basis for narrowing down purely semantic explanations allowing for more subtle discriminations as to the way in which interpretation is

built up. The challenge is to see whether the logic framework can characterize in full why and where *wh*-gap construal and ellipsis constructions overlap.

4.2 Wh-*gap dependency: a proof-theoretic reconstruction*

To get to the point where we can meet this challenge, we have to expand the LDS$_{NL}$ account to take in NP-construal and relative clauses, and the LDS$_{NL}$-basis for explaining island effects. The structures so far considered consist only of single clauses built up by simple steps of Modus Ponens, each step of Modus Ponens corresponding to functional application as reflected in the labelling algebra. The result is binary branching trees built up in the labels. However, as has been well-known since early work in Montague grammar (cf. Montague 1974, Partee 1976a) not all constructs can be expressed as straightforward functional application – in particular cross-clausal relations such as relative clause constructions. For these and other adjunct types, there are two possible routes in LDS terms – increase the complexity of type assignments and preserve the correlation between the operations on the labels and type deduction (as in categorial grammar) or use the labelling algebra alone, independent of any application of Modus Ponens to define ways in which separately projected local tasks of reasoning (corresponding to clauses) can be combined to form a composite whole. The LDS$_{NL}$ analysis chose the latter route, taking as its analogy the temporal system of natural deduction for which the LDS framework was first defined.

In temporal systems, reasoning has to be defined both relative to a single point in time, and across points in time. Reasoning relative to each point in time is presented as discrete databases of premises, each point in time providing a label for the database of premises true at that point. Schematically, we might have:

$$s_1- - - - - s_2- - - - - s_3$$

| s_1:P | s_2:P | s_3:$P \to Q$ |
| s_1:$P \to Q$ | s_2: $\neg Q$ | s_3: $\neg Q$ |

Cross-time generalisations are then expressed, while preserving the simple nature of time-local reasoning, by defining special additional rules within the labelling algebra for licensing transfer from one point in time to another (cf. Finger & Gabbay 1993). Similarly, in the projection of natural language structure we can define the projection of individual clauses through independent local goal-directed reasoning tasks onto α:t and then define separately (through the labelling algebra) the particular way in which such local databases may be put together, with rules dictating how information can be moved from one such local database to another. Relative clauses are just one such case, as in (32):

(32)   John saw Mary, who Sue liked.

Relative clause structures are a means of putting together two independent pieces of information – that presented by the main clause and that presented by the relative – by projecting agreement between the *wh*-element and the head of the relative. Informally speaking, (32) projects two items of information "John saw Mary" and "Sue liked Mary", and information about Mary is carried down to the relative clause through stipulated agreement that who = Mary. In the LDS framework outlined here (Gabbay and Kempson 1992), this is reconstructed directly through a process linking databases by unifying separate labels internally to the two databases. Two databases are said to be linked iff some variable of the labelling algebra in each is replaced by some common unifier:[6]

(32′) s_1 | John:**e** saw:**e** → (**e** → **t**)   Mary:**e** |

LINK (s_1(Mary:**e**), s_2(**y**:**e**), **y**/Mary)

s_2 | Sue:**e** liked:**e** → (**e** → **t**) **y**:**e** |

The result of building database-internal structure and relations between databases by two independent types of process is that we now have a composite logic system with two discrete subsystems, the structures defined by the local database-internal system, here a → Logic, and a global system defining relations between databases, defined exclusively through the labelling algebra. The LINK operation defined as a unification process on two labels and the consequent step of inference resulting from the linkage are both defined as parts of the global system specifying how the inferential domains defined by the → Logic are to be put together. Seen in this light, the information projected by the *wh*-expression is an encoded instruction to initiate the building of such a composite structure, driving the construction of linking two databases and fixing the internal structure in the second. We want the words in (32) to project (32′). The task at the point of introducing the *wh*-item involves a particular goal specification projected by the *wh*-item – not merely to build some arbitrary clause α:**t**, but the more detailed specification that the new database project a particular output label which contains a variable linked to the label Mary. It provides, that is, a look-ahead device as to the kind of structure required.

The force of this type of analysis for *wh*-initial expressions is that the process of projecting an interpretation to a *wh*-initial string can be seen to follow from general properties of goal-directed reasoning. The prototypical properties of goal-directed reasoning are: (i) the goal imposed is a filter on the outcome which is licensed from that database – neither the goal itself nor any element contained in it are part of the proof until those elements are assumed or derived as steps of the proof, (ii) the goal determines the form of subordinate routines which have to be entered into in arriving at that goal, (iii) the overall goal can, indeed must, be satisfied through such subordinate routines set up within its own database and not via some independent task of reasoning.

The pattern is displayed formally using a labelling system which manipulates a "metabox discipline" in which the nature of the goals to be reached is explicitly represented at each stage. Proofs with conditional conclusions exemplify the pattern.

III

$$P \rightarrow (Q \rightarrow R) \vdash Q \rightarrow (P \rightarrow R)$$

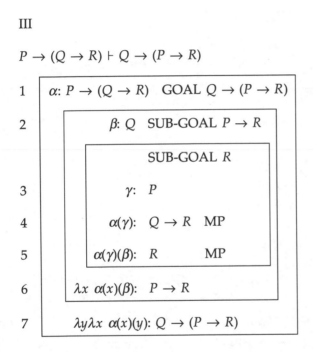

1	α: $P \rightarrow (Q \rightarrow R)$ GOAL $Q \rightarrow (P \rightarrow R)$
2	β: Q SUB-GOAL $P \rightarrow R$
	SUB-GOAL R
3	γ: P
4	$\alpha(\gamma)$: $Q \rightarrow R$ MP
5	$\alpha(\gamma)(\beta)$: R MP
6	$\lambda x\ \alpha(x)(\beta)$: $P \rightarrow R$
7	$\lambda y \lambda x\ \alpha(x)(y)$: $Q \rightarrow (P \rightarrow R)$

In III, Q, P, R are not elements of the proof in virtue of the presentation of the goal at step 1 – they only enter into the proof at steps 2, 3, and 5 respectively. The form of the overall goal, $Q \rightarrow (P \rightarrow R)$ also dictates all subroutines that are entered into, first the assumption of Q and the new subgoal $P \rightarrow R$, and secondly the assumption of P and the second subgoal of deriving R. In a discipline requiring explicit representation of all such subroutines, the information can be seen to be percolating down through the proof tree as the subgoals needed are progressively unpacked from the initial overall goal.

It is just this pattern which is displayed by *wh*-initial structures. The information projected by the *wh* is not itself part of the interpretation – it provides a licence for constructing some assumption later on. It is, rather, the position of the gap from which the interpretation of the *wh* is projected, and not its sentence-initial position. Furthermore the information projected by the *wh* needs to be carried down through the tree by successive sub-goal specifications to the position at which this "gap" assumption can be constructed. *Wh* is accordingly analysed in Gabbay and Kempson (1992) as a device which initiates the building of a new database with a goal specification that the resulting label α contain a metavariable created by assumption and linked to the label constituting the point of departure for the building of this new database.[7] The long-distance dependency as in (33) of a *wh* in initial position and the point of its construal at some arbitrary later point in the string will be derived as an immediate consequence:

(33)   John touched Mary, who smiled.

(33')   step

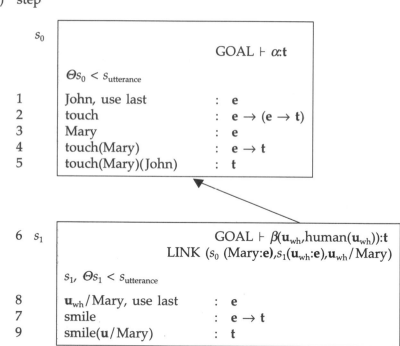

This analysis assumes a three-part procedure: (i) the presentation of the goal specification, *wh*; (ii) the LINK operation unifying the assumed variable with the chosen α; (iii) the construction of the required assumption (the gap). The point at which this goal specification is satisfied is not specified when this information is projected from the lexicon (step 6). It is determined by lexically imposed requirements on the structure of the database, in (33) that the predicate *smile* requires a premise immediately before it in the database (step 7).

With no such premise lexically projected, the requisite assumption of the premise $\mathbf{u}_{wh}$:e imposed by the target specification is created at step 8. The result, with $\mathbf{u}_{wh}$ linked to "Mary", is a linked labelled database.

(34) displays how the target specification projected from the *wh*-expression is carried down the tree by the requirements of the metabox discipline. Each successive subroutine that is entered carries down this goal specification that some assumption of the form $\mathbf{u}_{wh}$:e be constructed through the proof-tree database by database until such point as the lexical specifications of provided words license its construction. Satisfaction of some such subgoal will by successive steps of → Elimination then guarantee success in fulfilling all containing goals:

(34) John upset Mary, who Sue thought Bill had reassured

(34') s_0

	GOAL ⊢ α:t
	$\Theta s_0 < s_{\text{utterance}}$
1	John, use last : e
2	upset : e → (e → t)
3	Mary : e
4	upset(Mary) : e → t
5	upset(Mary)(John) : t

6   s_1

	GOAL ⊢ $\beta(\mathbf{u}_{wh},\text{human}(\mathbf{u}_{wh}))$:t
	LINK(s_0(Mary:e),s_1($\mathbf{u}_{wh}$:e),$\mathbf{u}_{wh}$/Mary)
	$\Theta s_1 < s_{\text{utterance}}$
7	Sue,use last : e
8	think : t → (e → t)
	s_2 : t

9   s_2

	GOAL:$\beta'(\mathbf{u}_{wh})$:t
	LINK (s_0(Mary:e),s_2($\mathbf{u}_{wh}$:e),$\mathbf{u}_{wh}$/Mary)
10	Bill, use last : e
11	reassure : e → (e → t)
12	$\mathbf{u}_{wh}$/Mary : e
13	reassure($\mathbf{u}_{wh}$/Mary) : e → t
14	reassure($\mathbf{u}_{wh}$/Mary)(Bill) : t

15	think(s_2:reassure($\mathbf{u}_{wh}$/Mary)(Bill) : e → t
16	think(s_2:reassure($\mathbf{u}_{wh}$/Mary)(Bill)(Sue) : t

4.2.1   *Restrictive relatives and a proof-theoretic account of determiners*

This analysis has been introduced with respect to nonrestrictive construals of the relative clause. To extend it to restrictive construals, we need to consider what account to give to determiners in general. As in the analysis of *wh* itself we shall see that the proof-theoretic format is essential to the analysis and not a mere reflection of semantic properties and so eliminable.

The extension turns on a proof-theoretic account of noun phrases as all projecting names of one kind or another. The initial evidence for this move comes from definite and indefinite determiners. Recall that definite NPs, like pronouns, display a range of anaphoric effects (examples from section 1). This suggests that the definite article, like a pronoun, should be analysed as projecting a metavariable requiring instantiation, with a lexical specification that it project

$$\mathbf{u}_{the} : \mathbf{e}$$

the choice of value for $\mathbf{u}_{the}$ being sensitive to its own locality requirements (reflecting binding principle C considerations). More surprisingly, indefinite NPs also can, indeed should, be analysed in like manner. Intuitively, in characterising the interpretation of a sentence containing mixed quantification with an existential quantifier construed as internal to a universal as in

(35)   Every professor refereed a book

under the interpretation

(35)   a. $(\forall x, \text{professor}(x))\ (\exists y, \text{book}(y))\ \text{referee}(y)(x)$

we must capture the implication that the set of books about which an assertion is made is dependent on the set of professors – the assertion is that for each professor taken in turn there is at least one book that he/she refereed. This is characterised in predicate calculus notation only implicitly, through the linear order in which the formula is written. Moreover this notation is misleading since only some orderings of quantifiers give rise to such dependency. In the reversed order of quantifiers "$(\exists y\ \text{book}(y))\ (\forall x\ \text{professor}(x))\ \text{read}(y)(x)$", the set of professors is invariant no matter what set is denoted by "$\exists y\ \text{book}(y)$" because by assertion it is the total set of professors that is picked out. We can explicitly represent the dependency intrinsic to the interpretation (35a) by introducing terms for functions into the logical language, defining a skolem function which maps the set of entities universally quantified over onto some new set, and thereby capturing the force of narrow-scope existential quantification. Taking first a simple formula with unrestricted variables

$\forall x\ \exists y\ G(y)(x)$
(equivalently written as "$\forall x\ \exists y\ G(x,y)$")

we can represent the content expressed by this formula as

$\forall x\ G(f(x))(x)$
(equivalently "$\forall x\ G(x,\ f(x))$")

What was expressed as y in the earlier formulation with its own quantifier $\exists y$ is in this alternative formulation expressed as $f(x)$ – "the result of applying the function f to x". Our representation of the interpretation (35a) can be recast in this format:

$(\forall x,\ \text{professor}(x))\ \text{referee}(f(x),\ \text{book}(f(x)))(x)$

– "for some function f mapping every professor x onto a book, x read $f(x)$" ("book$(f(x))$" expresses the range of f). The composite form of the term "$f(x)$, book$(f(x))$" explicitly records the dependency between the set of books picked out and the set of professors.

This analysis may seem to have little advantage to a linguist since the same analysis appears not to be available for the wide-scope interpretation of indefinites, as in the other interpretation of (35), viz.

(35)   b. $(\exists y,\ \text{book}(y))\ (\forall x,\ \text{professor}(x))\ \text{referee}(y)(x)$

However in the LDS framework in which everything bears a label, the database of premises which makes up the proposition also bears a label, and following the model of Finger and Gabbay (1993), this label carries information about the unit(s) of time at which the proposition holds. For each Δ, Δ a database of labelled premises leading to α:t, we shall have s_i: Δ mapped onto s_i, α:t, to be read as "α is construed as holding at some world-time unit s_i". This will have the immediate consequence that there is an additional element in the projection of a database configuration which can be used for defining dependencies on which to base the construal of indefinites. And having made the concept of scope dependency explicit, no longer needing to use linear order to express scope, we have opened up the possibility of expressing dependencies on any construct as part of the dependent term itself. We can thus project an additional interpretation for (35) as:

(35)   b'. s_i: $(\forall x,\ \text{professor}(x))\ \text{referee}(f(s_i),\ \text{book}(f(s_i)))(x)$

– "for some function f mapping a unit of time s_i onto a book $f(s_i)$, every professor x read $f(s_i)$". But this is equivalent to (35b) in which an existential quantifier is independent of the following universal quantifier and contains it within its scope. So by adopting an extension of the concept of skolem function, we can represent the very same interpretation using a dependent term "$f(s_i)$" without any movement of that term onto some level of representation in which it precedes "$\forall x$, professor(x)" but follows s_i. Given the presence of database labels, an indefinite can indeed always be represented as projecting a name which is dependent on some other expression in the database configuration (either on one paired with type **e** or on a database label). So interpretations that are more standardly analysed as involving wide-scope existential quantification will here be modelled as dependency on some world-time unit represented as a database label. If we take one step further and incorporate an element of under-determinacy into the analysis of indefinite expressions in natural language, we can represent indefinites as invariably projecting a dependent name of $f(\alpha)$ for some α, with a choice of α having to be made by the hearer as part of the process of utterance interpretation, exactly analogous to anaphoric resolution. The indefinite determiner will thus project a place-holding meta-variable whose value must be a dependent name, constructed new for the database into which it projects a name, but construed as dependent on some other previously specified entity.[8]

It is then a simple step to generalise this analysis, and assume that all quantifying expressions project a metavariable, with the choice in a case such as *every* being the trivial choice of some arbitrary free variable out of some set of variables. The projection of NP meanings is thus uniform: all determiners project a metavariable of some distinguished form with varying restrictions as to what type of label must be used to instantiate that metavariable (a free variable in the case of *every*, a dependent name in the case of the indefinite, either of these or names in the case of *the* and pronouns). This analysis may seem to fly in the face of all standard accounts of determiners as corresponding to predicate logic quantifiers, but there is no conflict at all in a model which builds interpretation as a proof process with words projecting premises in a natural deduction task. For invariably the first step in using a quantified formula in a predicate-logic proof has to be a step eliminating the quantifier, replacing it with a name. The proof then proceeds over such constructed names. In analysing determiners as mapping onto names of one kind or another, we are simply following the proof methodology adopted, bypassing the step of constructing the now unnecessary intermediate step of extracting the quantified expression out of its position in the clausal sequence to create a predicate logic structure as the input to interpretation. No step of quantifier raising is needed, and no account of indefinites as highly exceptional determiners need be invoked (contra Reinhart 1992). All that is required is that interpretation is not defined as semantic evaluation of a predicate logic-like formula. It is defined as the process of building a structure via steps of natural deduction. In setting the background for an analysis of ellipsis, we thus already see emerging a representation of natural-language content in a proof-theoretic format which provides just the right degree of added richness to solve what are currently seen as puzzles.[9]

This analysis of determiners makes available an account of the distinction between restrictive and nonrestrictive construals of relative clauses which directly reflects the step-by-step process whereby these interpretations are set up, and as a result we can begin to see the relation between database-internal relations and cross-database relations. In nonrestrictive relatives, the choice of value for the variable assigned to the determiner (or name) is chosen before the construction of the linked labelled database. In restrictive relatives, the linked labelled database is for the purpose of building a complex predicate necessary to the identification of the variable to be assigned to the determiner, and the value for this variable is chosen only after this database with its linked metavariable has been constructed. Schematically we have the two interpretations (37') and (37") of (37):

(37)   The idiot who took cocaine is ill

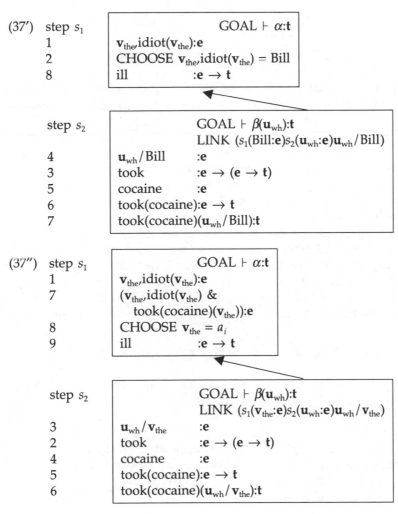

$(37')$ step s_1

1	$\mathbf{v}_{the}$, idiot$(\mathbf{v}_{the})$:e
2	CHOOSE $\mathbf{v}_{the}$, idiot$(\mathbf{v}_{the})$ = Bill
8	ill :e → t

GOAL ⊢ α:t

step s_2

GOAL ⊢ β$(\mathbf{u}_{wh})$:t
LINK $(s_1$(Bill:e)$s_2(\mathbf{u}_{wh}$:e)$\mathbf{u}_{wh}$/Bill)

4	$\mathbf{u}_{wh}$/Bill :e
3	took :e → (e → t)
5	cocaine :e
6	took(cocaine):e → t
7	took(cocaine)$(\mathbf{u}_{wh}$/Bill):t

$(37'')$ step s_1

GOAL ⊢ α:t

1	$\mathbf{v}_{the}$, idiot$(\mathbf{v}_{the})$:e
7	$(\mathbf{v}_{the}$, idiot$(\mathbf{v}_{the})$ &
	took(cocaine)$(\mathbf{v}_{the})$):e
8	CHOOSE $\mathbf{v}_{the}$ = a_i
9	ill :e → t

step s_2

GOAL ⊢ β$(\mathbf{u}_{wh})$:t
LINK $(s_1(\mathbf{v}_{the}$:e)$s_2(\mathbf{u}_{wh}$:e)$\mathbf{u}_{wh}$/$\mathbf{v}_{the}$)

3	$\mathbf{u}_{wh}$/$\mathbf{v}_{the}$:e
2	took :e → (e → t)
4	cocaine :e
5	took(cocaine):e → t
6	took(cocaine)$(\mathbf{u}_{wh}$/$\mathbf{v}_{the}$):t

(37′) and (37″) display not only the difference in choice point in the two interpretation processes, but also exemplify a step of inference defined over databases as units. In (37″) one extra step of inference is needed over and above the system of type-deduction and the choosing of values for variables – the linked database has to be used at step 7 as the basis for defining a complex predicate on the metavariable which is the general unifier and so to create:

$$(\mathbf{v}_{the}, idiot(\mathbf{v}_{the}) \ \& \ took(cocaine)(\mathbf{v}_{the})) : \mathbf{e}$$

With this predicate the hearer can establish what name to assign $\mathbf{v}_{the}$ (either as someone so identified, e.g. Bill, or as a constructed logical name, here a_i, whose semantic property is that it uniquely picks out the individual so described. We need a step of inference of the form:

$$\frac{(\mathbf{v}, \ \psi(\mathbf{v})):\mathbf{e} \qquad \Delta'(\mathbf{u}_{wh}:\mathbf{e})}{(\mathbf{v}, \ \psi(\mathbf{v}) \ \& \ \varphi(\mathbf{v})) : \mathbf{e}} \qquad \begin{array}{l} \text{LINK} \ (\Delta((\mathbf{v}, \psi(\mathbf{v})):\mathbf{e}),\Delta'(\mathbf{u}_{wh}:\mathbf{e}),\mathbf{u}_{wh}/\mathbf{v}) \\[2mm] \text{where } \Delta' \vdash \varphi(\mathbf{u}_{wh}/\mathbf{v}): \mathbf{t} \end{array}$$

The rule has the effect of flattening the database structure into a predicate algebra format for which standard procedures of semantic evaluation are available. It is this rule which has been applied at step 7 in (37″), thereby absorbing into the restriction on the metavariable $\mathbf{v}_{the}$ the label derived from the linked database s_2 but not its internal configuration. The rule, though a specifically defined rule of inference and hence a stipulation, is part of a general pattern. The purpose of building such database structures is, exclusively, to recover the proposition expressed by the string (or sub-string). They serve no other purpose. In particular they have no status in the resulting truth-theoretic content. The process of interpretation is thus a progressive two-stage building of linked labelled database-structure. First, by type-deduction, the individual databases are derived, and second, by rules of database-inference, the content which they make available can be derived. The framework is thus a mixed system of deduction – type-deduction over individual declarative units, and deduction defined over databases as these units become established.

4.2.2   Wh *and the precluded dependency into relative clauses*

A surprising confirmation of this composite natural-deduction perspective comes from the explanation it provides for regular syntactic constraints, where it provides the basis for discriminating between different types of relative-clause structure. With a proof-theoretic analysis of NPs, and initial *wh* treated as a special case of projecting a goal specification for database-building, two consequences emerge. First, relative clauses are predicted to preclude any *wh*-gap dependency across the clausal boundary. Second, we predict that some relative clauses might constitute exceptions. These two predictions together will then extend to bare-argument ellipsis and its partial parallelism with *wh*-construal. Consider (38):

(38) *John has reviewed that book which Bill dislikes everyone who read

(38')

s_0

	GOAL ⊢ α:t
John, use last :	e
reviewed :	e → (e → t)
$\mathbf{u}_{that}$, book($\mathbf{u}_{that}$):	e

s_1

	GOAL ⊢ $\beta(\mathbf{v}_{wh})$:t
	LINK $(s_o(\mathbf{u}_{that}, book(\mathbf{u}_{that}):\mathbf{e}), s_1(\mathbf{v}_{wh}:\mathbf{e}), \mathbf{v}_{wh}/(\mathbf{u}_{that}, book(\mathbf{u}_{that})))$
Bill	: e
dislikes	: e → (e → t)
x,human(x)	: e

s_2

	GOAL ⊢ $\beta'(\mathbf{u}_{wh})$:t
	LINK $(s_1(x, human(x):\mathbf{e}), s_2(\mathbf{u}_{wh}:\mathbf{e}), \mathbf{u}_{wh}/x)$
$\mathbf{u}_{wh}/x$	: e
read	: e → (e → t)
$\mathbf{v}_{wh}$	: e

(38) is ill-formed because the interpretation cannot get beyond the construal of "...Bill dislikes everyone". In s_1 the relative *wh* induces the building of a linked database, subject to the further restriction on the goal to be achieved in that database, that the outcome be a formula $\beta(\mathbf{v}_{wh})$: **t**, the metavariable $\mathbf{v}_{wh}$ to be linked on line to the point from which the *wh* initiated the building of this new database. The problem in s_1 is that this required outcome is not fulfillable, for the two place-predicate *dislike* allows for two minor premises both of which are independently provided. Moreover, because the database s_2 is not nested within s_1 as a label to one of the formulae of s_1, the construction of some requisite labelled assumption in s_2 will not be able to count as satisfying the goal specification imposed on s_1. A local reasoning task has to be fulfilled locally to the database in which the goal was imposed, and in (38') the goal is imposed on a particular reasoning domain defined by the → Logic, to wit s_1. Satisfying the task itemised in s_1 in some independent database s_2 will not do, as the task is imposed as a goal on successfully deducing a conclusion in s_1, and s_2 is not a subpart of s_1. The restriction turns out to be a restriction of the dynamics of the composite proof system and hence inviolable.

This analysis might appear to face immediate counterexamples, since some languages license at least some dependencies from a *wh*-expression into a relative clause, suggesting that whatever the basis of the restriction, it cannot be one which stems from a restriction of the logic. Even in English we have the peripheral (39)–(41) exactly mimicking comparable data in Swedish:

(39)   The Mercedes is the car which I know someone who will rent
(40)   The drug which I know someone who died from an overdose of is pethadrine.
(41)   A theory we need someone who will work on is DRT.

It is here however that the proof-theoretic analysis of indefinites as dependent names (carrying a record of their source of dependency) comes into its own. For it turns out that in all languages in which these constructions are licensed, such "extractions" from relative clauses demand a head which has either a definite or indefinite article and a construal of that head as functionally dependent on the gap itself (cf. Maling and Zaenen 1982). All we have to say of these languages is that presence of a name recorded as dependent on some constructed *wh*-licensed assumption counts as fulfilling the target set by the initial *wh*-element. (39′) displays the solution graphically.

(39′)

Step	s_1	GOAL α:t
1		Mercedes: **e**
2		is:**e** $\rightarrow$ (**e** $\rightarrow$ **t**)
3		$(\mathbf{v}_{the}\mathrm{car}(\mathbf{v}_{the}))$: **e**

	s_2	
4		GOAL $\beta(\mathbf{x}_{wh}/(\mathbf{v}_{the},\mathrm{car}(\mathbf{v}_{the}))){:}\mathbf{t}$
		LINK $(s_1((\mathbf{v}_{the},\mathrm{car}(\mathbf{v}_{the})){:}\mathbf{e}),\ s_2(\mathbf{x}_{wh}{:}\mathbf{e}),\ \mathbf{x}_{wh}/(\mathbf{v}_{the},\mathrm{car}(\mathbf{v}_{the})))$
5		I: **e**
6		know: **e** $\rightarrow$ (**e** $\rightarrow$ **t**)
7		$(\mathbf{u}_{dependent},\mathrm{person}(\mathbf{u}_{dependent})){:}\mathbf{e}$
13		$(\mathbf{u}_{dependent},\mathrm{person}(\mathbf{u}_{dependent})\ \&\ \mathrm{rent}(\mathbf{x}_{wh}/\mathbf{v}_{the}\mathrm{car}(\mathbf{v}_{the}))(\mathbf{u}_{dependent}\mathrm{person}(\mathbf{u}_{dependent}))){:}\mathbf{e}$
14		CHOOSE $(\mathbf{u}_{dependent},\mathrm{person}(\mathbf{u}_{dependent})) = f_{RENT}(\mathbf{x}_{wh}/\mathbf{v}_{the}\mathrm{car}(\mathbf{v}_{the})))$

	s_3	
8		GOAL $\beta'(\mathbf{y}_{wh}/(\mathbf{u}_{dependent},\mathrm{person}(\mathbf{u}_{dependent}))){:}\mathbf{t}$
		LINK $(s_2((\mathbf{u}_{dep},\mathrm{person}(\mathbf{u}_{dep})){:}\mathbf{e}),s_3(\mathbf{y}_{wh}{:}\mathbf{e}),\ \mathbf{y}_{wh}/(\mathbf{u}_{dep},\mathrm{person}(\mathbf{u}_{dep})))$
9		$(\mathbf{y}_{wh}/\mathbf{u}_{dependent},\mathrm{person}(\mathbf{u}_{dependent})){:}\mathbf{e}$
10		rent:**e** $\rightarrow$ (**e** $\rightarrow$ **t**)
11		$(\mathbf{y}_{wh}/\mathbf{v}_{the}\mathrm{car}(\mathbf{v}_{the})){:}\mathbf{e}$
12		$\mathrm{rent}(\mathbf{x}_{wh}/\mathbf{v}_{the}\mathrm{car}(\mathbf{v}_{the}))(\mathbf{y}_{wh}/\mathbf{u}_{dependent},\mathrm{person}(\mathbf{u}_{dependent})){:}\mathbf{t}$

s_1 is the database projected from *The Mercedes is the car*; s_2 is the database projected from *I know someone*, s_3 projected from *who will rent*. At step 7 the presence of the indefinite *someone* projects the presence of a dependent name, whose value and source of dependency has to be established. The significance of steps 8–12 is that the relative clause sequence is used to construct a predicate from which the dependent name can be identified – the predicate of "renting the car". At step 14 with this predicate, the dependent variable ($\mathbf{u}_{dependent}$ person ($\mathbf{u}_{dependent}$)) is identified as the name "the one who will rent the car" – "$f_{RENT}(\mathbf{x}_{wh}/(\mathbf{v}_{the},car(\mathbf{v}_{the})))$" – literally, a function of renting which when applied to a car yields the one who rents it. The critical property of this name is that it contains as a subpart the representation "$\mathbf{x}_{wh}/(\mathbf{v}_{the},car(\mathbf{v}_{the}))$" specified in the goal for s_2. So the hearer has effectively used the instruction to build a predicate on some dependent name as a means of identifying what that name should be, and by this means has established an occurrence of the constructed *wh*-assumption, "$\mathbf{x}_{wh}/(\mathbf{v}_{the}, car(\mathbf{v}_{the}))$", in the right place, viz. within the domain s_2 where its presence is necessary for a successful conclusion. Given the presence of the words *I*, and *someone*, which fill all available premises licensed as the requisite number for combining with "know:$\mathbf{e} \rightarrow (\mathbf{e} \rightarrow \mathbf{t})$", this strategy is indeed the only way of meeting the goal specification imposed on s_2 at step 4.

Notice the pattern here. The requirement of an assumption as licensed by the initial *wh* must in general be met by the construction of that assumption, as indeed the goal-directed natural-deduction system leads us to expect. However there is another process which plays a role in these locally defined domains – the process of anaphoric resolution here modelled as the choosing of labels. What is happening in these cases is that a target imposed on a given proof domain is being satisfied by this other process, the process of label choice. We can now see how languages might differ over the availability of this option. In order for the target specification imposed by the presence of the first relative pronoun in such sentences as (39)–(41) to be satisfied by such database structures as these, the language in question must allow this form of indirect satisfaction of that target specification – through a process analogous to anaphora resolution. It is this which is the source of the parametric variation, not variation according as the language does or does not constitute a counterexample of the general logic discipline. We would expect moreover that the predicted intermediate data would be displayed by NPs with a definite determiner as well as indefinites because definites, by analysis, are underdetermined and can take as value any name, hence equally a dependent or regular name. Pronouns on the other hand, despite similarity to definite NPs, do not license any such dependent construals, because they do not allow the linked database construction which gives rise to the complex predicate that provides the basis for identifying the lexically projected metavariable as dependent on the "gap" assumption. So the jigsaw puzzle of predicting island constraint effects and why they might be sensitive, against all conventional assumptions, to idiosyncratic semantic properties of determiners, is solved by the proof-theoretic methodology of bringing semantic and syntactic information together in a single format.

4.3 Bare-argument fragments and the island effects

We now have in place the pieces necessary to explain the extent to which ellipsis and *wh*-construal should pattern together. Consider (42), and the impossibility of interpreting the fragment as (42′)

> (42)   The woman who likes Bill visited Joan. And Mary too.
> (42′)   The woman who likes Mary visited Joan′:

(42′)

s_1

	GOAL $\vdash s_i$, α:t

Mary : **e**

s_2

	GOAL $\vdash s_i$, α:t	
($\mathbf{u}_{the}$, woman($\mathbf{u}_{the}$)), use last	: **e**	
($\mathbf{u}_{the}$, woman($\mathbf{u}_{the}$) & like(Bill)($\mathbf{u}_{the}$)), use last : **e**		
visit	: **e → (e → t)**	
Joan	: **e**	: **t**
visit(Joan)	: **e → t**	
visit(Joan)($\mathbf{u}_{the}$, woman($\mathbf{u}_{the}$) & like(Bill($\mathbf{u}_{the}$)) : **t**		

s_3

	GOAL $\vdash \beta(\mathbf{v}_{wh})$:**t**
LINK ($s_2(\mathbf{u}_{the}$, woman($\mathbf{u}_{the}$):**e**), $s_3(\mathbf{v}_{wh})$, $\mathbf{v}_{wh}/(\mathbf{u}_{the}$, woman($\mathbf{u}_{the}$)))	
($\mathbf{v}_{wh}/\mathbf{u}_{the}$, woman($\mathbf{u}_{the}$)), use last : **e**	
like : **e → (e → t)**	
Bill : **e**	
like(Bill) : **e → t**	
like(Bill)($\mathbf{v}_{wh}/\mathbf{u}_{the}$, woman($\mathbf{u}_{the}$)) : **t**	

(42′) represents the reconstruction of the interpretation up to the point at which a choice has to be made as to which premise Mary:**e** is to be substituted in place of. The problem in (42′) is that Bill must not be selected as a point of substitution for Mary:**e**. Consider the problem of doing so, given the reconstruction of substitution as a process of → Introduction. → Introduction by definition licenses the removal of an assumption α:**e** from some database Δ_i if the creation of that assumption has led **by step(s) of Modus Ponens** in that database to some conclusion $\beta(\alpha)$:**t** (cf. Section 4.1). But the presence of Bill in s_2 is not the result of any step of reasoning derivable by the local logic. To the contrary, it critically involved a step of the global discipline relating databases, a step which is not characterised within the → Logic. Indeed Bill:e is not a premise of s_2 at all. It is a label contained in s_2 in virtue of an operation defined solely through the labelling algebra for two independent databases, with no alteration to the premise structure of the host database. But a local logic contained within some global logic framework is by definition blind to any steps of that global discipline. → Introduction will accordingly not be able to apply to the output of any process unless it is a process licensed within the local logic. An element in some database as the result of any LINK operation will not therefore be able to provide the basis for interpreting a fragment by this process of substitution.

As with *wh*-gap dependencies, we shall however predict that substitution is possible into relative clauses if the determiner head which provides the point of linkage between the two databases is construed as dependent on the item being replaced. And this is exactly the restriction on which relative clause constructions appear to allow reconstruction across the relative clause boundary. Exactly as in the process of relative-clause construal, a well-formed interpretation of an elliptical fragment across such a boundary is possible only if the name which the indefinite/definite is taken to project is identified as dependent on the element being replaced, for it is this identification which guarantees that the element to be substituted is in a proof domain which licenses substitution by the newly presented premise – hence the asymmetry between (21)–(22) and (29)–(31). As with *wh*-gap construals, all such reconstruction across relative clause boundaries requires this form of interpretation.[10]

This parallelism does not extend to the other "island" configurations of sentential subjects, *wh*-islands and *that*-trace configurations. In each of these cases, as with complement clauses, the database is contained within the overall database, and the logical restriction debarring the construction of the requisite assumption in an independent linked database will not apply. The preclusion of *wh*-gap dependency has to be seen as due to restrictions on the process of building the database configuration within which the licensed assumption is to be made. The sentential subject restriction for example debars (23) but not (43)

(23) *Who is that John dotes on obvious?
(43) Who is it obvious that John dotes on?

What distinguishes (43) from (23) is that in (43) the incremental filling of the successive databases proceeds step by step, with each database being filled with data immediately following the instruction to set up such a structure. What happens in (23), to the contrary, is that, having assigned a goal to the initial database in the presence of *who*, the hearer proceeds to add to its label information about how it is to be construed in a flow of time. But then, before a single item of data has been put in the database, the instruction given by *that* requires the building of a new and nested database. All we have to do is impose on the construction algorithm the intuitively correct restriction that at all stages the construction process must generate minimally well-formed databases (a database being by definition a construct with premises in it), and the sentential subject restriction will duly follow. Violation of such a restriction will notably not arise in ellipsis construal, as there is no incremental process of database-building in projecting an interpretation for the fragment – merely a step of substitution carried out on a well-formed and complete database. So the restriction always to build some minimal database will not preclude the possibility of substituting the fragment premise into such an initial position in a database. Hence the asymmetry between (23) and (26) (repeated here):

(26)   That John dotes on Mary is obvious. Sue too.

The *wh*-island and *that*-trace effects are due to similar but weaker and language-specific prohibitions on the process of database building. The result is that the analysis of the interpretation process as a proof-theoretic procedure – driven not merely by the logical type specifications of the component parts but also by the dynamics of the proof discipline by which these parts are put together – provides a basis not only for describing the parallelism between interpretation of a severely impoverished fragment and a *wh*-initial structure, but also for predicting in what respect this parallelism will be only partial. Moreover it derives this parallelism as a consequence of general principles of the system.[11] We thus reach the conclusion that the content of a natural-language expression as projected from the lexicon is a set of procedures for building proof structures from which some truth-theoretic content of the string in which the expression is contained can be derived.

5   The Dichotomies Blurred

This success in explaining the partial parallelism between ellipsis construal and structural properties of *wh*-gap dependencies has led us, finally, to an unambiguous and representationalist answer to the question of the nature of natural-language interpretation. The proof-theoretic aspect of the explanation blurs the syntax and semantics dichotomy in an essential way. In the light of this general stance, the process of → Introduction was then used as a syntactic means of defining a predicate out of what had already been established in the discourse context in order to reconstruct ellipsis interpretation as a pragmatic process mapping some under-determined input specification onto a full determination of propositional content according to the proof-theoretic assumptions about utterance interpretation already set up. But it was this assumption that a semantic predicate-creating process should be subject to the limitations of the → Logic within which that predicate was defined that was essential to predicting that the limitation on that process would parallel the so-called island constraints. It was moreover just this assumption of a structure-building process of interpretation (with its specific use of goal-directed type-driven natural deduction over defined local domains) which gave rise to the prediction that ellipsis phenomena and *wh*-gap dependency phenomena would display similar though not identical properties. It was the very same proof-theoretic assumption which provided the analysis of indefinites that captures the basis by which semantic properties of elements may affect what is otherwise the strong universally-displayed restriction that relative clauses preclude construal of *wh*-gap dependency across their boundary. The systematic success in explaining a complex interacting web of data from general principles provides strong confirming evidence not merely of the structural nature of natural-language interpretation but of the precise form of natural deduction stance adopted.

This parallelism between ellipsis and *wh*-gap construal cannot be reconstructed with the same ease adopting either situation-theoretic or DRS assumptions about the nature of natural-language content, for both of these reconstruct the phenomenon of context-dependence solely against monolithic and set-theoretic assumptions about the nature of natural-language content. In situation theory, the resolution of all under-determinacy involves a process of fixing parameters against situation-theoretic constructs defined in the (rich) semantic algebra specified within situation theory. But despite the richness of that vocabulary, there is no reason to expect parallelism between ellipsis construal and *wh*-gap dependency phenomena, for this latter is subject to syntactic stipulation prior to any definition of semantic construal. In DRT, underdeterminacy resolution involves manipulation of the DRS structure. But since this is at heart model-theoretic in nature, there is no basis here for predicting parallelism with *wh*-gap dependency phenomena. The same paradox arises. Phenomena classified as syntactic are characterised prior to any form of semantic explanation and thus preclude generalisations between syntactic phenomena and phenomena which form part of the interpretation process. It is only in the LDS$_{NL}$ model in which ALL interpretation involves the proof-theoretic reconstruction of structure that we can explain the similarity between *wh*-gap dependency and ellipsis construal, while retaining the explanation of ellipsis in terms of some under-determined input plus an enrichment process of interpretation. And the heart of the LDS$_{NL}$ model is its definition of natural language interpretation as a composite proof-theoretic process of building a structure (through the dynamics of the goal-directed reasoning task) whose output is then subject to classical methods of model-theoretic construal. According to this model, natural-language strings are truth-theoretically interpreted only indirectly through the building of an inference structure. The intrinsic content of the words themselves is defined solely as the input specification to this structure-building process.

Looking back we can now see a pattern to analyses of context-dependent phenomena. Some phenomena for which a putative analysis in terms of some under-determined input might be available may arguably be analysed away as instances of ambiguity. Some context-dependent phenomena may be equivalently analysed as semantic or proof-theoretic processes. But only a proof-theoretic construal of natural-language interpretation is rich enough to explain both anaphora and ellipsis in terms of an incompletely specified input and a context-dependent process of interpretation which nevertheless captures the degree of parallelism between the interpretive process of fragment construal and the syntactic properties of a *wh*-gap sequence.

The consequence of adopting this particular representationalist model of natural language understanding is not merely a confirmation of representational assumptions about natural language content, but a radical reshuffling of familiar boundary assumptions. It suggests that the first step in the assignment of an interpretation to natural language strings is the incremental inferential procedure, whereby as part of the parsing process a hearer creates a configuration which represents some propositional content. So semantics and pragmatics are in part brought together. Furthermore, the preliminary assignment of interpretation is itself a structure directly reflecting the configurational properties of the string. So semantics, pragmatics and syntax are all brought together. The assignment of structure to the string in the LDS framework is thus a characterisation of syntactic properties of the string as well as an integral part of the explanation of its semantic and pragmatic properties. The full consequences of this blurring of boundaries remain to be explored, but there is a resulting need to review the relation between the language faculty and other cognitive faculties such as reasoning. For the result of modelling utterance interpretation as a natural deduction task set within a labelled deductive system has involved the reduction of encoded properties of language to properties general to an independently motivated family of reasoning systems.[12]

NOTES

1 Dynamic theories of anaphora have been proposed in terms of a general theory of context change (cf. Groenendijk and Stokhof 1991), but these involve solutions specific to the problem of pronominal anaphoric dependence and are not readily generalisable. Even in Discourse Representation Theory, the solutions are individual to anaphora, and are not extended to a general theory of the gap between lexically projected content and the interpretation assigned in context.

2 We define a family of Modus Ponens relative to a range of labelling restrictions, one such being a form of modus ponens sensitive to some restriction on the label that it be applicable only if the outcome be **A:t**.

3 Names also project incomplete labels requiring identification, but for simplicity I assume incorrectly that linguistic names are logical proper names.

4 The general LDS framework bears a close formal resemblance to the formal constructions of situation theory (cf. Gabbay 1993). Construed as a set of formal algebras, the latter is readily convertible into the former.

5   Reinhart's argument is based on the fallacious assumption that all fragment construal is homogeneous. Cf. Kempson 1991, Lappin, this volume, for further arguments that *except* phrases are distinct from other bare argument fragments.

6   First-order unification is defined over quantifier-free formulae with variables assumed to be universally quantified. Unification is a process of substitution for two expressions with no variables in common. The most general unifier is a set of substitutions (of variables by constants or by other variables) such that when the substitution is applied to both expressions, the two become identical. This process is central to the semantics of Prolog, and to all theories which involve combining a pair of feature specifications to yield a specification of the two in combination as a single collection of features.

7   No detailed lexical specifications are given here (cf. Kempson 1995).

8   This analysis predicts the apparently exceptional behaviour of indefinites in allowing a wide range of scope-differentiated interpretations without any respect for subjacency restrictions, (i) for example allowing at least four interpretations according as the indefinite is interpreted with narrow scope with respect to the context in which it occurs, maximally wide scope, or a range of intermediate interpretations:

> (i)   Every professor believed that John had submitted two reports that a friend of mine had cheated.

The precedence restriction on the choice of the source of dependency has however to be lifted in English when the dependent name occurs as subject, in the face of conflict with the language-specific restriction that subjects occur in database-initial position.

9   With there being no generally applicable proof-theoretic account of generalised quantifiers, this analysis is at present restricted to singular quantification only. The extension of these results to the full range of generalised quantifiers thus remains a considerable research project. Cf. van Lainbalgen 1991 for proof-theoretic accounts of a sub-set of generalised quantifiers.

10   Data such as

> (i)   A: "Bill has interviewed the suspect who is accused of stealing diamonds"
>   B: "You mean, rubies"
> (ii) A: "I will give 20,000 ecus to someone who can obtain money from a European company"
>   B: "Which European company?"

might suggest that there is no configurational restriction at all, vindicating a semantic account which precludes the possibility of syntactically imposed restrictions. However these data involve negotiation between speaker and hearer about a single database to be projected from the initiating speaker's words (in the first case involving correction, in the second case, expansion). What the proof-theoretic analysis of fragments predicts is that any process of substitution which involves taking a database as a whole and using it as a basis for building an additional different database will not allow substitution into a position in a linked-in database. This prediction is not challenged by these data.

11   As this account would predict, ellipsis reconstruction in the Scandinavian languages is possible (and borderline in English) across a relative clause boundary in exactly the same type of case as licensing *wh*-gap dependencies. Thus acceptable in Swedish and Norwegian, as in English, is the structure corresponding to:

   (i)   Bulgarian I know someone who speaks. But not Albanian.

12   This conception of natural language content stems directly from Sperber & Wilson 1986, whose insights this LDS$_{NL}$ was initially set up to capture. I remain indebted to Deirdre Wilson for the direction in which my ideas have developed over the last ten years. The role of natural deduction in natural language interpretation, and the particular development of this LDS$_{NL}$ model is being carried out with Dov Gabbay, and the formal framework behind this account of ellipsis is due to him. Without him, the framework which made these results possible would never have happened. The detailed linguistic results owe much to conversations with Shalom Lappin, and the pleasure of co-teaching a course on ellipsis with him. These three thus deserve more than just a vote of thanks. Thanks are also due to the various people who have helped these ideas along with their comments: Wilfried Meyer-Viol, Dick Oehrle, Michael Moortgat, Glyn Morrill, Chris Tancredi, David Wescoat, Johan van Benthem, Megumi Kameyama, Andrew Simpson, Asli Göksel, Akiko Yoshimura, audiences at Amsterdam, Osaka, Tokyo, the FOLLI summer school at Essex University, Utrecht, Rome, Paris, and my students Jiang Yan, Julia Capritsa, Stavroula Tsiplakou, Sean Jensen, Lutz Marten, David Swinburne, Keiko Abe, Denise Perrett, and many others. As usual however, no-one but myself can take the blame.

22 Semantics in Linguistics and Philosophy: An Intensionalist Perspective

JERROLD J. KATZ

1 Backgrounds

Once there was no semantics in linguistics and no linguistics in semantics. That was the forties, fifties, and early sixties. Linguistics was dominated by the taxonomic theory of grammar. On that theory, the study of a natural language is the study of speech. Linguistic description is segmentation of the utterances in a corpus and classification of the segments into phonological and syntactic categories on the basis of their distributional characteristics. Semantics had no place in such a study because meaning is too abstract to be captured in such acoustically focused description. Bloomfield (1933, 1936), the architect of the taxonomic theory, thus relegated semantics to associationist psychology.

Philosophy at the time, being in the throes of the so-called "linguistic turn" was, in contrast, absorbed with language and in particular its semantics. But as it was dominated by Ordinary Language Philosophy and Logical Empiricism, philosophy did not look outside itself to see what linguistics might have to say about language. Ordinary language philosophers concerned themselves with describing the use of words in natural language with little concern for either theory or linguistics. (Shortly before his death, Austin became interested in Chomsky's *Syntactic Structures*, but with him gone nothing changed.) Logical empiricists, inspired by Frege's revolutionary work in logic and the philosophy of logic, concerned themselves with the development of artificial languages based on Frege's (1879) blueprint for a logically perfect conceptual notation. They inherited Frege's disdain for natural languages as mine fields of logical imperfections.

The events which brought semantics into linguistics and linguistics into

semantics was Zellig Harris's (1954, 1957, 1965) development of transformational theory and Noam Chomsky's (1957, 1965) development of generative
grammar. Chomsky's theory of generative grammar brought the downfall of
Bloomfieldian taxonomic theory. Chomsky conceived of grammars as formal
systems like those in logic, but with sentences as theorems. Instead of
Bloomfield's physicalistic interpretation of grammars as taxonomies of actual
speech, Chomsky introduced a psychological interpretation of grammars as
theories of the ideal speaker's knowledge of the language, what Chomsky
(1965, pp.3–9) called "linguistic competence".

Two aspects of Chomksy's theory combined to create a place for semantics
in the grammar of a natural language. One was the notion of generativeness
itself and the other was the notion of a grammar as a system with levels of
grammatical structure underlying the surface structure of sentences, which
resulted from Chomsky's recasting of Harris's transformational theory in generative terms. What had been too abstract to have a place in a "bottom up"
taxonomic description of acoustic phenomena now has a place in the generative rules which determine representations at an underlying level of grammatical structure. Semantic representations, which interpret syntactic structures
in terms of meaning, take their natural place alongside phonological representations, which interpret them in terms of pronunciation.

However, Chomsky's (1957) initial statement of generative theory in *Syntactic Structures* contained no account of semantics. There he takes a skeptical
attitude towards semantics, first, because he associated semantics with the
view that syntactic categories rest on meaning, and hence saw semantics as a
threat to his conception of the autonomy of syntax, and, second, because,
under the influence of Goodman's (1952) skepticism about meaning, he thought
that meaning is intrinsically too confused to be a fit subject for scientific, and
in particular formal, study within generative grammar.

Fodor and I (1963), had no such misgivings. We saw the semantic component of generative grammar as necessary to complete the picture of the ideal
speaker's knowledge as knowledge of the sound/meaning correlation in the
language. We thus undertook to fill the semantic gap in the theory of generative grammar. With the conception of phonological and syntactic components
as a model, we developed a conception of the semantic component on the
basis of a number of ideas imported from the intensionalist tradition in the
philosophy of language, among them such things as Frege's (1952) sense/
reference distinction, Kant's definition of analyticity, and the principle of
compositionality.

On the conception we developed, the semantic component is a system of
generative rules which assign sentences formal representations of their sense
structure. Such representations were called "semantic markers" in analogy to
phrase markers which are formal representations of syntactic structure. Semantic markers are designed to explain the sense properties and relations of
sentences, e.g. their meaningfulness or meaninglessness, their ambiguity, their
synonymy or antonymy, and their analyticity, in much the way that syntactic

rules are designed to explain syntactic properties and relations like well-formedness, subject and direct object relations, agreement relations, and the relation between actives and their passives. Further, extending the parallelism with syntax, we took the speaker's intuitions about sense properties and relations as providing the evidence for semantic rules.

Our interest in linguistics and in plugging the semantic gap in the theory of generative grammar was philosophical. We had become dissatisfied with both the ordinary language and logical empiricist approaches to problems in the philosophy of language. Fodor and I (1962) criticized the atheoretical outlook of the former and the unscientific outlook of the latter. We hoped that, in designing a semantic theory to fit into the generative theory of grammar, we would produce a scientific semantic theory of natural language which might be brought into philosophy where it could be used to address philosophical issues about language and meaning that neither ordinary language philosophy nor logical empiricism had adequately addressed.

Fodor and I were neither the only nor the first philosophers to approach linguistics with a philosophical axe to grind. Even before we looked into Chomskyan linguistics to see what it might offer philosophy, Quine had turned to Bloomfieldian linguistics with much the same aim. As an uncompromising empiricist, Quine was critical of notions of meaning and analyticity in logical empiricism because the semantics underlying them lead to a rationalist position on *a priori* knowledge. Quine, in the spirit of his later doctrine of science as first philosophy, set about to show that the thinking underlying the formal semantics of the logical empiricists was mistaken because it did not square with the science of language. To show this, he (1953d) developed a rational reconstruction of the methodology of Bloomfieldian linguistics and then, on that basis, he (1953b) argued that intensionalist semantics is scientifically bogus.

Quine's importing of the methodological ideas of taxonomic linguistics into philosophy in order to undercut the liberal wing of contemporary empiricism and Fodor's and my importing of traditional intensionalist ideas from philosophy into linguistics in an attempt to construct a semantic theory in generative grammar opened a communication channel between linguistics and philosophy. Over the years, much two-way traffic has flowed through it. In slightly over three decades, American linguistics went from a discipline with no semantics to one in which semantic issues occupy a significant place, and philosophy of language went from an area which ignored the scientific study of natural language to one which increasingly requires knowledge of formal linguistics to understand philosophical discussions of language and meaning.

2 The Quinean Legacy

On the whole, the ideas which entered linguistics from philosophy and those which entered philosophy from linguistics have shed light on semantic phenomena in those fields. But the ideas going back and forth between the fields have also led to fundamental problems. These problems have clouded central questions in both linguistic and philosophical semantics, particularly the question of what linguistic meaning is.

Perhaps the most influential ideas to enter linguistics in the late fifties and early sixties were Quine's criticisms of the theory of meaning. His message was that philosophers and linguistic semanticists who wish to put their subject on a genuinely scientific footing ought to abandon the study of meaning and take up the study of reference instead. That change, Quine argued, would amount to a change from mythology to science: explanations of linguistic phenomena with meanings are, in his view, the counterpart of early explanations of the natural phenomena which invoke Homeric gods. Quine's criticisms received a very sympathetic hearing, ultimately undermining the development of the theory of meaning in both linguistics and philosophy.

On the constructive side, Quine made two proposals about the nature of a properly scientific linguistic semantics. One was his (1960) theory of stimulus meaning which modeled linguistic semantics on Skinnerian psychology. That proposal was assured less than an entirely warm reception in linguistics by the publication one year earlier of Chomsky's (1959) devastating critique of Skinner's (1957) psychology of language.

The other was Quine's (1953c) proposal that linguistic semantics be modeled on Tarski's theory of truth in logic. The proposal was that Tarski's theory of truth for artificial languages serve as a paradigm for the construction of a semantics for natural languages. Comparing the theory of meaning with Tarski's theory of reference, Quine (1953c, pp.137–138) extolled the latter as the true paradigm for the study of natural language semantics, remarking on how badly the theory of meaning fares in comparison with the theory of reference (in the light of his criticisms of the former theory). Eventually, this proposal was adopted by a significant number of linguists working in formal semantics, particularly in the form it took in Davidson's (1967b) program.

Davidson's program is to develop a referential semantics for natural language having the form of a Tarskian theory of its truth predicate. As Davidson (1967b, p.309) put it: "What we require of a theory of meaning for a language L is that without appeal to any (further) semantical notions it place enough restrictions on the predicate 'is T' [in the schema (T) *s is T if and only if p*] to entail all sentences got from T when 's' is replaced by a structural description of sentence of L and 'p' by that sentence". Sharing Quine's aversion to the notions of possibility and necessity, Davidson restricted the referential domain of natural languages to the actual world. On this approach, semantic interpretations of expressions and sentences are statements of referential relations, functions from the actual world to the semantic values of expressions in it. The semantic value of "gorilla" are the gorillas in the actual world.

An alternative conception of referential semantics was developed in philosophy prior to and during the time Quine and Davidson were developing their conception. This was the conception of modal referential semantics due to Carnap (1965). Like Quine and Davidson, Carnap was concerned with the construction of a theory of truth and reference for natural languages, but, not sharing their scruples about possibility and necessity, he took the referential domain of natural languages to be possible worlds rather than just the actual world. The semantic value of "gorilla" in a possible world are the gorillas in that world, and the semantic values of the term are somehow supposed to consist in its semantic values in the range of possible worlds.

On this approach, too, semantic interpretations of expressions and sentences are statements of referential relations which also take the form of world-semantic value functions, only the range of worlds comprising the domain of the language is vastly larger. Carnap developed the idea of semantic interpretations of expressions and sentences as functions from possible worlds to the referential values of expressions and sentences in them, appropriating the traditional term "intension" for such extensional functions. (See also David Lewis's (1970) formulation of them as functions from parameters specifying a world, time, etc., to the extensions of expressions at those parameters.) As Hintikka (1973a) suggests, the core of the notion of a functional dependence of reference (with respect to a domain) on sense is contained in Frege's (1952) definition of the sense of an expression as the determiner of its referent, a rule which assigns each object in the domain of the language to either the extension of the expression or its anti-extension. Frege's notion of a sense becomes a Carnapian intension once we broaden the domain of the language to possible worlds and adopt something like Frege's notion that the referent of a sentence is its truth value. (In this connection, see Barwise and Perry (1983).)

Note that Carnapian intensions do not represent a departure from referential semantics as might appear from the use of the term "intension". On Carnap's use of the term "intension", it is simply a homonym of "intension" in the sense in which the term is traditionally used in the theory of meaning. Carnap's intensional apparatus does not involve the introduction of non-referential concepts or of senses to mediate the relation between language and the world. His intensions state such relations directly.

Quine's famous criticisms of Carnapian semantics as an account of meaning in natural language might also lead one to think that Carnapian intensions have a commitment to the theory of meaning that is Quine's target on other occasions. But when we look closely at Quine's criticisms, we see that the problem to which they point is that Carnap's intensions are merely a referential apparatus. As I (1990b, 1992) argued elsewhere, it is the exclusively extensional nature of Carnapian semantical rules that is responsible for their failing to explain the (intensional) property of analyticity – or the (intensional) relation of synonymy. It is precisely because meaning postulates are constraints on extensional structure – no different from logical postulates – that Quine is right in criticizing them for not explaining analyticity.

With traditional sense semantics under the cloud of Quine's criticisms and with the rich resources of formal logic to exploit, the Davidsonian and Carnapian conceptions of referential semantics have become the formal semantics of choice in both linguistics and philosophy. Both conceptions have influential adherents in linguistics (See Higginbotham (1985 and 1986) in connection with a Davidsonian conception of semantics within Chomsky's theory of generative grammar, and Partee (1975a) in connection with a conception of modal semantics within that theory). Moreover, both conceptions have been instrumental in increasing the sophistication of that discipline both logically and syntactically. But the considerable progress that has been made in formal semantics in linguistics and philosophy has occurred in spite of the fact that the work has often been done within a theoretical framework that involves a mistaken conception of the nature of meaning in natural language.

3   The Quinean Legacy Revisited

Quine's critique of the traditional theory of meaning in "Two Dogmas of Empiricism" provided the rationale for the widespread view that one or the other of the two referential conceptions is the right account of the semantics of natural language. But if, as I (1988, pp.227–252, 1990b, pp.199–202) have argued, Quine's critique does not show that no objective sense can be made of synonymy, analyticity, and other concepts of the traditional theory of meaning, then that view may well be false.

As we have already seen, Quine's criticisms of Carnap's logical explanation of analyticity and other concepts of the traditional theory of meaning are correct. But they are not enough. Quine's critique of the traditional theory of meaning also has to rule out a linguistic explanation of those concepts. *A priori*, it is just as reasonable to think we might explain those concepts in linguistics as it is to think we might explain them in logic. The problem with Quine's critique is that the criticisms designed to rule out a linguistic explanation fail.

Quine argued that linguistic methodology precludes a linguistic explanation of concepts in the theory of meaning. To construct such an argument, he required a criterion for successful linguistic explanation, and, for this purpose, he invoked the criterion in the linguistic methodology with which he was familiar from his examination of the Bloomfieldian theory of taxonomic grammar. On that methodology, the acceptability of a linguistic concept depends on there being a substitution procedure which operationally defines the concept in terms of concepts outside its family. Given this criterion, Quine proceeded to establish the conditional (C), showing that any attempt to provide substitution procedures for concepts in the theory of meaning is circular.

> (C)   If substitution procedures are the criterion for explaining concepts in linguistics, the concepts in the theory of meaning cannot be made objective sense of in linguistics.

However, establishing (C) does not go far enough to preclude a linguistic explanation of the theory of meaning. Quine has to detach the consequent of (C). To do that, he requires a reason to think that the existence of a substitution procedure is the right criterion for explaining concepts in linguistics. Here he presents no reason but simply relies on Bloomfieldian linguistics. That turned out to be a mistake because the generative revolution in linguistics undercut his overall argument. Once the restrictive criterion of definition in terms of substitution procedures is replaced by the liberal standard of theoretical definition in a generative grammar, there is nothing circular about the conceptual connections which arise when the members of a family of linguistic concepts are defined with respect to one another within a system of formal rules. The more connections among the concepts, the merrier. Such interconnections reveal the systematic relations among the concepts. Furthermore, there is nothing arbitrary about such definitions, since the adequacy of the theoretical definition can be judged by whether its consequences are confirmed on the basis of linguistic facts.

There is, then, no grounds for detaching the consequent of (C), and, hence, no argument that we cannot make objective sense of the theory of meaning. Quine now seems to agree, and thus to have retreated from his earlier position that there is a philosophical argument showing that analyticity and the theory of meaning generally are just dogma. Commenting on my objection, Quine (1990, pp.199–202; also Clark 1993) concedes that the concept of meaning might be no worse off now than the concept of the gene forty or so years ago.

Quine's indeterminacy thesis does not provide a criticism of the theory of meaning to replace the criticisms in "Two Dogmas of Empiricism". His (1960, pp.72–79) claim is that there is no right answer to a question of translation "independent of choices among mutually incompatible manuals of translation" because such manuals "can be set up in divergent ways, all compatible with the totality of speech dispositions". Quine thinks that reflection on radical translation shows that the evidence concerning the application of a foreign term like "Gavagai" cannot in principle distinguish between incompatible hypotheses such as that it translates as "rabbit", that it translates as "undetached rabbit part", and that it translates as "rabbit stage". The argument against the theory of meaning is that, if we cannot obtain the evidence which favors the choice of one among such alternative hypotheses, we cannot determine what intension a sentence expresses.

As I (1988, 1990b, 1994a) have argued elsewhere, Quine simply begs the question. He puts forth radical translation as if it were an unobjectionable idealization of actual translation, one which merely abstracts away from irrelevant complications like "historical or cultural connections". But the "idealization" is constructed so that it lacks exactly the evidence necessary to break the evidential symmetry which is used to show that we cannot determine what intension a sentence expresses. Since the issue is whether translation involves evidence about *sense* properties and relations which might be used to determine intensions, Quine cannot, first, assume an "idealization" in which the only evidence available is evidence about *referential* properties and relations, and, then, argue from the absence of evidence about sense properties and relations to evidential symmetry and indeterminacy of translation.

Apart from that "idealization", there is no reason to think that we cannot choose between the alternative hypotheses for translating "Gavagai". The linguist could ask informants not only when they will and will not say "Gavagai" in reference to something, but also what judgments they can make about its sense properties and relations. Since bilingualism is as much a possibility as monolingualism, this option is available, and the former evidential symmetry is broken. Thus, informant judgments about the sense properties and relations of "Gavagai" can provide evidence which is, in principle, sufficient to rule out the hypotheses that incorrectly translate "Gavagai". For example, if informants say that "Gavagai" bears the same relation to some word in their language that "finger" bears to "hand", there is evidence that distinguishes among the hypotheses. There is, then, no reason not to think that intensional semantics is on a par with the gene theory forty or so years ago.

Quine's criticisms in "Two Dogmas of Empiricism" are the linch-pin of his entire case against the theory of meaning. Had they worked, there would be no possibility of evidence about sense properties and relations, Quine's "idealization" would be legitimate, and translation indeterminate. There is, then, no small irony that linguists and philosophers working in the Chomskyan framework have taken Quine as having cleared the way for referential semantics. In doing so, they rest their position on arguments which depend on the very theory of grammar that Chomsky had to refute in order for semantics to become part of linguistics.

4   Other Grounds?

Quine's indeterminacy thesis does not provide grounds for taking an exclusively referential direction in linguistic semantics. But there have been other arguments over the last thirty years that look *prima facie* as if they might provide independent grounds for taking an exclusively referential direction in semantics. In fact, however, so enormous was Quine's influence that those arguments turn out to depend on his criticisms of the theory of meaning and hence to be inadequate, too.

Such dependency is most clearly seen in the grounds Davidson (1967b, p.309) offers for replacing the intensionalist paradigm "'s' means *p*" with the extensionalist paradigm (*T*), namely, that the replacement is necessary to escape being "enmeshed in the intensional".

(*T*)   "*s*" is *T* if and only if *p*.

No doubt, one thing Davidson has in mind in speaking about being "enmeshed in the intensional" is the problems Quine's criticisms are supposed to have raised for the theory of meaning. Those problems, as we have seen, are nothing to worry about.

But, in the same context, Davidson (1967b, p.309) remarks that ". . . wrestling with the logic of the apparently non-extensional 'means that' we will encounter problems as hard as, or perhaps identical with, the problems our theory is out to solve". These problems arise in connection with substitution into opaque contexts. As he (1967b, p.307) puts it, the problem "is that we cannot account for even as much as the truth conditions of [belief sentences] on the basis of what we know of the meanings of the words in them". This problem, which he refers to as "the standard problem", was first raised in Mates's (1952) "Synonymity". Thus, Davidson's argument for replacing the intensionalist paradigm with (T) seems to be that an otherwise unsolvable problem is avoided when we switch paradigms. This argument seems to be entirely independent of Quine.

But Church (1954) proposed a solution within intensionalism. If that solution works, there is no motivation to switch paradigms. The proposal, as I understand it, is to argue that inferences like that from "Everyone believes that bachelors are bachelors" to "Everyone believes that bachelors are unmarried men" are valid because, since "bachelor" means "unmarried man", believing "Bachelors are bachelors" *is* believing "Bachelors are unmarried men". Hence, someone who thinks (sincerely says, etc.) that they believe "Bachelors are bachelors" but not "Bachelors are unmarried men" *ipso facto* convicts themselves of a linguistic confusion or deficiency which disqualifies them as a competent source of linguistic evidence and hence removes them as a counterexample to such inferences. Given that the expressions are synonymous, we can no more put our semantic trust in someone who says they believe "Bachelors are bachelors" but not "Bachelors are unmarried men" than we can put our arithmetic trust in someone who says they believe "$12 + 3 = 15$" but not "$(5 + 7) + 3 = 15$".

Davidson has not overlooked Church's proposal. In a later paper, he (1968) tells us that he rejects the solution because it depends on synonymy and analyticity, and Quine has gotten rid of them. Davidson (1968, p.138) says that "the lesson" of indeterminacy was implicit in Mates's problem: "Church and Sellars responded [to Mates' argument] by saying the difficulty could be resolved by firmly distinguishing between substitutions based on the speaker's use of language and substitutions coloured by the use attributed to others. But this is a solution only if we think there is some way of telling, in what another says, what is owed to the meanings he gives his words and what to his beliefs about the world. According to Quine, this is a distinction that cannot be drawn." Here again Davidson's argument for replacing the intensionalist paradigm with convention (T) depends on Quine. Hence, it is inadequate as grounds for a purely referential approach to linguistic semantics.

Possible worlds semanticists also claim that we ought to replace the intensionalist paradigm " 's' means p" with an extensionalist paradigm having the form of a truth schema. In their case, the new paradigm is (T').

(T') "s" is T in a possible world w if and only if p in w.

They claim that their semantics is superior to Davidsonian semantics on the grounds that functions from possible worlds to referential values in them provide finer-grained identity conditions for meanings than Davidsonian's semantic interpretations. Thus, a possible worlds semantics for English can discriminate the meanings of contingently co-extensional expressions like "creature with a heart" and "creature with a kidney" on the basis of the fact that they have different extensions in some possible worlds.

This way of arguing is a two-edged sword. If there is another semantics with the still finer-grained identity conditions to discriminate the meanings of necessarily co-extensional but nonsynonymous expressions like "creature with two kidneys" and "creature with a number of kidneys equal to the even prime", then it will be superior to possible worlds semantics for exactly the same reason that the latter is superior to Davidsonian semantics. The traditional theory of meaning and the semantic marker reconstruction of it described in Section 1 are semantic theories with just such finer-grained identity conditions for meanings. Given that the branching structure in semantic markers represents the way senses are constructed from their sense components, the identity conditions for meanings in such a semantics require both sameness of component senses and sameness of construction. Being as fine-grained as synonymy in natural language, those identity conditions will discriminate necessarily co-extensive, nonsynonymous expressions.

Hence, possible worlds semantics requires an argument against such theories to over-ride their advantage in the areas of semantic distinctions. What is needed is an argument, independent of Quine, which shows that there are no finer-grained identity conditions for meanings than those in possible worlds semantics. Lewis (1972, pp.169–170) presents an argument that seems at first to meet this need. He objects to semantic marker representations of sentences on the grounds that they are completely unrevealing about semantic structure because such representations accomplish no more than a translation of the sentences into another language, Markerese. Translating uninterpreted English sentences into uninterpreted Markerese sentences is no better than translating them into Latin. Dowty, Wall, and Peters (1981, pp.4–5) have canonized Lewis's argument in their text on Montague semantics.

Surprisingly, the argument is also popular outside possible world semantics. Searle (1974, p.27) uses a version of it, and so do Evans and McDowell (1976, pp.vii–viii). Its popularity is surprising because it has such a glaring fallacy. The crux of Lewis's (1970, p.169) argument is that Markerese representations are uninterpreted strings of symbols because they are not, as he puts it, "real semantics", that is, they are not interpreted referentially. What sanctions the inference from the fact that semantic marker formalism is not interpreted in terms of truth and reference to the conclusion that it is uninterpreted? What about an interpretation in terms of sense? In fact, I have always taken pains to provide exactly that interpretation. My presentations of the semantic marker theory specify the aim of the symbolism as representing the decompositional and compositional structure of senses and predicting meaningfulness, ambiguity, synonymy, redundancy, analyticity, and other sense properties and relations on the basis of such descriptions.

Those who use the argument seem somehow to have failed to recognize that. The charitable construal is to understand that failure not as a scholarly lapse but to suppose that the philosophers who use Lewis's argument think that there is no such alternative way of interpreting semantic marker formalism because Quine had discredited senses, synonymy, analyticity, and the other notions required for such an interpretation. But if that is what is behind the claim that semantic marker formalism is uninterpreted, then, like Davidson, Lewis relies on Quine, and, like Davidson, Lewis's argument is left without support.

Donnellan (1962), Putnam (1962, 1970, and 1975), and Kripke (1972) are not proponents of an exclusively referential semantics, but the form of argument they developed against the Fregean account of names and natural kind terms can be used on behalf of an exclusively referential semantics. Moreover, that form of argument seems to depend on no more than an exercise of the imagination, and hence it seems to be independent of Quine's arguments. Consider Putnam's (1962) original argument to show that an allegedly paradigm case of an analytic sentence like (1) cannot really be analytic.

(1)   Cats are feline animals.

He asks us to imagine that the objects to which everyone has been applying the term "cat" turn out to be robots which look and behave like cats. We can, and so it has to be acknowledged as a possibility that those things are actually robots. Putnam then argues that it couldn't be that (1) is analytic, since that would mean that "cat" had the sense "feline animal" and, in that case, it would have been impossible for literal uses of "cat" to refer to non-animals.

Although this line of argument seems to be independent of Quine's criticisms of the theory of meaning, it, too, turns out to depend on them. Since the form of argument appears in a number of different versions, the best I can do here is to explain the dependency in the case of the above version and refer the reader to other works of mine (1990b, pp.216–232) in which the other versions are discussed.

The problem with the argument is the step from the proposition that (1) is analytic – "cat" means "feline animal" – to the proposition that the referents in literal uses of the term "cat" must be animals. The only thing that can sanction that step is Frege's principle that sense determines reference. The argument's dependency on this principle goes unnoticed because it is widely supposed that, if there is any intensionalism at all, it is intensionalism based on Frege's definition of sense. But that supposition, as I (1986, 1992) have argued elsewhere, is simply false. Semantic marker theory is an intensionalist theory, but has no commitment to Frege's definition of sense as the determiner of reference. It defines sense as the aspect of the grammatical structure of expressions which explains their sense properties and relations, their meaningfulness, ambiguity, synonymy, antonymy, redundancy, analyticity, and so on. Sense is the determiner of sense properties and relations, not referential properties and relations. With this definition, we can have an intensionalism with the weaker principle that sense is necessary but not sufficient for reference.

The mere existence of such an intensionalism shows that the step in question is unsupported. On the alternative intensionalism, if it is a fact that (1) is analytic, then that fact consists in nothing more than that "cat" has a complex sense one component of which is the sense of "animal". Since Putnam can no longer claim that a commitment to the analyticity of (1) entails a commitment to literal uses of "cat" referring only to animals, he cannot use the possibility of literal uses of "cat" referring exclusively to robots as a basis for denying the analyticity of (1).

Moreover, the uses of "cat" to refer to robots can be explained as reference under a false description, exactly like the reference in Donnellan's (1966) famous case of the woman who refers to a man drinking sparkling water in a use of (2).

(2)   The man in the corner drinking champagne is tall.

In both cases, the context falsifies the belief of the speaker(s) on the basis of which the description was chosen – in the one case, the belief that the man in the corner is drinking champagne and in the other the belief that there are feline animals and that they are things which appear and behave in the way the robots do. Nonetheless, a man drinking sparkling water and robots are, respectively, the referents in the two cases because they are clearly what the speakers had in mind and of whom they have the false belief. Given that Putnam's case works like Donnellan's, it is one in which robots have been referred to as "cat" under the false description "feline animal". Hence, Putnam's case can be no more of a counterexample to the claim that "cat" analytically entails "animal" than Donnellan's case can be a counterexample to the claim that "man in the corner drinking champagne" analytically entails "man drinking an alcoholic beverage".

The only way to save Putnam's argument is to deny that there is an alternative intensionalism, and the only way to do that is to show that the sense properties and relations on which its definition of sense rests cannot be made objective sense of. Quine's arguments would have come in very handy.

5   Referential Semantics Without Quine's Arguments

Quine's arguments will also be sorely missed by those who claim that referential semantics is semantics enough for natural language not only because their arguments depend on Quine's arguments, but also because his arguments have shielded referential semantics from criticism. That criticism is based on the fact, noted above, that extensional semantic interpretations, whether they take the actual world as the domain of the language or all possible worlds, do not provide identity conditions for meanings fine-grained enough to handle meaning in natural language. Once Quine's arguments are blocked and notions like meaningfulness, synonymy, and analyticity are no longer under a cloud, purely referential theories of the semantics of natural language can be criticized for having identity conditions for meanings that are too coarse-grained to provide the best account of meaningfulness, synonymy, analyticity, etc. Theories with finer-grained identity conditions for meanings, like the traditional theory of meaning and its semantic marker reconstruction, challenge the view that referential semantics is semantics enough for natural language.

Consider some examples. Davidson (1967b) noted certain counter-intuitive consequences of adopting convention (T) as our paradigm for the semantic analysis of natural language. He observed that it is counter-intuitive to treat (4) as an account of the meaning of (2) on a par with (3).

(3)   Snow is white.
(4)   "Snow is white" is *T* iff snow is white.
(5)   "Snow is white" is *T* iff grass is green.

English would thus seem to contain only two meanings, since the truth-conditions for every true sentence of English can be given on the basis of any true sentence, and the truth-conditions for every false sentence can be given on the basis of any false sentence. Davidson (1967b, p.312) tried to mitigate this counter-intuitiveness by arguing that

> ... the grotesqueness of [(5)] is in itself nothing against a theory of which it is a consequence, ... if [(5)] followed from a characterization of the predicate "is true" that led to the invariable pairing of truths with truths and falsehoods with falsehoods – then there would not, I think, be anything essential to the idea of meaning that remained to be captured.

He would be quite right to dismiss these counter-intuitive consequences if Quine's arguments were available to show that there is no maximally fine-grained notion of sameness of meaning. But without Quine's arguments, Davidson cannot dismiss the grotesqueness of those consequences on the grounds that nothing essential remains to be captured once all extensional work is done. Those consequences are nothing but a sample of the old objections to a purely extensional semantics. Their reappearance shows that the extensionalist paradigm of meaning analysis does not do the necessary intensional work. For example, there is no way to distinguish between terms like "unicorn" and "centaur" or between sentences like (6) and (7).

(6)   A creature with a heart is a creature with a heart.
(7)   A creature with a heart is a creature with a kidney.

(As shown in Katz 1990b (pp.204–220), Davidson's attempts to mitigate these problems are unsuccessful.)

Essentially the same problems arise for possible worlds semantics. This should not be surprising, since the only advantage of introducing a domain of possible worlds is to distinguish the propositions expressed by different contingent truths and the propositions expressed by different contingent falsehoods. (6) and (7) become distinguishable because the former but not the latter is true in every possible world, but that victory over Davidsonian approaches is pyrrhic. Possible worlds semantics has essentially the same grotesque consequences in connection with sentences that express necessary truths and necessary falsehoods. For example, possible worlds semantics is unable to distinguish (8) and (9), surely as counter-intuitive as any of the grotesque consequences of Davidson's semantics.

(8)   Two is two.
(9)   Two is the even prime.
(10)   Kindergarten children know that two is two.
(11)   Kindergarten children know that two is the even prime.

No one would paraphrase or translate (8) and (9) in the same way. Nor would anyone take them to contribute the same semantic content to sentences in which they appear as constituents: the necessary equivalence of (8) and (9) does not entail the necessary equivalence of (10) and (11). Furthermore, whereas on Davidsonian semantics there are only two meanings for the sentences of a natural language, on possible worlds semantics, there are only two meanings for the sentences expressing necessary statements.

Lewis (1970, pp.182–186) acknowledges that "intensions for sentences cannot be identified with meanings", but, exploiting Carnap's (1965, pp.56–64) idea of intensional isomorphism, he argues that the fine-grainness of meanings can be captured using the intensions assigned to the syntactic constituents of a sentence, e.g. "Snow is white or it isn't" differs finely in meaning from "Grass is green or it isn't" because of the difference in intension between the embedded sentences "Snow is white" and "Grass is green". But, as Katz and Katz (1977; see also Pitt 1994) argue, such an attempt to extensionally mimic sense structure fails because syntactically simple constituents – morphemes – have complex meanings which are also the compositional meanings of syntactically complex expressions. If referential semanticists follow Lewis and take sameness and difference of the Carnapian intensions assigned to the constituents of expressions as sufficient for the expressions to be synonymous or nonsynonymous, they will wrongly mark synonymous expressions like "square" and "a parallelogram having four equal sides and four right angles" as nonsynonymous. If they do not follow Lewis and count only sameness and difference of the Carnapian intensions assigned to the expressions as a whole as sufficient for them to be synonymous or nonsynonymous, they will wrongly mark nonsynonymous but necessarily co-referential expressions like "two" and "the even prime" as synonymous. The intensional denizens of the theory of meaning cannot be captured by tracking their extensional footprints across possible worlds. All footprints of necessity look the same.

Let us now turn to Donnellan's and Kripke's extensionalism on proper names. Frege (1952) claimed that identity sentences and sentences involving opaque contexts, such as belief sentences, require us to recognize that names and other referring expressions have sense as well as reference. He argued that, if reference were the only semantic value for proper nouns, (12) would not express a trivial truth while (13) expresses a surprising discovery, and (14) would not have different truth value from (15).

(12) Clark Kent is Clark Kent.
(13) Clark Kent is Superman.
(14) Lois Lane believes that Clark Kent is a wimp.
(15) Lois Lane believes that Superman is a wimp.

Frege's explanation of such semantic differences was that proper nouns have sense just like common nouns. If "Clark Kent" means "the mildest mannered reporter working for the Daily Planet" and "Superman" means "the man of steel", we can explain the difference in cognitive significance between (12) and (13) and the difference in truth value between (14) and (15).

Kripke (1980) realized that this explanation commits Fregeans to the dubious claim that the sense of a proper name is an identifying property which is true of its bearer in all counterfactual situations. Kripke presented a wide range of examples which show the claim is false. It is possible that Clark Kent was never employed as a reporter for the Daily Planet. Perry White perpetrated an elaborate deception on him. But, even so, we do not think that the mildest mannered reporter working for the Daily Planet, Casper Milquetoast, is Clark Kent, or that (13) is true because Milquetoast is Superman. Such Kripke-style examples show that something has gone radically wrong with Frege's explanation.

Kripke, Donnellan, and the other proponents of the new theory of reference diagnose the trouble as the supposition that proper names have sense and adopt a Millian extensionalism according to which the semantic value of a name is just its bearer. The reference of a name is thus direct, and not determined by the sense of the name. Unsurprisingly, this extensionalism concerning names lands neo-Millians back with the problems Frege attempted to solve when he posited senses for names. The problems about (12)–(15) rearise in a variety of forms. One example is Kripke's (1979) case of Pierre who, though epistemically blameless, comes to believe the apparently inconsistent propositions (16) and (17). Sentences like (18)–(20) pose another problem. Since

"Superman" and "Batman" have no referent, Millians have to say that (18)–(20) are entirely meaningless.

(16)   Londres est jolie.
(17)   London is not pretty.
(18)   Superman does not exist.
(19)   There is no Superman.
(20)   Batman does not exist.

But the intuition that (18)–(20) are meaningful is clear, as are other intuitions which imply their meaningfulness like the intuition that (18) is synonymous with (19) but not with (20).

Donnellan (1974) and Kripke (1973) have tried to solve these problems, but, as I (1994b) have argued, without notable success. Because they have to count sentence types as meaningless, their solutions take the form of explanations of how we express truths in uses of sentences like (12)–(15) and (18)–(20) in spite of the fact that the sentences themselves are meaningless. This means the neo-Millians write off the entire range of semantic facts about such English sentences. Thus, what are to most of us intuitively clear facts about the meaningfulness, synonymy, analyticity, and other sense properties and relations of sentence types with vacuous names are to them a grammatical mystery.

Salmon (1986) makes an interesting attempt to cope with such Fregean problems. He introduces the notion of a guise to provide Frege-style explanations of how a use of (14) and a use of (15) can have different truth values. But no such explanation is available to neo-Millians at the level of sentence types because guises are creatures of context. That, from a Millian standpoint, is their major selling point. It is what enables the neo-Millian to use them in the manner of Fregean modes of presentation consistent with their doctrine that proper names have no sense in the language. But, restricted to context, guises are of no help with Fregean problems about sentence types like (12)–(15).

Elsewhere, I (1994b) have discussed the shortcomings of explanations of how tokens of sentences like (12)–(15) and (18)–(20) make statements when the speaker is assumed to have no knowledge of the sense of their types. I cannot review that discussion here. But, regardless of the status of those explanations, even if such pragmatic explanations are quite plausible, if there is a theory that can do justice to the semantic facts at both the level of language and the level of language use, then the existence of a grammatical mystery at the level of language condemns Millian extensionalism on names.

The semantic marker theory which reconstructs the traditional theory of meaning is such a theory. It can agree with Frege that bearerless names and occurrences of names in opaque contexts demonstrate the indispensability of sense while disagreeing with his view about the nature of sense. It can agree with Kripke that Frege's semantics mistakenly claims that the sense of a proper name is an identifying property which is true of its bearer in all counterfactual situations while disagreeing with Kripke's view that proper nouns have no sense. Sense is indispensable, but Frege's referential definition of it is not. If we replace Frege's definition with the notion of linguistic meaning in semantic marker theory, we can maintain intensionalism regarding names while denying that their sense functions as an identifying description.

Since, on that notion of linguistic meaning, the sense of a proper name does not have to determine its referents, we can say that the sense of a name "N" is simply a meta-linguistic condition of the form (21).

(21)   The thing which is a bearer of "N"

Although I cannot argue it here, an account of names based on (21) avoids Kripke's counterexamples to Fregean descriptionism. (See Katz (1990a and 1994b).) Part of the reason it does can be seen from the fact that, without real properties in the sense of "Clark Kent", Clark Kent will not be identified with whoever in counterfactual situations satisfies contingent descriptions like "the mildest mannered reporter working for the Daily Planet".

With our new intensionalism, we can solve the problems which returned when Millian extensionalism replaced Fregean intensionalism. Since, on (21), the occurrences of the names in (12) have the same sense but the occurrences of the names in (13) do not, (12) is trivial and (13) is not. The different senses of the names in (14) and (15) account for the different beliefs they ascribe to Lois Lane. (14) says (truly) that she believes the contextually definite thing which is a bearer of "Clark Kent" is a wimp, while (15) says (falsely) that she believes the contextually definite thing which is a bearer of "Superman" is a wimp. Similarly, the different senses of "London" and "Londres" mean that (16) and (17) express different and consistent *de dicto* propositions, which exonerates Pierre of the charge of having inconsistent beliefs. Finally, (18)–(20) are meaningful, and the synonymy of (18) with (19) but not (20) can be explained with minor attention to their syntactic relations. (See Katz (1990a and 1994b) for a full discussion.)

6   Semantics in Linguistics and Philosophy

Since the early sixties, there has been a good deal of semantics in linguistics and a good deal of linguistics in semantics. However, investigation in both linguistic and philosophical semantics has been skewed in the direction of the theory of reference, owing principally to Quine's criticisms of the theory of meaning having generally persuaded linguists and philosophers that no objective sense can be made of meaning, but also owing to Frege's having gotten intensionalism off on the wrong foot with his referential definition of sense. Referential semantics now enjoys something of a hegemony in linguistics and philosophy.

In linguistics, Quine's criticisms have enabled referential semanticists to avoid the problems which arise because extensional structure cannot provide sufficiently fine-grained identity conditions for meanings. In spite of the fact that those problems pose a fundamental challenge to the hegemony of purely referential semantics, they are treated as marginal questions best postponed until the final, mopping up stage in the semantic study of natural language – when they will no doubt sort themselves out somehow. Thus, virtually everyone now working in linguistic semantics pursues one or another referentialist program, concentrating on topics like co-reference and quantificational structure that are more tractable within an exclusively referential framework. (Exceptions are Katz (1972, 1977, and 1987), Katz, Leacock, and Ravin (1985), Ravin (1990), and Jackendoff (1990).) Since meaningfulness, synonymy, antonymy, analyticity, and other sense properties and relations are at the very heart of linguistic meaning, their neglect is a sad commentary on the present state of linguistic semantics.

In philosophy, the situation is different. The same referentialist programs enjoy the same hegemony, but questions about meaningfulness, synonymy, and analyticity cannot be marginalized. For one thing, too many of the central issues in the philosophy of language and logic are framed in terms of questions about those notions. For another, too many issues in epistemology, metaphysics, and other areas outside philosophy of language and logic hang on the answers to such questions. Quine clearly recognized the centrality of those questions in his attack on the *a priori*, necessity, and non-naturalistic conceptions of philosophy. The hegemony of referentialist programs together with the centrality of questions about meaningfulness, synonymy, and analyticity have created a situation in which philosophical semantics is plagued with problems – such as those mentioned in the last section – which some of the best contemporary philosophers see as precipitating a crisis in philosophy. Kripke (1972, 1980, p.21) has described some of those problems as "so vexing" as to question whether "the apparatus of 'propositions' does not break down in [the] area [of knowledge and belief]".

If the argument in the present essay is correct, those problems do not pose the threat of a breakdown of our semantic apparatus, but rather reveal the necessity of a break up of the Fregean amalgamation of the theories of sense and reference. The problems also reveal the limitations of globally extensionalist programs like Davidson's (1967b) and Lewis's (1970) and locally extensionalist programs like Kripke's (1980). Recognition of the inadequacy of Quine's arguments and the dispensability of Frege's definition opens the way for a more balanced investigation of semantics in both linguistics and philosophy. Among the benefits to be expected are, on the one hand, linguistic inquiries which face up to the central problem of meaning in natural language, and, on the other, philosophical inquiries which are no longer beset with difficulties that senses were originally introduced to solve.

References

Abney, S. (1987) *The English noun phrase in its sentential aspect*. PhD Dissertation, MIT.

Abusch, D. (1994) The scope of indefinites. *Natural Language Semantics*, 2, 83–136.

—— (1988) Sequence of tense, intensionality and scope. *WCCFL 7*, Stanford: Stanford University.

Aczel, P. and Lunnon, R. (1991) Universes and parameters. In Barwise et al. (eds) *Situation Theory and its Applications*, Vol. 2. Stanford, CA: CSLI Lecture Notes.

Aczel, P., Israel D., Katagiri, Y. and Peters, S. (eds) (1993) *Situation Theory and its Applications*, Vol. 3, Stanford, CA: CSLI Lecture Notes.

Ajdukiewicz, K. (1935) Die syntaktische Konnexitaet. *Studia Philosophica*, 1, 1–27. [Syntactic connexion]. In S. McCall (ed.) (1967), *Polish Logic*, 207–31. Oxford: Clarendon Press.

Allen, J. (1994) *Natural Language Understanding*. Walham, MA: Addison-Wesley.

Altham, J. E. J. and Tennant, N. W. (1975) Sortal quantification. In *Formal Semantics for Natural Language*. E. L. Keenan (ed.), Cambridge: Cambridge University Press.

Anderson, A. H., Bader, M., Bard, E. G., Boyle, E. H., Doherty, G. M., Garrod, S. C., Isard, S. D., Kowtko, J. C., McAllister, J. M., Miller, J., Sotillo, C. F., Thompson, H. S. and Weinert R. (1991) The HCRC map task corpus, *Language and Speech*, Vol. 34, 351–66.

Apresjan, Ju. D. (1973) Regular polysemy. *Linguistics*, 142, 5–32.

—— (1992) *Lexical semantics*. Ann Arbor, MI: Karoma.

Åqvist, L. (1965) *A New Approach to the Logical Theory of Questions*. Tübingen: Narr.

Armstrong, S. L., Gleitman, L. and Gleitman, H. (1983) On what some concepts might not be. *Cognition*, 13, 263–308.

Aronoff, M. (1976) *Word-formation in Generative Grammar*. Cambridge, MA: MIT Press.

Asher, N. (1987) A typology for attitude verbs and their anaphoric properties. *Linguistics and Philosophy*, 10, 127–89.

Atkins, B. T. and Levin, B. (1991) Admitting impediments. In U. Zernik (ed.), *Lexical Acquisition: Exploiting on-line Resources to Build a Lexicon*, 233–62. Hillsdale, NJ: Lawrence Erlbaum Associates.

Atlas, J. D. (1975) Frege's polymorphous concept of presupposition and its role in a theory of meaning. *Semantikos*, 1, 29–45.

—— (1979) How linguistics matters to philosophy: presupposition, truth, and meaning. In C.-K. Oh and D. A. Dinneen (eds), (1979) *Syntax and Semantics 11: Presupposition*. New York: Academic Press, 265–81.

—— (1989) *Philosophy Without Ambiguity*. Oxford: Oxford University Press.

Austin, J. L. (1950) Truth. In G. J. Warnock et al. (eds), *Austin: Philosophical Papers.* Oxford: Oxford University Press.

—— (1954) Unfair to facts. In Warnock et al. (eds), *Austin: Philosophical Papers.* Oxford: Oxford University Press.

Bach, E. (1968) Nouns and noun phrases. In E. Bach and R. T. Harms (eds), *Universals in Linguistic Theory*, 91–124. New York: Holt, Rinehart, and Winston.

—— (1976) An extension of classical transformational grammar. In *Problems of Linguistic Metatheory* (Proceedings of the 1976 Conference): Michigan State University.

—— (1979a) Control in Montague grammar. *Linguistic Inquiry*, 10: 515–31.

—— (1979b) Montague grammar and classical transformational grammar. In S. Davis and M. Mithun (eds), *Linguistics, Philosophy, and Montague Grammar.* Austin: University of Texas Press.

—— (1983) Generalized categorial grammars and the English auxiliary. In F. Heny and B. Richards (eds), *Linguistic Categories: Auxiliaries and Related Puzzles II*, 101–20, Dordrecht: Reidel.

—— (1984) Some generalizations of categorial grammars. In F. Landman and F. Veltman (eds), *Varieties of Formal Semantics*, 1–24, Dordrecht: Foris.

—— (1986a) Natural language metaphysics. In R. Barcan Marcus, G. J. W. Dorn, and P. Weingartner (eds), *Logic, Methodology and philosophy of Science VII*, 573–95, Amsterdam: North-Holland.

—— (1986b) The algebra of events, *Linguistics and Philosophy* 9, 5–16.

—— (1989) *Informal Lectures on Formal Semantics.* Albany: State University of New York Press.

—— (1993) On the semantics of polysynthesis. In J. S. Guenter, B. A. Kaiser, and C. C. Zoll (eds), Proceedings of the Nineteenth Annual Meeting of the Berkeley Linguistics Society, 361–8, Berkeley: Berkeley Linguistics Society.

Bach, E. and Wheeler, D. (1981) Montague phonology: a first approximation. In W. Chao and D. Wheeler (eds), *University of Massachusetts Occasional Papers 7.* Amherst: GLSA.

Bach, E., Jelinek, E., Kratzer, A. and Partee, B. H. (eds) (1995) *Quantification in Natural Languages.* Dordrecht: Kluwer.

Bach, K. and Harnish, R. W. (1979) *Linguistic Communication and Speech Acts.* Cambridge, MA: MIT Press.

—— (1987) Relevant questions. *Behavioral and Brain Sciences*, 10, 711–12.

Baker, C. L. (1966) *Definiteness and Indefiniteness in English.* MA Thesis, University of Illinois.

—— (1970) Double negatives. *Linguistic Inquiry*, 1, 169–86.

Bar-Hillel, Y. (1953) A quasi-arithmetical notation for syntactic description. *Language*, 29, 47–58.

—— (1954) Logical syntax and semantics. *Language*, 30, 230–7.

Bartsch, R. (1987) Frame representations and discourse representations, *Theoretical Linguistics*, 14, 65–117.

Barwise, J. (1979) On branching quantifiers in English. *Journal of Philosophical Logic*, 8, 47–80.

—— (1981) Scenes and other situations, *Journal of Philosophy*, 78, 369–97.

—— (1986) Conditionals and conditional information. Reprinted in *The Situation in Logic.* CSLI Lecture Notes. Stanford: CSLI.

—— (1987) Noun phrases, generalized quantifiers, and anaphora. In P. Gärdenfors (ed.), *Generalized Quantifiers*, 1–29. Dordrecht: Reidel.

—— (1989a) Situations, facts, and true propositions. In *The Situation in Logic.* Stanford, CA: CSLI Lecture Notes.

—— (1993) Constraints, channels and the flow of information. In Aczel, Kategiri, Israel and Peters (eds).

Barwise, J. and Cooper, R. (1981) Generalized quantifiers and natural language. *Linguistics and Philosophy*, 4, 159–219.

—— (1991) Simple situation theory and its graphical representation. Indiana University Logic Group Preprint No. IULG–91–8, and in Seligman (1991).

—— (1993) Extended Kamp notation: a graphical notation for situation theory. In Aczel, Israel, Katagiri and Peters (eds) (1993), 29–54.

Barwise, J. and Etchemendy, J. (1987) *The Liar*. Oxford: Oxford University Press.

—— (1990) Information, infons and inference. In Cooper et al. (eds).

Barwise, J. and Feferman, S. (eds) (1985) *Model-Theoretic Logics*. New York: Springer-Verlag.

Barwise, J. and Perry, J. (1983) *Situations and Attitudes*. Cambridge, MA: MIT Press.

Barwise, J. and Seligman, J. (1994) The rights and wrongs of natural regularity. In Tomberlin (ed.), 331–65.

Barwise, J., Gawron, J. M., Plotkin, G. and Tutiya, S. (eds) (1991) *Situation Theory and its Applications*, Vol. 2, Stanford, CA: CSLI Lecture Notes.

Bäuerle, R. (1979) Questions and answers. In Bäuerle et al.

Bäuerle, R., Egli, U. and von Stechow, A. (eds) (1979) *Semantics from Different Points of View*. Berlin: Springer Verlag.

Bealer, G. (1982) *Concept and Object*. Oxford: Oxford University Press.

—— (1989) Fine-grained type-free intensionality. In G. Chierchia, B. H. Partee, R. Turner (eds).

Beaver, D. I. (1992) *The Kinematics of Presupposition* No. LP-92-05. ITLI Prepublication Series for Logic, Semantics and Philosophy of Language.

Beghelli, F. (1992) Comparative quantifiers. In P. Dekker and M. Stokhof (eds), *Proc. of the 8th Amsterdam Colloquium*. ILLC University of Amsterdam.

—— (1993) Structured quantifiers. To appear in M. Kanazawa and C. Piñon (eds), *Dynamics, Polarity and Quantification*. Stanford, CA: CSLI Lecture Notes.

Belletti, A. and Rizzi, L. (1981) The syntax of *ne*: Some theoretical implications. *The Linguistic Review*, 1–2, 117–54.

—— (1988) Psych-verbs and theta-theory. *Natural Language and Linguistic Theory*, 6, 291–352.

Belnap, N. (1982) Questions and answers in Montague grammar. In S. Peters, and E. Saarinen (eds), *Processes, Beliefs, and Questions*, 165–98. Dordrecht: Reidel.

Belnap, N. and Steel, T. (1976) *The Logic of Questions and Answers*. New Haven: Yale University Press.

Bennett, M. (1975) *Some Extensions of a Montague Fragment of English*. PhD Dissertation, University of California at Los Angeles. Distributed by Indiana University Linguistics Club, Bloomington.

—— (1976) A variation and extension of a Montague fragment of English. In B. H. Partee (ed.), *Montague grammar*. New York: Academic Press, 119–63.

van Benthem, J. (1983) Determiners and logic. *Linguistics and Philosophy*, 6, 447–78.

—— (1984) Questions about quantifiers. *Journal of Symbolic Logic*, 49, 443–66.

—— (1986) *Essays in Logical Semantics*. Dordrecht: Reidel.

—— (1989) Polyadic quantifiers. *Linguistics and Philosophy*, 12, 437–64.

—— (1991a) General dynamics. *Theoretical Linguistics*, 17, 159–201.

—— (1991b) Language in Action. *Studies in Logic*, Vol. 130. Amsterdam: North-Holland.

van Benthem, J. and ter Meulen, A. (eds) (1985) *Generalized Quantifiers in Natural Language*. Dordrecht: Foris.

Berlin, B., and P. Kay (1969) *Basic Color Terms: Their Universality and Evolution*. Berkeley: University of California Press.

Berman, S. (1987) Situation-based semantics for adverbs of quantification, *WCCFL* 6.

—— (1990) Towards the Semantics of open sentences: Wh-phrases and indefinites. In M. Stokhof and L. Torenvliet, *Proc. of 7th Amsterdam Colloquium*, Amsterdam: ITLI.

620   References

—— (1991) *On the Semantics and Logical Form of wh-clauses*. PhD Thesis, University of Massachusetts at Amherst.

—— (1994) *Wh-clauses and Quantificational Variability: Two Analyses*. IMS, Universität Stuttgart Ms.

Bierwisch, M. (1967) Some Semantic universals of German adjectivals. *Foundations of Language*, 3, 1–36.

—— (1969) On certain problems of semantic representation. *Foundations of Language*, 5, 153–84.

—— (1981) Basic issues in the development of word meaning. In W. Deutsch (ed.), *The Child's Construction of Language*, 341–87. London, New York: Academic Press.

—— (1982) Formal and lexical semantics. *Linguistische Berichte*, 80, 3–17.

—— (1992) *Where is What and What is Where?* Manuscript, Berlin: Max-Planck-Arbeitsgruppe für Strukturelle Grammatik.

Bierwisch, M. and Lang, E. (eds) (1989) *Dimensional Adjectives: Grammatical Structure and Conceptual Interpretation*. Berlin: Springer-Verlag.

Bloom, P. (1994) Possible Names: the role of syntax-semantic mappings in the acquisition of nominals. *Lingua*, 92, 297–329.

Bloomfield, L. (1933) *Language*. New York: Holt, Rinehart, and Winston.

—— (1936) Language or ideas? *Language*, 12, 89–95.

Blutner, R. (1993) Dynamic generalized quantifiers and existential sentences in natural languages. *Journal of Semantics*, 10, 33–64.

Boër, S. (1978) Toward a theory of indirect question clauses. *Linguistics and Philosophy* 2, 307–46.

Boër, S. and W. Lycan (1985) *Knowing Who*. Cambridge, MA: MIT Press.

Bolinger, D. (1978) Yes/no questions are not alternative questions. In Hiz (ed.), (1978).

Boolos, G. (1981) For every A there is a B. *Linguistic Inquiry*, 15, 465–7.

Bouma, G. and van Noord, G. (1993) Head-driven parsing for lexicalist grammars: experimental results. In *Proc. of 6th European ACL*, 71–80. Utrecht.

Bouton, L. (1970) Antecedent-contained pro-forms. *Papers from the 6th Regional Meeting, Chicago Linguistic Society*, 154–65. Chicago: Chicago Linguistic Society.

Bowerman, M. (1974) Learning the structure of causative verbs: A study in the relationship of cognitive, semantic, and syntactic development. *Papers and Reports on Child Language Development 8*. Stanford: Stanford University Department of Linguistics.

—— (1978) Systematizing semantic knowledge: Changes over time in the child's organization of word meaning. *Child Development*, 49, 977–87.

—— (1989) Learning a semantic system: What role do cognitive predispositions play? In M. L. Rice and R. C. Schiefenbusch (eds), *The Teachability of Language*. Baltimore: Paul H. Brooks.

Brody, M. (forthcoming) *Lexico-Logical Form: A Radically Minimalist Theory*, Cambridge, MA: MIT Press.

Brown, P. and Levinson, S. (1987) *Politeness*. Cambridge: Cambridge University Press.

Brown, R. (1973) *A First Language: The Early Stages*. Cambridge, MA: Harvard University Press.

Brugman, C. (1981) *Story of Over*. Bloomington, Indiana: Indiana University Linguistics Club.

Burton-Roberts, N. (1989) *The Limits to Debate: A Revised Theory of Semantic Presupposition*. Cambridge: Cambridge University Press.

Burzio, L. (1986) *Italian Syntax: A Government-Binding Approach*. Dordrecht: Reidel.

Carey, S. (1985) *Conceptual Change in Childhood*. Cambridge, MA: MIT Press.

Carlson, G. (1977a) Amount relatives. *Language*, 53, 520–42.

—— (1977b) *Reference to Kinds in English*. PhD Dissertation: University of Massachusetts at Amherst.

—— (1984) Thematic roles and their role in semantic interpretation. *Linguistics*, 22, 259–79.

—— (1987) Same and different: some consequences for syntax and semantics. *Linguistics and Philosophy*, 10.

Carlson, L. (1980) *Plural Quantification*. ms., MIT.

—— (1983) *Dialogue Games*. Dordrecht: Reidel.

Carnap, R. (1947) *Meaning and Necessity*. Chicago: University of Chicago Press.

—— (1952) Meaning postulates. *Phil. Studies*, III, 65–73.

—— (1956) *Meaning and Necessity, 2nd. edition with Supplements*. Chicago: University of Chicago Press.

—— (1965) *Meaning and Necessity (2nd edition)* Chicago: University of Chicago Press.

Carpenter, B. (1992) *The Logic of Typed Feature Structures*. No. 32 Tracts in Theoretical Computer Science. Cambridge: Cambridge University Press.

Carroll, J. and Tanenhaus, M. (1975) Prolegomena to a functional theory of word formation. *Papers from the Parasession on Functionalism*, 47–62. Chicago: CLS.

Carston, R. (1985) *A Reanalysis of Some Quantity Implicatures*. Unpublished ms., University of London.

—— (1988) Implicature, explicature, and truth-theoretic semantics. In Kempson, R. (ed.), *Mental Representations: The Interface between Language and Reality*, 155–81. Cambridge: Cambridge University Press.

—— (1993) Conjunction, juxtaposition and relevance. *Lingua*.

Carter, R. J. (1976) Some constraints on possible words. *Semantikos*, 1, 27–66.

—— (1988) *On Linking: Papers by Richard Carter*, B. Levin and C. Tenny (eds), Lexicon Project Working Papers 25. Cambridge, MA: Center for Cognitive Science, MIT.

Cavedon, L. and Glaskey, S. Outline of an Information-Flow Model of Generics. Forthcoming in *Acta Linguistica*.

Chao, W. (1988) *On Ellipsis*. New York: Garland Outstanding Dissertations Series.

Chierchia, G. (1982) Nominalisation and Montague grammar. *Linguistics and Philosophy*, 5, 303–55.

—— (1984) *Topics in the Syntax and Semantics of Infinitives and Gerunds*. PhD Dissertation, Amherst: University of Massachusetts.

—— (1988) Dynamic generalized quantifiers and donkey anaphora. In M. Krifka (ed.), *Genericity in Natural Language*, Univ. of Tübingen.

—— (1988) Dynamic generalized quantifiers and donkey anaphora. In M. Krifka (ed.), *Proceedings of the 1988 Tübingen Conference*. Seminar für Natürliche Sprachliche Systeme der Universität Tübingen, November.

—— (1992) Anaphora and dynamic binding. *Linguistics and Philosophy*, 15, 111–83.

—— (1993) Questions with quantifiers. *Natural Language Semantics*, 1, 181–234.

—— (1994) Intensionality and context change. *JOLLI3*, 141–68.

Chierchia, G. and Rooth, M. (1984) Configurational notions in discourse representation theory. In C. Jones and P. Sells (eds), *Proceedings of NELS 14*. Amherst, MA: University of Massachusetts GLSA.

Chierchia, G. and Turner, R. (1988) Semantics and property theory. *Linguistics and Philosophy*, 11, 261–302.

Chierchia, G., Partee, B. H. and Turner, R. (eds) (1989) *Properties, Types and Meaning, Vol. II: Semantic Issues*. Dordrecht: Kluwer.

Choi, S. and Bowerman, M. (1991) Learning to express motion events in English and Korean: The influence of language specific lexicalization patterns. *Cognition*, 41, 83–121.

Chomsky, N. (1955) Logical syntax and semantics: Their linguistic relevance, *Language*, 31, 36–45.

—— (1957) *Syntactic Structures*. The Hague: Mouton.

—— (1959) Review of verbal behavior. *Language*, 35, 26–58.

—— (1965) *Aspects of the Theory of Syntax*. Cambridge, MA: MIT Press.

—— (1971) Deep structure, surface structure, and semantic interpretation. In D. Steinberg and L. Jakobovits (eds), *Semantics: An Interdisciplinary Reader in Philosophy, Linguistics, and Psychology*. Cambridge: Cambridge University Press, 183–216.

—— (1973) Conditions on transformations. In S. Anderson, and P. Kiparsky (eds), *A Festschrift for Morris Halle*. New York: Holt, Rinehart, and Winston. Reprinted in Chomsky (1977), 81–160.

—— (1975) Questions of form and interpretation, *Linguistic Analysis*, 1, 75–109; also in R. Austerlitz (ed.) (1975), *The Scope of American Linguistics*, 159–96. Lisse: Peter de Ridder Press.

—— (1976) Conditions on rules of grammar. *Linguistic Analysis*, 303–51.

—— (1977) *Essays on Form and Interpretation*. Amsterdam: North Holland.

—— (1981) *Lectures on Government and Binding*. Dordrecht: Foris.

—— (1986a) *Barriers*. Cambridge, MA: MIT Press.

—— (1986b) *Knowledge of Language: Its Nature, Origin and Use*. New York: Praeger Publishers.

—— (1993) A minimalist program for linguistic theory. In K. Hale and S. J. Keyser (eds), *The View from Building 20: Essays in Linguistics in Honour of Sylvain Bromberger*. Cambridge, MA: MIT Press, 1–52.

—— (1995) Bare phrase structure. In G. Webelhath (ed.) *Government and Binding Theory and the Minimalist Program*, Oxford, Blackwell, 383–439.

Chomsky, N., Huybregts, R. and van Riemsdijk, H. (1982) *The Generative Enterprise*. Dordrecht: Foris.

Church, A. (1940) A formulation of the simple theory of types. *Journal of Symbolic Logic*, 5, 56–68.

—— (1951) A formulation of the logic of sense and denotation. In P. Henle, H. Kallen, and S. Langer (eds), *Structure, Method, and Meaning: Essays in Honor of H. M. Sheffer*. New York.

—— (1954) Intensional isomorphism and the identity of belief. *Philosophical Studies*, 5, 65–73.

Clark, C. (1993) *Meaning, Skepticism. and Truth in the Immanent Naturalism of W. V. Quine*. PhD Dissertation. Graduate Center, CUNY.

Clark, E. V. (1973) What's in a word? On the child's acquisition of semantics in his first language. In T. E. Moore (ed.), *Cognitive Development and the Acquisition of Language*, 65–110. New York: Academic Press.

Clark, E. V. and Clark, H. H. (1979) When nouns surface as verbs. *Language*, 55, 547–90.

Clark, H. (1973) Space, time, semantics, and the child. In T. E. Moore (ed.), *Cognitive Development and the Acquisition of Language*, 27–64. New York: Academic Press.

—— (1987) Relevance to what? *Behavioral and Brain Sciences*, 10, 714–15.

Clark, H. and W. Chase (1972) On the process of comparing sentences against pictures. *Cognitive Psychology*, 3, 472–517.

Clark, H. and Schaefer, E. (1989) Contributing to discourse. In: H. Clark, *Arenas of Language Use*, Stanford: CSLI publications, CSLI.

Clark, R. (1992) Scope assignment and modification. *Linguistic Inquiry*, 23, 1–28.

Cole, P. (ed.) (1978) *Syntax and Semantics 9: Pragmatics*. New York: Academic Press.

—— (ed.) (1981) *Radical Pragmatics*. New York: Academic Press.

Cole, P. and Morgan, J. L. (eds), (1975) *Syntax and Semantics 3: Speech acts*. New York: Academic Press.

Coleman, L. and Kay, P. (1981) Prototype semantics: The English verb lie. *Language*, 57, 26–44.

Comrie, B. (1985) *Tense*. Cambridge: Cambridge University Press.

Contreras, E. (1984) A Note on parasitic gaps. *Linguistic Inquiry*, 15, 704–13.

—— (1993) On null operator structures. *Natural Language and Linguistic Theory*, 11, 1–30.

Cooper, R. (1975) *Montague's Semantic Theory and Transformational Grammar*. PhD Dissertation. Amherst: University of Massachusetts, University of Massachusetts Graduate Linguistics Students Association.

—— (1979) The interpretation of pronouns. In F. Heny and H. S. Schnelle (eds), *Syntax and Semantics 10: Selections from the Third Groningen Round Table*, 61–92. New York: Academic Press.

—— (1983) *Quantification and Syntactic Theory*. Dordrecht: Reidel.

—— (1986) Tense and discourse location in situation semantics. *Linguistics and Philosophy*, 9, 17–36.

—— (1987) Preliminaries to the analysis of generalized quantifiers in situation semantics. In P. Gärdenfors (ed.) *Generalized Quantifiers: Linguistic and Logical Approaches*. Dordrecht: Reidel.

—— (1990) *Classification-based Phrase Structure Grammar: an Extended Revised Version of HPSG*. PhD Thesis. Edinburgh: Centre for Cognitive Science.

—— (1991) Persistence and structural determination. In Barwise, Gawron, Plotkin and Tutiya (eds) (1991), 295–309.

—— (1991) Three lectures on situation theoretic grammar. In Filgueiras, Damas, Moreira and Tomás (eds), 101–40.

—— (1992) A working person's guide to situation theory. In Hansen and Sørensen (1992), 7–38.

—— (1993a) Generalized quantifiers and resource situations. In Aczel, Israel, Katagiri and Peters (eds) (1993), 191–212.

—— (1993b) Towards a general semantic framework, In R. Cooper (ed.), *Integrating Semantic Theories*. DYANA–2 Deliverable R2.1.A.

Cooper, R. and Ginzburg, J. (1994) A compositional situation semantics for attitude reports. Forthcoming in J. Seligman (ed.), *Language, Logic and Computation: The 1994 Moraga Proceedings*. CSLI Lecture notes. Stanford: CSLI.

Cooper, R. and Parsons, T. (1976) Montague grammar, generative semantics, and interpretive semantics. In B. H. Partee (ed.), *Montague Grammar*, 311–62. New York: Academic Press.

Cooper, R. and Poesio M. (1994a) Generalized quantifiers and scope: situation semantics. In Cooper et al. (1994b).

—— (1994b) Situation semantics. In Cooper et al. (1994a).

Cooper, R., Crouch, R., van Eijck, J., Fox, C., van Genabith J., Jaspers, J., Kamp, H., Pinkal M., Poesio, M., Pulman, S. and Vestre, E. (1994b) *The State of the Art in Computational Semantics: Evaluating the Descriptive Capabilities of Semantic Theories*. FraCaS Deliverable D9, Centre for Cognitive Science, University of Edinburgh.

Cooper, R., Mulai, K. and Perry, J. (eds) (1990) *Situation Theory and its Applications*. Vol. 1. Stanford: CSLI Lecture Notes 22.

Coppola, Francis F. (1973) *The Conversation*.

Cormack, A. (1985) VP anaphora: variables and scope. In F. Landman and F. Veltman (eds), *Varieties of Formal Semantics*. Dordrecht: Foris.

Coseriu, E. (1979) *Probleme der Strukturellen Semantik*, Tübingen.

Cresswell, M. J. (1973) *Logics and Languages*. London: Methuen.

—— (1978) Semantic competence. In M. Guenthner-Reutter and F. Guenthner (eds), *Meaning and Translation: Philosophical and Linguistic Approaches*. London: Duckworth.

—— (1985) *Structured Meanings*. Cambridge, MA: MIT Press.

—— (1988) *Semantical Essays: Possible Worlds and their Rivals*. Dordrecht: Kluwer.

Cresswell, M. J. and von Stechow, A. (1982) *De re* belief generalized, *Linguistics and Philosophy*, 5, 503–35.

Crimmins, M. (1993) *Talk about Beliefs*. Cambridge, MA: MIT Press.

Curry, H. and Feys, R. (1958) *Combinatory Logic*. Amsterdam: North-Holland.

Dalrymple, M. (1991) *Against Reconstruction in Ellipsis*. ms., Palo Alto, CA: Xerox-PARC.

Dalrymple, M., Shieber, S. and Pereira, F. (1991) Ellipsis and higher-order unification. *Linguistics and Philosophy*, 14, 399–452.

Daneš, F. (1957) *Intonace a veta ve Spisovné cestiné* (*Intonation and Sentence in Standard Czech*). Praha.

Davidson, D. (1967a) The logical form of action sentences. In N. Rescher (ed.), *The Logic of Decision and Action*. Pittsburgh, PA: University of Pittsburgh Press.

—— (1967b) Truth and meaning. *Synthese*, XVII, 304–23.

—— (1968) On saying that. *Synthese*, XIX, 130–46.

—— (1970) Semantics for natural languages. In B. Visentini et al. (eds), *Linguaggi nella Società e nella Tecnica*. Milan: Edizioni di Comunità.

—— (1984) Inquiries into Truth and Interpretation. Oxford: Oxford University Press.

Davidson, D. and Harman, G. F. (eds) (1972) *Semantics of Natural Language*. Dordrecht: Reidel.

Davis, A. (1995) *Linking and the Hierarchical Lexicon*. PhD Thesis, Stanford University.

De Morgan, A. (1847) *Formal Logic*. London: Taylor and Walton.

de Swart, H. (1991) *Adverbs of Quantification: a Generalized Quantifier Approach*. PhD Dissertation, Rijksuniversiteit Groningen.

Dekker, P. (1992) An update semantics for dynamic predicate logic, in P. Dekker and M. Stokhof (eds), *Proceedings of the Eighth Amsterdam Colloquium*, 113–32. Amsterdam: ILLC, University of Amsterdam.

—— (1993a) Existential disclosure. *Linguistics and Philosophy*, 16, 561–88.

—— (1993b) *Transsentential Meditations. Ups and Downs in Dynamic Semantics*, PhD Thesis. Amsterdam: ILLC/Department of Philosophy, University of Amsterdam.

Dennett, M. (1987) *The Intentional Stance*. Cambridge, MA: MIT Press.

Devlin, K. (1991) *Logic and Information*. Cambridge: Cambridge University Press.

Diesing, M. (1990) *The Syntactic Roots of Semantic Partition*. PhD Dissertation. Amherst: University of Massachusetts.

—— (1992) *Indefinites*. Cambridge, MA: MIT Press.

Dokulil, M. and Daneš, F. (1958) Semantic and grammatical structure of the sentence. (in Czech) In O *Vedeckem Poznaní Soudobých Jazyku*, 231–46, Prague: Nakladatelstvi ČSAV. English trans. in P. Luelsdorff, J. Panevová and P. Sgall (eds) (1994), *Praguina 1945–1990*, 21–37, Amsterdam, Benjamins.

Donnellan, K. (1962) Necessity and criteria. *The Journal of Philosophy*, LIX, 647–58.

—— (1966) Reference and definite descriptions. *The Philosophical Review*, LXXV, 281–304.

—— (1974) Speaking of nothing. *The Philosophical Review*, LXXXIII, 20–1.

van der Does, J. (1992) *Applied Quantifier Logics*. Dissertation. University of Amsterdam.

van der Does, J. and van Eijck, J. (eds) (forthcoming) *Quantifiers in Natural Language*. Stanford, CA: CSLI Lecture Notes.

Dowty, D. (1972) *Studies in the Logic of Verb Aspect and Time Reference in English* (= Studies in Linguistics 1) Austin: University of Texas.

—— (1978) Governed transformations as lexical rules in a Montague grammar. *Linguistic Inquiry*, 9, 393–426.

—— (1979) *Word Meaning and Montague Grammar*. Dordrecht: Reidel.

—— (1982a) Grammatical relations and Montague grammar. In P. Jacobson and G. K. Pullum (eds), *The Nature of Syntactic Representation*, 79–130. Dordrecht: Reidel.

—— (1982b) Tenses, time adverbs, and compositional semantic theory. *Linguistics and Philosophy*, 5, 23–55.

—— (1986) A note on collective predicates, distributive predicates and all. In Marshall (ed.), *ESCOL*, 86. Columbus: Ohio State University.

—— (1987) Type raising, functional composition, and non-constituent conjunction. In R. Qehrle, E. Bach, and D. Wheeler (eds), *Categorial Grammars and Natural Languages Structures*, 153–98. Dordrecht: Reidel.

—— (1989) On the semantic content of the notion thematic role. In B. Partee, G. Chierchia, and R. Turner (eds), 69–130.

—— (1991) Thematic proto-roles and argument selection. *Language*, 67, 547–619.

—— (1992) Variable-free syntax, variable-binding syntax, the natural deduction Lambek calculus, and the crossover constraint. In *Proceedings of the 11th Meeting of the West Coast Conference on Formal Linguistics*. Stanford, CA: CSLI Lecture Notes.

—— (1994) The role of negative polarity and concord marking in natural language reasoning. In M. Harvey and L. Santelmann (eds), *SALT IV: Proceedings of the 4th conference on Semantics and Linguistic Theory*. Ithaca, NY: Cornell University, Dept. of Modern Languages and Linguistics.

Dowty, D., Wall, R. E. and Peters, S. (1981) *Introduction to Montague Semantics*. Dordrecht: Reidel.

Dretske, F. (1972) Contrastive statements. *Philosophical Review*, 81, 411–37.

Dummett, M. (1977) *Elements of Intuitionism*. Oxford: Clarendon Press.

Dunn, J. M. (forthcoming) Star and perp: two treatments of negation. In J. Tomberlin (ed.), *Philosophical Perspectives: Philosophical Logic*. Vols. 7–8.

Edelberg, W. (1986) A new puzzle about intentional identity. *Journal of Philosophical Logic*, 15, 1–25.

van Eijck, J. (1993) The dynamics of description. *Journal of Semantics*, 10, 239–67.

—— and Cepparello, G. (forthcoming) Dynamic modal predicate logic. In M. Kanazawa and C. Piñon (eds), *Dynamics, Polarity and Quantification*. Stanford: CSLI.

van Eijck, J. and de Vries, F.-J. (1992) Dynamic interpretation and Hoare deduction. *Journal of Logic, Language and Information*, 1, 1–44.

—— (forthcoming) Reasoning about update logic. *Journal of Philosophical Logic*.

van Eijck, J. and Francez, N. (1994) Verb phrase ellipsis in dynamic semantics. In M. Masuch and L. Polos (eds), *Applied Logic: How, What and Why?* Dordrecht: Kluwer.

van Eijck, J. and Kamp. H. (forthcoming) Representing discourse in context. To appear in J. F. A. K. van Benthem and A. ter Meulen (eds), *Handbook of Logic and Language*. Amsterdam: Elsevier Science B. V.

Enç, M. (1981) *Tense without Scope: An Analysis of Nouns as Indexicals*. PhD Dissertation. University of Wisconsin-Madison.

—— (1986) Towards a referential analysis of temporal expressions. *Linguistics and Philosophy*, 9, 405–26.

—— (1987) Anchoring conditions for tense. *Linguistic Inquiry*, 18, 633–57.

—— (1990) *Tenses and Time Arguments*. Talk delivered at MIT Time Conference.

Enderton, H. B. (1972) *A Mathematical Introduction to Logic*. New York: Academic Press.

Engdahl, E. (1986) *Constituent Questions*. Dordrecht: Reidel.

Erteschek-Shir, N. and Lappin, S. (1979) Dominance and the functional explanation of island phenomena. *Theoretical Linguistics*, 6, 41–85.

Etchemendy, J. (1990) *The Concept of Logical Consequence*. Cambridge, MA: Harvard University Press.

Evans, G. (1977) Pronouns, quantifiers and relative clauses (I) *Canadian Journal of Philosophy*, 7, 467–536.

—— (1980) Pronouns. *Linguistic Inquiry*, 11, 337–62.

Evans, G. and McDowell, J. (1976) *Truth and Meaning: Essays in Semantics*. Oxford: Clarendon Press.

Farkas, D. (1993) *Modal Anchoring and Noun Phrase Scope*. Ms., University of California at Santa Cruz.

Fauconnier, G. (1975) Polarity and the scale principle. In R. E. Grossman, L. J. San and T. J. Vance (eds), *Proceedings of the 11th Meeting of the Chicago Linguistic Society*, 188–99.

—— (1979) Implication reversal in natural language. In F. Guenthner and S. Schmidt (eds), *Formal Semantics for Natural Language*. Dordrecht: Reidel.

—— (1985) *Mental Spaces*. Cambridge, MA: MIT Press.

Fenstad, J. E., Halvorsen, P.-K., Langholm, T. and van Benthem, J. (1987) *Situations, Language, and Logic*. Dordrecht: Reidel.

Fernando, T. (1991) *Mathematical Foundations of Situation Theory*. Stanford University PhD Dissertation.

Ferreira, F. and Clifton, C. (1986) The independence of syntactic processing. *Journal of Memory and Language*, 25, 348–68.

Fiengo, R. and May, R. (1993) The eliminative puzzles of ellipsis. In S. Berman and A. Hestvik (eds), *Proceedings of the Stuttgart Ellipsis Workshop*. Stuttgart.

—— (1994) *Indices and Identity*. Cambridge, MA: MIT Press.

Filgueiras, M., Damas, L., Moreira, N. and Tomás, A. P. (eds) (1991) Natural Language Processing, EAIA 90, Proceedings, *Lecture Notes in Artificial Intelligence*, No. 476. Springer Verlag.

Fillmore, Charles, J. (1968) The case for case. In E. Bach and R. T. Harms (eds), *Universals in Linguistic Theory*, 1–88. New York: Holt, Rinehart and Winston.

—— (1971) Types of lexical information. In D. Steinberg and L. Jakobovits (eds), *Semantics. An Interdisciplinary Reader in Philosophy, Linguistics, and Psychology*, 370–92. Cambridge: Cambridge University Press.

—— (1982) Towards a descriptive framework for spatial deixis. In R. Jarvella and W. Klein (eds), *Speech, Place, and Action*, 31–59. New York: Wiley.

Finger, M. and Gabbay, D. (1993) Adding a temporal dimension to a logic system. *Journal of Logic, Language and Information*, 1, 203–33.

von Fintel, K. (1993) Exceptive constructions. *Natural Language Semantics*, 1, 123–48.

—— (1994) Conditionals as Quantifier Restrictors. PhD Thesis. University of Massachusetts at Amherst.

Flickinger, D. and Nerbonne J. (1992) Inheritance and complementation: a case study of easy adjectives and related nouns. *Computational Linguistics*, 19, 269–309.

Flynn, M. (1981) *Structure Building Operations and Word Order*. Doctoral Dissertation. Amherst: University of Massachusetts. Distributed by Graduate Linguistic Student Association.

Fodor, J. A. (1975) *The Language of Thought*. Cambridge, MA: Harvard University Press.

—— (1983) *Modularity of Mind*. Cambridge, MA: MIT Press.

—— (1987) *Psychosemantics: The Problem of Meaning in the Philosophy of Mind*. Cambridge, MA: Bradford Books, MIT Press.

—— (1990) *A Theory of Content and Other Essays*. Cambridge, MA: MIT Press.

Fodor, J. A., Bever, T. and Garrett, M. (1974) *The Psychology of Language*. New York: McGraw-Hill.

Fodor, J. A., Garrett, M., Walker, E. and Parkes, C. (1980) Against definitions. *Cognition*, 8, 263–367.

Fodor, J. D. (1979) In defense of truth-value gaps. In C.-K. Oh and D. A. Dinneen (eds), 199–294.

—— (1980) *Semantics: Theories of Meaning in Generative Grammar*. Cambridge, MA: Harvard University Press.

—— (1982) The mental representation of quantifiers. In S. Peters and E. Saarinen (eds), *Processes, Beliefs, and Questions*. Dordrecht: Reidel.

Fodor, J. D. and Sag, I. (1982) Referential and quantificational indefinites. *Linguistics and Philosophy*, 5, 355–98.

Fraassen, B. van (1968) Presupposition, implication, and self-reference. *Journal of Philosophy*, 65, 136–57.

Frege, G. (1879) *Begriffsschrift, eine der arithmetischen nachgebildete Formelsprache des reinen Denkens*. Halle: Nebert. Translated by T. W. Bynum, in *Conceptual Notation and Related Articles*, Oxford: Clarendon Press.

—— (1892) Über Sinn und Bedeutung. *Zeitschrift für Philosophie und philosophische Kritik*, 100, 25–50. Translated as On sense and reference. In P. T. Geach and M. Black (eds), *Translations from the Philosophical Writings of Gottlob Frege*, 56–78. Oxford: Blackwell (1952).

—— (1953) *The Foundations of Arithmetic*. Oxford: Basil Blackwell. Berkeley: University of California Press.

French, P., Uehling, T. Jr. and Wettstein, H. (eds) (1979) *Contemporary Perspectives in the Philosophy of Language.* Minneapolis: University of Minnesota Press.

Gabbay, D. (1993) *Labelled Deductive Systems and Situation Theory.* Ms. Imperial College, London.

—— (forthcoming) *Labelled Deductive Systems.* Oxford: Oxford University Press.

Gabbay, D. and de Queiroz, R. (1992) *Labelled Deductive Systems: a synopsis.* Ms. London.

—— (1993) Extending the Curry–Howard–Tait interpretation to linear, relevant and other logics. *Journal of Symbolic Logic,* 56, 1139–40.

Gabbay, D. and Kempson, R. (1992) Natural-language content: a truth-theoretic perspective. In *Proceedings of the 8th Amsterdam Formal Semantics Colloquium.* Amsterdam: University of Amsterdam.

Gale, W., Church, K. and Yarowsky, D. (1992) A method for disambiguating word senses in a large corpus. *Computers and the Humanities,* 26, 415–440.

Gallin, D. (1975) *Intensional and Higher Order Modal Logic.* Amsterdam: North Holland.

Gamut, L. T. F. (1991) *Logic, Language and Meaning.* Chicago: University of Chicago Press.

García-Carpintero, M. (1993) The grounds for the model theoretic account of the logical properties. *Notre Dame Journal of Formal Logic,* 34, 107–31.

Gärdenfors, P. (1984) The dynamics of belief as a basis for a logic, *British Journal for The Philosophy of Sciences,* 35.

—— (ed.) (1987) *Generalized Quantifiers.* Dordrecht: Reidel.

Gardent, C. (1991) Dynamic semantics and VP-ellipsis. In J. van Eijck (ed.), *Logics in AI,* 251–67. Berlin: Springer.

Gawron, J. M. (1992) Focus and ellipsis in comparatives and superlatives: A case study. In C. Barker and D. Dowty (eds), *The Proceedings from the Second Conference on Semantics and Linguistic Theory: SALT II,* 79–98. Ohio State University Working Papers in Linguistics, Number 40. Department of Linguistics, Ohio State University.

Gawron, J. M. and Peters, S. (1990) *Quantification and Anaphora in Situation Semantics.* Standord, CA: CSLI Lecture Notes.

Gazdar, G. (1979) *Pragmatics.* New York: Academic Press.

—— (1980) A cross-categorial semantics for coordination. *Linguistics and Philosophy,* 3, 407–9.

—— (1982) Phrase structure grammar. In P. Jacobson and G. Pullum (eds), *The Nature of Syntactic Representation,* 131–86. Dordrecht: Reidel.

Gazdar, G., Klein, E., Pullum, G. and Sag, I. (1985) *Generalized Phrase Structure Grammar.* Oxford: Basil Blackwell.

Geach, P. T. (1962) *Reference and Generality: An Examination of Some Medieval and Modern Theories.* Ithaca: Cornell University Press.

—— (1967) Intentional identity. *Journal of Philosophy,* 64, 627–32.

—— (1971) A program for syntax. *Synthese,* 22, 3–17.

—— (1976) Back-reference. In A. Kasher, *Language in Focus.* Dordrecht: Reidel.

Gibb, R. (1987) The relevance of Relevance for psychological theory. *Behavioral and Brain Sciences,* 10, 718–19.

Gil, D. (1982) Quantifier scope, linguistic variation, and natural language semantics. *Linguistics and Philosophy,* 5, 421–72.

—— (1988) Georgian reduplication and the domain of distributivity, *Linguistics,* 26.

Gillon, B. (1987) The readings of plural noun phrases. *Linguistics and Philosophy,* 10.

Ginzburg, J. (1992) *Questions, Queries and Facts: a Semantics and Pragmatics for Interrogatives.* Stanford University PhD Dissertation.

—— (1993) Propositional and non-propositional attitudes. In Aczel, Katagiri, Israel and Peters (eds).

—— (1994a) Resolving questions. In Hans Kamp (ed.) DYANA Report R2.2.B *Ellipsis, Tense, and Questions.*

—— (1994b) Dynamics and the semantics of dialogue. To appear in J. Seligman (ed.), *Language, Logic and Computation: The 1994 Moraga Proceedings.* Stanford, CA: CSLI Lecture Notes.

—— (1994c) An update semantics for dialogue. In H. Bunt, R. Muskens, and G. Rentier (eds), *Proceedings of the International Workshop on Computational Semantics*. Tilburg: ITK.

—— (1995) The quantificational variability effect (QVE) to some extent defused and generalized. In J. Beckman (ed.), *Proceedings of NELS 25*, GLSA, University of Massachusetts.

—— (this volume). Interrogatives: Questions, facts and dialogue.

Goldberg, A. E. (1995) *Constructions: A Construction Grammar Approach to Argument Structure*. Chicago, IL: University of Chicago Press.

Goodman, N. (1952) On likeness of meaning. In L. Linsky (ed.), *Semantics and the Philosophy of Language*, 67–74. Urbana: University of Illinois Press.

Green, G. (1990) The universality of Gricean interpretation. *BLS* 16, 411–28.

Grice, H. P. (1961) The causal theory of perception. *Proceedings of the Aristotelian Society*, Supplementary Volume, 35, 121–52.

—— (1975) Logic and conversation. In P. Cole and J. Morgan (eds), *Speech acts: Syntax and Semantics*, 3, 41–58. New York: Academic Press.

—— (1989) *Studies in the Way of Words*. Cambridge, MA: Harvard University Press.

—— (1981) Presupposition and conversational implicature. In Cole, P. (ed.), *Radical Pragmatics*, 183–98. New York: Academic Press.

Groenendijk, J., Janssen, T. and Stokhof, M. (eds) (1981) *Formal Methods in the Study of Language*. Amsterdam: Mathematisch Centrum.

Groenendijk, J. and Stokhof, M. (1983) Interrogative quantifiers and skolem functions. In K. Ehlich and H. van Riemsdijk (eds), *Connectedness in Sentence, Discourse and Text*. Tilburg: Tilburg Studies in Language and Literature 4.

—— (1984) *Studies on the Semantics of Questions and the Pragmatics of Answers*. Unpublished doctoral dissertation. Amsterdam: University of Amsterdam,.

—— (1988) Context and information in dynamic semantics. In B. Elsendoorn and H. Bouma (eds), *Working Models of Human Perception*, 457–88. New York: Academic Press.

—— (1989) Type-shifting rules and the semantics of interrogatives. In G. Chierchia et al. (eds), *Properties, Types, and Meaning, Volume II: Semantic Issues*, 21–68. Dordrecht: Kluwer.

—— (1990a) Dynamic Montague grammar. In L. Kalman and L. Polos (eds), *Papers from the Second Symposium on Logic and Grammar*, 3–48. Budapest: Akademiai Kiado.

—— (1990b) Partitioning logical space. *2nd ESLLI lecture notes*, Leuven.

—— (1990c), Two theories of dynamic semantics. In J. van Eijck (ed.), *Logics in AI*, 55–4. Berlin: Springer.

—— (1991) Dynamic predicate logic. *Linguistics and Philosophy*, 14, 39–100.

—— (1993) Interrogatives and adverbs of quantification. In K. Bimbo and A. Mate (eds), *Proceedings of the 4th Symposium on Logic and Language*, Budapest.

Groenendijk, J., Stokhof, M. and Veltman, F. (this volume). Coreference and Modality.

—— (forthcoming) Coreference and contextually restricted quantification. In *Proceedings SALT V*. Austin.

Groeneveld, W. (1994) Dynamic semantics and circular propositions. *Journal of Philosophical Logic*, 23, 267–306.

Gruber, J. S. (1965) *Studies in Lexical Relations*. PhD Dissertation, MIT, Cambridge, MA. Also published in J. Gruber (1976) *Lexical Structures in Syntax and Semantics*. Amsterdam: North-Holland.

Hacking, I. (1979) What is logic? *Journal of Philosophy*, 76, 285–319.

Haddock, N. (1988) *Incremental Semantics and Interactive Syntactic Processing*. PhD Thesis, Edinburgh.

Haegeman, L. and Zanuttini, R. (1990) *Negative Concord in West Flemish*. Ms. University of Geneva.

Haik, I. (1984) Indirect binding, *Linguistic Inquiry*, 15, 185–223.

—— (1987) Bound variables that need to be. *Linguistics and Philosophy*, 11, 503–30.

Haiman, J. (1980) *Hua: A Papuan Language of the Eastern Highlands of New Guinea.* Studies in Language Companion Series 5. Amsterdam: John Benjamins.

Hajičová, E. and Sgall, P. (1987) The ordering principle. *Journal of Pragmatics*, 11, 435–54.

Hajičová, E., Partee, B. and Sgall, P. (in preparation) *Topic-Focus Articulation, Tripartite Structures, and Semantic Content.*

Halliday M. A. K. (1967) Notes on transitivity and theme. *Journal of Linguistics*, 3, 199–244.

Halvorsen, P.-K. (1983) Semantics for lexical-functional grammar. *Linguistic Inquiry*, 14, 567–615.

—— (1988) Situation semantics and semantic interpretation in constraint-based grammars. In *Proceedings of the International Conference on Fifth Generation Computer Systems*, FGCS-88, 471–8. Tokyo. Also published, as CSLI Technical Report CSLI-TR-101, Stanford University (1987).

Halvorsen, P.-K. and Ladusaw, W. A. (1979) Montague's 'Universal grammar': An introduction for the linguist. *Linguistics and Philosophy*, 3, 185–223.

Hamblin, C. L. (1970) *Fallacies.* Methuen: London.

—— (1973) Questions in Montague grammar. *Foundations of Language*, 10, 41–53. Reprinted in B. H. Partee (ed.) (1976), *Montague Grammar*, 247–59. New York: Academic Press.

Hamilton, Sir W. (1860) *Lectures on Logic, Volume I.* Edinburgh: Blackwood.

Hand, M. (1988) The Dependency Constraint – Global constraint on strategies in Game-Theoretical Semantics, *Linguistics and Philosophy*, 395–413.

Hankamer, J. and Sag, I. (1976) Deep and surface anaphora. *Linguistic Inquiry*, 7, 391–428.

Hansen, S. L. and Sørensen, F. (eds) (1992) *Topics in Semantic Interpretation.* Frederiksberg: Samfundsliteratur.

Hardt, D. (1991) A Discourse model approach to VP-ellipsis. *Proceedings of the AAAI Symposium on Discourse Structure in Natural Language Understanding and Generation.* Asilomar, CA.

—— (1992) VP ellipsis and semantic identity. In S. Berman and A. Hestvik (eds), *Proceedings of the Stuttgart Ellipsis Workshop*, Arbeitspapiere des Sonderforschungsbereichs 340, Bericht Nr. 29. Heidelberg: IBM Germany.

—— (1993) *Verb Phrase Ellipsis: Form, Meaning, and Processing.* Unpublished PhD Dissertation. Philadelphia, PA: University of Pennsylvania.

Harris, R. A. (1993) *The Linguistics Wars.* New York and Oxford: Oxford University Press.

Harris, Z. (1954) Distributional structure. *Word*, 10, 146–62.

—— (1957) Co-occurrence and transformation in linguistic structure. *Language*, 33, 283–340.

—— (1965) Transformational theory. *Language*, 41, 363–401.

—— (1968) *The Mathematics of Language.* Dordrecht: Reidel.

Hausser, R. (1983) On questions. In F. Kiefer (ed.).

Hausser, R. and Zaefferer, D. (1979) Questions and answers in a context dependent Montague grammar. In Guenthner and Schmidt (eds), *Formal Semantics and Pragmatics for Natural Languages.* Dordrecht: Reidel.

Heim, I. (1982) *The Semantics of Definite and Indefinite Noun Phrases*, PhD. Thesis. University of Massachusetts at Amherst. Published (1989) New York: Garland.

—— (1983) On the projection problem for presuppositions. In M. Barlow, D. Flickinger and M. Wescoat (eds), *Second Annual West Coast Conference on Formal Linguistics*, 114–25. Stanford University.

—— (1984) A note on negative polarity and downward entailingness. In C. Jones and P. Sells (eds), *Proceedings of NELS*, 14, 98–107.

—— (1990) E-Type pronouns and donkey anaphora. *Linguistics and Philosophy*, 13, 137–77.

—— (1992) Presupposition projection and the semantics of attitude verbs. *Journal of Semantics*, 9, 183–221.

Heim, I. and Kratzer, A. (unpublished) [textbook on formal semantics, title unknown],

Hendriks, H. (1987) Type change in semantics: the scope of quantification and coordination. In E. Klein and J. van Benthem (eds), *Categories, Polymorphism and Unification*, 96–119. Edinburgh: Centre for Cognitive Science and Amsterdam: ITLI, University of Amsterdam.

—— (1993) *Studied flexibility: Categories and types in syntax and semantics*. ILLC Dissertation Series 1993–5. Amsterdam: Institute for Logic, Language and Computation, University of Amsterdam.

Hepple, M. (1990) *The Grammar of Processing of Order and Dependency: A Categorial Approach*. PhD Dissertation, University of Edinburgh.

Herburger, E. (forthcoming) Focus on noun phrases. In P. Spaelti, D. Farkas and E. Duncan (eds), *Proc. of WCCFL 12*. Stanford: CSLI.

Herskovits, A. (1986) *Language and Spatial Cognition: An Interdisciplinary Study of the Prepositions in English*. Cambridge: Cambridge University Press.

Higginbotham, J. (1983) The logic of perceptual reports: an extensional alternative to situation semantics, *Journal of Philosophy*, 80, 100–27.

—— (1985) On semantics. *Linguistic Inquiry*, 16, 547–93.

—— (1986) Davidson's program in semantics. In E. Lepore (ed.), *Truth and Interpretation*, 29–48. Oxford: Basil Blackwell.

—— (1991) Interrogatives I. *MIT Working Papers in Linguistics*, XV, 47–76.

—— (1993) Interrogatives. In Hale, K. and Keyser, S. J. (eds), *The View from Building 20: Essays in Linguistics in Honor of Sylvain Bromberger*, 195–227. Cambridge, MA: MIT Press.

—— (this volume) The Semantics of Questions.

Higginbotham, J. and May, R. (1978) A General theory of crossing coreference. *CUNYForum: Proceedings, NELS IX*, 328–36. New York: Graduate Center of the City University, New York.

—— (1981) Questions, quantifiers and crossing. *Linguistic Review*, 1, 41–79.

Hilbert, D. and Ackermann, W. (1938) *Principles of Mathematical Logic* (2nd edition, trans. L. M. Hammond, et al.). New York: Chelsea. (1st German ed. 1928.)

Hindle, D. and Rooth, M. (1993) Structural ambiguity and lexical relations. *Computational Linguistics*, 19, Special issue on using large corpora, I. 103–20.

Hinrichs, E. (1985) *A Compositional Semantics for Aktions arten and NP-Reference in English*. Dissertation. Columbus: Ohio State University.

Hintikka, K. J. J. (1962) *Knowledge and Belief*. Ithaca: Cornell University Press.

—— (1969) *Models for Modalities: Selected Essays*. Dordrecht: Reidel.

—— (1973a) Carnap's semantics in retrospect. *Synthese*, 25, 372.

—— (1973b) Quantifiers vs. quantification theory. *Dialectica*, 27, 329–58.

—— (1976a) Answers to questions. In H. Hiz (ed.) (1978).

—— (1976b) The semantics of questions and the questions of semantics. *Acta Philosophica Fennica*, 28, 4. Amsterdam: North-Holland.

—— (1983a) New foundations for a theory of questions and answers. In F. Kiefer (ed.) (1983) *Questions and Answers*. Dordrecht: Reidel.

—— (1983b) *The Game of Language*. Dordrecht: Reidel.

Hintikka, K. J. J. and Hintikka, M. B. (1989) *The Logic of Epistemology and the Epistemology of Logic*. Dordrecht: Kluwer.

Hintikka, K. J. J. and Kulas, J. (1985) *Anaphora and Definite Descriptions: Two Applications of Game-Theoretical Semantics*. Dordrecht: Reidel.

Hintikka, K. J. J., Moravcsik, J. M. E. and Suppes P. (eds) (1973) *Approaches to Natural*

Language: Proceedings of the 1970 Stanford Workshop on Grammar and Semantics. Dordrecht: Reidel.

Hirschberg, J. (1985) *A Theory of Scalar Implicature.* University of Pennsylvania dissertation.

Hiz, H. (ed.) (1978) *Questions.* Dordrecht: Reidel.

Hoeksema, J. (1983) Negative polarity and the comparative. *Natural Language and Linguistic Theory*, 1, 403–34.

—— (1986) Monotonicity phenomena in natural language. *Linguistic Analysis*, 16, 25–40.

—— (1988) The semantics of non-Boolean *and. Journal of Semantics*, 6.

—— (1991) The semantics of exception phrases. In J. van der Does and J. van Eijk (eds), *Generalized Quantifiers and Applications, Dutch Network for Language, Logic, and Information*, 245–74. Amsterdam.

Hoekstra, T. (1984) *Transitivity.* Dordrecht: Foris.

—— (1988) Small clause results. *Lingua*, 74, 101–39.

—— (1992) Aspect and theta theory. In I. M. Roca (ed.), *Thematic structure: Its Role in Grammar*, 145–74. Berlin: Walter de Gruyter.

Horn, L. (1969) A presuppositional theory of only and even. *CLS*, 5. Chicago Linguistic Society.

—— (1972) *On the Semantic Properties of Logical Operators in English.* UCLA dissertation. Distributed by Indiana University Linguistics Club (1976).

—— (1984) Toward a new taxonomy for pragmatic inference: Q-based and R-based implicature. In Schiffrin, D. (ed.), *Meaning, Form, and Use in Context: Linguistic Applications (GURT 84)*, 11–42. Washington: Georgetown University Press.

—— (1985) Metalinguistic negation and pragmatic ambiguity. *Language*, 61, 121–74.

—— (1986) Presupposition, theme and variations. *Papers from the Parasession on Pragmatics and Grammatical Theory, CLS* 22/2, 168–92.

—— (1989) *A Natural History of Negation.* Chicago: University of Chicago Press.

—— (1990a) Showdown at truth-value gap: Burton-Roberts on presupposition. *Journal of Linguistics*, 26, 483–503.

—— (1990b) Hamburgers and truth: why Gricean inference is Gricean. *BLS* 16, 454–71.

—— (1991) Duplex negatio affirmat . . . : The Economy of Double Negation. In *Papers from the Parasession on Negation, CLS* 27/2, 80–106.

—— (1992) The said and the unsaid. *SALT II: Proceedings of the Second Conference on Semantics and Linguistic Theory*, 163–92. Columbus: Ohio State University, Department of Linguistics.

—— (1993) Economy and redundancy in a dualistic model of natural language. In Shore, S. and M. Vilkuna (eds), *1993 Yearbook of the Linguistic Association of Finland*, 33–72.

Hornstein, N. (1977) Towards a theory of tense. *Linguistic Inquiry*, 8, 521–57.

—— (1990) *As time goes by.* Cambridge, MA: MIT Press.

—— (1994) An argument for minimalism: The case of antecedent-contained deletion. *Linguistic Inquiry*, 25, 455–80.

Houghton, G. and Isard, S. (1986) Why to speak, what to say and how to say it: modelling language production in discourse. In P. Morris (ed.), *Modelling Cognition.* London: John Wiley.

Householder, F. (1971) *Linguistic Speculations.* Cambridge: Cambridge University Press.

Houtman, J. (1994) *Coordination and Constituency: A Study in Categorial Grammar.* PhD Thesis, Rijksuniversiteit Groningen.

Huang, J. (1982) *Logical Relations in Chinese and the Theory of Grammar.* Unpublished doctoral dissertation. Cambridge, MA: MIT Press.

Hughes, G. H. and Cresswell, M. J. (1968) *An Introduction to Modal Logic.* London: Methuen.

Hull, R. (1975) A semantics for superficial and embedded questions in natural language. In E. L. Keenan (1975).

Indurkhya, B. (1992) *Metaphor and Cognition: an Interactionist Approach*. Dordrecht: Kluwer.
Jackendoff, R. (1972) *Semantic Interpretation in Generative Grammar*, Cambridge, MA: MIT Press.
—— (1976) Toward an explanatory semantic representation. *Linguistic Inquiry*, 7, 89–150.
—— (1978) Grammar as evidence for conceptual structure. In M. Halle, J. Bresnan and G. Miller (eds), *Linguistic Theory and Psychological Reality*, 201–28. Cambridge, MA: MIT Press.
—— (1981) On Katz's autonomous semantics. *Language*, 57, 425–35.
—— (1983) *Semantics and Cognition*. Cambridge, MA: MIT Press.
—— (1987a) *Consciousness and the Computational Mind*. Cambridge, MA: MIT Press.
—— (1987b) The status of thematic relations in linguistic theory. *Linguistic Inquiry*, 18, 369–411.
—— (1990) *Semantic Structures*. Cambridge, MA: MIT Press.
—— (1992) *Languages of the Mind*. Cambridge, MA: MIT Press.
Jackendoff, R. and Aaron, D. (1991) Review of Lakoff and Turner (1989). *Language*, 67, 320–38.
Jacobs, J. (1983) *Fokus and Skalen*. Tübingen: Niemeyer.
—— (1988) Fokus-hintergrund-gliederung und Grammatik. In H. Altman (ed.), *Intonationsforschungen*, 183–216. Tübingen: Niemeyer.
Jacobson, P. (1992a) Antecedent contained deletion without logical form. In C. Barker and D. Dowty (eds), *Proceedings of the Second Conference on Semantics and Linguistic Theory*. Columbus: The Ohio State University.
—— (1992b) Bach–Peters sentences in a variable-free semantics. In P. Dekker and M. Stokhof (eds), *Proceedings of the Eighth Amsterdam Colloquium*. Amsterdam: University of Amsterdam Institute for Logic, Language, and Computation.
—— (1992c) Flexible categorial grammar: questions and prospects. In R. Levine (ed.), *Formal Grammar: Theory and Implementation*, 168–242. Oxford: Oxford University Press.
—— (1994) i-within-i effects in a variable free semantics and a categorial syntax. In P. Dekker et al. (eds), *Proceedings of the 9th Amsterdam Colloquium*. Amsterdam: University of Amsterdam Institute for Logic, Language, and Computation.
—— (this volume). The syntax/semantics interface in categorial grammar.
—— (forthcoming) The locality of interpretation: The case of binding. In F. Hamm and A. von Stechow (eds), *Proceedings of the Blaubeuren Symposium on Recent Developments in Natural Language Semantics*. Tübingen: University of Tübingen.
Janssen, T. M. V. (1983) *Foundations and Applications of Montague Grammar*. Amsterdam: Mathematisch Centrum.
Jespersen, O. (1924) *The Philosophy of Grammar*. London: George Allen and Unwin Ltd.
Johnsen, L. (1987) There-sentences and generalized quantifiers. In P. Gärdenfors (ed.), 93–107.
Johnson-Laird, P. N. (1983) *Mental Models: Towards a Cognitive Science of Language, Inference, and Consciousness*. Cambridge, MA: Harvard University Press.
Joshi, A. K. (1985) How much context-sensitivity is necessary for characterizing structural descriptions – Tree Adjoining Grammars. In D. Dowty, L. Karttunen and A. Zwicky (eds), *Natural Language Processing – Theoretical, Computational, and Psychological Perspectives*. Cambridge: Cambridge University Press.
—— (1990) Phrase structure and intonational phrases: Comments on the Chapters by Marcus and Steedman. In G. T. M. Altmann (ed.), *Cognitive Models of Speech Processing*, 513–31. Cambridge, MA: MIT Press.
Joshi, A. K., Levy, L. S. and Takahashi, M. (1975) Tree adjunct grammars. *Journal of Computer System Science*, 10.
Kadmon, N. (1987) *On Unique and-Non-Unique Reference and Asymmetric Quantification*. Dissertation, University of Massachusetts at Amherst. Published (1993), New York: Garland.

—— (1990) Uniqueness. *Linguistics and Philosophy*, 13, 273–324.

Kadmon, N. and Landman, F. (1993) Any. *Linguistics and Philosophy*, 16, 353–422.

Kahn, K. M. (1987) Partial evaluation as an example of the relation between programming methodology and artificial intelligence. In R. Hawley (ed.), *Artificial Intelligence Programming Environments*, 131–42. Chichester: Ellis Horwood.

Kalish, D. and Montague, R. (1964) *Logic: Techniques of Formal Reasoning*. New York: Harcourt, Brace, Jovanovich.

Kamp, H. (1979a) Instants, events and temporal reference. In R. Bäuerle et al. (eds), *Semantics from Different Points of View*, 376–417. Berlin: Springer Verlag.

—— (1979b) Semantics vs. pragmatics. In F. Guenthner and H. Schmidt (eds), *Formal Semantics and Pragmatics for Natural Languages*, 255–88. Dordrecht: Reidel.

—— (1981) A theory of truth and semantic representation. In J. Groenendijk, T. Janssen and M. Stokhof (eds), *Formal Methods in the Study of Language: Proceedings of the Third Amsterdam Colloquium. Mathematical Centre Tracts*, 277–322. Amsterdam. Reprinted in J. Groenendijk, T. M. V. Janssen and M. Stokhof (eds) (1984), *Truth, Interpretation and Information*, GRASS 2. Dordrecht: Foris.

—— (1990a) Comments on J. Groenendijk and M. Stokhof, 'Dynamic predicate logic'. In J. van Benthem and H. Kamp (eds), *Spatial and Dynamic Semantics*. DYANA Deliverable R2.1.A, University of Edinburgh Centre for Cognitive Science.

—— (1990b) Prolegomena to a structured theory of belief and other attitudes. In Anderson et al. *Propositional Attitudes*. Stanford: CSLI.

Kamp, H. and Partee, B. (forthcoming) Prototype theory and compositionality. To appear in *Cognition*.

Kamp, H. and Reyle, U. (1993) *From Discourse to Logic*. Dordrecht: Kluwer.

Kanazawa, M. (1994) Weak vs strong readings of donkey sentences and monotonicity inference in a dynamic setting. *Linguistics and Philosophy*, 17, 109–48.

Kanger, S. (1957a) The Morning Star paradox. *Theoria*, 23, 1–11.

—— (1957b) A note on quantification and modalities. *Theoria*, 23, 133–4.

Kaplan, D. (1964) *Foundations of Intensional Logic*. PhD Dissertation, University of California at Los Angeles.

—— (1977) Demonstratives. Widely circulated UCLA Ms.

—— (1979) The logic of demonstratives. In French et al. (eds) (1979), *Contemporary Perspectives in the Philosophy of Language*. Minneapolis: University of Minnesota Press.

—— (1989) Demonstratives. In J. Almog, J. Perry and H. Wettstein (eds), *Themes from Kaplan*. Oxford: Oxford University Press.

Kaplan, R. (1987) Three seductions of computational psycholinguistics. In P. Whitelock, M. M. Wood, H. Somers, R. Johnson and P. Bennett (eds), *Linguistic Theory and Computer Applications*, 149–88. London: Academic Press.

Kaplan, R. and Bresnan, J. (1982) *The Mental Representation of Grammatical Relations*. Cambridge, MA: MIT Press, 173–281.

Karttunen, L. (1969) Pronouns and variables. In *Papers from the Fifth Regional Meeting of the Chicago Linguistic Society*, 108–15. University of Chicago Linguistics Department.

—— (1971) Implicative verbs. *Language*, 47, 340–58.

—— (1973) Presuppositions of compound sentences. *Linguistic Inquiry*, 4, 169–93.

—— (1974) Presuppositions and linguistic context. *Theoretical Linguistics*, 1, 181–93.

—— (1976) Discourse referents. In J. D. McCawley (ed.), *Syntax and Semantics*, 7, 363–85. New York: Academic Press.

—— (1977) Syntax and semantics of questions. *Linguistics and Philosophy*, 1, 3–44.

Karttunen, L. and Peters, S. (1979) Conventional implicature. In C.-K. Oh and D. A. Dinneen (eds), *Syntax and Semantics*, 11, 1–56. New York: Academic Press.

Kasher, A. (ed.) (1991) *The Chomskyan Turn*. Oxford: Basil Blackwell.

Kasper, R. T. (1994) Adjuncts in the Mittelfeld. In J. Nerbonne, K. Netter, and C. Pollard (eds), *German Grammar in HPSG*, 39–69. Stanford: CSLI.

Kasper, R. T. and Rounds., W. C. (1986) A Logical semantics for feature structures. In *Proc. of the 24th Annual Meeting of the Association for Computational Linguistics*, 257–66. Columbia University.

Katz, F. M. and Katz, J. J. (1977) Is necessity the mother of intension? *The Philosophical Review*, LXXXVI, 70–96.

Katz, J. J. (1966) *The Philosophy of Language*. New York: Harper and Row.

—— (1972) *Semantic Theory*. New York: Harper and Row.

—— (1977) *Propositional Structure and Illocutionary Force*. New York: T. Y. Crowell. Reprinted, Cambridge, MA: Harvard University Press.

—— (1981) *Language and Other Abstract Objects*. Totowa, NJ: Rowman and Littlefield.

—— (1986) Why intensionalists ought not be Fregeans. In E. LePore (ed.), *Truth and Interpretation*, 59–91. Oxford: Basil Blackwell.

—— (1987) Common sense in semantics. In E. LePore (ed.), *New Directions in Semantics*, 157–233. London: Academic Press.

—— (1988) The refutation of indeterminacy. *The Journal of Philosophy*, LXXXV, 227–52.

—— (1990a) Has the description theory of names been refuted?. In G. Boolos (ed.), *Meaning and Method: Essays in Honor of Hilary Putnam*, 31–61. Cambridge: Cambridge University Press.

—— (1990b) *The Metaphysics of Meaning*. Cambridge, MA: MIT Press.

—— (1992) The new intensionalism. *Mind*, 101, 689–720.

—— (1994a) Symposium on the metaphysics of meaning. *Philosophy and Phenomenological Research*, LVI, No. 1, 127–83.

—— (1994b) Names without bearers. *The Philosophical Review*, 103, No. 1, 1–39.

Katz, J. J. and Fodor, J. A. (1962) What's wrong with the philosophy of language? *Inquiry*, 5, 197–237.

—— (1963) The structure of a semantic theory. *Language*, 39, 170–210.

Katz, J. J. and Postal, P. M. (1964) *An Integrated Theory of Linguistic Descriptions*. Cambridge, MA: MIT Press.

Katz, J. J., Leacock, C. and Ravin, Y. (1985) A decompositional approach to modification. In E. LePore and B. McLaughlin (eds), *Actions and Events*. Oxford: Basil Blackwell.

Katz, N., Baker, E. and Macnamara J. (1974) What's in a name? A study of how children learn common and proper names. *Child Development*, 45, 469–73.

Kay, M. (1984) Functional unification grammar: a formalism for machine translation. In *Proceedings of the 10th International Conference on Computational Linguistics*, 75–8. Stanford, CA: Stanford University Press.

—— (1992) Unification. In M. Rosner and R. Johnson (eds), 1–29.

Kayne, R. (1984) *Connectedness and Binary Branching*. Dordrecht: Foris.

Keenan, E. L. (1971) Two kinds of presupposition in natural language. In Fillmore, C. and Langendoen, D. T. (eds), *Studies in Linguistic Semantics*, 45–54. New York: Holt.

—— (1971a) Names, quantifiers, and a solution to the sloppy identity problem. *Papers in Linguistics*, 4.

—— (1971b) Quantifier structures in English. *Foundations of Language*, 7, 225–84.

—— (1974) The Functional principle: Generalizing the notion of 'subject of'. *CLS*, 10, 298–309.

—— (1975) (ed.) *Formal Semantics of Natural Language*. Cambridge: Cambridge University Press.

—— (1987a) A semantic definition of indefinite NP. In E. J. Reuland and A. ter Meulen, (eds) (1987) *The Representation of (In)Definiteness*. Cambridge, MA: MIT Press, 286–317.

—— (1987b) Unreducible n-ary quantifiers in natural language. In P. Gärdenfors (ed.), *Generalized Quantifiers: Linguistic and Logical Approaches*, 109–50. Dordrecht: Reidel.

—— (1987c) Multiply-headed NPs. In *Linguistic Inquiry*, 18, 481–91.

—— (1992) Beyond the Fregean boundary. *Linguistics and Philosophy*, 15, 199–221.

—— (1993) Natural language, sortal reducibility and generalized quantifiers. *The Journal of Symbolic Logic*, 58, 314–25.

—— (this volume) The Semantics of determiners.

Keenan, E. L. and Faltz, L. (1985) *Boolean Semantics for Natural Language*. Dordrecht: Reidel.

Keenan, E. L. and Hull R. (1973) The logical presuppositions of questions and answers. In D. Franck and J. Petöfi (eds), *Präsuppositionen in der Linguistik und der Philosophie*, Athenäum, Kronberg.

Keenan, E. L. and Moss, L. (1985) Generalized quantifiers and the expressive power of natural language. In J. van Benthem and A. ter Meulen (eds), 73–124.

Keenan, E. L. and Stavi, J. (1986) A semantic characterization of natural language determiners. *Linguistics and Philosophy*, 9, 253–326.

Keenan, E. L. and Westerståhl, D. (forthcoming) Generalized quantifiers in linguistics and logic. In J. van Benthem and A. ter Meulen (eds), *Handbook of Language and Logic*. Holland: Elsevier.

Kehler, A. (1993) The effect of establishing coherence in ellipsis and anaphora resolution. In *Proceedings of the Association for Computational Linguistics*.

Keil, F. C. (1979) *Semantic and Conceptual Development: An ontological Perspective*. Cambridge, MA: Harvard University Press.

—— (1989) *Concepts, Kinds, and Cognitive Development*. Cambridge, MA: MIT Press.

Keisler, H. J. (1970) Logic with the quantifier 'there exist uncountably many'. *Annals of Mathematical Logic*, 1, 1–93.

Kempson, R. (1975) *Presupposition and the Delimitation of Semantics*. Cambridge: Cambridge University Press.

—— (1986) *Ambiguity and the semantics-pragmatics distinction*. In Travis, C. (ed.), *Meaning and Interpretation*, 77–103. Oxford: Blackwell.

—— (1988) Logical form: the grammar cognition interface. *Journal of Linguistics*, 24, 393–431.

—— (1991) Wh-gap binding and ellipsis – a grammar for an input system. *Nordic Journal of Linguistics*, 14, 41–64.

—— (1995) Ellipsis as labelled natural deduction. In Kempson, R. (ed.), *Language and Deduction*. Special issue of *Bulletin of Interest Group of Pure and Applied Logics*. London.

—— (this volume) Semantics, pragmatics, and natural language interpretation.

Kempson, R. and D. Gabbay (1993) How we understand sentences. And fragments too? in M. Cobb (ed.), *SOAS Working Papers in Linguistics and Phonetics*, 3, 259–336.

Kiefer, F. (ed.) (1983) *Questions and answers*. Dordrecht: Reidel.

Kiparsky, C. and Kiparsky, P. (1971) Fact. In Steinberg and Jacobovitz (eds), *Semantics: an Interdisciplinary Reader*. Cambridge: Cambridge University Press.

Kiparsky, P. (1983) Word-formation and the lexicon. In F. Ingemann (ed.), *Proceedings of the 1982 Mid-America Linguistics Conference*, 47–78. University of Kansas Department of Linguistics.

Kitigawa, H. (1991) Copying identity. *Natural Language and Linguistic Theory*, 9, 497–536.

Klima, Edward (1964) Negation in English. In J. A. Fodor and J. Katz (eds), *The Structure of Language*, 246–323. New York: Prentice-Hall.

Klopstra, R. (1993) *Incremental Interpretation*. Masters Thesis, Alfa–informatica, Rijksuniversiteit Groningen. Also BCN poster, Theme Day 2/94.

König, E. (1989) Parsing as natural deduction. In *Proceedings of the Annual Meeting of the Association for Computational Linguistics*.

Koster, J. and E. Reuland (eds) (1991), *Long-Distance Anaphora*. Cambridge: Cambridge University Press.

Kratzer, A. (1977) What *must* and *can* must and can mean. *Linguistics and Philosophy*, 1.

—— (1981) The notional category of modality. In H. J. Eikmeyer and H. Rieser (eds), *Words, Worlds and Contexts*, 38–74. Berlin: de Gruyter.

—— (1989a) Stage-level and individual-level predicates. In E. Bach, A. Kratzer and B. H. Partee (eds), *Papers on Quantification*. University of Massachusetts.

—— (1989b) An investigation of the lumps of thought. *Linguistics and Philosophy*, 12, 607–53.

—— (1991) The representation of focus. In A. von Stechow and D. Wunderlich (eds), *Semantik/Semantics: An International Handbook of Contemporary Research*, 804–25. Berlin: de Gruyter.

Krifka, M. (1987) *Nominal Reference and Temporal Constitution: towards a semantics of quantity*. University of Tübingen.

—— (1989) *Boolean and non-Boolean and*. Ms. Austin: University of Texas.

—— (1990a) Four thousand ships passed through the lock: object-induced measure functions on events. *Linguistics and Philosophy*, 13.

—— (1990b) Polarity phenomena and alternative semantics. M. Stokhof and L. Torenvliet (eds), *Proceedings of the 7th Amsterdam Colloquium*, 277–302. Amsterdam: ITLI.

—— (1991a) A compositional semantics for multiple focus constructions. In S. Moore and A. Z. Wyner (eds), *Proceedings from Semantics and Linguistics Theory I*. Cornell Working Papers in Linguistics.

—— (1991b) Some remarks on polarity items. In D. Zaefferer (ed.), *Semantic Universals and Universal Semantics*, 150–89. Groningen-Amsterdam Studies in Semantics 12. Berlin and New York: Foris.

Kripke, S. (1959) A completeness theorem in modal logic. *Journal of Symbolic Logic*, 24, 1–14.

—— (1963) Semantical considerations on modal logic. *Acta Philosophica Fennica*, 16, 83–94.

—— (1980) *Naming and Necessity*. Cambridge, MA: Harvard University Press.

—— (1973) Kripke's Shearman Lectures and John Locke lectures (circulated but unpublished).

—— (1979) A puzzle about belief. In A. Margalit (ed.), *Meaning and Use*, 239–83. Dordrecht: Reidel.

Ladusaw, W. A. (1979) *Polarity Sensitivity as Inherent Scope Relations*. PhD Dissertation. Austin: University of Texas.

—— (1980) On the notion affective in the analysis of negative polarity items. *Journal of Linguistic Research*, 1, 1–16.

—— (1983) Logical form and conditions on grammaticality. *Linguistics and Philosophy*, 6, 389–422.

—— (1992) Expressing negation. In C. Barker and D. Dowty (eds), *Salt II: Proceedings of the Second Conference on Semantics and Linguistic Theory*. Columbus: Linguistics Department, Ohio State University.

—— (this volume) Negation and Polarity Items.

Lahiri, U. (1991) *Embedded Interrogatives and the Predicates that Embed Them*. Unpublished doctoral dissertation. Cambridge, MA: MIT Press.

van Lainbalgen, M. (1991) Natural deduction for generalized quantifier. In J. van der Does and J. van Eijck (eds), *Generalized Quantifiers and Applications*, 143–54. Amsterdam: Dutch Network for Language, Logic and Information.

Laka Mugarza, M. I. (1990) *Negation in Syntax: on the Nature of Functional Categories and Projections*. PhD Dissertation, MIT.

Lakoff, G. (1968) *Pronouns and Reference, Parts I and II*. Bloomington: Indiana University Linguistics Club.

—— (1971) On Generative semantics. In D. Steinberg and L. Jacobovits (eds), *Semantics*, 232–96. Cambridge: Cambridge University Press.

—— (1972) Linguistics and natural logic. *Synthese*, 22. Reprinted in Davidson, D. and G. F. Harman (eds), *Semantics for Natural Language*, 545–665. Dordrecht: Kluwer.

—— (1987) *Women, Fire, and Dangerous Things*. Chicago: University of Chicago Press.

—— (1990) The Invariance hypothesis: Is abstract reasoning based on image-schemas? *Cognitive Linguistics*, 1, 39–74.

Lakoff, G. and Johnson, M. (1980) *Metaphors We Live By*. Chicago, IL: University of Chicago Press.

Lakoff, G. and Turner, M. (1989) *More Than Cool Reason: A Field Guide to Poetic Metaphor*. Chicago: University of Chicago Press.

Lakoff, R. (1969) Some reasons why there can't be any some-any rule. *Language*, 45, 608–15.

Lambek, J. (1958) The mathematics of sentence structure. *American Mathematical Monthly*, 65, 154–69.

Landau, B. and Gleitman, L. (1985) *Language and Experience: Evidence from the Blind Child*. Cambridge: Harvard University Press.

Landau, B. and Jackendoff, R. (1993) "What" and "where" in spatial language and spatial cognition. *Behavioral and Brain Sciences*, 16, 217–38.

Landman, F. (1981) A note on the projection problem. *Linguistic Inquiry*, 12, 467–77.

—— (1986a) Conflicting presuppositions and modal subordination. In *Proceedings of CLS 22*, Chicago Linguistic Society.

—— (1986b) *Towards a Theory of Information: The Status of Partial Objects in Semantics*. PhD Dissertation, University of Amsterdam, published as GRASS 6. Dordrecht: Foris.

—— (1989a) Groups I. *Linguistics and Philosophy*, 12, 559–605.

—— (1989b) Groups II. *Linguistics and Philosophy*, 12, 723–44.

—— (1991) *Structures for Semantics*. Dordrecht: Kluwer.

—— (1992) The progressive. *Natural Language Semantics*, 1.

—— (1994) *Events and Plurality: the Jerusalem Lectures*. Ms. Cornell and Tel Aviv University.

Langacker, R. (1987) *Foundations of Cognitive Grammar, Vol. 1*. Stanford: Stanford University Press.

—— (1991) *Foundations of Cognitive Grammar, Vol. 2*. Stanford: Stanford University Press.

Langendoen, T. (1978), The logic of reciprocity. In *Linguistic Inquiry*, 9.

Lappin, S. (1982) On the pragmatics of mood. *Linguistics and Philosophy*, 4, 559–78.

—— (1984) VP anaphora, quantifier scope, and logical form. *Linguistic Analysis*, 13, 273–315.

—— (1988a) The semantics of "many" as a weak determiner. *Linguistics*, 26, 977–98.

—— (1988b) (ed.) The syntax and semantics of NPs. Special issue of *Linguistics*, 26–6.

—— (1989) Donkey pronouns unbound, *Theoretical Linguistics*, 15, 263–86.

—— (1991) Concepts of logical form in linguistics and philosophy. In A. Kasher (ed.), 300–33.

—— (1993a) The Syntactic basis of ellipsis resolution. In S. Berman and A. Hestvik (eds), *Proceedings of the Stuttgart Ellipsis Workshop, Arbeitspapiere des Sonderforschungsbereichs 340*, Bericht Nr. 29–1992. Stuttgart: University of Stuttgart.

—— (1993b) Ellipsis resolution at S-structure. In Amy Schafer (ed.), *Proceedings of NELS 23*, 255–69. Amherst, MA: University of Massachusetts.

—— (1995a) *Computational approaches to ellipsis*. Tutorial presented at the 7th Annual Conference of the European Chapter of the Association for Computational Linguistics, University College, Dublin.

—— (1995b) Generalized quantifiers, exception phrases and logicality. *The Bulletin of the Special Interest Group for Pure and Applied Logic*, 3, 203–22.

—— (this volume) The Interpretation of ellipsis.

Lappin, S. and Francez, N. (1994) E-type pronouns, I-Sums, and donkey anaphora. *Linguistics and Philosophy*, 17, 391–428.

Lappin, S. and McCord, M. (1990) Anaphora resolution in slot grammar. *Computational Linguistics*, 16, 197–212.

Lappin, S. and Reinhart, T. (1988) Presuppositional effects of strong determiners: a processing account. *Linguistics*, 26, 1021–37.

Larson, R. (1986) Lambda conversion and antecedent contained deletion. Ms. Cambridge, MA: MIT.

—— (1987) Missing prepositions and the analysis of English free relative clauses. *Linguistic Inquiry*, 18, 239–66.

Lasersohn, P. (1988) *A Semantics for Groups and Events*. Dissertation. Columbus: Ohio State University.

—— (1993) Existence presuppositions and background knowledge. *Journal of Semantics*, 10, 113–22.

Lasnik, H. (1976) Remarks on coreference. *Linguistic Analysis*, 2, 1–22.

Lasnik, H. and Saito, M. (1992) *Move Alpha: Conditions on its Applications and Output*. Cambridge, MA: MIT Press.

Lerdahl, F. and Jackendoff, R. (1983) *A Generative Theory of Tonal Music*. Cambridge, MA: MIT Press.

Lesniewski, S. (1929) Grundzuege eines neuen Systems der Grundlagen der Mathematik. *Fundamenta Mathematicae*, 14, 1–81.

Levelt, W. (1984) Some perceptual limitations in talking about space. In A. van Doorn, W. van de Grind, and J. Koenderink (eds), *Limits in Perception*. Utrecht: Coronet Books.

Levin, B. (1991) Building a lexicon: The contribution of linguistic theory. *International Journal of Lexicography*, 4, 205–26. Re-published in M. Bates and R. Weischedel (eds) (1993), *Challenges in Natural Language Processing*, 76–98. Cambridge: Cambridge University Press.

—— (1993) *English Verb Classes and Alternations: A Preliminary Investigation*. Chicago, IL: University of Chicago Press.

—— (1995) Approaches to lexical semantic representation. In D. Walker, A. Zampolli, and N. Calzolari (eds), *Automating the Lexicon I: Research and Practice in a Multilingual Environment*, 53–91. Oxford: Oxford University Press.

Levin, B. and Rapoport, T. (1988) Lexical subordination. *CLS*, 24, 275–89.

Levin, B. and Hovav, M. Rappaport (1991) Wiping the slate clean: A lexical semantic exploration. *Cognition*, 41, 123–51.

—— (1992) The lexical semantics of verbs of motion: The perspective from unaccusativity. In I. M. Roca (ed.), *Thematic Structure: Its Role in Grammar*, 247–69. Berlin: Walter de Gruyter.

—— (1995) *Unaccusativity: At the Syntax-Lexical Semantics Interface*. Cambridge, MA: MIT Press.

Levin, L. (1986) *Operations on Lexical Forms: Unaccusative Rules in Germanic Languages*. PhD Dissertation. Cambridge, MA: MIT.

Levinson, S. (1983) *Pragmatics*. Cambridge: Cambridge University Press.

—— (1987a) Minimization and conversational inference. In J. Verschueren and M. Bertuccelli-Papi (eds), *The Pragmatic Perspective*, 61–129. Amsterdam: John Benjamins.

—— (1987b) Pragmatics and the grammar of anaphora: a partial pragmatic reduction of binding and control phenomena. *Journal of Linguistics*, 23, 379–434.

—— (1991) Pragmatic Reduction of the Binding Conditions Revisited. *Journal of Linguistics*, 27, 107–61.

—— (1992) *Language and Cognition: The Cognitive Consequences of Spatial Description in Guugu Yimithirr*. Working Paper No. 13, Cognitive Anthropology Group. Nijmegen: Max Planck Institute for Psycholinguistics.

Lewis, D. (1968) Counterpart theory and quantified modal logic. *Journal of Philosophy*, 65.

—— (1969) *Convention: A Philosophical Study*. Cambridge, MA: Harvard University Press.

—— (1970) General semantics. *Synthese*, 22, 18–67. Reprinted in D. Davidson and G. F. Harman (eds) (1972), 169–218.

—— (1973) *Counterfactuals*. Cambridge, MA: Harvard University Press.

—— (1975) Adverbs of quantification. In E. L. Keenan (ed.), 3–15, Cambridge: Cambridge University Press.

—— (1979) Scorekeeping in a language game. *Journal of Philosophical Logic*, 8, 339–59.

—— (1986) *On the Plurality of Worlds*. Oxford: Blackwell.

Lewis, D. and Lewis, S. (1975) Review of Olson and Paul (1972). *Theoria*, xii, 39–60.

Liberman, A. and Studdert–Kennedy, M. (1977) Phonetic Perception. In R. Held, H. Leibowitz and H.-L. Teuber (eds), *Handbook of Sensory Physiology, Vol. VIII, Perception*. Heidelberg: Springer-Verlag.

Lindström, P. (1966) First order predicate logic with generalized quantifiers. In *Theoria*, 32, 186–95.

Linebarger, M. (1980) *The grammar of negative polarity*. PhD Dissertation, MIT.

—— (1987) Negative polarity and grammatical representation. *Linguistics and Philosophy*, 10, 325–87.

—— (1991) Negative polarity as linguistic evidence. In L. Dobring, L. Nichols and R. Rodriguez (eds), *CLS, 27 – II Papers from the Parasession on Negation*. Chicago: Chicago Linguistic Society.

Link, G. (1979) *Montague-Grammatik. Die Logische Grundlagen*. Munich: Wilhelm Fink Verlag.

—— (1983) The logical analysis of plurals and mass terms: A lattice-theoretical approach. In R. Bäuerle et al. (eds), *Meaning, Use, and Interpretation*, 302–23. Berlin: de Gruyter.

—— (1984) Hydras. On the logic of relative clause constructions with multiple heads. In F. Landman and F. Veltman (eds), *Varieties of Formal Semantics*. GRASS 3. Dordrecht: Foris.

—— (1987a) Algebraic semantics of event structures. In Groenendijk, Stokhof and Veltman (eds), *Proceedings of the Sixth Amsterdam Colloquium*, Amsterdam: ITLI.

—— (1987b) Generalized quantifiers and plurals. In P. Gärdenfors (ed.), 151–180.

—— (1991) Plural. In Wunderlich, D. and von Stechow, A. (eds), *Semantics: an International Handbook of Contemporary Research*. Berlin: de Gruyter.

Lønning, J. (1989) *Some Aspects of the Logic of Plural Noun Phrases*, COSMOS-report 11. University of Oslo.

Lyons, J. (1968) *Introduction to Theoretical Linguistics*. Cambridge: Cambridge University Press.

—— (1977) *Semantics*. Cambridge: Cambridge University Press.

Macnamara, J. (1982) *Names for Things*. Cambridge, MA: MIT Press.

—— (1986) *A Border Dispute*. Cambridge, MA: Bradford/MIT Press.

Maling, J. and Zaenen, A. (1982) A phrase structure account of Scandinavian extraction phenomena. In P. Jacobson and G. Pullum (eds), *The Nature of syntactic representation*, 229–83. Dordrecht: Reidel.

Manzini, R. (1994) Locality, minimalism, and parasitic gaps. *Linguistic Inquiry*, 25, 481–508.

Marantz, A. P. (1992) The *way* construction and the semantics of direct arguments in English. In T. Stowell and E. Wehrli (eds), *Syntax and Semantics 26: Syntax and the Lexicon*, 179–88. New York: Academic Press.

Markman, E. (1989) *Categorization and Naming in Children*. Cambridge, MA: MIT Press.

Marr, D. (1982) *Vision*. San Francisco: Freeman.

Martinich, A. P. (1980) Conversational maxims and some philosophical problems. *Philosophical Quarterly*, 30, 215–28.

Mates, B. (1952) Synonymity. In *Semantics and the Philosophy of Language*, 111–38.

—— (1973) Descriptions and reference. *Foundations of Language*, 10, 409–18.

May, R. (1977) The Grammar of Quantification. PhD Dissertation. MIT.

—— (1985) *Logical Form: Its Structure and Derivation. Linguistic Inquiry Monograph*, 12. Cambridge, MA: MIT Press.

—— (1989) Interpreting logical form. *Linguistics and Philosophy*, 12, 387–435.

—— (1991a) Syntax, semantics and logical form. In A. Kasher (ed.).

—— (1991b) Linguistic theory and the naturalist approach to semantics. In D. J. Napoli and J. Kegl (eds), *Bridges Between Psychology and Linguistics: A Swarthmore Festschrift for Lila Gleitman*. Hillsdale, New Jersey: Lawrence Erlbaum Associates.

McCarthy, T. (1981) The idea of a logical constant. *Journal of Philosophy*, 78, 499–523.

McCawley, J. D. (1968) Lexical insertion in a grammar without deep structure. In *Papers from the 4th Regional Meeting of the Chicago Linguistic Society*, 71–80. Chicago. Reprinted in McCawley (1973), 155–66.

—— (1970) Where do noun phrases come from? In R. Jacobs and P. Rosenbaum (eds), *Readings in English Transformational Grammar*, 183. Waltham: Ginn and Co.

—— (1971) Where do noun phrases come from?. In D. Steinberg and L. Jakobovits, (eds), *Semantics. An Interdisciplinary Reader in Philosophy, Linguistics, and Psychology*, 217–31. Cambridge: Cambridge University Press.

—— (1973) *Grammar and Meaning: Papers on Syntactic and Semantic Topics*. Tokyo: Taishukan. Reprinted (1976) New York: Academic Press.

—— (1978) Conversational implicature and the lexicon. In Cole (ed.) (1978), 245–59.

—— (1979) Presupposition and discourse structure. In C.-K. Oh and D. A. Dinneen (eds), 225–34.

—— (1981) *Everything that Linguists Have Always Wanted to Know About Logic But Were Ashamed to Ask*. Chicago: University of Chicago Press.

Mill, J. S. (1867) *An Examination of Sir William Hamilton's Philosophy* (3rd edition). London: Longman.

Miller, G. and Johnson-Laird, P. (1976) *Language and Perception*. Cambridge, MA: Harvard University Press.

Millikan, R. (1984) *Language, Thought, and Other Biological Categories*. Cambridge, MA: MIT Press.

Milsark, G. (1977) Toward an explanation of certain peculiarities of the existential construction in English. *Linguistic Analysis*, 3, 1–29.

Minsky, M. (1975) A framework for representing knowledge. In P. H. Winston (ed.), *The Psychology of Computer Vision*. New York: McGraw-Hill.

Mitchell, D. C. (1994) Sentence parsing. In M. A. Gernsbacher (ed.), *Handbook of Psycholinguistics*, 375–409. Orlando: Academic Press.

Mitchell, J. (1986) *The Formal Semantics of Point of View*. PhD Dissertation. University of Massachusetts. Amherst, MA: University of Massachusetts, GLSA.

Moltmann, F. (1992) Reciprocals and same/different: towards a semantic analysis. *Linguistics and Philosophy*, 15.

—— (1993) Resumptive quantifiers in exception sentences. In H. de Swart, M. Kanazawa, and C. Piñon (eds), *Proceedings of the CSLI Workshop on Logic, Language, Computation*. Stanford, CA.

—— (forthcoming) Exception sentences and polyadic quantification. *Linguistics and Philosophy*.

Montague, R. (1968) Pragmatics. In R. Klibansky (ed.), *Contemporary Philosophy: A Survey*, 102–22. Florence, La Nuova Italia Editrice. Reprinted in Montague (1974), 95–118.

—— (1969) On the nature of certain philosophical entities. *The Monist*, 53, 159–94. Reprinted in Montague (1974), 148–87.

—— (1970a) Pragmatics and intensional logic. *Synthese*, 22, 68–94. Reprinted in Montague (1974), 119–47.

—— (1970b) English as a formal language. In B. Visentini et al. (eds), *Linguaggi nella Società e nella Tecnica*, 189–224. Milan: Edizioni di Comunità. Reprinted in Montague (1974), 188–221.

—— (1970c) Universal grammar. *Theoria*, 36, 373–98. Reprinted in Montague (1974), 222–46.

—— (1973) The proper treatment of quantification in ordinary English. In K. J. J. Hintikka, J. M. E. Moravcsik and P. Suppes (eds), *Approaches to Natural Language*, 221–42. Dordrecht: Reidel. Reprinted in Montague (1974), 247–70.

—— (1974) *Formal Philosophy: Selected Papers of Richard Montague*. Edited and with an Introduction by Richmond H. Thomason. New Haven and London: Yale University Press.

Montague, R. and Kalish, D. (1959) That. *Philosophical Studies*, 10, 54–61. Reprinted in Montague (1974), 84–94.

Moore, R. C. (1989) Unification-based semantic interpretation. In *Proc. of the 27th Annual Meeting of the Association of Computational Linguistics*, 33–41.

Moore. S. (1993) Eventual objects. In *ESCOL*, 93.

Moortgat, M. (1987) Mixed composition and discontinuous dependencies. In R. Oerhle, E. Bach and D. Wheeler (eds), 319–48.

—— (1988) *Categorial Investigations: Logical and Linguistic Aspects of the Lambek Calculus*. Dordrecht: Foris.

Morgan, J. L. (1973) *Presupposition and the Representation of Meaning: Prolegomena*. PhD Thesis, University of Chicago.

—— (1978) Two types of convention in indirect speech acts. In Cole (ed.) (1978), 261–80.

Mostowski, A. (1957) On a generalization of quantifiers. *Fundamenta Mathematicae*, 44, 12–36.

Mullally, J. P. (1945) *The Summulae Logicales of Peter of Spain*. Notre Dame: University of Notre Dame Press.

Muskens, R. (1989a) Going partial in Montague grammar. In R. Bartsch, J. van Benthem and P. van Emde Boas (eds), *Semantics and Contextual Expression*, 175–220. Dordrecht: Foris.

—— (1989b) *Meaning and Partiality*. Unpublished PhD Dissertation. Amsterdam: University of Amsterdam.

—— (1989c) A relational reformulation of the theory of types. *Linguistics and Philosophy*, 12, 325–46.

—— (1991) Anaphora and the logic of change. In J. van Eijck (ed.), *Logics in AI*, 412–27. Berlin: Springer Verlag.

—— (forthcoming) Tense and the logic of change. In U. Egli et al. (eds), *Interface Aspects of Syntax, Semantics and the Lexicon*. Amsterdam/Philadelphia: Benjamins.

Nam, S. (forthcoming) Another type of negative polarity item. In M. Kanazawa and C. Piñon (eds), *Dynamics. Polarity and Quantification*. Stanford: CSLI Lecture Notes.

Neale, S. (1990) *Descriptions*, Cambridge, MA: MIT Press.

—— (1992) Paul Grice and the philosophy of language. *Linguistics and Philosophy*, 15, 509–59.

Neeijt, A. (1979) *Gapping: A Contribution to Sentence Grammar*. Dordrecht: Foris.

Nerbonne, J. (1992a) Constraint-based semantics. In P. Dekker and M. Stokhof (eds), *Proc. of the 8th Amsterdam Colloquium*, 425–44. Institute for Logic, Language and Computation. Also DFKI RR-92-18.

—— (1992b) Natural language disambiguation and taxonomic reasoning. In J. Heinsohn and B. Hollunder (eds), *DFKI Workshop on Taxonomic Reasoning (DFKI D-92-08)*, 10–47. Saarbrucken: DFKI.

—— (1993) A feature-based syntax/semantics interface. *Annals of Mathematics and Artificial Intelligence*, 107–32. ed. by A. Manaster-Ramer and W. Zadrozny, *Proceedings of the Second International Conference on the Mathematics of Language*.

—— (1994) Review of M. Rosner and R. Johnson (eds), Computational linguistics and formal semantics. *Computational Linguistics*, 20, 131–6.

Nerbonne, J., Laubsch, J., Diagne, A. K. and Oepen, S. (1993) Software for Applied Semantics. In C.-R. Huang, C. X. hui Chang, K. jiann Chen, and C.-H Liu (eds), *Proc. of Pacific Asia Conference on Formal and Computational linguistics*, 35–56. Taipei: Academica Sinica. Also available as DFKI Research Report RR 92-55.

Newmeyer, F. J. (1980) *Linguistic Theory in America*. New York: Academic Press.

Nikanne, U. (1990) *Zones and Tiers: A Study of Thematic Structure*. Helsinki: Suomalaisen Kirjallisuuden Seura.

Oehrle, R. (1991) Categorial frameworks, coordination, and extraction. In A. Halpern (ed.), *The Proceedings of the 9th West Coast Conference on Formal Linguistics*, 411–25. Stanford: Center for the Study of Language and Information.

Oehrle, R., Bach, E. and Wheeler, D. (eds) (1988) *Categorial Grammars and Natural Language Structures*. Dordrecht: Reidel.

Ogihara, T. (1989) *Temporal Reference in English and Japanese*. Doctoral dissertation. Austin: University of Texas.

Oh, C.-K. and Dinneen, D. A. (1979) (eds) *Syntax and Semantics 11: Presupposition*. New York: Academic Press.

Pagin, P. and Westerståhl, D. (1993) Predicate logic with flexibly binding operators and natural language semantics. *Journal of Logic, Language and Information*, 2, 89–128.

Parsons, T. (1972a) *An Outline of a Semantics for English*. Unpublished manuscript. Amherst, Massachusetts.

—— (1972b) Some problems concerning the logic of grammatical modifiers. In D. Davidson and G. Harman (eds) (1972) *Semantics of Natural Language*, 127–41. Dordrecht: Reidel.

—— (1985) Underlying events in the logical analysis of English. In E. LePore and B. McLaughlin (eds), *Actions and Events: Perspectives on the Philosophy of Donald Davidson*, 235–67. London: Basil Blackwell.

—— (1990) *Events in the Semantics of English: A Study in Subatomic Semantics*. Cambridge, MA: MIT Press.

Partee, B. H. (1973a) Comments on Montague's paper. In K. J. J. Hintikka, J. M. E. Moravcsik and P. Suppes (eds), *Approaches to Natural Language*, 243–358. Dordrecht: Reidel.

—— (1973b) Some structural analogies between tenses and pronouns in English. *Journal of Philosophy*, 70, 601–9.

—— (1973c) Some transformational extensions of Montague grammar, *Journal of Philosophical Logic*, 2, 509–34. Reprinted in B. H. Partee (ed.) (1976), 51–76.

—— (1975a) Montague grammar and transformational grammar, *Linguistic Inquiry*, 6, 203–300.

—— (1975b) Comments on C. J. Fillmore's and N. Chomsky's papers. In R. Austerlitz (ed.) (1975), *The Scope of American Linguistics*, 197–209. Lisse: Peter de Ridder Press.

—— (1976a) (ed.) *Montague Grammar*. New York: Academic Press.

—— (1976b) Semantics and syntax: the search for constraints. In C. Rameh (ed.) *Georgetown University Round Table on Languages and Linguistics*, 99–110. Georgetown: Georgetown University School of Languages and Linguistics.

—— (1979a) Constraining Montague grammar: a framework and a fragment. In S. Davis and M. Mithun, (eds), *Linguistics, Philosophy, and Montague Grammar*, 51–101. Austin: University of Texas Press.

—— (1979b) Semantics – mathematics or psychology? In R. Bäuerle, U. Egli and A. von Stechow (eds), 1–14.

—— (1980) Montague grammar, mental representation, and reality. In S. Ohman and S. Kanger (eds), *Philosophy and Grammar*, 59–78. Dordrecht: Reidel.

—— (1982) Belief sentences and the limits of semantics. In S. Peters and E. Saarinen (eds), *Processes, Beliefs, and Questions*, 87–106. Dordrecht: Reidel.

—— (1984) Compositionality. In F. Landman and F. Veltman (eds), *Varieties of Formal Semantics. Proc. of the 4th Amsterdam Colloquium*, 281–311. Dordrecht: Foris.

—— (1985) Ambiguous pseudoclefts with unambiguous be. In S. Berman, J.-W. Choe and J. McDonough (eds), *Proceedings of NELS 16*, 354–67. Distributed by Graduate Linguistic Student Association. Amherst: University of Massachusetts.

—— (1987) Noun phrase interpretation and type-shifting principles. In J. Groenendijk et al. (eds), *Studies in Discourse Representation Theory and the Theory of Generalized Quantifiers*, GRASS 8, 115–43. Dordrecht: Foris.

—— (1989a) Possible worlds in model-theoretic semantics: A linguistic perspective. In S. Allén (ed.), *Possible Worlds in Humanities, Arts, and Sciences: Proceedings of Nobel Symposium 65*, 93–123. Berlin and New York: Walter de Gruyter.

—— (1989b) Binding implicit variables in quantified contexts. *CLS*, 25.

—— (1991a) Adverbial quantification and event structures. In *Proceedings of the Berkeley Linguistic Society 1991 General Session and Parasession on the Grammar of Event Structure*, 439–56. Berkeley: Berkeley Linguistic Society.

—— (1991b) Topic, focus, and quantification. In S. Moore and A. Z. Wyner (eds), *Proceedings from Semantics and Linguistics Theory I*. Cornell Working Papers in Linguistics.

—— (1992) Naturalizing formal semantics. In *Proceedings of the XVth World Congress of Linguists*: Texts of Plenary Sessions, 62–76. Quebec: Laval University.

—— (1993a) Quantificational domains and recursive contexts. In *Proceedings of the Thirty-First Annual Meeting of the ACL*, 224–5, Columbus, OH: Association for Computational Linguistics.

—— (1993b) Semantic structures and semantic properties. In E. Reuland and W. Abraham (eds), *Knowledge and Language, Vol II: Lexical and Conceptual Structure*, 7–29. Dordrecht: Kluwer.

Partee, B. H. and Rooth, M. (1983) Generalized conjunction and type ambiguity. In R. Bäuerle, C. Schwarze and A. von Stechow (eds), *Meaning, Use, and the Interpretation of Language*, 362–83. Berlin: Walter de Gruyter and Co.

Partee, B. H. ter Meulen, A. and Wall, R. E. (1990) *Mathematical Methods in Linguistics*, Dordrecht: Kluwer.

Paul, H. (1880) *Prinzipien der Sprachgeschichte*, eighth edition (1970). Tübingen: Niemeyer.

Peacocke, C. (1976) What is a logical constant? *Journal of Philosophy*, 73, 221–40.

Pereira, F. (1990) Categorial semantics and scoping. *Computational Linguistics*, 16, 1–10.

—— (1991) Deductive interpretation. In E. Klein and F. Veltman (eds), *Natural language and speech*, 117–34. Heidelberg: Springer-Verlag.

Pereira, F. and Pollack, M. (1991) Incremental interpretation. *Artificial Intelligence*, 50, 37–82.

Pereira, F. and Shieber, S. (1987) *Prolog and Natural Language Analysis*. CSLI, University of Chicago Press.

Perlmutter, D. M. (1978) Impersonal passives and the unaccusative hypothesis. *BLS*, 4, 157–89.

—— (1989) Multiattachment and the unaccusative hypothesis: The perfect auxiliary in Italian. *Probus*, 1, 63–119.

Perlmutter, D. M. and Rosen, C. (eds) (1984) *Studies in Relational Grammar 2*. Chicago, IL: University of Chicago Press.

Pesetsky, D. (1982) *Paths and Categories*, Unpublished PhD Dissertation. Cambridge, MA: MIT.

—— (1987) Binding problems with experiencer verbs. *Linguistic Inquiry*, 18, 126–40.

—— (1995) *Zero syntax: Experiencers and Cascades*. Cambridge, MA: MIT Press.

Piaget, J. (1970) *Genetic Epistemology*. New York: Columbia University Press.

Pinker, S. (1984) *Language Learnability and Language Development*. Cambridge, MA: Harvard University Press.

—— (1989) *Learnability and Cognition: The Acquisition of Argument Structure*. Cambridge, MA: MIT Press.

Pitt, D. (1994) *In Defense of Definition*. PhD Dissertation, PhD Program in Philosophy. CUNY Graduate Center.

Poesio, M. (1991) Relational semantics and scope ambiguity. In J. Barwise, J. M. Gawron, G. Plotkin and S. Tutiya (eds).

—— (1993) A situation-theoretic formalization of definite description interpretation in plan elaboration dialogues. In Aczel et al. (1993).

—— (1994) *Discourse Interpretation and the Scope of Operators*. Unpublished PhD Dissertation, Rochester: University of Rochester.

Poesio, M. and Zucchi A. (1992) On telescoping. In C. Barker and D. Dowty (eds), *The Proceedings of SALT II*, 347–66. The Ohio State University Department of Linguistics.

Pollard, C. (1984) *Generalized Phrase Structure Grammars, Head Grammars, and Natural Languages*. PhD Dissertation, Stanford University.

Pollard, C. and Sag, I. (1987) *Information-Based Syntax and Semantics Vol 1: Fundamentals*. Stanford: CSLI Lecture Notes No. 13.

—— (1994) *Head-Driven Phrase Structure Grammar*. Chicago, IL: CSLI, University of Chicago Press.

Portner, P. (1992) *Situation Theory and the Semantics of Propositional Expressions*. PhD Dissertation. Amherst: University of Massachusetts.

—— (1993) *The semantics of Mood, Complementation, and Conversational Force*. Ms. Washington, D.C.: Georgetown University.

Postal, P. (1994) Parasitic and pseudoparasitic gaps. *Linguistic Inquiry*, 25, 63–117.

Prior, A. (1967) *Past Present and Future*. Oxford: Oxford University Press.

Progovac, L. (1993) Negative polarity: entailment and binding. *Linguistics and Philosophy*, 16, 149–80.

—— (1994) *Negative and Positive Polarity: a binding approach*. Cambridge: Cambridge University Press.

Pullum, G. (1988) Citation etiquette beyond thunderdome. *Natural Language and Linguistic Theory*, 6, 579–88.

Pulman, S. (1992) An equational approach to the semantics of focus. Ms. Cambridge: SRI International.

Pustejovsky, J. (1991) The generative lexicon. *Computational Linguistics*, 17, 409–41.

—— (1992) *Linguistic Constraints on Type Coercion*. Ms. Brandeis University.

Putnam, H. (1962) It ain't necessarily so. *The Journal of Philosophy*, LIX, 647–58.

—— (1970) Is semantics possible? *Metaphilosophy*, 1, 189–201. Reprinted (1975) in *Mind, Language and Reality: Philosophical Papers, Vol. 2*. Cambridge: Cambridge University Press.

—— (1975) The meaning of meaning. In Gunderson, K. (ed.), *Language, Mind, and Knowledge: Minnesota Studies in the Philosophy of Science*, 131–93. Minneapolis: University of Minnesota Press. Reprinted (1975) in *Mind, Language and Reality: Philosophical Papers*, Vol. II.

Quine, W. V. (1953a) *From a Logical Point of View*. Harper and Row: New York.

—— (1953b) Two dogmas of empiricism. In *From a Logical Point of View*, 20–46.

—— (1953c) Notes on the theory of reference. In *From a Logical Point of View*, 130–8.

—— (1953d) The problem of meaning in linguistics. In *From a Logical Point of View*, 47–64.

—— (1960) *Word and Object*. Cambridge, MA: MIT Press.

—— (1961) *From a Logical Point of View*. Cambridge, MA: MIT Press.

—— (1966) Variables Explained Away. In Quine, W. V., *Selected Logic Papers*. New York: Random House.

—— (1969) Existence and quantification. *Ontological Relativity and Other Essays*, 91–113. New York: Columbia University Press.

—— (1970) *Philosophy of Logic*. Englewood Cliffs: Prentice-Hall.

—— (1981) What price bivalence? *Journal of Philosophy*, 78, 90–5.

—— (1990) Comment on Katz. In R. Barrett and R. Gibson (eds), *Perspectives on Quine*, 198–99. Oxford: Basil Blackwell.

Rappaport, M. and Levin, B. (1988) What to do with theta-roles. In W. Wilkins (ed.), *Syntax and Semantics 21: Thematic Relations*, 7–36. New York: Academic Press.

Ravin, Y. (1990) *Lexical Semantics without Thematic Roles*. Oxford: Oxford University Press.

Reichenbach, H. (1947) *Elements of Symbolic Logic*. New York: Macmillan.

Reinhart, T. (1981) Pragmatics and linguistics: an analysis of sentence topics. *Philosophica*, 27, 53–94.

—— (1983a) Coreference and bound anaphora: a restatement of the anaphora question. *Linguistics and Philosophy*, 6, 47–88.

—— (1983b) *Anaphora and Semantic Interpretation*. London: Croom Helm.

—— (1991) Elliptic conjunctions – non-quantificational QR. In A. Kasher (ed.), 360–84.

—— (1992) Interpreting Wh-in-situ. In *Proceedings of the 8th Amsterdam Colloquium*.

Rescher, N. (1969) *Many-valued Logic*. New York: McGraw-Hill.

Reyle, U. (1993) Dealing with ambiguities by underspecification: construction, representation and deduction. *Journal of Semantics*, 10, 123–79.

Rizzi, L. (1982) Negation, WH-movement, and the null subject parameter. *Issues in Italian Syntax*, 117–84. Dordrecht: Foris.

—— (1990) *Relativized Minimality*. Linguistic Inquiry Monographs 16. Cambridge, MA: The MIT Press.

Roberts, C. (1987) *Modal Subordination, Anaphora, and Distributivity*, PhD Dissertation. Amherst: MA University of Massachusetts. Revised (1990) Garland Press.

—— (1989) Modal subordination and pronominal anaphora in discourse. *Linguistics and Philosophy*, 12, 683–721.

—— (1991) Distributivity and reciprocal distributivity. In S. Moore and A. Wyner (eds), *SALT* 1. Ithaca: Cornell University.

—— (1993) *Uniqueness in Definite Noun Phrases*. Ms. The Ohio State University.

—— (1994) *If and when: The Semantics of Conditional and Temporal Subordinating Conjunctions*. Ms. The Ohio State University.

—— (this volume) Anaphora in intensional contexts.

—— (1995) Domain restriction in dynamic interpretation. In E. Bach, E. Jelinek, A. Kratzer and B. H. Partee (eds).

Roberts, L. (1991) Relevance as an explanation of communication. *Linguistics and Philosophy*, 14, 453–72.

Rooth, M. (1985) *Association with Focus*, PhD Dissertation. Amherst, MA: University of Massachusetts.

—— (1987) Noun phrase interpretation in Montague grammar, file change semantics, and situation semantics. In Peter Gärdenfors (ed.), *Generalized Quantifiers*, 372–468. Dordrecht: Reidel.

—— (1992) A theory of focus interpretation. *Natural Language Semantics*, 75–116.

—— (this volume) Focus.

Rosch, E. (1973) On the internal structure of perceptual and semantic categories. In T. E. Moore (ed.), *Cognitive Development and the Acquisition of Language*, 111–44. New York: Academic Press.

—— (1975) Cognitive reference points. *Cognitive Psychology*, 7, 532–47.

—— (1978) Principles of categorization. In E. Rosch and B. Lloyd (eds), *Cognition and Categorization*, 27–48. Hillsdale, NJ: Erlbaum.

Rosch, E. and Mervis, C. (1975) Family resemblances: studies in the internal structure of categories. *Cognitive Psychology*, 7, 573–605.

Rosch, E., Mervis, C., Gray, W., Johnson, D. and Boyes-Braem, P. (1976) Basic objects in natural categories. *Cognitive Psychology*, 8, 382–439.

Rosen, C. (1981) *The Relational Structure of Reflexive Clauses*: Evidence from Italian. PhD Dissertation. Cambridge, MA: Harvard University.

—— (1984) The interface between semantic roles and initial grammatical relations. In D. M. Perlmutter and C. Rosen (eds) (1984), 38–77.

Rosetta, M. T. (1994) *Compositional Translation*. Dordrecht: Kluwer.

Rosner, M., and Johnson, R. (1992) *Computational Linguistics and Formal Semantics*. Cambridge: Cambridge University Press.

Ross, K. (1981) *Parsing English Phrase Structure*, PhD Dissertation. Amherst: University of Massachusetts. Distributed by GLSA, University of Massachusetts, Amherst.

Rothstein, S. (1988) Conservativity and the syntax of determiners. In *Linguistics*, 26–6, 999–1021.

—— (1992) Case and NP licensing. *Natural Language and Linguistic Theory*, 10, 119–39.

Russell, B. (1905) On denoting. *Mind*, 14, 479–93.

—— (1918) The philosophy of logical atomism. In D. Pears (ed.), *Russell's Logical Atomism*. London: Fontana.

Sacks, H. and Schegloff, E. (1973) Opening up closings. *Semiotica*, 8.

Sag, I. (1976) *Deletion and Logical Form*. PhD Dissertation. Cambridge: MIT. Distributed by the Indiana University Linguistics Club, Bloomington.

Salkoff, M. (1988) Analysis by fusion. *Linguisticae Investigationes*, 12, 49–84.

Salmon, N. (1986) *Frege's Puzzle*. Cambridge, MA: MIT Press.

Sanchez Valencia, Victor (1991) *Studies on Natural Logic and Categorial Grammar*. University of Amsterdam dissertation.

van der Sandt, R. A. (1990) *Anaphora and Accommodation*. Paper presented at a workshop on presupposition, lexical meaning and discourse processes of ESPRIT working group 3315.

—— (1992) Presupposition projection as anaphora resolution. *Journal of Semantics*, 9, 333–77.

van der Sandt, R. A. and Zeevat, H. (1992) Editorial introduction to second special issue on presupposition, *Journal of Semantics*, 9, 287–8.

Scha, R. (1981) Distributive, collective and cumulative quantification. In J. Groenendijk, T. Janssen and M. Stokhof (eds). Reprinted in J. Groenendijk, M. Stokhof and T. Janssen (eds), *Truth, Interpretation and Information*, GRASS 2. Dordrecht: Foris.

Schabes, Y. (1990) *Mathematical and Computational Aspects of Lexicalized Grammars*. Ph.D. Thesis, University of Pennsylvania.

Schank, R. (1973) Identification of conceptualizations underlying natural language. In R. Schank and K. Colby (eds), *Computer Models of Thought and Language*, 187–248. San Francisco: Freeman.

Schank, R. and Abelson, R. (1975) *Scripts, Plans, Goals, and Knowledge*. Hillsdale, NJ: Erlbaum.

Schein, B. (1993) *Plurals and Events*. Cambridge, MA: MIT Press.

Schulz, S. (1993) Modal situation theory. In Aczel, Katagiri, Israel and Peters (eds).

Schwarzschild, R. (1991) *On the Meaning of Definite Plural Noun Phrases*, Dissertation. Amherst: University of Massachusetts.

—— (1992) Types of plural individuals. *Linguistics and Philosophy*, 15.

Searle, J. (1965) What is a speech act? In Black, M. (ed.), *Philosophy in America*, 221–39. Ithaca: Cornell University Press.

—— (1969) *Speech Acts*. Cambridge: Cambridge University Press.

—— (1974) Chomsky's revolution in linguistics. In G. Harman (ed.), *On Noam Chomsky*, 2–23. New York: Anchor Books.

—— (1975) Indirect speech acts. In Cole and Morgan (eds), 59–82.

Seligman, J. (ed.) (1991) *Partial and Dynamic Semantics III*. DYANA Deliverable R2.1.C, Centre for Cognitive Science, University of Edinburgh.

Seligman, J. and Barwise J. (in preparation) *Channel Theory: Notes Toward a Mathematical Theory of Information*, Department of Philosophy, University of Indiana, Bloomington.

Seuren, P. A. (1985) *Discourse Semantics*, Oxford: Blackwell.

Sgall, P. (ed.) (1984) *Contributions to Functional Syntax, Semantics and Language Comprehension*. Praha: Academia.

Sgall, P., Hajičová, E. and Panevová, J. (1986) *The Meaning of the Sentence in its Semantic and Pragmatic Aspects*. Edited by Jacob Mey. Dordrecht: Reidel.

Sher, G. (1989) A conception of Tarskian logic. *Pacific Philosophical Quarterly* , 70, 341–69.

—— (1990) Ways of branching quantifiers. *Linguistics and Philosophy*, 13, 393–422.

—— (1991) *The Bounds of Logic: a Generalized Viewpoint*. Cambridge, MA: MIT Press.

—— (forthcoming) Did Tarski commit 'Tarski's fallacy'? *Journal of Symbolic Logic*.

Shieber, S. M. (1986) *An Introduction to Unification-Based Approaches to Grammar*. CSLI Lecture Notes 4. Stanford: CSLI.

Shieber, S. M. and Johnson, M. (1993) Variations on incremental interpretation. *Journal of Psycholinguistic Research*, 22, 287–318.

Shieber, S. M., Uszkoreit, H., Pereira, F., Robinson, J., and Tyson, M. (1983) The formalism and implementation of PATR-II. In *Research on Interactive Acquisition and Use of Knowledge*. Menlo Park, CA: Artificial Intelligence Center, SRI International.

Siegel, E. A. (1976) *Capturing the Adjective*, PhD Dissertation. Amherst: University of Massachusetts.

Sigwart, C. ([1889]1895) *Logic, Vol. 1* (2nd edition) (trans. H. Dendy) New York: Macmillan.

Sikkel, K. (1993) *Parsing Schemata*. PhD Thesis. University of Twente.

Simpson, J. (1983) Resultatives. In L. Levin, M. Rappaport, and A. Zaenen (eds), *Papers in Lexical-Functional Grammar*, 143–57. Bloomington, IN: Indiana University Linguistics Club.

Sinclair, J. M. (ed.) (1987) *Looking up: An Account of the COBUILD Project in lexical computing*. London: Collins.

Skinner, B. F. (1957) *Verbal Behavior*. Appleton-Century-Crofts, Inc.

Smiley, T. (1960) Sense without denotation. *Analysis*, 20, 125–35.

Smith, C. S. (1970) Jespersen's move and change class and causative verbs in English. In M. A. Jazayery, E. C. Polomé, and W. Winter (eds), *Linguistic and Literary Studies in Honor of Archibald A. Hill: Descriptive linguistics (vol. 2)*, 101–9. The Hague: Mouton.

—— (1978) The syntax and interpretation of temporal expressions in English. *Linguistics and Philosophy*, 2, 43–100.

Soames, S. (1979) A projection problem for speaker presupposition. *Linguistic Inquiry*, 10, 623–66.

—— (1982) How presuppositions are inherited. *Linguistic Inquiry*, 13, 483–545.

—— (1987) Semantics and semantic competence. In S. Schiffer and S. Steele (eds), *Thought and Language: Second Arizona Colloquium on Cognitive Science*. Tucson, Arizona: University of Arizona Press.

—— (1989) Presupposition. In Gabbay, D. and Guenthner, F. (eds), *Handbook of Philosophical Logic, IV*, 553–616. Dordrecht: Reidel.

Sperber, D. and Wilson, D. (1986) *Relevance: Communication and Cognition*. Oxford: Blackwell.

—— (1987a) Precis of relevance. *Behavioral and Brain Sciences*, 10, 697–710.

—— (1987b) Authors' response. *Behavioral and Brain Sciences*, 10, 736–51.

Stabler, E. P. (1991) *Principle-Based Parsing: Computation and Psycholinguistics*. Cambridge: MIT Press, 199–237.

—— (1992) *The Logical Approach to Syntax*. Cambridge: MIT Press.

Stalnaker, R. C. (1968) A theory of conditionals. In N. Rescher (ed.), *Studies in Logical Theory*, 98–112. Oxford: Blackwell.

—— (1974) Pragmatic presuppositions. In M. Munitz and P. Unger (eds), *Semantics and Philosophy*, 197–214. New York: New York University Press.

—— (1978) Assertion. In Peter Cole, (ed.), *Syntax and Semantics, Vol. 9: Pragmatics*, 315–32. New York: Academic Press.

—— (1984) *Inquiry*. Cambridge, MA: Bradford Books/MIT Press.

Stechow, A. von (1982) *Structured Propositions*. Technical report, Sonderforschungsbereich 99, Universität Konstanz.

—— (1985/89) Focusing and backgrounding operators. *Technical Report 6*, Fachgruppe Sprachwissenschaft, Universität Konstanz.

—— (1991) Current issues in the theory of focus. In A. von Stechow and D. Wunderlich (eds), *Semantik/Semantics: An International Handbook of Contemporary Research*, 804–25. Berlin: Walter de Gruyter.

—— (1991) Syntax und Semantik. In A. von Stechow and D. Wunderlich (eds), *Semantik/Semantics: An International Handbook of Contemporary Research*, 90–148. Berlin: Walter de Gruyter.

Steedman, M. (1985) Dependency and coordination in the grammar of Dutch and English. *Language*, 61, 523–68.

—— (1987a) Combinatory grammars and human language processing. In J. Garfield (ed.), *Modularity in Knowledge Representation and Natural-Language Understanding*, 187–205. Cambridge, MA: MIT Press.

—— (1987b) Combinatory grammars and parasitic gaps. *Natural Language and Linguistic Theory*, 5, 403–40.

—— (1990) Gapping as constituent coordination. *Linguistics and Philosophy*, 13, 207–63.

—— (1991) Syntax, intonation and focus. In E. Klein and F. Veltmann (eds), *Natural Language and Speech: Proceedings of the Symposium, ESPRIT Conference, Brussels*, 21–38. Berlin: Springer Verlag.

Stein, M. (1981) *Quantification in Thai*. PhD Dissertation. Amherst, MA: University of Massachusetts; GLSA.

Stenius, E. (1967) Mood and language game. *Synthese*, 17, 254–74.

Stockwell, R., Schachter, P., and Partee, B. (1973) *The Major Syntactic Structures of English*. New York: Holt, Rinehart, and Winston.

Stowell, T. (1981) *Origins of Phrase Structure*. PhD Dissertation. Cambridge, MA: MIT.

—— (1987) Subjects, specifiers, and X-bar theory. In M. Baltin and A. Kroch (eds), *Alternative Conceptions of Phrase Structure*. University of Chicago Press.

—— (1991) Determiners in NP and DP. In K. Leffel and D. Bouchard (eds), *Views on Phrase Structure*. Dordrecht: Kluwer.

Strawson, P. F. (1950) On referring. *Mind*, 59, 320–44.

—— (1952) *Introduction to Logical Theory*. London: Methuen.

—— (1964) Identifying reference and truth-values. *Theoria*, 30, 96–118.

Stump, G. T. (1985) *The Semantic Variability of Absolute Constructions*. Dordrecht: Reidel.

Svartvik, J. and Quirk, R. (1980) *A Corpus of English Conversation*. Lund: Liber Laromedel Lund.

Szabolcsi, A. (1981) The semantics of topic-focus articulation. In J. Groenendijk, T. Janssen and J. Stokhof (eds), 513–40.

—— (1987a) Bound variables in syntax: Are there any? In J. Groenendijk et al. (eds), *Proceedings of the 6th Amsterdam Colloquium*. Amsterdam: University of Amsterdam ITLI.

—— (1987b) Functional categories in the noun phrase. In I. Kenesei (ed.), *Approaches to Hungarian 2. Theories and Analyses*. Szeged: Jozsef Attila University.

—— (1992) Combinatory categorial grammar and projection from the lexicon. In I. Sag and A. Szabolcsi (eds), *Lexical Matters*. Stanford, CA: CSLI Lecture Notes.

Talmy, L. (1975) Semantics and syntax of motion. In J. P. Kimball (ed.), *Syntax and Semantics*, 4, 181–238. New York: Academic Press.

—— (1978) The relation of grammar to cognition. In D. Waltz (ed.), *Proceedings of TINLAP-2: Theoretical Issues in Natural Language Processing*. Urbana: University of Illinois.

—— (1980) Lexicalization patterns: Semantic structure in lexical forms. In T. Shopen (ed.), *Language Typology and Syntactic Description: Grammatical Categories and the Lexicon (vol. 3)*, 57–149. Cambridge: Cambridge University Press.

—— (1983) How language structures space. In H. Pick and L. Acredolo (eds), *Spatial Orientation: Theory, Research, and Application*. New York: Plenum Press.

—— (1985) Force dynamics in language and thought. In *Papers From the Twenty-First Regional Meeting, Chicago Linguistic Society*. University of Chicago, Chicago, IL. Also in *Cognitive Science*, 12, 49–100 (1988).

—— (1991) Path to realization: A typology of event conflation. *Buffalo Papers in Linguistics*, 147–87. State University of New York.

Tarski, A. (1933) The concept of truth in formalized languages (with a later postscript) In Tarski (1983), 152–278.

—— (1936a) On the concept of logical consequence. In A. Tarski (1983), 409–20.

—— (1936b) The establishment of scientific semantics. In A. Tarski (1983), 401–8.

—— (1983) *Logic, Semantics, Metamathematics* (trans. J. H. Woodger, 2nd ed., ed. J. Corcoran). Indianapolis: Hackett.

—— (1986) What are logical notions? (ed. J. Corcoran), *History and Philosophy of Logic*, 7, 143–54. (1966 lecture.)

Tenny, C. (1987) *Grammaticalizing Aspect and Affectedness*. PhD Dissertation. Cambridge, MA: MIT.

—— (1994) *Aspectual Roles and the Syntax-Semantics Interface*. Dordrecht: Kluwer.

ter Meulen, A. and Reuland, E. (eds) (1987) *The Representation of (In)Definiteness*. Cambridge, MA: MIT Press.

Tharp, L. H. (1975) Which logic is the right logic? *Synthese*, 31, 1–21.

Thomason, R. (1974) Introduction to Montague, Richard (1974). *Formal Philosophy: Selected Papers of Richard Montague*, 1–69. New Haven: Yale University Press.

—— (1976) Some Extensions of Montague Grammar. In B. H. Partee (ed.) (1976), 77–118.

—— (1981) Deontic logic as founded on tense logic. In R. Hilpinen (ed.), *New Studies in Deontic Logic*. Dordrecht: Reidel.

Thomason, R. and Stalnaker, R. (1973) A semantic theory of adverbs, *Linguistic Inquiry*, 4, 195–220.

Thysse, E. (1983) On some proposed universals of natural language. In A. ter Meulen (ed.) *Studies in Model Theoretic Semantics*, 19–36. Dordrecht: Foris.

Tomberlin, J. (ed.) (1994) *Philosophical Perspectives*. Ridgeview, CA.

Traum, D. and Allen, J. (1994) Discourse obligations in dialogue processing. In *Proceedings of ACL 1994*.

Turner, R. (1983) Montague semantics, nominalization, and Scott's domains. *Linguistics and Philosophy*, 6.

—— (1984) *Logics for A.I.* Ellis Horwood Series in A.I. New York: John Wiley.

—— (1986) Formal semantics and type-free theories. In J. Groenendijk, D. de Jongh and M. Stokhof (eds) *Studies in Discourse Representation Theory and the Theory of Generalized Quantifiers* (= GRASS No. 8), 145–59. Dordrecht: Foris.

—— (1987) A theory of properties, *Journal of Symbolic Logic*, 52, 455–72.

—— (1989) Two issues in the foundations of semantic theory. In G. Chierchia, B. H. Partee and R. Turner (eds).

—— (forthcoming) Types. To appear in J. van Benthem and A. ter Meulen (eds), *Handbook of Logic and Language*. Amsterdam: Elsevier.

Ultan, R. (1972) The nature of future tenses. In *Working Papers on Language Universals*, 8, 55–96. Stanford: Stanford University.

Van Valin, R. D., Jr. (1990) Semantic parameters of split intransitivity. *Language*, 66, 221–60.

Vandeloise, C. (1986) *L'espace en Français*. Paris: Editions du Seuil. English translation: *Spatial Prepositions*. Chicago: University of Chicago Press (1991).

Veltman, F. (1981) Data semantics. In J. Groenendijk, T. Janssen and M. Stokhof (eds), 541–65. Reprinted in J. Groenendijk et al. (eds) *Truth, Information and Interpretation. Selected Papers from the Third Amsterdam Colloquium*. GRASS 2, 43–63. Dordrecht: Foris.

—— (forthcoming) Defaults in update semantics. *Journal of Philosophical Logic*.

Veltman, F., Klein, E. and Moens, M. (1990) Default reasoning and dynamic interpretation of natural language. In *Esprit 90. Proceedings of the Annual ESPRIT Conference 1990*. Dordrecht: Kluwer.

Vendler, Z. (1967) Causal relations. *Journal of Philosophy*, 64, 704–13.

—— (1972) *Res Cogitans*. Ithaca, NY: Cornell UP.

Verkuyl, H. and van der Does, J. (1991) *The semantics of Plural Noun Phrases*. ITLI prepublication. Amsterdam: ITLI.

Vermeulen, C. F. (1993) Sequence semantics for dynamic predicate logic. *Journal of Logic, Language and Information*, 2, 217–54.

—— (1994a) *Explorations of the Dynamic Environment*. PhD Thesis. Utrecht: OTS/Utrecht University.

—— (1994b) Update semantics for propositional texts. In M. Masuch and L. Pólós (eds), *Applied Logic: How, What and Why?* Dordrecht: Kluwer.

—— (forthcoming a) Incremental semantics for propositional texts. *Notre Dame Journal of Formal Logic*.

—— (forthcoming b) Merging without mystery. Variables in dynamic semantics. *Journal of Philosophical Logic*.

Vinay, J.-P. and Darbelnet, J. (1958) *Stylistique Comparée du Français et de l'Anglais*. Paris: Didier.

Visser, A. (1994) Actions under presuppositions. In J. van Eijck and A. Visser (eds), *Logic and Information Flow*. Cambridge, MA: MIT Press.

Wasow, T. (1985) Postscript. In P. Sells, *Lectures on Contemporary Syntactic Theories*, 193–205. Stanford, CA: Center for the Study of Language and Information, Stanford University.

Webber, B. L. (1979) *A Formal Approach to Discourse Anaphora*. New York: Garland Publishing Co.

Wegener, P. (1885) *Untersuchungen über die Grundfragen des Sprachlebens*. Halle.

Weinreich, U. (1966) Explorations in semantic theory. In T. Sebeok (ed.), *Current Trends in Linguistics, Vol. 3*. The Hague: Mouton. Reprinted in U. Weinreich (1980) *On Semantics*, 99–201. Philadelphia: University of Pennsylvania Press.

Welker, K. A. (1994) *Plans in the Common Ground: Towards a Generative Account of Conversational Implicature*. PhD Dissertation. Ohio State University.

Wertheimer, M. (1923) Laws of organization in perceptual forms. In W. D. Ellis (ed.), *A Source Book of Gestalt Psychology*, 71–88. London: Routledge and Kegan Paul.

Westerståhl, D. (1984) Some results on quantifiers. In *Notre Dame Journal of Formal Logic*, 25, 152–70.

—— (1985) Logical constants in quantifier languages. In *Linguistics and Philosophy*, 8, 387–413.

—— (1989) Quantifiers in formal and natural languages. In D. Gabbay and F. Guenthner (eds), *Handbook of Philosophical Logic, Vol. IV*, 1–131. Dordrecht: Reidel.

—— (1990) Parametric types and propositions in first order situation theory. In Cooper et al. (eds).

Wheeler, S. (1983) Megarian paradoxes as Eleatic arguments. *American Philosophical Quarterly*, 20, 287–95.

Wierzbicka, A. (1980) *Lingua Mentalis*. Sydney: Academic Press.

—— (1985) *Lexicography and Conceptual Analysis*. Ann Arbor: Karoma.

—— (1987) *English Speech Act Verbs: A Semantic Dictionary*. New York: Academic Press.

—— (1988) *The Semantics of Grammar*. Amsterdam: Benjamins.

Wilkins, D. P. and Van Valin, R. D., Jr. (1993) *The Case for a Case Reopened: Agents and Agency Revisited, Technical Report 93–2*. Buffalo: Center for Cognitive Science, State University of New York at Buffalo.

Wilkinson, K. J. (1991) *Studies in the Semantics of Generic Noun Phrases*. PhD Dissertation. Amherst: University of Massachusetts.

Wilks, Y. (1975) A preferential, pattern-seeking semantics for natural language inference. *Artificial Intelligence*, 6, 53–74.

Williams, E. (1977) Discourse and logical form. *Linguistic Inquiry*, 8, 101–39.

—— (1978) Across-the-board rule application. *Linguistic Inquiry*, 9, 31–43.

Wilson, D. and Sperber, D. (1986) Pragmatics and modularity. In A. Farley, P. T. Farley and K.-E. McCullough (eds), *Papers from the Parasession on Pragmatics and Grammatical Theory, CLS*, 22, 67–85.

Wittgenstein, L. (1918) *Tractatus Logico-Philosophicus* (trans. D. F. Pears and B. F. McGuinness). London: Routledge and Kegan Paul (1961).

—— (1953) *Philosophical Investigations*. Oxford: Blackwell.

van der Wouden, T. (1994a) Polarity and illogical negation. M. Kanazawa and C. J. Piñon (eds), *Dynamics, Polarity, and Quantification*. Stanford, CA: Center for the Study of Language and Information. 1745.

—— (1994b) *Negative Contexts*. Groningen dissertations in Linguistics, Dutch Department. Groningen: Dutch Department, Rijksuniversiteit Groningen.

van der Wouden, T. and Zwarts, F. (1993) A semantic analysis of negative concord. Utpal Lahiri and Adam Zachary Wyner (eds), *Proceedings from Semantics and Linguistic Theory III*, 202–19. Ithaca, NY: Cornell University, Dept. of Modern Languages and Linguistics.

Yavaş, F. (1982) Future reference in Turkish. *Linguistics*, 20, 411–29.

Zadrozny, W. (1994) From compositional to systematic semantics. *Linguistics and Philosophy*, 17, 329–42.

Zaenen, A. (1993) Unaccusativity in Dutch: Integrating syntax and lexical semantics. In J. Pustejovsky (ed.), *Semantics and the Lexicon*, 129–61. Dordrecht: Kluwer.

Zanuttini, R. (1991) *Syntactic Properties of Sentential Negation: a Comparative Study of Romance Languages*. PhD Dissertation. University of Pennsylvania.

Zeevat, H. (1989) A compositional approach to discourse representation theory. *Linguistics and Philosophy*, 12, 95–131.

—— (1992) Presupposition and accommodation in update semantics, *Journal of Semantics*, 9, 379–412.

Zimmermann, T. E. (1981) Einfuehrungen in die Montague-Grammatik. *Linguistische Berichte*, 75, 26–40.

—— (1993) Zu Risiken und Nebenwirkungen von Bedeutungspostulaten. *Linguistische Berichte*, 146, 263–82.

Zucchi, A. (1989) *The Language of Propositions and Events: Issues in the Syntax and Semantics of Nominalization*. Unpublished PhD Dissertation. Amherst: University of Massachusetts.

Zwarts, F. (1981) Negatief polaire uitdrukkingen I. *Glot*, 4, 35–132.

—— (1986) *Categoriale Grammatica en Algebraische Semantiek*, Doctoral Dissertation. University of Groningen.

—— (1993) Three types of polarity. University of Groningen Ms. Forthcoming in F. Hamm and E. Hinrichs (eds), *Semantics*. Dordrecht: Kluwer.

—— (forthcoming) The syntax and semantics of negative polarity. In S. Busemann (ed.), *Views on the Syntax-Semantics Interface II*.

Zwarts, J. and H. Verkuyl (1994) An algebra of conceptual structure: An investigation into Jackendoff's conceptual semantics. *Linguistics and Philosophy*, 17, 1–28.

Index

A-bound 150
A-chains 157
A-quantifiers 518
A-structures 523
Aaron, D. 557
Abelson, R. 542
Abney, S. 44
aboutness 407
Aboutness-Set 395
abstract domains of thought 554–7
absurd states 189
Abusch, D. 284
accessibility, anaphoric 216
accommodation 215, 224, 227–34, 236, 237–42, 243
de facto vs. de jure 308
global 228, 231, 232–3, 234, 241, 242, 308
local 223, 228, 232–3, 241, 308
presupposition 307, 308, 309
ACE structures *see* antecedent contained ellipsis
actual world, and logical consequences 530–1
Aczel, P. 404, 409
adjectively restricted dets 46
adjectives, semantics of 22, 34
adjuncts
and computational semantics 467–8, 470–2
phrases 145
adverbs
focusing 272–3, 276, 279–80
quantificational 216, 217, 218, 219, 220, 229, 272–3, 402–3
affirmation, and negation 323, 324

affirmative polarity items 326–7, 332–3
agentivity 500–2
Ajudiewicz, K. 23, 89
algebra
labelling 570, 580, 593
semantic 29–32, 566
syntactic 16
algorithms 462
incremental processing 478–81
Allen, J. 413
alternative semantics 276–7, 278–9, 280–2, 285, 290–1, 296
and negation 294
versus existential presupposition 291–5
Altham, J. E. J. 41
ambiguity
and context-dependence 565, 566, 577
and incremental processing 474–5, 478
and noncompositional constraints 466, 467–8, 468
and sense properties 609, 610
analyticity 600, 601, 603, 604, 605, 609, 610, 611, 614, 616
anaphora 3, 30, 32
and binding 216, 217, 241
cross-sentential 198
in discourse 216–17, 241, 242
donkey 198, 210
formal structure of 133
and identity 117–44
in intensional contexts 215–44
intersentential 210
pronominal 3, 242, 566, 573
and quantification 248–9
anaphoric accessibility 216

anaphoric agreement   239–40
anaphoric resolution   592
Anderson, A.   77
answers
  elliptical   414, 415–16
  exhaustive   392, 395, 400, 407
  to questions   369–71, 374–6, 377, 387
Antecedent Contained Deletion, in
  categorial grammar   103–5
antecedent contained ellipsis (ACE
  structures)   147, 148–9, 153–4, 155,
  156, 159, 168
antecedents, syntactically non-matching
  156–9
antonymy   610, 616
approximate dets   45
Apresjan, J. D.   503
Aqvist, L.   389
Argument Lift   97–8, 102
arguments, syntactic expression of
  487–8
Aristotle   300, 302, 303, 305
Aronoff, M.   315
artificial intelligence   179, 180, 181, 461
artificial languages   599, 602
Asher, N.   228
assertion   417–18, 419
assignment, and information growth   188
Atkins, B. T.   491
Atlas, J. D.   304, 315, 563
atomic domains   456–7
atomicity, and mass/count distinction
  28–9
attribute-value representation   463
Austin, J. L.   599

Bach, E.   12, 15, 18, 22, 23, 24, 28, 29,
  32, 34, 91–2, 456, 550, 564
Baker, C. L.   217, 326, 327
Baker, E.   542
Bar-Hillel, Y.   89
bare argument ellipsis   145, 148, 159–62
  and the island constraints   574–9
  LF movement and higher-order
    unification   159–61, 162
  and subjacency   161–2
  and *wh*-construal   592–5
Barsch, R.   210
Barwise, J.   2, 3, 20, 29, 33, 41, 65, 66,
  68, 70, 71, 73–4, 75, 82, 163, 216,
  219, 266, 324, 603
  and the characterization of questions
    404, 405

and context-dependence   566, 567
and generalized quantifiers   526, 527,
  528
basic predicates   428–9, 432
Bealer, G.   404
Beaver, D. I.   240, 243, 252
Beghelli, F.   44, 58
Belletti, A.   495
Belnap, N.   363, 376, 377, 378, 391, 392,
  395
Bennett, M.   19
van Benthem, J.   41, 55, 163, 211, 527,
  528, 569
Berlin, B.   542, 548
Berman, S.   29, 219, 402
Bever, J. A.   542
Bierwisch, M.   542, 543, 547, 549
bilingualism   606
binary quantification   425–6, 451
binding   106–13
  across the board, and Right Node
    Raising   112–13
  and anaphora   216, 217, 241
  anaphora and identity   121–2, 124,
    126, 132, 134
  and dynamic semantics   206
  and functional questions without
    traces   110–12
  lambda   283, 284
  and scope   216, 221
  by tense   354
  with and without variables   106–10
Bloom, P.   542
Bloomfield, L.   599, 600, 604
Blutner, R.   210
Boolean semantics   3
  and negation   294, 295, 322
Boolean truth functions   515, 516
Boolos, G.   528
bottom-up evaluation, for semantic
  processing   473–4, 476–8, 479
bound variables, and focus   289–90
bounding dets   46
Bouton, L.   103
Bowerman, M.   542, 547
brain instantiation   541
Bresnan, J.   32, 462, 478
broken vase, case of the   200–1
Bromberger, S.   131, 132
Brown, K.   84
Brown, P.   311
Brown, R.   542
Brugman, C.   542, 552

Burton-Roberts, N. 300, 306
Burzio, L. 489, 490, 492, 495, 499

CARD (cardinal) DETS 45, 57–8, 61
cardinality quantifiers 521–22, 526
Carey, S. 542, 558
Carlson, G. 220, 244, 390, 413, 425, 433, 438, 456
Carnap, R. 5, 13, 14, 17, 22, 34, 362, 603, 604, 612
Carpenter, B. 462
Carston, R. 315, 563
Carter, R. J. 487, 488, 501
Case components 157
categorial grammar (CG) 3, 6, 32
   antecedent contained deletion 103–5
   applications 100–6
   binding and variable-free semantics 106–13
   conjunction in 93–4
   elaborations in 94–100
   flexible 21, 477–81
   and functional composition 98–100
   hypothesis of direct surface compositionality 89, 101–2
   NP meanings and type lifting 94–8
   quantifier scopes 100–2
   semantic types and semantic composition 92–3
   syntactic categories in 90–2
   syntax/semantics interface in 89–116
   unbounded 'extraction' constructions 102–3
   Wrap operations 91–2
categories
   empty 151, 152
   with graded boundaries 548–9
categorization, and I-semantics 548–52, 557–8
causative alternation, and verbs of sound/manner of motion 499–500
Causer Linking Rule 501–2
Cepparello, G. 211
CG *see* categorial grammar
Chao, W. 157, 159, 566, 573
Chase, W. 542
Chierchia, G. 22–3, 27, 30, 32, 210, 236, 250, 404, 566, 573
children, research on semantic development in 542
Choi, S. 547
Chomsky, N. 1, 18, 19, 26–7, 91, 121, 149, 281, 289, 314, 365, 487, 490, 602, 606

and generative grammar 12, 600, 604
   semantics and cognition 539
Church, A. 14, 17, 607
Clark, C. 605
Clark, E. 542
Clark, E. V. 315
Clark, H. 542
Clark, H. H. 315
clauses
   ellipsis and non-restrictive relative 155–6
   matrix 243, 353
   relative 157–8, 579–80, 589–92, 594
Clifton, C. 233
'cluster' concepts 549–50
CO-INT (co-intersective) Dets 56–61
cognitive linguistics (cognitive grammar) 542
cognitive psychology 561, 562–3
coherence, updating information states 192–3
coindexing
   and coreference 122, 124–34
   and syntactic identity 134, 138
Coleman, L. 550
collective predication 428, 429–31, 433, 441
collective readings 451, 454
   and cumulative readings 436–7
   Lakoff's theory of 445–9
   second (cover) readings 452–6
collectivity criterion, in plurality 432–3, 434–5, 437
Combinatory Logic 106
common ground
   and dialogue dynamics 413–15, 417
   and modal subordination 237, 241–2
   and presupposition 305–6, 307, 308
complement clauses 243
complementizers 363–5
complex verbs 153
compositional semantics
   in categorial grammar 89–90
   and exception phrases 168
compositionality 16, 21, 24–5, 26–7, 600
   and computational semantics 465, 466–8, 472–3
   and meanings for interrogatives 407–8
   and natural language interpretation 564
   of semantic vocabulary 544–6
   surface 89, 101–2, 110, 113, 390

computational model of semantic
interpretation 4–5
computational semantics 461–84
constraint-based view 461, 464–72
feature-based theories 462–4
noncompositional constraints 466–72
noncompositional processing 472–81
computer science 5
Comrie, B. 345, 347, 348, 357
CON (conservative) DETs 54–6, 60
concept acquisition, and I-semantics 541
conceptual categories, noncategorical
nature of 548–52
conceptual dependencies 542
conceptual parallelism 556
conceptual structures 5
conjoined dets 46
conjunctions
in categorial grammar 93–4
updating information states 191
conservative generalized quantifiers 163
conservativity, and generalized
quantifiers 527
consistency, updating information states
192–3
constancy, and generalized quantifiers
527
constituents, incomplete 145–8
constraint-based view, of computational
semantics 461, 464–72
context, and grammar 118
context-change potential, and
presupposition 306
context-dependence 7, 30
of natural language interpretation
564–73, 574, 577, 596
of polarity licensing 329, 331
and resource situations 80
context-sensitive meaning assignment,
and negative concord 339–40, 341
continuity, and generalized quantifiers
527
contradictory negation 322
contrary negation 321
Contreras, E. 149, 154
conversational implicature 4, 274
Cooper, R. 3, 19, 20, 32, 33, 41, 65, 66,
68, 70, 71, 75, 79, 81, 101, 163, 166,
283, 324
and anaphora 566, 573
and the characterization of questions
404, 405
and generalized quantifiers 526, 527

Cooperative Principle, in implicature
311, 312
coordination, and flexible categorial
grammar 478
Coppola, Francis Ford 274
coreference
grammatically determined 122
and modality 198–205
and non-coreference 119–34
Cormack, A. 104
counterfactual reasoning 272–3
counterfactual sentences, and tense 347
cover readings 452–7
cover roles 452–4
Cresswell, M. J. 16, 17, 19, 22, 23, 24,
228
cross-reference sentences 527
cumulative readings 4, 426–7, 435–7, 451
and collective readings 436–7, 454
Curry, H. 106
currying, in incremental processing
476–7

Dalrymple, M. 104, 146, 147, 472, 574,
576
Danes, F. 273
Darbelnet, J. 504
Davidson, D. 5, 29, 602, 603, 606–7,
609, 611–12, 616
Davis, A. 469
De Morgan, A. 312
de Queiroz, R. 568, 569
de Swart, H. 219
de Vries, F.-J. 211
declarative detonations 391
declarative embedding predicates 396
decompositional lexical conceptual
structures 7
decreasing NPs 53–4
default logic, and cluster concepts 550
definite dets 45
deictic demonstratives 209
Dekker, P. 182, 210, 217, 243
Delacruz, E. 19
Dennett, M. 563
deontic modality 356
deotonics 235, 241
dependency grammar 33
dependent domains of quantification
260–2
determinators see Dets
detonation conditions, and meaning
108, 179

detonation domains, of DLF 251–2
Dets (natural language determinators)
41–63
constraints on determiner denotations
54–6
definite 61–2
extensional 47–8
generalizations 44–5, 48–62
'logical' 61
monotonicity generalizations 48–54
subclasses 56–61
terminology 42–4
types of in English 45–8
development questions, and I-semantics
541
Devlin, K. 566
dialogue dynamics 411–20
Diesing, M. 33
disambiguated syntax 465
discourse anaphora 216–17, 241, 242
discourse information 183, 184, 185
discourse processing 4
Discourse Representation Structure
(DRS) 572–3
Discourse Representation Theory (DRT)
2, 30, 33, 572–3
and presupposition 309
displaced exception phrases 162–7
distributive dependency 446
distributive predication 428
distributive quantifying in 444
distributive readings 451
distributive scope generalization 444,
447, 452
distributivity 426–8
and collectivity 435
and partial distributivity 433–5
division of pragmatic labor 314
DLF (Dynamic Logic Fragment) 250–4
DNP (determined NPs) 48
van der Does, J. 41, 452
Domain Restriction 56
domain selection problem 565
donkey anaphora 198, 210
'donkey-sentences' 30
Donnellan, K. 609, 610, 613, 614
downward entailing 324, 328–9
Dowty, D. 17, 19, 23, 24, 26, 34, 91,
105, 106, 340, 468, 608
and lexical semantics 490, 500, 501, 502
and plurality 426, 429, 431, 432, 433
doxastic alternatives 226–7
Dretske, F. 273–4

dynamic domains of quantification
260–66
dynamic interpretation 179–81
Dynamic Logic Fragment (DLF) 250–4
Dynamic Montague Grammar 2, 30
dynamic semantics 3, 5–6, 181–3
and information 183–95
and modality 195–205
dynamics, of dialogue 411–20

E-language (externalized language) 539
E-semantics 539–40, 541, 551, 559
Eckhard, R. 295
Edelberg, W. 218, 237
van Eijck, J. 41, 182, 210, 211
EKN (Extended Kamp Notation) 66
elaborations, in categorical grammar
94–100
elided structures 145
elided VPs 158
ellipsis 135–41, 573
answer 414, 415–16
bare argument 145, 148, 159–62,
574–9
construal 592–5, 596
and dialogue dynamics 411, 412
higher-order unification 146–7, 148,
159–61
interpretation of 145–75
resolution 3, 146–8, 157–9
see also VP ellipsis
embedded (indirect) questions 259,
379–81
embedded present tense 351–5
embedded statements 362
empiricism
logical 599, 601
Quine's two dogmas of 604–6
empty operators 150, 154, 155
Enç, M. 243, 347, 353, 357
encyclopaedic knowledge 546
Engdahl, E. 110
entailment
in modal subordination 227–31, 235,
237
and presupposition 300, 303–4
updating information states 193, 194
epistemic modal statements, update of
197–8
epistemic modality 356
equivalence, updating information states
193–5
Erteschek-Shir, N. 577

ET (Existential There) Ss (sentences)
    59–60
Etchemendy, J.   404, 525, 528, 530, 532
Evans, G.   119, 121, 127, 236, 566, 573, 608
evolutionary questions, and I-semantics
    541, 542
exception dets   46
exception phrases   145, 147, 168
    displaced   162–7
    interpretation of   162–5
Excluded Middle, Law of the   322, 324
exhaustive answers   392, 395, 400, 407
existential closure   443, 446
existential presupposition   291–5
    and alternative semantics   291–5
existential quantification   82, 191, 198,
    202, 586
explicature   315
exponibilia   300
EXT (extension) Dets   55–6
extension, and information growth
    188–9
extensional dets   47–8
extensionalism
    and proper names   613–15
    and theories of meaning   5–6, 603,
        607, 611–12, 615, 616
externally caused eventualities   501–2

factives
    declaratives   403, 411
    predicates   388–9, 393, 395, 396–7
    propositional case with   411
facts
    logical and mathematical   558
    questions and propositions   399
Faltz, L.   93, 322
family resemblance, and cluster concepts
    549
Farkas, D.   242
Fauconnier, G.   52–3, 329, 336, 542
feature-based theories, of computational
    semantics   462–4
Fenstad, J. E.   463
Fernando, T.   404
Ferreira, F.   233
Feys, R.   106
Fiengo, R.   3, 147, 573
figural objects   553, 554
Fillmore, C.   12, 487, 488, 542, 549
Finger, M.   579, 585
first-order logic   12, 14, 16, 19–20, 21,
    25, 29–30

Flexible Categorial Grammar   21,
    479–81
Flickinger, D.   469
Flynn, M.   23
focus   4, 271–97
    adverbs   272, 276, 279–80
    and alternative semantics   276–7,
        278–9, 280–2, 285, 290–5, 296
    and bound variables   289–90
    compositional semantics of   280–91
    and conversational implicature   274
    and existential presupposition   291–5
    multiple, and multiple focus operators
        286–8
    and negation   293–5
    nested   284–6, 287
    and quantification   248, 249, 255,
        262–3, 289
    and question–answer congruence
        271–2
    reasons and counterfactuals   273–5
    recursive definition of   282, 284, 287
    and restrictiveness   277–80
    and semantics   275–7
Fodor, J. A.   12, 18, 21, 22, 24, 33, 305,
    542, 545, 559, 563, 564, 566, 567, 600,
    601
formal semantics   2, 7, 561–2, 604
formality, and logical consequence   529,
    532
van Fraasen, B.   303
fragments
    exception phrases   147, 168
    method of   17
Francez, N.   210
Frege, G.   12, 13, 22, 179, 299, 301, 302,
    303, 309, 514, 599, 600, 603, 609–10,
    616
function-argument structure   14
functional composition, in categorical
    grammar   98–100
functional questions, binding
    applications   110–12
futurity   349–50
fuzziness, in category boundaries   548

Gabbay, D.   159, 568, 569, 570, 574, 579,
    580, 582, 585
Gallin, D.   17–18, 31
game-theoretical semantics   33
Gamut, L. T. F.   17, 24, 27, 31, 562
Gärdenfors, P.   41, 181
Gardent, C.   210

Garrett, M. 542, 545
Gawron, M. 4, 65, 68, 70, 254, 405, 566, 573
Gazdar, G. 21, 25, 32, 90, 93, 94, 304, 308, 309, 312, 462
Geach, P. 30, 100, 134, 218, 236
Geach rule 100
  and the binding of pronouns 109
generalization, and identifiers 209–10
generalized quantifiers (GQs) 3, 5, 19, 20
  dets 42
  and exception phrases 163–5
  linguistic theory of 526–8
  and negation 322, 324
  NPs as 94–6, 163–5
  role of situations in 65–86
  see also quantifier relations
generative grammar 12, 35, 542, 600, 601, 604, 605
  focus in 271, 274
  and intersectivity 59–61
  and negative polarity items 325–37
  and unbounded 'extraction' constructions 102
generative semantics 12, 18, 20, 21
  and quantifier scope ambiguities 101
generic quantification 81–2
Gibb, R. 564
Gil, D. 425
Gillon, B. 452, 454
Ginzburg, J. 4, 385, 389, 405, 409, 412, 419
Gleitman, L. 542
global accommodation 228, 231, 232–3, 234, 241, 242, 308
global repair strategy 231–2
goal-directed reasoning 581
Goldberg, A. E. 493
Goodman, N. 600
Government-Binding framework 490
GPSP, and categorial grammar 91
graduality, and generalized quantifiers 527
grammar
  and computational linguistics 481–2
  and cumulative readings 426
  HPSG (head-driven phrase structure grammar) 464, 469, 470, 475
  and plurality 440–4
  unification grammars 32
  Universal Grammar 545
  see also categorial grammar; generative grammar; Montague Grammar

Green, G. 306
Grice, H. P. 233, 299, 307, 309–11, 312, 313–14, 563
Groenendijk, J. 2, 3, 27, 30, 110, 182, 210, 211, 217, 243, 250, 251, 363
  and interrogative semantics 394–5, 396, 399
Groenveld, W. 211
Gruber, J. S. 488, 552, 553, 554
guises 614

Hacking, I. 528
Haddock, N. 477
Haegman, L. 339
Haik, I. 148
Halliday, M. A. K. 271
Halvorsen, P.-K. 33, 464
Hamblin, C. L. 19, 277, 366–7, 369
  semantics of questions 390–1, 392, 402–3, 413
Hamilton, Sir William 312
Hankamer, J. 104
Hardt, D. 158
Harnish, R. W. 550, 564
Harris, Z. 18, 20
Hauser, R. 387
Heim, I. 2, 16, 30, 32, 33, 70, 181, 216, 217, 219, 220, 223, 224, 225, 226, 227, 228, 229, 230, 240, 243
  and accommodation 308
  and anaphora 566
  and negative polarity 328–9, 330, 331, 332, 336
  projection theory 308
  The Semantics of Definite and Indefinite Noun Phrases 238, 250
Hendriks, H. 21, 102, 283
Hepple, M. 106, 569
Herskovits, A. 542, 552
Higginbotham, J. 4, 29, 41, 119, 363, 425, 526, 527, 604
higher-order unification 146–7, 148, 159–61, 162, 167–8
Hinrichs, E. 456
Hintikka, J. J. J. 33, 219, 389, 528, 603
Hirschberg, J. 312
Hoeksema, J. 166–7, 328, 432
Hoekstra, T. 492, 493, 495, 498
holes, and presuppositions 307
homomorphism, Montague's requirement of 15, 16
Horn, L. 276, 302, 303, 305, 309, 312, 313, 314, 316, 322, 323, 324, 327, 336, 451

Hornstein, N.   345, 347, 350–1
Houghton, G.   413
Householder, F.   312
Houtman, J.   478
HPSG (head-driven phrase structure
    grammar)   464, 469, 470, 475
Huang, J.   284, 365
Hull, R.   387

I-language (internalized language)   539,
    541
I-semantics   539–59
  and abstract domains of thought
    554–7
  counterpart of theory of reference in
    557–9
  and spatial expressions   552–4
  truth and reference in   543–4
idealized cognitive models   550
idempotency, in dynamic semantics
    196
identifiers, need for   208–10
identity
  and anaphora   117–44
  and identification   205–10
ignorance, state of   189
IL *see* intensional logic
imagistic encodings   551–2
implicature   299, 309–17
  cancellation   233–4
  conventional   310
  conversational   310–12
  generalized vs. particularized   310–11
  negative   331
  scalar (quantity-based)   233, 235–6,
    274, 312
in-situ application   442–3, 446
incomplete constituents   145–8
incremental processing   474–81
indexical identity   121
indexicality, and context   118
individual commitment slate   413
individual situations   69, 72–5, 84–5
individuals, and quantifiers   517, 533
inductive definition, of well-formed
    formulas   512
inferences
  and exception phrases   164
  and implicature   310, 312
information   183–90
  about the world   183, 184, 185
  changing   181, 182, 183
  content   182
  discourse   183, 184, 185

growth   188–90
  and modality   197–8
  states   185–8, 250, 255
  updating information states   190–5
initial states   189
instantiation, and identifiers   209–10
INT (intersective) Dets   56, 60, 61
intensional contexts, anaphora in   3,
    215–44
intensional identity   236, 237
  statements of   218
intensional isomorphism   612
intensional logic (IL)   4, 5, 13, 14, 16,
    30, 183
  and the semantics of questions   363,
    366, 388
intensional predicates   220, 221, 227,
    241
intensional subordination   221
intensionalism   5–6, 32, 603, 610, 615
intensionalist paradigm   607
intensionality
  in I-semantics   541, 558–9
  in categorial grammar   92
  possible-worlds bias in   26
interpretive semantics   21
interrogative embedding predicates   393
interrogatives
  embedding relations   394–5
  meanings for   407–10
  questions and   385–6
  resolutive   403, 410–11
  situation-theory analysis of   4,
    385–422
  see also questions
intersectivity, and generative grammar
    59–61
invariance conditions
  and logical terms   523
  and polyadic quantifiers   528
Isard, S.   413
islands, syntactic   161
isomorphism, and logical terms   520,
    521

Jackendoff, R.   1, 5, 6, 7, 18, 217, 249,
    271, 275, 293, 295, 488, 493, 501, 616
  semantics and cognition   542, 543,
    544, 548, 550, 551, 552, 557, 559
Jacobs, J.   275, 276
Jacobson, P.   3, 91, 92, 104, 106
Janssen, T. M. V.   27
Jespersen, O.   347, 348
Johnson, R.   461, 478, 542, 547, 556

Johnson-Laird, P. 21, 26, 542, 550, 552
Joshi, A. K. 32, 478

Kadmon, N. 332, 335, 336, 451, 566
Kahn, K. M. 473
Kalish, D. 14, 362
Kamp, H. 2, 6, 17, 27, 29, 30, 34, 70, 84,
  181, 216, 250, 564, 566, 572
Kanger, S. 13
Kant, I. 600
Kaplan, D. 14, 17, 117, 462
Karttunen, L. 12, 19, 30, 217, 224, 225,
  226, 227, 290, 292, 305, 307, 309, 310
  analysis of questions 366-71, 381,
    389-2, 392-3, 399
Kasper, R. T. 471
Katz, F. M. 612
Katz, J. J. 5-6, 12, 18, 24, 33, 542, 546,
  547, 549, 558, 612, 616
Katz, N. 542
Kay, P. 542, 548, 550
Keenan, E. L. 3, 5, 19, 41, 43, 47, 58,
  59, 60, 93, 94, 162, 322, 387, 526,
  527, 528
Kehler, A. 157
Keil, F. C. 542, 558
Kempson, R. 5, 159, 304, 315, 566, 568,
  569, 570, 573, 574, 580, 582
Kiparsky, P. 315
Klein, E. 90, 94
Klima, E. 51, 326, 327
Konig, E. 569
Kratzer, A. 16, 29, 32, 33, 219, 221, 222,
  223, 244, 290, 349, 356
Krifka, M. 34, 276, 286-7, 329, 336-7,
  437, 439, 456
Kripke, S. 13, 219, 609, 613-15, 616

Labelled Deductive System *see* LDS
labelling algebra 570, 580, 593
Laduslaw, W. A. 48, 52-3, 324, 328,
  329, 332, 333, 335, 338, 339, 341
Lahiri, U. 391, 402-3
Laka Mugaraza, M. I. 338, 340
Lakoff, G. 12, 27, 101, 217, 218, 224,
  225, 227, 336
  and cognitive linguistics 542
  semantics and cognition 544, 547,
    548, 550, 556, 557, 558, 559
  theory of scope and plurality 445-9
lambda abstraction
  and bare argument ellipsis 159, 160
  and plurality 437
lambda binding 283, 284, 290

lambda operators 281, 289, 290
Lambek, J. 89
Landau, B. 542, 551, 552
Landman, F. 4, 31, 308, 332, 335, 336,
  427, 428, 432, 433, 434, 437, 438, 441,
  456, 457
  theory of scope and plurality 449-51,
    455
Lang, E. 543, 549
Langacker, R. 542, 552, 556
Langendoen, T. 425
Lappin, S. 41, 47, 566, 573, 577, 578
Lasersohn, P. 305, 429, 430
Lasnik, H. 118-19, 284
lattice structures, in semantics of nouns
  28-9, 34
Law of Contradiction 321, 324
Law of the Excluded Middle 322, 324
LDS (Labelled Deductive System)
  568-9, 570, 573, 574, 579, 590, 585-6
Leacock, C. 616
left-corner (LC) parsing 479-81
Leibniz' law 207
Lerdahl, F. 550
Lesneiwski, S. 23
Levelt, W. 542
Levin, B. 5, 488, 491, 492, 493, 495, 497,
  498, 499, 500, 501, 502, 504
Levin, L. 490, 492, 495, 498
Levinson, S. 307, 313, 314, 413, 542, 563
Lewis, D. 4, 17, 19, 22, 23, 26, 72, 73,
  76-7, 215, 241, 306-7, 308, 565, 603,
  608, 612, 616
lexical ambiguity 466, 467-8
lexical conceptual structures 5, 7
lexical decomposition 545
lexical dets 45
lexical semantics 5
  representation 488-9
  and syntactic structure 487-507
lexicalization patterns 488-9
LF (Logical Form) 6, 113, 511
  of focus 283, 288-9, 290-1, 294, 295
  and the interpretation of ellipsis
    147-8
  movement analysis of bare argument
    ellipsis 159-61, 162
  movement vs. NP storage 166-7
  and multiple questions 365
  and quantifier scopes 100-2
  reconstruction at 150-5
  and reconstruction problems 134
LFG (Laduslaw-Fauconnier
  Generalization) 52-3

Liberman, A.   550
Lindstrom, P.   41, 520, 521, 524, 525,
    528, 531, 534, 535
Linebarger, M.   329, 330–1, 332, 333–5,
    336
Link, G.   17, 28, 34, 426–7, 432, 456
linking rules   487, 491, 500–2
local accommodation   223, 228, 232–3,
    241, 308
locality conditions
    on parasitic gap chains   150, 154–5
    on pseudo-gapping   153
logic   5
    default   550
    developing adequate   29–32
    formal presuppositional   304–5
    formal semantics and   12–13, 19
    mathematical   179
    for quantification domains   250–60
    and semantics   511–37
    see also first-order logic; intensional
        logic; LF (logical form)
logical connectives, criterion for   515
logical consequences   513–14, 528–32,
    535
    proof theoretical definition   529–30,
        531
    syntactic definition   530–1
logical empiricism   599, 601
logical terms
    constructive definition of   521–6
    and extra (non) logical terms   515,
        516, 521, 528, 528–34, 535
    in Tarskian semantics   514–15, 516,
        533–4
logical truths   514, 528, 531
Lonning, J.   437
Lunnon, R.   404, 409
Lyons, J.   23

McCarthy, T.   528
McCawley, J.   20, 72, 73, 75, 101, 217,
    218, 224, 226, 227, 236–7, 238, 240,
    314
McDowell, J.   608
Macnamara, J.   542, 558
Maling, J.   590
Marantz, A. P.   493
Markman, E.   542
Marr, D.   550, 551
'masked ball' circumstance   119, 120, 125
mass domain   456
mass partition   455, 456
Mates, B.   607

matrix clauses   243, 353
matrix verbs   153, 154, 155, 349
maxims of conversation   311–13, 314,
    563
May, R.   3, 21, 41, 101, 147, 148, 151,
    339, 363, 425, 526, 527, 528, 573
meaning
    and I-semantics   540
    identification with human concepts
        542–3
    image-like components of   551–2
    in natural language   616
    Quine's criticisms of theory of   602,
        604–5, 615
    and semantics   600
    theories of   5–6, 603, 607, 611–12, 615
meaning shift, and variable behavior
    verbs   502–5
meaningfulness   609, 610, 611, 614, 615,
    616
meaninglessness   614
Mervis, C.   542, 549
metaphor   556–7
MG *see* Montague Grammar
Mill, J. S.   312
Miller, G.   542, 550, 552
Millikan, R.   549
Milsark, G.   60
Minsky, M.   542, 550
Mitchell, J.   30
modal auxiliaries   220, 222, 229, 234
modal bases   222, 229, 234, 238, 241
modal context   243
modal force   243
modal referential semantics   602–3
modal semantics   604
modal subordination   197–8, 203–5, 210,
    215–43
modality   195–8
    and coreference   198–205
    and information   197–8
    and tense   4, 345–58
modals
    and focusing   272–3
    and tense   4, 354, 355, 356
model structures   29–32
model theories   2, 6, 17, 20
model-theoretic semantics   13, 25, 35,
    511, 561–2
model-theoretical interpretation
    in categorial grammar   89
    and natural language   571–2
    of surface structures   100
Moltmann, F.   47, 165

monotone decreasing 324
monotonicity generalizations 48–54
Montague Grammar (MG) 2, 6, 15–27, 32, 33, 35, 579
  and negative concord 338, 339
  and plurality 440, 443
  questions and propositions 389, 390, 394
Montague, R. 1, 11, 12, 14, 23, 26, 41, 70, 89, 92, 93, 94, 95, 96, 217, 218, 219, 579
  and computational semantics 464, 465
  and Kalish, D. 362
Montague semantics 13–18, 26, 511
mood 241
Moore, R. C. 456, 457, 463
Moortgat, M. 92, 94
Morgan, J. L. 217
Moss, L. 3, 43, 47, 58
Mostowski, A. 5, 41, 516–21, 526, 528, 535
Mullally, J. P. 300
Muskens, R. 31, 210

n-place cardinality quantifiers 521–2
natural language
  anaphora in discourse 216–17
  and compositionality 467
  and context-dependence 564–73
  and dynamic semantics 181–3
  and formal semantics 562
  and logical empiricism 599
  meaning in 616
  and negation 323–4
  referent systems 185–6
  and referential semantics 610–11
  tense 345
natural language determinators *see* Dets
natural language interpretation
  context-dependence of 564–73
  as structure-building 573–95
natural language metaphysics 12–13, 28–9
natural language semantics 117–18, 516, 602
  relation of human concepts to 546–7
necessitation 303–4
Neeijt, A. 577
negated dets 46
negation 4, 321–41
  and affirmation 323, 324
  antiadditive operators 325, 328, 331
  antimorphic operators 325, 328, 331

configurational expression of 340
contradiction 307
contradictory 322
contrary 321
descriptive and metalinguistic 323
external 302, 303
  and focus 293–5
hierarchy of strengths of 324–5
as a hole to presuppositions 307
internal 302, 303
intra- and inter-domain 323–4
law of double 324
metalinguistic use of 313
multi-domain nature of 322–3
propositional 322
and questions 367
semantics of 321–5
negative concord 4, 337–40
negative polarity items 4, 48, 51–3, 325–37, 340, 341
  licensee marking question 326, 329–33
  licensee relation question 326, 333–5
  licensor question 326, 327–9
  status question 326, 335–7
neo-Davidsonian theory, of events and plurality 437–9, 442, 443
Nerbonne, J. 4–5, 461, 463, 469, 474
nested focus 284–6, 287
Newmeyer, F. J. 18
Nikanne, U. 543
nomenclature terms 131–2
nominalization, and indirect questions 379–80, 382
Non-Constituent Conjuction *see* Right Node Raising
non-restrictive relative clauses, and ellipsis 155–6
noncompositional constraints, and computational semantics 466–72
noncompositional processing 472–81
nouns, mass semantics of 28–9
NP (noun phrases)
  anaphoric accessibility between 21
  coindexed non-coindexed 124, 125, 131
  decreasing 53–4
  and dets 42, 43–4, 48–51, 60, 61–2
  and exception phrases 163–5
  as generalized quantifiers 526
  indefinite 30, 217–18, 223, 238, 241, 248, 566, 584
  interpretation of 19–21
  meanings and type lifting 94–8

NP (noun phrases) (*cont.*)
  modal anchoring of   242
  non-quantificational   441, 445, 449–50
  and plurality   441–2, 451, 454
  quantificational   248, 441–2, 443, 445
  and resource situations   70–1, 74
  storage   166–7, 168

Oehrle, R.   23
Ogihara, T.   350, 357
operators, empty   150, 154, 155
order matters, in dynamic semantics
    195–6
orders, and quantifiers   517
Ordinary Language Philosophy   599

Pagin, P.   210
paradigm boundaries, in current
    semantic theory   2
parasitic gaps   149–50, 154–5, 159
Parkes, C.   545
parsing   474, 481
  left-corner (LC)   479–81
parsing-as-deduction models   569–70
Parsons, T.   17, 19, 22, 29, 32, 437, 440,
    443, 501
Partee, B.   6, 17, 18, 19, 24, 26, 27, 28,
    30, 33, 34, 78, 93, 94, 96, 243, 248,
    262, 352, 442
  and I-semantics   545
  and modal semantics   604
  and natural language interpretation
    564, 579
partial information   462
partial resolutives   402–3
partial specifications, in incremental
    processing   476, 477
partitions, of a propositional space
    371–4, 382
partitive dets   46
partivity   456–7
PATR-II   462–3
Paul, H.   275
Peacocke, C.   528
Pereira, F.   104, 166, 569, 570
Perlmutter, D. M.   489, 490, 492, 495
Perry, J.   2, 32, 70, 71, 73–4, 75, 219,
    405, 566, 567, 603
Pesetsky, D.   488, 566, 576
Peters, S.   4, 65, 68, 70, 254, 292, 307,
    308, 310, 405, 566, 573, 608
philosophy   5, 599, 616
  formal semantics and   12, 19, 35,
    604

phonetic perception, and cluster
    concepts   550
phrases
  adjunct   145
  exception   145
Piaget, J.   552
pied piping   365
Pinker, S.   488, 489, 542, 543, 547
Pitt, D.   612
plugs, and presuppositions   307
plural partition   455, 456
plural predication   428, 429, 431, 439,
    441, 545
plural roles   439, 452
plurality   4, 425–57
  collective predication   428, 429–31,
    433, 441
  collective readings   436–7, 445–9, 451,
    454
  collectivity criterion   432–3, 437
  and cover readings   452–7
  cumulative readings   4, 426–7, 435–7,
    451, 454
  distributivity   426–8, 433–5, 435
  and grammar   440–4
  neo-Davidsonian theory   437–9, 442,
    443
  non-thematic predication   431–2,
    440–1, 455
  partial distributivity   433
  thematic predication   428–33, 440–1,
    455
  thematic roles   438–9
  theories of scope and   444–51, 454–7
Poesio, M.   65, 76, 77, 79, 219, 242
Pollard, C.   23–4, 92, 463, 464, 469, 470,
    475
Portner, P.   29, 33, 34, 244
possession   555, 557
possessive dets   46
possibilities, in information states   186–8
possible-worlds bias, in intentionality   26
possible-worlds semantics   511, 608
post-Montague semantics   35
Postal, P.   18, 21, 24
potential-resolvedness   407
pragmatic labor, division of   314
pragmatics   5, 546, 562–4
  and negative polarity structures   4, 336
  and semantics   315
Prague School   33
predicate decompositions   488
predicate-centred theories, of lexical
    semantic representation   488

predicates
  basic 428–9, 432
  declarative embedding predicates 396
  factive 388–9, 393, 395, 396–7
  intensional 218, 219, 225, 241
  interrogative embedding 393
  lexical decomposition of 390
  propositional attitude 396
  question predicates 393, 395, 397
  questions and propositions 388–90
  resolutive 389, 393, 395, 396–7, 401
  scopal and non-scopal derived 449
  TF predicates 397, 398
  of type 520–1
predication
  collective 428, 429–31, 433, 441
  non-thematic 431–2, 440–1, 455
  plural 428, 429, 431, 439, 441, 455
  singular 428, 429, 431, 439
  thematic 428–33, 440–1, 455
preference rule systems 550
present tense, embedded 351–5
presupposition 4, 225, 238, 243, 299–309
  anaphoric account of 309
  existential 291–5
  pragmatic 305, 307, 308, 310
  resolvedness 417
  semantic (logical) 304–5, 310
presuppositions, of a question 374–6
Prior, A. 352
processing
  'noncompositional' 472–81
  semantic 7, 482
Progovac, L. 327, 335
projection problem, for presupposition 307
promotion, of partially ordered domains 457
pronominal anaphora 566, 573
  in intensional contexts 3, 242
pronouns
  anaphoric possibilities in modal contexts 3
  binding of 20–1, 107–10, 121–2
  E-type 30, 236
  familiarity presuppositions 234, 235
  indexical and anaphoric 118–34
  of laziness 236
  model subordination 203–5
proper names 613–15
properties
  ascription of 555
  of propositions 392
  in quantifier relations 65–8

property recovery, ellipsis resolution through 146–7, 156–7
property theory 31–2, 404
proportionality dets 46, 57
propositional attitude predicates 396
propositional attitudes 219, 220, 226, 234, 235, 397–8
propositions
  characterizing 406
  and questions 388–95, 399
pseudo-gapping 152, 153–4, 156, 168
psychology, formal semantics and 5, 11
Pullum, G. 90, 94, 489
Pustejovsky, J. 543, 549
Putnam, H. 548, 551, 609, 610

Q Principle 313–14, 316
QR *see* Quantifier Raising
quantification 247–67
  dynamic domains of 260–6
  and focus 248, 249, 255, 262–3, 289
  logic for quantificational domains 250–60
quantificational adverbs 216, 217, 218, 219, 220, 229
  focusing 272–3
  and interrogatives 402–3
quantificational NPs 248, 441–2, 443, 445
quantificational situations 69, 72–5, 82, 83–5
quantificational subordination 264–6
Quantifier Lowering (QL) 21, 445
Quantifier Raising (QR) 21, 445, 446, 449
quantifier relations
  individual situations 69, 72–5, 84–5
  quantificational situations 69, 72–5, 82, 83–5
  resource situations 69, 70–82
  types and properties 65–8
quantifier scopes, in categorical grammar 100–2
quantifier storage 281
quantifiers
  A-quantifiers 519
  existential 517–18
  generalization of logical 514, 516–21
  n-place cardinality 521–2
  polyadic 526, 527–8
  predicate logic 586–7
  standard 519
  universal 517–18
  see also generalized quantifiers

quantifying, in questions 276–9
quantifying in 443–4, 449
QUD downdate principle 416–17, 418
querying 415–17
question predicates 393, 395, 397
question–answer congruence 271–2, 279
questions
  and answers 369–71, 374–6, 377, 387
  characterizing 406–7
  constructing meanings 409–10
  direct (root interrogatives) 361, 363
  indirect (embedded interrogatives)
    361, 379–81
  as interrogative forms 361, 362–3
  and interrogatives 385–6
  and meta-linguistic interaction
    418–20
  and N-ary relations 386–8, 395
  partial resolutives 402–3
  and partitions 371–4
  presuppositions of 374–6
  and propositions 388–95, 399
  quantifying in 276–9
  and resolvedness 389, 392, 395, 396,
    399–404, 407, 412
  resolving when and where 401–2
  semantics of 4, 361–83, 366–76
  syntactic elements 363–6
  test questions 381
  y/n 391, 394
  see also interrogatives; *wh*-questions
Quine, W. V. 5, 13, 17, 22, 106, 305,
  514, 529, 601–6, 607, 608, 609,
  610–11, 615, 616

R Principle 313–14, 316
Rappaport Hovav, M. 492, 493, 495,
  497, 498, 499, 500, 501, 502, 504
Ravin, Y. 616
reconstruction, syntactic 3
  problems 135–41
  of VP ellipsis 150–5, 156, 157–8, 159
recursive method, and Tarskian
  semantics 511–13
reference, sense/reference distinction
  600, 603, 606, 610, 613, 614–15
reference objects 553, 554
referent systems 185–6
referential semantics 602–4, 609,
  610–15, 616
Reichenbach, H. 12, 167
Reinhart, T. 127–9, 147, 159, 160, 161,
  166, 368, 566, 573, 576, 577, 586

relative clauses
  non-restrictive, and ellipsis 157–8
  substitution into 594
  and *wh*-gap dependency 579–80,
    589–92
relevance, principle of 563–4
Relevance Theory 4, 315, 316, 566
resolutive predicates 389, 393, 395,
  396–7, 401
resolvedness conditions, and questions
  389, 392, 395, 396, 399–404, 407, 412
resource situations 69, 70–82
Restriction Logic (RL) 254–60
  dependent domains of quantification
    260–2
  and quantificational subordination
    264–6
  semantics of 257–60
  syntax of 256–7
restrictive relatives, and a proof-
    theoretic account of determiners
    584–9
restrictor adjuncts 471–2
resultative construction, variable
    behavior of verbs of sound 493–6
Reuland, E. 41, 60
Reyle, U. 2, 572
Right Node Raising (Non-Constituent
    Conjunction) 105–6, 478
  and across the board binding 112–13
Rizzi, L. 334, 339–40, 495
RL *see* Restriction Logic
Roberts, C. 3, 203, 219, 222, 236, 243,
  244
  and plurality 426, 432, 433, 436–7,
    448–9
Roberts, L. 564
Rodman, R. 19
role-centered theories, of lexical
    semantic representation 488
root interrogatives (direct questions)
    361, 363, 380
root statements 362
Rooth, M. 93, 94, 96, 216, 247, 249, 262,
  263, 267, 276, 278, 282, 289, 442
Rosch, E. 542, 549
Rosen, C. 488, 492, 495, 498, 499
Rosetta, M. T. 16
Rosner, M. 461
Ross, J. R. 365
Ross, K. 23
Rothstein, S. 47, 488
Russell, B. 179, 301–3, 514

S-structures, and VP ellipsis resolution 148, 150–5, 156
Sacks, H. 413
Sag, I. 24, 90, 94, 103, 104, 105, 463, 464, 469, 470, 475, 566
Saito, M. 284
Salkoff, M. 493
Salmon, N. 614
Sánchez Valencia, V. 328
van der Sandt, R. 240, 243, 309
satisfaction, recursive definition of 513
scalar implicatures 231, 233–4, 274, 312
Scha, R. 426–7, 429, 431, 433, 437, 447, 451, 452, 455
Schabes, Y. 474
Schank, R. 542
scheduling activities 555
Schegloff, E. 413
Schein, B. 437
Schwartzchild, R. 433, 434, 438, 452, 454–5
scopal quantifying in 444
scope
  and anaphoric accessibility 238
  and binding 216, 217, 220
  constraint on anaphoric relations 216, 221, 241
  dependencies 445, 586
  distributive scope generalization 452
  inverse scope readings 447
  islands 283–6, 289, 290
  and negative polarity items 333–4
  and quantifying in 443, 449
  scoping of focused phrases 289–90
  sentential scope constraint 216, 220, 221, 241
  theories of plurality and 444–51, 454–7
scope ambiguity 464
scope domain principle 440, 442, 446
scopeless readings 442
Scott, D. 14, 17
Searle, J. 180, 314, 608
Seligman, J. 82
semantic class shift 496–500
semantic composition, in categorial grammar 92–3
semantic/conceptual primitives 545–6
semantic decomposition 544
semantic markers 600–1, 608–9, 614–15
semantic pluralization 426–7, 455
semantic predicates, in natural language 117

semantic representations 21–2
semantic types, in categorial grammar 92–3
semi-E-semantics 539–40, 559
semilattices, atomic and non-atomic 28–9, 34
sense/reference distinction 600, 603, 606, 610, 613, 614–15
sentential formatives 136
sentential scope constraint 216, 220, 221, 241
sentential subjects 594
set-abstraction 437
sets
  dets 42–3
  NPs as 163
  objects as members of 535
  and resource situations 75–7
Seuren, P. A. 181
Sher, G. 521, 527, 528
Shieber, S. 104, 462, 463, 478
Siegel, E. A. 19
Sigwart, C. 300–1
Simpson, J. 493, 499
Sinclair, J. M. 491
singular predication 428, 429, 431, 439
situation semantics 29, 33
  dets 42
  and generalized quantifiers 65–86
  meanings for interrogatives in 407–8
  and meta-linguistic interaction 419
situation theory
  and natural language interpretation 571–2
  and propositions 406
  and reconstruction of context 566–7
Skinner, B. F. 602
Smiley, T. 303
Smith, C. S. 347
SOA-abstracts 405–6, 411
Soames, S. 26, 305, 308
SOT (sequence of tense) 350–1
space of possibilities, and partitions 371–4, 382
spatial expressions 552–4
spatial location and motion 555
spatial representation 551
speech act theory 180
  and statements 362–3
Sperber, D. 4, 311, 315, 316, 563, 564, 568
Stabler, E. P. 469
Stalnaker, R. 19, 26, 30, 180, 225, 299, 305, 306, 307, 308, 411, 413, 563

state of ignorance   189
statements   361–3
Stavi, J.   3, 41, 162, 526, 527
Steedman, M.   94, 99, 102, 284, 477, 478
Steel, T.   363
Stein, M.   27, 29
Stokhof, M.   2, 3, 27, 30, 110, 182, 210,
    211, 217, 243, 250, 251, 363
  and interrogative semantics   394–5,
    396, 399
storage
  and the scope domain principle   443
  semantic operation of NP   166–7, 168
Stowell, T.   44, 487
Strawson, P. F.   299, 302–3, 304, 305,
    312
structural semantics   35
Studdert-Kennedy, M.   550
subcategorization, and computational
    semantics   467, 468, 470, 475
subjacency   148, 149, 155
  and bare argument ellipsis   161–2,
    578
subsistence, and information growth
    189–90
support, updating information states
    192
surface compositionality   89, 101–2, 110,
    113, 390
synonymy   603, 609, 610, 611, 614, 615,
    616
syntactic categories   3
  in categorical grammar   90–2
syntactic identity   141
  and coindexing   134, 138
syntactic islands   161
syntactic properties   601
syntactic reconstruction *see*
    reconstruction, syntactic
Syntactic Structures (Chomsky)   599, 600
syntax licensing   562
syntax–phonology interface   547
syntax–semantics interfaces   3, 463–4,
    472, 474
Szabolcsi, A.   44, 106, 296

Talmy, L.   488, 503, 504, 542, 547, 549,
    552, 554, 556
Tarski, A.   13, 14, 22, 511, 525, 528, 529,
    602
Tarskian semantics   5, 511–16, 533–6
taxonomic theory   600, 601, 604
telescoping   219, 242
telicity   500–2

temporal interpretation   345
Tennant, N. W.   41
Tenny, C.   500, 502
tense
  embedded present tense   351–5
  evaluation time   353–4
  futurity   349–50, 357
  and modality   345–58
  past tense   345–6, 356–7
  semantics of   4
  sequence of (SOT)   350–1
tense logic   13, 14
ter Meulen, A.   41, 60
test questions   381
TF predicates   397, 398
Tharp, L. H.   528
that-trace configurations   594, 595
thematic predication   428–33, 440–1, 455
Theme Linking Rule   502
Thomason, R.   17, 18, 19, 25, 222, 235
3-D model structure   551
total information, states of   189
trace, *wh*-trace   150, 152, 154–5
Traum, D.   413
truth
  and I-semantics   543–4
  logical   514, 528, 531
  recursive definition   512, 513–14
  Tarskian definition of   515–16, 534–5,
    543
truth-conditions   12, 13, 17, 22
  and I-semantics   544, 548
  and anaphora in discourse   217
  and coreference   133–4
  and implicature   310, 315
  and individual situations   84–5
  and intensionalism   607
  and meaning   179, 180
  and metaphor   556
  and negation   322
  and presupposition   305, 308
  questions and resolvedness conditions
    400–1
  and the semantics of natural language
    117–18
  and the semantics of questions   366
  and sets   76
  and statements   362, 363
truth-functional connectives   514,
    515–16
truth-theoretical evaluation, of natural
    languages   658
truth-value gaps, and presupposition
    303, 304, 307

truth-values 42, 515
  and guises 614
  and interrogative forms 363, 382
  and logical forms 524
  and negation 321, 322
  and proper names 613, 614
  and quantifiers 526–7
  and root clauses 380
Turner, R. 31, 32, 404, 542
type lifting, and NP meanings 94–8
type raising 283
type shifting theory 442–3, 453
type theory 6, 19, 27, 31
  and interrogatives 388
  and partitions 372
  two-sorted 31
types
  and logical terms 522–3, 524
  in quantifier relations 65–8
  and quantifiers 517–21

Ultan, R. 348
Unaccusative Hypothesis (UH) 489,
  490–1, 492, 505
unbounded 'extraction' constructions, in
  categorial grammar 102–3
underspecification of semantics 465
unification 5
  and compositionality 466
  higher-order 146–7, 148, 159–61, 162,
  167–8
unification grammars 32
uniformity, and generalized quantifiers
  527
Unique Role Requirement 438
Universal Grammar 545
universality
  in lexical semantics 545
  and logical terms 522, 532–3
update semantics 191, 193, 195
utterance formatives 136
utterance processing, deductive model
  of 568–72
utterances
  and meanings for interrogatives
  407–8
  and meta-linguistic interaction 419
  verbalizations of 139–40

valid prefix property 474
value judgement dets 46
Van Valin, R. D. 490, 495, 498, 500
Vandeloise, C. 542, 552

variable behavior verbs 491, 493–6,
  502–5
variable-binding *see* binding
vehicle change 151
Veltman, F. 210, 211, 221, 250
Vendler, Z. 396
verb phrases, ellipsis 135–41
verbs 5
  and bare argument ellipsis 160
  complex 153
  of directed motion 495, 496, 497–8,
  504–5
  and futurity 349
  lexicalization patterns 488–9
  of manner of motion 489, 498–500,
  502–4, 505
  matrix 153, 154, 155, 349
  and plurality 440–1
  propositional attitude 234, 235
  of sound 489, 491–8, 499–50, 501,
  502–3, 504–5
  and the Unaccusative Hypothesis
  (UH) 489, 490–1, 492, 505
  variable behavior 491, 493–6, 502–5
  see also VP ellipsis
Verkuyl, H. 452, 543
Vermeulen, C. F. 211
Vinay, J.-P. 504
Visser, A. 211
visual perception, and cluster concepts
  550
von Fintel, L. 47
Von Stechow, A. 16, 32, 275, 276, 281
VP ellipsis 145, 148–59, 168
  antecedent contained (ACE) 147,
  148–9, 153–4, 155, 156, 159, 168
  elided 158
  and non-restrictive relative clauses
  155–6
  in parasitic gap constructions 149–50
  reconstruction 150–5, 156, 157–8, 159
  without syntactically matched
  antecedents 156–9

Walker, E. 545
Wall, R. E. 608
Wasow, T. 487
Webber, B. L. 160
Wegener, P. 275
Weinreich, U. 542
Welker, K. A. 233
Wertheimer, M. 550
Westerstahl, D. 41, 47, 210, 404, 527
wh-gap construal 595

wh-gap dependencies 577, 578, 579–92, 595, 596
wh-islands 594, 595
wh-phrase meaning 408–10
wh-questions 361, 364, 365–6, 367–70, 376, 377, 380
  bijective 527
  and propositions 394
wh-trace 150, 152, 153, 154–5
Wheeler, D. 23
Wierzbicka, A. 543
Wilkinson, K. J. 220, 244
will
  and different modalities 348–9
  dual of 355–6
  and futurity 349–50, 355, 356
  and the past tense 353
  and sequence of tense 350–1
Williams, E. 167

Wilson, D. 4, 311, 315, 316, 563, 564, 568
Wittgenstein, L. von 179, 532, 549
world-creating predicates 217
van der Wouden, T. 325, 328, 340
Wrap operations, in categorial grammar 91–2

y/n questions 391, 394
Yavas, F. 347, 348, 349

Zadrozny, W. 467
Zaefferer, D. 387
Zaenen, A. 490, 498, 500, 590
Zanuttini, R. 338, 339, 340
Zeevat, H. 121, 309
Zimmerman, T. E. 17, 34
Zucchi, A. 29, 219, 242
Zwarts, F. 325, 328, 340
Zwarts, J. 52, 54, 543